BAJA
HANDBOOK

BAJA
HANDBOOK

JOE CUMMINGS

MOON
PUBLICATIONS INC.

BAJA HANDBOOK

Please send all comments,
corrections, additions,
amendments, and critiques to:

**JOE CUMMINGS
c/o MOON PUBLICATIONS
722 WALL STREET
CHICO, CA 95928 USA**

Published by
Moon Publications, Inc.
722 Wall Street
Chico, California 95928 USA
tel. (916) 345-5473

PRINTING HISTORY

First Edition—February 1992
Reprinted August 1992

Printed by
Colorcraft Ltd., Hong Kong

Library of Congress Cataloging in Publication Data

Cummings, Joe

    Baja Handbook / Joe Cummings
        p.   cm.
    Includes bibliographical references and index
    ISBN 0-918373-69-7 : $13.95
    1. Baja California (Mexico)—Description and Travel—Guide-books
    I. Title.
    F1246.C99 1992   91-38313
    917.2'204835—dc20   CIP

All color photos by Joe Cummings

Cover photo: Terrence Moore

*The very air here is miraculous,
and outlines of reality change with the moment.*
—John Steinbeck,
The Log from the Sea of Cortez

TABLE OF CONTENTS

LIST OF MAPS

MAP SYMBOLS

MEX. FEDERAL HIGHWAY	INTERNATIONAL BORDER	POINT OF INTEREST
MEX. STATE HIGHWAY	STATE BORDER	ACCOMMODATION
U. S. STATE HIGHWAY	FREEWAY	TOWNS / VILLAGES
U. S. HIGHWAY	MAIN HIGHWAY	CITIES
	OTHER ROADS	TOLL GATE
U. S. INTERSTATE	UNPAVED ROADS	MISSION
PEMEX GAS STATION	BRIDGE	CAMPSITE
	RAILROAD	MOUNTAIN
	WATER	

LIST OF CHARTS

ABBREVIATIONS

a/c—air-conditioned   pp—per person
B & B—bed and breakfast   RT—roundtrip
d—double occupancy   RV—recreation vehicle
OW—one way   s—single occupancy
km—kilometers   t—triple occupancy

ACKNOWLEDGEMENTS

Guidebook writers are only as good as their support networks, and for *Baja Handbook* I was fortunate to be able to assemble one of the best. Most especially I must thank the national, state, and local representatives of the Secretaría de Turismo (SECTUR) for their invaluable assistance in providing information on Baja California destinations and ongoing logistical support.

Gringos and *mexicanos* near and far were of immeasurable assistance during the research phases of this book, including, Eduardo Amezcua, Javier Rivas Garcia, Joel Ramiro Alvarez, Cinthya Cazares and the Tijuana Tourism and Conventions Bureau, Mario D'Avila, Cecilia Haugen, Gerardo Murray Acedo and the Holiday Inn Mexicali, José Salinas, Cesar Palomar Meza, Luis Armando Camalich, Guadalupe Salas Osuna, Ruben Chavez Hernandez and Cervecería Cuauhtémoc, Alex Vernon and Laura Luna of the Colegio de Idiomas, *mi madre mexicana* Gloria Beltrán, Hugo Torres Chabert and the Rosarito Beach Hotel, José Hernandez Limón, Patricia Hernandez Mota, Julian Souza Legorreta, Inocencio Enrique Ruíz, Stouffer Presidente Hotels, Hoteles La Pinta del Prado, Gus Robertson, Eric Hiss and the GCI Group, Norbert Beatty and M. Silver Associates, John Utley and Carlos Chabert of the *Baja Times,* John Shepard, Mike Nelson, surf dragon and fellow bluesbreaker Tony McCormick, and adventurer Graham Mackintosh.

Production

When former Moon managing editor Mark Morris approached me with the idea for this guidebook, I tried to talk him into getting someone else. But he persisted—thanks, Mark, for opening up proverbial new vistas. Thanks also to patient, eagle-eyed editor Beth Rhudy, efficient cartographers Bob Race and Brian Bardwell, laconic Dave Hurst for a nice cover, Mark Voss for layout, and to everyone else at Moon who has had a hand in shaping (and shipping) this volume.

IS THIS BOOK OUT OF DATE?

Between the time this book went to press and the time it got onto the shelves, hotels have opened and closed, restaurants have changed hands, and roads have been repaired (or fallen into disrepair). Also, prices have probably gone up; because of this, all prices herein should be regarded as approximations and are not guaranteed by the publisher or the author.

We want to keep this book as accurate and up-to-date as possible and would appreciate hearing about any errors or omissions you may encounter while using *Baja Handbook*.

If you have any noteworthy experiences (good or bad) with establishments listed in this book, please pass them along to us. If something is out of place on a map, tell us; if the best restaurant in town is not included, we'd like to know. Found a new route to a mission ruins site or palm oasis? Share it with other Baja travelers. All contributions will be deeply appreciated and properly acknowledged. Address your letters to:

> Joe Cummings
> c/o Moon Publications
> 722 Wall Street
> Chico, CA 95928

FOREWORD

If you're thinking of visiting Baja California and are hesitating . . . don't! There will never be a better time than now. Certainly, don't be put off by the thought of bandidos, Mexican jails, or *turista*. Before I ventured into Baja 12 years ago I was subjected to every horror story imaginable—mostly from Southern Californians who had never been there.

Now a veteran of a score of Baja adventures, and having spent two years walking alone around her beautiful coastline, I have to look back and wonder at the origin of the "stories" and declare that in all my time below the border I have never had a problem with anyone. My abiding memories are of incredible vistas, fascinating wildlife, and a people as warm and hospitable as any in the world.

Whatever attracts you to Baja—fishing, surfing, seafood, desert flora, cave paintings, whales, Spanish missions, sun-filled days—you won't be disappointed. Although this "forgotten peninsula" has been discovered and every year brings more development and better facilities, much of it remains a true frontier with an attendant frontier ethos. Don't be surprised to find a seemingly impoverished fisherman or rancher coming to your aid and then politely refusing a fistful of pesos in return, declaring sincerely, "Out here we are all brothers."

Joe Cummings's impressively researched and comprehensive *Baja Handbook* will not only assist you around Baja's border cities and down the main highways, but will also open your eyes to the "real" Baja of remote villages, fish camps, empty beaches, and rugged islands. Together with courtesy and common sense, this excellent guide will go a long way toward getting you safely to wherever you want to go; then, as many of us have found, the biggest danger is you may not want to come back.

Graham D Mackintosh

Graham Mackintosh, author
Into A Desert Place

INTRODUCTION

The first maps of Baja California, drawn by 16th-century Spanish explorers, depicted it not as a peninsula but as an island. Lured by tales of gold cities and a kingdom of warrior women, the conquistadors were among the first in a long line of seekers who have approached Baja's shores with a sense of mystery. Though the maps have long since been corrected, a legion of explorers—Latinos and gringos alike—continue to tramp the peninsula with dreams of finding Shangri-la in a hidden canyon or secluded cove.

Scattered along Baja's natural and artificial borders are outward concessions to the modern world (including Mexico's fifth-largest city),

as well as sufficient recreational opportunities to satisfy the most hedonistic refugees from that same world. This is one Baja; a peninsula wedged between one of the world's wealthiest and most technologically advanced countries and one struggling to develop with dignity.

But another Baja remains an island, in spite of 20th-century mapping. For four centuries, this Baja has stubbornly resisted the efforts of conquistadors, missionaries, miners, developers, and tourist boards to bring "civilization" into its rugged interior. The intrepid few who make it to the cultural and geographic heart of the peninsula will find it belongs to an era long-ago lost to most of North America.

THE LAND

BIRTH OF A PENINSULA

Baja California is the fourth-longest peninsula in the world after the Kamchatka (U.S.S.R.),

Malay (S.E. Asia), and Antarctic, but its landmass wasn't always scissored from the rest of Mexico. At one time its entire length was attached to a broad tropical plain along Mexico's Pacific coast; about two-thirds of the area was

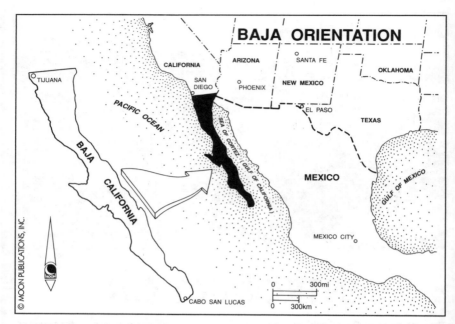

beneath the ocean. The 23-ton duck-billed hadrosaur roamed the region (its fossilized bones have been found near El Rosario) as did mammoth, bison, hyracotherium (a small, primitive horse), and camel. The peninsula's eventual divergence from the mainland came about as a result of the continual shifting of massive sections of the earth's surface, a process known as plate tectonics.

Like much of coastal Alta California to the north, Baja California is part of the North Pacific Plate, while the rest of the North American continent (including most of Alta California and Mexico) belongs to the North American Plate. The boundary line between these two plates is the San Andreas Fault, which extends northward through the center of Mexico's Sea of Cortez and into Alta California, where it parallels the California coast on a southeast-northwest axis before veering off into the Pacific Ocean, near San Francisco. The Pacific and North American plates have been shifting along this gap for millions of years, with the Pacific plate moving in a northwesterly direc-

tion at a current rate of about one to two inches a year.

This movement eventually tore basins in the earth's crust which allowed the Sea of Cortez (also known as the Gulf of California) to form, thus separating the land area west of the fault zone from land to the east. At one time the Sea of Cortez extended as far north as Palm Springs in Alta California; the sea would have continued moving northward at a gradual pace had it not met with the Colorado River. Silting in the Colorado River delta reversed the northward movement of the basins, holding the northern limit of the Sea of Cortez at a point well below what is now the U.S.-Mexican border. Alta California's Salton Sea is a remnant of the northernmost extension of the Sea of Cortez cut off by delta sedimentation.

As the peninsula moved slowly northwestward (257 km from the mainland by the time the Sea of Cortez became a stable feature—about five million years ago), the coastal plains tipped toward the west, creating a series of fault-block mountain ranges that now form one of Baja California's most outstanding topographic features. Volcanism further contributed to the peninsular and island geography, as seen in the massive lava flows east of San Ignacio (where the Tres Vírgenes volcanos erupted as recently as 1746), the basaltic geology south of Bahía de los Angeles, the various cinder cones near San Quintín, and the volcanic islands of Isla Raza, Isla Guadalupe, and Isla San Luis. At Laguna de los Volcánes in northeastern Baja, boiling mud pits and steam vents are the most visible signs of recent volcanic activity.

A third topographical contributor, sedimentation, has created the salient features of Baja's larger valleys and southwestern coastal plains. Prehistoric Mexican rivers, cut off from their mainland sources upon the creation of the Sea of Cortez, deposited sediments west of Mexicali to form the vast Laguna Salada. The fertile Valle de Mexicali, like Alta California's Imperial Valley, holds silt from the Colorado River—much of it comprised of geologic elements once contained in the Grand Canyon. The low coastal plain that forms the western portion of the Vizcaíno Desert region contains sedimentary deposits up to 16 km thick, a combination of sierra river deposits and material left over from the period 15 million years ago when this area was underneath the Pacific Ocean.

GEOGRAPHY

Size And Area

Baja California extends 1,300 km (806 miles) from the U.S.-Mexico border to the peninsula's southernmost tip—a hundred miles longer than Italy and twice the length of Florida. (If the coastline could be straightened, it would reach a distance equivalent to that between Tijuana and Juneau, Alaska.) Its widest girth, measured across land only, is at the 193-km (120-mile) border. Measuring across land and water to include Bahía de Sebastian Vizcaíno, the widest point is about 230 km (144 miles), from Punta Eugenio on the west coast to Punta San Francisquito on the east. The peninsula reaches its narrowest at a section 161 km (100 miles) above the southern

tip, where it's only 45 km (28 miles) between the Pacific Ocean and Bahía de La Paz.

The total land area of the states of Baja California (or Baja California Norte) and Baja California Sur is about 144,000 square km (55,000 square miles)—add another 2,460 square km (930 square miles) for the dozens of islands and islets nearby. The coastline created by the Pacific Ocean, the Sea of Cortez, and the dozens of bays, lagoons, coves, and inlets totals about 4,800 shore km (3,000 miles).

Mountain Ranges

Baja's most striking geographical feature is the spine of mountain ranges, or sierras, that run down its center from northwest to southeast. For the most part, Baja's sierras are a continuation of a mountain system that stretches southward from Alaska's Aleutian Islands to the spectacular rock formations at Cabo San Lucas. There are 23 named ranges in all; most are of fault-block origin while a scattered few are volcanic.

Because of the way in which the underground fault blocks tipped to create these sierras, they tend to slope gradually toward the west and fall off rather dramatically toward the east. The Cape Region's Sierra de la Laguna is the major exception. Like Alta California's Sierra Nevada, Baja's high sierras typically feature granitic peaks topped by conifer forests. The eastern escarpment, facing the Sea of Cortez, is dissected by stream-eroded canyons and arroyos (stream beds that are dry most of the year).

The four most substantial mountain ranges are the **Sierra Juárez** and **Sierra de San Pedro Mártir** in the north, the volcanic **Sierra de la Giganta** in the upper south, and the **Sierra de la Laguna** in the center of the southern cape. Baja's highest peak, **Picacho del Diablo** (3,086 meters/10,154 feet), is in the Sierra de San Pedro Mártir; during the winter its snowcapped peak can be seen from the Mexican mainland 225 km (140 miles) away.

Deserts

On a simple meteorological basis, about 65% of Baja California's total land area can be

BAJA CALIFORNIA MOUNTAIN RANGES
OVER 1,500 METERS (5,000 FEET)

Range	Highest Peak(s)
Sierra Juárez	Cerro Torre Blanco 1,794 meters (5,904 feet)
Sierra de San Pedro Mártir	Picacho del Diablo 3,086 meters (10,154 feet)
Sierra la Asamblea	Cerro Dos Picachos 1,653 meters (5,438 feet)
Sierra San Borja	Pico Echeverria 1,902 meters (6,258 feet)
Sierra de San Francisco	Pico Santa Monica 2,098 meters (6,904 feet)
Sierra de Guadalupe	Monte Thetis 1,635 meters (5,380 feet)
Sierra de la Giganta	Cerro la Giganta 1,760 meters (5,792 feet)
Sierra de la Laguna	Picacho de la Laguna 2,155 meters (7,090 feet)

classified as desert since these portions average less than 25 cm (10 inches) of rain per year. From a botanical perspective, Baja's desert lands belong to the Sonoran Desert, which extends across northwestern Mexico into parts of southeastern Alta California and southern Arizona. However, there are so many endemic plant species in Baja (see "Flora and Fauna," p. 14) that these areas probably deserve a classification all their own.

Any visitor who has previously traveled in the Sonoran Desert lands of northern Mexico, southeastern Alta California, or southern Arizona will note many subtle differences among their Baja counterparts. Because of the peninsula's numerous sierras and its location between two large bodies of water, the aridity of any given area along the peninsula can vary considerably. Following this variation in elevation and aridity, Baja's deserts can be divided into four subregions, each distinguished by its own unique geography and the resultant dominance of one group of plant species over another.

San Felipe Desert: This southwestern extension of Alta California's Colorado Desert is wedged between the eastern escarpment of the northern sierras and the coastal plains of the Sea of Cortez. The peninsula's driest desert, it averages only five cm (two inches) of rainfall a year. Most of the topography is a mixture of salt flats, rocky plains, sand dunes, arroyos, and extinct volcanic craters.

The Valle de Mexicali is part of the San Felipe Desert, but is made productive by an irrigation system fed by the Colorado River. The large Isla Angel de la Guarda and nearby islands also belong to this region. The dominant plant species throughout the sparsely vegetated area is bursage (*huizapol* in Spanish) and creosote bush *(hediondilla),* along with a variety of succulents and hardy trees.

Gulf Coast Desert: This narrow subregion stretches along the Sea of Cortez from just below Bahía de los Angeles to the tip of the peninsula near San José del Cabo. On average, the elevation is substantially higher here (with peaks up to 1,500 meters) than in the San Felipe Desert to the north, and the terrain is marked by several broken sierras of granitic and volcanic rock. These sierras contain numerous arroyos and a few perennial streams which allow for pockets of subsistence farming. The underground stream at Mulegé supports intensive cultivation in the surrounding valley.

The southern reaches of the Gulf Coast Desert receive a bit of extra precipitation from the occasional tropical storm that blows in from the south. As a result of the added moisture and elevation, many more trees and flowering cacti are found here than in the San Felipe Desert, including **torote, palo blanco, ocotillo, cholla,** and **cirio** (the "boojum tree"). Sea of Cortez islands to the east have a similar terrain although the endemic vegetation varies from island to island due to isolation.

Vizcaíno Desert: After a worldwide search for the perfect desert habitat, the designers of **Biosphere II,** a self-contained ecological research laboratory in Arizona, modeled their dome's desert biome on the Vizcaíno Desert. The largest desert area in Baja, this subregion lies along the Pacific coast from a point just north of El Rosario to the Magdalena Plains some 1,000 km (600 miles) southward. Its eastern boundary is the eastern escarpment of the central sierras. This positioning means that it's just out of reach of the northwestern rains, so important to coastal Alta California and northwestern Baja, as well as the southern tropical storms that bring water to the Cape Region and to the lower Gulf Coast Desert.

In spite of the lack of measurable precipitation, desert plants proliferate here. The entire region is sparsely populated because of the lack of dependable water sources, but the desert vegetation, especially **yucca,** thrives on night and morning fog from the Pacific Ocean. The whimsical-looking **cirio** is another of the dominant succulents in the Vizcaíno Desert; toward the Pacific coast it's often draped with ball moss. Other common species here include **agave, mesquite, cholla, prickly pear,** and **pitaya.**

The major coastal feature in this subregion is Laguna Ojo de Liebre, also called Scammon's Lagoon, one of several bays favored by wintering gray whales. The most substantial inland water source is the Río San Ignacio, which flows westward from a large date palm oasis in the heart of the peninsula into the open desert near the coast.

Magdalena Plains (Llano Magdalena): Beginning below the Vizcaíno Desert and bounded by the Pacific coast on the west and by the central and southern sierras on the east, the Magdalena Plains (or Llano Magdalena) extend southward until they come to an abrupt halt at the northwestern escarpment of the Sierra de la Laguna. The main feature of the Pacific side is Bahía Magdalena, Baja's largest bay, which is sheltered by the huge,

(MIKE WELLINS)

© MOON PUBLICATIONS, INC.

L-shaped Isla Magdalena to the northwest, and the equally large Isla Santa Margarita to the southwest. The Canal Gaviota connects Bahía Magdalena with Bahía Almejas to the immediate south. Other saltwater bays and lagoons along the Pacific coast include Bahía de Ballenas and Laguna San Ignacio; all are used as calving areas by migrating whales.

Other coastal features include mangrove swamps, dunes, and small sandbar islands. The only inland waterway of note is the Río La Purísima, which drops westward from the Sierra de la Giganta to Punta San Gregorio on the Pacific coast. Large underground aquifers in the vicinity of Ciudad Constitución support intensive agriculture in the area. The aquifer is becoming increasingly saline, however, as the fresh water is pumped out faster than it is replenished. A number of arroyos on the west side of the Sierra de la Giganta supply water to the area when rainfall is sufficient.

Cactus varieties are abundant throughout the Magdalena Plains and there are stands of **date palms, palo verde, torote, mesquite,** and **palo blanco** along the riverine corridors and upland arroyos.

The Vizcaíno Desert and the Magdalena Plains are sometimes referred to as one entity, the **Central Desert.**

Californian Region

Most of northwestern Baja California bears the same topography, climate, and ecosystems as are found in southwestern Alta California. These conditions extend almost as far south as El Rosario, near the Pacific coast, and eastward to the eastern escarpment of the Sierra Juárez and Sierra de San Pedro Mártir. Within this region are three subregions; they are for the most part defined by changes in elevation from the coast to the highest mountain peaks in the center of the peninsula.

Conifer Forests: This subregion begins at an elevation of about 1,500 meters (4,920 feet) in the Sierra Juárez and from about 2,400 meters (7,872 feet) in the Sierra de San Pedro Mártir. The granitic substrata of these fault-block mountains becomes more apparent the higher you go, as rocky ledges poke through the soil and sediment accumulated over the

eons. Abundant precipitation supports lush forests and meadows along the flats, ridges, and plateaus of both ranges. During the winter, snow is the most common source of moisture in the higher elevations, and peaks are often snowcapped.

Dominant trees in the Sierra Juárez include the **canyon live oak, juniper, piñon pine,** and **Jeffrey pine.** The forests of the Sierra de San Pedro Mártir also feature **incense cedar, white fir,** and **sugar pine,** and at least three tree types not found in either the Sierra Juárez or San Diego County farther north in Alta California—quaking aspen, lodgepole pine, and the endemic **San Pedro Mártir cypress.** Along the streams and meadows at slightly lower elevations are **manzanita, Indian paintbrush, hedgehog cactus, snowberry,** and a number of other flowering plants.

Pine-Juniper-Oak Woodlands: On the intermediate slopes of the two sierras, at elevations of about 900 to 1,500 meters (3,000 to 5,000 feet), are stands of pine, oak, and juniper. The lower southern reaches of the Sierra de San Pedro Mártir display a Darwinian salad of conifer, chaparral, and desert species, mixing pines and juniper with **blue fan palm, Mojave yucca, palmita, sagebrush, sand verbena,** and **barrel cactus.**

Chaparral: At just below 900 meters on either side of the mountain ranges, the woodlands give way to chaparral, a dense shrub community that supports **sagebrush, scrub oak, wild lilac, manzanita, coast live oak, chaparral ash** and other hardy species with deep-branching root systems. Interspersed with the chaparral are boulders of varying size; some of the larger are used as billboards by Bajacalifornios who paint them with political slogans, declarations of love, and religious messages.

The **palm canyons** of the eastern slopes are at chaparral elevation, but because of the abundance of year-round water, they feature unique terrains of their own. Eroded by mountain streams that terminate in the San Felipe Desert, these steep and steep-walled arroyos shelter picturesque groves of **California fan palm** and the endemic **blue fan palm.** Volcanic activity on the eastern side of the peninsula has resulted in underground geothermal reservoirs; hot springs can be found in some of the canyons where the water seeps from the surface.

Coastal Sage Scrub: On the Sea of Cortez side of the northern mountain ranges, the chaparral subregion gives way to the arid San Felipe Desert. On the Pacific side, chaparral fades into the rolling hills of the coastal plains. The terrain is rocky, with a blend of chaparral vegetation and the low-lying shrubs that dominate the coastal sage-scrub biome. Common species include **chamise, barrel cactus, agave, ash, cholla, flat-top buckwheat, hedgehog cactus, jimson weed, margarita, buckeye, jojoba, saltbush,** and a variety of grasses.

Cape Region

In many ways, Baja California's Cape Region has the most distinctive geography on the peninsula. The Sierra de la Laguna, in the center of the cape itself, runs north to south rather than northwest to southeast; unlike other ranges in the southern half of the peninsula, it's granitic rather than volcanic. Yet in contrast to the granitic, fault-block ranges of northern Baja, it tips eastward so that its steepest slopes face west. It is also more lushly vegetated than the northern sierras. Arroyos on the eastern slopes of Sierra de la Laguna are water-filled much of the year, enabling this area to support pockets of fruit and vegetable farming.

The entire region receives substantially more rainfall than any other part of Baja California, save for the Californian Region in the northeast. Most of the rain falls in the highland areas, however, leaving the coastal lowlands fairly dry and highly attractive to beach-going tourists. About a fourth of the Cape Region falls below the Tropic of Cancer; the combination of dry coastal areas, moist uplands, and tropical latitudes has created two unique subregions.

Cape Oak-Piñon Woodlands: The Sierra de la Laguna has been called an "island in the sky" because of its remarkable isolation from the Central Desert to the north and the Gulf Coast Desert to the east. At its very top, the peaks receive up to 100 cm (40 inches) of annual rainfall; at higher elevations are extensive stands of **Mexican piñon pine** and endemic oaks such as **madroño** or **palmita.** Oaks are also found on the higher slopes of the Sierra de la Giganta to the north, which falls within the Cape Region as well.

Cape Arid Tropical Forest: The coastal areas of the Cape Region as well as the lower slopes of la Laguna and la Giganta sierras share characteristics typical of both tropical and arid biomes, hence the seemingly oxymoronic term "arid tropical forest. Like tropical forests worldwide, the lower Cape forests produce trees, shrubs, and undergrowth of varying heights that create a canopied effect. Mixed with this tangled growth are a profusion of succulents more associated with arid climes, including the **cardón-barbón,** a shorter cousin of the towering cardón found throughout Baja's deserts.

Much of the vegetation in the Cape Arid Tropical Forest is normally associated with the tropical thorn forests of coastal Colima and Guerrero on the Mexican mainland. Prominent marker plants unique to the Cape subregion include the native **Tlaco palm, wild fig** *(zalate), mauto,* and the alleged aphrodisiac herb **damiana.**

Coastal Wetlands Region

Wetland pockets can be found in numerous spots along the peninsular coast; they lie in shallow areas along bays and lagoons and aren't limited to any particular longitude or latitude. In Baja, these wetlands usually consist of **salt marshes,** which contain high concentrations of salt-tolerant plants such as cordgrass, eelgrass, saltwort, and salt cedar, or **mangrove** *(mangle)* communities containing one or more of the five species common in Baja—black mangrove, white mangrove, red mangrove, buttonwood mangrove, and sweet mangrove. Within any given wetland, there can be considerable variances in salinity, temperature, and wetness; hence, an extensive variety of plants and animals can adapt to wetland areas. Because of this environmental variation, salt marshes and mangrove wetlands represent the most concentrated biomass areas on the planet. For most visitors, the main attraction of the wetlands is the abundant presence of waterfowl.

Areas with substantial wetlands include Bahía San Quintín (salt marshes), Laguna Ojo de Liebre (saltwater estuarine marshes), Laguna San Ignacio (salt marshes, mangrove forests), Bahía Magdalena (salt marshes, mangrove forests), Bahía de la Paz (mangrove forests), Río Mulegé (mixed saltwater/freshwater estuarine marshes), Estero San Bruno (mangrove forests), Bahía de los Angeles (salt marshes, some mangrove), and Bahía San Luis Gonzaga (salt marshes).

Islands
Around 50 islands and islets surround the Baja peninsula, with the great preponderance of them on the Sea of Cortez side. Many of the Sea of Cortez islands were created as the peninsula broke away from mainland Mexico

PHYSIOGRAPHIC REGIONS

SAN DIEGO
TIJUANA — MEXICALI
ENSENADA
SAN FELIPE
SAN QUINTIN
EL ROSARIO
CATAVIÑA
BAHÍA DE LOS ANGELES
GUERRERO NEGRO
SAN IGNACIO — SANTA ROSALÍA
MULEGÉ
PACIFIC OCEAN
LORETO
CIUDAD CONSTITUCIÓN
LA PAZ
CABO SAN LUCAS

UNITED STATES
MEXICO

SEA OF CORTEZ

0   100mi
0   100km

= CALIFORNIAN REGION
= SAN FELIPE DESERT
= VIZCAÍNO DESERT
= GULF COAST DESERT
= MAGDALENA PLAINS
= CAPE REGION

© MOON PUBLICATIONS, INC.

and hence are "land-bridge" or "continental" islands rather than true oceanic islands. Because of their low elevation, these islands don't snag much of the rain that moves up from the south in summer. As a result, they're quite arid although the larger islands harbor a number of endemic plant and animal species. Among the largest of these islands are Isla Angel de la Guarda, Isla Espíritu Santo, and Isla Cerralvo. The smaller Isla San Luis and Isla Raza are of volcanic origin.

On the Pacific side, Baja's islands tend to have semi-moist Californian Region climates on their northwestern (windward) shores and desertic conditions on their southeastern (leeward) shores. Isla Guadalupe, about 250 km (155 miles) west of the Pacific coast, is one of the few islands of volcanic (hence, oceanic) origin. It's rarely visited by cruising boats because of its steep (up to 450 meters) shores but is an important habitat for the endemic **Guadalupe fur seal** and **northern elephant seal,** as well as various species of endemic pine, cypress, and palm.

Other Pacific islands of note are the much closer Islas de Todos Santos, just 10 miles (16 km) southwest of Ensenada. These twin isles are well known among surfers for having the highest surf (up to 30 feet high in winter) on the entire North American west coast. Isla Cedros, 24 km (15 miles) north of the Vizcaíno Peninsula, is one of the few Baja islands inhabited by humans, as it's used as a transshipment port for salt from the huge Guerrero evaporative saltworks.

THE SEA OF CORTEZ

The Sea of Cortez was apparently named by Francisco de Ulloa after he sailed the entire perimeter of this body of water in 1539 and 1540 at the command of the most infamous of all Spanish conquistadors, Hernán Cortés (who had himself sailed the sea in an aborted attempt to colonize the peninsula four years previously). The name Mar de Cortés henceforth appeared intermittently on maps of the region, alternating with Mar Vermejo (Vermillion Sea, in reference to the color reflected from huge numbers of pelagic crabs) until the

Mexican government officially renamed it the Gulf of California (Golfo de California) early in this century. Sailors, writers, and other assorted romanticists, however, have continued to call it by its older name.

The sea is roughly 1,125 km (700 miles) long, with an average width of 150 km (93 miles). Oceanographers have divided it into four regions based on the prominent characteristics—depth, bottom contours, and marine productivity—of each zone. The northern quarter of the gulf, between the Colorado River delta and the Midriff Islands, is shallow in relation to the zones farther south because of silt deposited by the Colorado River, which has also rounded the bottom contours. The sea here is highly saline due to evaporation and there is a tidal range of up to 31 feet. Before the Colorado River was dammed, the tidal bore created when the seaward river currents met the incoming tide was powerful enough to sink ships.

The second region south encompasses the Midriff Islands, where basins reach depths of 820 meters (2,700 feet) and strong currents bring nutrients up from the bottom while aerating the water. This leads to a unusually high level of biological productivity, otherwise known as "good fishin'."

From the Midriff Islands to La Paz, basin depth doubles, silting is minimal, and water temperatures begin decreasing dramatically. The final sea zone below La Paz is oceanic, with trenches and submarine canyons over 3,600 meters (12,000 feet) deep. Around the tip of the cape, the Sea of Cortez meets the Pacific Ocean, a point at which the currents from each meet to produce some wicked riptides. This means that although the tip of the cape is the warmest area on the peninsula during the winter months, the beach swimming can be rather treacherous in places.

The Sea of Cortez is biologically the richest body of water on the planet, with over 800 species of marine vertebrates and over 2,000 invertebrates at last count. The reported number rises with the publication of each new marine study.

CLIMATE

In satellite photographs of the North American continent taken a hundred miles above the earth, Baja California invariably jumps off the plate. The rest of the continent north and east may be obscured by whorls of clouds while the shores, plains, and mountains of Baja are carved into the photographic image, remarkably clear. In 1991, the truth-in-travel magazine *Condé Nast Traveler* named Baja California the best dollar value per hour of sunshine for any North American living west of Denver—according to their survey, the chances of a day without rain in the winter are 95% in Baja (beating out Hawaii's 84% and Florida's 87%).

How does Baja California get so much sunshine? The simple answer is that it's positioned almost out of reach of the two major weather systems that influence climate in western North America and along the Pacific coast of mainland Mexico. Northwesterly storms from Eurasia and the Arctic bring rain and snow to the American Northwest and Midwest all winter long, while tropical storms roll across the South Pacific from Asia, dumping loads of rainfall along the lower Mexican coast and Central America in the summer.

Baja is only slightly influenced by the outer edges of these systems. Anchored between the warm, fish-filled waters of the Sea of Cortez and the heaving Pacific Ocean, bisected by plains and cordilleras, the peninsula's isolated ecosystems range in climate from Mediterranean to desert to tropical. In some areas, overlapping microclimates defy classification, combining elements of semiarid, arid, subtropical, and tropical climes.

WET AND DRY

The "Land of Little Rain," as Baja has been called by one fanciful author, isn't unique in its aridity since most of the earth's desert areas are found between 15° and 30° latitude either north or south of the equator. (Baja is positioned roughly between 23° and 31° N latitude.) Global convection currents in the atmosphere create a more or less permanent high-pressure shield over these zones, insulating them from the low-pressure fronts that bring rain clouds.

Only about two-thirds of Baja California can be classified as true desert (less than 25 cm of annual precipitation), and even the driest areas receive occasional rain. In the peninsula's Central Desert this may be as little as an inch a year, while in the interior of the Cape Region's Sierra de la Laguna annual rainfall may appoach 100 cm (40 inches). Since mountain peaks trap rain clouds, Baja's higher elevations invariably receive more rain than the low-lying coastal zones.

Variation in rainfall also occurs on a seasonal basis. For the northwestern peninsula, the wettest months are Dec.-April (with about 7½ cm per month in Ensenada, more in the mountains) while in the Cape Region rain usually arrives Aug.-Nov. (an average 5.8 cm in September for Cabo San Lucas and La Paz). The central peninsula, including both coasts, is relatively dry all year long, receiving only brief spurts of rain from the north (in the winter) or south (late summer, early fall).

The driest coastal area in all of Baja is along the northwestern shores of the Sea of Cortez—San Felipe records an average annual precipitation of only two inches, with no measurable rainfall most months. At the other extreme, the peaks of the Sierra de San Pedro Mártir are often covered with a three- to four-foot snowpack during the winter.

HOT AND COLD

Three variables influence temperatures at any given Baja California location: elevation, latitude, and longitude. In plain talk, that means the higher you climb, the cooler it gets; the farther south you go, the warmer it gets; and it's always cooler on the Pacific side of the peninsula and warmer on the Sea of Cortez side.

ESTIMATING TEMPERATURE CHANGES

For every degree of latitude farther south you travel, figure a temperature increase of 2° C (3.5° F). For each 100-meter increase in elevation, figure a temperature drop of 2° C.

Pacific Coast

Because of prevailing ocean currents, the Pacific coast shows the least overall variation in temperatures, staying relatively cool year-round. From March to July, the California Current flows southward along the coast, bringing cooler temperatures from the north that moderate seasonal atmospheric warming, while in December and January the coast is warmed a bit by the northward movement of the Davidson Current. These seasonal currents stabilize the air temperatures so that Ensenada, for example, averages 12° C (54° F) in January and 20° C (70° F) in August, a range of only 8° C (16° F). Along much of the central Pacific coast during the summer, the cool air brought by the California Current meets warm air from the interior of the peninsula, resulting in fog masses that can sweep as far inland as 32 km (20 miles).

Sea Of Cortez

The Sea of Cortez has its own set of currents (sometimes lumped together as the Gulf Current), fed by tropical waters of the South Pacific that travel in a counterclockwise direction north along the mainland's upper Pacific coast and then south along the peninsular coast. As a result, the Sea of Cortez enjoys an average annual surface temperature of 24° C (75° F), significantly warmer than the Pacific's 18° C (64° F). The high rate of evaporation at the north end of the sea also contributes to warmer air temperatures; this combination of warm air and water temperatures means the Sea of Cortez can be classified as "tropical" over its entire length.

The weather along this coast is warm and sunny all winter long with average January temperatures ranging from 13° C (55° F) in

San Felipe to 18° C (64° F) in Loreto. In August, average temperatures are 28° C (82° F) in San Felipe and 31° C (88° F) in Loreto, although daily high figures in the summer, at either locale, can easily reach 38° C (100° F) or more. La Paz is usually warmer than San Felipe but cooler than Loreto.

Chubascos, Coromuels,* And *Cordonazos
Monthly average wind velocities for Baja California as a whole are quite low. From mid-May to mid-Nov., however, tropical storms from the south or east, known as *chubascos,* can bring high winds and rain to the coasts of the Cape Region. Although they usually blow over quickly, local mythology has it that if a chubasco lasts more than three hours, it will last a day; if it lasts more than a day, it will last three days, and if more than three days, it'll be a five-day blow.

Another Sea of Cortez weather pattern is the *cordonazo,* a small but fierce summer storm that originates locally and is usually spent within a few hours. A more welcome weather phenomenon is the *coromuel* of Bahía de La Paz, a stiff afternoon breeze that blows from offshore during the hot summer and early fall months. This wind was named for the English Lord Protector Cromwell, identified with English pirates who took advantage of the wind's regular occurrence for the plunder of ships trapped in the bay.

BEST SEASONS FOR TRAVEL

Northwestern Baja: Tijuana, Tecate, Rosarito, And Ensenada
This area lies within the Californian Region and is affected by the mild Pacific climate. Hence, it's fairly comfortable all year-round—very much like Alta California's San Diego County. Although rain is almost never heavy or frequent, even in the winter months, you can usually avoid all rain by planning visits here for anytime from May to October. The beaches between Rosarito and Ensenada are warmest in July, August, and September, when they are most visited by Southern Californians. To get away from the crowds and enjoy low-season prices, visit between Oct. and April.

High Sierras
For those who like to travel light, the summer months are best for mountain hiking; even in July everything above 1,500 meters (5,000 feet) will feel like spring. From mid-Oct. to mid-April, come prepared for winter camping for hikes at similar elevations.

To appreciate the beauty of spring flowers, the best hiking season is just after the end of the rainy seasons. For the northern ranges, i.e., Sierra Juárez and San Pedro Mártir, this means April and May. For the Sierra de la Laguna in the Cape Region, October or early November is best (the Cape's rainy season occurs from late summer to early fall).

Deserts
Inland desert explorations should be absolutely avoided May-Oct. when daytime temperatures are fierce. The remaining cooler months are usually fine, although in the Central Desert, January daytime temperatures may be a bit on the cool side in areas exposed to high coastal winds or at higher elevations. The San Felipe and Gulf Coast deserts are usually warm and comfortable throughout the winter. Keep in mind, however, that desert nights can be cold at any time of year.

Sea Of Cortez
Along Baja's Sea of Cortez coasts, temperatures are moderate Oct. through mid-June. High tourist season is Nov. through March, even though the north coast is a bit too cool for swimming, for most people, during these months. Days and nights grow progressively warmer as one moves south, so that water sports are enjoyable from Loreto down, even in the winter.

From mid-June through Sept., the entire coast can be uncomfortably hot; the fishing, however, is usually very good during these months and out on the sea it's usually breezy. But if you don't fish, forget it. One of the best times to visit the Sea of Cortez coast is April to mid-June, when the weather is balmy and few tourists are about.

Cape Region
The flat end of the peninsula from San José del Cabo to Cabo San Lucas is warm year-

round. Pacific influences generally moderate the heat July-Sept. while the tropic waters of the Gulf Current make this stretch the warmest coastal zone on the peninsula during winter months. Except for the occasional chubasco in late summer, the climate seems darn near perfect here, which is why "Los Cabos" has become such a popular vacation destination. Cabo San Lucas receives about 45% of its measurable annual rainfall (a total of 15-18 cm a year) in September, so if there's a month to be avoided for weather reasons, this is the one.

The two months when you're least likely to have Los Cabos beaches to yourself are December and January, when large numbers of North Americans come here seeking respite from rainstorms and blizzards.

FLORA AND FAUNA

Had Charles Darwin happened to explore the peninsula and islands of Baja California instead of Ecuador's Galapagos Islands, he might well have arrived at the same conclusions about evolution. Baja's unique environment—an arid-to-tropical slice of mountains and plains isolated between two large bodies of water—has led to superlative endemism, or what one naturalist called "a high degree of freakishness," among its plant and animal species.

A thorough examination of all the plants and creatures of interest in Baja California would take volumes. The following sections cover only a few of either the most remarkable or the most common forms of plant and animal life found in Baja. In truth, the peninsula and its islands remain relatively unexplored with regard to the complex interconnecting ecosystems responsible for the high number of solitary species. Several botanists, marine biologists, zoologists, and paleontologists have undertaken solo research in the area, but only in the last two years has the first interdisciplinary team (sponsored by a Canadian university) begun studying the region.

In many ways, these researchers are heir to the Spanish fortune-seeker tradition of nearly five centuries ago. As George Lindsay, director of the California Academy of Sciences has said, "For the scientist, Baja California is a treasure chest, just barely opened."

VEGETATION

Botanists have estimated that over 4,000 varieties of plants have made Baja California their home. The most complete reference available on Baja vegetation, Dr. Ira L. Wiggins's *Flora of Baja California,* lists 2,958 species among 155 families and 884 genera. Another good source of information is Norman C. Roberts' recently published *Baja California Plant Field Guide,* which covers over 550 notable species and provides excellent photos of about half of these.

Cactus And Succulents

Many visitors find the desert plants of Baja the most exciting simply because they're often the most exotic-appearing forms of life in the region. Like Alice in *Through The Looking Glass,* they find that the farther they travel into the interior, the "curiouser and curiouser" the landscape becomes. The seemingly bizarre appearance of many succulents is due to the evolutionary gymnastics they've had to perform in order to adapt themselves to an environment where water is scarce.

Cactaceae: Around 120 species of cactus have been identified on the peninsula and its surrounding islands, more than anywhere else on the planet; almost three-fourths of them are unique to Baja.

One of the most common cacti throughout Baja is the towering **cardón** *(Pachycereus pringlei),* the world's tallest species of cactus. Individuals can reach as high as 18 meters (60 feet) or more and weigh 12 tons (not counting the root system), though more commonly they top out at seven to nine meters. The giant, pale green trunks feature 11-17 vertical ribs and may measure one meter thick. The cardón is often confused with the smaller saguaro cactus of Sonora and Arizona; one major difference is that the branches of the cardón tend to be more vertical than those of the saguaro.

The cardón is near-endemic to Baja California, found throughout the peninsula (outside of the Californian Region) and islands, and also along the coast of Sonora. The hardwood cores of cardón columns have been used by Bajacalifornios for centuries as building beams and fence posts. Among Baja residents, a cardón forest is called a *cardonal*.

Another extremely common and highly visible cactus is the *biznaga* or **barrel cactus** (genus *Ferocactus*). There are at least 15 species in Baja, most of which are endemic. Its English name refers to its shape, which is short and squat like a barrel—the most common varieties reach about waist-height. One variety, however, *Ferocactus diguettii*, which grows only on a few Sea of Cortez islands, easily reaches four meters (13 feet) in height and a meter (3.28 feet) in diameter. The spines of this cactus are often tinged red; from March to June the tops bloom with gorgeous yellow to red flowers. The indigenous Indians of Baja reportedly used hollowed-out biznaga as Dutch ovens by inserting food into the cavity along with heated stones, and then sealing the cactus off till the food was cooked. The sturdy, curved spines also served as fishhooks in native fishing expeditions.

Among Baja's original populations, another of the most important cacti was the *pitahaya dulce,* known among Anglos as **organ pipe cactus.** The spiny, orange-size fruit of the pitahaya (also spelled pitaya) contains a sweet, juicy, pleasant-tasting pulp the color of red watermelon. According to Spanish mission accounts, the Pericú Indians figured their yearly calendar according to the harvest of the ripe fruit in late summer and early fall. During this season, the Indians engaged in a veritable fruit orgy, gorging themselves on the pulp until they fell asleep and then waking to begin eating it again. The early Spanish explorers took it along on long sea journeys to prevent scurvy.

The pitahaya dulce has slender, vertical ribs that grow in clusters and is commonly found on the peninsula south of the Sierra de San Borja, on several Sea of Cortez islands and in Sonora and southern Arizona. A similar spe-

cies, *pitahaya agria (agria* means "sour" in Spanish; *dulce* is "sweet"), branches more densely and lower to the ground, hence its English name **galloping cactus;** it grows throughout the peninsula and on most Sea of Cortez islands. The fruit of the pitahaya agria is quite similar in appearance to that of the pitahaya dulce but, as implied by the Spanish name, it's less sweet, more acidic. Both types of pitahaya fruit remain popular among Baja residents and travelers.

Another cactus variety that's well represented throughout Baja is the genus *Opuntia,* which includes all types known as **cholla** as well as the *nopal* (or **prickly pear).** Cholla are a bane to Baja hikers because they're so prolific and the spines on any given plant are especially numerous. All true chollas belong to the subgenus *Cylindropuntia* and are multi-branched, multi-jointed, and cylindric-stemmed. The typical branch looks somewhat like braided or twisted rope. Historically speaking, cholla has had few domestic uses although a tea made from the roots of the fuzzy-looking **teddy-bear cholla** (also called "jumping cholla" for its propensity to cling to the lower legs of hikers), found along the east coast of the peninsula, is reportedly used by the Seri Indians as a diuretic.

In contrast, the much-loved prickly pear cactus (subgenus *Platyopuntia)* has broad, flat stems and branches and a sparser distribution of spines. In Spanish the prickly pear is known as *nopal,* and in northern Mexico and Baja its fleshy pads are a dietary staple. The most highly prized parts of the nopal are the young stem shoots, called *nopalitos,* and the ripe fruits or *tuna.* The flavor of the pads is a bit bland—like a cross between bell pepper and okra. The fruit, on the other hand, is juicy and sweet; when it's in season, many Baja markets sell the fruit. If you want to taste it in the wild, remove the tunas carefully, cut them lengthwise with a sharp knife, and scoop out the insides with a spoon. Nine species of nopal are found in Baja, including the endemic *tuna tapona* found south of Loreto.

Agavaceae: One of the most common and most striking desert plants is the **yucca,** which occurs in several varieties throughout Baja. Yuccas belong to the Agave family, of which

Baja has 19 species, including 11 endemics. The largest is the **tree yucca** *(Yucca valida),* called *datilillo* or "little date" in Spanish for its resemblance to a date palm. The average datilillo grows in clusters three to seven meters tall, the dagger-like blades supported by long woody trunks. This endemic is found throughout the desert plains and chaparral subregions of the peninsula—just about anywhere except in the mountains. The best place to view it in numbers is on the Pacific side of the Vizcaíno Desert where it's the dominant plant.

Yuccas are extremely useful plants for rural Bajacalifornios. The fruit and flowers are edible (a candy called *colache* is made from the cooked flower buds), the roots can be boiled to make soap or leather softener, and the tough leaf fibers are used to make cordage, sandals, baskets, and mats. In some parts of central Baja you may see fences made from packed-together datilillo stalks, which often take root and produce a "living fence."

Very similar to yucca is another member of the Agave family called *sotol* (genus *Nolina*). The leaves of a sotol are narrower and softer than those of a yucca; some sotols also produce long flower stalks similar to those of the century plant except that flower buds occur along the entire length of the stalk instead of only at the top.

Perhaps the most spectacular variety of sotol in Baja is the endemic *Nolina beldingii,* sometimes called *palmita* because of its resemblance to a small palm tree. Taller individuals reach up to seven meters, with a complex of thick leaf clusters branching from a short, woody trunk. The palmita grows most commonly along the higher elevations of the Cape Region; isolated stands can also be found in mountain areas northwest of Mulegé, north of Bahía de los Angeles, and on Volcán Las Tres Vírgenes.

More common in Baja are the many varieties of *maguey,* commonly called the century plant in English. Yet another member of the sizable Agave family, the maguey has broad, closely clustered leaves that grow at ground level without a visible trunk. In most species, the plant only flowers once in its lifetime, sending up a tall, slender stalk after maturation (typically 5-20 years, depending on the variety and the locale); early Anglo settlers in the southwestern U.S. spread the myth that agaves bloomed only once in a hundred years, hence the fanciful name "century plant."

The maguey was a very important food source to certain aboriginal populations who harvested the plant just before it bloomed, when it is full of concentrated nutrients. Trimmed of its leaves, the heart of the plant was baked in an underground pit for one to three days, then eaten or stored. Some ranchers still prepare the agave in this manner today; as with datilillo, the leaf fibers are used as cordage for weaving various household goods.

Fouquieriaceae: This family of succulents contains what many travelers consider to be the plant most symbolic of Baja—the *cirio* or "boojum tree." Most naturalists describe the cirio by likening it to an inverted carrot, since the plant's tall stalk is thickest near the ground and very gradually tapers along its height until it reaches a skinny point at the top. The Spanish name *cirio* ("candle") seems far more evocative when one compares the plant to the slender wax tapers typically found on mission altars. In times of abundant rain, the cirio even puts forth at its tip a golden bloom that resembles a flaring candle flame.

In height, the cirio is second only to Baja's cardón cactus, with mature plants extending 12-15 meters (40-50 feet) high from a base that's 30 centimeters or so in diameter. Since a cirio on average grows only three cm a year (or a foot every 10 years), a 15-meter individual is around 500 years old!

The whimsical name "boojum" was bestowed ad hoc upon the cirio by Arizona botanist Godfrey Sykes during a 1922 expedition to Baja. Sykes had apparently been reading Lewis Carroll's *Hunting of the Snark,* a tale which mentioned the imaginary boojum without describing it except to say that it inhabited "distant shores." In this sense Sykes's spontaneous epithet was descriptive since the cirio only grows in a relatively narrow, 200-mile-wide band between the 30th and 27th parallels on the Baja peninsula. (There is also a small cirio colony near La

Libertad in Sonora, at the same latitude.) Although the cirio is abundant within this area, the area itself is rather distant from the tourist centers of northwestern Baja, Loreto, and Los Cabos.

Because of its uniqueness, some botanists award the cirio with its own genus, *Idria,* within the Fouquieria family (so the Latin name can appear as either *Fouquieria columnaris* or *Idria columnaris).* Like all plants in this family, the white-barked cirio sprouts tiny leaves over the entire plant surface when there is sufficient rainfall. During long periods of dry weather, the leaves drop off to conserve the internal water supply.

Much more common throughout Baja's desert lands are two other members of the Fouquieria family, the ocotillo and *palo adán* ("Adam's tree"). The **ocotillo** *(Fouquieria splendens)* has long, whip-like branches that radiate directly from the ground in a shape that has been compared to an exploding shell. In the southwestern U.S., it's sometimes known as "coachwhip." As with the cirio, tiny leaves come and go on ocotillo stems according to changing weather conditions. After a good rainfall, a mature (two meters or more) plant puts forth droopy red blossoms at the end of each branch.

Ocotillo grows profusely in all the desert regions of Baja north of the 28th parallel (and as far northeast as New Mexico and Texas) and occasionally as far south as Bahía Concepcíon. A rare endemic species *Fouquieria burragei (ocotillo de flor* in Spanish, distinguished by its salmon-pink flowers) also grows between Bahía Concepcíon and La Paz and on a few Sea of Cortez islands. *Rancheros* use ocotillo branches for fencing, shade ramadas, and as bracing in adobe construction.

At about the point on the peninsula where ocotillo begins fading, its cousin the **palo adán** *(Fouquieria diguetti)* begins making an appearance. Looking like a larger ocotillo, the Adam's tree has considerably thicker branches that radiate from a short, woody trunk. The leaves, when present, are slightly larger while the flowers are smaller. In the Bahía de los Angeles area, ocotillo and Adam's tree often grow side by side. The latter is also popular as a fencing material and makes excellent firewood when dry.

Trees
Palms: Seven varieties of palm grow wild in Baja California; four are native to the peninsula and islands while three are introduced species. Palms are very important to the local economy of the southern half of the peninsula, where they're most common. The long, straight trunks are used as roof beams, the leaves are used in basketry and for roof and wall thatching, and the fruits provide a source of nutrition.

Among the most handsome Baja palm trees is the endemic **blue fan palm** or *palma azul,* which reaches up to 24 meters (78 feet) tall and sports bluish, fan-shaped leaves at its crown. The 4½-meter flower stalks, which usually appear Feb. through March, often extend well below the shag (the thatch of dead leaves below the crown). The blue fan palm typically grows in the canyons and arroyos of the Sierra Juárez and in similar locales as far south as San Ignacio.

Another native variety, the **Tlaco palm** (also called *palma palmia* and *palma colorado),* is common in the canyons and arroyos of the Cape Region sierras below Loreto. The smooth, slender trunks, crowned by fan-shaped leaves, stand up to 20 meters (65½ feet) tall. A closely related species, the **Guadalupe Island palm,** is native to Isla Guadalupe; its self-shedding trunk (leaving little or no shag) has made it highly popular as a cultivated palm in southern Alta California.

Baja's tallest palm variety is the endemic **Mexican fan palm** (also Baja California fan palm, skyduster, or *palma blanca)* which reaches heights of 27-30 meters (90-100 feet). As the name implies, its leaves are fan-shaped; the length of the trunk means the tree is highly productive for local construction use although it's not as durable as the Tlaco palm. The tree's native habitats are the Sierra de la Giganta and Isla Angel de la Guarda, but it has also spread west of Cataviña as well and has been imported to southern Alta California as an ornamental. More common in the northern peninsula is the similar, but shorter, **California fan palm.**

Two palm varieties were imported to Baja for their fruit value. The **date palm** was introduced to Baja by Jesuit missionaries and is now common near former mission sites, including Loreto, Comondú, Mulegé, San Ignacio, and San José del Cabo. The tree typically reaches 15-20 meters tall at maturity; the oblong fruit grows beneath feather-shaped leaves in large clusters, turning from pale yellow to dark brown as it ripens. Baja dates are eaten locally and shipped to mainland Mexico but are generally not considered of high enough quality for export. The 30-meter, feather-leafed **coconut palm** commonly grows along coastal areas of the Cape Region as far north as Mulegé and is an important local food source.

Elephant Trees: At least two different species from completely different plant families have been given the name "elephant tree." The first, which some Baja experts claim is the only "true" elephant tree, is the sumac family's *Pachycormus discolor,* called either *copalquín* or *torote blanco* in Spanish. The English name refers to the thick, gray, gnarled-looking trunks and branches of the tree. Travelers who have been to East Africa may note a resemblance to the baobab tree.

The papery bark of the elephant tree continually peels off in sheets to reveal the dark green, spongy inner trunk. Drought-deciduous leaves form on the branches when rainfall is sufficient; between May and Sept. small pink flowers may bloom for a few weeks, casting a pink glow over the whole. This endemic species is often seen in the same central desert areas that feature cirios. It's particularly prolific in volcanic soils, and in lava flows like the one off the highway to Bahía de los Angeles where it's the dominant species.

The second elephant tree, very similar in appearance to the *Pachycormus* but belonging to the torchwood family, is the *Bursera odorata*. Like the other elephant tree, the *Bursera* has thick, gnarled trunks and branches; the thin bark also peels off in papery sheets. The inner trunk is yellow, however, rather than dark green. This one grows south of Bahía

Concepcíon and on the Mexican mainland only. The Spanish name for the tree is the same as for the "true" elephant tree, *torote blanco*. A close relative, the *torote colorado* (another *Bursera*), has a reddish bark. It's found throughout the deserts of Baja and on many Sea of Cortez islands, as well as in the Alta California's Anza-Borrego Desert.

Conifers: The high sierras of Baja support a surprising number and variety of conifers (see "Mountain Ranges," p. 3) including species of cypress, cedar, juniper, fir, and pine. Among the most interesting because of their relative confinement to the Baja region are the **Tecate cypress** (found on the western slopes of the Sierra Juárez and in the Valle San Vicente, as well as in southern Alta California north to Orange County), the **San Pedro Mártir Cypress** (eastern escarpment of the Sierra de San Pedro Mártir only), the **Cedros Island Pine** (found only on Isla Cedros), and the **Guadalupe Island Pine** (only on Isla Guadalupe).

Other, more common conifer varieties found at higher elevations include **incense cedar, Mormon tea, white fir, piñon pine, Jeffrey pine, sugar pine, bishop pine,** and **lodgepole pine.**

Oaks: Varieties of oak *(encino* in Spanish) abound along the Pacific slopes of the northern sierras and in the canyons, arroyos, and meadows of the two Cape Region sierras. Of the many species found in Baja, four are known to be endemic: the **cape oak** (found in canyons and arroyos of the Cape Region sierras), **black oak** (lower slopes in the Cape Region), **Cedros Island oak** (Isla Cedros, and from San Vicente south to Sierra San Borja), and **peninsular oak** (lower slopes of the northern and central sierras). Other common oaks are the **coast live oak, canyon live oak, white oak, scrub oak, mesa blue oak,** and **Palmer oak.**

Mimosas: This subfamily of the Leguminosae or pea family represents dozens of genera common to arid and semiarid zones all over the world. Characterized by linear seed pods and double rows of tiny leaves, common varieties in Baja include the **mesquite** and various endemic kinds of **acacia.**

Indians have used the trunk, roots, leaves, beans, and bark of the mesquite tree for hundreds of years for a variety of purposes from lumber to medicine. Ground mesquite leaves mixed with water form a balm for sore eyes—a remedy still used by *curanderos* ("healers") in rural Mexico today—and chewing the leaves relieves toothache. Mesquite gum has also been used by various tribes as a balm for wounds, a ceramic glue, a dye, and a digestive.

Mesquite beans are a good source of nutrition—a ripe bean pod grows as long as nine inches, contains roughly 30% glucose, and is high in protein. Many animals and birds savor the beans—horses will eat them until they're sick, if allowed. Rural Mexicans grind the dried pods into a flour with which they make bread and a kind of beer. The Seri Indians, who live along the Sonoran coast of the Sea of Cortez, have separate names for eight different stages of the bean pod's development.

One of the prettiest endemic mimosas is the **palo blanco,** which has a tall, slender trunk with silver-white bark and a feathery crown that produces small, white, fragrant blossoms March-May. This tree can be found the length of the peninsula although it is most easily seen in the Sierra de la Giganta or in the vicinity of Loreto.

Wild Figs: Three *Ficus* trees *(zalate* in Spanish), one of which is endemic, are common in peninsular Baja. Most are found in rocky areas of the Cape Region. In the village of La Playita, east of San José del Cabo, is a venerable stand of zalates of impressive stature.

Willows: Various cottonwoods *(alamo)* and willows *(sauz)* grow in higher elevations throughout the peninsula. The endemic *huerivo (Populus brandegeei)* is a beautiful endemic cottonwood found in the canyons and arroyos of the Cape Region Sierras. The tall, straight trunks reach heights of 30 meters and are highly valued as lumber for construction and furniture-making.

An unlikely Baja find is the **quaking aspen** *(Populus tremuloides),* which grows in high mountain meadows of the Sierra de San Pedro Mártir and nowhere else in Baja or southern Alta California. The name comes from the fluttering effect created when the small leaves begin to turn yellow in the fall and shimmer against the white bark of the tree. In Spanish this tree is called *alamillo* or "little cottonwood."

Herbs

Most herbs (shrubs with culinary, medicinal, or religious value) thrive in arid climates, and in Baja California they grow in some abundance. To get an idea of the variety, visit any *botanica* (herb shop) on the peninsula and ask to see *yerbas indígenas.* Most likely your query will turn up the following herbs, plus a dozen others not mentioned below.

One of the most common plants in northern Baja is **Great Basin sagebrush,** named for the area of the western United States where it's a dominant species. In Baja it's called *chamizo blanco* and is found in chaparral and

cirio (JOE CUMMINGS)

damiana   (KAREN WHITE)

piñon-juniper zones throughout the foothills of the northern sierras. Despite its name, the bluish, evergreen shrub isn't a true sage but a member of the mayweed tribe. Like sage, however, its leaves are sometimes used by Mexican herbalists in medicinal teas.

True sages or *salvia* belong to the mint family and are readily identified by the savory aroma of their crushed leaves. **White sage** proliferates on rocky hillsides from southern Alta California to as far south as Punta Prieta near the turnoff for Bahía de los Angeles. The grayish-green shrub grows up to three meters tall, and between March and July it produces pale lavender flowers along its stalks. Several varieties of white sage are endemic to the peninsula and islands. A tea of sage will mitigate the symptoms of a sore throat; the crushed leaves are also used to flavor cooked meats.

The much sought-after ***chia*** is a species of sage that grows only in the desert areas of Baja, Sonora, and the southwestern United States. The plant produces sizable rose-colored flowers and inch-wide nutlets containing seeds valued for their wakefulness-inducing properties.

Another psychoactive plant found in Baja is *datura* or **Jimson weed** *(toloache* in Spanish). A member of the potato family, a group which also includes nightshade and tobacco, Jimson weed produces large, fragrant, trumpet-shaped flowers that open in the evening and close by noon the following day. According to one folk remedy, the flowers will relieve insomnia if placed beside the pillow at night. All parts of the plant are considered toxic; in certain Yaqui Indian ceremonies, the seeds are eaten for their hallucinatory effect. Datura grows in abundance on rocky and sandy soils below 800 meters (2,600 feet) throughout the peninsula and on some Sea of Cortez islands.

More docile but also widespread in dry, lower elevations is the **creosote bush** (Spanish: *gobernadora),* which is found in the deserts of northern Mexico, Utah, and Texas as well. This venerable shrub originated near the lower Colorado River and has been around at least 17,000 years, cloning itself in rings that widen with time. It's a fairly inconspicuous-looking plant, with sparse evergreen branches that reach a maximum height of about 3½ meters. The English name derives from the creosote-like odor (dubbed "the smell of the desert" by admirers) that the shrub exudes after a rainfall, caused by the reaction of rainwater with a varnish-like resin on the outer skin of the plant. In periods of drought this resin protects the plant from dehydration.

The indigenous peoples of Baja California and northern Mexico have known about gobernadora's medicinal properties for ages. A tea made from the leaves relieves indigestion, coughs, and colds; a root tea is used to treat ulcers and a root poultice to treat arthritis. Rancheros wash their feet in a root solution to prevent foot odor caused by wearing boots all day. Pharmacologists are now experimenting with several different chemical components of the plant that have been shown to possess analgesic, diuretic, antihistaminic, expectorant, and antibacterial properties.

The homely **oregano** plant belongs to the same botanic family (Verbenaceae) as the creosote bush. The crushed leaves of this herb are mainly used in Mexico as a flavoring for stews and tomato sauces; an oregano tea is also used by some women to relieve menstrual pain. The small evergreen shrub is found on Isla Magdalena and along the peninsula near Bahía Magdalena, on many Sea of Cortez islands, and along the Sonora/Sinaloa coast on the Mexican mainland.

Probably the most well-known herb native to Baja is *damiana (Turnera diffusa)*, a small shrub with bright, five-petaled yellow or golden flowers. The plant's aphrodisiac properties are its main claim to fame; these are often derided as nonsense by self-appointed Baja analysts. But according to botanist Norman C. Roberts, damiana "stimulates the genito-urinary tract and is used in the treatment of sexual problems such as impotence, frigidity, sterility, and sexual exhaustion." Other benefits ascribed to the herb include its use as a sedative and as a diuretic.

Damiana grows most commonly in rocky areas of the Cape Region but is also found as far away as Sonora, Texas, and the West Indies. The two most common ways of ingesting the herb are in a sweetened tea made from the leaves or in a liqueur containing damiana extract. In resort areas a "Baja margarita" is one in which damiana liqueur is substituted for triple sec.

WILDLIFE

Mammals
Of the hundred or so species of mammals found in Baja California, around 28 are endemic.

Carnivores: One of the most widespread carnivores on the peninsula as well as on some Sea of Cortez islands is the **coyote**, which seems to be able to adapt itself equally well to mountain, desert, and coastal terrains. Anyone venturing into the interior of the peninsula is virtually guaranteed to spot at least one—in some areas they don't seem particularly afraid of humans although they always keep a distance of at least 15 meters between themselves and larger mammals. Coyotes have been seen fishing for crab—they place their furry tails in the water and wait for a crab

to grab on, then with a flick of the tail toss the crab onto the beach, pounce on it before it has a chance to recover from the shock, and then enjoy a crab feast.

Much more rarely sighted is the **mountain lion** (also called cougar, panther, or puma), which, like all cats, is a mostly nocturnal animal. These beautiful creatures have been known to attack humans on occasion, so a degree of advance knowledge about their habits is called for if you plan to hike in the sierras.

First, if you avoid hiking at night, you're much less likely to encounter a lion. Secondly, wildlife experts advise that if you do encounter one, convince the lion that you are not prey and that you may be dangerous yourself. You can do this by not running from the animal (this is an invitation to chase), and by shouting, waving your hands, and, if the lion behaves aggressively, throwing stones at it. If you're carrying a backpack, raise it above your shoulders so that you appear larger to the lion. One or more of these actions is virtually guaranteed to frighten the lion away—if not, grab the biggest, heaviest stick you can find and fight it out to avoid becoming cat food.

Smaller, less intimidating carnivores commonly encountered in Baja include the **kit fox, gray fox, northern fox, ringtail, bobcat, linx, skunk, raccoon,** and **badger.** Although there haven't been any recent sightings, it is thought that the **gray wolf** may still exist in small numbers in the central sierras. Up until the middle of this century the gray wolf was fairly common in Baja, but farmers and ranchers have made an unfortunate tradition of killing them on sight.

Various seals and sea lions flourish along Baja's coasts, including two species, the **elephant seal** (or sea elephant) and the **Guadalupe fur seal,** that only in recent years have come back from the brink of extinction. Both are native to the volcanic Isla Guadalupe, and were heavily hunted in the 19th century, the elephant seal for its oil and the Guadalupe fur seal for its furry skin.

The elephant seal is the largest seal on the planet; males reach five meters (16 feet) or more and weigh up to two tons, while females are typically around three meters and about

(continued on p. 25)

GRAY WHALES

Physiology And Behavior

The *Eschrichtius robustus* or gray whale, often called the "California gray whale," reaches 10-15 meters (35-50 feet) in length at maturity (the average length is 13 meters for males, slightly longer for females) and weighs 20-40 tons. Its skin is almost black in color at birth but mottling caused by barnacles and barnacle scars imparts an overall gray tone to the portion of the animal exposed when it breathes, the rostrum (the area of the head that's a combination upper jaw and nose). Bite scars on flukes and flippers from orca (killer whale) attacks are common—at least 20% of all grays are attacked at one time or another. Most survive—juveniles are the most common fatalities.

Unlike many other whale species which feed on plankton, the gray whale feeds mainly on amphipods, small crustaceans that live on the ocean floor. To get at them, the gray dives to the bottom, scoops water and sand into its mouth cavity, and then expels the water through its baleen (a whalebone "sieve" in the mouth), filtering out the amphipods. In spite of an esophagus that's only about four inches wide, one whale can ingest up to a ton of food per day.

Although gray whales may engage in mating behavior at any point along their migration route, females only conceive while at the north end, in the vicinity of the Bering Strait, and give birth at or near the southern end, Baja's Pacific lagoons. In a remarkable display of tribal rhythm, 90% of all gray whale conceptions take place within three weeks of 5 December. The female grays give birth after a gestation period of about 13 months, by which time the whales have arrived at the lagoons or are well on their way.

The females usually calve in water that's 3-15 meters deep, which is remarkably shallow considering that newborn grays are four to five meters long and weigh up to 1½ tons. Following birth, the main activity is fattening up and exercising the newborns so that they'll be strong enough for the migration north. A female gray has recessed nipples on her underside, but the calf doesn't actually suck the milk from the mammaries like other mammals; instead the calf takes the nipple in its mouth and after a watertight seal has formed, the mother discharges a stream of milk into the calf's throat.

Since whale milk is about 800% richer in fat than human milk, the calves gain weight rapidly. By the time the return migration begins roughly three months after birth, the young whales average six meters (20 feet) and 2½ tons.

Migration

At one time the gray whale swam the Atlantic Ocean, Baltic Sea, and North Sea as well as the Pacific, but it was decimated by Dutch, British, and American whalers in the North Atlantic by the beginning of the 19th century and now survives only in the Arctic-Pacific corridor. Currently numbering around 21,000, the grays spend their summers feeding in the Bering, Chukchi, and Beaufort seas in the vicinity of Alaska and Siberia, where the long Arctic days result in highly productive marine growth.

The gray's primary feeding grounds are in the Chirikof Basin, where they begin their annual

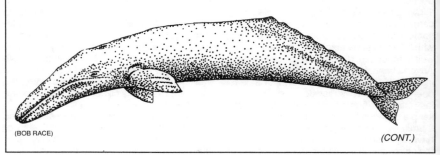

(BOB RACE)

(CONT.)

GRAY WHALES (CONT.)

migration south in mid-to-late fall. Swimming at an average four knots, the whales cover the 9,600-km (6,000-mile) journey to the southern Baja lagoons in about two months. Traveling in pods of three to four whales, they typically rest for a few hours each night. (When there's a full moon, they swim all night.)

On their way southward the grays follow the North American shoreline closely, taking the outside coast of major islands. By early January they begin arriving at protected bays and lagoons on the Pacific side of Baja, primarily Laguna Ojo de Liebre, Laguna San Ignacio, and Bahía Magdalena. (The grays used to winter farther north in Alta California's San Diego Bay, but heavy sea traffic has forced them to stay south.)

During the gray's winter sojourn in Baja, the females calve and nurse their young in the interiors of the lagoons, while the males tend to loiter at or near the lagoon entrances. Since female grays are fertile every other year, each available female (those not calving or nursing) has an average of two suitors at the lagoon entries at any given time. When they're not actively mating, the males seem content to watch their rivals coupling or else they seek out other females—fighting for access to a female is not a known whale behavior.

Calving season extends from Dec. to April, but because of individual differences in pacing, some whales begin migrating north as early as February while some may linger in the lagoons as late as June. The entire 19,300-km (12,000-mile) migration, the longest of any mammal on the planet (the humpback whale's Arctic-to-Hawaii migration ranks second), occurs within a period of seven to eight months. Apparently, adult whales don't eat during this entire interval.

The Rise And Fall Of Pacific Whaling

The Indians of Alta and Baja California as well as the Eskimos of Alaska were know to hunt whales for tribal consumption. But whaling as an industry didn't begin along the Pacific coast until the 19th century, when American whaleboats from New England and Hawaii began cruising Pacific waters in significant numbers. At first gray whales were for the most part left alone; because they're fiercely defensive when under attack, the grays are very difficult to kill using traditional harpooning techniques and they would often destroy attacking whaleboats.

The gray's destiny was altered in 1857, however, when Boston whaler Charles Melville Scammon followed a pod into Baja's Laguna Ojo de Liebre. Taking advantage of the local geography, Scammon figured out how to bomb the trapped whales with explosive harpoons while his whaleboats remained safely anchored in the shallows where larger whales couldn't reach them. Scores of whalers followed his example, and within less than 20 years following his discovery, an estimated 10,000 gray whales had been killed.

The slaughter quickened in the 20th century with the introduction of factory boats, which meant that the whales could be processed on site. By the 1930s the estimated number of grays was down to 250 from a pre-1850s population of 25,000. International fishing agreements signed in 1937 and 1946 forbade the killing of gray whales, but American whalers didn't comply until the U.S. government enacted the Marine Mammal Protection Act of 1972, by which time the gray whale was thought to be extinct. Their remarkable comeback as a species over the last 20 years has been one of the greatest successes of the environmental movement.

Whalewatching

The main reason the gray whale is a common target of whalewatching expeditions is that it has the greatest affinity for land and is therefore among the more accessible of large whale species. Other whale species tend to frequent deeper parts of the ocean, while the gray swims mostly in coastal shallows and seeks out lagoons for calving. Also, because it's a bottom feeder, the gray tolerates areas so shallow that its abdomen can rest on the sea bottom, a feat no other large whale can accomplish—most whales would suffocate in such a position. This means large grays can often be seen very close to shore.

A visit to one of the gray's calving lagoons can be exciting. Sometimes whales seem to be everywhere you look—"spouting" (clearing their

(CONT.)

GRAY WHALES (CONT.)

blowholes with pneumatic blasts that send vapor spumes high into the air), "breaching" (leaping out of the sea and arching through the air), "spyhopping" (poking their heads, eyes, and mouths vertically out of the water, possibly for a peek at the nonaquatic world), "tail lobbing" (slapping their flukes on the water surface), or just floating by asleep on the tide. At other times the whales are relatively inactive—choppy water seems to occasion more activity.

Grays can be spotted almost anywhere along Baja's peninsula coast, from Punta Banda near Ensenada right around to the Sea of Cortez, but the best place to see them up close and in large numbers is in one of three protected bays in Baja California Sur: Laguna Ojo de Liebre (Scammon's Lagoon) near Guerrero Negro; Laguna San Ignacio, southwest of San Ignacio; and Bahía Magdalena (or adjacent Bahía Almejas), southwest of Ciudad Constitución. Of these three areas, Laguna San Ignacio seems to attract the greatest number of "friendlies," gray whales that actively approach whalewatching boats for human contact.

Although whales can be seen fairly easily in Baja waters from the beginning of January through the end of March, February is the month when they're generally present in greatest numbers. At any given lagoon, whales can be viewed from three vantage points: shore, air, or water. Viewing them from shore can be frustrating since even the closest whales are usually at least 100 meters or more distant; also, since the closest whales usually are in the shallowest water, they're less likely to perform their most exciting maneuvers like spyhopping or breaching. From the air, distance is also a problem since you can't approach too closely without endangering the whale's life as well as the lives of those in the plane—and, of course, to consider whalewatching from the air you must either own a small plane, know someone who does, or charter one.

The optimum place to experience the world of the gray whale, then, is from the water. Any boat entering an area where whales are protected (including in all three of the bays mentioned above) during the calving season must have a special whalewatching permit issued by the Mexi-

can government on a year-to-year basis. Ordinarily only boat-owners with registered whalewatching concessions and academic researchers from approved institutions are issued these permits.

The least expensive whalewatching trips are those you arrange on your own from the shores of the aforementioned lagoons. During the season, licensed Mexican boatmen install themselves and their pangas at approved launching points in each lagoon; all you have to do is drive out to one of these points, park your vehicle, and pay the going price—which varies with the distance the boats must go to reach the whales and the number of hours they stay out.

In Guerrero Negro and San Ignacio, a couple of local hotels can arrange trips that include roundtrip ground transport to the lagoons—prices are usually quite reasonable since they're based on group sign-ups. Next up in price are the trips arranged in major tourist towns like Ensenada, Mulegé, Loreto, and Cabo San Lucas. The problem with locally hired whalewatching tours is that the guides are often not very knowledgeable about the whales or can't speak enough English to communicate their knowledge to non-Spanish-speakers.

Some whalewatchers prefer the convenience and expertise of whalewatching cruises sponsored by scientific or environmental organizations. This sort of trip costs a great deal more than arranging it on your own, but you'll have the advantage of having every contingency planned in advance and will be able enjoy the ongoing commentaries of experienced naturalists. Three well-established organizations in the U.S. that operate Baja whalewatching expeditions are:

Baja Expeditions
P.O Box 3725
San Diego, CA 92103
tel. (619) 297-0506

Biological Journeys
1696 Ocean Dr.
McKinleyville, CA 95521
tel. (800) 548-7555 (outside CA)
(707) 839-0178 (in CA)

(CONT.)

GRAY WHALES (CONT.)

Oceanic Society Expeditions
    Fort Mason Center, Bldg. E
    San Francisco, CA 94123
    tel. (415) 441-1106

Sven-Olof Lindblad's Special Expeditions
    720 Fifth Ave.
    New York, NY 10019
    tel. (800) 762-0003 (outside New York)
    (212) 765-7740 (in New York)

    Biological Journeys, Oceanic Society Expeditions, and Special Expeditions also operate programs in the Sea of Cortez that focus on other marine mammals, including dolphins as well as humpback, fin, and blue whales.

    Footnote: Charles Melville Scammon, the New England whaler whose understanding of the gray whale's habits led to their near extinction, became a naturalist of some note during the latter part of his career. His book *The Marine Mammals of the Northwestern Coast of North America* is considered a classic of amateur zoology and remains one of the most important reference works on whales and the whaling industry.

---

half a ton. The male's thick, flexible proboscis resembles a bobbed elephant's trunk. To scare off rivals in breeding season (Dec.-Feb.), the male places the tip of his trunk into his mouth and blows, producing a roaring snort. If the rival doesn't flee, a bloody fight ensues until one bull surrenders.

When the seal-hunting era began in the early 19th century, the elephant seal's range extended all the way north to Alta California's Point Reyes, near San Francisco. By 1911 seal-hunters had wiped out all the elephant seals once living in Alta California's waters and reduced the elephant's numbers on Isla Guadalupe to 125. After the Mexican government enacted a ban on seal-hunting in 1922, the seals began repopulating Isla Guadalupe and nearby islands. The current population is estimated to be around 15,000, most of which live on Pacific islands of Baja California; the elephant seal is gradually working its way back up the Alta California coast as well.

The smaller Guadalupe fur seal has had a more difficult time recovering from the seal-hunting era. It was believed to be extinct by the end of the 1800s but in 1926 a small herd of around 60 living on Isla Guadalupe was discovered by American angler William Clover. Clover captured a pair of the seals and sold them to the San Diego Zoo, but following a quarrel with the zoo's director, he returned to the island and attempted to kill and skin the entire remaining population. After selling the skins in Panama he met his just demise in a barroom brawl. Fortunately he missed some of the seals in his massacre and the current population on the island is estimated at around 500.

Artiodactyls: This order encompasses all creatures with split hooves, including deer, sheep, pigs, and cattle. One of the largest of these beasts still roaming wild in Baja is the **mule deer,** of which there is an endemic peninsular variety. Mule deer are most commonly seen on mountain slopes below 1,500 meters. A lesser number of **white-tail deer** is usually found above this elevation. Deer are a popular source of meat for ranchers living in the sierras; they also use deerskin to make soft, homemade boots called *teguas.*

At one time herds of **desert bighorn sheep** *(borrego)* lived throughout the peninsular deserts, but big-game hunting in the '20s and '30s reduced their numbers to a few small groups now living in remote areas of the Central Desert. The Mexican government still allows an occasional bighorn hunt for the handful of wealthy hunters who can afford a US$12,000 special permit. The elegant **pronghorn antelope** *(berrendo)* is also an endangered species—less than a hundred are still hanging on in the Vizcaíno Desert and they are now under the official protection of the Mexican government.

In the central Baja sierras are a smattering of wild horses and many wild cattle. Every five years or so local vaqueros gather in the El Arco area to round up wild, unbranded cattle.

Rabbits: At least four varieties of rabbit are hopping around in Baja, the **brush rabbit, desert cottontail, black-tailed jackrabbit,** and the rare, endemic **black jackrabbit.** Each is especially adapted to its particular habitat; the long, upright ears of the black-tailed jackrabbit, for example, enable it to hear sounds from quite a distance, a necessity for an animal that is prey for practically every larger animal (including coyotes, eagles, hawks, and bobcats) in the Cape Region. The more delicate ears of the desert cottontail act as radiators on hot desert days, allowing the rabbit to release excess body heat into the air.

The endemic black jackrabbit *(Lepus insularis)* is found only on Isla Espíritu Santo. Zoologists haven't been able to explain why the fur of this rabbit is mostly black, or why a cinnamon-red coloring occurs along the ears and underparts.

Rodents: The Californian Region and sierras of Baja support a wide variety of common and not-so-common rodents—the **white-tailed antelope squirrel, marsh rice rat, Botta's pocket gopher,** and **piñon mouse** to name a few—but what may be a surprise to some travelers is how many varieties manage to survive in the desert lands. Among these are the **little desert pocket mouse, cactus mouse, desert wood rat,** and five endemic species of **kangaroo rat.**

The kangaroo rat, which you may see hopping in front of your headlights at night (its long tail acts as a powerful spring), is built so that it doesn't need to drink water, ever. It derives moisture from seeds that it eats, from the air deep inside its burrows where the relative humidity is 30-50%, and from condensation in its nasal passages (its nostrils are much cooler than the rest of its body). Its efficient kidneys excrete uric acid in a concentrated paste, rather than in liquid form. Because its body is so full of moisture, it is an especially prized quarry for larger desert mammals and birds of prey. Backcountry rancheros occasionally trap them for fiesta food.

Cetaceans: The protected lagoons of Baja California's Pacific coast and the warm waters of the Sea of Cortez were practically made for whales and dolphins. Twenty-five species of cetaceans frequent Baja seas, from the **blue whale,** the largest mammal on the earth, to the **common dolphin** *(Delphinus delphis),* which is sometimes seen in the Sea of Cortez in pods as large as 10,000.

Whale species known to visit Baja or make it their year-round habitat include **Minke, fin, Sei, Bryde's, humpbacked, gray, goose-beaked, sperm, dwarf sperm, false killer, killer,** and **pilot.** Commonly seen dolphins are the **Pacific white-sided, bottle-nosed, spotted, Risso's, spinner,** and **striped.** The *vaquita,* a rare type of harbor porpoise, is endemic to the northern Sea of Cortez.

The marine mammal usually of most interest to Baja travelers is the **gray whale,** which migrates some 19,300 km (12,000 miles) a year between its feeding grounds above the Arctic Circle and its calving grounds in the Pacific lagoons of southern Baja California. The gray is the easiest of the whales to view since it frequents shallow coastal waters. For details on whalewatching and on the gray itself, see "Gray Whales" on p. 220.

Fishes

The seas surrounding Baja California on three sides contain a truly amazing variety of marinelife. In the Sea of Cortez alone, around 800 varieties of fish have been identified. Marine biologists estimate there to be a total of around 3,000 species (including invertebrates) between the Golfo de Santa Clara at the north end of the sea and the southern tip of Cabo San Lucas, which would make it the richest sea (or gulf, depending on your definition) in the world. The wide spectrum of aquatic environments along both coasts is largely responsible for this abundance and has led to Baja's reputation as a mecca for fishing and diving enthusiasts (see "Sports and Recreation," p. 66 and p. 79 respectively), and for *mariscos* aficionados (see "Food and Drink," p. 95).

About 90% of all known Baja fish varieties can be found close to the shores of the peninsula or its satellite islands. The Midriff Islands area in the center of the Sea of Cortez is especially rich in life—tidal surges aerate the water and stir up nutrients, supporting a thick food chain from plankton to fish and birds to sea lions. The Cortez, in fact, has acted as a giant fish trap that has collected an assortment of marine species over thousands of years from the nearby Pacific, the more distant equatorial zones of South America, and even the Caribbean (through a now-extinct water link that once existed between the two seas).

The information below represents only a brief overview of the many fishes of common, everyday interest to Baja visitors and residents in contact with the aquatic world.

Billfish: Baja is known as the world capital for sailfish and marlin fishing; just about every serious saltwater angler eventually considers a pilgrimage to La Paz or Cabo San Lucas to test his or her mettle. Six billfish species exist here in some numbers: **swordfish, sailfish,** and **striped, blue,** and **black marlin.** All are strong fighters, though the sailfish and striped marlin are generally the most "acrobatic." Billfish occur in a wide range of offshore Pacific and Sea of Cortez waters south of Bahía Magdalena and the Midriff Islands, although the swordfish is found mostly on the Pacific side.

Corvinas and Croakers: About 30 species in Baja belong to this group of small- to medium-size fish that make croaking sounds. Among the largest is the **totuava,** formerly one of the most famous game fishes in the upper Sea of Cortez. Over-fishing has led to a scarcity of these silvery 35- to 250-pounders and it's now illegal to take or possess them in Mexico. The totuava is reportedly one of best-tasting of all game fish; others in this category, found inshore to onshore in a variety of coastal waters, include **white seabass, Gulf corvina, yellowfin croaker, orangemouth corvina, spotfin croaker,** and **California corvina.**

Jack: Popular jacks include **yellowtail** (one of the most popular fishes for use in *tacos de pescado),* **Pacific amberjack,** various **pompanos, jack crevalle,** and the strong-fighting **roosterfish,** named for its tall dorsal "comb." These jacks are most prevalent in inshore to onshore areas in the Sea of Cortez and in the Pacific south of Magdalena.

Dorado, Mackerel, and Tuna: Among the more sought-after of the food fishes, found offshore to inshore throughout parts of both seas, are the **dorado** (sometimes called "dolphinfish"—though it isn't related to mammalian dolphins or porpoises—or by its Hawaiian name *mahi mahi),* **sierra** (especially good in *ceviche* or marinated seafood salad), the knife-shaped **wahoo** (one of the fastest of all fishes, reaching speeds of 50 knots), **Pacific bonito,** and three kinds of tuna—the **bluefin, albacore,** and highly prized **yellowfin.** Yellowfins can reach up to 180 kilograms (400 pounds) and are one of the best tasting of all tunas.

Bass: Sea bass are basically an inshore fish; different species dominate different Baja waters and very commonly find their way into Mexican seafood restaurants. In Spanish, the larger ones are generally called *garropa* (groupers), the smaller *cabrilla.* Popular finds are the **leopard grouper** (Sea of Cortez near San Felipe), **Gulf grouper** (up to 90 kilograms/200 pounds, San Felipe to the Midriff Islands), **giant sea bass,** (San Quintín round to above the Midriff Islands), **spotted cabrilla** (Isla Cedros round to upper Sea of Cortez), **flag cabrilla** (lower Sea of Cortez), **kelp bass** (northwest Pacific coast), and **spotted sand bass** (Pacific coast north of Magdalena, upper Sea of Cortez).

Bottomfish: These smaller bottom-feeding fishes (13 kilograms or less) favor the inshore Pacific above Magdalena and include the **lingcod, sculpin,** and **rockfish.**

Surf Fish: Most of the 25 or so species weigh less than two kilograms and are found along the Pacific coast since there's no surf to speak of in the Sea of Cortez. Popular catches among gringos (this isn't a popular category among Mexican anglers) are the **barred surfperch, rubberlip surfperch,** and **sargo.** The sargo also frequents the upper Sea of Cortez coast.

Flatfish: These include flounder and halibut, usually called *lenguado* in Spanish. The most common variety found on the Pacific side is the **California halibut,** on the other side it's the **Cortez halibut.** Both are good eating and often used for *tacos de pescado* in tourist areas.

Snapper: Generally found south of Magdalena and round the Cape as far north as the upper Sea of Cortez, the locally popular snappers include **red snapper, yellow snapper, barred pargo,** and **dog snapper.** All snappers are called *pargo* in Spanish, except for the red snapper, which is *huachinango*. All are common food fish.

Sharks and Rays: Although over 60 species of sharks are found in Baja waters, some are rather rare while most stay clear of humans. The more common species are found offshore to inshore from Magdalena to the Midriff, including the **smooth hammerhead, common thresher, bonito, sand, blue, blacktip,** and the world's largest fish (reaching up to 18 meters and 3,600 kilograms), the **whale shark.** Shark-fishing is an important activity in Baja, supplying much of the seafood eaten locally. Hammerhead, thresher, bonito (mako), and leopard shark filets are all very tasty (see "Sharks: Myth vs. Fact," p. 78 for more information).

Rays are quite common in warmer offshore to inshore waters throughout Baja. Many varieties have barbed tail-spines that can inflict a painful wound when the ray feels threatened.

manta ray

(KAREN WHITE)

(Contrary to myth the barb is not actually venomous, although a ray "sting" easily becomes infected.) Experienced beachgoers know to perform the "stingray shuffle" when walking on sandy bottoms. If you bump into a ray resting on the bottom, it will usually swim away; if you step on one, it's likely to give you a flick of the barb. Common smaller rays found inshore include the **butterfly ray** and the aptly named **shovelnose guitarfish,** a ray with thick tail and flat head.

Two species of rays are sometimes called "devilfish" because of their horn-like pectoral fins: the **mobula** and the huge **Pacific manta ray.** The Pacific manta has a "wingspan" of up to seven meters (23 feet) across and can weigh nearly two tons. Another fairly large ray, the **bat ray,** is sometimes confused with the manta but it doesn't have the characteristic pectoral fins of the latter. A friendly manta will allow scuba divers to hitch rides by hanging on to the base of the pectorals.

Elongated Fishes: These varieties have long, slender bodies and beak-like jaws in common. The sharp-toothed **California barracuda** swims in the Pacific from the border down to Cabo San Lucas while a smaller, more edible variety is found in the Sea of Cortez. In spite of their somewhat frightful appearance, barracudas rarely attack humans.

The silvery **flying fish** can be seen leaping above offshore waters throughout the Pacific and the lower Sea of Cortez. It is not generally considered a food fish. The most edible of the elongated fishes is probably the acrobatic **Mexican needlefish,** or *agujon,* which reaches two meters in length and has green bones!

Shellfishes: Baja's shores abound with deep-water and shallow-water shellfish species, including multiple varieties of **clams, oysters, mussels, scallops,** and **shrimp,** many of which have disappeared from coastal Alta California to the north. But Baja's most famous shellfish is undoubtedly the **spiny lobster,** which appears on virtually every *mariscos* menu on the peninsula.

Challenges to the Marine Environment: One of the major problems facing Baja's fisheries is illegal fishing by unlicensed Japanese and Korean boats. Despite Mexico's ban on the netting of gamefish, many foreign vessels still use huge dredge nets to harvest marlin, swordfish, dorado, and other species legally reserved for sportfishing only, not to mention protected species such as porpoises and dolphins.

Novelist John Steinbeck, in his 1941 account of a scientific marine expedition into the Sea of Cortez accompanying marine biologist Ed Ricketts (inspiration for Steinbeck's novel *Cannery Row)*, described how he watched six Japanese shrimpers—weighing at least 600 tons each—purse-dredge the sea bottom, killing hundreds of tons of fish that were merely discarded after each dredging. One of his reactions: "Why the Mexican government should have permitted the complete destruction of a valuable food supply is one of those mysteries which have their ramifications possibly back in pockets it is not well to look into."

With government corruption apparently on the wane, Mexico is taking steps to curtail many of the commercial enterprises on the Sea of Cortez; expanding budgets mean it should become easier to enforce new regulations. One can only hope that intervention is soon enough and strong enough to preserve Mexico's great marine resources.

Birds

Hosting around 300 known species of birdlife, the peninsula and islands of Baja California are one of the most concentrated and undisturbed aviary habitats in North America. Ornithological research focused on Baja, however, is rather difficult to come by as well as incomplete; one of the most up-to-date references available is Peterson and Chalif's *A Field Guide to Mexican Birds,* last published in 1973.

Although numerous varieties thrive in the desert lands, the vast majority of Baja's native and migrating species are either coastal or open-sea (pelagic) birds. The Sea of Cortez islands are particularly rich in birdlife; the Mexican government has designated 49 of the Midriff Islands as wildlife refuges to protect the many rare and endangered species here. The most famous of these islands among birders

is Isla San Pedro Mártir, home to the rare and clownish **blue-footed booby** and its more common cousins the **brown booby** and the **masked booby.**

Isla de Raza, tiny guano-covered Midriff island of only 250 acres, is another birding mecca. Every April this island is the site of territorial "wars" between **Heermann's gulls,** and **elegant terns** (see "Bahía de los Angeles," p. 247).

Common throughout the coastal areas of southern Baja is the **magnificent frigate,** called *tijera* (scissors) in Mexico because of its scissor-shaped tail. In spite of their seafood diet, frigates can't swim or even submerge their heads to catch fish—instead they glide high in the air on boomerang-shaped wings, swooping down to steal fish from other birds (especially slow-witted boobies).

Among the more commonly seen birds along the Sea of Cortez coast is the **brown pelican,** which in global terms is not so common. The pelican species go back 30 million years; paleontologists use the modern pelican as a model for creating visual representations of the pteranodon, an extinct flying reptile with an eight-meter wingspan. Brown pelicans, the only truly marine species among the world's seven pelican species, dive 10-30 meters (30-100 feet) under water to catch fish. Other pelicans only dip their beaks beneath the surface (and they tend to frequent inland waterways rather than marine habitats). Browns have disappeared entirely from the U.S. shores of the Gulf of Mexico, and are almost gone from the coastal islands of Alta California—apparently due to the pesticide content of the Pacific Ocean. Baja's Cortez and Pacific coasts are among the last habitats where the brown pelican thrives.

Another rather special bird along the coast is the **fisher eagle,** which, as its name implies, catches and eats fish. The fisher eagle is also occasionally seen along freshwater rivers and around the Pacific lagoons.

Other coastal birds of note are two species of **cormorant,** the **long-billed curlew,** four species of **egret,** four species of **grebe,** 10 species of **gull,** three species of **heron,** the **belted kingbird,** two species of **ibis,** three

THE BURRO

Long-eared, slow-plodding, dim-witted, the quintessential beast of burden: this is the city person's image of *Equus asinus*. But to rural Mexicans the donkey, or burro, is an image of strength and sure-footedness. Compared to its taller, more graceful-appearing cousin the horse, the burro is a far more useful animal in mountainous or arid domains. On slopes, rocky surfaces, and sand it moves with more agility and is able to keep a load—whether human or inanimate—more balanced. Standing only about a meter high at the shoulder, burros can also cover greater distances than horses on less water and food; they actually seem to prefer rough forage such as dead cactus or thorny palo verde over nutrient-rich (and scarce, in Baja) grasses.

Although a burro's coloring may vary from light to dark brown, its withers are almost always marked with a cross of darker hair. Mexican mythology says this cross is a symbol of divine protection for having carried Mary and the infant Christ from Egypt to the Holy Land. Amid Baja's desert palms, a burro certainly takes on a biblical aura.

An unknown number of wild burros roams the interior of the peninsula, particularly in the area between the Sierra la Asamblea and Sierra San Borja. Ranchers or *campesinos* will occasionally capture a wild burro for domestic use as they are fairly easy to tame. (The burro's legendary stubbornness can often be attributed to mistreatment by its owner; a well cared for animal is usually quite loyal.) The wild male burro, or "jack," is considered to be the best stud for producing a mule, so ranchers occasionally turn mares loose to breed with them. Mules produced from such a union are especially hardy.

(BOB RACE)

Mountain trekkers occasionally hire burros or mules as pack animals in Baja's sierras. For long forays, it is sometimes cheaper to purchase one rather than pay a daily hire rate; purchase prices range from around US$40 for a poor animal to around US$75 for an exemplary one—if you can find a rancher willing to sell one. If the price doesn't include a *burriqueta,* a saddle-like wooden frame for carrying cargo, you'll have to buy one or have one made—they're quite inexpensive. If possible, have a veterinarian inspect the animal for diseases before agreeing on a purchase.

species of **loon,** the **osprey,** the **American oystercatcher,** six species of **plover,** six species of **sandpiper,** the **tundra swan,** and seven species of **tern.**

Certain fish-eating birds are usually seen only by boaters since they tend to swim over open ocean. These pelagics include two species of **albatross,** the **black-legged kitti-**wake, the **red phalarope,** three species of **shearwater,** the **surf scoter,** the **south polar skua,** five species of **storm petrel,** the **black tern,** and the **red-billed tropicbird.**

Another type of waterfowl in Baja frequents only freshwater ponds, *tinajas* (springs), lakes, streams, and marshes, among them two species of **bittern,** the **American coot,** two species of **duck,** the **snow goose,** the **northern harrier,** six species of **heron,** the **white-faced ibis,** the **common moorhen,** two species of **rail,** five species of **sandpiper,** the **lesser scaup,** the **shoveler,** the **common snipe,** the **sora,** the **roseate spoonbill,** the **wood stork,** three species of **teal,** the **northern waterthrush,** and the **American wigeon.** Some of these birds are native, others are only winter residents.

In Baja's sierras you may find the **golden eagle,** the **western flycatcher,** the **lesser goldfinch,** the **black-headed grosbeak,** the **red-tailed hawk,** two species of **hummingbird,** the **pheasant,** the **yellow-eyed junco,** the **white-breasted nuthatch,** the **mountain plover,** four species of **vireo,** eight species of **warbler,** the **acorn woodpecker,** and the **canyon wren.**

Common over desert and/or open country are three species of **falcon** (peregrine, prairie, and Cooper's), three species of **flycatcher,** six species of **hawk,** the **black-fronted hummingbird,** the **American kestrel,** the **merlin,** two species of **owl,** the **greater roadrunner,** eight species of **sparrow,** two species of **thrasher,** the **vernon,** the **turkey vulture,** the **ladder-backed woodpecker,** and the **cactus wren.**

Reptiles And Amphibians

Among the slippery, slimy, scaly, crawly things that live in Baja California are around 30 species of lizards (including two endemics), five species of frogs and toads (none endemic), six turtles, and around 35 different kinds of snakes (one endemic).

Lizards: Four-legged reptilians of note include the **chuckwalla,** which is found on certain islands in the Sea of Cortez and grows up to nearly a meter long. The chuckwalla drinks freshwater when available, storing it in sacs that gurgle when it walks; when a freshwater source is not available, the lizard embibes saltwater, which it is able to process through a sort of internal desalinator. Another good-sized lizard in Baja is the **desert iguana,** found throughout the Gulf Coast Desert and possibly farther north. The larger iguanas are sometimes eaten in ranchero stews and are said to taste better than chicken. The **coast**

horned lizard, similar to the "horny toad" of the American Southwest, is another Baja endemic.

Turtles: Of the six turtle varieties known to Baja, five are sea turtles: the **leatherback, green, hawksbill, western Ridley,** and **loggerhead.** Because their eggs, meat, and shells are highly valued among coastal Mexican populations, all of these turtles are on the endangered species list. The Mexican government has declared turtle-hunting and turtle egg-collecting illegal; the decimation of the turtles has slowed but it hasn't yet been stopped. Bajacalifornios say they're upholding the laws but that fishermen along the mainland coast of the Sea of Cortez are still taking sea turtles.

The main culprit has apparently been Japan, which is the world's largest importer of sea turtles including the endangered Ridley and hawksbill (both of which the Japanese use for meat, turtle leather, and turtle-shell fashion accessories). In 1991 the Japanese government announced a ban on the importation of sea turtles, so perhaps the Sea of Cortez populations will soon be making a comeback.

Snakes: The rocky desert lands and chaparrals of Baja seem like perfect snake country. The bad news is that about half of the known species are venomous; the good news is that they rarely come into contact with humans. Scorpion bites, in fact, far outnumber the incidents of snakebite in Baja. Harmless species include the **western blind snake,** the **rosy boa,** the **Baja California rat snake,** the **spotted leaf-nosed snake,** the **western patch-nosed snake,** the **bullsnake,** the **coachwhip,** the **kingsnake,** the **Baja sand snake,** and the **California lyre snake.**

The venomous kinds fall into two categories, one of which contains only a single snake species, the **yellow-bellied sea snake.** Sea snakes usually flee the vicinity when they sense human presence—as a general precaution, don't grab anything in the water that looks like a floating stick (that's how sea snakes deceive their prey).

As for rattlesnakes, there are supposedly 18 species known in Baja, the most common of which is the near-endemic **Baja California rattler** *(Crotalus enyo),* whose range includes the lower three-fourths of the peninsula—look for scaly mounds over the eyes if you care to make an identification. The **red diamondback** *(Crotalus ruber)* frequents the northern deserts and chaparral and is also fairly common. The most dangerous of the rattlers in Baja is the **Western diamondback,** simply because it's the largest and therefore has the most potential to deliver fatal or near-fatal doses of venom. The diamondback is mostly confined to the canyons of the northern sierras. All of the other rattlesnakes in Baja are more of a nuisance than an actual threat to your continuing existence since they overwhelmingly tend toward the injection of non-fatal doses of venom. For Graham Mackintosh, the Briton who hiked almost the entire perimeter of the Baja peninsula (and wrote a book about his experiences, *Into A Desert Place),* rattlesnake became a welcome part of his desert diet.

The only rattler fully endemic to Baja is also the strangest. The **rattleless rattlesnake** *(Crotalus catalinensis)* was first discovered in 1952 on Isla Santa Catalina, a small mountainous Sea of Cortez island south of Loreto. Fortunately Santa Catalina is the only habitat for this snake, whose lack of a warning signal might otherwise keep most of us away from the peninsular deserts forever.

The general all-inclusive Spanish term for snake is *serpiente;* a nonvenomous snake is referred to as *culebra,* the venomous kind is a *vípera.* A rattlesnake is *un serpiente de cascabel* or simply *un cascabel.* For tips on how to avoid snakebite, see "Snakebite Prevention and Treatment," p. 110. An encouraging factoid: According to Spanish records, no missionary ever died of snakebite during the 300-year period of Spanish colonization of the New World.

HISTORY

PRE-COLUMBIAN HISTORY

Because Baja California lacks spectacular archaeological remains such as those of the Mayan and Aztec cultures in the southern reaches of mainland Mexico, it has largely been ignored by archaeologists. It is highly likely, however, that the Baja California peninsula was inhabited by human populations well before the rest of Mexico, since it was the logical termination for the coastal migration route followed by Asian groups who crossed the Bering Strait land bridge between Asia and North America beginning around 50,000 B.C.

San Dieguito And La Jolla Cultures

The earliest known Baja inhabitants were members of the San Dieguito culture who migrated southward into northern Baja approximately 7,000 years ago. (Evidence of their presence in Alta California, however, dates back 9,000 years.) The San Dieguito people spent much of the year wandering in small migratory bands of 15-20, guided by freshwater sources and the availability of game. Their simple economy was based on hunting, fishing, and the gathering of edible wild plants. Archaeological remains include circles of stones, stone tools—choppers, raspers, knives, spear points, axe heads, mortars (*metates*)—and simple pottery.

Evidence suggests that the San Dieguitos coexisted, at least for a time, with the Jollanos (or the La Jolla Culture), about whom little is known except that they lived by gathering fish and shellfish, seeds, roots, and wild vegetables. If so, their northern Baja peregrinations must have intersected and there may have been cultural interaction between the two groups.

The Yumanos

The San Dieguito culture either developed into or was superseded by that of the Yumanos, whose archaeological signature (rock paintings, petroglyphs) indicates their presence on the peninsula around 2,500 years ago. The Yumanos made use of more sophisticated hunting equipment as well as fishing nets; they also seem to have developed ceramics well before their counterparts in the American Southwest. Upon the arrival of Spanish in the 16th century A.D., some Yumano groups were practicing cultivation in the Río Colorado floodplains of northern Baja, including the Cucapá, Tipai, Paipai (or Pa'ipai), Kumyai, and Kiliwa.

Like many of the less aggressive Indian groups throughout Mexico and Mesoamerica, the Yumano tribes didn't last very long under the influences of missionization—those who weren't killed by European-borne diseases or executed for rebelling against the padres were assimilated. All that is left of the Yumano culture today are scattered galleries of petroglyphs and rock paintings found throughout northern Baja.

A Yumano rock painting near La Rumorosa indicates they must have had a rudimentary knowledge of astronomy as it depicts a winter solstice celebration. One of the figures in the painting, a 12-inch red human caricature that may represent a shaman, catches light only on 21 Dec. for about 20 minutes beginning at sunrise.

The Cochimís And Guaycuras

Indian groups living in the central and southern reaches of the peninsula when the Spanish arrived were apparently much less advanced technologically than the Yumanos. Because of the lack of archaeological research in these areas, the only record we have of these Indians is the one left us by Spanish accounts, which were undoubtedly biased in light of their purposes in subordinating the peoples of the New World. Mission histories are full of lurid tales of Indian customs, many of which were probably written with the intention of proving to the Spanish crown how desperately the natives needed missionizing. Nevertheless, the Indians of central and southern Baja appeared to be among the

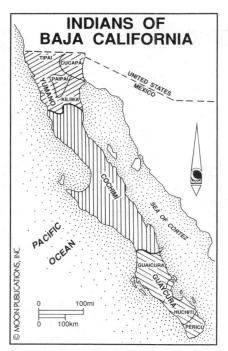

INDIANS OF BAJA CALIFORNIA

TIPAI
CUCAPA
PAIPAI
YUMANO
KILIWA
UNITED STATES
MEXICO
COCHIMI
SEA OF CORTEZ
PACIFIC OCEAN
GUAICURA
GUAYCURA
HUCHITI
PERICU
MOON

0   100mi
0   100km

© MOON PUBLICATIONS, INC.

woven grasses or twigs suspended from the front and animal skins in the back, which were sometimes painted with bright colors. The tips of their arrows and spears were generally of sharpened hardwood only, though chipped stone points were also occasionally used. A reed blowgun was also in use among the Guaycuras. The most important time of year among these Indians was when the fruit of the pitahaya cactus ripened; the fruit was so abundant during this season that the Indians allegedly abandoned all other activities save for sleeping and eating.

Neither the Guaycuras nor the Cochimís apparently left behind any artwork for posterity's sake. This has been attributed to the fact that because their living environment was so harsh, they had little time or energy to spare for artistic pursuits. However, in the inland areas of the peninsula inhabited by the Guaycura/Cochimí tribes are numerous rock-art sites. The Cochimís told the Spanish that this rock art was created by a race of giants who had preceded them. Almost nothing is known about this lost Indian culture whom Baja rock-art expert Harry Crosby has dubbed "The Painters" (see "The Prehistoric Murals of Baja California," p.262).

more "primitive" of the tribes encountered by the Spanish in Mexico or Mesoamerica—in modern archaeological terms, they hadn't progressed beyond the Paleolithic epoch.

According to these accounts, the Cochimís (central peninsula) and Guaycuras (Cape Region—includes the Pericú, Huchiti, and Gauicura tribes) spent most of their daylight hours searching for food; the men hunted small game or gathered shellfish while the women gathered fruit, seeds, and roots. If game was scarce, they subsisted on a variety of insects and would even eat dried animal skins, including (according to reports) the leather boots of the conquistadors.

The southern Indians generally lived in the open and sought shelter only in the severest of weather conditions. Men went naked "or nearly so," but the women wore leather or yucca-fiber thongs around the waist with

SPANISH CONQUEST OF MEXICO

Following 700 years of conflict with the Moors over control of the Iberian peninsula, Spain in the 15th century emerged as the most powerful nation in Europe. Convinced that a Roman Catholic God was destined to rule the world with Spain as His emissary, the Spanish monarchy sent Christopher Columbus in search of a new route to the Far East. His mission was to establish contact with a mythical "Great Khan" in order to develop an alternate trade route with the Orient, since Arabs controlled the overland route through the Middle East. Along the way as many pagans as possible were to be converted to Christianity. Once the Arab trade monopoly was broken, the Holy Land would be returned to Christian control.

Columbus's landing in the West Indies in 1492 was followed by Pope Alexander VI's historic 1493 decree which gave the Spanish rights to any new land discovered west of the Azores, as long as the Spanish made "God's name known there." Hence, the Spanish conquest of the New World started as a roundabout extension of the Holy Crusades.

Following a succession of Spanish expeditions into the Caribbean and Gulf of Mexico, the conquest of Mexico and Central America was rapidly achieved. Conquistador Hernán Cortés subdued the Valley of Mexico Aztecs in three years (1519-21) and the allegiance (or decimation) of other Aztecs and Mayans followed quickly.

Early California Explorations
When the Spanish conquistadors came to the western edge of mainland Mexico and looked beyond toward the landforms they could see above the sea in the distance, they concluded that Baja California was a huge island and that the as-yet-unnamed Sea of Cortez led to the Atlantic. (The idea of a "northwest passage" to the Atlantic persisted for years, even among seasoned Pacific explorers like Cabrillo, Drake, and Vizcaíno.) Cortés himself directed four voyages that targeted the island of La California from the mainland in 1532, 1533, 1535, and 1539—although he only actually accompanied the third. The history of these early expeditions exposes the enmity and extreme sense of competition among the conquistadors who were supposedly working toward a common cause.

The first voyage never made it to the peninsula as the ships were captured in the Sea of Cortez by Nuño Guzman, an arch-rival of Cortés operating farther north in Mexico. The second expedition, under Capt. Diego Becerra of the *Concepción,* suffered a mutiny in which the captain was killed. Basque pilot Fortún Jiménez took charge and the ship landed in Bahía de la Paz in early 1534. Thus the first European visitors to reach Baja California, a group of mutineers, arrived there just 42 years after Columbus touched down in the West Indies and nearly a century before the Pilgrims landed at Plymouth Rock.

Jiménez and 22 of his crew were killed by Indians while filling their water casks at a spring near the bay before they had a chance to explore much of the vicinity. The survivors managed to sail the *Concepción* back to the mainland, where most were promptly captured by Guzman. One of the escapees, however, managed to reach Cortés with tales of rich caches of pearls on a huge island with "cliffs and headlands and rocky coasts" as in the California of popular myth (see "What's in a Name?" below).

Cortés, inspired by these stories, organized and led a third expedition (partially financed by his own personal wealth) consisting of three ships and a group of 500 Spanish colonists that included women and children. The colonists landed at the northeast end of Bahía de la Paz (which Cortés named Santa Cruz) in May of 1535, the same year that New Spain was officially established. Although Cortés apparently found pearls in abundance, his attempt to colonize the peninsula lasted only two years, by which point disease, hostile Indians, and *chubascos* (tropical storms) had driven the colonists back to the mainland.

The fourth attempt by Cortés to establish a Spanish foothold on California soil was led by the highly competent Capt. Francisco de Ulloa, who had accompanied Cortés on the failed Santa Cruz expedition. Cortés stayed behind on this one, hoping that Ulloa's expedition would be able to find a more hospitable California beachhead. Ulloa's two ships (he started with three but abandoned the smallest shortly after departure) set sail from Acapulco in July 1539, and over the next eight months he managed to explore the entire perimeter of the Sea of Cortez, reaching the mouth of the Río Colorado and rounding the Cape along the Pacific coast as far north as Isla Cedros.

Upon reaching Isla Cedros, Ulloa is reported to have sent one ship back to Acapulco for supplies, but it isn't known for certain what happened to the other vessel. According to some historical accounts, Ulloa found his way back to the mainland and was murdered by one of his own crew near Guadalajara; other accounts simply say he disappeared north of Isla Cedros. At any rate, his written report of the voyage—which indicated that Baja was not an island but a peninsula—didn't surface

Manila galleon (BOB RACE)

until a hundred years later. His biggest contribution to the geography of the times was the naming of the Mar de Cortés, now the Sea of Cortez or Gulf of California.

After squandering most of his wealth in an attempt to explore Baja California with nothing to show for it, Cortés was recalled to Spain in 1541, never to return to Mexican shores. In his place, Spain dispatched experienced Portuguese navigator Juan Rodríguez Cabrillo to explore the Pacific coast in 1542. Starting from the southern tip of the peninsula, his expedition made it as far north as the Oregon coast and mapped several major bays along the way, including those of San Diego and Monterey. Cabrillo himself never made it past Alta California's Santa Barbara Islands, however, where he reportedly died following a mysterious fall.

Manila Galleons And Privateers

Meanwhile on the other side of the globe, events were unfolding that were to influence Baja California's history for the next 250 years. Although the Portuguese world-navigator Ferdinand Magellan had reached the Philippines (where he was killed) in 1521, it wasn't until

1565 that Lopez de Legaspi was able to defeat the archipelago's native defenders. Immediately thereafter, Esteban Rodríguez and Padre Andrés de Urdaneta pioneered a ship route from Manila to the New World that took advantage of the 14,500-km-long (9,000-mile-long) Japanese Current across the northern Pacific, thus establishing a trade connection between the Orient and New Spain.

The ships that made the annual roundtrip voyages between Manila and Acapulco beginning in 1566 came to be called "Manila galleons." The lengthy sea journey was very difficult, however, because of the lack of fresh water during the final weeks of the five-to seven-month eastward crossing. This provided further impetus for establishing some sort of settlement in lower California where the ships could put in for water and supplies.

A California landfall became even more desirable when in 1572 the Manila galleons started carrying shipments of gold, silks, and spices to New Spain—the ships were so heavy they became easy prey for faster pirate vessels. By 1580, England's Sir Francis Drake had entered the Pacific via the Straits of Magellan and circumnavigated the globe, thus ending Spanish dominion over the seas. Drake plundered Spanish ships with regularity (although he never boarded a Manila galleon), and as news of the treasure-laden ships spread, other English as well as Dutch privateers were lured into the Pacific.

Their raids on Spanish ships became an embarrassment to the crown and a drain on Spanish wealth, so the Spaniards were forced to seek out harbors along Baja's Cape Region where they could hide. Since the first land sighting on the east Pacific leg of the Manila-Acapulco voyage was below the peninsula's mid-point, the Cape Region was the logical choice for a landing. Following much experimentation, the two harbors that came to be most frequently used were at Bahía San Lucas and Bahía de la Paz.

Eventually, however, the keen privateers figured out how to trap Spanish ships in the very bays their crews sought for protection. Thomas Cavendish (the second Englishman to circumnavigate the globe) plundered the Manila galleon *Santa Ana* at Cabo San Lucas

WHAT'S IN A NAME?

The name "California," as applied to what was orginally thought to be an island northwest of Mexico, made its first appearance in the diary of a seaman on the 1539-40 Francisco de Ulloa expedition. The term began appearing on maps shortly thereafter but at the time its derivation was never explained. Until the late 18th century, there were two competing suppositions. One theory said that the oppressive heat of the peninsula led the Spanish to call it Calida Fornax, Latin for "hot furnace," and that "California" was a corrupted version of this phrase (but any historical linguist would barbecue this theory on a skewer). Another explanation claimed that it derived from a mixture of the Spanish *cala,* or "little bay," and the Latin *fornix,* meaning "arch," and that it was a reference to the arch at Bahía San Lucas. This didn't make much sense either since Bahía San Lucas wasn't a favored harbor in the early days of peninsular exploration.

The true origin of the word wasn't discovered until 1862 when Edward Everett Hale of New England came across the word in a four-part Spanish novel, *Las Sergas de Esplandián ("The Adventures of Esplandian"),* first published in 1500. In the fourth tale of this extremely popular 16th-century novel, the fictional California was:

> an island on the right hand of the Indies very near the terrestrial Paradise, peopled by black women among whom there was not a single man. They had beautiful, robust bodies, spirited courage and great strength. Their island was the most impregnable in the world with its cliffs and headlands and rocky coasts. Their weapons were all of gold . . . because in all the island there was no metal except gold.

In the tale the warrior women are known as Amazons (a name later bestowed upon South America's most famous river) and the island's name is a compound of Califia, their queen (from the Greek *kalli,* "beautiful"), and *ornix,* the Greek word for "bird"—a reference to the 500 griffins who supported the Amazons in battles.

Since this novel was widely read during the years of the Spanish conquest of Mexico, the California myth probably joined other gold-tinged stories circulating among the conquistadors. In the novel the Amazons were pagan allies of a Persian king, so the story dovetailed well with the conquistadors' promise to the Vatican to convert the heathen hordes.

At first the name California was applied to all lands west of the Colorado River; the distinction between Baja ("Lower") and Alta ("Upper") California wasn't made until the late 1700s. For the next hundred years or so, if you said "California," it was understood that you meant Baja California, since this was where the first California missions were established. Even after California became a U.S. state in 1850, the "Alta" persisted—in the 1880s, San Franciscans were still publishing a newspaper called the *Daily Alta Californian.*

Today whenever you get a quorum of Baja aficionados around a table of cervezas, you've got the raw material for a name debate. Are the peninsula and islands properly called "Baja California" or is just "Baja" okay? What about "the Baja" (which seems to be particularly popular among Canadians—perhaps because they relate it to "the Yukon")? Bajacalifornios (the preferred term for residents of Baja California) will often pretend to be rankled at the abbreviated form, yet you may occasionally catch them using it themselves.

For the purposes of this book—and supported by common English usage—the author has decided to use "Baja California" and "Baja" interchangeably throughout the text. On the other hand, to make it clear which California is meant (and perhaps to make up for using "Baja" so frequently), all references to the U.S. state will appear as "Alta California" or "the U.S. state of California."

The official names of the two Mexican states separated by the peninsula's 28th parallel are "Baja California" (BC) and "Baja California Sur" (BCS), but many Bajacalifornios refer to the northern state as "Baja California Norte" (BCN) to distinguish it from the southern state. In this book the latter practice will be followed so as not to confuse the northern state with the whole peninsula.

in 1587, and so many ships were captured in Bahía de la Paz that the landfall there, originally called Santa Cruz by Cortés, eventually earned the name Pichilingue, a Spanish mispronunciation of Vlissingen, the provenance of most of the Dutch pirates.

Pirating continued off the Baja coast throughout the entire 250-year history of the Manila-Acapulco voyages. One of the more celebrated English privateers in the later years was Woodes Rogers, who arrived in the Pacific in 1709 and captured the Manila galleon *Encarnación* off Cabo San Lucas. On his way to Baja California that same year Rogers had rescued Alexander Selkirk, a sailor who had been marooned on an island off the coast of Chile for four years; Selkirk served as shipmaster on Rogers's vessel and later became the inspiration for Daniel Defoe's 1719 novel, *Robinson Crusoe*.

Further Exploration And Colonization Attempts

As the need for a permanent settlement in California grew more dire, coastal explorations were resumed after a hiatus of over 50 years. Cabrillo was succeeded by merchant-turned-admiral Sebastián Vizcaíno, who in 1596 landed at the same bay on the southeast coast chosen by his predecessors, Jiménez and Cortés. This time, however, the natives were friendly—perhaps because it was pitahaya fruit season when they arrived—and Vizcaíno named the site La Paz ("Peace"). Loading up on pitahaya fruit (which were effective for preventing scurvy) and pearls, Vizcaíno continued northward along the Sea of Cortez coast, stopping to gather more pearls before returning to the mainland after two months.

In 1602 Vizcaíno commanded a second, more ambitious expedition that sailed along the Pacific coast to near present-day Mendocino in Alta California. His names for various points and bays—San Diego, for example—along the coasts of both Californias have superseded most of those bestowed by Cabrillo or Cortés.

Upon his return Vizcaíno told his superiors that the Monterey Bay area of Alta California was well suited to colonization. However, be-

cause he was no longer in favor with New Spain's fickle viceroys, no one paid much attention to Vizcaíno's findings and he was reassigned to an obscure Sinaloa port. The cartographer for the voyage, Gerónimo Martínez, was beheaded for forgery although his maps of the Californias remained the best available for the next 200 years.

This neglect of Alta California's potential enabled an Englishman to put first claim to the territory. Sir Francis Drake, who landed at what is now Drake's Bay in northern Alta California during his 1578-80 voyage, christened the land "New Albion" on behalf of the English crown. Like the Spanish maps of the time, his maps depicted California as an island.

For a time Spain left both Californias unexplored. In 1615 Capt. Juan de Iturbi obtained the first official concession for pearl-diving along the peninsula but no land settlement was established. After two of his ships were captured by Dutch privateers off Cabo San Lucas, de Iturbi's remaining vessel sailed northward in the Sea of Cortez as far as the 28th parallel, harvesting pearls along the way. Because of dwindling provisions, however, they were forced to turn back to the mainland after only a few months.

The peninsula remained unconquered by the Spanish for another 80 years. In 1683 Spain's Royal Council for the Indies authorized an expedition under Admiral Isidor Atondo y Antillón and Padre Eusebio Francisco Kino which managed to occupy an area of La Paz for 3½ months before being driven back to the mainland by native hostility and short provisions. After two months of rest and provisioning on the mainland, they crossed the Sea of Cortez again, this time establishing a mission and presidio just above the 26th parallel at a place they named San Bruno. Supported by a friendly Indian population, the mission lasted 19 months, but lack of water and food—they had to rely upon supply ships from the mainland during the entire period—forced Kino and Atondo back to the mainland.

Kino never returned to Baja California but later became very famous for his missionary efforts in northwestern Mexico and Arizona, where he is said to have converted thousands of Indians to the one true faith, Roman Catholicism. In 1701 he accompanied an expedition from the northwest of Sonora to the mouth of the Río Colorado that confirmed Ulloa's claim that Baja California was a peninsula. He died in Sonora in 1711.

THE MISSION PERIOD

The Founding Of The Jesuit Missions

In Baja California, where Kino failed to extend his spiritual empire, Padre Juan María Salvatierra finally succeeded in giving Spain and the Church what they wanted—a permanent Spanish settlement on the peninsula. Backed by the mainland missionary system, a 30,000-peso annual subsidy from the Royal Council of the Indies, and a contingent of Spanish soldiers, Salvatierra landed in San Bruno in October 1697, located a better water source 24 km south of the original presidio, and pro-

ceeded to establish the mother of all California missions, Nuestra Señora de Loreto.

The founding of the Loreto mission initiated what Baja historians usually call "the Jesuit missionary period," lasting from 1697 to 1767. During this interval, the Jesuits established 20 missions stretching from the southern tip of the peninsula to near present-day Cataviña in central Baja. For a 70-year period, that wasn't a spectacular accomplishment compared with the progress of mainland colonization, but lower California was a much more difficult area to colonize. It had taken 167 years from the time the first Spaniard had set foot on her shores until the first successful settlement was established on Baja California soil.

The Spanish mission system basically worked like this: the padres, always in the company of armed escorts, approached a groups of natives and offered them the protection of the Church and the Spanish crown in return for a willingness to undergo religious instruction. Those natives who agreed were congregated at a suitable spot and directed to build a mission. The mission in turn became a refuge for the Indians and a place for them to learn European farming techniques and other trades, as well as Catholic ways. Once pacification was complete, the mission became a secularized church community (pueblo) and the missionaries moved on to new areas.

The system worked well among the docile Indians of Central Mexico but was often unsuccessful among the nomadic, fiercely independent Indians of Northern Mexico and Baja. Elsewhere in Mexico and Latin America, the norm was to secularize the missions after 10 years; in Baja, the Spanish Church never voluntarily secularized the missions.

Amateur historians like to say that the Californias were missionized by the cross, not the sword. This was actually no more true in Baja than it was for the mainland, although the military presence was indeed less (but only because the Jesuits were given greater administrative power in Baja and had to finance themselves—and their militia—through Church funds). The conversion techniques were the same: natives who obeyed the padres were rewarded with land and protection,

MISSIONS (1697-1856)

those who rebelled were punished, and those who organized rebellions were executed. Apologists claim that the padres never endorsed violence, but if this were true, they wouldn't have brought along the militia in the first place (which most especially in the case of Baja, they weren't required to do).

A contemporary report of the founding of Misión San Juan Bautista (translated from a book published in 1739 by historian Miguel Venegas) describes how Padres Salvatierra and Pedro de Ugarte approached the natives of Liguí in 1703:

> The two Padres, the soldier who accompanied them and two Christian Indians were given a real fright by a large band of Indians who fired a shower of arrows toward them, but after the soldier . . . discharged his musket into the air the Indians threw down their weapons and prostrated themselves on the earth, presently sitting up to await the coming of the Padres. Through an interpreter, Padre Salvatierra explained to them the purpose of their visit, and distributed among them some small gifts, expressing the hope that Padre Pedro de Ugarte might return later and be welcomed by them. Before leaving they brought 48 Indian children for baptism.

Indian Revolts, Disease, And The Decline Of The Jesuits

Several times during the Jesuit period, groups of Indians revolted against missionization. The most significant rebellion occurred in 1734-36 among the Pericú Indians of the southern peninsula. Apparently the revolt was triggered by an injunction against polygamy—long a practice among the Pericús and Guaycuras because women outnumbered men among them—delivered by Padre Nicolás Tamaral of Misión San José del Cabo. The punishment of a Pericú shaman under the injunction doubled the perceived assault on native culture and a group of disaffected Indians organized themselves against the entire mission structure.

In October 1734, the Pericús attacked and burned the missions at Santiago and San

José del Cabo, killing Padre Tamaral and his counterpart at Santiago; they also set fire to the mission in Loreto although the padre there escaped unharmed and was able to send to the mainland for assistance. The provincial governor of Sinaloa, after receiving letters describing the uprising from Loreto, dispatched a ship from the mainland with 60 Yaqui warriors and a number of Spanish soldiers who marched from mission to mission, meeting little resistance from the poorly equipped Pericús.

Unrest among the Pericús is said to have continued for another two years, a situation that led to the founding of a large presidio at San José del Cabo. As a further precaution, the garrisons at every mission in the south were expanded by 10 soldiers each. Besides reinforcing the missions, this increased military presence encouraged Manila galleons to make Cabo San Lucas a regular stop on their return voyages from the Orient.

In the years to follow, epidemics of smallpox, syphilis, and measles—diseases borne by the Europeans for which the Indians had no natural immunity—decimated the Indian population. In 1538 Padre Jacobo Baegert of Misión San Luis Gonzaga estimated the Baja Indian population at about 50,000. In three outbreaks of smallpox in 1742, 1744, and 1748, an estimated 42,000, or five-sixths of the Indian population, perished. Gathering the natives into mission settlements only hastened their demise by intensifying the spread of contagions. A significant number of Indians also lost their lives in continued rebellions against the padres. The La Paz mission was abandoned in 1748; by 1767 only one member of the entire Huchiti branch of the Guaycura nation had survived.

As the southern Indians died out, the missionaries moved northward more quickly in an effort to find new sheep for their flocks. The last four missions established by the Jesuits, Santa Gertrudis (1752), San Borja (1762), Calamajué (1766), and Santa María (1767) were scattered widely in northern Baja in an obvious push toward Alta California.

In 1767 King Charles III ordered the expulsion of the Jesuit Order from all Spanish dominions, including Baja California. Accounts of the expulsion disagree as to the reasons behind the action. According to crown representatives, it was because the Jesuits had become too power-hungry and could no longer be held accountable for their actions. The Jesuits themselves claimed it was because they had dared to criticize corruption among the nobility and royalty of Europe. Whatever the true reason, in 1768 the 16 Jesuit padres of Baja found themselves herded onto a ship and taken to the mainland port of San Blas, where the same ship received a contingent of Franciscan padres sent to replace them on the peninsula.

The Franciscans And Dominicans

The 14 Franciscan padres who arrived in Loreto in 1768 included among them Padre Junípero Serra, often misleadingly dubbed the "Father of California" (that title really belongs to Padre Salvatierra, who established the first California—Baja California, that is—mission 72 years prior to Serra's arrival at San Diego). To counter the flow of non-Spanish Europeans toward Alta California—the English across the south and middle of North America, the French across Canada, and the Russians south from Alaska along the coast—Serra was under orders to establish missions and presidios as quickly as possible in a northward direction.

Serra and the Franciscans only established one mission in Baja before moving on to Alta California. This was San Fernando Velicatá, founded in 1769 about 64 km southeast of today's El Rosario. Apparently the main reason for the founding of the Velicatá mission was so that it could be used as a staging area for expeditions to upper California. There were to be two initial expeditions, one by sea from La Paz and one by land from Velicatá, and they were to rendezvous at San Diego Bay. Padre Serra accompanied the land expedition, led by Capt. Gaspár de Portolá, and established Alta California's first mission at San Diego, the first in a chain of 20 missions that stretched along the upper California coast as far as Sonoma, north of San Francisco.

The ambitious Serra, realizing that the arid, underpopulated peninsula did not have the empire-building potential of Alta California, wrote to Mexico City with a proposal that the administration of the Baja California (at this time called Antigua or "Old" California) missions be released to the Dominican Order, who had been clamoring for a place in California missionary action. The viceroy approved Serra's request in 1772 and the first Dominican priests arrived on the peninsula in 1773 under the direction of Padre Vicente Mora.

The first new Dominican mission, Nuestra Señora del Rosario Viñaraco, was founded in the valley now known as Arroyo del Rosario in 1774. Eight more missions and one visiting chapel were established by the Dominicans between 1774 and 1834, all of them north of El Rosario. The northernmost was Misión El Descanso (between modern-day Ensenada and Rosarito), built on the edge of Arroyo del Descanso, the official boundary line separating the respective California domains of the Dominican order to the south and the Franciscan order to the north. This boundary also served to separate the New Spain provinces of Alta and Baja California, as officially designated in 1777. (The current border between Baja California and the U.S. state of California was created by the Treaty of Hidalgo at the end of the Mexican-American War in 1848.)

By the end of the 18th century it was clear that Spain and the Church could not afford to support the Baja missions much longer. The peninsula's Indian population had dwindled to less than 5,000 by 1800, and, without an abundance of free native labor, maintaining a colony wasn't an easy task. The Alta California missions seemed much more promising—water was more available and the Indian labor force was more docile and plentiful—and the growing unrest in Mexico placed the peninsula even lower on Spain's list of priorities.

Independence From Spain

The Catholic Church in Mexico had amassed huge amounts of wealth by the beginning of the 19th century and had become lenders to the colony's growing entrepreneurial class. At the other end of the economic spectrum, the increasing numbers of mestizos (Mexican-born residents of mixed Spanish and Indian ancestry) were denied land ownership and other rights, and were generally treated as second-class citizens.

Fearing that the Church was becoming too powerful, King Charles III of Spain decreed in 1804 that all church funds be turned over to the royal coffers, and as padres all over Mexico were forced to comply with the decree (calling back large sums of money that had been lent out to entrepreneurs), economic chaos ensued. Mexicans blamed their economic and social problems on Spain's remote rule; when Napoleon invaded Spain in 1808, limiting authority to Spanish loyalists in Mexico City, the disaffected clergy began planning a revolt.

Mexico's struggle for independence from Spain began on 16 Sept., 1810, a date that's celebrated annually as Diez y Seis or Mexican Independence Day, when Padre Miguel Hidalgo y Costilla issued a call for independence entitled the Grito de Dolores ("Dolores Cry") in the mainland province of Guanajato. Although the rebels who gathered around Hidalgo soon captured Zacatecas, Valladolid, and San Luis Potosí, Mexico wasn't completely free of Spanish rule for another 11 years. When Hidalgo was captured and executed by loyalists, another padre took his place and the fighting continued until Mexico City acceded to the demands of the rebels in 1821.

The 1821 Plan de Iguala treaty between Spain and Mexico guaranteed three political underpinnings of the new regime: the religious dominance of the Catholic Church, a constitutional monarchy, and equal rights for mestizos as well as Mexican-born Spaniards. Former Viceroy Agustín de Iturbide was appointed emperor of the new republic, but his reign only lasted two years before he was overthrown by another junta that established a short-lived federal republic called Los Estados Unidos de México—the United States of Mexico—in 1824.

Over the next six years the Mexican republic endured two more coups; it wasn't until 1829 that all Spanish troops were expelled from Mexico. In 1832 all non-Dominican missions in Baja were secularized and converted to parish churches. The Dominican missions of the northern peninsula were allowed to remain because they were considered the only outposts of civilization north of La Paz and Loreto and as such were important links with prospering Alta California. Another change in policy involved the encouragement of Anglo-American immigration to the northeastern Mexican state of Coahuila y Texas.

The Mexican-American War

In 1833 Antonio López de Santa Anna, a megalomaniac general in charge of enforcing the expulsion of Spanish troops, seized power and revoked the Constitution of 1824, thus initiating a series of events that eventually led to a war with the U.S. and the resultant loss of huge amounts of territory. During the first 30 years of Mexican independence, Mexico changed governments 50 times; Santa Anna—who called himself the "Napoleon of the West"—headed 11 of these regimes.

Mexican citizens everywhere were angry at the revocation of their republican constitution by a self-appointed dictator. But none were more frustrated than the Anglo-American immigrants who had voluntarily abandoned their U.S. citizenship in order to take Mexican citizenship under the Constitution of 1824 and live in the northern half of Coahuila y Texas. In 1836 the "Texicans" declared an independent Republic of Texas, fought and lost San Antonio's infamous Battle of the Alamo, and then routed Santa Anna's defending troops in San Jacinto, Texas.

Defeated and captured, Santa Anna signed the Velasco Agreement, which guaranteed Texas independence and recognized the Rio Grande as the border between Mexico and the new Texan republic. There matters lay until the U.S. granted statehood to the near-bankrupt republic in 1845. Santa Anna's government refused to recognize the Velasco Agreement, claiming that Texas only extended as far south as the Nueces River (about 160 km north of the Rio Grande at the widest gap). When the U.S. Army moved into the area south of the Nueces, Santa Anna retaliated by sending troops across the Rio Grande, thus initiating the Mexican-American War.

After a series of skirmishes along the Rio Grande, U.S. President James Polk ordered the army to invade Mexico. In Baja California, Mexican and American forces engaged at Santo Tomás, Mulegé, La Paz, and San José del Cabo. Mexico City finally fell to U.S. troops in March 1847 and Santa Anna signed the Treaty of Guadalupe Hidalgo in 1848. In the treaty, Mexico conceded not only the Rio Grande area of Texas but part of New Mexico and all of Alta California for a payment of US$25 million (US$10 million for South Texas and US$15 million for New Mexico and Alta California) and the cancellation of all Mexican debt.

In retrospect, it is likely that the annexation of Texas was part of a U.S. plan to provoke Mexico into declaring war so that the U.S. could gain more of the Southwest. The war so damaged Mexico's already weakened economy that in 1853 Santa Anna sold Arizona and southern New Mexico (the Mesilla Valley) to the U.S. for another US$10 million. During that same year, American freebooter William Walker sailed to La Paz and declared himself "President of Lower California." He and his mercenary troops fled upon hearing that Mexican forces were on the way and he was later tried (and acquitted) in the U.S. for violation of neutrality laws. Walker was executed during a similar escapade in Nicaragua two years later.

For the Mexican population, already strongly dissatisfied with Santa Anna, this additional loss and threatened loss of territory was the final straw; in 1855 Santa Anna was overthrown by populist Benito Juárez.

Depopulation Of The Peninsula, Civil War, And Reform

The second half of the 19th century was to be even more turbulent for Mexico than the first. At the end of the Mexican-American War, the California Gold Rush of 1849 lured many Mexicans and Indians away from the peninsula to seek their fortunes in Alta California, lowering Baja's already scant population even further and leaving it to become a haven for bandits, pirates, and an assortment of other outlaws and misfits. Only six Dominican padres remained on the peninsula by the 1880s.

Meanwhile back on the mainland, a civil war (called the "War of Reform" in Mexico) erupted in 1858, following the removal of Santa Anna, in which self-appointed governments in Mexico City and Veracruz vied for national authori-

Benito Juárez   (KAREN WHITE)

ty. Once again, Church wealth was the principal issue. The liberals, under Zapotec Indian lawyer Benito Juárez, had promulgated a new constitution in 1857 and passed a law further restricting the financial powers of the Church—all Church property save for church buildings had to be sold or otherwise relinquished. A reactionary opposition group took control of Mexico City and fighting continued until 1861, when the liberals won and Juárez was elected president.

Juárez immediately had to deal with the 1862 French invasion of Mexico, which came in response to Mexico's nonpayment of debts to France. Napoleon's first invading force was defeated at Puebla on the Gulf of Mexico coast, but the following year the French captured the port and continued onward to take Mexico City, where they installed Austrian Ferdinand Maximilian as emperor of Mexico. Under U.S. pressure, the French gradually withdrew from Mexico and Juárez was back in power by 1867.

Over the next four years Juárez initiated many economic and educational reforms. Upon his death in 1872, political opponent Porfirio Díaz took over and continued reforms begun by Juárez, albeit in a much more authoritarian manner. Díaz and/or his cronies ruled for the next 28 years, suspending political freedoms but modernizing the country's education and transportation systems.

Foreign Investment In Baja California
In Baja, Díaz and the "Porfiriato" encouraged foreign investment on a large scale, and in the 1880s vast land tracts were sold to American or European mining, farming, manufacturing, and railway concessions. All but the mining concessions met failure within a few years, mainly because the investors weren't prepared for dealing with the demanding climate and lack of transportation on the peninsula. A Connecticut company invested US$5 million (as a down payment on US$16 million) for extensive land holdings in Ensenada and San Quintín which they planned to develop with farmlands, railways, and seaports. When their first wheat crop succumbed to lack of rain, they sold out to a similar English development syndicate which also failed.

Mineral excavation in turn-of-the-century Baja, however, enjoyed a boom—gold, silver, copper, and gypsum were the main finds, along with graphite, mercury, nickel, and sulfur. One of the most successful mining endeavors was that of Compañía del Boleo, a French mining syndicate in Santa Rosalía which for many years was the largest copper-mining and smelting operation in Mexico.

The Mexican Revolution And U.S. Prohibition
By the early 1900s, it was obvious that the gap between rich and poor in Mexico was becoming increasingly wide due to the extreme pro-capitalist policies of the Díaz regime and the lack of a political voice for workers and peasants. In response to the situation, a liberal opposition group formed in exile (using Texas as a base) and organized strikes throughout the country, which forced Díaz to announce an election in 1910. His opponent was Francisco Madero, a liberal from Coahuila, but as it

became clear that Madero was garnering mass support, Díaz imprisoned him on trumped-up charges.

Upon his release, Madero fled to Texas and began organizing the overthrow of the Díaz government. The rebels, with the assistance of the colorful, bandit-turned-revolutionary Pancho Villa and peasant-hero Emiliano Zapata, managed to gain control of the northern Mexican states of Sonora and Chihuahua. Unable to contain the revolution, Díaz resigned in May of 1910 and Madero was elected president. The opposition, however, broke into several factions—the Zapatistas, Reyistas, Vasquistas, and Felicistas (named for the leaders of each movement)—and Madero was executed in 1913. Baja California had its own faction, the Magónistas, who briefly held Tijuana in 1911.

For the next six years the various factions played musical chairs with national leadership, and Mexico remained extremely unstable until revolutionary leader Venustiano Carranza emerged as president. Carranza held a historic convention that resulted in the Constitution of 1917 (the current Mexican constitution), which established the *ejido* program to return lands traditionally cultivated by the Indian peasantry, but taken away by rich ranch and plantation owners under Díaz, to local communities throughout Mexico. Three years later opponent Álvaro Obregón and his supporters overthrew Carranza.

Obregón managed to hang onto the office for four years and establish important educational reforms, and he was followed by Plutarco Elías Calles in 1924. Calles instituted wide-reaching agrarian reforms, including the redistribution of three million hectares of land. He also participated in the establishment of the National Revolutionary Party (PNR), the forerunner of the Institutional Revolutionary Party (PRI), Mexico's dominant party today.

In the same year that Obregón took power in Mexico City, the U.S. government amended its own constitution to make the consumption, manufacture, and sale of alcoholic beverages a federal offense. This proved to be a disastrous experiment for the U.S. (ushering in an era of organized crime) but was a boon to Baja California development as Americans began rushing across the border to buy booze from the restaurants, cantinas, and liquor stores of northern Mexico.

Tijuana and Mexicali added casinos and brothels to the assortment of liquor venues and became so prosperous that the municipal leadership was able to lobby successfully for the division of Baja California into northern and southern territories. On the negative side, the two cities became renowned as world sleaze capitals. Their reputations persisted long after Prohibition had ended in 1933 and the Mexican government had outlawed gambling (prostitution remained legal) in 1938, even though the cities wisely managed to channel much of their unexpected revenue into manufacturing, agriculture, and other non-tourist-related development.

Nationalist Reforms And World War II

The year 1938 proved a turning point in modern Mexican history as PNR candidate Lázaro Cárdenas ascended to the presidency. (With Mexico's legacy of election-fixing, it's difficult to use the word "elect" in the usual democratic sense—see "Government," below.) Cárdenas, a mestizo with a Tarascan Indian heritage, instituted the most sweeping social reforms of any national leader to date, effecting significant changes in education, labor, agriculture, and commerce.

His land reforms included the redistribution of 46 million acres among newly created *ejidos* or agricultural collectives in which land is owned jointly by peasant communities—a legacy that is as hot a topic for debate today as it was then. Foreign-owned oil interests were expropriated and a national oil company, Petróleos Mexicanos (PEMEX), was established. These reforms frightened off foreign investors for many years and it has been only very recently that Mexico has been able to reattract foreign capital. Cárdenas also reorganized the PNR as the Mexican Revolution Party (PRM—Partido de la Revolución Mexicana), which soon changed its name to the Institutional Revolutionary Party (PRI—Partido Revolucionario Institucional).

During WW II, Mexican troops fought in the Pacific on the Allied side. The Mexican economy was boosted by the increased demand for materials and labor in the U.S. and also by the scarcity of imported goods in Mexico, which forced the nation to increase domestic production. In 1942 the U.S. instituted the Bracero Program, which permitted Mexicans to work north of the border for short periods of time; the program lasted until 1962 and had a profound effect on urban development along the U.S.-Mexico border.

Baja Statehood And The Transpeninsular Highway

After the war Mexico continued to industrialize and the economy stayed on a more-or-less even keel under one PRI president after another. In 1952 the Territory of (Northern) Baja California was declared Mexico's 29th state as its population moved past the required 80,000 criterion for statehood. Northern Baja was, in fact, better off economically than most of the rest of the country by this time. The boomtowns of Tijuana and Mexicali were servicing a fast-growing border economy and Valle de Mexicali farming was competing well with California's Imperial Valley. In 1958 it was determined that Baja was second only to Mexico City in the number of autos per capita.

Throughout the 1960s most of Baja south of Ensenada remained benevolently neglected, which led travel writers of the time to employ the famous catchphrase, "the forgotten peninsula." The population of the Territory of Southern Baja California was stagnating, perhaps even decreasing; except for La Paz, it was limited to tiny collections of hardy souls here and there who scratched out a living as rancheros or *pescadores* (fishermen). Even La Paz was just a step above a sleepy back-water port although its status as a duty-free port was beginning to attract a steady trickle of mainland Mexicans.

By the 1970s it was obvious that southern Baja wasn't going to catch up with northern Baja unless transportation between the south, north, and the mainland was upgraded. Travel between Tijuana and La Paz took up to 10 days via rough dirt tracks. Construction on the Transpeninsular Highway (Mexico 1) was finally completed in 1973, connecting Tijuana with Cabo San Lucas for the first time. In less than a year following the completion of the highway, the population of Baja California Sur passed the 80,000 mark and the territory became Mexico's 30th state.

The 1,700-km-long Transpeninsular Highway has greatly contributed to the modernization of one of Mexico's last frontiers. Fishing and agricultural cooperatives now have a way to transport their products to the border or to the ports of Santa Rosalía, Guerrero Negro, and La Paz. The highway has also brought Americans, Canadians, and Europeans deep into the peninsula in greater numbers than ever before, and the revenue from their visits has provided another means of livelihood for the people of Baja.

Like the border visitors of the Prohibition years, those foreigners who come to Baja in the 1990s are seeking something that's scarce in their own countries. For some it may be the unfenced desert solitude, for others the pristine beaches or historic mission towns. The challenge of the future for Baja's fledgling tourist industry is how to develop and maintain an adequate infrastructure without sacrificing those things that make Baja California unique.

GOVERNMENT

POLITICAL BOUNDARIES

The 28th parallel divides the peninsula into two states, officially named Baja California (abbreviated BC) above the parallel and Baja California Sur (BCS) below. Unofficially, the northern state is often called Baja California Norte (BCN); a debate is continually simmering about whether or not to make this version official. (In this book, BCN is used so as not to confuse the northern state with the whole peninsula.)

Mexicali is BCN's state capital, which governs four *municipios* (similar to counties in the U.S.): Tijuana, Ensenada, Mexicali, and Tecate. Besides its southern border with BCS, BCN shares a northern border with the U.S. and a western border, formed above the Sea of Cortez by the Colorado River, with the Mexican state of Sonora.

Baja California Sur is also divided into four municipios: La Paz, Cabo San Lucas, Mulegé, and Comondú; La Paz is the capital.

POLITICAL SYSTEM

As Mexican states, BCN (since 1952) and BCS (1974) are part of Mexico's federal system *(Estados Unidos Mexicanos* or United Mexican States), which allows for some degree of autonomous rule by state governors and their legislatures. Both states are considered among the most socially progressive states in the nation. (All of Mexico's 12 orphanages, for example, are located in Baja.) BCN is the only state with a non-PRI governor, Ernesto Ruffo Appel, a PAN (Partido Acción Nacional or National Action Party) candidate who defeated PRI's Margarita Ortega Villa in 1989 state elections—the first time in PRI's 60-year history it had conceded an electoral loss. In that same election PAN took nine of 19 state legislative seats and the mayoral seats of Tijuana and Ensenada. PAN is sometimes described as a conservative party because it favors private over government ownership, yet in the context of Mexican politics it is more reform-minded than PRI. As elsewhere in the world, political labels and their meanings shift with time.

The PAN victory is considered by some to be a watershed in Mexican politics, which has been notorious for election fraud ever since it adopted a republican system in 1917. Many Bajacalifornios remain skeptical, however, and see the PRI concession as a one-time occurrence. Hard-boiled cynics insist that all high political offices are part of a ruling dynasty extending outward from the presidency in Mexico City (even municipal mayors in Mexico are called *el presidente* and the local seat of government is the *palacio municipal).* Wags point out other symbolic evidence—the President wears an imperial sash and sits upon a throne when making official proclamations— and the fact that political candidates endorsed by the incumbents always win succeeding elections.

The *presidentes municipales* appoint city *delegados* to represent federal power at the local level; smaller communities may even have *subdelegados.* These delegados and subdelegados are the highest authority within their jurisdictions and are part of a chain of command that reaches back to the president of Mexico.

ECONOMY

INCOME

Agriculture, fishing, and tourism are Baja's main revenue-earners, followed by manufacturing and services in the border area. Per capita income figures for either BCN or BCS are well above the Mexican national average (which is US$1860 per year, just below Brazil, ahead of Fiji, and on a par with Mongolia) and second within the nation only to that of Mexico D.F. (Distrito Federal).

Most of the large-scale farming is centered in the Río Colorado delta (Valle de Mexicali), Valle de Guadalupe, Valle de San Quintín, and the Magdalena Plains surrounding Ciudad Constitución. Fishing boats work both coasts, but the Sea of Cortez produces the largest catch and La Paz is the main fishing center. Tourism is for the most part concentrated in Tijuana, Rosarito-Ensenada, Mulegé-Loreto, La Paz, and Los Cabos (San José del Cabo and Cabo San Lucas).

The stars of the manufacturing sector are the *maquiladoras,* or in-bond industries, which combine third-world labor costs with first-world capital and management. These are predominantly located in special export-processing zones in the Tijuana area, although nearby Tecate and Mexicali are also developing industrial parks. Although wages at the maquiladoras are far below comparable wages in the U.S., they are about twice Mexico's current minimum daily wage of US$4.65 a day.

THE SYSTEM

On a macroeconomic level, Baja finds itself caught between two economic systems. Because it's so isolated from the rest of Mexico, the regional economy has tended to be American-influenced yet subject to the same vicissitudes of the national Mexican economy as the rest of the country, most pointedly a weak currency and high inflation. Although the country's current-account balance rose from a deficit US$6.2 billion in 1982 to a surplus of US$4 billion in 1987, the inflation rate that same year hit 146%. Because of its regional ties to the U.S., particularly Alta California, the Baja economy weathered this period better than many areas in Mexico.

Since the election of President Carlos Salinas de Gortari (a Harvard University economics graduate), however, the nation has moved closer to a U.S.-style supply-side economics, thus lessening the schizoid nature of Baja's regional economy. In 1988 the Bank of Mexico was able to slow the runaway devaluation of the Mexican peso to almost a halt; the national currency is now losing less than a peso a day against the U.S. dollar, a considerable improvement over the 1976-87 period in which it slid from eight pesos to the dollar to over 2,000.

One of the biggest steps taken by the Salinas government has been the reprivatizing of the national banking system and several other state industries—PEMEX is the major exception. The current policy is to open all sectors of the Mexican economy to private investment save for "below-ground" resources, i.e., petroleum and minerals.

Inflation is now running at about 20-25% per annum, foreign exchange reserves are rising (US$220 billion in exports for 1990-91), and the current-account deficit is at US$5.5 billion. GNP growth is a respectable 3.9% per annum (four times that of the U.S. at this writing) and an increase to 5% is a reasonable projection within the next few years. Some optimistic economists predict that if Mexico continues its current economic reforms, it may become the world's fastest growing economy by the year 2000. Growth in Baja will probably be slower, however, since much of the current and projected growth is in areas of Mexico that are "catching up" with Baja.

Ejidos

One of the most unique features of the Mexican economy is the *ejido* institution. An ejido is a land tract, held in common by a peasant community, that includes not only cultivated fields but also school properties, urban zones, water and forest resources, and any other facilities or resources either native to the land or produced by collective efforts. Ejidos are granted to *ejidatarios* by the government without rents or fees of any kind and are nontransferrable, nonattachable, and inalienable (i.e., ejido lands cannot be sold, used as loan collateral, or taken away by local, regional, or national legal bodies).

According to Mexican law, ejidos are considered neither state property nor private property but are entities of the "social interest sector." How they are used is solely the concern of the peasant communities that hold them, but around 95% of them are "individual" ejidos in which the common holdings are divided into individual plots and cultivated by individual ejidatarios and their families. The remaining 5% are "collective" ejidos which pool all land resources for collective production.

The ejido came into being under the Constitution of 1917 as a way of restoring Indian lands that had been taken from them by rich *hacendados* (big ranchers and plantation-owners) during Spanish colonization and early Mexican independence. The number and total acreage of Mexico's ejidos is not well documented but by 1970 it was estimated that they encompassed around 46% of national farm-lands.

Various bits of legislation enacted since the ejido's 1917 inception have alternately strengthened and weakened the ejido program. In recent years laws have passed that allow ejidatarios to lease their lands to neighboring private estates for agricultural or livestock purposes.

Has the ejido program been successful? On the one hand, it has kept hereditary lands in the hands of peasant communities who have worked the lands for hundreds of years—without them, many ejidatarios would probably become landless migrant workers. On the other hand, because ejido production is notoriously low (as are fixed prices for agricultural products), the need for cash to survive in Mexico's cash economy has forced many ejidatarios to work as laborers on private neighboring lands. As a result, economists estimate that ejidatarios are among the poorest and most exploited of Mexico's rural workers. All ejidatarios are automatic members of PRI's peasant division, but because of their overall lack of education and political experience, they're easily manipulated by PRI leaders in Mexico City and are hence relatively powerless.

THE PEOPLE

The people of Baja California are in many ways a breed apart from their compatriots on the mainland. As Mexico's last frontier, the peninsula continues to attract residents seeking something they haven't been able to find on the mainland, whether it's the rugged, independent life of the interior deserts and sierras, the tropical ambience of La Paz or Cabo San Lucas, or the promising multicultural world where the two Californias meet in Tijuana and Mexicali.

For the rest of Mexico, Baja California occupies a place in the national psyche somewhat analagous to that of Hawaii for many Americans. It's seen as a place that's part of the nation yet almost out of reach—an exotic destination which most of the population will never have an opportunity to see. Hence, mainlanders typically regard people native to Baja California as somehow "different" from themselves. (It works the other way, too.)

POPULATION

The current population of the entire peninsula is approximately 2,850,000, about 87% of which live above the 28th parallel in Baja California Norte. Well over half of Baja's population live in Mexicali and Tijuana alone, and 13% in Ensenada. As is obvious from these figures, most of the peninsula is very sparsely populated—the average density, even if these and all other Baja cities are included in the estimate, is only 1½ persons per square km (about four persons per square mile). Outside the three most populated cities it's less than one person per 26 square km (one body per 10 square miles)!

Mexico's population growth rate is currently estimated at 1.9% per annum, relatively low for a developing country. The average for Baja California is probably somewhat higher than the national average because of immigration. Baja California Sur is the country's least populated state.

ORIGINS

The residents of Baja California, *bajacalifornios,* are an unusually varied lot. Elsewhere in Mexico, the "average" citizen is a mix of two heritages, Spanish and Indian. In Baja, the mix is typically more complicated, mainly because it has remained a frontier area much longer than most of the mainland. Hence it has attracted people who arrived in the New World long after the Spanish colonized the Mexican mainland. In fact, it was 167 years after the conquest of Mexico before the Spanish were able to maintain a permanent settlement on the peninsula. By this time, tales of the Californias were on the tongues of adventurers throughout the world.

By the end of the 19th century the peninsula had become a favorite spot for sea-weary sailors to jump ship since the eastern shores of the peninsula were so placid, and there was little chance they'd be rounded up and incarcerated by local militia (who were very scarce then, and remain scarce to this day). Most of the ex-sailors who "retired" to Baja in this manner were English, but during WW I a few Germans and other Europeans came ashore and put down roots. Their ship captains might have considered them cowardly deserters, but survival in Baja in the 19th and early 20th centuries was possible for the brave, hardy, and resourceful only.

Other immigrants who pioneered the Baja frontier included Chinese workers, who came via the Mexican mainland and eventually flourished in the Mexicali area, Russian viniculturists who settled the Valle de Guadalupe, French miners in Santa Rosalía and Mulegé, and Mexican intellectuals and dissidents fleeing political oppression on the mainland (and gravitating toward La Paz, Ensenada, or Tijuana). Many of these newcomers intermarried and their descendants have added much to the peninsula's multicultural spirit.

Since in a very real sense much of Baja is still a frontier area—with more immigrants wandering in year by year—Baja's demographics have yet to solidify into recognizable pie-graph proportions. About 2% of the population aren't even citizens; many of them are North Americans or Europeans who have retired in Baja at the end of their work careers. A lesser number are gringos who have simply dropped out of the rat race, and, with the recent relaxation of investment and trade laws, a growing number of nonnationals are also setting up businesses on the peninsula.

Bajacalifornios

If there is a personality trait common to all "true" Bajacalifornios (definitions vary, the most popular being those whose forebears came to the peninsula before WW II), it is a do-or-die spirit that says "I belong here because my family was tough enough to survive in Baja back when this was the toughest place in Mexico to survive." A self-adopted nickname for Bajacalifornios, particularly popular in northern Baja, is *cachanilla* (sometimes spelled *cachania*), taken from a hardy desert plant *(Pluchea sericea,* arrowweed) that produces rose-colored flowers under even the harshest of conditions.

The Bajacalifornio loves to rant about how the peninsula was neglected by the mainland for centuries, and how they cultivated Baja for themselves, without any help from Mexico City. Now that the Transpeninsular Highway is complete and the economic infrastructure is expanding, the Bajacalifornios say, the weak mainlanders are coming to harvest the fruits of Baja's development. A special scorn is reserved for *chilangos,* a derogatory term used by Bajacalifornios for Mexico City politicians or businesspeople who come to Baja and tell the cachanillas how to run things.

Indians

Of the estimated 50,000 Indians who inhabited the peninsula when the Spanish estab-

lished their first Baja mission of any duration in 1697, at least 80% were wiped out by disease or colonial violence within a hundred years. None of the Guaycura tribes of the south (Guaicura, Pericú, and Huchiti) survived the Spanish occupation, but small numbers of the central and northern Cochimí and Yumano tribes still reside in the valleys and sierras of BCN.

According to Mexico's 1980 census, the Paipai (Pa'ipai) are the largest surviving native tribe, numbering only around 300; most are concentrated in the vicinity of Santa Catarina and San Isidoro. About 165 Kumyai live in Valle de Guadalupe and Juntas de Neji, 200 Cochimí in Valle Ojos Negros and San Antonio Necua, 200 Kiliwa (Quilihua) in Ejido Tribu Quilihua, and about 200 Cucapá in Cucapá El Mayor in the Río Colorado delta.

The Mexican government has set aside tracts of land in BCN for each tribe; the Paipais, for example, own 160,000 acres from the Alamo plain eastward. For the most part, Baja's native tribespeople make their living on small ranches and farms; the livestock trade in particular has been a primary source of income ever since they acquired horses, burros, cattle, goats, and sheep from Spanish missionaries. Little is known about the extent to which *los indígenos* have preserved tribal traditions since, as in the American Southwest, many customs and ceremonies have gone "underground" due to a deep and understandable suspicion of outsiders.

Outnumbering the Indians native to Baja are the thousands of Indians from Sonora, Oaxaca, and Chiapas who have come to Baja to work as migrant laborers. They're most numerous in the Valle de San Quintín but are also commonly found in the Ensenada area. Migrant Indians who have not been able to find agricultural jobs can often be seen hawking blankets and other handicrafts on the streets of the tourist districts in Tijuana, Ensenada, and Cabo San Lucas.

LANGUAGE

As in the rest of Mexico, Spanish is the most widely spoken language in Baja California. English is occasionally spoken by merchants, hotel staff, and travel agents in Tijuana, Mexicali, Ensenada, Loreto, La Paz, San José del Cabo, and Cabo San Lucas—but even in these cities, you can only count on finding English-speaking Mexicans within each city's tourist districts. Outside of the tourist areas, and even in smaller border towns like Tecate, it is somewhat rare to encounter anyone who speaks more than a few words of English.

Hence it is incumbent upon the non-Spanish-speaking visitor to learn at least enough Spanish to cope with everyday transactions. Knowing a little Spanish will not only go a long way toward mitigating communication problems, it will also bring you more respect among the local Mexicans, who quite naturally resent foreign visitors (usually Americans) who expect Mexicans to abandon their mother tongue whenever a gringo approaches. A popular sign seen in tourist restaurants reads "We promise not to laugh at your broken Spanish if you won't laugh at our broken English." Out of courtesy, you should at least attempt to communicate in Spanish whenever possible. After all, it's the third-most-spoken language in the world after English and Chinese.

The type of Spanish spoken in Mexico is usually referred to as "Latin-American Spanish" (in contrast to the Castilian Spanish spoken in Spain) although the Spanish here differs significantly from that of even other Spanish-speaking countries in the Western Hemisphere. In Baja California especially, many Anglicisms have crept into the language. For example, the common Latin-American Spanish term for "car" is *coche,* but in Baja you'll more often hear *carro.* Signs at automotive stores may read *auto partes* rather than *refacciones; yonke* (junk) is also commonly seen, and refers to new and used auto parts rather than junked cars.

LANGUAGE STUDY

Dictionaries And Phrasebooks

One of the best dictionaries of a portable size for the Spanish student is the paperback *University of Chicago Spanish-English, English-Spanish Dictionary,* which emphasizes New World usages and contains useful sections on grammar and pronunciation. If even this small volume is too large for your backpack, the *Collins Gem Dictionary: Spanish-English, English Spanish* comes in a tiny 4-by-3½-by-1-inch size with a sturdy plastic cover and over 40,000 entries.

Berlitz's *Latin-American Spanish For Travellers* is a small phrasebook divided by topics and situations (e.g., grammar, hotel, eating out, post office). Not all of the phrases and terms it contains are used in Baja, but it's better than nothing.

One of the best references for off-the-road adventurers is Burleson's and Riskind's *Backcountry Mexico: A Traveler's Guide and Phrase Book* (University of Texas Press). Although it's rather bulky for carrying in a backpack and is oriented toward travel in northern mainland Mexico, it contains many words and phrases that could be of value to Baja hikers and campers if studied before taking an extended backcountry trip.

Advanced Spanish learners may be able to improve their command of idiomatic Spanish with Frances de Talavera Berger's ¡Mierda! (Plume, New York). Subtitled *The Real Spanish You Were Never Taught in School,* the book's copious *vulgarismos* or slang expressions have a decidedly scatological slant and should probably be aired in public only after practice with a trusted native speaker.

Schools In Baja

Those who plan to spend an extended period of time in Baja should seriously consider enrolling in an intensive Spanish course. Night classes at an adult community school or summer university courses are a fine introduction, but the most time-and-cost-effective study programs are those that immerse you in the language and culture within the country of the target language. Although there are Spanish language schools at several locations in mainland Mexico, it's also possible to study in Baja. Hence if Baja is your travel focus, it would be prudent to investigate schools on the peninsula.

Since the '60s, a number of language schools have opened and closed in Tijuana, Ensenada, and La Paz. One well-established school with a good reputation is the family-owned **International Spanish Institute of Ensenada (Colegio de Idiomas)** (tel. 6-01-09, 6-65-87) at 337 Blvd. J.A. Rodriguez in Ensenada. This school offers a choice of one-day, weekend, and six-day (or longer) courses, with six hours of language class per day. Tuition is US$20 per day (a bargain at less than US$4 an hour) and classes are always limited to five or fewer persons. For an additional US$20 per day, they can arrange a homestay with a local Mexican family that includes a private room and three meals per day. This is considerably cheaper than staying in even the cheapest hotel and eating out; staying with a Mexican family also gives students plenty of opportunity to practice Spanish after class. ISIE can also be contacted through Kathy Luna (tel. 619-472-0600), 5329 Ruby St., Unit C, Torrance, CA 90503.

Another long-running language program is the Spanish conversation course offered by Glendale Community College's Baja California Field Studies Program. The course is held for 12 days in late August at the GCC's rustic field studies center in Bahía de Los Angeles. Students sleep on cots in the center itself. The course costs around US$400, including roundtrip transport between GCC and Bahía de los Angeles, dormitory-style accommodation, and meals. For further information, contact Dr. José Mercadé, Glendale Community College, 1500 N. Verdugo Rd., Glendale, CA 91209.

USEFUL WORDS AND PHRASES

Consonants

c:	before a, o, or u, like c in "cat," before e or i, like s
d:	as d in "dog," except between vowels, then like th in "that"
g:	before e or i, like the ch in Scottish "loch" elsewhere like g in "get"
h:	always silent
j:	like the English h in "hotel" except stronger
ll:	like the y in "yellow"
ñ:	like the "ni" in "onion"
r:	always pronounced as strong r
rr:	trilled r
v:	similar to the b in "boy" (not as English v)
z	like s in "same"

b, f, k, l, m, n, p, q, t, as in English

Vowels

a:	as in "father" except shorter
e:	as in "hen"
i:	as in "machine"
o:	as in "phone"
u:	usually as in "rule"; when it follows a q the u is silent; when it follows an h or g it is pronounced like w except when it comes between g and e or i, when it is also silent

Greetings And Civilities

¡Hola!	Hello!
Buenos dias.	Good morning.
Buenas tardes.	Good afternoon.
Buenas noches.	Good evening, good night.

(CONT.)

USEFUL WORDS AND PHRASES (CONT.)

Buenas	can be used when you're not sure of the time of day
¿Cómo está?	How are you?
Muy bien.	Fine
Así así.	So-so.
Muchas gracias.	Thank you very much.
De nada.	It's nothing.
Si.	Yes.
No.	No.
Yo no sé.	I don't know.
Está bien.	It's fine; okay
Bueno	Good; okay
Por favor	Please
¡Salud!	(To your) health! (used in toasting or after someone sneezes)
Dispénseme.	Excuse me.
Perdóneme.	Pardon me.
Lo siento.	I'm sorry.
Adios	Goodbye (can also be used as a passing hello).
¿Mande?	What? (as in "Could you repeat that?")

Communication Problems

No hablo bien español.
  I don't speak Spanish well.

No entiendo.
  I don't understand.

Hable más despacio, por favor.
  Speak more slowly, please.

Repita, por favor.
  Repeat, please.

¿Cómo se dice . . . en español?
  How do you say . . . in Spanish?

¿Entiende el inglés?
  Do you understand English?

¿Se habla inglés aquí?
  Is English spoken here? (Does anyone here speak English?)

Getting Directions

¿Dónde está . . . ?
  Where is . . . ?

¿Qué tan lejos está a . . . ?
  How far is it to . . . ?

de . . . a . . .
  from . . . to . . .

¿Conduce a . . . este camino?
  Does this road lead to . . . ?

la carretera	highway
el camino	road
la calle	street
la cuadra	block
kilómetro	kilometer
milla	mile (commonly used in Baja)
el norte	north
el sur	south
el oeste	west
el este	east
al derecho or *adelante*	straight ahead
a la derecha	to the right
a la izquierada	to the left

At A Hotel

¿Hay un hotel cerca de aquí?
  Is there a hotel near here?

¿Puedo (podemos) ver un cuarto?
  Can I (we) see a room?

¿Cuál es el precio?
  What is the rate?

¿Están incluídos los impuestos?
  Does that include taxes?

¿Acepta tarjetas de credito?
  Do you accept credit cards?

(CONT.)

USEFUL WORDS AND PHRASES (CONT.)

un cuarto solo	single room
un cuarto doble	a double room
con camas gemelas	with twin beds
con una cama de matrimonio	with a double bed
casa de huéspedes	guesthouse
posada	inn
con baño	with bath
sin baño	without bath

agua caliente	hot water
agua fria	cold water
calentador	heater
aire acondicionado	air conditioning
toalla	towel
jabón	soap
llave	key
cubierta or *manta*	blanket
papel higiénico	toilet paper
hielo	ice

Post Office
la oficina de correos
   post office
Quiero unas estampillas
   I'd like some stamps.
Quiero mandar esto . . . .
   I'd like to send this . . . .
por correo aéreo
   by air mail
certificado
   certified mail
Quiero mandar este paquete.
   I'd like to send this parcel.
¿Hay correo para mí? Me llamo . . .
   Is there any mail for me? My name is . . .

Telephone
caseta de teléfono	telephone office

Quiero llamar a . . .	I want to make a call to . . .
por cobrar	collect call
persona a persona	person-to-person
una llamada de larga distancia	a long-distance call
Quiero hablar con . . .	I want to speak with . . .
¿Está . . . ?	Is . . . there?
No está.	S/he's not here.
La linea está ocupada.	The line is engaged.

Changing Money
Quiero cambiar dinero.
   I want to change money.
cheques de viajero.
   traveler's checks
¿Cuál es el tipio de cambio?
   What's the exchange rate?
¿Hay comisión?
   Is there a commission?
banco	bank
casa de cambio	currency exchange office

Making Purchases
Necesito . . . .
   I need . . . .
Deseo . . . . or *Quiero . . . .*
   I want . . . .
¿Hay . . . aquí?
   Is/are there any . . . here?
   (Do you have . . . ?)
¿Cuánto cuesta?
   How much does it cost?
¿Puedo ver . . . ?
   Can I see . . . ?
ésta	this one
ésa	that one
Me llevo éste.	I'll take this one.
caro	expensive
barato	cheap

(CONT.)

USEFUL WORDS AND PHRASES (CONT.)

Driving

Lleno, por favor.
   Full, please (at a gasoline station).

Se me ha descompuesto el carro.
   My car has broken down.

Necesito un remolque.
   I need a tow.

¿Hay un garage cerca?
   Is there a garage nearby?

¿Puedo pasar con este carro (troca)?
   Is the road passable with this car (truck)?

¿Con doble tracción?
   With four-wheel drive?

No hay paso.	It's not passable.
el semáfora	traffic light
el señal	traffic sign
gasolina	gasoline (petrol)
gasolinera	gasoline station
aceite	oil
agua	water
llanta desinflada	flat tire
llantera	tire repair shop

Auto Parts

banda de ventilador	fan belt
batería	battery
bomba de gasolina (agua)	fuel (water) pump
bujía	spark plug
carburador	carburetor
distribuidor	distributor
eje	axle
embrague	clutch
empaque, junta	gasket
filtro	filter
frenos	brakes
llanta	tire
manguera	hose
marcha, arranque	starter
radiador	radiator
regulado de voltaje	voltage regulator

Public Transport

la estación del autobus
   bus stop

central camionera
   main bus terminal

el aeropuerto
   airport

la terminal del transbordador
   ferry terminal

Quiero un boleto a . . . .
   I'd like a ticket to . . . .

Quiero bajar en . . . .
   I want to get off at . . . .

¡Aquí, por favor!
   Here, please!

¿Cuánto le debo?
   What do I owe?

Hiking And Camping

¿Dónde empieza la vereda (el sendero)?
   Where does the trail (path) start?

¿Se puede acampar aquí (allá)?
   Is camping permitted here (there)?

¿Hay agua potable?
   Is there drinking water?

¿Hay agua allá?
   Is there water there?

Quiero rentar (comprar) . . . .
   want to rent (buy) . . . .

la tinaja	water hole
el ojo de agua	spring
el pozo	well
la mochila	backpack
la bolsa de dormir	sleeping bag
la carpa	tent
la leña	firewood
el carbón	charcoal
el fuego	fire
los cerrillos or *los fósforos*	matches
el cruce	crossing
a pie	on foot

(CONT.)

USEFUL WORDS AND PHRASES (CONT.)

a bestia	by horse, mule, or burro	15	quince
un burro	a burro	16	diez y seis
un caballo	a horse	17	diez y siete
una mula	a mule	18	diez y ocho
		19	diez y nueve
Geography		20	veinte
la isla	island	21	veinte y uno
el cerro or la colina	hill	30	treinta
la montaña	mountain	40	cuarenta
la sierra	mountain range	50	cincuenta
el bosque	forest	60	sesenta
el cañon	canyon	70	setenta
el arroyo	stream bed, wash	80	ochenta
el valle	valley	90	noventa
la catarat	waterfall	100	cien
el río	river	101	ciento y uno
la laguna	lagoon or lake	200	doscientos
bahía	bay	1000	mil
el mar	sea	2000	dos mil
la playa	beach	20,000	veinte mil
la punta	point, headland	million	millión

Numbers

zero	cero
one	uno (masculine)
	una (feminine)
two	dos
three	tres
four	cuatro
five	cinco
six	seis
seven	siete
eight	ocho
nine	nueve
10	diez
11	once
12	doce
13	trece
14	catorce

Days Of The Week

domingo	Sunday
lunes	Monday
martes	Tuesday
miércoles	Wednesday
jueves	Thursday
viernes	Friday
sábado	Saturday

Time

¿Qué hora es?	What time is it?
la una	one o'clock
las dos	two o'clock
a las dos	at two o'clock
las tres y diez	10 past three
las seis	6 a.m. (0600)
a la mañana	

(CONT.)

USEFUL WORDS AND PHRASES (CONT.)

las seis a la tarde	6 p.m. (1800)
el mediodia	noon
la medianoche	midnight
hoy	today
mañana	tomorrow
ayer	yesterday
esta noche	tonight
anoche	last night
esta semana	this week
la semana pasada	last week
el próximo año	next year
el mes pasado	last month

Miscellaneous

yo	I
usted	you (formal)
tu	you (familiar)
él	he/him
ella	she/her
nosotros	we/us
ustedes	you (plural)

ellos	they/them (all male or mixed gender)
ellas	they/them (all female)
señor	Mr., sir
señora	Mrs., madam
señorita	miss, young lady
más	more
menos	less
mejor	better
un poco	a little
un poquito	a very little
grande	large
pequeño	small
caliente	hot (temperature)
picante	hot (spicy)
frío	cold
rapido	quick
malo	bad
dificil	difficult
facil	easy

RELIGION

Census-takers report that approximately 89% of Baja California's population are Roman Catholics, 4.2% are Protestant, .06% are Jewish, and 4% "have no religion." The original inhabitants of Mexico were indoctrinated in the ways of Roman Catholicism by Spanish missionaries between the 16th and 19th centuries. That Catholicism is now the majority religion in Mexico is an amazing achievement considering that it was laid over a vast variety of native belief systems in existence for perhaps thousands of years, and also given the fact that the Mexicans eventually forcefully expelled the Spanish from their country.

Mexican Catholics tend to be devout practitioners of their faith. Mexican Catholicism, however, has its own variations that distinguish the religion from its European predecessors. Some can be traced to preexisting Indian spiritual traditions that were absorbed by the Catholic faith, and as such are localized according to tribe.

One variation that is common to all of Mexico is the Virgin of Guadalupe cult, which began in 1531 when a dark-skinned Virgin Mary appeared before Indian peasant Juan Diego in a series of three visions at Tepeyac, near Mexico City (which coincidentally was a sacred Aztec site dedicated to the goddess To-nantzin). Many Mexican churches are named for Our Lady of Guadalupe, who has become so fused with Mexican identity that the slogan ¡Viva Guadalupe! is commonly used at political rallies. The official feast day for Guadalupe, December 12, is fervently celebrated throughout the country.

At one time all of the peninsula was under the ecclesiastical jurisdiction of the Guadalajara diocese; now there are regional dioceses centered in Tijuana, Mexicali, and La Paz. Since there are fewer churches per capita in Baja than on the mainland, a church (iglesia) will sometimes hold as many as 18 masses a day. In southern Baja it isn't uncommon for a parish priest to hail from abroad (usually Italy), since there is a chronic shortage of priests on the peninsula.

Roadside Religion

Along Baja's roadways you'll occasionally see small roadside crosses (sometimes in clusters) or shrines. Often placed at fatal accident sites, each cross marks a soul's point of departure from this world. Larger shrines containing Christ or Virgin figures have been erected to confer blessings or protection on passing motorists. They can vary from simple enclosures made of vegetable oil cans to elaborate sculptural designs.

cave painting of a figure
(BOB RACE)

ENTERTAINMENT

Most visitors to Baja California come for the beaches, mountains, deserts, fishing, or water sports, not for what would normally be called "entertainment." Nonetheless it's not necessarily bedtime when the sun goes down, except in the most remote areas. The larger cities—Tijuana, Mexicali, Rosarito, Ensenada, La Paz, and Cabo San Lucas—offer a variety of museums, theaters, cinemas, concert halls, bars, and discos. For specific recommendations regarding these types of entertainment venues, see the destination sections of this book.

MUSIC

When most North Americans think of Mexican music they think of brass-and-violins mariachi music, which is a style from the state of Jalisco on the Mexican mainland. In Baja, mariachi music is generally reserved for weddings and tourists as is the music of the so-called Baja Marimba Band. (Marimba music also hails from elsewhere in Mexico.) The most commonly heard music on the peninsula is la *música norteña,* a style that's representative of ranchero life yet has a wide appeal throughout northern Mexico and the southwestern United States. Everyone from urban truckers in Tijuana to pescadores in Bahía Agua Verde seems to play norteña tapes on their boom boxes.

Norteña music is very similar to—and shares common roots with—the Tex-Mex or *conjunto* music enjoyed in Texas and New Mexico and made famous by Flaco Jimenez, Ramon Ayala, and, among Anglos, Doug Sahm's Sir Douglas Quintet. It's typically played by an ensemble led by an accordion and *bajo sexto,* a large Mexican 12-string guitar. Originally, these two instruments were supported by a string bass and sometimes a trap drum set; later, electric bass and guitar were occasionally added, along with alto sax and keyboards (though most norteña bands maintain the traditional accordion, bajo sexto, and acoustic bass line-up). The music itself encompasses an exciting mix of Latinized polkas and waltzes, *rancheras* (similar to American country and western), and *corridos* (Mexican ballads) as well as modern Latin forms like *cumbias* and salsa.

The most popular norteña band among Bajacalifornios in recent years has been Los Tigres del Norte, who, although based in San Jose, Alta California, are *superestrellas* (superstars) in Mexico. Like many norteña bands, Los Tigres sing songs that reflect the daily lives and sentiments of northern Mexican peasants, often with a political edge. Some of the songs recorded by Los Tigres and other norteña groups have been banned by the Mexican government and can only be heard from bootleg tapes that circulate at cantinas or local fiestas. In 1988, Los Tigres won a Grammy award (Mexican music category) in the U.S. for their album *¡Gracias! America Sin Fronteras* (Thank You! America Without Borders).

Live norteña music can often be heard at fiestas throughout Baja and in Mexican bars and cantinas in larger towns and cities. Strolling *trobadores,* for example, wander from bar to bar playing norteña music along Calle Ruiz in Ensenada most evenings—it's not the nicest area of town to hang out at but it's an opportunity for the musically curious to hear some local sounds.

BULLFIGHTS

One type of entertainment you won't find north of the border is the bullfight. Variously called *la corrida de toros* (the running of bulls), *la fiesta brava* (the brave festival), *la lidia de toros* (the fighting of bulls), or *sombra y sol* (shade and sun), the bullfight can be perceived as a sport, an art, or a gory spectacle, depending on the social conditioning of the observer.

To the aficionado, the lidia is a ritual drama which rolls courage, fate, pathos, and death together into a symbolic event. No matter how one may feel toward the bullfight, it is undeniably an integral part of Mexican history and culture. Every town of any size has at least one *plaza de toros* or bullring; in Baja California you'll find two major stadiums in Tijuana (one of which is the second largest in the world) and one in Mexicali. Occasionally a small bullring will be improvised for a rural fiesta.

History

Ritualistic encounters with bulls have been traced as far back as 3000 B.C., when the Minoans on the Greek island of Crete would perform ritual dives over the horns of attacking wild bulls. A closer antecedent developed around 2000 B.C. on the Iberian peninsula, where a breed of fierce, wild bulls roamed the plains. Iberian hunters—ancestors of the Spanish and Portuguese—figured out how to evade the dangerous bulls at close quarters while delivering a fatal blow with an axe or spear. When the Romans heard about this practice they began importing wild Spanish bulls and accomplished bullfighters for their colosseum games—possibly the first public bullfights.

During the Middle Ages, bullfighting became a royal sport practiced on horseback by both the Spanish and the occupying Moors, who used lances to dispatch the wild bulls. As the *toreros* (bullfighters) began dismounting and confronting the bulls on the ground, the game eventually evolved into the current *corrida* as performed in Spain, Portugal, Mexico, and throughout much of Latin America.

In the early years the only payment the torero received was the bull's carcass after the event. Nowadays bullfighters receive performance fees that vary according to their status within the profession.

El Toro

The bulls used in the ring, *toros de lidia* (fighting bulls), are descendants of wild Iberian bulls that have been specially bred for over four centuries for their combative spirit. They're not trained in any way for the ring, nor goaded into viciousness, but as a breed are naturally quick to anger. The fighting bull's neck muscles are much larger than that of any other cattle breed in the world, making the animal capable of tossing a torero and his horse into the air with one upward sweep.

Bulls who show an acceptable degree of bravery by the age of two are let loose in huge pastures (averaging 10,000 acres per animal) to live as wild beasts until they reach four years, the age of combat. By the time *el toro* enters the ring, he stands around 125 centimeters high at the withers (higher at the shoulder, but they aren't measured here because the neck muscle expands to varying degrees

norteña musicians
(MIKE WELLINS)

when the bull is preparing to attack) and weighs 450 kilograms (a half ton) or more.

The carcass of a bull killed in the ring does not go to waste, at least not from a meat-eater's perspective. Immediately after it's taken from the ring, it's butchered and dressed, and the meat is sold to the public.

El Torero

The bullfighter is rated by his agility, control, and, as surprising as it may seem to the uninitiated, his compassion. The torero who teases a bull or who is unable to kill it quickly when the moment of truth arrives is considered a cruel brute. In order to be judged a worthy competitor by the spectators, he must excel in three areas: *parar,* or standing still as the bull charges (as opposed to stepping away from the bull, even as little as an inch)—only the cape and the torero's upper body should move; *templar,* or timing and grace—the movements must be smooth, well timed,

and of the right proportion; and *mandar,* or command—the degree to which he masters the entire lidia through his bravery, technique, and understanding of the bull, neither intimidating the animal nor being intimidated by it.

Standard equipment for the torero is the *capote de brega,* the large cape used in the first two thirds of the lidia, the *muleta,* a smaller cape used during the final third, the *estoque* or matador's sword, and the *traje de luces* or "suit of lights," the colorful torero's costume originally designed by the Spanish artist Goya.

Although it's usually the bull who dies in a lidia, toreros are also at great risk. Over half of all professional matadors on record worldwide during the last 250 years have been gored to death in the ring.

La Lidia

The regulated procedures *(suertes)* followed in a bullfight date from 18th-century Spain. Anywhere from four to eight bulls may appear in a corrida (typically six), with one torero on hand for every two bulls scheduled. The order of the appearance for the toreros is based on seniority. Toreros who have proven their skills in several bullfighting seasons as *novilleros* (novice fighters) are called *matadores de toros* (bull killers). Ordinarily each torero will fight two bulls; if he is gored or otherwise put out of action, another torero will take his place even if it means facing more than his allotment of bulls.

(MIKE WELLINS)

Each lidia is divided into three *tercios,* or "thirds." In *el tercio de varas,* the bull enters the ring and the matador performs *capeos* (cape maneuvers that don't expose the matador's body to the bull's horns, meant to test the bull or lead it to another spot in the ring) and *lances* (cape maneuvers that expose the matador's body to the horns and bring the bull closer to him) while two horsemen receive the bull's charge with eight-foot *varas* or lances. The varas have short, pyramid-shaped points which are aimed at the bull's neck muscle and do not penetrate very deeply on contact.

The purpose of the encounter is to force the bull to lower its horns and to give the bull the confidence of meeting something solid so it won't be frustrated by the emptiness of the cape as the lidia proceeds. Usually only two vara blows are administered, but more are permitted if necessary to produce the intended effect (the lowering of the head). The crowd protests, however, when more than two are applied, as they want the matador to face a strong bull.

In *el tercio de banderillas,* the bull's shoulders receive the banderillas, 26-inch wooden sticks decorated with colored paper frills, each tipped with a small, sharp, iron barb. They can be placed by the matador himself or more often by hired assistant toreros (called *banderilleros* when performing this function). The purpose of the banderilla placement is to "correct" the bull's posture; the added punishment also reportedly makes the bull craftier in his charges. Placed in pairs, up to six banderillas may be applied to the bull, varying in number and position according to the needs of the individual animal.

At the end of the tercio de banderillas, signaled by a bugle fanfare, the matador takes up his muleta and sword and walks before the box of the *juez* (judge) presiding over the lidia. He looks to the juez for permission to proceed with the killing of the bull and, after receiving a nod, the matador offers his *brindis* (dedication). The brindis may be made to an individual spectator, to a section of the plaza, or to the entire audience. If the dedication is to an individual, he will present his *montera* (matador's hat) to that person (who will return it, with a present inside, to the matador after the lidia). Otherwise, he tosses his hat onto the sand after waving it at the crowd; he remains hatless for the final tercio, a gesture of respect for the bull during its final moments alive.

The final round of the lidia is called *el tercio de muerte* (the third of death). The main activity of this tercio is *la faena* (literally, "the work") involving cape and sword, during which a special set of passes lead to the killing of the bull. The first two tercios have no time limit; for the last, however, the matador has only 15 minutes within which to kill the bull, or else he is considered defeated and the bull is led from the ring (where it is killed immediately by the plaza butcher).

In a good faena, a matador will tempt fate over and over again, bringing the bull's horns close to his own heart. The time for the kill arrives when the bull has so tired from the faena that it stands still, forelegs squared as if ready to receive the sword. Then, with his cape, the matador must draw the bull into a final charge while he himself moves forward, bringing the sword out from under the cape, sighting down the blade, and driving the blade over the horns and between the animal's shoulders. A perfect swordthrust severs the aorta, resulting in instant death. If the thrust is off, the matador must try again until the bull dies from one of the thrusts.

It is not necessary to kill the bull in one stroke (quite an extraordinary accomplishment); the matador's honor is preserved as long as he goes in over the horns, thus risking his own life, every time. If the bull falls to its knees but isn't dead, another torero on hand immediately comes forward and thrusts a dagger *(puntilla)* behind the base of the skull to sever the spinal cord and put the beast out of its misery. When the bull is dead, the lidia is over. If the matador has showed bravery and artistry, the crowd will let him know with their applause; an unusually dramatic performance will see hats and flowers thrown into the ring. In cases of outstanding technique or bravado, the juez will award the bull's ears and/or tail to the matador.

Practicalities

It's usually a good idea to buy tickets for a corrida in advance if possible—check with the local tourist office to find out where they're available—since it's not unusual for an event to sell out. In the event of a sellout, you may still be able to buy a ticket—at higher prices—from a scalper or *revendedor*. In a large stadium, the spectator sections are divided into the *sol* (sunny side) and *sombra* (shaded side), then subdivided according to how close the seats are to the bullring itself. The *sol* tickets aren't bad, since the corrida doesn't usually begin until around 4 p.m., as long as you bring a hat, sunglasses, and sunscreen, plus plenty of pesos to buy beverages—tequila and beer are usually available, along with soft drinks.

SPORTS AND RECREATION

Baja California's major attractions largely fall under this heading—from trekking in the Sierra de San Pedro Mártir to scuba diving off Cabo Pulmo. An added bonus is that, for the most part, Baja's outdoor recreation can be enjoyed at little or no cost simply because user demand is so low; when fees are involved they're usually quite reasonable.

HIKING AND BACKPACKING

National Parks, Natural Areas, And Wildlife Preserves

Baja has two national parks (Parque Nacional de Sierra San Pedro Mártir and Parque Nacional Constitución de 1857), three natural parks (Parque Natural del Desierto Central de Baja California, Parque Natural Isla Angel de la Guarda, and Parque Natural de la Ballena Gris), two wildlife sanctuaries (Isla Guadalupe and the Midriff Islands), and two underwater marine parks (Arrecife Pulmo and Bahía Cabo San Lucas). At the two national parks, public facilities are few and rudimentary—in the other government-protected areas they're virtually nonexistent. These public lands are described in some detail in later sections of this guidebook.

Trails

Hiking trails are plentiful in the northern sierras, from fairly wide, 150-year-old paths created by Indians or shepherds to smaller, more recent trails worn by hikers. In the smaller central sierras, which are more arid, trails are much more scarce—it's a good idea to scout an area first and ask questions locally about the best way to get from point A to point B. Although it's sometimes tempting to venture off established trails, this is a good way to get lost; it can also add to the destruction of delicate ecosystems. Light trails that don't seem to go anywhere may be coyote trails, which connect surface water sources.

Maps

Topographic maps, which chart trails and elevation differential, are essential for extended hiking and backpacking. **Map Centre** (tel. 619-291-3830, 2611 University Ave., San Diego, California, 92104-2894) carries a complete line of Baja topo maps in three scales (1:1,000,000, 1:250,000, and 1:50,000) that are sold separately (around US$6 each) according to region. Map Centre will mail out a Baja map listing on request.

A San Diego publisher has recently issued the useful *Baja Explorer Topographic Atlas Directory.* Besides the 239 topo maps contained therein, the atlas includes several reference sections on accommodations, campgrounds, and other services. Available for US$28 from Baja Explorer Atlas (tel. 800-669-2252), P.O. Box 81385, San Diego, CA 92138-1385.

Equipment

Day Hikes: For hikes of a day or less, all you need is sturdy footwear (light, high-topped hiking boots are preferable to sneakers in rocky terrains) and whatever food or water you plan to consume for the day (count on at least two liters of water per person for chaparral or lower sierra hiking, more if the weather is hot).

Overnight Hiking/Backpacking: Longer hikes obviously require more preparation and more equipment. Whether in the desert or the mountains, bring enough clothing along to remain comfortable at both ends of the thermometer since throughout the peninsula days tend to be warm, nights chilly. A light sleeping bag (for temperatures down to -4° C/25° F in the high sierras) and a backpacking tent (with plenty of ventilation for camping at lower elevations) are necessities for coping with potentially harsh environments.

Good hiking boots are essential. Thick lug soles with steel shanks are preferable, as they provide protection from sharp rocks and desert plants. (Graham Mackintosh's *Into A Desert Place* documents how Baja terrains eat up hiking boots.) Bring along a first-aid kit that includes an elastic bandage for sprains and snakebite treatment (see "Snakebite Prevention and Treatment" on p. 111 for more detail) and a pair of tweezers for removing thorns and cactus spines. Also bring a flashlight, compass, waterproof matches, knife, flashlight with extra batteries, foul-weather gear, and a signal device (mirror or whistle). A handy addition, if you'll be hiking near Baja's shoreline, is a "telescoping" fishing rod, along with light tackle, as surf fish are usually plentiful. (See below, for details on what to catch).

Water and Food: Always carry plenty of water—a minimum of four liters per person per full day of walking during hot weather, three liters in winter. Although there are springs and tinajas in the sierras, the water level varies considerably and you shouldn't count on finding water sources along the way. If you need drinking water from one of these sources, always boil it first for at least 10 minutes or treat it with iodine or with a water filter designed to remove impurities. Bring enough food for the duration of your hike, plus one or two days extra.

Campsites: In addition to all the usual rules for choosing campsites, add: don't camp beneath coconut palms (a falling coconut could knock down your tent in or fracture your skull) or in arroyos (danger of flash floods).

Fires and Waste Disposal: Open fires are permitted just about anywhere in Baja except within city limits. Even in the desert, fuel is plentiful (dried ocotillo and cactus skeletons make excellent fuels), but imitate the locals and keep your fires small so as not to waste any. Never leave hot coals or ashes behind—smother with sand (or water if you can spare it) till cool to the touch.

Pack out all trash that won't burn (including cigarette butts—they take 10-12 years to decompose), bury human waste six inches down, and don't use soap in streams or springs.

Desert Hiking

For hikes in Baja's desert lands, special precautions are appropriate in addition to those outlined above. Water is the number-one concern; desert hiking requires at least four liters of water per day per person—some people recommend at least eight liters per day for hikes that span the mid-day hours. On extended excursions of more than a night or two, the weight of anything beyond eight liters (water weighs about one kilogram per liter) is prohibitive and it will be necessary to ascertain water locations from reliable sources in advance. While hiking, keep your mouth closed and breath through your nose to keep the mouth and throat from drying out. This will keep you cooler, as the nasal cavities are designed to moderate outside air temperatures as air passes into your lungs.

Sun protection is especially essential in the desert. Wear long- sleeved clothing with light, reflective colors (white is best), sunglasses, a wide-brimmed hat, and sunscreen. Between 1100 and 1500, it's best to take shelter from the sun if possible, especially during the hotter months. Most of Baja's deserts have plenty of shade in the form of mesquite trees, overhanging cliffs, or leaning boulders. But it's also a good idea to carry your own shade—a light, opaque tarp. (A poncho can double as a tarp and rain protection—yes, it does rain in the desert occasionally.) The Vizcaíno Desert is the most barren of the peninsular deserts, but also the coolest because of the tendency for fog to form when the hot desert air meets cool Pacific breezes.

Anyone contemplating an extended desert hike for the first time might consider reading at least one of the books on desert travel listed in the "Booklist." These contain important information on a variety of desert survival topics, from how to test the edibility of plants to making your own water with an improvised solar still.

FISHING

Baja's reputation as one of the best sportfishing regions in the world is well deserved. Nowhere else will you find as many varieties of fish in an area as compact and accessible as the waters of Baja. Although it's most famous for the acrobatic billfish (marlin, sailfish, and swordfish) of the Cape area and other deep-sea fishing, Baja also has opportunities for surf casters, small-boaters, and sport divers as well as for folks who don't yet know a rod from a reel.

Onshore Fishing

Most accessible to travelers, since it doesn't require a boat, is the onshore or surf fishing, which can be enjoyed anywhere along the coast where you can get a line into the water (unless you see a rare *Prohibido Pescar* sign). Surf fishing is best along the Pacific coast between El Rosario and Bahía Magdalena, and on the Sea of Cortez between San José del Cabo and La Paz, but fish can be taken just about anywhere along Baja's 4,800-km (3,000-mile) shoreline. Common onshore fishes include surfperch, cabezon, sand bass, ladyfish, halibut, corvinas, opaleye, leopard shark, triggerfish, and croakers. Submarine canyons along the shore of the East Cape can actually yield onshore catches of roosterfish, California yellowtail, and yellowfin tuna for anglers using the right tackle; shore-caught dorado (dolphinfish) and even marlin are not unknown. All of these except the marlin are excellent food fishes.

One fish commonly caught onshore, the puffer, is *not* a good food fish; the meat of the puffer is toxic to humans and can cause poisoning. The two puffer species common to Baja can be easily identified, as their bodies expand like balloons when they're disturbed. Further identifiers: the bullseye puffer has a brownish body with black spots; depending on its stage of maturity, the golden puffer is either all golden or a dark purple-black with white spots and white fin trim. In Mexico this fish is called *bolete*.

Inshore Fishing

Anyone with access to a small boat, either a skiff trailered in or a rented *panga* (an open fiberglass skiff that's usually five to six meters long and powered by a 40-60 hp outboard motor), can enjoy inshore fishing at depths of up to around 50-100 meters. Common inshore catches include many of the surf fishes mentioned above, plus various kinds of groupers, sea bass, bonito shark, sculpin (scorpionfish), barracuda, rockfish, lingcod, sierra, pompano, amberjack, red and yellow snapper, pargo, and cabrilla. (Cabrilla must be released if caught, however—see "Legal Requirements" below.) Larger gamefish that may occasionally be taken inshore are the bluefin and yellowfin tuna, yellowtail, dorado, jack crevalle, and roosterfish. Again, all fishes mentioned here are good eating.

Offshore Fishing

The bigger game fish are found in deeper waters—over 200 meters (100 fathoms)—and require bigger tackle and more technique (e.g., specialized trolling methods prescribed for each type of fish). Larger boats—fishing cruisers—are usually necessary simply because of the distances involved from shore to fishing areas. In the Cape area, however, depths of over a 200 meters can be reached less than 1½ km offshore in places and can be reached by skiff or panga. (Strong seasonal currents can be a problem here, however, and a larger outboard motor may be required.) Contrary to the popular image of Cabo San Lucas sportfishing, it isn't necessary to use a boat equipped with fighting chairs to catch the big ones, although it's undoubtedly more comfortable.

Because of the special tackle and techniques involved in offshore fishing, many Baja

pangas
(JOE CUMMINGS)

visitors hire local fishing guides (who usually provide boats and tackle) to take them to offshore fishing grounds. A sometimes less-expensive alternative is to sign up for fishing cruises which take groups of tourist anglers out on big power boats.

Most offshore anglers are after striped, blue, or black marlin, sailfish, swordfish, wahoo, dorado, roosterfish, yellowtail, and tuna. All of these fish are large, powerful fighters and require a certain skill in handling rod and line. The billfish are known as the most acrobatic, performing high leaps and pirouettes when hooked, although the wahoo and roosterfish will also "greyhound," performing a series of long, low jumps while swimming rapidly in one direction.

Of the billfish, none except for the swordfish are considered particularly good eating; the other billfishes are traditionally thought of as trophy fish to be stuffed and mounted in someone's den or living room. To their increasing credit, more and more sportfishers these days are tagging and releasing billfish after the fight is over; many sportfishing outfitters, in fact, discourage (or even forbid) the taking of these beautiful creatures unless a fish has been badly damaged in the fight.

The wahoo, dorado, roosterfish, yellowtail, and various tunas all make excellent eating. For more information on all types of fish common to Baja, see "Fishes," p. 26; for common Spanish fish names, see "Fish Translator," below.

Fishing Seasons

Fish are biting somewhere in Baja waters all year-round. Water temperature, ocean currents, weather patterns, fish migrations, and other changing variables, however, mean that you usually won't find the same type of fish in the same spot in December, say, as in July. All the variables interact to provide a complex set of fishing conditions that not only vary from month to month but from year to year. An unusually dry year in the American Southwest, for example, can lessen the outflow of nutrients from the Colorado River into the Sea of Cortez, thus diminishing the proliferation of plankton and other small marine creatures at the bottom of the Cortez food chain. This, in turn, will affect populations of larger fish from sea bass to whale sharks (a Cortez resident, the largest fish on the planet). All the various "fishing calendars" in print can serve only as general guidelines.

Some calendars, however, are more accurate than others. The best this author has seen is the set of calendars devised by Tom Miller in his *Angler's Guide to California,* which divides the Baja coast into 10 fishing zones, with a calendar for each zone. Even if you have a set of detailed calendars in hand, however, it is wise to seek the counsel of local fishing

FISH TRANSLATOR

Bajacalifornio guides who lead sportfishing trips often use the local Mexican terms for gamefish, and when they don't, the English terms aren't always correct. This works the other way, too—many gringos use the incorrect Spanish names for Baja fishes, which can cause confusion when asking about local fishing conditions. Here is a key to some of the more common translations:

English	Spanish
albacore tuna	albacora
blue marlin	marlín azul
bluefin tuna	atún de aleta azul
dolphinfish (mahi mahi)	dorado
grouper (generic)	garropa
halibut	lenguado
hammerhead shark	cornuda
jack crevalle	toro
ladyfish	sabalo
mackerel	sierra, makerela
manta ray	manta
octopus	pulpo
Pacific amberjack	pez fuerte
perch (generic)	mojarra
puffer (generic)	bolete (the flesh of this fish is poisonous to humans)
red snapper	huachinango
roosterfish	papagallo, pez gallo
sea bass (cabrilla)	cabrilla
shark (generic)	tiburon
sting ray (generic)	raya
sailfish	pez vela
squid	calamar
striped marlin	marlín rayado
swordfish	pez espada
triggerfish	cochi
wahoo	sierra wahoo, peto
whale shark	pez sapo
white seabass	corvina blanca
yellowfin tuna	atún de aleta amarilla
yellowtail	jurel

guides or other anglers on the scene before investing all your time and money toward catching a particular type of fish in a particular area.

A few generalizations with regard to fishing seasons are possible. The greatest variety and number of offshore, onshore, and inshore fishes are swimming the widest range of Baja waters April-Oct., when the water temperatures are relatively warm. During the winter, many species migrate south and are available only off the Cape.

Fortunately for winter anglers farther north, however, exceptions abound. The widely distributed California yellowtail, for example, is present year-round, migrating up and down the Sea of Cortez (La Paz and the East Cape in the winter, central to northern Cortez in the summer) as well as the lower Pacific coast. Barred perch and rock cod are present year-round on the northern Pacific coast, while peak season for sierra is winter, when they can be found in abundance near Bahía Magdalena. Wahoo generally spend Dec. through April at the Cape, moving up toward Bahía Magdalena and the southern Cortez in the warmer months.

The following generalized summary may be of some assistance in planning a fishing expedition. If your trip has to be between Dec. and April, head for the Cape; from May to Nov. you can choose anywhere along a horseshoe-shaped loop that extends from Bahía Magdalena on the Pacific side around to Mulegé on the Cortez side. Yes, you can fish farther north on both coasts, especially in the summer, but if sportfishing is your reason for traveling to Baja, you're more likely to be satisfied by heading to those areas. As a final caveat, remember that an unusually warm winter will mean better fishing all over Baja; likewise a particularly cold winter will force many fish quite far south, making even Cabo San Lucas, the "fisherman's paradise," less productive than average.

Equipment
Although bait and tackle are available at shops in Ensenada, San Felipe, Loreto, Mulegé, La Paz, and Cabo San Lucas, you can't count on finding exactly what you want since supplies

are variable. Therefore you ought to have your gear squared away, according to the type of fishing you plan on trying, before arrival in Baja.

A full fishing kit that contained tackle for every conceivable Baja sportfishing possibility would probably weigh in excess of 70 kilograms. Seasoned Baja anglers, however, claim you can get by in just about any situation with four basic rigs: two trolling rods with appropriate reels and 50- to 80-pound test monofilament line (for offshore fishing), one medium-duty eight- or nine-foot rod and spinner with 30-pound mono (for surf casting and onshore fishing), and a six-foot light spinning rig loaded with four- to eight-pound line (for bait fishing, freshwater fishing, or light surf casting). Two trolling rigs are recommended because these are the ones used against the fish most likely to yank your outfit into the sea; it's always best to have a spare.

No matter how many rods you bring into Mexico, you are legally permitted to fish with only one at a time. Electric reels are permitted for use by handicapped persons only.

Bait: What a fish will take at any given moment is highly variable, hence the properly equipped angler comes ready to fish with an array of natural and artificial bait. Live or frozen bait (including everything from squid to mackerel to clams) is usually available near the more frequented fishing areas; you can also catch your own quite easily with a light rig. A cooler is necessary for keeping bait fresh—hired boats will usually supply them. Among the vast selection of artificial lures available, the most reliable seem to be those perennials that imitate live bait, such as spoons, leadheads, candybars, swimmers, and, for offshore fishing, trolling heads. Bring along a few of each in different colors and sizes, and you'll be ready for just about anything. A few highly specialized lures, such as marlin heads and wahoo specials, can be purchased in Loreto and Cabo San Lucas.

Other: Serious onshore-inshore anglers will want to bring along a set of current tide tables so they can decide what time to wake up in the morning. (For information on where to obtain Pacific and Cortez tables, see "Boating," above)

Legal Requirements

The red tape surrounding fishing in Mexico is minimal. The basic requirement is that anyone over 16 who intends to fish must have a Mexican fishing license; technically, this includes all persons aboard boats equipped with fishing tackle, whether they plan to fish or not. This is important to remember for anyone going along on fishing trips as a spectator.

A single license is valid for all types of fishing, anywhere in Mexico, and is issued for periods of one day, one week, one month, or one year. A license is usually included in the price of sportfishing cruises, but not necessarily on panga trips—if you don't have a license, be sure to ask if one is provided before going out on a guided trip. The cost of the Mexican license has been rising steadily over the last few years but remains less expensive than most fishing licenses in the U.S. or Canada.

Fishing licenses are available from a number of sources, including tackle shops and Mexican insurance companies near the U.S.-Mexico border. They can be obtained by mail from the **Mexico Department of Fisheries** (tel. 619-233-6956, 1010 2nd Ave., Suite 1605, San Diego, CA 92101) or from California branches of the **American Automobile Association** (AAA). **Mexico West Travel Club** (tel. 619-585-3033, P.O. Box 1646, Bonita, CA 92002-1646) also issues Mexican fishing licenses.

Mexican Regulations: The general daily bag limit is 10 fish per person, including no more than five of any one species. Certain fish varieties are further protected as follows (per day limits): one full-grown marlin, sailfish, or swordfish; two dorado, tarpon, roosterfish, or shark. Extended sportfishing by boat is limited to three consecutive days if the daily bag limit is reached each of the three days.

Bag limits are the same for divers as for rod-and-reelers; only hand-held spears and band-powered spearguns (no gas guns or powerheads) are permitted. A further weight limitation permits no more than 25 kilograms (55 lbs) to be taken in a day's catch of five specimens, or one specimen of unlimited weight. Gill nets, purse nets, and every other kind of net except for handling nets are pro-

WORLD FISHING RECORDS SET IN BAJA

The nonprofit International Game Fish Association (IGFA) keeps track of world records set for each species of game fish according to weight, weight/test ratio (fish weight to line test), place where the catch was made, and other significant record details. World-record catches achieved by Baja anglers for specific line classes include those for the following fishes: Pacific blue marlin, striped marlin, Pacific sailfish, swordfish, roosterfish, dolphinfish (dorado), gulf grouper, California yellowtail, Pacific bonito, bigeye trevally, spotted cabrilla, spearfish, giant sea bass, white sea bass, California halibut, Pacific jack crevalle, black skipjack, yellowfin tuna, Pacific bigeye tuna, and chub mackerel.

Baja anglers hold all-tackle records (highest weight of any fish species regardless of line test) for gulf grouper (48 kg/106 lb), roosterfish (51.8 kg/114 lb), Pacific amberjack (93 kg/104 lb), white seabass (37.7 kg/83 lb), Pacific jack crevalle (11 kg/24 lb), chub mackerel (2.16 kg/4 lb, 12 oz), and California yellowtail (35 kg/78 lb).

For information on IGFA membership and record entries, write to IGFA, 3000 East Las Olas Blvd., Fort Lauderdale, FL 33316. Membership includes a copy of the IGFA's annual *World Record Game Fishes Book,* which contains a list of all current fishing records, as well as the bimonthly *International Angler* newsletter.

---

hibited for use by nonresident aliens, as are traps, explosives, and poisons.

The taking of shellfish (clams, oysters, abalone, shrimp, and lobster) by nonresident aliens is officially prohibited; however, it is generally recognized that taking a reasonable amount of these (no more than can be eaten in a meal or two) is customarily permitted. This regulation is in place to protect the Mexican fishing unions; even buying shellfish from local sources is prohibited unless purchased from a public market or *cooperativa,* in which case you should obtain a receipt to show in case of an inspection.

Totuava, sea turtles, and cabrilla are protected species which cannot be taken by anyone. Mexican fishing regulations are subject to change at any time—be sure to check with the Mexico Department of Fisheries for the latest version before embarking on a fishing expedition.

Two areas off limits to all fishing are Bahía Cabo San Lucas harbor and Pulmo Reef, the only official fish sanctuaries along the peninsular coast. Many other areas perhaps ought to be protected for educational and recreational purposes, since the government-regulated bag limits help to preserve fish species but not fish habitats. Fishing, boating, diving, and other aquatic activities can have long-

term effects in lagoons and on delicate reef systems—use special care when traversing these places. Never drop an anchor or a fishing line on a coral reef as such contact can cause irreversible damage to reef systems.

U.S. Customs and California State Regulations: Once you've bagged a load of fish in accordance with Mexican fishing limits, you still have to conform to U.S. Customs regulations if you cross the U.S.-Mexico border with your catch. Fortunately, the U.S. regulations conform with Mexican bag limits, so that whatever you've legally caught south of the border may be transported north of the border. The U.S. state of California further requires anyone transporting fish into the state to present a completed California Declaration of Entry form, available at the border. In order to facilitate the identification of the transported fish, some part of each fish—head, tail, or skin—must be left intact. (In other words, you can't just show up at the border with a cooler full of anonymous fish fillets.)

HUNTING

The Mexican government allows licensed hunting in season, as regulated by the Secretaría de Desarrollo Urbano y Ecologia

(SEDUE). Hunting is popular in Baja among foreigners and Mexicans alike but is for the most part restricted to various species of rabbit, quail, dove, pheasant, and waterfowl (ducks, widgeons, and geese). White-tail deer and mule deer are also hunted but permits are limited in number and quite expensive by Mexican standards. Occasionally a special hunt for the rare desert bighorn sheep *(borrego cimmarón)* is held; bighorn permits cost around US$12,000 and aren't usually issued to foreigners. (Earlier in this century, bighorn hunting by foreigners nearly wiped out the entire population.)

Permits come in six types: Type I—waterfowl, Type II—doves, Type III—other birds, Type IV—litter mammiferous, Type V—limited, and Type VI—special. Hunting regulations, which include bag (size and number) limits, are strictly enforced. Signs that say *Prohibido Cazar* mean "Hunting Prohibited." To apply directly to the Mexican government for a permit, contact SEDUE (tel. 61-74-91), Calle Lic. Alfonso Garcia Gonzalez 555, Distrito Profesores Federales, Mexicali, BCN. The office is open Mon.-Fri. 0900-1430 and 1730-2000, Sat. 0900-1300.

In addition to the SEDUE hunting permit, foreign hunters need a consular certificate, special visa, and military gun permit. The consular certificate may be obtained from any Mexican consulate upon presentation of a letter from the hunter's local police or sheriff's office verifying that the hunter has no criminal record. This certificate is also necessary for obtaining the military gun permit, which is issued by the army garrison in Tijuana or Mexicali. Once hunters have the consular certificate, gun permit, and hunting permit in hand, they can bring their guns across the border, where they will receive a special hunter's visa.

If you don't speak Spanish, you might be better off arranging all the necessary paperwork through a U.S. broker service. This costs a bit more than applying directly through SEDUE because you have to pay either membership dues or a surcharge, but the procedure is guaranteed to be smoother. One organization dedicated to helping hunters obtain Mexican permits is the **Mexican Hunting Association** (tel. 213-421-1619), 3302 Josie Ave., Long Beach, CA 90808. Another permit broker is **Romero's Mexican Service** (tel. 714-548-8931), 1600 West Coast Hwy., Newport Beach, CA 92663.

BOATING

Recreational boating along Baja's peninsular and island coastlines has been popular since at least the 1950s. In the days before the Transpeninsular Highway was built, it was one of the safest, if slowest, ways of traveling from Alta California to the southern peninsula. In spite of the recently achieved ease of highway travel, however, interest in getting out on Baja waters has only increased. The main difference now is that smaller vessels can be trailered or car-topped down the peninsula, saving days and weeks that might otherwise have been used just to reach your cruising destination.

An extremely wide range of pleasure boats are in use at any one time in Baja, from sea kayaks to huge motor yachts. The most heavily navigated areas are along the northwest coast between San Diego and Ensenada and in the Cabo San Lucas to La Paz corridor, but even these waters are relatively uncrowded compared to the marinas and bays of Alta California. Cabo San Lucas, the most popular southern Baja harbor, only checks in a thousand foreign-owned vessels or so per year, an average of less than 2.7 arrivals per day.

The Pacific Vs. The Sea Of Cortez

Although a number of visitors circumnavigate the entire Baja peninsula each year, the vast majority of boaters select one area to cruise in and transport their crafts to that area by land. Because of the relative safety of Sea of Cortez boating, it's the most popular coast, particularly for smaller craft—kayaks, skiffs, and motor- or sail-powered vessels under 10 meters (35 feet). The Cortez waters are relatively calm most of the time, the late summer and early fall being the exceptions, when chubascos or hurricanes can whip up some sizable and sometimes treacherous swells. The Pacific coast, on the other hand, is prone to high winds and challenging swells throughout the year.

The major difference between the two coasts is the number of available, safe anchorages. The Pacific side features about 30 anchorages along the peninsula as well as island shorelines that provide protection when northwest winds prevail; this number is reduced to approximately 12 anchorages during prevailing southwesterlies (common July through September). Over on the Cortez side are more than 60 protected anchorages—roughly 35 along the peninsula and 30 more on islands just off the peninsular coast. Obviously, the Sea of Cortez offers not only safer boating waters but a wider selection of places to drop anchor on a whim.

Open-ocean Pacific sailing is not for the novice and it shouldn't be attempted along Baja's Pacific coast without plenty of prior open-ocean experience. The relative absence of assistance and boat-repair facilities (see "Emergencies," below) in Baja make Pacific boating south of Ensenada an especially risky venture for first-timers.

It is now possible for boaters to navigate from ports in Alta California, British Columbia, or Alaska to the Ensenada marina and then arrange for overland transport of their boats (on hired trailers) from Ensenada to San Felipe on the Cortez side. The Ensenada tourist office (tel. 6-22-22, 6-37-18, 1350B Lopez Mateos Ave., PRONAF Bldg., Ensenada, BCN) has details on this newly established service.

Car-topping

The most popular boats for short-range cruising, fishing, and diving are those that can be transported on top of a car, RV, or truck (e.g., aluminum skiffs in the 12- to 15-foot range). The primary advantage of this type of boat is that it can be launched just about anywhere. Larger, trailered boats are restricted to boat launches with trailer access. The most appropriate outboard motor size for a boat this size is 15- to 20-horsepower—larger motors are generally too heavy to be carried separately from the boat (a necessity for car-topping).

If you decide to transport a skiff (or sea kayak) on top of your vehicle, be sure to use a sturdy, reliable rack or loader with a bow line to the front bumper and plenty of tie-downs. The rough road surfaces typical of even Baja's best highways can make it difficult to keep a boat in one place; crosswinds are also a problem in many areas. Frequent load checks are necessary.

Trailering

Larger boats that must be trailered because of their weight, and then floated from the trailer at a launch site, are much less versatile than car-top boats. On the entire peninsula fewer than 20 launches (five or six on the Pacific side, the remainder on the Sea of Cortez) have trailer access. Another disadvantage to boat trailering is that Baja road conditions can make towing a slow, unpleasant task. On the other hand, if one of these spots happens to be your destination and you plan to stay awhile, then the added cruising range of a larger vessel might be worthwhile.

Ocean Cruising

The typical ocean cruiser on Baja's Pacific side is a 12- to 24-meter (40- to 80-foot) power boat; on the Cortez side, 10- to 18-meter (35- to 60-foot) sailboats are popular. Properly equipped and crewed, these types of boats can navigate long distances and serve as a home-away-from-home. Smaller motor-powered vessels are usually prevented from Baja ocean cruising simply because of the lack of available fueling stations—their smaller fuel capacities greatly diminish cruising range. Sailboats smaller than nine meters (30 feet) have a similar problem because of the lack of storage space for food and water.

If you want to try your hand at ocean cruising, a Florida outfit with a base in Puerto Escondido on the Sea of Cortez can arrange bareboat sailing cruises on their 38- to 50-foot sailing yachts. Contact **The Moorings** (800-535-7289 or 813-535-1446), 19345 U.S. Hwy. 19 North, Suite 402, Clearwater, Florida 34624-3193. Another charter outfit is **Cortez Yacht Charters** (tel. 619-469-4255), 7888 Ostrow St., San Diego, CA 92111.

Charts And Tide Tables

The best nautical charts available for Baja waters are those originally published by the U.S. government. They come in two series: the Coastal Series, which covers the entire Pacific and Cortez coastlines in three large charts (numbers 21008, 21014, and 21017) with a scale of around 1:650,000 each (they vary a bit from chart to chart); and the Golfo de California Series, which offers much larger-scale maps (from 1:30,000 for La Paz to 1:290,610 for the entire Cape Region) of selected areas along the Cortez coast and around the Cape. The nautical surveys that resulted in both series were carried out between 1873 and 1901, so many of the place names are out of date.

The charts can be purchased individually from the **Defense Mapping Agency** (tel. 800-826-0342 or 301-227-2495), Washington, DC 20315-0010. Two of the Coastal Series are out of print, however, and others may eventually drop from sight as well. A much better, and less expensive source of these charts is *Chart-Guide: Mexico West,* a compilation of all the U.S. nautical charts from San Diego to Guatemala, including those currently unavailable from the DMA. ChartGuide has extensively updated the U.S. charts by marking anchorages, boat ramps, hazards, even fishing and diving spots. The spiral-bound volume costs US$58 and can be ordered from **ChartGuide** (tel. 714-533-1423), 300 N. Wilshire No. 5, Anaheim, CA 92801. It is also available in many Alta California marine supply stores.

Tide tables are published annually; to cover the entire Baja coastline you'll need two sets, one that pertains to the Pacific tides and one for the Sea of Cortez tides. Either or both can be ordered from the **Map Centre** (tel. 619-291-3830, 2611 University Ave., San Diego, California, 92104-2894) or purchased from marine supply stores.

Legal Requirements

Boat Permits: Any nonresident foreigner operating a boat in Mexican waters who intends to fish from the boat is required to carry a Mexican boat permit as well as a fishing permit. Even if you transport a boat to Baja with no fishing tackle and no plans to fish, it's a good idea to obtain a permit anyway; first, because you might change your mind when you see all the fish everyone else is pulling in, and, second, because you never know when you might end up carrying a passenger who has fishing tackle. *All* boats used for fishing require a permit, whether car-topped, trailered, carried inside a motor vehicle, or sailed on the open seas.

The permits can be obtained by mail from the Mexico Department of Fisheries or from the Mexico West Travel Club (see "Fishing," above, for the phone numbers and addresses of each). A boat permit is valid for 12 months; fees vary according to the length of the craft.

Temporary Import Permits: These aren't necessary for Baja but are required if you plan to take a boat to mainland Mexico, whether by land or water. The permit can be obtained from ferry offices in La Paz or Santa Rosalía or from a Registro Federal de Vehiculos office in Tijuana, Mexicali, Ensenada, or La Paz.

Port Check-ins: If you launch a boat at a Mexican port, specifically within the jurisdiction of a Captain of the Port (COTP), you must comply with official check-in procedures. This simply involves reporting to the COTP office and filling in some forms; the only time it's a hassle is when the Captain isn't present—you may have to wait around a few hours. Some ports have filing fees of up to US$15.

Anytime you enter another COTP's jurisdiction, you're required to check in. Checking out is not required except when you leave the port of origin (i.e., the port at which you first launched). Current COTPs in Baja are centered at Ensenada, Guerrero Negro, Bahía Magdalena (San Carlos), Cabo San Lucas, San José del Cabo, La Paz, Puerto Escondido, Loreto, Mulegé, Santa Rosalía, Bahía de los Angeles, and San Felipe.

Fuel, Parts, And Repairs

At present only five permanent marinas offer fuel year-round: Ensenada, Cabo San Lucas, La Paz, Puerto Escondido (fuel promised by early 1992), and Santa Rosalía. Elsewhere you must count on your own reserves or try your luck at canneries, boatyards, and fish camps along the way. (Prices at these sources will probably be above the official PEMEX rates.) Often at places other than marinas you'll have to go ashore and haul your own fuel back to the boat—come prepared with as many extra fuel containers as you can manage.

Finding marine supplies and repairs in Baja is much more challenging than finding fuel. Ensenada and La Paz are the best places for both—there's usually someone around who can work minor miracles. To a limited extent, parts—but not necessarily competent repair—are also available for established-brand (e.g., Johnson, Mercury, Evinrude) outboard motors in San Felipe, Loreto, Mulegé, and Cabo San Lucas. As with all other motorized conveyances in Baja, it's best to bring along plenty of spare parts (especially props, filters, water pumps, shear pins, hoses, and belts) to avoid getting stuck "in the middle of nowhere." Don't forget to bring along at least one life jacket per person—statistics show that in 80% of all boating fatalities, the victims weren't wearing PFDs (personal flotation devices).

Watermakers: Ocean cruisers might consider equipping their boats with a desalinator in order to avoid relying totally on stored fresh water. **Recovery Engineering** (tel. 800-548-0406 in the U.S. and Canada) has developed a new line of reverse-osmosis desalinators that run off 12-volt power sources and produce as much as 12½ liters of drinking water per hour from sea water. They also manufacture a hand-pumped survival version that weighs just over one kilogram for life rafts.

Emergencies

The U.S. Coast Guard monitors VHF radio channel 16 and can pick up transmissions as far south as the Ensenada area. In the north end of the Sea of Cortez, the Cholla Bay Sportsmen's Club in Lukesville, Arizona can respond to pleas for emergency assistance on VHF 16 with their own search-and-rescue team. Elsewhere along the Baja coastline, many Mexican agencies also monitor this channel, including the Mexican Navy, all COTPs, ferry vessels, and commercial ships.

Citizen-band (CB) radio is commonly used as a substitute for a telephone system in the more remote areas of the peninsula; it's also heavily used by RVers, the Green Angels, CB clubs, and other boaters, so it's one of the quickest ways to get attention. As in the U.S. and Canada, channel 9 is the most used, but channels 1, 3, 4, 7, 9, and 10 are also monitored. Special radio permits for foreign visitors are no longer required for CB radios with a transmission power of five watts or less.

SEA KAYAKING

Kayaking is one of the best ways to experience coastal Baja, bar none. Coves, inlets, water caves, and beaches inaccessible to skiffs or 4WD vehicles are easily approached in a kayak, especially on the Sea of Cortez. The Cortez is, in fact, a truly world-class kayaking environment, as more and more kayakers are discovering every year. It's also an excellent place to learn sea-kayaking skills, since the seas are generally calm.

The most popular kayaking areas on the Cortez coast are between Mulegé and Loreto and between Puerto Escondido and La Paz. (Bahía de los Angeles, protected by Isla Angel de la Guarda, is a favorite among novice kayakers.) The Gulf Current, which runs counterclockwise around the Cortez, favors trips planned in a north-south direction, with pickup arranged at the south end. A few intrepid kayakers have accomplished voyages across the currents from Bahía de los Angeles to the Mexican mainland by using the "Stepping Stones" route from island to island. (Seri Indians once followed the same route in reed canoes.) Extended Cortez trips are fairly easy when the weather's good, since campsites can be chosen from a huge selection of beaches and coves. If you bring along some light fishing gear, you're virtually guaranteed not to go without food.

Kayaking on the Pacific side, on the other hand, is for the experienced paddler only. Bahía Magdalena is the most popular area since it's large and fairly protected—whalewatching is also a big attraction here. Gray whales have been known to use their enormous tails to toss kayaks around, however, so your first Mag Bay outing in whale season should be in the company of someone who understands whale behavior. (Rule one: Never paddle directly toward a nearby whale; instead, run parallel to the whale's course.) Elsewhere on the Pacific coast, high surf and strong currents require equal quantities of strength and expertise. Finding a potential beach campsite isn't that difficult, but getting to it through the surf can be.

Equipment

There are four basic types of sea touring kayaks, each with several variations to choose from. All are in the 4½- to 5½-meter (15- to 18-foot) range necessary for extended paddling. The traditional closed-cockpit, hardshell boat comes in single (one-person) and double (two-person) models and is made either of plastic (molded polyethylene) or fiberglass. A "glass" boat is lighter and faster; a polyethylene boat is a bit heavier and slower, but holds up to Baja's rocky beaches much better. This type of kayak is easily car-topped, but a sturdy, secure rack is necessary on Baja's rough roads. Touring models can carry up to 115 kilograms of gear in built-in hatches, an attribute that makes them a good choice for extended overnight kayaking. Because of the sealed cockpits, they're also very good in cold waters (e.g., in the Pacific or the northern Cortez during the winter).

Folding kayaks are much easier to transport and are popular among kayakers who fly to their destinations, or who want to keep boats inside their vehicles rather than on top. The disadvantages are that they cost a bit more than a standard kayak and are a bit slower because of a wider beam (up to 86 cm/34 inches, compared with a 60- cm/24-inch beam on a hardshell boat). Assembling and disassembling them (the hull is usually hypalon, a synthetic rubber, stretched over aluminum tubing) is not as easy as their sales representatives usually claim. For carrying convenience, however, they can't be beat. The wider beams also mean they can carry up to twice the payload of a hardshell.

Gaining popularity in recent years, especially in Baja, are open-cockpit kayaks. The advantage to these is that the paddler sits on top of the deck rather than underneath it, which makes it much easier to exit and thus somewhat safer overall. Like the closed-cockpit variety, at least one model (the Scupper Pro) has hatched stowage compartments that carry up to 115 kilos. Open-cockpit kayaks are easier to paddle than the traditional kayak as well—just about anyone can paddle one with little or no practice—but they're a bit slower because of a wider beam and higher center of gravity. They also cost several hundred dollars less than the closed-deck version, making them the ideal kayak for the Baja visitor for whom kayaking is just one among several recreational activities; they make excellent dive stations for short scuba- or free-diving trips. (One model, the Scupper Scrambler, is designed specifically to carry scuba gear.) As with other hardshell kayaks, they're easily car-topped.

Inflatables are the lightest of the touring kayaks, which makes them even easier to transport than folding kayaks. However, inflating one requires an air compressor or electric air pump since the craft's rigidity depends on an air pressure of two to four pounds per square inch. Like the folding kayak, their main advantage is ease of storage and transport.

Accessories: Paddle styles are very much a personal choice although as a general rule, Aleuts or asymmetrical paddles are useful on the windy Pacific side, traditional shapes on the Cortez side—but whatever you do, bring a spare. Other essentials include a paddle leash, a 15-meter (50-foot) parachute-cord towline, a waterproof flashlight, and—in the winter—a wetsuit. A detachable two-wheel cart or "skate" for the stern is helpful for transporting a kayak short distances on land and can easily be stored in one of the hatches.

Foot-controlled rudders are really not necessary for Sea of Cortez kayaking during most of the year since winds and currents are usually moderate (the exception is from Nov. to March when wind and swells are up); also since there are no kayaking facilities in Baja, parts and service for a broken rudder are virtually nonexistent. On the Pacific side, or if you're going to attempt a cross-Cortez route to the mainland, a foot-controlled rudder is a good idea—but bring along spare parts.

If you can afford the extra weight, bring along a kayak sail rig to give your arms a rest when a good breeze (common in the Cortez as well as the Pacific) comes along.

Maps and Tide Tables: Nautical charts are of little use for kayak navigation—a better choice would be 1:50,000-scale topo maps, available from the Map Centre (see "Hiking and Backpacking," above for phone number and address). Tide tables are also invaluable (see "Boating," above for sources).

Organized Kayak Trips

A great way to learn the skills of sea kayaking in Baja is to join an organized trip led by experienced kayakers. One of the most established is **Sea Trek** (tel. 415-332-4457, 85 Liberty Ship Way, Sausalito, CA 94965), which specializes in one-week Sea of Cortez trips Dec.-May. They also occasionally offer special Bahía Magdalena trips during gray whale migrations. **Paddling South** (tel. 707-942-4550, 4510 Silverado Trail, Calistoga, CA 94515) is another reputable Baja specialist. The venerable standby **Baja Expeditions** (tel. 619-581-3311, 2625 Garnet Ave., San Diego, CA 92109) offers kayaking trips to Mag Bay and to the Midriff Islands.

Several universities and community colleges in the U.S. state of California sponsor kayaking programs in Baja open to nonstudents. The UC Aquatic Center at the University of California, Berkeley, for example, recently began offering a 10-day Sea of Cortez trip for only US$450 per person, about US$300 less than most private tour companies. (Call 415-642-4000 for further information on this particular program.)

WINDSURFING

The Sea of Cortez is a windsurfer's paradise from Nov. through March, particularly from the central coast southward. Bahía de los Angeles and Bahía Concepción are perfect for beginning and intermediate board-sailors while the high winds of the East Cape will delight those in the advanced class. Any of the channels between the peninsula's east coast and the larger offshore islands (e.g., Canal de Cerralvo, Canal San José, Canal de Ballenas) usually see good sideshore wind action, although sometimes that goes together with strong currents. If you don't see other sailboards out, try to find someone who knows the currents before launching.

La Paz is also a very good area, even in the summer, when a strong breeze called El Coromuel comes in just about every afternoon. The best spots here are along the mostly deserted beaches on the peninsula northeast of town— Punta Balandra to Punta Coyote. When nothing's blowing in the Bahía de la Paz vicinity, dedicated windsurfers can shuttle west across the peninsula to check out the action at Punta Marquéz on the Pacific side, only 72 km (45 miles) away.

Los Barriles on Bahía de Palmas, along the East Cape, is one of the more accessible windsurfing areas in southern Baja from Mexico Highway 1. The wind is a steady 18-30 knots here all winter long and wave-sailing is possible in some spots. During the season, uphauling is usually out of the question due to chop and high winds, so ability to waterstart is a prerequisite for board-sailing in this area.

Los Barriles is also home to the **Baja Vela Highwind Center** (tel. 800-223-5443 in the U.S. and Canada, or 415-322-0613), which offers highly rated instruction and package deals from mid-Nov. through mid-March. Even if you're not a participant in one of their windsurfing vacations, you may be able to arrange for service and parts here during the season. Every January, Vela cosponsors (with equipment manufacturer O'Neill) the Baja Windsurfing Championships at Los Barriles. (For more information on the Center, see "Los Barriles," under "Cape Region," p. 289.)

The Pacific side of Baja generally demands a more experienced board-sailor. Those who can handle high surf along with strong winds will love it. Novices and intermediate windsurfers can enjoy the larger bays (Bahía de San Quintín, Bahía Magdalena, Bahía Almejas), which are protected from major swells in all but the worst weather. Board-sailors with sturdy transport—4WD or high-clearance trucks—can choose from dozens of smaller bays connected to Mexico Hwy. 1 by dirt roads of varying quality.

SURFING

Baja is one of the last refuges of "soul surfing," an experience that has all but disappeared from the crowded surfing beaches of Alta California. Instead of fighting for a wave, Baja surfers will typically take turns, making sure that everyone gets a ride now and then. Two reasons account for the laid-back atmosphere: Baja attracts a lot of older Alta California surfers who are either fed up with the agro scene up north or are simply investigating new territory (or both); fewer surfers are seen on Baja beaches, hence heated competition is simply less imperative.

From the border all the way down to Cabo, most of the good surf areas are below *puntas* (points) that offer right point breaks stoked by prevailing northwesterlies during the winter months. Even without any advance tips on Baja surfing, a surfer has only to drive down the Transpeninsular with a good road map in hand, turning west wherever the map shows a side road leading off to "Punta X." As with all other coastal recreation, more places are accessible to those with high clearance vehicles or 4WD, although many good surf spots are easily accessed by ordinary passenger car as well.

In the summer the surf's mostly small to flat except when a tropical storm comes up from the south. When this happens, there's usually high surf at Cabo and at the southern end of many offshore Pacific islands, the most notorious being Isla Natividad (under "South Central Baja," p. 253) and Islas de Todos Santos ("Tijuana to Ensenada," p. 160).

Surf Locations
The number of surfers diminishes as you proceed south of Ensenada or north of Cabo San Lucas since any point between these two destinations involves some serious road travel. In fact, even when the surf's really pumping in this middle zone, you stand a good chance of sharing monster breaks with only a handful of others—or even having them all to yourself—since there are no "surf hotlines" for central and southern Baja. (San Diego surf reports can be generalized only as far south as Ensenada.) This means serendipity is a major element in Baja surfing safaris—those that have the most time to scout the coastline will find the best wave action.

In the Ensenada area, the main spot is San Miguel (also known as "Rincon"), a small bay just south of the last toll gate on the Tijuana-Ensenada toll road. A number of surfers live

dawn patrol
(JOE CUMMINGS)

SHARKS: MYTH VS. FACT

The word "shark" usually evokes an initial reaction of fear or loathing. Such a reaction is somewhat irrational, however, considering that of the 360 identified species of shark, only four (bull, tiger, white, and ocean whitetip) are known to attack humans. Around 60 shark species swim the Pacific and Sea of Cortez waters of Baja California, and of these the most common are smooth hammerhead, common thresher, bonito, sand, blue, and blacktip.

The shark's killer image is based on its quite real, natural prowess as a predator—sharks may, in fact, have been the world's first predators, having first appeared about 400 million years ago (200 million years before the dinosaurs). Sharks can hear the sounds of other fish in the water from up to a mile away; they can smell blood from a similar distance and sense faint electrical fields transmitted by other animals that indicate whether an animal is in distress. A special lens in the shark's eye intensifies light so that it can see prey in almost total darkness. All of these attributes form the perfect combination for quick, silent surprise attacks. Most sharks, however, feed on small fish. The largest of all, the whale shark, which reaches up to 18 meters (60 feet) long and may weigh as much as four tons, feeds on tiny plankton. (The magnificent whale shark is occasionally seen in the Sea of Cortez.)

As animals at or near the top of the marine food chain, sharks play a similar role in the sea to that of lions on land—helping to maintain an ecological balance by weeding out sick or feeble fish that can spread disease or bad genetics among their own or other marine populations. The shark's greatest natural enemy is humans, whose appetite for shark meat is fast depleting shark populations around the world (especially in the Pacific).

About 100 million sharks a year—about the same quantity as tuna—are taken by hook or net, an amount that marine biologists caution is 9,000 tons more than the shark population can tolerate without serious decrease. As a result, many shark species are on the brink of endangerment, a trend that doesn't bode well for other species in marine ecosystems because of the shark's important place in the food web.

Shark Attacks
Most sharks are under two meters in length and are much more likely to flee from a swimmer or diver than to attack. The most dangerous is the great white shark, which can reach over six meters and weigh up to 2½ tons, and is the fastest and most powerful of the sharks. Its sharp, serrated teeth are set in jaws that hinge widely for the largest possible bite. Although not common, they occasionally cruise the deeper waters of the Pacific and account for most fatal attacks on humans.

Surfers are usually at a greater risk than swimmers or divers because the great white is more likely to confuse the profile of a surfer's dangling limbs with relatively small fish. When a shark can see the entire body of a swimmer, it is more likely to consider the prey too large to attack. Murky waters diminish general visibility and can add to potential confusion; hence, many shark attacks on humans occur in murky waters (often caused by abrupt changes in weather conditions). If an area is known for the presence of large sharks *(tiburones)*, it might be best for surfers to avoid unclear waters, especially at offshore breaks.

Searching the water's surface for shark fins is a relatively useless activity since a shark will have pinpointed your location long before you've become aware of any shark activity. Besides avoiding murky water conditions, a more obvious precaution for surfers with open wounds is to stay out of the water since blood may attract sharks.

here year-round and others make weekend trips from southern Alta California, so at times it's a bit on the crowded side. The winter break here is usually quite reliable, pumping for weeks at a time. And when the surf's too small onshore, you can always climb in a panga and cruise 20 km (12 miles) out to Islas de Todos Santos, home of the biggest breaks on the entire west coast of North America. When San Miguel's nearly flat, Todos Santos waves may hit three to four meters (10-12 feet); when San Mig's ripping at 2½-3½ meters (8-10 feet), the pros will be out at northern Todos on their nine-foot guns, tearing down 30-foot Waimea-style walls. The southern island of the twin Islas de Todos Santos produces a good left break during summer swells.

Several spots can also be found between Ensenada and the border in and around La Fonda, La Misión, and Rosarito, especially Punta Descanso, Punta Mesquite, and Punta Salsipuedes. South of Ensenada to the Cape are perhaps dozens of places with intermittent point breaks, but the most reputable for accessibility and steady surf are at Punta San José, Punta Baja, Punta Santa Rosalillita, Punta Abreojos, Punta El Conejo, and beaches in the vicinity of Todos Santos (the Baja California Sur town, not the islands).

For important shark information relevant to surfers in Baja waters, see "Sharks: Myth vs. Fact," above.

Equipment

Surfing is one of the most low-tech sports of modern times, so fortunately the scarcity of surf shops in Baja is not a major problem. For any extended trip down the coast, carrying both a short- and a long-board (or a gun for the northwest shores of Isla Natividad or Islas de Todos Santos in winter) would prepare one for the wide variation in surf. Besides wax and a cooler, about the only other items you need bring are a first-aid kit for routine surf injuries (most surf spots are far from medical assistance—don't forget butterfly bandages) and a fiberglass-patching kit for bad dings. Boards can also be repaired at just about any boat-yard on the coast, since most Mexican pangas are made of fiberglass and require a lot of patching.

Small surf shops in Ensenada and Cabo San Lucas sell boards, surfwear, and accessories. You can buy Mexican-made boards—San Miguel and Cactus brands—in Ensenada for about US$50 to US$75 less than what they cost north of the border (about US$100 less than retail for a comparable American or Japanese board).

Organized Trips

Surfers aren't usually big on organized travel but for one destination in Baja, Isla Natividad,

some make an exception. Getting to Natividad ordinarily involves driving to Punta Eugenia on the Vizcaíno Peninsula, an ordeal in itself, and then chartering a boat to the island (when a boat can be found). **Scorpio Surfing Tours** (tel. 619-425-8154, P.O. Box 4184, Chula Vista, CA 91909) provides a much easier alternative.

Scorpio has a special concession for the famous "Open Doors" break at Isla Natividad for six months per year. They offer a package surf trip to the island from July through Sept. (peak time for the south swell) that includes roundtrip airfare from Ensenada, lodging on Natividad, and two meals per day for rates ranging from US$350 for a weekend to US$550 for a full week. Tours are limited to 12 persons. For more information on the island, see "Isla Natividad," p. 258.

SNORKELING AND SCUBA DIVING

The semitropical Sea of Cortez coral reefs at the southern tip of the Cape Region are among the most well-known dive locations in Baja—simply because they're so close to shore—but many spots of interest along much of the 4,800-km coastline's entire length are accessible to divers with good boat transportation and the necessary diving skills. For the most part, Pacific diving is for experienced offshore scuba divers only while the Cortez coast and islands are excellent for inshore novice divers as well as snorkelers.

Marinelife—the usual object of a diver's attention—is concentrated in Baja among three types of environments: kelp fields, reefs (both rock and hard coral), and shipwrecks. The latter develop into artificial reefs with time and are particularly plentiful in Baja waters. Some of the sunken vessels that can be explored are Liberty ships, junks, steamers, tuna clippers, submarines, yachts, ferryboats, tugs, and full-rigged barques.

Pacific Diving

The most dived areas of all are in the northwest—Islas Todos Santos and Islas Coronados—because of their accessibility to day-tripping southern Alta Californians. As at most of

Baja's Pacific islands, the west and southwest sides of these islands offer the greatest proliferation of sealife, including kelp beds, rock reefs, and encrusted sea pinnacles amid scenic sand flats. Both the Todos Santos and the Coronados are popular among spearfishing enthusiasts because of the large yellowtail populations that feed in the vicinity of these island groups. Halibut, various sea basses, and bonito are also common, as is lobster. (The latter are illegal for nonresident aliens to take.) The cold, fast-running currents mean that visibility is usually quite good in offshore areas.

Farther south at Bahía Rosario (off the coast near the town of El Rosario) are some large kelp beds and the Sacramento Reef. Along with an abundance of marinelife, this four-km-long reef features so many shipwrecks that it's been dubbed the "Graveyard of the Pacific." The reef (named for the paddlewheeler *Sacramento* that ran aground here in 1872) is also home to a population of large lobsters dubbed *burros* (donkeys) or *caballos* (horses) locally. Isla San Gerónimo, 2½ km northwest of the reef, is known as an excellent spearfishing location.

The next diving area south is off the tip of the Vizcaíno Peninsula at Islas San Benito, Isla Cedros, and Isla Natividad. This group of islands features kelp beds, sea pinnacles, shoals, and rock reefs. Bahía Magdalena, much farther south, is of interest for its shallows teeming with sealife, including sea turtles, sharks, manta rays, seals, and whales. Heavy swells and surging along the Pacific coast mean that it should only be tackled by experienced scuba divers or under the guidance of an experienced underwater guide. Ensenada has three dive shops, but southward along the Pacific coast there are none before Cabo San Lucas.

Sea Of Cortez Diving

Because the Sea of Cortez has one of the richest marine ecosystems in the world, the underwater scenery is especially vivid and varied. Sea lions, numerous whale and dolphin varieties, colorful tropical species, manta rays, and schooling hammerhead sharks are all part of a thick food chain stimulated by cold-water upwellings amid the over 100 islands and islets that dot the Cortez. The largest proportion of Cortez sealife are species of tropical Panamic origins that have found their way north from Central and South American waters.

The northern Cortez is avoided by many divers because of strong tidal surges, speedy currents, and overall lack of underwater marine variety (relative to the central and southern Cortez). In general, the northernmost diving area is Bahía de los Angeles, where tidal conditions and visibility are suitable for recreational diving. The offshore islands are the main attractions here; two small hotels can service divers and arrange guided trips.

Next south are the Midriff Islands, which require long-range boats and an experienced appraisal of local currents and tidal changes. Rock reefs are abundant throughout these islands. Below the Midriffs, tidal conditions calm down considerably and the water is generally warmer. Marinelife is plentiful and varied, and spearfishing is excellent in many areas.

In the central Cortez, divers are serviced by Mulegé Divers, one of the better dive-shop operations in Baja. Many of the nearby islands, bays, and points are suitable for snorkeling as well as scuba diving; Isla San Marcos, Punta Chivato, Islas Santa Inés, and Bahía Concepción are among the most well-known areas. Loreto, a bit farther south, also has a dive shop and several popular diving areas nearby: Isla Coronado, Punta Coyote, Isla del Carmen, and Isla Danzante. Rock reefs, boulders, volcanic ridges, and sand flats are common throughout. Farther east in the Cortez are vast submarine canyons as well as more remote volcanic and continental islands best explored by experienced scuba divers.

From La Paz south, onshore water temperatures usually hover between 21° C (70° F) and 29° C (85° F) year-round, making the southern Cortez the most popular diving destination on this side of Baja. The area is most known for the Pulmo Reef, the only hard coral reef in the Sea of Cortez. Water visibility is best from July through Oct., when it exceeds 30 meters (100 feet); this is also when the air temperature is warmest, however, often reaching well over 32° C (90° F).

La Paz has several dive shops; popular local dive sites are numerous and include Playa Balandra (mostly snorkeling), Roca Suwanee, Isla Espíritu Santo, Isla Partida, the *Salvatierra* shipwreck, El Bajito Reef, Los Islotes, and the El Bajo Seamount. El Bajo is famous for its summer population of giant manta rays, who seem unusually disposed toward allowing divers to hitch rides on their *allas* (pectoral fins). Schooling hammerhead sharks are also common during the summer months—they are very rarely aggressive toward divers while swimming in schools, so El Bajo is an excellent area for observing them.

The Cabo Pulmo and Los Cabos (San José del Cabo and Cabo San Lucas) areas are served by several small dive operations in Cabo San Lucas. Pulmo Reef in Bahía Pulmo consists of a series of eight volcanic ridges inhabited by profuse coral life. The coral attracts a wide variety of fish of all sizes and colors, and other, smaller reefs as well as shipwrecks are in the general vicinity. Because most of the underwater attractions are close to shore, this area is good for diving from small boats or open-cockpit kayaks.

Several coves along the coast toward Cabo San Lucas are good snorkeling sites. Bahía Cabo San Lucas itself is a protected marine park; the rocks and points along the bayshore are suitable for snorkeling and novice scuba diving while the deep submarine canyon just 45 meters offshore attracts more experienced thrill-seekers. This canyon is known for its intriguing "sand falls," streams of falling sand channeled between rocks along the canyon walls. Nearby Playa Santa María, on the way east toward San José del Cabo, is a popular snorkeling area with coral at either end of a large cove.

Equipment

Divers shouldn't count on finding the equipment they need in Baja, even in the resort areas; since most equipment sold or rented at the dive shops is imported from the U.S., stock can vary from season to season. Purchase prices are also generally higher in Mexico than north of the border.

For Pacific diving south to Punta Abreojos, a full quarter-inch wet suit is recommended year-round; from Punta Abreojos south lighter suits are sufficient in the summer. At Cabo San Lucas and around the Cape as far north as the central Cortez, a light suit may be needed from late Nov. through March, shorties or ordinary swim suits the rest of the year. From the Midriff Islands north in the Sea of Cortez, heavier suits are necessary Dec. through early April.

Because divers and anglers occasionally frequent the same areas, a good diving knife is essential in case you have to deal with wayward fishing line; in fact, bring two knives so you'll have a spare. Bring extra CO_2 cartridges for flotation vests, rubber slings for spearguns, O-rings, and a wet-suit patching kit.

Air

Dependable air for scuba tanks is usually available in Ensenada, Mulegé, Loreto, La Paz, and Cabo San Lucas. Always check the compressor first, however, to make sure it's well maintained and running clean to lessen the risk of a contaminated air supply. Divers with extensive Baja experience will usually carry a portable compressor not only to avoid contaminated air, but so they can travel to areas where tank refills aren't available.

Recompression Chambers

The nearest full-time, dependable recompression facility is the **Hyperbaric Medicine Center** (tel. 619-543-5222) at the University of California Medical Center in San Diego. The HMC is open Mon.-Fri., 0730-1630, and for emergencies. Emergency air transport to the facility can be arranged by calling Life Flight (tel. 619-297-4356) or by contacting one of the air evacuation organizations that service Baja. Several commercial diving facilities on Baja's Pacific coast also have recompression chambers but they're often suffering from disuse and disrepair.

Organized Diving Trips

Two Alta California outfits operate dive trips in Baja waters: **Baja Expeditions** (tel. 619-581-3311, 2625 Garnet Ave., San Diego, CA 92109) leads scuba diving excursions to the

La Paz area in the Sea of Cortez; **Diving Charters** (tel. 619-224-4997, P.O. Box 6374, San Diego, CA 92106) specializes in trips off Baja's Pacific coast—including the Coronados and Isla Guadalupe.

In Baja, divers will find skilled diving guides in Ensenada, Bahía de los Angeles, Mulegé, Loreto, La Paz, and Cabo San Lucas. Most of the Baja dive outfits also offer instruction and scuba certification at quite reasonable rates.

RACE AND SPORTS BETTING

During the U.S. Prohibition era of the 1920s, casinos were a major part of the Baja high life in Tijuana, Mexicali, the Coronado Islands, and Ensenada. Although the Mexican government outlawed casino gambling in the 1930s, it has allowed race and sports book to continue in Baja California Norte and today it's a major source of foreign revenue for the state.

The heir to Tijuana's lavish El Casino de Agua Caliente is the **Caliente Race and Sports Book,** with locations at the famed Caliente Race Track in Tijuana as well as in Ensenada, Rosarito, Mexicali, and San Felipe. The Caliente Race Track hosts weekly horse and greyhound racing (see "Tijuana," p. 139 for details) but at all Caliente Race and Sports Book locations you can bet on basketball, football, baseball, and other sports as well. Caliente has an information hotline in Alta California: (619) 231-1910 (or 231-1919). **LF Race and Sports Book** operates a similar chain in Tijuana, Rosarito, and Ensenada. The Caliente and LF betting lounges also feature bars and restaurants; betting is not required if patrons just want to have a drink or a meal while watching sports events on multiple screens.

In Tijuana you have the alternative of betting on live jai alai matches at the Fronton Jai Alai on Av. Revolución (see "Tijuana" for further information).

HOLIDAYS, FESTIVALS, AND EVENTS

Mexicans love a fiesta and Bajacalifornios are no exception. Any occasion will suffice as an excuse to hold a celebration, from a birthday or promotion to a lobster harvest. Add to all the civic possibilities the vast number of Mexican Catholic religious holidays, and there's potential for some kind of public fiesta at least every week of the year, if not all 365 days. Besides the national religious holidays, Mexico has feast days for 115 Catholic saints per year (9 or 10 each month). Any town, pueblo, ejido, or colonia named for a saint (e.g., Santo Tomás, San Javier, Santa Catarina, San José, San Ignacio, etc.) will usually hold a fiesta on the feast day of its namesake. Individuals named for saints, too, will often host parties on their *día de santo* (saint's day).

The primary requisites of a fiesta are plenty of food (especially tamales, considered a festive dish), beer and liquor, music, and dancing. More elaborate celebrations will include parades, exhibitions, *charreadas* (Mexican rodeos), and occasional fireworks.

Some of the more memorable yearly events and public holidays observed throughout Baja are highlighted below by month. Smaller festivals and events held locally are mentioned later in the text along with the respective destination. Actual dates may vary from year to year, so be sure to check with the appropriate tourist office in advance if you need current dates for the time of your visit.

Government offices and some businesses close on national holidays. These closings are not always mentioned in the text; you may want to call ahead to find out.

January
New Year's Day, 1 Jan., is an official holiday.

Día de los Santos Reyes, 6 January. See *Las Posadas* under December.

February
Constitution Day, 5 February, is an official holiday.

Carnaval: This pre-lenten festival is held in late February or early March as a last celebration of the carnal pleasures Catholics are supposed to forego during the 40-day lent season preceding Easter. (The fiesta's name derives from the Italian *carne vale*, "flesh taken away.") In Mexico, Carnaval is traditionally observed only in port towns; in Baja the festival is celebrated most grandly in La Paz and Ensenada. Like New Orleans's Mardi Gras, Carnaval features lots of music, dancing, costumes, parades, and high-spirited revelry. See "Ensenada," p. 172 for more information.

Flag Day, 24 February, is an official holiday.

March
Birthday of Benito Juárez, 21 March, is an official holiday.

Spring Break: Not a Mexican holiday at all, this is an annual ritual for American college and university students (mostly southern Alta Californians and Arizonans) who go on the rampage in Rosarito, Ensenada, San Felipe, and Los Cabos. The spring break season usually straddles late March and early April. Unless you're one of the revelers, these towns should be avoided at all costs during these weeks.

April
Semana Santa: "Holy Week," or Easter Week (the third week in April), is second only to Christmas as the most important holiday period of the year. One of the most prominent Semana Santa customs is breaking *cascarones,* colored eggs stuffed with confetti, over the heads of friends and family. Besides attending mass on Good Friday and Easter Sunday, many Mexicans take this opportunity to go on vacations. Baja resorts (particularly Rosarito, Ensenada, San Felipe, and Los Cabos) can be overcrowded this week since the peninsula receives a large influx of both Mexican mainlanders and North Americans.

Rosarito-Ensenada 50-Mile Bicycle Ride: A yearly event since 1987, the ride takes place on the last Saturday in April and attracts as many as 10,000 participants, making it one of the largest cycling events in the world. The route follows the coast with an elevation differential of around a 300 meters (a thousand feet). The same ride is repeated in the fall with even larger crowds (up to 16,000). Sponsored by **Bicycling West** (tel. 619-583-3001, P.O. Box 15128, San Diego, CA 92175-0128).

Newport-Ensenada Yacht Race: Reportedly the world's largest international yachting regatta, held the last weekend in April. Boats race from Newport Beach, Alta California, to Ensenada. Sponsored by the Newport Ocean Sailing Association (tel. 714-640-1351, fax 714-640-1628).

May

International Workers' Day, 1 May, is an official holiday.

Cinco de Mayo: Held on 5 May, this festival commemorates the defeat of an attempted French invasion at Puebla de los Angelos, on Mexico's Gulf of Mexico coast, in 1862. Features music, dance, food, and other cultural events.

Mother's Day (Día de las Madres) is held on 10 May.

Feast of Corpus Christi: A religious holiday celebrated 60 days after Easter to honor the Body of Christ and the Eucharist. Cornhusk figurines and miniature mules are displayed in stores and homes.

June

Navy Day, 1 June, is an official holiday.

September

Día de Nuestra Señora de Loreto: Held in Loreto on 8 September to commemorate the founding of the first mission in the Californias. Special masses, processions, music, dancing, and food.

Mexican Independence Day (Fiesta Patria de la Independencia): Also called Diez y Seis, since it falls on 16 Sept., this holiday celebrates the country's independence from Spain, as announced in 1821 in the town of Dolores. Festivities actually begin on the 15th and last two days. The biggest celebrations are centered in the state capitals of Mexicali and La Paz, and include fireworks, parades, charreadas, music, and folk-dance performances.

Rosarito-Ensenada 50-Mile Bicycle Ride is held on the last Saturday in September; see description under "April."

October

Día de la Raza: Celebrated as Columbus Day north of the border, 12 Oct. in Mexico commemorates the founding of the Mexican race as heralded by the arrival of Columbus in the New World.

November

Día de los Muertos: The "Day of the Dead" is Mexico's third-most important holiday, corresponding to Europe's All Saints Day except that it's celebrated on the 1st and 2nd of Nov. instead of only the 1st. Some of the festivities are held in cemeteries where children clean the headstones and crucifixes of their deceased relatives *(los difuntos)* and play games unique to this fiesta. Roadside shrines throughout Baja are laid with fresh flowers and other tributes to the dead. Offerings of *pan de los muertos* (bread of the dead) and food and liquor are placed before family altars on behalf of deceased family members along with papier-mâché skulls and skeletons.

Baja 1000: In the second or third week of November the most famous desert race in North America, the Baja Mil, draws a dedicated crowd of off-road fanatics and automotive manufacturers hoping to gain advertising copy like "Baja 1000 Winner" or at least "Baja 1000-Tested" if their products manage to finish the race. These days the course follows established auto trails (still quite challenging) to avoid further damage to Baja's fragile desert lands; the course alternates from year to year between a full 1,000-mile (1,600-km) race between Ensenada and La Paz and a 1,000-km race that loops through the northern state only. The race runs in several classes from dirt bikes to 4WD trucks; an average of 300 drivers (about 120 motorcycle and 180 car/truck entries) compete. Sponsored by SCORE (tel.

818-889-9216, 31125 Via Colinas, Suite 908, Westlake Village, CA 91362).

Anniversary of the 1910 Revolution is held on 20 Nov. (official holiday).

December

Día de Nuestra Señora de Guadalupe: The feast day of the Virgin of Guadalupe, Mexico's patron saint, is 12 Dec.; special masses are held that day throughout Mexico and the nearest Sunday to the 12th also features special events such as mariachi masses, food booths, and games. The celebrations at the border town of Tecate are particularly well attended.

Las Posadas: Beginning on 16 Dec., Mexicans hold nightly *posadas*—candlelight processions terminating at elaborate, community-built nativity scenes—in commemoration of the Holy Family's search for lodging. The processions continue for nine consecutive nights. Other activities include piñata parties where children break open hanging papier-mâché figures filled with small gifts and candy.

Churches large and small hold continuous Christmas masses beginning at midnight on the 25th (Día de la Navidad).

Las Posadas culminates on 6 Jan., which is Día de los Santos Reyes, (literally, "Day of the King-Saints," referring to the story of the Three Wise Men). On this day Mexican children receive their Christmas gifts, and family and friends gather to eat a wreath-shaped fruitcake called *rosca de reyes* (wreath of the kings) baked especially for this occasion. Hidden inside each *rosca* is a small clay figurine *(muñeco)* that represents the infant Jesus. While sharing the rosca on this day, the person whose slice by chance contains the muñeco is obliged to host a *candelaría*, or Candlemas party, on 2 Feb. for everyone present.

At the candelaría (which commemorates the day the newborn Jesus was first presented at the Temple in Jerusalem), the host traditionally displays a larger Christ-infant figure and serves tamales and *atole* (a thick, hot grain drink flavored with fruit or chocolate).

CUSTOMS AND CONDUCT

CROSS-CULTURAL COMMUNICATION

Time And Appointments

Of the many common myths about Mexican culture, the one about the Mexican sense of time being highly flexible is probably the most accurate. The whys and wherefores attached to this concept are too numerous and too complex for the context of this book. (Read Octavio Paz's *The Labyrinth of Solitude* for a glimpse of an explanation.) However, it's important to realize that the so-called *mañana* attitude is nothing more than a generalization; in many cases Mexican individuals may be every bit as punctual as North Americans (especially when it comes to doing business with North Americans). Furthermore, Bajacalifornios, it is said, tend to be more punctual than their mainland counterparts.

If you make an appointment with a Bajacalifornio for dinner, a party, or other social engagement, you should figure that the actual meeting time will be around two hours later than verbally scheduled. As with business engagements, if the person involved has dealt frequently with North Americans, this might not *always* be the case. Also, Mexicans will typically accept an invitation rather than say no, even if they don't plan to attend the scheduled event. This is because, within the Mexican social context, it is usually worse to refuse an invitation than it is not to show up. To avoid disappointment, prepare yourself for any of these scenarios.

When hiring a fishing boat or any sort of guide in Baja, you can expect a modicum of punctuality since Mexicans in the tourist industry have usually adapted themselves to the expectations of North American and European tourists. Again, note the difference between business and social appointments.

Siesta: The stereotypical siesta, where everyone goes off to sleep for a couple of hours in the afternoon, is fast becoming history throughout Mexico. Nevertheless, a vestige of the siesta has been preserved in the opening and closing hours for offices and small businesses, typically closed from two to four or three to five in the afternoon. The first hour is reserved for *comida,* the midday meal, while the second hour is for relaxing or taking care of personal business. While to North Americans two hours may seem like a long lunch hour, the fact is that Mexican offices and businesses generally stay open much later than in the U.S. or Canada (until seven or eight in the evening).

No matter what hours are posted for small businesses, the actual opening and closing times may vary with the whims of the proprietors. This is also true for tourist information offices, but banks usually follow their posted hours to the minute.

Meal Times: If you'll be meeting Mexican acquaintances for meals, whether at a restaurant or in their homes, you should be aware that customary eating times differ from those in North America or northern Europe.

The first meal of the day, *desayuno* (breakfast), is usually taken at about the same time as the average North American breakfast, say between 0600 and 0800. On a working weekday, there may be another light breakfast/early lunch at around 1100 called *almuerzo* (on weekends and holidays this may be a much larger feed), or nothing at all until around 1400 or 1500 when the *comida,* the largest meal of the day, is eaten. In small towns, workers often go home for this meal, not returning to the workplace until around 1600 or 1700.

After work, at anywhere from around 2000 to 2200, *la cena,* the final meal of the day, is eaten. Cenas are usually as light and informal as desayunos, so it is not often that guests are invited to a home for this meal. On weekends and holidays, the cena may become a grander occasion.

Terms Of Address

Mexicans frequently use titles of respect when addressing one another. At a minimum, "señor" will do for men, "señora" for married women, and "señorita" for unmarried women or girls. When in doubt about a woman's marital status, "seño" can be used.

Professional titles can also be used for variety and to show additional respect. *Maestro* (master) or *maestra* (mistress) are common and can be used to address skilled workers (cobblers, auto mechanics, seamstresses, etc.) and any teacher except those at secondary schools and college or university (who are *profesores)*. Attorneys or persons with graduate degrees are *licenciado* (men) or *licenciada* (women), while doctors are *doctor* or *doctora*.

Body Language

Mexicans tend to use their arms and hands more during verbal communication than do their North American or North European counterparts. Learning to read the more common gestures (but not necessarily imitate them) can greatly enhance your comprehension of everyday conversations, even when you don't understand every word being spoken.

One of the more confusing gestures for North Americans is the way Mexicans beckon to other persons by holding the hand out, palm down, and waving in a downward motion. This looks similar to a farewell gesture in the U.S. and Canada but means "come here" in Mexico. Holding the palm upward and crooking the fingers toward the body, the typical North American gesture for "come here," is a vaguely obscene gesture in Mexico.

Extending the thumb and forefinger from a closed hand and holding them about a half-inch apart means "a little bit" in North America but in Mexico usually means "just a moment" or "wait a minute" (often accompanied by the utterance *momentito* or *poquito)*.

The wagging of an upright forefinger means "no" or "don't do that." This is a good gesture to use when children hanging around at stoplights or gasoline pumps begin wiping your windshields and you don't want them to. Don't overdo it, though—they only need to see a few seconds of the wagging finger—otherwise you'll look out of control.

Handshakes and Abrazos: Mexicans commonly greet one another with handshakes, which are used between the sexes and among children and adults—in fact, with everybody. Mexican males who are friends will sometimes greet one another with an *abrazo* (embrace) and urban women may kiss one another on the cheek. Foreigners should stick to the handshake until they establish more intimate relationships with Bajacalifornios. Handshakes are also used upon parting and saying farewell.

Dress

Compared to their mainland counterparts, who tend to be more conservative, Bajacalifornios are relatively tolerant about the way visitors dress. Nonetheless, invisible lines exist which, out of respect for Mexican custom, shouldn't be crossed. Number one is that beachwear is not considered suitable dress for town visits. Rosarito, Cabo San Lucas, and San Felipe are the most obvious exceptions to this general rule since during peak tourist seasons tourists outnumber the locals in these towns, so the locals are quite habituated to gringo foolishness. In Ensenada, however, beachwear will result in indignant stares if you wander far from the Avenida Lopez Mateos tourist strip. In La Paz and other Baja towns, you're disrespecting local custom if you wear a bathing suit anywhere other than the beaches.

Churches: Upon entering a church or chapel in Baja, men are expected to remove their hats. (Many Mexican males will also remove their hats when passing in front of a church.) More tradition-minded Bajacalifornio women will cover their heads when inside a church, but younger women usually don't and foreign females aren't expected to. Shorts, sleeveless shirts/blouses, sandals, or bare feet are considered improper dress (for both men and women) in churches, even for brief sightseeing visits.

LEGAL MATTERS

All foreign visitors in Mexico are subject to Mexican legal codes, which are based on Roman and Napoleonic law. The most distinctive features of the Mexican judiciary system, compared to Anglo-American systems, are that the system doesn't provide for trials by jury (the judge decides) nor writs of habeas corpus (though you must be charged within 72 hours of incarceration). Furthermore, bail is rarely granted to an arrested foreigner—for many offenses, not even Mexican nationals are allowed bail. Hence, once arrested and jailed for a serious offense, it can be very difficult to arrange release. The lesson here is: Don't get involved in matters that might result in your arrest—this primarily means anything having to do with drugs or guns.

The often-repeated saw that in Mexico an arrested person is considered guilty until proven innocent is no more true south of the border than north. As in Canada or the U.S., an arrested person is considered a criminal *suspect* until the courts confirm or deny guilt. You have the right to notify your consulate if detained.

Mexican federal police *(federales)* occasionally set up roadblocks to conduct searches for drugs, mostly under pressure from the United States. Such roadblocks have become increasingly rare in Baja, however, due to complaints from tourists who drive regularly on the peninsula. If your vehicle is stopped by a roadblock, be as cooperative as possible. If there are any irregularities or if you object to the way in which the procedure is carried out, make note of the incident (including whatever badge numbers, names, or license tag numbers you can obtain discreetly) and later file a report with the Mexican Attorney General for Tourist Protection (see "In Case of Arrest" below for more details).

La Mordida
In the past, Mexican police had a reputation for hassling foreigners, especially those who drove their own vehicles in Mexico. Tales of the legendary *mordida* or minor bribe (literally, "bite"), supposedly a necessary part of navigating one's way around Mexico, swelled way out of proportion to reality but were nonetheless based on real incidents.

For several years now, the Mexican police have for the most part ceased singling out foreigners for arrest, partly as a result of anti-corruption efforts by the federal government but more importantly because of a conscious

effort to attract more tourists. Most foreign visitors who drive in Baja these days complete their trips without any police hassles. (See "Getting Around," p. 126 for tips on traffic laws and dealing with traffic police).

In Case Of Arrest
If you get into trouble with Mexican law, for whatever reason, you should try to contact your nearest consulate in Baja (when there is one—embassies and consulates for each town are listed under the respective destination chapters). The state of Baja California Norte has established a special Attorney General for Tourist Protection (Procuraduria de Protección al Turista) with representatives in Tijuana (tel. 81-94-92), Rosarito (tel. 2-02-00) Ensenada (tel. 6-22-22, 6-37-18), Tecate (tel. 4-10-95), Mexicali (tel. 52-57-44, 52-97-95) and San Felipe (tel. 7-11-55). They also can be contacted at the local offices of the Secretary of Tourism—see the sections on each town for phone numbers and addresses. In Baja California Sur, the Secretary of Tourism office in La Paz may be able to help. These agencies routinely handle emergency legal matters involving visiting foreigners; you stand a much better chance of resolving legal difficulties with their assistance.

SAFETY

Statistics clearly show that violent crime is much less common in Mexico than anywhere in the U.S. In Baja California crime statistics are about 90% lower than the U.S. national average! Yet Americans themselves seem to be the most paranoid of all visitors to Mexico.

Historical reasons, to a large degree, account for this paranoia (although Mexicans historically have even more reason to fear Americans), the primary one being the general border lawlessness that was the norm very early in this century. The turn of the century and early 1900s was an era of border disputes and common banditry on both sides of the border, all the way from the Texas gulf coast to California's Pacific coast. Americans living in these areas came to fear *banditos* who stole livestock and occasionally robbed the Anglo ranchers themselves, while the Mexicans in turn feared American cattle rustlers, horse thieves, gunslingers, and the infamous Texas Rangers, a private militia whose conduct at the time fell somewhere between that of the Hell's Angels motorcycle gang and the Los Angeles Police Department.

Soon after this era had begun to cool down, as politics on both sides of the border stabilized, the U.S. Prohibition experiment sent millions of Americans scrambling into Mexican border towns to get booze. In the illicit atmosphere, boozers were soon rubbing elbows with gamblers and whoremongers, and it wasn't long before Mexican border towns gained an even more unsavory reputation.

Once Prohibition was lifted, Americans had no reason to come to Mexico solely for drinking purposes and the border towns began cleaning up their act. Among the uninformed and inexperienced, however, the border-town image remains and sadly mixes with the equally outdated bandito tales to prevent many Americans from enjoying the pleasures of life south of the border.

To add a personal testimony to statistics, neither the author nor anyone in the author's acquaintance has ever been robbed in Baja (or, for that matter, anywhere in Mexico). On one occasion, however, the author left behind two shirts and a pair of slacks in a hotel closet in Loreto, BCS, one morning and didn't remember them until arriving in La Paz in the evening. A phone call that same day and a visit to the hotel a week later were unsuccessful in retrieving the clothes—the management claimed they were never turned in by the cleaning staff. The moral of the story: the author now tries to be extra careful about not leaving things behind in hotel rooms.

Precautions: In general, visitors to Baja should take the same precautions they would when traveling anywhere in their own countries or abroad. Keep money and valuables secured, either in a hotel safe or safety deposit box, or in a money belt or other hard-to-get-at place on one's person. Keep an eye on cameras, purses, etc., to make sure you don't leave them behind in restaurants, hotels, or campgrounds. At night, lock the doors to your hotel room and vehicle.

Private campgrounds usually have some kind of security (if only a night watchman) to keep out intruders. Secluded beach campsites seem to be safe due to their seclusion—in Baja it is rare for crime to occur in such areas. Nonetheless, don't leave items of value lying around outside your tent, camper, or RV at night.

ACCOMMODATIONS

Places to stay in Baja run the gamut from free campgrounds to plush resort hotels. Camping spots are actually much more numerous than hotels or motels (smaller towns may only have one or two motels), so visitors who bring along camping gear will have a greater range of possibilities at any given location. Larger cities—Tijuana, Ensenada, Mexicali, La Paz, and Cabo San Lucas—have dozens of hotels to choose from.

HOTELS AND MOTELS

At many hotels and motels, midweek rates are lower than weekend rates. In northern Baja, some places charge high-season rates from May through Oct.; in southern Baja it's generally the opposite (winter rates are highest). To save money on accommodations, try traveling in the off-season for each region; except for the inland deserts, most of the peninsula is livable year-round. Summer temperatures of 37° C/100° F on the Cortez coast are usually mitigated by sea breezes and relatively low humidity.

Whatever the rack rate is, you can usually get the price down on a hotel room by bargaining (except during peak periods, e.g., Christmas, spring break, and Easter). Be sure to clarify whether or not the room rate includes meals when checking in—occasionally it does. Asking for a room without meals *(sin comidas)* is an easy way to bring the rate down, or simply ask if there's anything cheaper *(Hay algo mas barato?)*.

Economic

Hotels and motels in Baja are considerably less expensive than their counterparts in the U.S., Canada, or Europe, but slightly more expensive than equivalent accommodation in mainland Mexico. In the economic range, you'll find simple but clean rooms with private bath and double bed for around US$15-20 a night (up to US$35 in Tijuana, Ensenada, Mexicali, or Cabo San Lucas). Soap, towels,

toilet paper, and purified drinking water are usually provided but in some places you may have to ask. Rooms in this price range usually don't have air conditioners or heaters. In northern Baja you can often obtain a *calentador* or space heater on request for especially cool nights.

Lodging under US$15 per night is rare unless you stay at a youth hostel, *casa de huéspedes,* or *pensión* (described separately below), where bathrooms are usually shared.

Medium-priced

The largest number of hotels and motels in Baja fall into the US$40-60 range. Some are older Mexican-style hotels just a bit larger than those in the economic range while others are American-style motels; most everything in this price range will come with heating and air-conditioning.

La Pinta Chain

Straddling the line between mid-range and luxury hotels is the Hotel La Pinta chain, a joint venture between the Mexican government and Del Prado Inns. In Baja their hotels are located in Ensenada, San Quintín, Cataviña, San Ignacio, and Loreto; some formerly belonged to the El Presidente chain (which has since been taken over by a multinational corporation and upgraded).

La Pinta hotels are all very similar in appearance and facilities; the Las Cazuelas restaurant at each features the same menu, though the food quality varies according to the talents of the local kitchen staff. Room rates are exactly the same throughout the chain: US$58 s, US$69 d (including 15% tax, if paid in pesos—if you pay in dollars, the low exchange rate will cost extra).

Like most hotel or motel chains, the most you can say for La Pinta is that there are few surprises when moving from one hotel in the chain to another. All have PEMEX pumps conveniently located on the hotel grounds, and between Ensenada and Loreto they are the only hotels which accept credit cards for room and meal charges. (Mulegé's Hotel Serenidad will also accept credit cards, but adds a 6% surcharge for this service.)

Mexico Resorts International can arrange reservations for any La Pinta hotel via their toll-free U.S. number, (800) 336-5454, or you can write MRI, P.O. Box 120637, Chula Vista, California, 92012, USA. In Baja, reservations can be made by calling the chain's central office in Ensenada at (667) 6-26-01.

Luxury And Resort Hotels

Higher-end places are found in or near Tijuana, Rosarito, Ensenada, San Felipe, La Paz, San José del Cabo, and Cabo San Lucas. Prices in Baja for "international-class accommodation" average around US$75 to US$120. (A few Cape resorts charge as high as US$250 for particular rooms or suites.) Some of these places are good values in this range, while others are definitely overpriced. When in doubt, stick to the less-expensive hotels.

GUESTHOUSES AND HOSTELS

Casas De Huéspedes And *Pensiónes*

The *casa de huéspedes* (guesthouse) and *pensión* (boarding house) are the cheapest places to stay in Baja (aside from free or very basic campgrounds) but unfortunately for budgeters they aren't very plentiful. They are most numerous in Baja California Sur towns (especially Guerrero Negro, Santa Rosalía, Mulegé, and La Paz). The typical casa de huéspedes offers rooms with shared bath for US$5-8 or US$8-10 with private bath. A pensión costs about the same but may include meals. At either, most lodgers are staying for a week or more but the proprietors are usually quite happy to take guests by the night.

The main difference between these and budget hotels/motels (besides rates) is that they are usually located in old houses or other buildings (e.g., convents) that have been converted for guesthouse use. Soap, towels, toilet paper, and drinking water are usually provided, but as with budget hotels and motels you may have to ask.

Youth Hostels

Baja has one youth hostel *(villa deportivas juvenile* or "youth sports villa") each in Tijuana, Mexicali, La Paz, and Cabo San Lucas. Accommodation is in shared dormitory-style rooms where each guest is assigned a bed and a locker. Bathing facilities are always communal and guests must supply their own soap and towels. Rates are US$4 per night in the BCS hostels, US$5 in BCN, and food is available at hostel cafeterias (BCS only) for US$2-2.50 per meal.

Staying at youth hostels in Baja is a great way to meet young Mexicans and improve your Spanish—English is rarely spoken. About the only drawback is that the hostels tend to be inconveniently located some distance from the center of town so transport can be a problem if you don't have your own wheels. For the fitness-oriented, on the other hand, they're ideal; sports facilities usually include a gym, swimming pool, and playing courts for basketball, volleyball, and tennis.

CAMPING

Baja has more campgrounds, RV parks, and other camping areas for its size than anywhere else in Mexico. Because the population density of the peninsula is so dramatically low, it's easy to find off-the-beaten-track campsites that offer idyllic settings and precious solitude (often for free). For travelers who like the outdoors, it's also an excellent way to slash accommodation costs.

Campgrounds And RV Parks

The Baja peninsula has roughly 100 campgrounds on (perhaps 125 if you count Sea of Cortez fish camps) that charge fees ranging from around US$1.50 for a place with virtually zero facilities to as high as US$15 for a developed RV park with full water, electrical, and sewage hookups plus recreation facilities (e.g., boat ramps). Most campgrounds charge around US$3-5 for tent camping, US$6-12 for full hookups.

If you can forego permanent toilet and bathing facilities, you won't have to pay anything to camp in Baja since there's a virtually limitless selection of free camping spots, from beaches to deserts to mountain slopes. You won't necessarily need 4WD to reach these potential campsites, as plenty of turnouts and graded dirt *ramals* (branch roads) off the main highways can be negotiated by just about any type of vehicle.

FOOD AND DRINK

Much of what Bajacalifornios eat can be considered northern Mexican cuisine. Because northern Mexico is generally better suited to ranching than farming, ranch-style cooking tends to prevail in rural areas, which means that ranch products—meat and dairy foods—are highly favored.

Unlike the northern mainland, however, just about any point in Baja is only a couple of hours drive from the seashore, so seafood predominates here more than elsewhere in northern Mexico (or anywhere else in Mexico for that matter). In fact, in most places on the peninsula, seafood is more common than meat or poultry. If there's anything unique about Baja cuisine, it's the blending of ranch cooking with coastal culture, which has resulted in such distinctive Baja creations as the *taco de pescado* (fish taco).

WHERE TO EAT

Your selection of eating venues in Baja depends largely on where you are on the peninsula at any given moment. The most populated areas are at either end of the peninsula, where you'll find the greatest range of places to eat. Baja's larger towns and cities—Tijuana, Mexicali, Ensenada, and La Paz—offer everything from humble sidewalk taco stands to four-star hotel restaurants.

Between Ensenada and La Paz the choices are fewer and more basic. Along certain lengthy stretches of the Transpeninsular Highway in central Baja, about the only places to eat are *ranchos* that serve whatever's on the stone hearth that day. Usually ranchos that take paying diners will hang a sign out front or post an arrow along the highway that says *Lonchería, Café, Comedor, Comida,* "Eat," or "Food." A few post no signs and are known only by word of mouth.

In small towns there may be only two or three restaurants *(restaurante, restorán)* that serve basic Mexican dishes or, if near the coast, *mariscos* (seafood). Most hotels in Baja have restaurants and in small towns they may be among the best choices. While the Hotel La Pinta chain's restaurants are not known for their culinary excellence, in the town of San Ignacio it's just about the only place where you can count on getting a full meal. Sometimes the best meals on the road come from what you improvise yourself after a visit to a local *tienda de abarrotes* (grocery store).

Back in the city, one of the main non-restaurant choices is the *taquería,* a small, inexpensive diner where tacos are assembled before your eyes (sort of the Mexican equivalent to the old-fashioned American hamburger stand). Taquerías tend to be found in areas where there's a lot of foot traffic (near bus terminals, for example); the good ones will be packed with taco-eaters in the early evening.

Another economical choice is anything called a *lonchería,* which is a small, café-style place that usually serves *almuerzo* (late breakfast/early lunch) and *comida* (the main, midday meal). Lonchería hours are typically 1100 to 1700. Municipal markets in Baja often have a row of loncherías where basic meals and *antojitos* (snacks or one-plate dishes) are quite inexpensive. Some loncherías offer *co-*

mida corrida, a daily fixed-price meal that includes a beverage, an entree or two, plus side dishes and possibly dessert.

A *comedor* is usually a more basic version of a lonchería; they aren't as common in Baja as on the mainland but are seen occasionally. Cafés are similar to loncherías except that they may open earlier and serve *desayuno* (breakfast) in addition to other meals.

Ordering And Paying

You really don't need much Spanish to get by in a restaurant. Stating what you want, plus *por favor,* (please) will usually do the trick (e.g., *dos cervezas, por favor,* "two beers, please"). Don't forget to say *gracias* (thank you). The menu is called *el menú* or, much less commonly in Baja, *la carta.* As a last resort, you can always point to what you want on the menu (if you want to look stupid instead of sound stupid).

La cuenta is the bill. A tip *(la propina)* of about 15% is expected at any restaurant with table service; look to see if it has already been added to the bill before placing a tip on the table.

WHAT TO EAT

Tortillas

A Mexican meal is not a meal without tortillas, the round, flat, pancake-like disks eaten with nearly any non-dessert dish, including salads, meats, seafood, beans, and vegetables. Both wheat-flour and cornmeal tortillas are commonly eaten throughout Baja, although flour tortillas *(tortillas de harina)* are the clear favorite. Corn tortillas *(tortillas de maíz)* are more common in southern Mexico, where Indian populations (the first corn cultivators) are larger, while flour tortillas are more popular among the ranching areas of northern Mexico. Among northern Mexicans, it is said that meat and poultry dishes taste best with flour tortillas while vegetable dishes go best with corn. Most restaurants will offer a choice of the two. (If you order tortillas without specifying, you may get *¿de harina o de maíz?* as a response.)

Although prepackaged tortillas are available in *supermercados* (supermarkets), most

---

ANTOJITOS
(COMIDA TÍPICOS)

burrito—a flour tortilla rolled around meat, beans, or seafood fillings; Baja's lobster burritos are legendary

chalupa—a crisp, whole tortilla topped with beans, meat, etc. (also known as a *tostada)*

chiles rellenos—mild poblano chiles stuffed with cheese, deep-fried in an egg batter, and served with a *ranchero* sauce (tomatoes, onions, and chiles)

enchilada—a corn tortilla dipped in chile sauce, then folded or rolled around a filling of meat, chicken, seafood, or cheese and baked in an oven

flauta a small corn tortilla roll, usually stuffed with beef or chicken and fried

picadillo—a spicy salad of chopped or ground meat with chiles and onions (also known as *salpicón)*

quesadilla—a flour tortilla folded over sliced cheese and grilled; ask the cook to add *chiles rajas* (pepper strips) for extra flavor

taco—a corn tortilla folded or rolled around anything and eaten with the hands; *tacos de pescado,* or "fish tacos," are the closest thing Baja has to a regional specialty

tamal—cornmeal *(masa)* dough wrapped in a corn husk and steamed; sometimes stuffed with corn, olives, pork, or turkey

torta—a sandwich made with a Mexican-style roll *(bolillo* or *birote);* one of the most popular is the *torta de milanesa,* made with breaded, deep-fried veal or pork

---

Bajacalifornios buy them fresh from neighborhood *tortillerías* or make them at home. Many restaurants and cafés in Baja, and virtually all loncherías and taquerías, serve only fresh tortillas (tortillas made the same day, or at most the night before). If you're used to prepackaged tortillas (which is what most Mexican eateries in the U.S. or Canada serve), you're in for a pleasurable surprise when you raise a fresh, hot, homemade tortilla to your nose for the first time.

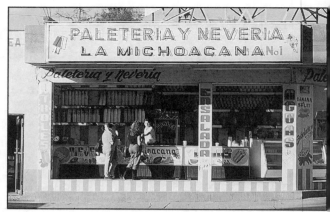

Paleteria y Neveria
(JOE CUMMINGS)

Incidentally, a tortilla has two sides, an inside and an outside, that dictate which direction the tortilla is best folded when wrapping it around food. The side with the thinner layer (sometimes called the *panzita*—belly) should face the inside when folding the tortilla. If you notice the outside of your tortilla is cracking and pieces are peeling off onto the table, it's probably because you've folded it with the panzita outside instead of inside (where the food would have kept it from flaking off).

Antojitos

This word literally means "little whims," thus implying "snacks" to many people. However, it also refers to any food that can be ordered, served, and eaten quickly—in other words, Mexican fast food (like burgers and hot dogs in North America). Typical antojitos include tamales, enchiladas, burritos, flautas, chiles rellenos, chalupas, picadillo, quesadillas, tortas, and tacos.

Breakfasts

Menus at tourist restaurants are often confusing because some of the same "breakfast" dishes may end up on more than one section of the menu. Mexicans have two kinds of breakfasts, an early one called *desayuno*, eaten shortly after rising, and a second called *almuerzo* that's usually taken around 1100. To further confuse the issue, Spanish-English dictionaries usually translate almuerzo as "lunch," while bilingual menus often read "breakfast."

The most common Baja desayuno is simply *pan dulce* (sweet pastry) and/or *bolillos* (torpedo-shaped, European-style rolls) with coffee and/or milk. Cereal is also sometimes eaten for desayuno, e.g., *avena* (oatmeal), *crema de trigo* (cream of wheat), or *hojuelas de maíz* (corn flakes).

The heavier eggs-and-frijoles dishes known widely as "Mexican breakfasts" in the U.S. and Canada are usually taken as almuerzo, the late breakfast (which is most typically reserved for weekends and holidays). Eggs come in a variety of ways, including *huevos revueltos* (scrambled eggs), *huevos duros* (hard-boiled eggs), *huevos tibios* (soft-boiled eggs), *huevos estrelladas* (eggs fried "sunny side up"), *huevos a la mexicana* (also *huevos mexicanos*, eggs scrambled with chopped tomato, onion, and chile), *huevos rancheros* (fried eggs served on a tortilla), and *huevos con chorizo* (eggs scrambled with ground sausage), *con tocino* (with bacon), or *con jamón* (with ham). All egg dishes usually come with frijoles and tortillas.

One of the cheapest and tastiest almuerzos is *chilaquiles*, tortilla chips in a chile gravy with crumbled cheese on top. Eggs and/or chicken can be added to chilaquiles as options.

Entrees

The main dish or *el plato fuerte* of any meal can be a grander version of an antojito, a regional specialty from another part of Mexico *(mole poblano,* for example), or something the *cocineros* (cooks) have dreamed up themselves. The most typical entrees are centered around meats, seafood, or poultry.

Meat and Poultry: Common meats include *carne de res* (beef), *puerco* (pork), and *cabrito* (kid goat). Jamón (ham), chorizo (sausage), and tocino (bacon) are usually reserved for almuerzo. Steak may appear on menus as *bistec, bistek, biftec,* or steak. *Venado* (deer meat or venison) and *conejo* (rabbit) are commonly served on ranchos. Poultry dishes include *pollo* (chicken), *pavo* (turkey), and, less frequently, *pato* (duck) and *codorniz* (quail).

Seafood: Mariscos entrees on the menu are often seasonal or dependent on the "catch of the day." Often just the word *pescado,* along with the method of cooking (e.g., *pescado al mojo de ajo),* will appear. If you need to know exactly what kind of fish, just ask *(¿Hay cuál tipo de pescado?),* although in some cases the only response you'll get is something generic like *pescado blanco* ("white fish"). For specific fish names, see "Fish Translator," p. 68.

Baja's number-one seafood specialty is the *taco de pescado* (fish taco). If you haven't ever tried one, you're most likely wondering "What's the big deal—a fish taco?" Eat one, though, and you're "hooked" for life. Short, tender, fresh fish filets are battered and fried quickly, then folded into a steaming corn tortilla with a variety of condiments including *salsa fresca* (chopped tomatoes, onions, chiles, and lime juice), marinated cabbage (similar to cole slaw in the States), *guacamole* (a savory avocado paste), and sometimes a squirt of mayonnaise. *¡La última!* Any kind of white-fleshed fish can be used—the best fish tacos are those made from yellowtail *(jurel)* or halibut *(lenguado).*

Shellfish are also quite popular on Baja menus: *ostiones* (oysters), *almejas* (clams), *callos* (scallops), *jaiba* (small crab), *cangrejo* (large crab), *camarones* (shrimp), *langosta* (lobster), *langostina* (crayfish, also called *cucarachas),* and *abulón* (abalone). They can be ordered as *cocteles* (cocktails—steamed or boiled and served with lime and salsa), *en sus conchas* (in the shell), or in many of the ways listed below.

Carnitas: This dish belongs in a category all its own and is usually sold only at butcher shops or at restaurants specializing in it. The usual method for producing carnitas is to slowly braise an entire pig in a huge cauldron, along with a variety of flavorings which are a closely guarded secret among carnitas purveyors. The results are chopped into thin slices and eaten with stacks of tortillas, pickled vegetables and chiles, guacamole, and various salsas.

Carnitas are almost always sold by weight. You can order by the *kilo,* (one kilogram, about 2.2 pounds), *medio* (half kilo), *cuarto* (one-fourth kilo), or sometimes in 100-gram increments *(cien gramos).* Figure on a quarter kilo

COOKING METHODS

Entree items, whether meat, poultry, or seafood, are most commonly prepared in one of the following styles:

adobo, adobada—marinated or stewed in a sauce of vinegar, chiles, and spices
a la birria—roasted on a spit (usually goat)
a la parilla—broiled
albóndigas—meatballs
al carbón—charcoal-grilled
a la veracruzana—seafood (often huachinanga—red snapper) cooked with tomatoes, onions, and olives
al mojo de ajo—in a garlic sauce
al pastor—slowly roasted on a vertical spit
al vapor—steamed
asada—grilled
barbacoa—pit-roasted
con arroz—steamed with rice
encebollado—cooked with onions
entomado—cooked with tomatoes
empanizada—breaded
frito—fried
guisado—in a spicy stew
machaca—dried and shredded

(about a half pound) per hungry person and you shouldn't have much left over.

Other Dishes

Beans: The beans most preferred in Baja, as on the northern mainland, are pinto beans, usually dried beans *(frijól)* boiled until soft, then mashed and fried with lard or vegetable oil (usually the former) to make *frijoles.* Often this preparation is called *frijoles refritos,* or "refried beans," although they're not really refried except when reheated! Sometimes the beans are served whole, in their own broth, as *frijoles de ollas* (boiled beans) or with bits of roast pork as *frijoles a la charra* (ranch-style beans). Frijoles can be served with any meal of the day, including breakfast.

Cheese: Even the lowliest rancho will usually have some cheese around, so if you're appetite isn't stimulated by the *iguana guisada* simmering on the hearth, you can usually ask for *chiles rellenos* (mild poblano chiles stuffed with cheese and fried in an egg batter) or *quesadillas* (cheese melted in folded flour tortillas). A meal of beans, tortillas, and cheese provides a complete source of protein for travelers who choose to avoid meat, poultry, or seafood for health, economic, or moral reasons.

Many ranchos produce their own *queso fresco,* "fresh cheese" made from raw cow's, goat's, or sheep's milk. To make queso fresco, the rancheros first cure the milk with homemade rennet (from a calf's fourth stomach) until the milk separates, and then press the curds with weights (sometimes under flat rocks lined with cloth) to remove excess moisture. In more elaborate operations, the initial pressing is then ground up and repressed into small round cakes. If you want to buy some queso fresco, look for *Hay queso* signs as you pass ranchos. If you're very fortunate, you might even come across *queso de apoyo,* an extra-rich cheese made from heavy cream.

Soup: The general menu term for soup is *sopa* although a thick soup with lots of ingredients is usually a *caldo.*

Vegetables: Although vegetables are sometimes served as side dishes with *comidas corridas,* with restaurant entrees, or in salads *(ensaladas),* they're seldom listed separately on the menu. When they do appear on menus, it's usually at restaurants in towns which are near farming areas in northern Baja or else in the La Paz-Los Cabos area, where many vegetables come over by boat from the mainland. The best place to add vegetables to your diet is at a market or grocery store.

Salsas And Condiments

Any restaurant, café, lonchería, taquería, or comedor will offer a variety of salsas with the food they serve. Sometimes only certain salsas are served with certain dishes, while at other times one, two, or even three salsas are stationed on every table. Often each place has its own unique salsa recipes—canned or bottled salsas are rarely used.

There are as many types of salsas as there are Mexican dishes—red, green, yellow, brown, hot, mild, salty, sweet, thick, thin, blended, and chunky—that it would take a separate book to describe them all. The most typical is the *salsa casera* (house salsa), a simple, fresh concoction of chopped chiles, onions, and tomatoes mixed with salt, lime juice, and cilantro. This is what you usually get with the complimentary basket of *totopos* (tortilla chips) served at the beginning of every Mexican meal (including almuerzo). Another common one is *salsa verde,* "green sauce," made with a base of *tomatillos* (a small, tart, green tomato-like vegetable). Some salsas are quite *picante* (spicy hot—also *picosa),* so it's always a good idea to test a bit before pouring it over everything on your plate.

Whole pickled chiles are sometimes served on the side as a condiment, especially with tacos and carnitas. Salt *(sal)* is usually on the table, although it's rarely needed since Mexican dishes tend to be prepared with plenty of salt. Black pepper is *pimiento negro,* and if it's not on the table it's normally available for the asking. Butter is *mantequilla,* sometimes served with flour tortillas.

In taquerías, *guacamole* (mashed avocado blended with onions, chiles, salt, and sometimes other ingredients), is always served as a condiment. In restaurants it may be served as a salad or with tortilla chips.

Desserts And Sweets

The most popular of Mexican desserts, or *postres,* is a delicious egg custard called *flan.* It's listed on virtually every tourist restaurant menu, along with *helado* (ice cream). Other sweet alternatives include pastries found in *panaderías* (bakeries) and the frosty offerings at the ubiquitous *paleterías.* Strictly speaking, a paletería serves only *paletas,* flavored ice on sticks (like American popsicles except with a much wider range of flavors), but many also serve *nieve,* literally "snow," flavored ice served in bowls or cones like ice cream.

Another common street vendor food is *churros,* a sweet fried pastry which is something like a donut stick sprinkled with powdered sugar. One of the best places to sample churros is at La Bufadora at Punta Banda, just south of Ensenada—nowhere else in Baja are there so many churro vendors in one place.

Dulcerías are candy shops where a huge variety of sticky Mexican sweets, usually wrapped individually, are sold. Often brightly decorated, dulcerías are oriented toward children and sometimes carry inexpensive toys as well as sweets. The larger ones sell piñatas, colorful papier-mâché figures filled with candy and small gifts and hung at parties; on special occasions, children are allowed to break them with sticks, thus releasing all the goodies inside. Traditionally, piñatas are crafted to resemble common animals but these days you'll see all kinds of shapes, including "Teenage Mutant Tortugas de Ninja."

BUYING GROCERIES

The cheapest way to feed yourself while traveling in Baja is the same way you save money at home, by buying groceries at the store and preparing meals on your own. While they may not have any dining spots to speak of, even the smallest towns in Baja will have a little grocery store or corner market. A ripe avocado, a chunk of queso fresco, and a couple of bolillos can make a fine, easy-to-fix meal.

The humblest stores are the small family-owned *tienda de abarrotes,* usually recognizable by the single word *abarrotes*—"groceries"—printed somewhere on the outside *(tienda* means "store"). These will have the basics—tortillas, dried beans, flour, herbs and spices, bottled water, a few vegetables, possibly *bolillos* and queso fresco—as well as limited household goods like soap and laundry detergent. Like the 7-11 back home, the food at the average tienda de abarrotes is not particularly inexpensive.

A better deal, when you can find them, are the government-sponsored CONASUPO (an acronym for Compañía Nacional de Subsistencias Populares). CONASUPOs carry many of the same items as a tienda de abarrotes, but at government-subsidized prices. Not every item is cheaper, however, so it pays to shop around. A large, supermarket-style CONASUPO is called CONASUPER. Even less expensive are markets operated by ISSTE (Instituto de Seguridad y Servicios Sociales para Trabajadores del Estado).

Privately run supermarkets (e.g., Calimax, Giganta) can be found in larger towns throughout the peninsula and are usually called *supers* or *supermercados.* Like their North American counterparts, they're usually well stocked with a wide variety of meats, baked goods, vegetables, household goods, beer and liquor, and so on. Supermarket prices are often better than in smaller grocery stores.

Several towns and cities in Baja have *mercados municipales* (municipal markets), large warehouse-type structures where meat, fruit, and vegetable producers sell their goods directly to the public. Prices are often very good at these markets but it helps if you know how to bargain. Although they're usually centrally located, sometimes municipal markets are difficult to find simply because they look so inconspicuous on the outside—you may have to ask around.

Another common tienda is the *ultramarinos,* which is primarily a place to buy beer and liquor but which also usually sells a few deli-style food items.

Panaderías: A few bakery items can often be purchased at all of the above-named stores, but the best place to buy them, naturally, is at their source—a *panadería* (literally, "breadery," i.e., bakery). Many of the panaderías in Baja still use wood-fired *hornos* (ovens), which make the *bolillos* (Mexican rolls), *pastels* (cakes), and *pan dulce* (cookies and sweet pastries) especially tasty. *Pan de barra,* American-style sliced bread, is also occasionally available but it never measures up to crusty bolillos. To select bakery items from the shelves of a panadería, simply imitate the other customers—pick up a pair of tongs and a tray from the counter near the cash register and help yourself, cafeteria-style.

Tortillerías: Unless you make them yourself, the best place to buy tortillas is where they make them fresh every day. Restaurants, tiendas, and home cooks will purchase from the local tortillería to avoid spending hours at a *metate* (grinder) and *tomal* (griddle). The automated process at a tortillería uses giant electric grinders and conveyor belts to transform whole corn into fresh tortillas, which you purchase by weight, not number. A kilo will yield about 40 average, 12-cm tortillas; you can order by the *cuarto* or *medio* (quarter or half kilo). The government-subsidized prices are quite low.

DRINKING

Nonalcoholic Beverages

Cold Drinks: The water and ice served in restaurants in Baja is always purified—it's not necessary to order *agua mineral* (mineral water) unless you need the minerals. Likewise, the water used as an ingredient in "handmade" drinks, e.g., *licuados* or *aguas frescas,* is also from purified sources.

Licuados are similar to American "smoothies—fruit blended with water, ice, honey or sugar, and sometimes milk or raw eggs to produce something like a fruit shake. In Baja, *tuna* (not the fish but the prickly-pear cactus fruit) licuados are particularly delicious. Any place that makes licuados will also make orange juice, *jugo de naranja.* Orange juice is very popular in Baja and you'll often see street vendors who sell nothing but fresh-squeezed OJ.

Aguas frescas are the colorful beverages sold from huge glass jars on the streets of larger cities, or at carnivals, usually during warm weather. They're made by boiling the pulp of various fruits, grains, or seeds with water, then straining it and adding large chunks of ice. *Arroz* (rice) and *horchata* (melon-seed) are two of the tastiest aguas.

American soft drinks *(refrescos)* like 7-Up, Coke, and Pepsi are common; their Mexican equivalents are just as good. An apple- flavored soft drink called Manzanita is quite popular.

Hot Drinks: Coffee is served in a variety of ways. The best (when you can find it—ranchos sometimes serve it) is traditional Mexican-style coffee, which is made by filtering near-boiling water through fine-ground coffee in a slender cloth sack. Instant coffee *(nescafé)* is often served at small restaurants and cafés—a jar of instant coffee may be sitting on the table for you to add to hot water. When there's a choice, a request for *café de olla* (boiled coffee) should bring you real brewed coffee. One of the better Mexican brands found in supermarkets is Café Combate.

Café con leche is the Mexican version of café au lait, i.e., coffee and hot milk mixed in near-equal proportions. *Café con crema* (coffee with cream) is not as available; when it is, it usually means a cup of coffee with a packet of non-dairy creamer on the side.

Hot chocolate *(chocolate)* is fairly common on Baja menus. It's usually served very sweet and may contain cinnamon, ground almonds, and other flavorings. A thicker version made with cornmeal—almost a chocolate pudding—is called *champurrado.*

Black tea *(té negro)* is not popular among Bajacalifornios although you may see it on tourist menus. Ask for *té helado* if you want iced tea. At home many Mexicans drink *té de manzanilla* (chamomile tea) or *té de yerba buena* (mint tea) in the evenings.

Alcoholic Beverages

Drinking laws in Mexico are quite minimal. The legal drinking age in Mexico is 15 years, and it's illegal to carry open containers of alcoholic beverages in a vehicle. Booze of every kind is widely available in bars, restaurants, grocery stores, and *licorerías* (liquor stores). *Borracho* means both "drunk" (as an adjective) and "drunkard."

Cerveza: The most popular (and most available) beer brand in northern Baja is Tecate (brewed in Tecate, BCN), while in the south it's Pacifica (from Mazatlan, just across the Sea of Cortez from Cabo San Lucas). Both are good-tasting, light- to medium-weight brews, with Tecate holding a slight edge (more hops) over Pacifica. You can't compare either of these with their export equivalents in the U.S., since Mexican breweries produce a separate brew for American consumption that's lighter in taste and lighter on the alcohol content. It's always better in Mexico.

Other major Mexican brands such as Corona, Dos Equis, Superior, Carta Blanca, Bohemia, and Negro Modelo are available in tourist restaurants, but you'll notice that the

TEQUILA

Mexico's national drink has been in production since at least the time of the Aztecs—the Spaniards levied a tax on tequila as early as 1608. The liquor's name was taken from the Ticuila Indians of Jalisco who mastered the process of distilling an extract from the *Agave tequiliana,* or **blue agave,** a process still employed by tequila distilleries today. Native to Jalisco, this succulent is the only agave that produces true tequila as certified by the Mexican government. (Look for the initials DGN—for *Dirección General de Normas*—on the label.)

Much of the tequila-making process is still carried out *a mano* (by hand). In the traditional method, the mature heart of the tequila agave, which looks like a huge pineapple and weighs 20-60 kilograms, is roasted in a pit for 24 hours, then shredded and ground by mule- or horse-powered mills. After the juice is extracted from the pulp and fermented in ceramic pots, it's distilled in copper stills to produce the basic tequila, which is always clear and colorless, with an alcohol content of around 40%.

"Gold" tequilas are produced by aging the tequila in imported oak barrels. After six months it can be bottled as *reposado* or "rested" tequila; after three years in barrels it's truly *añejo* or "aged."

José Cuervo, Sauza, and Herradura are well-established tequila labels with international notoriety. Of these three, Herradura is said to employ the most traditional methods, and hence tequila connoiseurs generally prefer it over the other two. But don't take their word for it, try a few *probaditos* ("little proofs" or shots) for yourself. One of the best places to experiment is Cabo San Lucas' Caballo Blanco Restaurant, where the bar stocks over 35 varieties of tequila—don't try tasting them all in one night or you'll probably never drink tequila again.

Mezcal And The Worm
The distillate of other agave plants (also known as *magueys* or century plants) is called *mezcal.* The same roasting and distilling process is used for mezcal as for tequila. (Tequila, too, is a mezcal, but no drinker calls it that, just as no one in a U.S. bar orders "whiskey" when they mean to specify scotch or bourbon.) The caterpillar-like grub you see floating at the bottom of a bottle of mezcal is the *gusano de maguey* (maguey worm), which lives on the maguey plant itself. They're safe to eat (just about anything pickled in mezcal would be), but not particularly appetizing. By the time you hit the bottom of the bottle, though, who cares?

Tequila Drinks
The most common way to drink tequila is straight up, followed by a water or beer chaser. Licking a few grains of salt before taking a shot and sucking a lime wedge afterward will make it go down more smoothly. (The salt raises a protective coating of saliva on the tongue while the lime juice scours the tongue of salt and tequila residues.)

Another popular way to drink tequila is in a margarita, a tart Mexican cocktail made with tequila, lime juice, and triple-sec (or Cointreau) served in a salt-rimmed glass. A true margarita is shaken and served on the rocks, but just about every gringo in Baja seems to drink frozen margaritas (in which the ice is mixed in a blender with the other ingredients). A "Baja margarita" substitutes Baja's own damiana liqueur for the triple-sec. The damiana herb is said to be an aphrodisiac (see "Flora and Fauna," p. 14).

locals stick pretty much to Tecate and Pacifica, perhaps out of regional loyalty.

The cheapest sources for beer are the brewery's agents or distributors (look for signs saying *agencia, subagencia, cervezería,* or *deposito),* where you can return deposit bottles for cash or credit. You can buy beer by the bottle *(envase),* can *(bote),* six-pack *(canastilla),* or case *(cartón).* Large, liter-size bottles are called *ballenas* ("whales") and are quite popular. When buying beer at an agencia or deposito, specify *fría* if you want cold beer, otherwise you'll get beer *al tiempo* (at room temperature).

Wine: Baja is one of Mexico's major wine production areas (see "Bajacalifornio Wine," p. 176) and Baja wines are commonly served in restaurants. Two of the more reliable labels are Domecq and Santo Tomás, both produced in northern Baja. A broad selection of varietals is available, including Cabernet Sauvignon, Chardonnay, Chenin Blanc, Pinot Noir, Barbera, and Zinfandel. These and other grapes are also blended to produce cheaper *vino tinto* (red wine) and *vino blanco* (white wine). When ordering wine in Spanish at a bar, you may want to specify *vino de uva* ("grape wine"), as *vino* alone can be used to refer to distilled liquors as well as wine. *Vino blanco,* in fact, can be interpreted as cheap tequila.

Liquor: Tequila is Mexico's national drink and also the most popular distilled liquor in Baja. The second most popular is brandy, followed closely by ron (rum), both of which are produced in Mexico for export as well as domestic consumption. A favorite rum drink in Baja is the cuba libre (Free Cuba), called cuba for short—a mix of rum, Coke, and lime juice over ice. Similar is the cuba de uva, which substitutes brandy for rum. Other hard liquors—gin, vodka, scotch, etc.—may only be available at hotel bars and tourist restaurants.

Cantinas and Bars: Traditionally speaking, a true cantina is a Mexican-style drinking venue for males only, but in modern Mexico the distinction between "bar" and "cantina" is becoming increasingly blurred. Is Hussong's Cantina in Ensenada a true cantina? Plenty of women are present each evening holding their own with the best of the machos, yet among locals it still has the reputation of a place where "nice" Mexican girls don't go.

A more typical Baja cantina is the kind of place you'll occasionally stumble upon in a small town, usually on the outskirts, where blinking Christmas lights festoon a palapa roof and palm-thatch or ocotillo walls. Inside are a few tables and chairs and a handful of borrachos; if any women are present, they'll either be serving the booze or serving as hired "dates." The only drink choices will be beer, Mexican brandy, and cheap tequila or *aguardiente* (moonshine—often when you order tequila in a place like this, you'll be served a large glass of aguardiente, considered an acceptable substitute).

Bars, on the other hand, will only be found in hotels and in the larger cities or resort areas, i.e., Tijuana, Mexicali, Ensenada, San Felipe, La Paz, and Cabo San Lucas. They have developed largely as social venues for tourists or for a younger generation of Mexicans for whom the cantina is passé. A bar, in contrast to a cantina, will offer a variety of beer, wine, and distilled liquor. By Mexican standards, bars are considered very up-market places to hang out, so they aren't extremely popular—many young Mexicans would rather drink at a disco where they can dance, too.

Incidentallly, a sign outside a bar reading "ladies bar" almost always means that the bar provides ladies for male entertainment, not that it admits women (although it may).

BAR LINGO

cantinero	bartender
cerveza	beer
una fría	a cold one
envase, botella	bottle
casco	empty bottle
una copita, uno tragito . . .	a drink
vaso, copa	glass
la cruda	hangover
sin hielo	without ice
con hielo	with ice
botanas	snacks

IMMIGRATION AND CUSTOMS

ENTRY REGULATIONS

U.S. And Canadian Citizens

U.S. and Canadian citizens visiting Mexico solely for tourism, transit, or study purposes are not required to obtain a visa. In fact, for Baja visits of less than 72 hours, all that's needed is proof of citizenship—a birth certificate (or certified copy), voter's registration card, certificate of naturalization, or passport.

All U.S. or Canadian citizens crossing the Mexican border for more than 72 hours or going farther south than Maneadero must carry a validated "tourist card" (Form FMT), which isn't actually a card but a slip of paper. These are available free of charge at any Mexican consulate or Mexican tourist office, from many travel agencies, on flights to Mexico, or at the border.

The tourist card is valid for stays of up to 180 days and must be used within 90 days of issuance. Your card becomes invalid once you exit the country (you're supposed to surrender it at the border), even if your 180 days hasn't expired. If you'll be entering and leaving Mexico more than once during your trip, you should request a multiple-entry tourist card, available from Mexican consulates.

Validation: Once you cross the border with your tourist card, it must be validated by a Mexican immigration officer. This can be arranged at any *migración* office in Baja (all *municipio* seats have them), but is most conveniently accomplished at the border crossing itself or at the immigration office in Ensenada (right around the corner from the tourist information booth on Blvd. Costero).

Minors: Officially speaking, children under the age of 18 who cross the border without one or both parents must carry a notarized letter granting permission from the absent parent (or both parents if both are absent) for travel to Mexico. In cases of divorce, separation, or death, the minor must carry notarized papers documenting the situation. In reality, minors with tourist cards are rarely asked for these documents. Children under 15 may be included on their parents' tourist card but this means that neither child nor parents can legally exit Mexico without the other.

Citizens From Other Countries

Tourists from countries other than the U.S. or Canada may need visas in advance of arrival in Mexico. Citizens of Australia, New Zealand, and most west European countries can usually obtain free, no-photo visas at the border; be sure to check with a Mexican embassy or consulate first—visa regulations change from year to year.

If you apply in person, the Mexican Consulate General in San Diego can usually issue tourist visas on the same day of application.

Pets

Dogs and cats may be brought into Mexico if each is accompanied by a **vaccination certificate** (which must show that the animal has been vaccinated or treated for rabies, hepatitis, pip, and leptospirosis) and a **health certificate** (the latter must be issued no more than 72 hours before entry) signed by a registered veterinarian. Upon recrossing the border into the U.S., the U.S. Customs Service will ask to see the vaccination certificate.

Inmigrante Rentista Visas

Special visas (FM-2 status) are issued to foreigners who choose to reside in Mexico on a "permanent income" basis. This most often applies to foreigners who decide to retire in Mexico, though it is also used by artists, writers, and other self-employed foreign residents. With this visa you're allowed to import one motor vehicle as well as your household belongings into Mexico tax-free.

The basic requirements for this visa are that applicants forego any kind of employment while residing in Mexico and show proof (bank statements) of a regular source of foreign-earned income amounting to at least

US$1,500 per month (plus US$500 for each dependent over the age of 15, e.g., US$2,000 for a couple). A pile of paperwork, including a "letter of good conduct" from the applicant's local police department, must accompany the initial application, along with an immigration tax payment (currently US$121) and various applications fee totaling around US$75. The visa must be renewed annually but the renewal can be accomplished at any immigration office in Mexico—there's one in every municipio. After five years in Mexico, an immigrant rentista is eligible to apply for *inmigrado* status, which confers all the rights of citizenship (including employment in Mexico), save the right to vote.

Similar to the FM-2 but easier to obtain is the FM-3, or *No Inmigrante Visitante,* visa, which requires an income of US$1000 a month plus US$500 for each dependent. Like the FM-2, the FM-3 is annually renewable for five years, at which point you must start the application process over again.

Many foreigners who have retired in Baja manage do so on the regular 180-day tourist visa; every six months they dash across the border and return with a new tourist card (issued at the border) on the same day. This method bypasses all the red tape and income requirements of the retirement visa.

Mexican Consulate In San Diego

San Diego's Mexican Consulate General (tel. 619-231-8414, 619-231-8427, 610 "A" St., San Diego, CA 92101) is relatively close to the Tijuana border crossing (about 30-45 minutes by car) and can assist with visas, immigration problems, special import permits, and questions concerning Mexican customs regulations. The consulate's hours are Mon.-Fri., 0900-1400.

BORDER CROSSINGS

Baja California's U.S.-Mexico border has five official border crossings along: Tijuana (open 24 hours a day), Otay Mesa (open 0600-2200), Tecate (0700-2000), Mexicali (24 hours), and Algodones (0700-2000). Tijuana is the largest and also the most heavily used since it connects Baja with U.S. Interstate 5, which extends all the way up the U.S. west coast to the Canadian border. Border officials are considering longer hours for the nearby Otay Mesa crossing to ease congestion at Tijuana.

At any of the border crossings, you'll find the shortest waits (15-30 minutes at Tijuana) are between 1000 and 1530 or after 1900 or 2000 on weekdays. Weekends are the worst days in either direction (except late at night or before dawn, when traffic is light). If you're on your way out of Baja and find yourself near the border rush hours, it might be best to find a restaurant or other spot on the Mexico side and wait it out. A Saturday or Sunday morning wait at the Tijuana crossing can be as long as two hours in either direction but it's always longer going north.

If you're on foot, crossing is usually a breeze. Public and chartered buses also get through more quickly than private vehicles because of special traffic lanes provided them.

CUSTOMS

Entering Mexico

Officially, tourists are supposed to bring only those items into Mexico that will be of use during their trip. This means that you can bring practically anything in as long as it doesn't appear to be in large enough quantities for resale. Firearms and ammunition, as well as boats, however, require special permits (see "Sports and Recreation," p. 71 and p. 69 respectively, for permit information).

Foreign-registered motor vehicles (cars, trucks, RVs, motorcycles, etc.) do not require permits for travel anywhere on the Baja California peninsula. However, if you plan to take a vehicle registered outside Mexico onto one of the vehicle ferries that sail from Baja to the mainland, you must obtain an auto permit before boarding. These are available from any Mexican consulate abroad or from the ferry offices in Santa Rosalía and La Paz. For further information on vehicle permits, see "Getting There," p. 120.

Into The U.S.

Visitors returning to the U.S. from Mexico may have their luggage inspected by U.S. Customs officials. The hassle can be minimized by giving brief, straight answers to their questions (e.g., "How long have you been in Baja?" "Do you have anything to declare?") and by cooperating with any requests to open your luggage, vehicle storage compartments, and anything else they want opened. Occasionally the officers use Dutch Malenoy dogs to sniff vehicles for contraband or illegal aliens.

Customs Duties: Nearly 3,000 items (including all handicrafts) made in Mexico are exempt from any U.S. customs duties. Adults over 21 are allowed one quart of alcoholic beverages and 200 cigarettes (or 100 cigars) per person. All other purchases or gifts up to a total value of US$400 within any 31-day period can be brought into the U.S. duty-free.

Plant And Animal Prohibitions

The following fruits and vegetables cannot be brought into the U.S. from Mexico: oranges, grapefruits, mangoes, avocados (unless the pit is removed), and potatoes (including yams and sweet potatoes). All other fruits are permitted (including bananas, dates, pineapples, cactus fruits, grapes, and berries of all types).

Other prohibited plant materials are straw (including packing materials and items stuffed with straw), hay, unprocessed cotton, sugarcane, and any plants in soil (this includes house plants).

Animals and animal products that cannot be imported include wild and domesticated birds (including poultry, unless cooked), pork or pork products (including sausage, ham, and other cured pork), and eggs. Beef, mutton, venison, and other meats are permitted up to 50 pounds total per person.

Customs regulations can change at any time, so if you want to verify the regs on a purchase before risking duties or confiscation at the border, check with a U.S. consulate in Baja before crossing. If the three-way free trade agreement currently under negotiation between the U.S., Canada, and Mexico is successful, expect sweeping changes in customs regulations—toward more leniency—in both directions.

MONEY, MEASUREMENTS, AND COMMUNICATIONS

MONEY

Currency

The unit of exchange in Mexico is the peso, which appears in coins of 50, 100, 500, and 1000 pesos, or in bills of 1000, 5000, 10,000, 20,000, and 50,000. Denominations of 20,000 and 50,000 pesos can be difficult to break, so try to get them changed at every opportunity in order to have a good supply of smaller notes.

The $ symbol is often used for indicating peso as well as dollar prices. While it is highly unlikely that you would ever confuse the two since the exchange ratio is so high, if in doubt, ask. Sometimes the abbreviation m.n. will appear next to a price—this means *moneda nacional* ("national money," or pesos). Mexican vendors will often abbreviate a verbal price quote by omitting the word *mil* (thousand) since few things cost less than 1000 pesos. Thus *doce cinco* can mean *doce mil cinco cien* (12,500 pesos).

Most places in Baja will take U.S. dollars as well as pesos. Paying with pesos, however, usually means a better deal when the price is fixed in pesos; if you pay in dollars for a purchase quoted in pesos, the vendor can determine the exchange rate. (For example, if a can of motor oil is marked at 6000 pesos, and the bank rate is 3000 pesos per dollar, you'll pay only US$2 for the oil with pesos changed at the bank. However, if you ask to pay in dollars, the vendor may charge US$2.50 since vendors have the right—by custom rather than law—to charge whatever exchange rate they want.) On the other hand, if you're bargaining for a price, it really doesn't matter which currency you use.

Some stores in smaller towns prefer not to take dollars since this means keeping track of two currencies and makes banking more complicated. PEMEX stations typically refuse dollars—attendants are usually too busy to stop and calculate the rates.

At press time, the U.S. dollar was buying roughly 3000 pesos at the official exchange rate (see below for caveats).

Deflation

The Mexican peso has been in a deflationary spin since 1976 when the government decided to allow the national currency to float on the international money market. From 1976 to 1987 the exchange rate slid from eight pesos to the dollar to over 2000. In 1988 the Bank of Mexico instituted measures to slow the decline so that it is now loses only about two to three pesos per week.

The relatively stable exchange rate means that changing money in Baja is much less stressful now than just a few years ago—there's no need to check the exchange rate every day (about once a week will do). The slower devaluation still works in favor of the dollar-holder; the dollar bought 11.6% more in 1990 than it did in 1989.

Changing Money

Banks: Banks offer the best exchange rate for buying pesos and they all offer the same rate, as set by the Bank of Mexico. This rate is usually posted behind the counter where foreign exchange is handled. They also accept a wide range of foreign currencies, including Swiss francs, German marks, English pounds, Japanese yen, and Canadian dollars. Either cash or traveler's checks are accepted. The main drawbacks with banks are the long lines and short hours (Mon.-Fri., 0900-1330); the foreign exchange service usually closes at noon or 1230.

Money-changers: The second best rate is at the *casa de cambio*o or private money-changing office. The casa de cambio will either knock a few pesos off the going bank rate or charge a percentage commission. It pays to

10,000 peso note

shop around for the best casa de cambio rates since some places charge considerably more commission than others. The rates are usually posted; *compra* refers to the buying rate for US$ (how many pesos you'll receive per dollar), while *venda* is the selling rate (how many pesos you must pay to receive a dollar). As with banks, the difference between the buying and selling rates is the money-changer's profit, unless they charge a commission on top of it.

Money-changers are usually open much later than banks; some even have evening hours, which makes them immeasurably more convenient than banks. U.S. dollar currency is generally preferred though many casas will also accept Canadian dollars. However, Canadians should always keep a reserve supply of U.S. dollars for instances where Canadian currency isn't accepted. Money changers will usually accept traveler's checks; some of the border-town casas, however, take only cash.

Only the larger towns and tourist centers have money-changing offices. In smaller towns you'll have to resort to a bank or local merchant. Many store-owners will be glad to buy dollars at a highly variable and sometimes negotiable rate. Few will take traveler's checks, however, unless you make a purchase.

Money changers at Mexican airports offer notoriously low rates. Try to buy pesos in advance of your trip if arriving by air, or pay with dollars until you can get to a bank or reasonable casa de cambio.

Hotels: Hotels, motels, pensiones, and other lodging places generally offer the lowest exchange rates. If you're trying to save money, avoid changing currency where you stay and pay for your room in pesos if possible, since the same low rate often applies to room charges paid in dollars.

Credit Cards

Plastic money (primarily Visa and Master-Card) is widely accepted in Baja at large hotels, at restaurants catering to tourists or businesspeople, at car rentals (you can't rent a car without a credit card), and at shops in tourist centers or large cities. Usually card displays at the cash register or on the door will announce that *tarjetas de credito* (credit cards) are accepted. If in doubt, flash one and ask *¿Se acepta tarjetas de credito?* or simply *¿Está bien?*

Credit cards are not accepted at PEMEX stations. The Mexican government has recently announced plans to introduce a special "tourist credit card" that will be valid at PEMEX outlets. If/when the plan is finally realized, travel agencies abroad will know the details.

Paying for goods and services in Baja with credit cards that are paid through U.S. or Canadian banks can save you money since the exchange rate will usually have dipped further in the dollar's favor by the time the transaction is posted at your bank. Many shops and some hotels, however, will add a 3-6% surcharge to bills paid with a card, which more than offsets the exchange rate differential.

Cash advances on credit card accounts—a very useful service for emergencies—are available at Mexican banks.

Estimating Costs

Inflation in Mexico is currently running at around 25% per annum, in large part due to the continued weakening of the peso on international markets but also because of a slight relaxation of wage and price controls. This means that when estimating your travel costs based on prices quoted in this book, some allowance must be made for ongoing inflation. Although peso prices will increase in direct proportion to the inflation rate, this isn't necessarily so for prices figured in dollars, since the dollar is continuing to gain in value against the peso.

Because of fluctuations in the peso-dollar ratio, and in an effort to keep prices more up-to-date, all prices in this book are quoted in dollars. This doesn't mean, however, that there won't be any increase in prices by the time you arrive, book in hand. A couple of phone calls to hotels or other services for price quotes should give you an idea how much rates have increased, if at all, and this difference can be applied as a percentage to all other prices for a rough estimate of costs.

Tipping

A tip of 15-20% is customary at restaurants with table service unless a service charge is added to the bill. Luggage handling at hotels or airports warrants a tip of US$.50, or the equivalent in pesos, per bag. (A few hotels have a no-tipping policy, which will be posted in your room.) The tipping of chambermaids is apparently optional according to Mexican custom.

PEMEX station attendants don't need to be tipped unless they wash your windows, check the oil, or perform other extra services beyond pumping gas—the equivalent of US$.25 to US$.50 in pesos is sufficient. When the change due on a gasoline purchase is less than 1000 pesos, however, it's customary to let the attendant keep the change.

MEASUREMENTS

Mexico, like most countries in the world, uses the metric system as the official system of weights and measures. This means the distance between Maneadero and San Quintín is measured in kilometers, cheese is weighed in grams or kilograms, a hot day in San Felipe is 32° C, gasoline is sold by the liter, and a big fish is two meters long. A chart at the end of this book converts pounds, gallons, and miles to kilos, liters, and kilometers (or vice versa).

Bajacalifornios used to dealing with American tourists will often use the Anglo-American and metric systems interchangeably. Even rancheros in remote areas occasionally use *millas* (miles) as a measure.

In this book, distances will be given in kilometers, often followed by miles in parentheses (for the benefit of American readers and for checking against American odometers), since all road markers in Baja employ the metric system. Dimensions and weight are usually quoted using the metric system, except when feet or pounds are culturally more appropriate (e.g., when prescribing monofilament fishing line).

COMMUNICATIONS

Time

Baja California Norte is part of the Pacific Time Zone along with the west coast of the U.S. and Canada, while Baja California Sur is in the Mountain Time Zone. This means you should set your timepiece an hour ahead when crossing the BCS state line going south or back an hour when crossing north. It isn't necessary to reset your watch from the last Sunday in April to the last Sunday in October, when BCN advances an hour for Daylight Savings Time and thus follows the same time as BCS (which does not observe Daylight Savings Time).

The time in Mexico is commonly expressed according to the 24-hour clock, from 0001 to

2359 (one minute past midnight to 11:59 p.m.) rather than the Anglo-American 12-hour system. A restaurant that posts hours of 1100-2200, for example, is open from 11 a.m. to 10 p.m. To conform to the Mexican system, all times in this guidebook follow the 24-hour clock.

Electricity
Mexico's electrical system is the same as those in the U.S. and Canada: 110 volts, 60 cycles, alternating current (AC). Electrical outlets are of the North American type, designed to work with appliances with standard double-bladed plugs. Small towns in some rural areas may experience brief interruptions of electrical service or periods of brownout (voltage decrease). In a few villages, gasoline-powered generators are the only source of electricity and they may be turned off during the day.

Postal Service
The Mexican postal service is quite reliable though relatively slow. Most towns in Baja have a post office *(oficina de correos)* where you can receive poste restante mail. Have correspondents address mail in your name (last name capitalized), followed by a/c Lista de Correos, the town name, and the state, e.g., Joe CUMMINGS, a/c Lista de Correos, La Paz, Baja California Sur, Mexico.

Many foreigners who are seasonal Baja residents have their mail sent in care of a hotel or RV park. You can rent boxes at larger Mexican post offices but the initial application process often takes several weeks. Tijuana, Tecate, and Mexicali have private mail companies (e.g., "Mail Boxes, Etc.") that also rent boxes but with minimal red tape.

For mail to the U.S., many residents in towns north of Ensenada or San Felipe save their letters and parcels until a friend or relative makes a trip across the border—the Chula Vista, CA post office probably handles more mail from Tijuana than from Chula Vista! (A letter mailed to Los Angeles from Tijuana will take a week or more while one mailed from Chula Vista will only take two days.) Old Baja hands usually do the same, handing over mail to other travelers who are going back to the States.

TELEPHONE CODES

To call a number in Mexico from outside the country, dial 011 + 52 + area code + number. Example: To call the number 2-4761 in La Paz from the U.S., dial 011 (international dialing code) + 52 (Mexico country code) + 682 (La Paz area code) + 2-4761 (the phone number in La Paz). Older Baja guidebooks often show a 706 "area code" for the peninsula; this number sequence is no longer functional—you must dial the country code and local area code before the local number.

In Mexico:

Information (national)	01
Long-distance operator (national)	02
Time	03
Information (local)	04
Mexico City area code	05
Police	06
Spanish-English emergency information	07
International operator	09

Long-distance Direct Dialing From Mexico:
station to station (in Mexico)
    91 + area code + number
person to person (in Mexico)
    92 + area code + number
station to station (to U.S. and Canada)
    95 + area code + number
person to person (to U.S. and Canada)
    96 + area code + number
station to station (to other countries)
    98 + area code + number
person to person (to other countries)
    99 + area code + number

Baja California Area Codes:

Tijuana	66
Rosarito	661
Ensenada	667
Mexicali	65
Tecate	665
San Felipe	657
Guerrero Negro/Mulegé	685
Loreto	683
La Paz/Todos Santos	682
San José del Cabo/Cabo San Lucas	684

ROAD SIGNS

stop

railroad crossing

parking

no parking

one way

two way

dip

dip

yield right of way

left turn only

bus stop

keep to the right

Telephone Services

The national telephone company, TelMex (part nationalized, part privately owned), has improved its services considerably over the last few years. Local phone calls are relatively cheap—a 100-peso coin, about US$.03, will pay for a phone-booth call—as are long distance calls within Mexico. Connections are usually good, though you may have to wait awhile to get through to the operator during busy periods (e.g., Sundays and holidays).

If you don't want to use a phone booth or a hotel/RV park phone (hotels and RV parks usually add their own surcharges to both local and long-distance calls), you can make a call during business hours from a TelMex office. Only large towns have TelMex offices with public telecommunications facilities; a small town may have a private telephone office (usually called *caseta de teléfono),* often set up in the corner of a local shop, where you can make calls. Like hotels, private telephone offices add surcharges to calls.

On the long stretch between Ensenada and Mulegé, few towns or villages have telephone service, much less a telephone office. There's no phone service in Bahía de los Angeles, for example—residents and visitors alike must drive to Guerrero Negro, some 129 km (80 miles) distant, to make a phone call. (Some residents maintain their own two-way radio stations for communication with the outside world.) Mulegé has only two public phone booths; visitors line up on Sundays to phone home.

Making International Calls: To direct dial an international call to the U.S. or Canada, dial 95 plus the area code and number for a station-to-station call or 96 plus area code and number for a person-to-person call. For other countries besides Canada and the U.S., dial 98 and 99 respectively. Long-distance international calls are heavily taxed and cost more than equivalent international calls from the U.S. or Canada.

Collect: For international service, calling collect saves money and hassles. In Spanish the magic words are *por cobrar* (collect), prefaced by the name of the place you're calling (e.g., *a los Estados Unidos, por favor—por cobrar).* This will get you connected to an English-speaking international operator. You're supposed to be able to obtain an international operator directly by dialing 09, but this number doesn't always work. Speak slowly and clearly for best results.

Local Numbers: Most telephone numbers in Baja consist of five digits (six digits in Tijuana and Mexicali). There's no standard way of hyphenating the numbers; a five-digit number may appear as 211-13, 2-1113, or 2-11-13 and a six-digit number may be written 341720, 341-520, 34-1720, or 34-17-20. For the sake of consistency, the latter forms are used in this book since they seem to be the most commonly used in Baja.

Business Hours
The typical small business will be open Mon.-Fri. (plus Sat. for retail businesses) from 0900 to 1400, then closed until 1600 or 1700, and then reopened until 1900 or 2000. Official government offices typically maintain an 0830-1530 schedule (although Secretary of Tourism offices will usually open again from 1700 to 1900).

Banks are open Mon.-Fri., 830-1330, but remember that the foreign exchange service usually closes around noon (probably to lock in the exchange rate before afternoon adjustments).

HEALTH

By and large, Baja California is a healthy place—sanitation standards are relatively high compared to many other parts of Mexico and the water quality in many areas is superior to that found in Alta California. The visitor's main health concerns are not going to be with food or water sources but with avoiding mishaps while driving, boating, diving, surfing, or otherwise enjoying Baja's great outdoor life. Health issues directly concerned with these activities are covered under the relevant sections in this book.

FOOD AND WATER

Visitors who use common sense will probably never come down with food- or water-related illnesses while traveling in Baja. The first rule is not to overdo it during the first few days of your trip—eat and drink in moderation. Shoveling down huge amounts of tasty, often heavy Mexican foods along with pitchers of margaritas or strong Mexican beer is liable to make anyone sick from pure overindulgence. If you're not used to the spices and different ways of cooking, it's best to ingest small amounts at first.

Second, take it easy with foods offered by street vendors, since this is where you're most likely to suffer from unsanitary conditions. Eat only foods that have been thoroughly cooked and are served either stove-hot or refrigerator-cold. Many gringos eat street food without any problems whatsoever (the author included), but it pays to be cautious, especially if it's your first time in Mexico.

Travel nags usually recommend that you avoid unpeeled fruit and vegetables in Baja, but since virtually all fruit is peeled before eating anyway, this is a somewhat useless suggestion. Peeled or not, as long as fruits and vegetables are washed and dried with a clean cloth before eating they're usually okay. After all, plenty of Mexican fruit is consumed daily in Canada and the U.S..

Hotels and restaurants serve only purified drinking water and ice to their customers (whether Mexican or gringo), so there's no need to ask for mineral water or to refuse ice. Tap water, however, should not be consumed except in hotels where the water system is purified—if so, there will be a notice over the washbasin in your room. Most grocery stores sell bottled purified water if you need it for the road. Water purification tablets, iodine crystals, water filters, etc. aren't necessary for Baja travel unless you plan to do extensive backpacking (see "Sports and Recreation," p. 64 for details).

Turista

People who have never traveled to a foreign country before may find there's a period of adjustment to the new gastrointestinal flora that comes with the new territory—there's really no way to avoid the differences wrought by sheer distances. Sometimes the adjustment is unpleasant.

Mexican doctors call gastrointestinal upset of this sort *turista* since it affects tourists but not the local population. The usual symptoms of turista (also known by the gringo tags "Montezuma's Revenge" and "the Aztec Two-Step") are nausea and diarrhea, sometimes with stomach cramps and a low fever. Again, eating and drinking in moderation will help prevent the worst of the symptoms, should they begin to appear. These symptoms rarely persist more than a day or two. (If it's any consolation, Mexicans often get sick the first time they go to the U.S. or Canada.)

Prevention and Treatment: Many Mexico travelers swear by a preventive regimen of Pepto-Bismol begun the day before arrival in country. Opinions vary as to how much P-B is necessary to ward off or tame the evil flora, but the average seems to be about a bottle a day (taking a couple of spoonfuls at intervals throughout the day) for the first week, tapering off over the second week until you stop using it altogether.

Another regimen that seems to be effective is a daily tablet of 100-milligram doxycycline (sold as Vibramycin in the U.S.), a low-grade antibiotic that requires a prescription in most countries. It works by killing all the bacteria in your intestinal tract—including the ones that reside there naturally and help protect your bowels from outside intruders as well as new arrivals. It's available without a prescription in Mexican *farmacias,* but you should check with your doctor first to make sure you're not sensitive to it—some people have problems with sunlight while taking doxycycline. Some physicians believe that when you stop taking this drug you're particularly susceptible to intestinal upset because there's no protective bacteria left to fight off infections. Hence, once you start it don't stop until you return home.

If you come down with a case of turista, the best thing to do is drink plenty of fluids (adults should drink at least three liters a day, a child under 80 pounds/37 kilos at least a liter a day—but no tea, coffee, milk, fruit juices, or booze), eat only bland foods (nothing spicy, fatty, or fried), and take it easy until it passes. Pepto-Bismol or similar pectin-based remedies usually help. Some people like to mask the symptoms with a strong over-the-counter medication like Immodium AD (loperamide is the active ingredient), but though it can be very effective, it isn't a cure—only time will cure traveler's diarrhea.

If the symptoms are unusually severe (especially if there's blood in the stools) or persist more than one or two days, see a doctor. Most hotels can arrange a doctor's visit or you can contact a Mexican tourist office or U.S. Consulate for recommendations.

SUNBURN AND DEHYDRATION

Sunburn probably afflicts more Baja visitors than all other illnesses and injuries combined. The sunlight in Baja can be quite strong, especially in the center of the peninsula and along the Sea of Cortez coast. For outdoor forays, sun protection is a must, whatever the activity—the longer you'll be in the sun, the more protection you'll need.

A hat, sunglasses, and plenty of sunscreen or sunblock make a good start. Bring along a sunscreen with a sun protection factor (SPF) of at least 25, even if you don't plan on using it all the time, for when your skin has had enough toasting. Apply it to *all* exposed parts of your body—don't forget the hands, top of the feet, and neck (and, men, any thinned-out or bald areas on your scalp). Sunscreen must be reapplied after swimming (no matter what the label says) or after heavy perspiring.

If you're going boating, don't leave shore with just a bathing suit—bring along an opaque shirt, preferably with long sleeves, along with a pair of long pants in case the sun gets to be too much. Since you can never know for certain whether your boat might get stranded or lost at sea for a period of time (if, for example, the motor conks out and you get caught in an offshore current), you shouldn't be without extra clothing for emergencies.

It's also important to drink plenty of water and/or nonalcoholic, non-caffeinated fluids when spending time in the sun to avoid dehydration (alcohol and caffeine—including the caffeine in iced tea and Coke—only increase your potential for dehydration). Symptoms of dehydration include darker-than-usual urine (or not being able to urinate), a flushed face, profuse sweating or an unusual lack thereof, and sometimes a headache, dizziness, and general feeling of malaise. Extreme cases of dehydration caused by hot weather can lead to heat exhaustion or less commonly heatstroke, in which the victim may become delirious and/or convulse. If either condition is suspected, get the victim out of the sun immediately, cover with a wet sheet or towel, and administer a rehydration fluid that replaces lost water and salts (sodium, potassium, chloride, and bicarbonate). If you can get the victim to a doctor, all the better—heat stroke can be very serious.

Rehydration Formula: If Gatorade or a similar rehydration fluid isn't available you can mix your own by combining the following ingredients: 1 liter (4 cups or 1 quart) purified water or diluted fruit juice; 2 tablespoons sugar or honey; ¼ teaspoon salt; and ¼ teaspoon bicarbonate of soda—if soda isn't available,

scorpion (BOB RACE)

use another ¼ teaspoon salt. A dehydration victim should drink this mixture at regular intervals until symptoms have subsided substantially—four or more quarts/liters may be necessary in moderate cases, more in severe cases.

MOTION SICKNESS

Visitors with little or no boating experience who join fishing cruises in Baja, especially on the Pacific side, are sometimes prone to motion sickness caused by the movement of a boat over ocean swells. This happens when the repeated pitching and rolling affects a person's sense of equilibrium to the point of nausea. Commonly known as "seasickness" *(mareado* in Spanish), it can be a very unpleasant experience not only for the green-at-the-gills but for fellow passengers (who will be anxious lest the victim spew on them at any moment).

The best way to prevent motion sickness is to take one of the preventives commonly available from a pharmacist: promethazine (sold as Phenergan in the States), dimenhydrinate (Dramamine), or scopolamine (Transderm Scop). The latter is available as an adhesive patch worn behind the ear—the time-release action is supposed to be more effective than tablets. These medications should be taken *before* boarding the vessel rather than after one feels seasick. It's also not a good idea to eat a large meal before getting on a boat.

If you start to feel seasick while out on the bounding main, certain actions can lessen the likelihood that it will get worse: 1) do not lie down, since often the first symptom of motion sickness is drowsiness—if you give in to the impulse you'll almost certainly guarantee a worsening of the condition; 2) stay in the open air rather than below decks—fresh air usually helps; 3) fix your gaze on the horizon—this will help steady your disturbed inner ear, which is the proximate cause of motion sickness.

INSECT BITES AND STINGS

Mosquitoes And *Jejenes*

Mosquitoes breed in standing water and since standing water isn't that common in arid Baja, neither are mosquitoes (exceptions include palm oases, estuaries, and marshes—when there isn't a strong breeze around to keep them at bay). The easiest way to avoid mosquito bites is to apply insect repellent to exposed areas of the skin and clothing whenever the mossies are out and biting (for most species, this means between dusk and dawn). The most effective repellents are those that contain a high concentration of DEET (N,N-diethyl-metatoluamide). Those with an aversion to applying synthetics to their skin can try citronella (lemongrass oil), which is also effective but requires more frequent application.

More common in Baja than mosquitoes are *jejenes,* tiny flying insects also known as "no-see-ums" among North Americans because you almost never see them while they're biting. The same repellents effective for mosquitoes will usually do the trick for jejenes.

For relief from the itchiness of mosquito bites, try rubbing a bit of hand soap on the affected areas. Jejene bites will usually stop itching in less than 10 minutes if you refrain from scratching them. Excessive scratching of either type of bite can lead to infection, so be mindful of what your fingers are up to.

In spite of the presence of the occasional mosquito, the U.S. Center for Disease Control has declared all of Baja California to be malaria-free.

SNAKEBITE PREVENTION AND TREATMENT

The overall risk of being bitten by a poisonous snake while hiking in Baja California is quite low, mainly because the rattlesnake (the only venomous land snake in Baja) avoids contact with all large mammals, including humans. Most of the unfortunate who are bitten by snakes in Baja are local ranchers who spend a great deal of time in snake habitats or small children who may not know to retreat from a coiled rattler.

Nonetheless, anyone spending time in the Baja outback, including campers and hikers, would be well-advised to follow a few simple precautions.

Prevention

First of all, use caution when placing hands or feet in areas where snakes may lie. This primarily includes rocky ledges, holes, and fallen logs. Always look first, and if you must move a rock or log, use a long stick or other instrument. Wear sturdy footwear when walking in possible snake habitats. High-top leather shoes or boots are best. *Rancheros* wear thick leather leggings when working in known snake territory; these are sometimes available for purchase at *zapaterias* (shoe stores) that sell boots or at leather and saddle shops.

Most snakes strike only when they feel threatened. Naturally, if you step on or next to a snake, it is likely to strike. If you see or hear a rattlesnake, remain still until the snake moves away. If it doesn't leave the vicinity, simply back away slowly and cautiously. Sudden movements may cause a snake to strike; rattlers rarely strike a stationary target. A rattler can't strike a target that is farther away than three-fourths of its body length; use this rough measure to judge when it may be safe to move away from one, leaving plenty of room for error.

If you'll be hiking in wilderness areas far from professional medical treatment, by all means carry an elastic bandage or two, the type used for sprains. The old "slice and suck" method of treating snakebite has been discredited by most medical experts.

Don't attempt to kill a rattler unless you have a genuine need to use it as food—as nasty as they may seem, snakes are as important to the desert ecosystem as the most beautiful flowering cactus.

Treatment

If bitten by a snake, it is important that you remain calm in order to slow the potential spread of venom in your body until you are able to discern whether the snake in question is a rattler, and so that you can follow the necessary steps for treatment in a cool-headed manner.

First, immediately following the bite, try to identify the snake (see "Flora and Fauna," p. 14, for descriptions of common Baja rattlers). At the very least, memorize the markings and physical characteristics so that a physician can administer the most appropriate antivenin. If you can kill the snake and bring it to the nearest treatment center, all the better, but this could expose you or your fellow hikers to the risk of another bite.

Second, examine the bite for teeth marks. A successful bite by a poisonous pit viper (which includes copperheads, cottonmouths, and rattlesnakes) will have one or two large fang punctures in addition to smaller teeth marks, while a bite by a nonpoisonous snake will not feature fang punctures. In general, nonpoisonous bites cause relatively small, shallow marks or scratches.

If it's suspected that the bite is poisonous, **immobilize the affected limb and wrap tightly in an elastic bandage.** This will slow the spread of venom through the lymph system and mitigate swelling. Be careful that the bandage isn't wrapped so tightly that it cuts off circulation—you should be able to insert a finger under it without difficulty. Keep the arm or leg below the level of the heart. The victim should avoid all physical activity if possible since increased circulation will accelerate the absorption of the venom. For this same reason, aspirin, sedatives, and alcohol should be avoided. Do not apply cold therapy—ice packs, cold compresses, and so on—to the bite area or to any other part of the victim's body.

Get the victim to a hospital or physician if possible. Where feasible, carry the victim to re-

SNAKEBITE PREVENTION AND TREATMENT (CONT.)

strict physical exertion. Even when wrapping the limb appears successful in preventing symptoms, the bite will need medical attention and a physician may decide that antivenin treatment is necessary. (However, it's possible for a poisonous snake to bite without injecting any venom—up to 20% of reported bites are "dry bites" like these.) Snakebite victims who require antivenin treatment will usually receive the broad-spectrum North American Antisnakebite Serum for pit viper poisoning—where available (not likely anywhere outside Tijuana, Mexicali, La Paz, or Cabo San Lucas). Your home physician may be able to provide a prescription for the serum in advance of your outdoor trip if convinced that you'll be in areas where antivenin is unavailable or medical treatment is inaccessible.

In cases where it's been determined that a bite is venomous and the serum isn't available, the best you can do is follow the treatment outlined above and keep the victim immobile and cool until the symptoms—pain in the affected limb, abdominal cramps, headache—have subsided. (For some bites, wrapping the limb in an elastic bandage will avoid all or most of the worst symptoms.) The victim should drink plenty of water. Don't panic—remember that few rattlesnake bites turn out to be fatal, even when untreated.

Wasps, Bees, And Hornets

Although stings from these flying insects can be very painful, they aren't of mortal danger to most people. If you're allergic to such stings and plan to travel in remote areas of Baja, you should consider requesting anti-allergy medication from your doctor before leaving home. At the very least, carry a supply of Benadryl or a similar over-the-counter antihistamine. Dramamine (dimenhydrinate) also usually helps mitigate allergic reactions.

Relief from a wasp/bee/hornet sting can be achieved by applying a paste of baking soda and water to the area. Liquids that contain ammonia, including urine, are also helpful in relieving pain. If a stinger is visible, remove (by scraping if possible, or with tweezers) before applying any remedies. If a stung limb becomes unusually swollen or if the victim exhibits symptoms of a severe allergic reaction (difficulty in breathing, agitation, hives), seek medical assistance.

Ticks

If you find a tick embedded in your skin, don't try to pull it off—this may leave the head and pincers under your skin and lead to infection. Covering the tick with petroleum jelly, mineral oil, alcohol, gasoline, kerosene, or alcohol will usually cause the tick to release its hold in order to avoid suffocation.

Burning the tick with a cigarette butt or hot match usually succeeds only in killing it—when you pull it out, the head and pincers may not come with it. Stay with the suffocation method and if it doesn't come out, use tweezers.

Scorpions

Scorpions (alacránes in Spanish) vary in the strength of their venom from individual to individual and species to species, but the sting is rarely dangerous to adults. It can be very painful, however, and can result in partial numbness and swelling that lasts up to several days. In Baja, the small yellow scorpions inflict more painful stings than the larger, dark-colored ones.

The best treatment begins with having the victim lie down and relax to slow the spread of the venom; keep the affected area below the level of the heart. Ice packs on the sting may relieve pain and mitigate swelling, and aspirin also helps.

Children who weigh less than about 13 kilos (30 pounds) should receive medical attention if stung by a scorpion. Doctors in Baja usually have ready access to scorpion antivenin (anti-alacrán), but it should only be administered under qualified medical supervision.

Avoiding Scorpions: Scorpions prefer damp, dark, warm places (e.g., dead brush, rock piles, and fallen logs), so exercise particular caution when placing your hands in or near such areas—hands are the scorpion's most common target on the human body. In fact, campers should wear gloves while handling firewood in Baja as an extra precaution against scorpion stings.

Other favorite spots for scorpions are crumpled clothing and bedding. In desert areas of Baja, always check your bedsheets or sleeping bag for scorpions before climbing in. In the same environments, shake out your shoes and clothing before putting them on.

POISONOUS SEA CREATURES

Various marine animals carry poisons in parts of their bodies that can inflict painful stings on humans. In Baja, such creatures include jellyfish, Portuguese man-of-war, cone shells, sting rays, sea urchins, and various fishes with poisonous spines.

The best way to avoid jellyfish and Portuguese man-of-war is to scope out the water before going in—if you see any nasties floating around, look for another beach. Sting rays can be avoided by shuffling your feet in the sand as you walk in shallow surf—this will usually cause rays resting in the sand to swim away.

To avoid cone shell and sea urchin stings, wear shoes in the water (several sport shoe manufacturers now produce specialized water shoes, e.g., Nike's Aqua Socks). You can also often spot cones and urchins in clear water, especially if you're wearing a diving mask.

Anglers should take care when handling landed fish to avoid poisonous spine wounds. If you don't know how to avoid the spines while handling a fish, let someone who is more experienced show you how.

The treatment for stings from all of the above is the same: remove all tentacles, barbs, or spines from the affected area; wash with rubbing alcohol or diluted ammonia (urine will do in a pinch) to remove as much venom as possible; and wrap the area in cloth to reduce the flow of oxygen to the wound until pain subsides. If an acute allergic reaction occurs, get the victim to a doctor or clinic as quickly as possible.

MEDICAL ASSISTANCE

The quality of basic medical treatment, including dentistry, is of a relatively high standard in Baja's cities and larger towns—ask at a tourist office or at your consulate for recommendations. Hospitals can be found in Tijuana, Mexicali, Ensenada, Guerrero Negro, Ciudad Constitución, and La Paz, and there are public clinics or Red Cross (Cruz Roja) stations in nearly every other town. In Tijuana, Ensenada, Mexicali, Rosarito, Tecate, and San Luis Río Colorado, the Red Cross can be reached by dialing 132 (toll-free) from any pay phone.

Emergency Evacuation

San Diego's **Air-Evac International** provides emergency 24-hour airlift service (or ground ambulance in the border areas) from Baja to U.S. hospitals in the San Diego area. Their emergency number is (619) 278-3822. Air-Evac will accept collect calls; payment for the air service can be made with a credit card or through your health insurance company. **Critical Air Medicine** (tel. 619-571-8944, 800-247-8325 in Alta California, 800-633-8326 elsewhere) provides a similar service.

Medical Air Services Association (tel. 817-430-4655, 800-643-9023, 9 Village Circle, Roanoke, TX 76262) offers a yearly membership plan that covers unlimited emergency air transport from anywhere in Mexico to anywhere in the U.S. or Canada. MASA membership rates are US$150 per year per family. The service is also available to Sanborn's Mexico Club members at a discount rate of US$90 annually (US$45 for individuals). For information on club membership, contact Sanborn's (see "Services and Information," p. 116, for phone, fax, and address).

SERVICES AND INFORMATION

Tourist Information

Mexico's federal tourist bureau, the Secretaría de Turismo (SECTUR), has state offices in Mexicali and La Paz. These in turn have branch offices in Tijuana, Ensenada, Tecate, Rosarito, San Felipe, and Loreto. These offices usually stock a variety of free brochures, maps, hotel and restaurant lists, and information on local activities, but some offices are better staffed to handle visitor queries than others. Tijuana, Ensenada, and Mexicali have convention and visitors bureaus in addition to state offices, so they are particularly well stocked with useful information. The addresses, phone numbers, and hours of each office are listed under the appropriate destination sections of the book.

If you would like to contact the national office directly, you can call or write the **Secretaría de Turismo de México** (tel. 250-01-51, 250-01-23, 250-04-93), Presidente Mazaryk No. 172, 11570 México, D.F. In the U.S., SECTUR maintains a toll-free information number, tel. (800) 262-8900.

Travel Clubs

Baja's popularity as a boating and RV destination has spawned two Alta California-based travel clubs that specialize in recreational travel on the peninsula as well as along the Pacific coast of mainland Mexico. Membership benefits include discounts (usually 10-20%) at various hotels, restaurants, and other tourist-oriented establishments in Mexico, discounted group auto and boat insurance, the opportunity to participate in club events (e.g., tours, fiestas), and a subscription to a newsletter that contains tips from other club members, short travel features, and the latest information on road conditions and Mexican tourism policy. The clubs can also arrange tourist cards, boat permits, and fishing licenses by mail.

The main differences between the two are that Mexico West specializes in road (especially RV) travel and publishes a monthly newsletter, while Vagabundos del Mar is more oriented toward boaters and publishes its newsletter every two months. Mexico West also maintains a telephone information "hotline." Contact **Mexico West** at 3450 Bonita Rd., Suite 107, Chula Vista, CA 91910 (tel. 619-585-3033; fax 619-422-2671), or write them at P.O. Box 1646, Bonita, CA 91902-1646. Write or call **Vagabundos del Mar** at P.O. Box 824, Isleton, CA 95641 (tel. 707-374-5511; fax 707-374-6843).

A third travel club, sponsored by Texas-based Sanborn's Mexico Insurance, offers similar benefits for all of Mexico, with the addition of custom-designed itineraries (prepared by long-time Mexico travel aficionado, "Mexico" Mike Nelson) for those who need guidance. For an extra charge of US$45 a year (US$90 for a family), Sanborn's Mexico Club members may also subscribe to a medical evacuation service covering all air transportation costs to the U.S. or Canada for medical treatment. For details, contact Sanborn's (tel. 512-686-0711, fax 512-686-0732), P.O. Box 310, McAllen, TX 78502.

MEDIA

Newspapers

Several Spanish-language newspapers are published in Baja; *El Mexicano,* published daily in Tijuana, has the highest circulation, closely followed by Mexicali's *La Voz de la Frontera* ("Voice of the Border"). Also of considerable interest is the progressive *Zeta* ("Z"), out of Tijuana.

Three English-language newspapers and one bilingual newspaper are published monthly in Baja, all of them heavily oriented toward tourists. Although not exactly pillars of journalism, they nonetheless contain much information of value to the visitor, not the least of which are up-to-date sketch maps. Typical features include restaurant reviews, cultural primers on upcoming festivals, Spanish lan-

(previous page) Río Mulegé; (top) agave;
(bottom left) Playa del Amor, Cabo San Lucas; (bottom right) palm and cardón

guage lessons, seasonal fishing recommendations, plus the occasional editorial on national or local tourism policies. The content of each is somewhat biased toward the town in which it is published.

Each of the two English-language newspapers based in northern Baja, the *Baja Sun* and the *Baja Times,* offer foreign and local subscriptions. Read their classified ads to find out about Baja real estate.

At newsstands in Tijuana, Ensenada, Mexicali, and La Paz you can also find *The News,* an English-language daily published in Mexico City. In tourist hotels in the north you'll often see day-old copies of the *San Diego Tribune* or the *Los Angeles Times.*

Radio And Television

In the border area of northern Baja, radios and TVs pick up a mix of broadcasts from Tijuana and San Diego. Farther south the San Diego stations begin to fade, followed by the Tijuana stations. South of Ensenada you'll need shortwave radio to pick anything up until you arrive in La Paz or Los Cabos, where TV and radio reception begins again.

Tapes and CDs: Because of the general lack of TV and radio reception in most of Baja, it would be rather foolish to pack an AM/FM radio or portable TV. An audio-cassette or portable CD player wouldn't be out of place, however. Many towns in Baja have shops that sell tapes and CDs, which are generally less expensive than in the U.S. or Canada. (North American and European releases—in addition to Latino recordings—often appear on Mexican labels.) Baja is a good place to pick up a selection of *música norteña* tapes.

MAPS

Among the many Baja California maps available to visitors, two are particularly well-suited to general-purpose Baja road travel. One is published by the Automobile Club of Southern California and is available from most AAA offices—maps are free to members. The excellent graphics on this map, which include topographic shading, make it easy to read,

BAJA NEWSPAPERS

Baja California News
Apartado Postal 31
Cabo San Lucas, BCS
(tel./fax 3-0969)

Baja Sun
Calle Sexta No. 995
Ensenada, BCN
or
P.O. Box 8530
Chula Vista, CA 92012

Baja Times
Centro Comercial
Hotel Rosarito
Rosarito, BCN
(tel. 2-12-44; fax 2-23-66)
or
P.O. Box 5577
Chula Vista, CA 91912
Los Cabos Times ("El Tiempo Los Cabos")
Blvd. Marina No. 20
Cabo San Lucas, BCS
(tel. 3-01-63, 3-05-46; fax 3-03-69)

and it's accurate and detailed enough for any border-to-cape auto trip.

Distances on the AAA map are marked in miles (scale: one inch = 12.4 miles or 20 km), which makes it convenient for anyone driving a vehicle purchased in the U.S. but frustrating for drivers of vehicles acquired anywhere else in the world, including Canada or Mexico. Even for American-market vehicles, it can be confusing trying to match map mileage with the Mexican roadside kilometer markers. The AAA map has a distance table with entries in both miles and kilometers, but this is of little use when trying to figure out distances between points not listed on the table. Perhaps in some future edition of its Baja map, AAA will add metric equivalents alongside the mile notations.

International Travel Map Productions (ITM) publishes a well-researched map that competes well with the AAA map. It's a bit harder to find, especially in the U.S.; map and travel stores may carry it, or it can be ordered from ITM, P.O. Box 2290, Vancouver, BC V6B 3W5, Canada. In spite of its smaller scale (one inch = 15.78 miles or 25.4 km) the ITM map is far more detailed than the AAA map and all distances are entered in kilometers as well as miles. Many dirt roads, trails, and destinations that aren't marked on the AAA map appear on the ITM map (e.g., Cañon Tajo in northern Baja). In addition, the map features contour lines in 200-meter intervals and is annotated with useful historical and sightseeing information. The main drawback of this map is that it's so detailed it can be difficult to read. In addition, the map's graphics scheme uses far too much red (all roadways are marked in red), a color which is particularly difficult to read in low light (e.g., at dusk, or under a vehicle's interior lights).

Topographical Maps

Since differences in elevation often determine backcountry route selection, hikers, kayakers, mountain-bikers, and off-road drivers should consider obtaining topographical maps in advance of their arrival in Baja. Topo maps are very difficult to come by in Baja itself. For information on what's available and where to get it, see "Hiking and Backpacking," under "Sports and Recreation," p. 64.

BUYING OR LEASING PROPERTY IN BAJA

The Mexican government allows both resident and nonresident foreigners to own Mexican real estate—both land and buildings—within certain restrictions. Under the Constitution of 1857, land ownership by direct title is only permitted in areas more than 100 km (62 miles) from any international border and 50 km (31 miles) from any sea coast. In Baja California, this limits prospective buyers to areas in the interior of the peninsula where services (water, electricity, sewage, telephone) are often nonexistent.

However, since 1973 the Mexican government has offered a way for foreigners to ac-

quire lots that fall outside the geographic limits, including coastal property. For transactions of this nature, the Ministry of Foreign Affairs issues permits to foreigners allowing them to create limited real estate trusts, administered by Mexican banks, with themselves as beneficiaries. Originally, these trusts were valid for 30-year nonrenewable terms only. In 1989 the government further liberalized real estate regulations so that the trusts (called *fideicomisos*) could be renewed at the end of each 30-year term for an additional 30-year term, with no limit on the number of renewals. Fideicomisos can be bought and sold among foreigners—at market rates—just like fee-simple property.

Needless to say, Baja real estate prices have increased substantially as a result of this change in policy. An estimated 40,000 foreigners are now residing in Baja California Norte alone, some of whom are Americans who commute to San Diego for work. The priciest coastal properties are those near the U.S.-Mexico border and on the Cape, but prices are still substantially below what's available in coastal Alta California.

Beach lots large enough for a two- or three-bedroom home in the La Paz area (less expensive than either the Cape or the Rosarito-Ensenada areas) can be had for US$15,000 and up. Survivalist types can find beach hideaways with no services for even less—in remote areas, total annual payments are as low as US$500-1000. With a desalinator, generator or solar cells, propane stove and refrigerator (and perhaps an airplane to get in and out) you can live in considerable style.

Before you rush off to grab Baja land, you should be aware that a lot of people get burned in Mexican real estate deals. It's best to deal through an established, reputable real estate agent. The American company Century 21 has opened a franchise in Baja, and although they generally represent only the more expensive properties, they can be very helpful with information on real estate trusts. Mexican tourist offices in Baja also often carry information on residential property.

Precautions: Many sellers will ask that the full purchase price be paid up front. Because a large number of gringos buy land in Mexico with cash, some Mexicans assume that this is customary for North Americans. Paying up front is *not* the typical procedure for Mexicans themselves, who usually make a down payment and then send in monthly time payments; mortgage terms similar to those found in Canada and the U.S. are available in Mexico. Even if you have the cash, don't hand over more than half the full amount until you have the fideicomiso papers in hand.

Time Shares

Time-share salesmen have become the scourge of the resort areas in Baja, especially in Cabo San Lucas where they hang out on street corners and in hotel lobbies, hounding every tourist that passes by. These hustlers, who are usually gringos, will try almost anything to convince you to sign on the dotted line, on the spot (including denying that what they're selling is a time-share). It pays to hold off on any decision until you've made inquiries among current time-share residents at the development and checked with your consulate to see if there have been any complaints.

Time-share developments typically begin selling when construction has just begun—sometimes they don't get finished, or when they do they may not shape up as promised. Also, keep in mind that from an investment perspective, time-shares don't appreciate in value (if they appreciate at all) as much as single-owner properties.

Other Problems: Because time-share owners aren't year-round residents, they usually lack a sense of community as well as any sense of responsibility toward the local environment. For the developer, time-shares mean huge profits since the same space is sold repeatedly in one-week segments. Since land in Baja is relatively inexpensive, considering the charming scenery and climate, it seems to attract a get-rich-quick type of developer who shows a decided lack of respect for the fragile Baja environment.

This is not to say that there aren't any good time-share opportunities in Baja. But in general, as with any real estate deal, it pays to proceed very cautiously—don't be cajoled into buying without considering all the options.

GETTING THERE

BY AIR

International Flights

Baja's most commonly used air gateway for flights from the U.S. (the only country with direct international flights to Baja) is Los Cabos (SJD), a modern airport about 15 km (nine miles) north of San José del Cabo. Daily direct flights to Los Cabos are offered from Los Angeles, San Diego, San Francisco, and Phoenix.

Loreto (LTO) also fields regularly scheduled flights from the U.S., but via Los Angeles only. International flights to La Paz (LAP) are out of Los Angeles and Tucson; the Tucson flight is direct but there's a brief stopover in Guaymas.

Tijuana International Airport (TIJ) is connected to only one U.S. city, Los Angeles. **Air L.A.** (800-933-5952 in the U.S.) flies jet-props five times weekly between Los Angeles and Tijuana. All flights depart from Los Angeles Airport's West Imperial Terminal; fares are US$69 one-way, US$99 roundtrip. If you're planning to pick up a rental car in Tijuana, arranging a connection through L.A. would be considerably easier than flying to San Diego and taking a taxi or bus to Tijuana.

San Felipe and Santa Rosalía each have airports reportedly equipped to handle international service but so far the only way to fly to either of these airports is by chartered plane. It's rumored that either Air L.A. or Aero California may be starting regular domestic service to these airports.

Private Planes

Baja is a popular destination among North American light-aircraft pilots. Entry procedures are minimal, air traffic over the peninsula is light, and nearly 200 airstrips take pilots and their passengers in a matter of hours to corners of Baja usually accessible only by days of driving. Most of these airstrips are unpaved and unstaffed—a significant attraction for those who consider themselves "bush pilots."

Private aircraft weighing less than 12,500 kilograms (27,500 pounds) and carrying fewer than 14 passengers are subject to the same customs procedures as automobiles and light trucks. (In cases where the plane's owner doesn't accompany the aircraft, flights are further restricted to single-engine craft with five or fewer passengers.) Cargo is restricted to the personal belongings of pilots and passengers.

Flight plans must be filed in advance with the Mexican airport nearest the point of entry—other than this original filing, no other flight plans are necessary. A stop on either side of the border is required in order for pilots and passengers to clear immigration and customs. For further information on flying regulations in Baja, contact a Mexican consulate or the Departmento de Transport Aéreo Internacional, Edificio Torre, Aeropuerto Internacional de la Ciudad de México, México, D.F.

For more information on flying conditions in Baja, see "Getting Around," below.

BY LAND

To San Diego

Whether they reach the U.S.-Baja California border by train, bus, or trolley, most visitors using public transport must first pass through San Diego, from where they can choose from several options to Tijuana or Mexicali. San Diego is connected to other points in the U.S. by frequent long-distance bus and rail service.

Bus: Intercity buses generally depart more frequently and are less expensive than trains. Greyhound Bus Lines is the major carrier into San Diego. If you're bussing a long distance to San Diego, a bus pass may be more economical than buying single-journey tickets. Outside North America, a Greyhound **Ameri-**

AIRLINES IN BAJA

Airline:	To:	Nonstop Flights From:	Connecting Flights From:
Aero California tel. (800) 258-3311	Loreto	Los Angeles, La Paz Los Cabos Phoenix, San Diego	Los Angeles, Mexico City,
	La Paz	Aguascalientes, Colima, Culiacán, Guadalajara, Loreto, Los Angeles, Los Mochis, Mexico City, Tijuana	
Aeromexico tel. (800) 237-6639	La Paz	Culiacán, Guaymas, Los Angeles,	Acapulco, Chihuahua, Mexico City, Puerto Vallarta, Tijuana Ciudad Juárez, Guadalajara, León, Monterrey, New York, Tucson
Air L.A. tel. (800) 933-5952	Tijuana	Los Angeles	
Alaska Airlines tel. (800) 426-0333	Los Cabos	Los Angeles, San Diego,	Portland, Seattle San Francisco
Mexicana Airlines tel. (800) 531-7921	Los Cabos	Los Angeles	
Noroeste tel. (83) 13-36 (in Tijuana)	Tijuana, Mexicali	(no nonstops)	El Paso, Las Vegas, Phoenix, Tucson, Ciudad Obregón, Hermosillo, Guaymas, La Paz, Mazatlán, Juárez

Note: All routings are subject to change; call the airlines for the latest information.

pass, which allows unlimited bus travel within specified dates, can be purchased from travel agencies at a discount (e.g., a seven-day pass bought outside the U.S. costs US$99; in the U.S., US$125). For Greyhound fare and schedule information in the U.S., dial (800) 942-5444.

Rail: The only long-distance passenger rail line to San Diego is Amtrak's San Diegan, which rolls between Los Angeles and San Diego nine times daily (US$30 roundtrip Mon.-Thurs.,

US$35 roundtrip on weekends, US$23 one way). Connections with a number of other Amtrak lines to points in the U.S. north or east of Los Angeles can be arranged. Amtrak has special one-way, roundtrip, or excursion fares on occasion—always ask before booking.

Outside North America, some international travel agencies sell a **USA Railpass** which allows unlimited rail travel within specified dates. For schedule information or bookings inside the U.S., call (800) 872-7245 (800-

USA-RAIL). A rail pass called **All Aboard America** is sold inside the U.S. at slightly higher prices.

Bus To Tijuana

Greyhound Trailways (tel. 619-239-9171 in San Diego, 213-620-1200 in L.A.) operates 18 buses a day between 0040 and 2340 from Los Angeles to Tijuana, via San Diego. The fare is US$20 one way from L.A., US$4.20 from San Diego. Buses leave from the downtown Greyhound Trailways terminals in each city and terminate at Tijuana's downtown terminal at Calle Comercio and Avenida Madero. The trip from San Diego is about 35 minutes when traffic is light; in the reverse direction it usually takes around 55 minutes. (Mexican Customs doesn't make everyone get off the bus at the border; U.S. Customs does.) From Los Angeles, the bus journey is about three hours. Boxed bicycles may accompany paying passengers at no extra charge.

Mexicoach (tel. 619-232-5040 in San Diego, 800-628-3745 toll-free in Alta California, 85-69-13 in Tijuana) runs five buses a day between 0900 and 1900 from San Diego's Amtrak depot (on Broadway at Kettner Blvd.) to the Mexicoach terminal next to the Fronton Jai Alai at Avenida Madero and Calle 7A. Drivers will also stop at the Tijuana Cultural Center on request. Mexicoach will take bicycles (preferably boxed) for no additional charge. The fare is US$5.25 one way, US$10 roundtrip.

Mexicoach also operates a shorter bus run from San Ysidro—just across the border on the U.S. side—to its Tijuana terminal. This trip takes about 20 minutes, costs US$2 each way, and includes a ticket to the museum at the Tijuana Cultural Center. From its Tijuana terminal Mexicoach now has direct buses to Rosarito (US$10 roundtrip—see "Rosarito Transport," under "Tijuana to Ensenada," p. 160, for details).

The cheapest bus transport to the border is San Diego Transit's city bus no. 932, which goes from the downtown area to San Ysidro every 30 minutes from 0500 to midnight for just US$1. Because it makes several stops along the way, however, it takes twice as long as the direct buses to reach San Ysidro. For schedule information, call (619) 233-3004.

Tijuana Trolley

The San Diego trolley system's train to San Ysidro, nicknamed the "Tijuana Trolley," is the second-cheapest form of public transport to the border after the city bus. San Ysidro-bound trains leave every 15 minutes from 0500 to 0100 from downtown San Diego and cost US$1.75 each way. Like the city bus, the trolley makes numerous stops along the way to San Ysidro—figure on about an hour from downtown. Bicycles may be taken on the trolley with certain restrictions (see "Bicycle Transport," under "Getting Around," p. 130). Call (619) 231-8549 for general trolley information or (619) 233-3004 for information on scheduling and stops.

Bus To Calexico

Calexico is opposite Mexicali on the U.S. side of the border. Greyhound Trailways operates several buses daily to Calexico from Los Angeles (US$29.65), San Diego (US$19.65), Tucson (US$31.75), Yuma (US$16.45), Phoenix (US$42.35), and El Paso (US$116.20). The Calexico Greyhound terminal is on 1st St., from where it's a short walk through the immigration and customs checkpoint into downtown Mexicali.

From Mainland Mexico

Transportes Norte de Sonora and **Autotransportes del Pacifico** operate long-distance express buses to Mexicali and Tijuana from various towns in Guanajuato, Nayarit, Sonora, Chihuahua, Michoacán, Jalisco, Sinaloa, Zacatecas, Querétaro, and México, D.F.

Train

Mexico's national rail service has its westernmost terminus in Mexicali. The Mexicali line connects with the Mexico City-Nogales line at Benjamin Hill, hence it's an alternative way to get to Baja from Nogales or Mexico City (or anywhere in between—although the ferry from Mazatlán or Topolobampo would be a more direct way to southern Baja). For details, see "Mexicali," p. 215.

In the U.S. and Canada, you can dial (800) 228-3225 for information on the Mexican rail system.

Driving To Baja

More people drive private vehicles across the U.S.-Mexico border at Tijuana than at any other point along its 1,600-km (1,000-mile) length (although Nuevo Laredo—opposite Laredo, Texas—gets more traffic overall if commercial vehicles are taken into account). If you find the traffic daunting, Tijuana can be avoided altogether by choosing any of four other Baja border crossings. The red tape for driving into Baja is extremely minimal and shouldn't prevent anyone from attempting it. In fact, no vehicle permits of any kind are required—no matter how long you stay in Baja—unless you plan to board one of the vehicle ferries from Santa Rosalía or La Paz to the mainland. For stays of less than 72 hours no farther south than Maneadero, U.S. and Canadian citizens don't even need a tourist permit for themselves—just some identification.

Insurance: Before driving into Baja, drivers should arrange for Mexican vehicle insurance. No matter what your own insurance company may tell you, the Mexican authorities don't recognize foreign insurance policies for private vehicles in Mexico.

Vehicle insurance isn't required by law in Mexico but it's a good idea to carry a Mexican liability policy anyway; without it, a minor traffic accident can turn into a nightmare. Short-term (as little as one day's worth) insurance can be arranged at any of several agencies found in nearly every border town (e.g., San Ysidro, Tecate, Calexico) between the Pacific Ocean and the Gulf of Mexico. One of the most popular, and reliable, is Sanborn's Mexico Insurance, which has offices in virtually every town along the U.S. Mexico border. Better deals, however, can usually be negotiated from sources specializing in Baja road travel, especially for drivers who will be making more than one trip into Mexico each year. Several agencies in Tijuana and Ensenada offer annual policies for which you're charged only for those days

you're actually in Mexico. Of course, this requires a trip south of the border in order to obtain such a policy in the first place, so you'll need a day's worth of border insurance beforehand.

One agency north of the border that can arrange Mexican liability insurance on a per-use basis is **Anserv Insurance Services** (tel. 619-233-5444, 800-262-1994 in Alta California, tel. 800-654-7504 elsewhere in the U.S. and Canada). Their rates are as low as US$1 a day based on 60 days (minimum) use per policy year. The Mexico West and Vagabundos del Mar travel clubs (see "Services and Information," p. 116 for addresses and phone numbers) offer low group insurance rates (for members only) which range from US$100 a year for liability only to US$135 a year for US$5000 worth of collision, fire, theft, and glass insurance—add another US$15-20 for each additional US$5000 in coverage. These group policies are offered on a yearly basis only (i.e., they can't be purchased by the day, week, or month).

Some insurance companies try to justify higher premiums by claiming their policies cover repairs performed in the U.S. or Canada, pointing out that less expensive insurance is valid only for repairs in Mexico. In most cases, such an argument is irrelevant; the primary reason you need Mexican insurance is to protect yourself against liability in the event of an accident. In cases where your vehicle is disabled, repairs will have to be performed in Mexico anyway. (Even if you obtain a policy that covers U.S./Canada repairs, chances are it won't cover transport of a disabled vehicle to the border.) However, North American visitors driving vehicles with difficult-to-obtain parts might want to consider a policy that's valid for U.S./Canada repairs.

Parking In San Ysidro

Another alternative is to drive to San Ysidro, park your vehicle in one of the guarded fee lots, and walk across the border at Tijuana (or take a Mexicoach bus as described above). San Ysidro parking lots charge US$7-8 per day or any portion thereof.

Green Tortoise

To those who have never traveled by Green Tortoise, it's difficult to describe the experience. Imagine a sort of youth hostel on wheels, with a bit of a '60s spirit (e.g., a communal meal fund), and you'll begin to get the idea. The buses are refurbished Greyhounds with convertible beds and tables, comfortable but a bit of a tight squeeze at night when everyone's lying down—that's also when the bus travels. Great way to meet people.

Green Tortoise operates nine-day and 14-day trips to Baja Nov.- April that begin in San Francisco (pick-ups in L.A. are possible) and range as far south as La Paz. Prices are very reasonable (less than full roundtrip fare alone between San Francisco and La Paz) and include roundtrip transport and lodging on the bus, plus guided hikes and sidetrips to off-the-beaten-track beaches in Baja. The food fund adds another US$5 per day to the trip; communal meals cover about 70% of the meals—some meals are left to the participants (e.g., in La Paz). The trips include an optional windsurfing and sailing program available for an additional fee. All things considered, it's a travel bargain and a novel introduction to Baja.

For further information, contact Green Tortoise Adventure Travel (tel. 800-227-4766), P.O. Box 24459, San Francisco, CA 94124.

BY SEA

Ferry And Jetfoil

Four ferry services are currently running to southern Baja from the Mexican mainland—three to La Paz and one to Santa Rosalía. The Cabo San Lucas to Puerto Vallarta passenger-vehicle service was terminated in 1989.

The new 3½-hour, passenger-only jetfoil service between La Paz and the mainland is destined to become popular among business travelers and tourists with tight schedules. It also provides a smoother crossing than the regular ferries, so persons prone to seasickness may want to spend the extra money to avoid turning green with *mareado*. The main drawback is that it moves so quickly (top speed 45 mph) that passengers get less of a chance to enjoy the abundant sealife of the Sea of Cortez. (Then again, the eastbound ferries sail at night so in that direction the jetfoil is a better marine-viewing choice.)

The larger passenger-vehicle ferries, on the other hand, are an excellent way for anyone driving on the mainland to reach southern Baja without having to make a time-consuming "U-turn" at the top of the peninsula. Many drivers from the North American west coast use the Baja ferry services as an alternative way of reaching the mainland, since it allows them to avoid Mexico 15 on the way to Mazatlán and points farther south.

Fares and Classes: The vehicle ferry system was recently privatized under the directorship of Grupo SEMATUR (Servicios Maritimos y Turisticos) de California, S.A., and fares are now market-priced rather than subsidized. Passenger fares are based on class: *salon* (reclining seats in various general seating areas), *turista* (shared bunk rooms), and *cabina* (private cabins with toilet facilities). Some ferryboats also have an additional *especial* class that features large, deluxe cabins. Vehicle fares are based on the length of the vehicle—the longer the rig, the higher the fare. All fares must be paid in pesos.

Note: Signs at the vehicle ferry ticket offices in Santa Rosalía and La Paz warn (in Spanish only) that passenger tickets will not be issued to pregnant women.

For jetfoil fares, see "Topolobampo-La Paz" below.

Reservations: Whether it was the fare increases or the reorganization of management under private auspices, ferry reservations are now much easier to make than they were several years ago. Generally speaking, if you show up at the ferry terminal one day in advance of your desired voyage, you should be able to get tickets. During holiday periods (especially Semana Santa—when you might want to avoid ferry service altogether) you should try to pick up your tickets at least a week or two in advance. If your Spanish is up to it, you can also make phone reservations by calling (91) (800) 6-96-96 (toll-free in Mexico).

Guaymas-Santa Rosalía

Ferries depart Guaymas every Monday, Tuesday, and Friday at 1000 and arrive at Santa Rosalía at 1800 the same day. In the opposite direction, ferries leave on Sunday, Monday, and Wednesday at 2300, arriving in Guaymas at 0600.

Passenger fares are US$10 salon, US$20 turista, US$30 cabina and US$40 especial. Vehicle fares range from US$77 for a car, truck, or van under five meters (about 15 feet) to US$263 for an auto-trailer combo totaling nine to 17 meters (roughly 27-51 feet). A full-size bus or motorhome costs US$131 and motorcycles are US$16.

Topolobampo-La Paz

Topolobampo is a small port town that serves the Los Mochis area. An interesting way to reach Baja from, say, Texas is to take the *Chihuahua al Pacifico* train via Creel and the Barrancos del Cobre (the Copper Canyon— Mexico's equivalent of the Grand Canyon) to Los Mochis, then the Topolobampo ferry or catamaran to La Paz.

Passenger-vehicle Ferry: The ferry leaves Topolobampo daily at 1000 and arrives in La Paz at 2000. Eastbound, the ferry departs La Paz at 2000, arriving at Topolobampo around 0600. Passenger fares are US$10 salon, US$20 turista, US$30 cabina, and US$40 especial. Vehicle fares are: auto, truck, or van to five meters US$67; with trailers to nine meters US$120 or to 17 meters US$230; buses and motorhomes US$114; motorcycles US$14.50.

Jetfoil: Baja Express (tel. 682-2-5-63-11, fax 682-5-63-10 in La Paz; 800-829-0510 or 213-578-9680 in the U.S.) has been operating a jetfoil catamaran service between La Paz and Topolobampo since 1990. It's much faster but also more expensive than the ordinary passenger-vehicle ferry. The vessel departs daily from Topolobampo at 1500, arriving in La Paz at 1830. From La Paz, it leaves at 1000 and arrives in Topolobampo at 1330.

Baja Express fares are US$31 for tourist class (285 seats on the lower deck) and US$45 for express seats (35 leather-upholstered seats on the upper deck, open bar). Both classes feature air-conditioning and videos. Tickets include a free shuttle service between Los Mochis and Topolobampo.

The company has tentative plans to establish Baja Express service from La Paz to Guaymas via Loreto at some point in the future. A San Diego-Ensenada route is also under consideration.

Mazatlán-La Paz

Ferries depart both ports daily at 1700, arriving on the other side at around 1030. Passenger fares are US$15 salon, US$30 turista, US$45 cabina, and US$60 especial. For vehicles, fares are: auto, truck, or van to five meters US$110; with trailers to nine meters US$143 or to 17 meters US$374; buses and motorhomes US$187; motorcycles US$24.

GETTING AROUND

Most North American visitors to Baja travel the peninsula with their own vehicles—cars, trucks, campers, RVs, or motorcycles. Alternative transport modes include domestic airlines, rented car, public bus, bicycle, and hitchhiking.

BY AIR

Domestic air travel in Baja (as well as the rest of Mexico) is generally less expensive than comparable distances flown on international flights from the U.S. to Baja. It's cheaper to fly from Tijuana to La Paz than from San Diego to Los Cabos (two trips of roughly equivalent distances), for example. Hence, especially for San Diego residents, the minor inconvenience of flying out of Tijuana could result in a considerable savings—if your destination is either La Paz or Loreto.

Aero California and Mexican Airlines each have flights between Tijuana and La Paz that cost around US$120 one way, US$215 roundtrip. Aero Mexico also flies between La Paz and Loreto for US$36 one way (US$72 roundtrip).

Local Airlines
Several small airlines in Baja specialize in short flights ("puddle-jumpers") to destinations—usually Pacific islands—inaccessible by land transport. **Aerolineas California Pacificos** flies between Guerrero Negro, Isla Cedros, and Bahía Tortugas. **Soc. Coop. de Producción Pesquera** (nicknamed "The Cannery") has scheduled flights from Ensenada's El Ciprés airfield to Isla Cedros and Bahía Tortugas. If enough passengers are on hand to make it profitable (or one passenger is very generous), this company will also fly to Isla Natividad.

Charter Flights
Two companies can arrange small-plane charters to any airfield in Baja from southern Alta California: Gunnell Aviation (tel. 213-452-

0999, 3100 McDonnell Douglas Loop North, Santa Monica, CA 90405) and Lundy Air Charter (tel. 619-562-4181, 1860 Joe Crosson Dr., El Cajon, CA 92020).

Private Flights
If you've got a pilot's license and a plane, you can fly to any of Baja's nearly 200 airstrips (around 20 paved, 150 dirt) on the peninsula as well as on nearby islands. Air traffic over Baja is very light and the paperwork for crossing the border is minimal. If that weren't enticing enough, aviation gas is significantly cheaper in Mexico than in the U.S. or Canada. Many pilots fill up on the less expensive stuff immediately after crossing the border (a Mexican customs check is required anyway) and then stop again before leaving Mexico. Another reason to take fuel at the border is because fuel is only available at or nearby a fraction of the "bush" strips; careful itinerary planning is required.

A San Diego area outfit calling itself Baja Bush Pilots (tel. 619-297-5587) publishes a 384-page guide, *Airports of Baja California and Northwest Mexico* by Arnold Senterfitt, which contains aerial photos, sketch maps, and descriptions of virtually every landing strip in Baja. While some pilots fly to Baja without this book, they're few and far between.

Another source of information is Flight Log, a members-only service for pilots interested in Baja flying. The US$25 membership fee covers a newsletter subscription, a copy of *Flying Baja: A Pilot's Primer,* and a telephone information service. This group also organizes group "adventure" flights to Baja destinations such as Mulegé, Loreto, Punta Chivato, Punta Colorada, and La Paz.

As with land vehicles, planes that fly into Mexico should carry Mexican liability insurance. Lewis and Lewis (tel. 213-657-1112, 8929 Wilshire Blvd. #200, Beverly Hills, CA 90211) offers inexpensive annual aircraft policies. In addition U.S. Customs requires an annual inspection for planes flying into the

U.S. whether American- or foreign-owned; the inspection costs US$25 but is good for an unlimited number of entries per year.

Further information on flying a private plane into Baja is covered under "Getting There," above.

Air Hitching

At any of the airstrips mentioned above, it may be possible to hitch rides to other points in Baja on private aircraft or small cargo planes. The overall best places to try for rides, however, are the small commercial airfields in Ensenada, Guerrero Negro, and Santa Rosalía.

BUS

Intercity bus transportation in Baja is quite reliable and covers everywhere from Tijuana to Cabo San Lucas. The longest direct ride available is the Tijuana-La Paz route (about 25-28 hours), operated by **Autotransportes Aguila** and **Tres Estrellas de Oro.** To make a bus trip all the way to Cabo, you'd have to disembark in La Paz and change to one of the many La Paz-Cabo San Lucas buses. In central and southern Baja are two other intercity bus companies, **ABC** (Autobuses Baja California) and **Autotransportes de La Paz. Transportes Norte de Sonora** operates buses between Tijuana, Tecate, Mexicali, and points farther west, including destinations on the Mexican mainland as far away as Mexico City.

Special express buses with hostess service and air-conditioning are used on long-distance trips. Shorter trips may or may not have air-conditioning, but the buses are always tolerably comfortable—with toilets on-board and reclining seats that usually work. (The infamous "chicken buses" of southern Mexico and Central America don't exist in Baja.)

Fares are inexpensive. A Tijuana-La Paz ticket on a *primera* or first-class bus costs about US$28 (half that in second class); La Paz to Cabo San Lucas is around US$6. Reservations aren't accepted for bus travel— buses usually depart several times daily, so you simply show up at the bus terminal around the time you want to leave. All the Spanish you need for riding a bus is *boleto* (ticket), the name of your destination (have a map handy just in case), and a reasonable command of spoken numbers for when they quote the fare (although the fare is always posted somewhere on the ticket office wall).

LOCAL TAXIS AND BUSES

City Buses And Route Taxis

Tijuana, Ensenada, Mexicali, and La Paz have comprehensive city bus systems with fares averaging US$.15 to US$.35 (in pesos only). City buses come in a variety of sizes and shapes, from 12-passenger vans to huge modern vessels with automatic doors. In Mexicali, painted school buses are the norm. The destination or general route (typically a street name) of the bus is usually painted somewhere on the front of the bus or displayed on a marquis over the front windshield.

Printed bus schedules are hard to come by or may be nonexistent. If you can't figure out which bus to take by comparing the destination sign with a map, you'll just have to ask other waiting bus passengers or, if your Spanish isn't up to that, make inquiries at the tourist office.

Route Taxis: These same cities also have *taxis de ruta,* specially licensed cars (usually large American station wagons that hold up to 12 passengers) which follow set routes similar and often paralleling the bus routes. Unlike the city buses, they can be flagged down anywhere along their route. The destination is usually painted in whitewash on the windshield but locals often distinguish the route by the taxis's two-tone color scheme (e.g., a *roja y crema* may run from the central bus station to a market on the outskirts of town while a *negro y azul* may go from the cathedral to the main shopping district). Other than the terminating points of the route at either end, there are no predetermined taxi stops so passengers must let the driver know where they want off. As on the city buses, route taxi fares are the same no matter where you disembark, and they're usually only a bit higher than bus fares (around US$.30-.35).

Hire Taxis: Regular hire taxis congregate at hotels and designated taxi stands in Tijuana, Mexicali, Ensenada, Mulegé, Loreto, La Paz, San José del Cabo, and Cabo San Lucas. Sometimes fares are posted at the hotel or taxi stand, but often you'll have to ask for a fare quote. If possible, try to find out the fare (from hotel staff or a friendly resident) in advance of approaching a taxi driver so you'll feel more secure about not getting ripped off. If the quoted fare doesn't match what you've been told in advance, you have the option of negotiating for something closer to the correct fare or trying another taxi driver. The author's experience, however, has been that Bajacalifornio city-taxi drivers usually quote the correct fare immediately.

In smaller towns with no buses or route taxis you may sometimes find a few regular hire taxis hanging out by the town plaza. They're generally used for reaching out-of-town destinations, since anyplace in Baja without a city bus system is small enough for getting around on foot. Although the locals pay a set fare based on distance, gringos are sometimes quoted a much higher fare. Dig in and negoti-

HAS THE TRANSPENINSULAR HIGHWAY RUINED BAJA?

Old Baja Hands like to grieve over the pre-1973 days when Baja was accessible only to the select few who were macho enough to brave 800 miles of rutted tracks or wealthy enough to own or charter their own planes. These folks will bore you—mostly, it seems, to bolster their own egos—with lengthy tales of iron nerves in the face of on-the-road hardships. According to the Old Hands, the completion of the Transpeninsular meant Baja's demise as an adventure.

In spite of all the ranting and raving, however, Baja has turned out to be more stubborn than these whiners ever imagined. A thin strip of asphalt hasn't yet defeated the peninsula—the Old Hand's nightmare of rampant development hasn't really made it much farther south than Ensenada or farther north than La Paz (with the exception of the Mulegé-Loreto area, which has been "on the verge" of a major tourist explosion for at least 15 years), and even in these parts it's confined to slim coastal areas. This represents only a small proportion of the peninsula.

Will the rest succumb in the foreseeable future? Probably not, since several obstacles remain—the lack of water being the major one along with the fact that engineers just won't be quick to tackle many parts of Baja. Most of the peninsula remains unaffected by big plans, leaving enough open wilderness for even the greediest Old Hands if they'd only take the time to leave their rigs and do a little hiking. (Keep your 4WDs off the desert, please.)

Proposed Border-Cape Toll Road

A La Paz consortium is proposing to construct a privately funded, four-lane toll road from the U.S.-Mexico border to the Cape. The proposed highway would follow the Pacific Coast closely rather than parallel the sometimes mountainous route followed by the current Transpeninsular Highway. The proposal suggests either a road-head at Mexicali or a link-up with the current Tijuana-Ensenada toll road—whether it would terminate at La Paz or Cabo San Lucas is still under debate. Funding would come from a variety of Mexican, U.S., and Japanese companies who would recoup their investments from vehicle toll charges on the highway itself over a period of 15-20 years. Construction of the road would take at least four years.

The Mexican government has already granted a concession to the consortium for engineering studies, but it remains to be seen whether or not this will be another Baja project that remains eternally in the planning stages. Many people hope it will never get off the ground, but business interests are wildly supportive. If it's ever completed, those of us who have only driven post-Transpeninsular-Highway Baja can join the ranks of the cranky Old Hands and say "You should have seen Baja before they built the Border-Cape Toll Road."

ate until it's reasonable—even if you can afford the higher fare, you owe it to other foreign visitors not to encourage price-gouging.

CYCLING

Among North American cyclists, Baja is the most popular area in all of Mexico, for a number of reasons—traffic is relatively light, the scenery is striking (which helps fight boredom), and cyclists can pull over and camp just about anywhere. Also, recreation-al cyclists on the North American west coast outnumber their counterparts farther east, and Baja just happens to be the nearest Mexican destination.

Touring or mountain bike? If you're only heading straight down the peninsula and back on the Transpeninsular, or doing the northern loop on Mexico 2, 3, and 5, a touring bike would be the best choice (lighter and faster than a mountain bike). On the other hand, the Baja peninsula has so many great off-road rides that anyone who really wants to see Baja (and has the time) should consider the mountain bike option, since off-road riding requires a stronger frame, higher clearance, and wider tires. In fact, many interesting trail rides are within 95 km (60 miles) of the U.S.-Mexico border. Parque Nacional Constitución de 1857, for example—less than 80 km (50 miles) southwest of Mexicali—has been called a "fat-tire heaven" by cycling editors at *Outside* magazine and offers rides through startling pine forests and subalpine meadows. The Cataviña Boulder Field in the Central Desert also features some excellent trails. (Don't forget the anti-puncture booting for that one.)

Popular paved touring routes include Tecate to Ensenada (116 km) and Ensenada to San Felipe (236 km), both on scenic Mexico 3, as well as the Cape loop on Mexico 1 and Mexico 19 (La Paz-Cabo San Lucas-Todos Santos-La Paz). Because the Baja sun can be particularly strong when you're on paved surfaces (which both reflect and radiate heat), you may find that an 1100-1500 siesta is necessary no matter what time of year you ride. Don't forget to bring sunglasses and plenty of high-SPF sunscreen.

Equipment And Repairs

Whether you're riding a mountain or touring bike, you'll need the same basic essentials to handle long-distance Baja riding. If you plan to camp along the way (often the only choice, even on Transpeninsular trips, since cyclists simply can't make the mileage from hotel to hotel in central Baja), you'll need the usual camping and first-aid gear, selected to fit your panniers. Helmets are particularly important since a head injury becomes even more serious when you're "in the middle of nowhere," and it will also keep direct sun off the top of your skull.

A rearview mirror is a must for keeping an eye on motorists coming from behind on narrow roads. A locking cable is preferable to a clunky U-lock for long-distance trips since they weigh less—bicycle theft isn't much of a problem in Baja. The only other security you might need is a removable handlebar bag for carrying camera and valuables—the bag can be taken with you when stopping off at restaurants or tiendas, and it's also a reachable spot for on-the-fly snacks.

Water will be an uppermost consideration on overnight trips. No matter what the time of year (spring and fall are the best pedaling seasons) cyclists should try to carry four one-liter bottles of water per day—so if one is punctured, all your water won't be lost. (The one-liter bottles used for cycling are also more puncture resistant than the typical water containers designed for camping.) Punctures are a concern in Baja because of all the trees and plants that bear spines.

Tires: The same puncture threat means that your bike should be outfitted with heavy-duty tires and tubes. Bring along two or three spare tubes, one spare tire, a tire gauge, and a complete tire repair kit. You should also carry duct tape and moleskin—or commercial plastic booting—to use as booting material against sidewall cuts caused by sharp rocks or cactus along the road.

Rack: Check nuts and bolts daily and retighten as necessary. Applying Locktite should lessen the need for retightening—carry a small supply along with extra nuts and bolts. Bailing wire can be used for improvised repairs if you run out of nuts and bolts or get a minor break—carry two or three meters along with wire cutters.

Other Repairs: Bike shops operate in Tijuana, Ensenada, San Quintín, Ciudad Constitución, La Paz, and Cabo San Lucas. Although the Mexicans who run these shops can sometimes perform miraculous repairs using nothing that resembles a bike's original parts, it's safer to come prepared with spares, especially for parts that aren't easily "jury-rigged." At a minimum, carry a spare freewheel, a rear derailleur, and all the wrenches and screwdrivers necessary to work on your bike. If in addition you bring along several extra spokes, cables, and a spare chain, you'll be ready for just about any repair scenario.

Bicycle Transport

Bikes can be taken on the **Tijuana Trolley** to San Ysidro and then walked over the border, but to get the bike on the trolley you first need a pass from the San Diego AYH Travel Store (tel. 619-226-1221), at 335 W. Beach St.—about three blocks from the Columbia St. trolley station. The pass costs US$3 and is valid for three years; it requires a photo but can be issued on the spot. Bikes aren't allowed on the trolley on weekdays during the hours of 0500-0900 and 1500-1800 (see "Getting There," above for further trolley details).

Mexicoach and **Greyhound** will take the bikes of paying passengers in their luggage compartments for no additional cost, but bikes should be boxed. For return trips from Baja, you should be able to pick up a box from bicycle shops in Tijuana or Ensenada (or build your own from discarded cardboard boxes).

DRIVING IN BAJA

The most heroic procedure for anyone who has decided to get a general idea of what the whole peninsula is like would be to set out from San Diego in a four-wheel-drive truck well loaded with food, water, camping equipment and reserve gasoline to carry him over the long stretches between the border and the Cape, where nothing is available. He should allow a minimum of ten days of hard driving (it may well take more) to cover the thousand road miles to the tip, and he must be prepared to assume all responsibilities for himself and his car.

The famous naturalist Joseph Wood Krutch wrote the above in his classic *The Forgotten Peninsula* as an introduction to a chapter entitled "Seeing Baja the Easy Way." It's obvious that not only was this written in a time (1961) when literary license allowed a writer to use masculine pronouns exclusively when speaking of heroic endeavors, but that it was well before the construction of La Carretera Transpeninsular Benito Juárez, otherwise known as the Transpeninsular Highway or Mexico 1.

Skeletons of cars, vans, and trucks that didn't make it, rusting among the ocotillo and cardón alongside Baja's highways, are visible reminders of this era. If you look closely, you'll notice that some of those decaying hulks are post-1973 models, testifying that a certain challenge remains in spite of the long strip of tarmac that winds down the peninsula.

For the most part, however, the 1973 completion of the Transpeninsular opened Baja travel up to ordinary folks who drive ordinary passenger cars, as long as they employ a little ordinary common sense. For the adventurer, there remains a stack of unpaved roads that will take you about as far from civilization as almost anybody would care to go. Such off-highway digressions are perfect for those who might agree with another of Krutch's fiats:

> Baja California is a wonderful example of how much bad roads can do for a country. Bad roads act as filters. They separate those who are sufficiently appreciative of what lies beyond the blacktop to be willing to undergo mild inconvenience from that much larger number of travelers which is not willing. The rougher the road, the finer the filter.

Baja Highways

A 1988 *Car and Driver* magazine story stated that driving in Baja compared with driving in North America "like hiking in the Rocky Mountains compares with walking on Madison Avenue," a more than slight exaggeration that was most likely added for color to an otherwise very accurate story. In terms of how it feels to drive in Baja, however, there's more than a small element of truth in this comparison—people who *really* like to drive will love driving in Baja.

In less romantic terms, driving the Transpeninsular Highway is somewhat similar to two-lane driving in some of the less populated areas of the American Southwest. The two main differences are: 1) there tends to be more variance (sometimes a lot) in road conditions from one section of highway to another; and 2) once you're well into the center of the peninsula you're farther from any significant population centers than on any comparable section of American highways, so that accidents or errors of judgment may have more ramifications. Drivers from western Canada may feel more at home than Americans on desolate sections of Baja highways—except that the terrain is completely different from anything in Canada!

Six paved national highways grace the Baja California peninsula: Mexico 1 (the Transpeninsular, from Tijuana to Cabo San Lucas), Mexico 2 (from Tijuana to Sonora), Mexico 3 (Tecate to El Sauzal, near Ensenada, and east to Crucero La Trinidad at Mexico 5), Mexico 5 (Mexicali to San Felipe), Mexico 19 (between Cabo San Lucas and San Pedro, via Todos Santos), and Mexico 22 (Ciudad Constitución to San Carlos). The only state highways are a small cluster of relatively short blacktops in the northeast corner above the Sea of Cortez (BCN 1, 2, 3, 4, and 8, which link farm communities in the Valle de Mexicali with Mexicali and the state of Sonora), BCN 23 (linking Mexico 1 with Punta Banda), and the solitary BCS 286 in the south between La Paz and San Juan de los Planes.

In addition, Mexico 1 has two alternate routings, a four-lane toll road between Tijuana and Ensenada and a two-lane digression to Bahía de los Angeles on the Sea of Cortez coast. All other roads in Baja are gravel, dirt, or some combination thereof.

Off-highway Travel

Like the highways, Baja's unpaved roads vary considerably, from rutted jeep tracks to elevated, graded, gravel boulevards. The trouble with the graded unpaved roads is that they tend to degenerate rather quickly between gradings into "washboard" surfaces impossible to drive on at anything but very low speeds (8-16 kph/5-10 mph)—unless you want to risk crushed vertebrae and a dropped transmission.

The effect of these unpaved roads on you and your vehicle depends a lot on what kind of vehicle you're driving. Some off-highway Baja navigators drive pickups with customized shocks and suspension that enable a driver to "float" over the worst washboard surfaces. Other drivers (like many of the local residents, who can't afford heavy-duty, customized rigs) learn to drive slowly and appreciate the scenery.

The best unpaved roads in Baja are probably those that have evolved more or less naturally (i.e., with little or no grading). When the weather's right (not wet) some of these roads ride better than the Transpeninsular. Roads

like this, however, will sometimes start out quite nicely but get increasingly worse with each passing mile to the point that even the most intrepid explorers are forced to turn around. At other times, a road will suddenly improve after a long stretch of cavernous potholes and caved-in sides. Weather is a big determining factor; even the best ungraded, unpaved roads are often impassable during or following a hard rain.

How do you know when to turn around? There's always an element of risk when driving down a dirt road for the first (or even the hundredth) time, but it helps to ask around before embarking on a road that doesn't see much traffic. A good road map can also assist with such decisions. The AAA map (see "Services and Information," p. 116) classifies unpaved roads into four categories: gravel, graded, dirt, and poor. The annotated ITM map uses a similar but more specific four-fold system: gravel, graded, unimproved dirt, and vehicular track. Although neither of these maps is entirely up-to-date (no published map could be) or 100% accurate, using one or the other in conjunction with local input will greatly enhance the decision-making process with regard to off-highway travel. A topographical map could be of considerable value to a 4WD navigator as well, since sometimes it's the steep canyon grades that call up defeat.

Getting Stuck: Even with the best planning there's always the possibility of getting stuck in muddy or sandy areas. Anyone engaging in serious off-highway driving should carry along a sturdy shovel for digging out mired wheels. Another handy trick for negotiating soft ground is to let the air out of your tires to a pressure of around 12-15 psi. This really works, but you should also carry along a 12- volt air compressor (one that will plug into the cigarette lighter) for pumping the tires back up after you're on firm ground again.

Driving Precautions

The first rule for Baja driving, no matter what kind of road you're on, is: *never* take the road for granted. Any highway in Baja, including the Transpeninsular, can serve up 100 meters of smooth, seamless blacktop followed immediately by 100 meters of contiguous potholes or large patches of missing asphalt. A cow, horse, or burro could be right around the next curve, or a large dog can leap out in front of your vehicle just as you fasten your eyes on a turkey vulture drying its wings on top of a tall cardón.

The speed limits set by the Mexican government—80 km per hour (48 mph) on most highways, 110 km (66 mph) on the Ensenada toll road—are very reasonable for Baja's highway conditions. Obey them and you'll be much safer than if you try to keep the speedometer needle in the spot you're accustomed to. Wandering livestock, relatively narrow highways widths (6-8 meters/19-25 feet max), and lack of consistent highway maintenance mean that you simply can't drive at U.S.-Canada speeds in this neck of the woods.

Most Baja roadways also suffer from a conspicuous lack of shoulders. This doesn't mean you won't find any places to pull off, as many Baja writers have implied—gravel turnouts appear fairly regularly, and in many areas you can drive directly onto the roadside from the highway—it just means that you can't count on a safe margin at one side of the highway or the other in case of an emergency situation. At the very least, an emergency turnout will raise a lot of rocks and dirt—small dangers in themselves—and in some spots (e.g., in the sierras on Mexico 3) leaving the highway will launch you and your vehicle into a thousand-foot (or greater) free fall. Guardrails may be flimsy or nonexistent.

Yet another reason not to take the road for granted is the high number of blind curves (sometimes unmarked) and blind hilltops in areas of varied elevation. Never assume a clear path around a curve or over a hilltop—potential obstructions include an 18-wheeler or bus passing in the opposite direction (oblivious to the risk of passing blind), wandering livestock, a rockslide, or a road washout. To be on the safe side, keep toward the outside edge of your own lane. Commercial trucks in Baja drive as if they're exempt from all speed limits, almost always flying at least 40 km over the posted limit.

Rule number two is never to drive on the highways at night. Except along portions of the

Ensenada toll road, highways have no lighting. In addition, reflectors and even painted lines are absent from many highway sections—even if no other vehicles besides your own were on the road at night, you could easily overshoot an unexpected curve. Add to this the fact that many poorly maintained local vehicles have nonfunctioning headlights, taillights, or brakelights and it should be obvious that trying to make highway miles after sundown is crazy. Some Bajacalifornios may do it, but they're used to local conditions and know the roads relatively well. Still, a high proportion of car accidents in Baja—around 80% according to insurance companies—occur at night in spite of local savvy.

Specific Hazards: When you see road signs marked Vado or Zona De Vados, slow down. The word *vado* is most often translated as "dip," but in Baja it usually means more than a simple dip in the road—it's any place where the road intersects an *arroyo* (dry stream wash). The danger lies not only in the sudden grade drop but in the potential for running into a recently accumulated body of water. Some vados have a measuring stick (marked in meters) next to them so that if water is present you'll know roughly how deep it is. If you come to a vado full of water with no measuring stick, get out of your vehicle and measure the depth yourself using an ocotillo branch or other suitable object before attempting to cross.

Vados aren't always signposted, so keep an eye out for them—they appear even in relatively flat terrains. Some vados are relatively mild road dips when dry, while others are particularly treacherous, even in dry weather. The vados south of San Felipe on the road to Puertecitos are deadly—crossing them at a high rate of speed can severely damage the undercarriage of a passenger car.

Another hazard to watch out for are **sand drifts** in the road, which often aren't visible until it's almost too late to avoid them. They're most common in the San Felipe area but can occur anywhere in Baja where a road runs through sandy terrain.

In towns, pueblos, ejidos, or anywhere else people live in Baja, you'll encounter *topes* (speed bumps). Often unpainted and unsign-

HOW MUCH FARTHER?

Kilometers (miles) from Tijuana, along the Transpeninsular Highway (using the Tijuana-Ensenada toll road), rounded off to the nearest kilometer (mile):

Ensenada	109 km (68 miles)
San Quintín	301 km (187 miles)
El Rosario	359 km (223 miles)
Cataviña	481 km (299 miles)
Punta Prieta	599 km (372 miles)
Bahía de los Angeles . .	654 km (406 miles)
Guerrero Negro	714 km (444 miles)
San Ignacio	856 km (532 miles)
Santa Rosalía	928 km (577 miles)
Mulegé	990 km (615 miles)
Loreto	1,125 km (699 miles)
Ciudad Constitución .	1,268 km (788 miles)
La Paz	1,483 km (922 miles)
Cabo San Lucas . .	1,704 km (1,059 miles)

posted, they can really sneak up on a driver. Some topes are real industrial-strength tire-poppers, so always take it very slow when traversing them.

Highway Signs
One of the pleasures of driving in Baja is the relative absence of signs cluttering the road side—billboards, in fact, are virtually nonexistent. The Mexican government does have a system of highway signs, however, based on common international sign conventions followed throughout most of the world (except for the U.S.); these can be very helpful as long as you know what they mean. Most display self-explanatory symbols (e.g., a silhouette of a man holding a shovel means "men working").

Along the Transpeninsular Highway as well as on many secondary roads, driving progress can be measured with the assistance of regularly spaced kilometer markers (usually black lettering on a reflective white background). In northern Baja these markers start at zero (K0)

in Tijuana and ascend in number as you proceed southward. Starting at paralelo 28 (the state borderline between BCN and BCS), however, the markers descend as you move southward, beginning with K220 in Guerrero Negro. These contrary directions can be traced to the original construction of the Transpeninsular, which started at either end of the peninsula and met in the middle. To further add to the confusion, sometimes the numbers run only as far as the next town and then start over. Still, the markers can be a significant navigational aid, especially when you want to take note of a remote off-highway spot for a future trip.

Cautionary sign captions are especially helpful, including: Curva Peligrosa ("Dangerous Curve"), Despacio ("Slow"), and Zona De Vados ("Dip Zone")—see "Specific Hazards" above. Other common signs along highways are: Desviacion ("Detour"); No Tire Basura ("Don't Throw Trash"), Conserve Su Derecha ("Keep to the Right"), Concida Cambio De Luces("Dim Your Lights"), No Rebase ("No Passing"), and No Hay Paso ("Road Closed").

If you're having tire trouble, look for homemade signs reading Llantera, which indicate tire repair shops.

Traffic Offenses
Although Mexican traffic police don't go out of their way to persecute visiting foreign drivers, it may appear that way when you're the foreigner being stopped. But if you're caught violating a traffic law, what can you expect? The more cautiously you drive, the less likely you'll inadvertently transgress local traffic codes. This would seem like obvious advice, but for some reason many visiting drivers in Baja drive as if they thought there were no traffic laws in Mexico (most of those who drive like this seem to have California plates).

If you are stopped by a *tránsito* (traffic cop), the first rule is to behave in a patient, civil manner—the officer might let you off with just a warning. Usually, if the officer decides to make a case of it, he'll ask you to follow him to the nearest police post or station, where a fine will be assessed and collected—a perfectly legal request. If the cop suggests (or hints at) being paid on the spot, he's going for *la mordida,* the minor bribe.

In Baja, mordida requests from foreigners—for traffic offenses, at least—have become increasingly rare and the government is trying hard to stamp it out altogether. But if you are confronted with such a situation, you have two choices. Mexico's Attorney General for the Protection of Tourists recommends that you insist on going to the nearest station to pay the fine, and that as you pay you request a receipt. Such a request may result in all charges being dropped. On the other hand, if you don't feel like taking the time for a trip to the station, you can choose to negotiate the "fine" on the spot. Doing so, however, won't contribute to the shrinking of the mordida phenomenon.

Along Mexico 1-D, the toll highway between Tijuana and Ensenada, the federal highway police have recently begun using radar speed detectors. Fines are assessed at a day's Mexican minimum wage (currently about US$4.65) for each kilometer over the speed limit the offender has been driving—the fine is the same for foreigners as for Mexican nationals. The offender's driving license is attached to the citation and delivered to the nearest Baja *transito* station, or to another Baja station chosen by the offender, where the license is returned upon payment of the assessed fine. If you're cited just outside Tijuana, for example, you can elect to settle your citation in Ensenada if that's your destination.

Aside from speeding on Mexico 1-D, driving the wrong direction on one-way streets and running stop signs are the two most common traffic violations among foreign drivers in Baja. In Ensenada, for example, the stop *(Alto)* signs almost seem to be intentionally hidden in places; also, several intersections display no vertical signs at all, only a broad stripe painted on the pavement indicating where vehicles are supposed to stop. The best practice is to assume you're supposed to stop at every single intersection in the city (which is pretty close to the truth). This can be generalized to most other urban areas on the peninsula.

In Mulegé only two streets in town are open to two-way traffic; all the others are supposed to be one-way, although they're not sign-posted at every intersection. Always look carefully at the cars driving or parked on a street to determine which direction is legal before turning.

Note to patriotic visitors: In Mexico it's illegal to display any foreign national flag unless over an embassy or consulate. A miniature flag flying from a vehicle's radio antenna provides Mexican police with a valid excuse to pull you over. (It may also invite vandalism—Mexicans are extremely nationalistic.) It's rarely a problem, but don't say you weren't warned.

Insurance

It's very important to carry a Mexican liability insurance policy on your vehicle while driving in Baja. In case of an accident, such a policy could keep you from going to jail. For details on Mexican insurance, see "Driving to Baja, " p. 123.

Fuel

The only automotive fuel commercially available in Baja is that sold at government-owned PEMEX stations. The total number of PEMEX stations in Baja varies from year to year, but they're always scarce outside of large cities. A good rule of thumb is to top off your tank whenever it reaches the half-empty mark and there's a PEMEX station at hand.

Three kinds of fuel are available: leaded ("Nova"), a higher-octane unleaded ("Magna Sin"), and diesel. All three are priced by PEMEX according to standard rates and shouldn't vary from station to station. All three fuels are cheaper in Mexico than their equivalents in the U.S. or Canada; the price is usually marked (in pesos) on the pump. The pump readout often accommodates only three or four digits, so a 25,000-peso sale may appear as 2500, 25.00, 250, or 25.0. (Although this may sound like it could be a problem when paying up, it's not once you're used to seeing it.) The author has never been shortchanged at any PEMEX station in Baja.

Rumors about the quality of PEMEX fuels sometimes suggest that an extra fuel filter or an additive are necessary. This may have been the case 10 or more years ago, but nowadays PEMEX fuel seems to perform well with all types of vehicles.

The main problem with PEMEX fuel remains its availability. Stations are sometimes widely spaced (or abandoned) and not all stations carry unleaded gasoline. In a pinch, leaded gas can be used in vehicles that are supposed to take only unleaded (i.e., those fitted with anti-smog catalytic converters) without an appreciative difference in performance. You shouldn't be forced to burn more than a tankful of leaded here and there, if at all, since roughly every other PEMEX station seems to dispense unleaded.

Other availability-related problems include long lines at small-town stations (the lines at the Mulegé PEMEX are legendary) and the occasional selling out of one or all types of fuel at a particular station. To notify customers, the hose will usually be draped over the top of a pump when it's empty. One of the main culprits for pump sell-outs are the North American RV caravans; if 10 or 15 RVs fuel up at a PEMEX station when it's between deliveries, the station may have to shut down until the next PEMEX tanker arrives.

Liquified Petroleum Gas (LPG): LPG fuel is available in Baja for those driving LPG-powered vehicles. The price per liter is about the same as for Magna Sin when bought for vehicular purposes. LPG sold for heating and cooking is subsidized and costs only about US$.16 per liter. The difficulty is finding it—look for signs reading *butano*.

Parts And Repairs

Good auto shops and mechanics are available in Tijuana, Mexicali, Ensenada, La Paz, and, to a lesser extent, in El Rosario, Mulegé, Loreto, and Cabo San Lucas. Elsewhere in Baja, if you have a breakdown, it's either do-it-yourself or rely on the mercy of passing drivers. In areas where you can find a mechanic, the following makes can usually be serviced: Chevrolet, Dodge, Ford, Nissan, Toyota, and Volkswagen. For anything other than these makes—even for short trips—you should carry spare filters, plugs, points, hoses, belts, and gaskets.

Oil: Motor oil is widely available at tiendas and PEMEX stations throughout Baja. If your vehicle takes anything lower than 30-weight, however, you'd better bring along your own since most places stock only 30- or 40-weight oil.

Green Angels: The Secretaría de Turismo operates a fleet of 275 green trucks called Angeles Verdes (Green Angels) that patrol Baja's highways and offer professional assistance to anyone with automotive problems. Each truck carries a first-aid kit, shortwave radio, and a variety of common auto parts as well as extra gasoline; they are usually staffed by two uniformed employees, one of whom may speak some English. The drivers will perform minor repairs for the cost of the parts and can provide towing for distances up to 24 km (15 miles). If they can't remedy the problem or tow your vehicle to a nearby mechanic, they'll give you a lift and/or arrange for other assistance.

The trucks supposedly patrol their assigned highway sections at least twice a day; the author's experience is that the Green Angels are much more commonly seen south of Santa Rosalía (where they're probably more needed because of the longer distances between towns) than anywhere north.

Ensenada Toll Road Assistance: Mexico's federal highway department has installed 29 roadside call boxes at approximate three-km intervals along the Tijuana-Ensenada toll road. Calls are free and bilingual operators are on duty 24 hours a day to help arrange emergency medical or automotive assistance.

Trailers And RVs

Baja is a popular destination among the trailer/RV crowd, since not only are there plenty of RV parks with services, but you can pull off the road and camp just about anywhere outside the cities, with few restrictions. The restrictions that do exist are largely physical—numerous places simply can't accommodate a wide trailer or motor home due to narrow roadways, steep grades, or sharp curves. Even the Transpeninsular is tight in some places. In fact, you shouldn't even attempt a Baja trip in any rig wider than three meters (nine feet).

Caravans: An RV caravan, in which a number of individual RV owners travel as an organized group with a caravan leader, is one way to accomplish an RV trip to Baja with little self-reliance. Average costs run about US$100 a day, not including food and gasoline. In theory, RV caravans are a great introduction to Baja for RVers apprehensive about going it alone the first time.

The reality, however, is that everyone else on the road hates RV caravans because they cause traffic jams, especially on winding, mountainous roads, and because they tend to suck the PEMEX stations dry. On top of that, they bring little money into the local economy since they bring in virtually all of their own supplies from North America. Finally, following natural group behavior, caravan participants tend to insulate themselves from Baja-californios as well as other foreign visitors. This writer's advice is to avoid caravans (except informal two- or three-vehicle caravans among friends) in order to maintain a better image of RV travel among the locals as well as the rest of us on the road.

Campers And Vans

Probably the rig most suited to Baja travel is a well-equipped camper or van. With a bed, two five-gallon water containers, a small propane stove and refrigerator, and a portable toilet, you can travel just as independently as someone driving a 40-foot motor home. Add a deep-cycle RV battery under the hood and you can run a variety of electrical appliances for at least a week without running your engine. For extra power, a solar panel can be mounted on top of the cab or camper.

As long as your tricking out your rig, consider installing oversize tires to get more traction and road clearance, overload shocks to protect your vehicle and its contents on rough roads, and a rollbar over the front seats. Whether or not you've got high clearance, skid plates under your fuel tank, engine, and transmission are a good idea if you plan any off-highway driving.

What's the perfect Baja rig? Such a beast doesn't really exist, of course, since we all have individual needs. (How about a kayak with wings?) Probably the nearest-to-perfect rig for enjoying most of what Baja has to offer would be one that combines features of a self-sufficient camper (as described above) with a rugged 4WD vehicle with a turning circle of six meters (20 feet) or less. Ambitious Baja hands have successfully tried everything from jeeps to three-ton diesel cabs as bases for custom-built campers. **Callen Camper** (tel. 619-442-3305) in El Cajon, Alta California specializes in custom-outfitting Baja camper rigs.

Car Rental

Cars can be rented in Tijuana, Mexicali, Ensenada, Loreto, La Paz, San José del Cabo, and Cabo San Lucas. In general, Tijuana, Cabo San Lucas, and San José del Cabo have the

---

AUTOMOTIVE EQUIPMENT

Although plenty of visitors drive the length of the Baja peninsula and back without so much as a spare tire, anyone driving long distances in Baja should consider bringing the following extras, regardless of the type of vehicle:

air filters
battery cables
brake, steering, and transmission fluids
fan belts
fuel filters
fuses
lug wrench and jack
radiator hoses
spare tire
spark plugs
water filters
one or two five-gallon gas cans
one five-gallon water container
emergency flares
fire extinguisher
18-meter (60-foot) tow rope
tire gauge
tube repair kit
12-volt air compressor

For a glossary of Spanish automotive terms, see "Language," p. 52.

least expensive rentals while Ensenada and Loreto have the most expensive. Various Volkswagen models are usually the only choice; most rental places charge a daily rate of around US$25 for a VW bug, US$45 for a Jetta, US$48-55 for a van plus per-kilometer fees ranging from US$.18 to US$.30 per kilometer. Rates include Mexican liability insurance, but not collision damage. For added collision coverage, figure an extra US$6-10 a day.

If you're planning on driving long distances, you can save money by arranging a flat rate with no kilometer costs. If you can rent by the week, the savings increase considerably. Currently the best long-distance deal in Baja is from the Avis agency in Tijuana (see "Tijuana," p. 139 for the address and phone number): a new, made-in-Mexico VW bug (no air-con or radio) for US$159 per week, with unlimited free kilometers.

Rentals out of San Diego are sometimes a bit cheaper, but those few agencies that allow their cars into Mexico won't allow them any further south than Guerrero Negro. They often add mandatory collision damage waivers to the cost as well. The VW bug, incidentally, is one of the best non-4WD passenger cars for Baja travel since the engine is air-cooled (no radiator boil-overs) and the road clearance is just a bit above average.

Motorcycles

Much of Baja is excellent motorcycle country. The winding sierra roads are especially challenging and since traffic is generally light you can really let it rip. Another advantage of motorcycle travel in Baja is that if your bike gets mired in soft ground, you can almost always extricate it without assistance.

As with automotive travel in Baja, pre-departure planning is important. You should be able to carry enough gear in two panniers and a backpack (tied down on the rear) for a trip all the way down the peninsula. (With just such an arrangement, a Japanese biker the author met in Baja was heading across the Sea of Cortez by ferry to the mainland and on to the Panama Canal—his second trip along this route.) Motorcycle mechanics in Baja are few and far between—you must be entirely self-reliant to make this trip safely and successfully. Besides the usual camping and first-aid gear, bikers should carry all tools needed for routine maintenance, spare brake shoes, a tire repair kit, spare levers, an extra battery, a clutch cable, spare light bulbs, a four-liter reserve gas can, and a spare helmet visor.

For a transpeninsular trip, any bike smaller than 600cc is too small. A four-stroke gets better mileage than a two-stroke, an important consideration given the situation with gas stations in Baja. Experienced Baja bikers replace standard fuel tanks with larger 20-liter tanks to extend their fuel range.

All of the same driving precautions that apply to four-wheel driving should be followed by bikers as well. Special care should be taken when negotiating blind curves since buses and trucks in Baja aren't used to seeing motorcycles on the highway. As with bicycle touring, motorcyclists may find that an 1100-1500 siesta is necessary to avoid the sun's worst rays.

(BOB RACE)

NORTHWESTERN BAJA

TIJUANA

With a population exceeding one million, Tijuana is the second-largest city along the Pacific seaboard of North and South America after Los Angeles and the fourth largest in Mexico. It's also one of Mexico's youngest cities, having been established as a line of defense against filibusteros following the Treaty of Guadalupe Hidalgo in 1848. During the U.S. Prohibition era, Tijuana developed a bawdy, rough-and-tumble reputation for its casinos, cantinas, and bordellos; for many North Americans, the image has outlasted the reality.

Today's Tijuana is a fast-modernizing, bicultural city where skyscrapers and shopping malls are replacing yesterday's shantytowns, and discos outnumber cantinas. A nearby industrial zone supports nearly 300 *maquiladora* or in-bond plants where international companies such as Sony, Kodak, and Mattel manufacture export products. Tijuana's colleges and universities (Colegio de la Frontera Norte, Iberoamericana University, Universidad Autonoma de Baja California) attract students from all over the peninsula as well as northwestern Mexico.

For some visitors, "TJ" is merely a gateway to Baja while for others—especially San Diegans—it's a destination in its own right. Like the rest of Baja, Tijuana enjoys duty-free status and hence one of its main attractions is shopping—everything from Casas Grandes pottery to Tequila Sauza to Luis Vuitton luggage is available at discount prices. Avenida Revolución, once the city's booze-and-gambling center, is now lined with restaurants, cafes, and boutiques. Bullfights are no longer the only cultural attraction; the Tijuana Cultural Center and other city venues host symphonies, theater, art exhibits, and other events, thus firmly establishing Tijuana as northern Baja's cultural heart.

CLIMATE

As in nearby San Diego, the climate in Tijuana is moderate all year round owing to the confluence of Pacific and desert environments. November-March, temperatures average 15° C (60° F) during the day, 12° C (53° F) at night. Rain is more likely this time of year than during any other time of year but generally amounts to less than 25 centimeters (10 inches) per annum—not enough to deter a visit.

June-Sept., daytime temperatures average 22-29° C (72-85° F), nighttime 18-21° C (65-70° F). It rarely rains during the summer months in the Tijuana area; on still days, however, a thin layer of smog may collect over the city (but never as bad as in Los Angeles, the smog's source). Fall and spring temperatures are in the low 20s C (70s F).

HISTORY

The Frontier

Before the Río Tijuana was designated as the westernmost portion of the U.S.-Mexico border at the end of the Mexican-American War in 1848, no town as such existed in the shallow river valley. Until the postwar border agreement, the border between Alta and Baja California had been about 20 miles farther south near El Descanso.

San Dieguito and Yumano Indian cultures intermittently occupied the area before the Spanish came in the late 17th century; the Yumano called the valley Ti-wan, meaning "Near-The-Sea." Early 19th-century maps refer to the Río Tijuana as Arroyo de Tijuan, obviously a Spanish rendering of the Yumano name. A local Mexican ranch in existence as early as 1809 was called Rancho Tia Juana—"Tijuan" had no Spanish meaning and "Tia Juana" ("Aunt Jane") was easier to pronounce. Anglo settlers in Alta California somehow latched onto this name and today many North Americans persist in calling the city "Tia-wana." (The pronunciation might have remained a southern California colloquialism if it hadn't been for the Kingston Trio's 1959 international hit, "The Tia Juana Jail.")

In the 1870s the Mexican government established a small customs house at the border, but Tijuana would probably have remained nothing more than a ranching area if it hadn't been for the development of San Diego across the border. In 1887 a savvy developer built the sprawling Hotel del Coronado, which advertised the locale's favorable year-round climate and quickly became a famous resort. A minor gold rush in the El Alamo area of northern Baja in 1888 brought added American attention to the border area.

The Mexicans, knowing that wherever Americans congregated along the border there was a danger of losing real estate—as proven more than once in the 19th century—created the "Pueblo de Tijuana" or "Town of Tijuana" in 1889. During the Spanish-American War in 1898, San Diego grew further with the establishment of a U.S. naval base, and following the war many Navy men and their families chose to remain in the San Diego area. By the turn of the century, local entrepreneurs had opened several small resort hotels in Tijuana to compete with those in San Diego.

U.S. attention was focused on Tijuana during a local revolution in the early 1900s. Following the 1910 Mexican revolution, a group of "wobblies" (International Workers of the World) affiliated with the Mexican Liberal Party briefly took control of the town under the leadership of Ricardo Magón in May 1911. Hundreds of San Diegans watched from the U.S. side of the border as Mexican federal troops entered Tijuana on June 22, 1911 and routed the Magonistas, killing 31 rebels in the process. For many Americans, this was the first time they'd heard of Tijuana.

Prohibition And Tourism

The town's frontier image was further enhanced in 1915 when the Tijuana Fair proffered bullfights, horse racing, boxing, cock fighting, and casino gambling. Curious San Diegans came in droves for the event, but Tijuana returned to its sleepy state once the fair was over. The city boomed practically overnight, however, when the San Diego city government banned cabaret dancing in 1917, and as Tijuana's casinos and cabarets multi-

Tijuana Cultural Center
(JOE CUMMINGS)

plied, the city began drawing visitors from Hollywood—only a three-hour drive away.

The 1920 grand opening of Tijuana's magnificent El Casino de Agua Caliente coincided with the announcement of the 18th Amendment to the U.S. Constitution, which prohibited the sale, manufacture, and consumption of alcoholic beverages. Well-heeled U.S. residents flocked to the plush new casino, which had no peer anywhere in the Americas at the time. The lavish interior blended art deco, Spanish colonial, Moorish, and French provincial designs; Hollywood glitterati such as Douglas Fairbanks, Jean Harlow, Rita Hayworth, Clark Gable, Dolores del Rio, and the Aga Khan danced on its Italian marble floors beneath Louis XV chandeliers.

As the Tijuana high life boomed, rich American investors poured millions of dollars into developing more racetracks, casinos, hotels, restaurants, and high-class bordellos. Mexicans from the interior of Mexico, hearing that the gutters of Tijuana ran with money (literally true inasmuch as drunk Americans were notorious for dropping change and greenbacks as they stumbled in and out of taxis), rushed to Tijuana as well.

Post-WW II Tijuana

Tijuana's golden sin days lasted until the repeal of U.S. Prohibition in 1933; the ensuing slump became a crash when President Lázaro Cárdenas outlawed casino gambling in 1938. Baja—and the rest of Mexico—was able to reverse its precipitous economic decline with the outbreak of WW II. To aid in alleviating unemployment in the border area, and to provide needed labor for the wartime U.S. economy, the U.S. and Mexico created the Bracero Program in 1942; this program gave Mexican workers the temporary right to work for American agricultural concerns in Alta California. Another action that prevented Tijuana from becoming a ghost town was the declaration of Baja California as a duty-free zone.

The expansion of San Diego's military presence during WW II brought a new prosperity to the San Diego-Tijuana area, and shopping gradually replaced boozing and gambling as the main Tijuana attraction. Many Alta Californians crossed the border regularly to purchase items rationed in the U.S. during the war, e.g., stockings, butter, meat, and gasoline. Eventually, however, Tijuana began to grow even faster than San Diego; between 1950 and 1970 the city's population grew 600%. This growth severely taxed the city's infrastructure as Tijuana became ringed by shantytowns practically overnight.

The situation of too many people and too few jobs created problems on both sides of the border. Although the U.S. had discontinued the Bracero Program in the early '60s, the flow of migrant labor to Alta California continued.

LA FRONTERA

The U.S. and Mexico share a thousand-mile border that has become more than just a political boundary. When residents on either side of the border refer to "La Frontera," they're talking about an area that extends as far as a hundred miles north and south from the Rio Grande. It's the center of a hybrid culture that's neither American nor Mexican; here first world meets third world, and north European, Protestant capitalism meets south European, Catholic feudalism. Despite the fact that Mexico is the U.S.'s third-largest trading partner, La Frontera is one of the poorest areas in either country.

The burgeoning twin-plant *(maquila* or *maquiladora)* industry along the border, in which American (or Canadian, European, or Japanese) technology and management exploits cheap Mexican labor, is said to be the hope of the future for the borderland. Goods produced at the plants are given special trade status since they're established in "export processing zones" using U.S. capital. As the number of *maquilas* increases, more unemployed Mexicans migrate to northern Mexico in hopes of landing steady, though low-paying, jobs. Once they're on the border there's the imminent attraction of higher-paying work just over the river, so labor tends to flow back and forth. Human taxis even wade across carrying passengers on their backs (25¢ a trip) during "commute" hours.

In spite of a multimillion-dollar U.S. Border Patrol budget, the border will probably remain effectively fluid far into the foreseeable future.

After all, 150 years ago all of the lower American Southwest was still part of Mexico.

Human Smuggling

A 27-km stretch along the border between the Otay Mountains and the Pacific Ocean, commonly called *la tierra de nadie* (no man's land), is estimated to be the busiest area of illegal human traffic in the world—90% of illegal entries into the U.S. state of California are said to occur here. Visitors driving south just north of the Tijuana international gateway can often see Mexicans running in and out of wooded areas alongside the freeway as they make their way into or out of Mexico—part of the daily commute.

For more permanent immigration, and to better avoid the U.S. Border Patrol, "coyotes" or *polleros* regularly lead small groups of seven to 10 *pollos* ("chickens," undocumented immigrants) across the border and deliver them to Los Angeles for fees of around US$300 per Mexican, US$400-500 per Central American; portions of these fees are used to pay safe houses and drivers along the way. Once they've arrived, the immigrants easily blend into the huge, ever-growing Hispanic population in Los Angeles.

A 1980s Rand Corporation report concluded that Mexican immigration, illegal or otherwise, did not pose a true economic or political crisis for the U.S. The evidence, in fact, clearly indicates that the influx of Mexican labor provides strong economic benefits for Southwestern states that greatly outweigh the undocumented immigrants' use of public facilities and services.

Sewage and garbage handling on both sides of the border threatened to turn the San Diego-Tijuana area into an environmental disaster. Periodic flooding of the Río Tijuana was a bane to communities living on either side as unchecked development came ever closer to the river.

Because there was simply no other alternative, U.S.-Mexico cooperation over the last 20 years has come a long way toward dealing successfully with these problems. The arrival of the in-bond plants or maquiladoras in the

'70s and '80s alleviated unemployment t some degree, and stricter law enforcement i halting much of the environmental damag caused by uncontrolled waste disposal. Chai nelization of the Río Tijuana at the borde under the auspices of the Internation Boundaries and Water Commission (IBWC has solved the flood problem.

More recent economic reform at the na tional level has allowed Tijuana a wider sele tion of resources, including foreign inves ment, with which to develop a livable cit

Visitors who haven't been to Tijuana for some time may be surprised to find that the city has made great strides during the last decade or so and now enjoys one of the highest standards of living of any city in Mexico. Conditions have improved to such a degree that many U.S. citizens who work in San Diego have chosen to reside in Tijuana, where living costs are at least a third lower than north of the border.

SIGHTS

Tijuana Cultural Center
("Centro Cultural Tijuana")

This huge, government-built complex at the intersection of Paseo de los Héroes and Av. Independencia is one of the most distinctive monuments in the city. Designed by the same architect responsible for Mexico City's Museum of Anthropology (Pedro Ramírez Vázquez), the centerpiece of the complex is the spherical **Space Theater,** meant to resemble the Earth emerging from a broken shell. Three Omnimax-style films are presented daily in the theater, but the main attraction is "The People of the Sun," a pan-Mexico travelogue that's shown daily at 1400 with English narration, and at 1600 on weekends with Spanish narration. Admission to the English version costs US$5.50; for the Spanish, US$2.30. The other two films change periodically. A Space Theater ticket entitles the holder to free museum admission.

The center's **Museum of Mexican Identities** features historical, anthropological, and archaeological displays focusing on various Mexican ethnic groups. The exhibits pack a lot of information into a relatively compact area that's negotiated by an ascending ramp—a pleasant change from the angular stairways found in most museums. Hours are 1100-2000; guided English-language tours are offered at 1400 weekdays, 1300 weekends. Museum admission is US$1.25.

Other Cultural Center facilities include a 1,000-seat performing arts theater where the National Symphony and Ballet Folklorico perform regularly, exhibit halls with rotating art exhibits, a restaurant serving *platillos típicos,* a bookstore that specializes in materials on

Baja California, and a shopping arcade with nine shops selling Mexican arts and crafts.

During the summer months an outdoor area features cultural performances by groups such as the Papantla Flyers, a music and dance troupe from Veracruz that performs 1,500-year-old ritual dances from the top of a 30-meter pole.

Mexitlán

Tijuana's latest tourist attraction, a new theme park on Av. Ocampo between Calle 2a and 3a, represents a "Mexico-in-miniature" concept. The focus of the 15,000 square-meter complex, built over a huge parking garage, is a permanent exhibit of around 200 scale replicas (1:25) of famous Mexican archaeological monuments, from Mayan to Spanish colonial to modern (the tallest model recreates the Mexicana Airlines building in Mexico City). Designed by Pedro Ramírez Vázquez, architect of the Tijuana Cultural Center as well as Mexico City's Museum of Anthropology and Aztec Stadium, the models are illuminated from sunset until midnight.

Shops on the street level offer ongoing arts-and-crafts demonstrations, while a stage on the terrace features folk dancing and various styles of Mexican music. Facilities include seven Mexican restaurants, purified water fountains, handicapped access to all areas, and locker, stroller, and wheelchair rentals.

Admission to Mexitlán is US$9.95 per adult, US$6.95 for children 3-12, US$7.95 over 60; U.S. dollar, pesos, and credit cards are accepted. The exhibits and restaurants are open Wed.-Mon. 1000-2200 during the summer, 1000-2000 the remainder of the year. For more information, call 81-82-94 or 81-82-95 in Tijuana, (619) 531-1112 in the U.S., or (800) 834-4939 in California.

Guadalupe Cathedral
("Catedral Nuestra Señora de Guadalupe")

At Calle 2a and Av. Constitución, this large, urban cathedral is only worth a visit if you're Catholic or if you've never seen a Mexican cathedral. The interior is perhaps more impressive than the exterior. Vendors on the adjacent sidewalks sell typical Catholic ritual paraphernalia.

Guerrero Park
("Parque Teniente Vicente Guerrero")

Tijuana doesn't have a zócalo or public square, but four blocks west of Av. Revolución off Calle 3a is a park where late-afternoon strollers may tarry for a few minutes or a few hours. It's dedicated to the heroes of the 1911 Tijuana battle against the Magonistas; the park's namesake, Lieutenant Guerrero, led the federal troops who quashed the rebellion.

Art Exhibits

Tijuana attracts artists from all over the country and in recent years has become known as an arts center for northern Mexico. The Tijuana Cultural Center is the main showcase for traveling exhibitions but modern artists' works can also be seen at several private galleries in the **Plaza Fiesta** center on Paseo de los Héroes (diagonally opposite the Cultural Center).

Popular Mexican mural art can be found throughout the city; the **Palacio Municipal** ("County Hall") on Paseo de Tijuana features

several examples. On the third-floor wall is a mural depicting the history of Mexico while on the second floor is a "Rebirth of Baja California" mural; other floors have murals as well.

ACCOMMODATIONS

Hotels And Motels

Plenty of rooms are available in Tijuana to accommodate those who choose to spend the night. The best hotel in town is the landmark **Hotel Fiesta Americana,** completed in 1986 as one of the Plaza Agua Caliente twin towers, the city's first skyscrapers. The 22-floor, 430-room, five-star hotel features several restaurants and discos, a race-and-sports betting lounge, and penthouse suites where visiting celebrities and politicos stay.

Many other tourist hotels and motels are strung out along Blvd. Agua Caliente, especially in the vicinity of the Caliente Race Track. For visitors on a budget, a handful of more economic places to stay can be found downtown—facilities are basic (no heating, a/c, or parking) but adequate. The "Tijuana Hotels and Motels" chart lists room rates and facilities.

Youth Hostel
Tijuana has one *villa juvenil* or youth hostel, located just north of the river between Via Oriente and Av. Padre Kino near the Cuauhtémoc Bridge (tel. 84-75-10). Rates for a bed and locker in a dorm-style room are US$5 a night. From the border, you can get here by taking any bus marked "Central Camionera"; from the downtown area, take a blue-and-white bus south on Av. Niños Héroes. The hostel is part of a large sports facility (look for the sign "Deportivas") off Av. Padre Kino.

Campgrounds And RV Parks
The nearest camping/RV facilities are on the coast between San Antonio del Mar and Rosarito, some 20-25 km south of Tijuana via Mexico 1-D. See "Rosarito," p. 162, for details.

FOOD

Some of Baja's best food is found in Tijuana—it's worth a stopover just for a meal or two. Menus in La Reforma (Av. Revolución) district list prices in both M.N. and US$ or US$ only—if you pay in pesos you'll almost always save a little money. Mexico has very lenient liquor laws, so virtually all of the restaurants described below serve at least beer; most offer full bars as well.

Downtown
$-$$ **Bol Corona** (tel. 85-79-40, Calle 2a and Av. Revolución, Plaza Revolución): Originally opened in 1934, this venerable institution was gutted by fire in 1990 but reopened after several months. The ground floor features a Mexican family-style coffee shop while the upper floor is more touristy. The menu features a wide selection of northern Mexican specialities, including carne asada and enchiladas verdes, but the restaurant is most known for its burritos (probably invented here); in fact, smaller branch restaurants called Burritos del

Bol Corona can be found all over town—great burritos cost from US$0.60 for a bean burrito to US$1.60 for shrimp or fajita burritos. Open daily for breakfast, lunch, and dinner.
$$-$$$ **Caesar's** (tel. 88-27-94, Hotel Caesar, Calle 5a and Av. Revolución): This continental restaurant is famous for its Caesar salad, which was invented here by Alex and Caesar Cardini in 1924. The original Caesar's recipe uses coddled eggs (eggs boiled for one minute) in the dressing rather than the customary raw egg yolks used in North America. Open daily for dinner.
$$ **Pedrin's** (tel. 85-40-62, Av. Revolución 1115): A branch of the long-established Pedrin's in Rosarito, this is one of the most popular seafood places in Tijuana. The cabrilla (seabass) is particularly reliable. Open daily for lunch and dinner. Pedrin's has two other Tijuana branches, at Calle 7a 150 and at Av. Sánchez Taboada and Blvd. Cuauhtémoc in the Zona Río.
$ **Restaurant Nelson** (tel. 85-77-50, Av. Revolución 100): This nondescript coffeeshop on the ground floor of the Hotel Nelson is one of the cheaper sit-down places to eat in La Reforma district, especially for breakfast. Open daily for breakfast, lunch, and dinner.
$ **Super Antojitos Jalisco** (tel. 88-08-36, Av. Constitución 1111): The menu here is limited but authentic Mexican fare, and prices are low. Open Mon.-Sat. for lunch and dinner. If Super Antojitos Jalisco is too crowded, plenty of other local favorites can be found along Av. Constitución. (Another Super Antojitos can be found in the Plaza Río shopping center on Paseo de los Héroes, Zona Río.)
$$ **Tia Juana Tilly's** (tel. 85-16-12, 85-25-24), Calle 7a and Av. Revolución (part of the Frontón Jai Alai): Tilly's started out as Café de Jai Alai in 1945, later became an elegant restaurant called La Puenta, and in the '70s settled into its current casual-but-polished image. Historic Tijuana photos line the walls, and TV screens to one side of the restaurant broadcast live sports and racing events (so bettors from the adjacent booking lounge can follow their fates). Although basically a tourist scene, the food at Tilly's—Mexican, steak, and seafood—is excellent (especially the *caldos,* served with *chipotle* salsa) as is the service.

TIJUANA HOTELS AND MOTELS

Add 15% hotel tax to all rates (some hotels may charge an additional 10% service charge).
Area code: 66
*Affiliated with the Best Western chain; reservations can be arranged
in the U.S. or Canada by calling (800) 528-1234

NAME	ADDRESS	TELEPHONE	RATES	FEATURES
Caesar	Av. Revolución 827	85-16-06	US$35	heat, a/c, restaurant
Centenario Plaza	Blvd. Agua Caliente 1426	81-81-03	US$55	a/c, pool, restaurants, parking
*Country Club	Calle Tapachula 1 (at Blvd. Agua Caliente)	81-77-33	US$45	heat, a/c, restaurant, pool, jacuzzi, sauna, parking
Del Mar	Calle 1 1948 (Articulo 123)	85-73-02	US$12	
El Conquistador	Blvd. Agua Caliente 1777 (P.O. Box 120637, Chula Vista, CA 92012)	81-79-55 (or in the U.S. 800-336-5454)	US$47	heat, a/c, laundry, pool, restaurant, coffee shop, parking
Fiesta Americana Tijuana	Blvd. Agua Caliente 4500		US$80	heat, a/c, laundry, tennis, pool, restaurants, disco, fitness center, jacuzzi, sauna, parking
*Hacienda del Río	Blvd. Sanchez Taboada 10606 (Zona Río)	84-86-44	US$60-65	restaurant, pool, parking
*La Mesa Inn	Blvd. Díaz Ordaz 50	81-65-22	US$55-70	heat, a/c, restaurants, coffee shop, pool, parking
La Villa de Zaragoza	Av. Madero 1120	85-18-32	US$33-39	heat, a/c, laundry, parking
Lucerna	Av. Paseo de los Héroes 10902	34-20-00 (in U.S. & Canada 800-LUCERNA)	US$60	laundry, restaurants, pool, gardens
Nelson	Av. Revolución 502	85-43-03	US$20-35	coffee shop
Padre Kino	Blvd. Agua Caliente 3	86-42-08	US$23-38	parking
Palacio Azteca	Av. 16 de Septiembre 213	81-81-00	US$50-55	heat, a/c, laundry, coffee shop, pool, parking

TIJUANA HOTELS AND MOTELS (CONT.)

NAME	ADDRESS	TELEPHONE	RATES	FEATURES
Paraíso Radisson Tijuana	Blvd. Agua Caliente 1	81-72-00 (in U.S. & Canada 800-333-3333)	US$74-84	heat, a/c restaurants, pool, jacuzzi, sauna, parking
*Plaza de Oro	Calle 2 & Av. D (Av. Martinez)	85-14-37	US$45-65	a/c, complimentary continental breakfast
Rey	Calle 4 (Díaz Miron) 2021	85-14-26	US$20	

Open noon-midnight, except Fri.-Sat. until 0300.

Tilly's has an outdoor section called **La Terraza** that's open noon-1900 Oct.-May, until midnight the remainder of the year.

$ **Woolworth's** 616 Revolución: Whether the claim that this is the largest Woolworth's in the world is true or not, the store's *lonchería* serves tasty *platillos típicos* and beer at low prices. Open Mon.-Sat. for breakfast, lunch, and dinner.

Agua Caliente

$$$ **Bocaccio's Nuevo Marianna** (tel. 86-18-45), Blvd. Agua Caliente 2500. A place where the local elite meet to eat, this kitschy Italian restaurant started out in 1927 at a downtown location and moved to the racetrack area after a 1957 fire. Some of the best menu items are seafood entrees, including crab claws, lobster, and abalone. Open daily for lunch and dinner.

$-$$ **Carnitas Uruapan** (tel. 81-61-81), Blvd. Díaz Ordaz 550, opposite Plaza Patria: A classic carnitas joint, where the pig is cooked on-site and sold by the kilo along with rice, beans, salsa, and guacamole. Other Mexican specialities as well as steak are on the menu. Breakfasts are good, too. Open 22 hours daily (closed 0500-0700).

$$-$$$ **Don Pepe** (tel. 84-90-86). Blvd. Fundadores 688 (about three km south of Blvd. Agua Caliente): This restaurant in south Tijuana has one of the most extensive seafood menus in the city; shellfish, freshwater fish, and saltwater fish are prepared in a variety of Mexican, American, and continental styles. Don Pedro's *postres* (desserts), including his renowned flan and cheescake, are made on the premises and are sold at other Tijuana restaurants. Open daily for lunch and dinner.

$$-$$$ **La Escondida** (tel. 81-44-58), Santa Monica 1 (east of the racetrack, off Blvd. Agua Caliente): This converted hacienda serves high-quality seafood, Mexican, and continental specialties in a variety of dining areas, both indoors and outdoors. Open daily 1100-midnight; Wed.-Sat. live music and dancing.

$$ **La Leña** (tel. 86-29-20), Blvd. Agua Caliente 4560: This restaurant near the Hotel Fiesta Americana and the racetrack specializes in mesquite-grilled Sonoran steaks and carne asada. Mexican plates and seafood are also available. Open daily for lunch and dinner. There is a second La Leña at Av. Revolución 816 (between Calle 4a and 5a) downtown.

$-$$ **Plaza Agua Caliente,** Blvd. Agua Caliente (adjacent to the Hotel Fiesta Americana): The ground floor of this office tower features an array of vendor-style restaurants, including one of the aforementioned Burritos del Bol Corona outlets as well as several other eateries offering Mexican antojitos, burgers, pizza, licuados, ice cream, and enough other alternatives to satisfy most food cravings.

Zona Río

$ **Giragril** (tel. 84-01-47), Blvd. Sánchez Taboada 9: Serves 14 different kinds of *giraespadas,* meats that are marinated, skewered, and barbecued. Prices include salad and a side dish. Open daily for lunch and dinner.

$-$$ **Los Mandilones de Tijuana** (tel. 84-02-60), Plaza Río Tijuana, Paseo de los Héroes: After a visit to this splendid little taco bar, you'll never patronize Taco Bell again. Open daily for lunch and dinner.

$-$$ **Plaza Fiesta,** Paseo de los Héroes and Av. Independencia: The architecture is inspired by old Guanajuato, but the many cafes, bars, restaurants, and panaderías here feature specialties from all over Mexico, Europe, and Latin America. At night the atmosphere can be quite festive, with outdoor music and occasional dancing. In spite of the convenient location, few tourists venture here—all the better for those of us seeking local ambience. Open nightly; some places are also open for lunch.

$-$$ **Sarita's Place,** Pueblo Amigo Shopping Center: Vegetarians can rejoice in the moderately priced soups, salads, and healthful vegetable cutlets here. The pineapple cheescake, though perhaps not as healthful as the rest of the menu, is excellent. Open daily 1300-1700 only.

$$ **Victor's** (tel. 84-02-04), Blvd. Sánchez Taboada and Calle Joaquin Clauser: This two-story Mexican restaurant features a full-menu dining room downstairs and a bar with specialty menu upstairs—both serve good food. Open for breakfast, lunch, and dinner.

Loncherías

Loncherías are often the least expensive and most characterful sit-down meal spots in Mexico, and Tijuana is full of them. Several are scattered along avenidas Constitución and Madero, often wedged between larger shops. Public markets also usually harbor a few—try the **Mercado Hidalgo** opposite the Cultural Center or the **Mercado de Todos** in the 1800 block of Blvd. Agua Caliente. Tacos, tortas, and other antojitos are the usual offerings—sometimes a comida corrida is available.

A few loncherías depart from the usual Mexican standards and serve regional specialities. **Lonchería Rinconcito Yucateco** (tel. 21-60-41) is a bit out of the way at Av. Los Arboles 16 in La Mesa district, but for *comida yucateca* fans it may be worth the trip. Besides food specialties made from Yucatan recipes, the lonchería serves León Negra beer—a rare find anywhere in Mexico outside the Yucatan peninsula.

Groceries

The northern Baja **Calimax** supermarket chain has several outlets in Tijuana. Food prices at Calimax are often lower than at smaller mom 'n' pop stores and the selection is huge. Probably the most accessible Calimax for those driving through the city is the one on the south side of Paseo de los Héroes just east of Blvd. Cuauhtémoc.

For bolillos, pan dulce, and other Mexican bakery items, your best choice is **Panificadora Suzette** opposite the Super Antojitos at Plaza Río Tijuana. Although Mexican bakeries don't usually stock tortillas (they're made and sold at tortillerías), Suzette's does. For decent European-style pastries and baked goods, stop by **La Baguette** on Blvd. Agua Caliente southeast of El Toreo bullring.

ENTERTAINMENT

Although Tijuana is considerably tamer now than it was during the 1920s Prohibition era, it still has some nightlife—albeit of a more polished sort. For the most part, the entertainment center has shifted from La Reforma district round Av. Revolución to the Zona Río along Paseo de los Héroes.

Discos

San Diegans mix with a mostly local crowd at several high-tech discos, most of which are in the Zona Río. The current top draws are: **Baby Rock** (tel. 84-94-38, Calle Diego Rivera 1482), **News** (tel. 82-49-67, Plaza Pueblo Amigo, Via Oriente), **Splash** (tel. 84-21-19, Calle Mina 3), **Bacarat** (tel. 81-70-00, Fiesta Americana Hotel), and the world-class **Oh! Laser Club** (tel. 84-02-67, Paseo de los Héroes 56). All these discos have dress codes that prohibit blue jeans or sneakers; most (top) San Felipe; (bottom) Playa Palmilla

(top) mosiac over entrance to Rosarito Beach Hotel;
(bottom left) roadside shrine; (bottom right) olives. Maneadero

nights a cover charge of up to US$10 per person is collected. The recorded music varies from international pop to Latin funk.

Bars

For those who prefer sitting and drinking to dancing, Av. Revolución offers a string of bars, from sleazy to posh, attracting an eclectic mix of cholos, punks, tourists, and the occasional American sailor. What was once the longest bar in the world, La Ballena, has been reduced to the **Cinco de Mayo,** on Av. Revolución between Calles 2a and 3a. In the early 1900s, before it was sold off piece by piece, the classic wooden bar here ran the entire length of the block—under a tent.

Another classic is the **Bar San Marcos,** attached to the Hotel Caesar (tel. 88-27-94, Calle 5a and Av. Revolución). The ultimate in Latin kitsch, the San Marcos features a 10-piece mariachi band on a semicircular platform over the glistening bar. The decor is '40s-'50s, and the clientele consists of day tourists from San Diego and local business people.

The **Plaza Fiesta,** on Paseo de los Héroes in the Zona Río, has a handful of bar/restaurants where drinks are reasonably priced and often accompanied by *botanas* (snacks). The plaza's **Tango Bar,** for example, offers Argentine atmosphere and food while **La Taberna Española** serves Spanish botanas.

Miscellaneous

Highbrow evening entertainment is available at the **Tijuana Cultural Center** (see "Sights" above for location). Mexico's National Symphony performs at the center on a regular basis, as does the Ballet Folklorico and other performing arts groups from around the country.

For lowbrows, a dwindling number of strip joints survive along Av. Revolución—vestiges of TJ's former life as a sleaze capital but rather tame and expensive. As for prostitution, the tourist bureau would like everyone to believe it disappeared from Tijuana with the casinos in 1938. The reality is bordello activity has moved to a motley collection of saloons and short-time hotels in the Zona Norte (often simply spoken of as "La Zona") on the outskirts of town—definitely not a tourist scene.

AVENIDA REVOLUCIÓN (DOWNTOWN TIJUANA)

SPORTS AND RECREATION

Hipódromo Caliente
("Caliente Race Track")

Tijuana's first racetrack was opened in 1916, just 400 meters south of the current border crossing, in response to a 1909 ban on pari-mutuel betting in Alta California. Business was good right from the start, and when U.S. Prohibition sent even greater numbers of Alta Californians south of the border, a larger track was needed. The Hipódromo Agua Caliente was constructed in 1929 following the highly successful 1928 opening of Tijuana's El Casino del Agua Caliente.

In 1931 Caliente became the first track in North America to become a "Hundred Grander," that is, to award US$100,000 to a single race winner. Following the 1938 Mexican ban on gambling, the track remained in operation even after the casino had closed, and after the re-legalization of pari-mutuel betting in Alta California in 1933, Caliente became an important training ground for young U.S.-owned thoroughbreds. Famous horses—Phar Lap (1932), Seabiscuit (1938), and Round Table (1958)—have run at Caliente.

Today, the *cupula* entrance to the Caliente Racetrack, a vestige of Tijuana's Prohibition-era splendor, preserves the 1920s Moorish style that has become the epitome of San Diego-Ensenada architecture. Closed for renovations throughout 1990, the refurbished (and renamed, dropping "Agua") facilities cover 160 acres and feature three tracks for thoroughbred and greyhound racing, three restaurants (Jockey Club, La Cupula, Turf Club), two Foreign Books (see "Race And Sports Book" below), as well as several bars and snack bars.

The racetrack is 12 km (eight miles) south of the international border on Blvd. Agua Caliente, just east of the Plaza Agua Caliente twin towers. Red-and-black route taxis marked "La Mesa" pass in front of the entrance, as do the green-and-cream city buses.

Racing Schedule: Thoroughbreds race year-round on Sat. and Sun.; post time is at noon Oct.-May, 1300 June-Sept. Greyhounds run nightly except Tuesday beginning at 1945; matinee dog races are held at 1430 on Mon., Wed., and Friday.

Wagering: Pari-mutuel wagers include daily doubles, quinielas, trifectas, exactas, pick-six (invented at this track), win, place, and show. Caliente claims it collects the lowest take of any racetrack in North America, 14.86%; the racetrack pays all taxes, so figures shown on the tote board are the actual win amount. (U.S. winners are expected to voluntarily submit the appropriate portion of

Caliente Racetrack
(COURTESY OF THE
CALIENTE RACETRACK)

their winnings to the IRS, unless they spend at least 11 months of the year outside the United States.) Bets are accepted in U.S. currency as well as pesos.

Race And Sports Book
Sporting folk don't have to go all the way out to Caliente Race Track to make a wager, as Tijuana has several venues for sports and off- track betting. These legal betting lounges offer plush bars and restaurants, plus banks of closed-circuit TV monitors so you can keep up with your wagers—or just watch for fun.

LF Race and Sports Book has locations at the Plaza Pueblo Amigo (Paseo de Tijuana, Zona Río), at the Hotel Fiesta Americana, and at the Jai Alai Palace. The similar **Caliente Foreign Book** has lounges at the Caliente Race Track and at Av. Revolución and Calle 4a. All book lounges keep the same hours: Wed.-Sun. 0900-2300, Tuesday 0900-2030.

Bullfights
The bullfight season in Tijuana is May through Sept., usually two corridas in May, one in June, and weekly thereafter except for the last week in Sept.; the corridas are held at 1600 Sundays. Current schedule and ticket information is available in Tijuana by calling 85-22-10. Ticket reservations are often necessary and can be obtained by calling 85-22-10 or at: 1) Ticketron outlets in the San Diego (tel. 619-231-3554) and Los Angeles (tel. 213-410-1062) areas; 2) Mexicoach Five Star Tours (tel. 619-232-5049) in San Diego or Tijuana; 3) the Hotel Fiesta Americana Tijuana (tel. 81-70-00); 4) the bullfight information booth at Av. Revolución 815 (Sonia Arcade, between Calle 4a and 5a). Depending on the seat and the matador lineup, ticket prices range from US$6 to US$15.

The city has two permanent bullrings. **El Toreo de Tijuana** (tel. 86-15-10, Agua Caliente Blvd. 100) is the older and more atmospheric of the two and is close to the city center. The **Plaza Monumental** (tel. 80-18-08, Paseo Monumental) is approximately 10 km (6 miles) west of the city, in the Playas

district next to the Pacific Ocean. Dubbed the "Bullring-by-the-Sea," this huge, stadium-like edifice is reportedly the second-largest bullring in the world (after Mexico City's); when the world's top matadors visit Tijuana, they always perform at the Plaza Monumental.

For a brief history and description of the corrida de toros, see "Bullfights," p. 60.

Charreada (Mexican Rodeo)
Although the *charreada* inspired the development of North American rodeo, it differs in significant ways. Competition is generally based on the *charro's* (cowboy's) performance style, rather than timed events, and the atmosphere is considerably more festive, featuring elaborate costumes and music. In Tijuana, occasional charreadas are held Saturdays or Sundays May through Sept. at *lienzos charros* (charreada rings) throughout the city, including **Lienzo Charro La Misión** (tel. 80-41-85, Av. Braulio Maldonado, Zona Misión). Easier to find is the **Cortijo San José** in the Playas Tijuana district near the Plaza Monumental bullring.

Smaller Tijuana lienzos arrange occasional rodeo events during fiestas. For the latest information on charreada schedules, call Tijuana's tourist information number (tel. 83-14-05) or contact the Charro Association's secretary (tel. 81-34-01, 81-26-11).

Jai Alai
Known as "the fastest ball-game in the world," jai alai (a Basque word meaning "merry festival," pronounced "HAI- lai") is descended from *pelota,* a 200-year-old Basque game which is also the forerunner of handball, squash, and racquetball. In the Basque country of northern Spain, the pelota (originally a goatskin ball, now hard rubber encased in goatskin) was originally bounced against church walls or *frontis;* it moved indoors to the *frontón* (playing court) in the late 18th century.

Jai Alai has come a long way from its humble beginnings as a goatherd's pastime. The Frontón Palacio Jai Alai de Tijuana, a landmark Spanish-style structure in the center of the city, is one of the San Diego-Tijuana area's major attractions. The palacio's facilities include the frontón itself (a three-walled court with hardwood floors and seating for 1500 spectators), one of the city's finest restaurants (Tia Juana Tilly's), a '50s-style burger-and-fries bar (Rock Ola), a sidewalk café (La Terraza), and a disco (Tilly's).

The *pelotaris,* or jai-alai players, who appear at the frontón mostly hail from France, Spain, and Mexico. A pelotari's uniform consists of a numbered, colored jersey, white pants, a red waist sash *(faja),* court shoes, a helmet, and a *cesta.* The cesta is an elongated wicker basket (imported from Spain at a cost of around US$200 each) strapped to the playing hand and used for throwing and catching the pelota. The curvature of the cesta combined with the throwing technique of a skilled pelotari allows the pelota to be pitched against the frontón walls as if shot from a cannon. Ball speeds can reach as high as a blistering 290 km per hour.

The Game: Pelotari teams of six to eight players play in singles or doubles in round-robin fashion. A printed program distributed to spectators every evening contains the name and jersey numbers of the pelotaris in each *juego* (match), along with his odds for scoring. The minimum wager is US$2 for win, place, or show, and there are also quiniela, exacta, trifecta, and daily double bets. If you've never wagered on jai alai before, it might be best to watch a round or two (12 juegos are usually played in an evening) before diving in. Bilingual staff are on hand to explain scoring and betting.

Admission: Doors to the palacio open at 1900 the pelotaris start warming up on the court around 1930, and play begins promptly at 2000. Jai alai matches are played nightly, year-round, except on Thursdays. General admission—at the top of the seating area—is US$3, reserved seating is US$4, and seats in the Cancha Club are US$5. Cancha Club seating is closest to the court, and offers seated bar service. Bars in the palacio lobby areas (three on the main floor, two on the mezzanine) serve other spectators.

Location and Information: The palacio is at the intersection of Av. Revolución and Calle 7a. For information call 85-78-33, 85-25-24, or 85-16-12 in Tijuana, (619) 260-0452 in San Diego.

El Béisbol

Tijuana has its own pro baseball team, Los Potros (Colts), who play other ball clubs in the Mexican-Pacific League as well as the occasional visiting team from North or Central America. Games are played at the exemplary, 15,000-seat **Estadio de los Potros** (tel. 25-10-56), off Blvd. Los Insurgentes near the Otay Mesa border crossing. The Mexican baseball season runs from about the end of the American World Series through late Jan.; game admission is around US$3.

Golf

The *Club Campestre Tijuana,* or **Tijuana Country Club** (tel. 81-78-55, off Blvd. Agua Caliente near the Caliente Race Track), has a decent 6,500-yard, par-72, 18-hole course where the Mexican Open is occasionally held. Nonmembers may tee off at the club for greens fees of US$20 weekdays, US$25 weekends. Carts and caddies may be hired at extra cost. A special "fiesta package" is available for US$65 weekdays, US$78 weekends and holidays, including green fees, cart rental, and lunch at the club for two persons.

SHOPPING

For North Americans, shopping is perhaps Tijuana's number-one attraction. Although both Baja California states have been designated duty-free zones by the Mexican government, Tijuana has the widest variety of merchandise to offer—everything from Mexican-Indian handicrafts to pharmaceuticals to top-of-the-line European clothing fashions.

Nearly everything is cheaper in Tijuana than it is north of the border. Some of the better bargains are found in leather goods, cosmetics, drugs (prescriptions aren't usually required, even for drugs normally dispensed by prescription in the U.S.), high-tag import items (e.g., designer fashions), cooking spices (vanilla costs a fraction of the U.S. price), handicrafts (especially blankets, rugs, basketry, and ceramics), and liquor.

Avenida Revolución

For individual shops and boutiques, Av. Revolución between Calle 2a and Calle 9a is one of the best window-shopping areas. **Sanborn's**, at the corner of Av. Revolución and Calle 8a, is a favorite department store among day-tripping San Diegans. Although not large, it's divided into books, arts and crafts, pharmacy, liquors, and restaurant sections.

For high-quality Mexican handicrafts, **Tolan** (opposite the Fronton Jai Alai on Av. Revolución, between Calle 7a and 8a), is among the best shops in the city. Farther north along Av. Revolución, at Calle 2a, is **Plaza Revolución,** a two-story mall with around 65 shops purveying arts and crafts, leather goods, jewelry, and other items. And don't overlook **Woolworth's,** at the same intersection, where everyday items are on sale at rock-bottom prices.

Except at department stores, pharmacies, and liquor stores, bargaining for a lower price than marked or quoted is acceptable. U.S. currency is accepted anywhere in the city; some shops accept credit cards. Most of the sales staff in Av. Revolución stores can speak some English.

Avenida Constitución

Few visitors seem to know it, but one block west of Av. Revolución is the major downtown shopping area for locals. Especially for shoes and boots, liquor, and pharmaceuticals, shops on Av. Constitución always beat the prices of their counterparts on Av. Revolución. And unlike at some shops on Revolución, bargaining (or Spanish language mastery) isn't necessary since prices are always marked and fixed.

Shopping Centers

Tijuana was the first city in Mexico to erect North American-style shopping malls; at last count, the city boasted 12 major *centro comerciales* (shopping centers), with more on the way.

Plaza Río Tijuana, on Paseo de los Héroes (between Via Poniente and Blvd. Cuauhtémoc) in the Zona Río, is the most highly acclaimed. Here you'll find over a hundred busi-

Fronton Jai Alai (JOE CUMMINGS)

nesses, including department stores, pharmacies, optometrists, banks, jewelry and gift stores, music shops, clothing stores, a bakery, a florist, a cinema, photo shops, travel agencies, bookstores, sporting goods, and even a chapel, all surrounded by a large parking lot.

Opposite Plaza Río is **Plaza del Zapato,** "Shoe Plaza." This is one of Tijuana's best bargain centers, with over 35 *zapaterías* (shoe stores) in one location. Shoes and boots, especially those made in Mexico, usually cost less than half what they would north of the border. Next to Plaza del Zapato is **Plaza Fiesta,** a mall featuring old Guanajuato-style architecture. Most of the businesses are restaurants, bars, or cafés, interspersed with a few specialty shops. **La Herradura de Oro (The Golden Horseshoe)** in Plaza Fiesta sells Mexican, Western, and English riding equipment—chaps, sombreros, rebozos, saddles, etc.—and can also produce custom leather work.

The **Tijuana Cultural Center** at Paseo de los Héroes and Av. Independencia has a shopping area with nine shops specializing in regional arts and crafts, including hand-crafted silver, gold, copper, brass, textiles, ceramics, jewelry, paintings, and sculptures.

Other Tijuana shopping centers of note include Plaza Patria (Blvd. Díaz Ordaz, east of

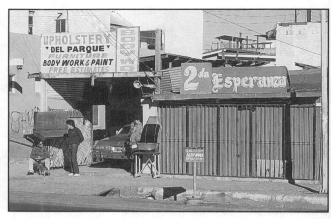

upholstery shop
(JOE CUMMINGS)

Caliente Race Track), Plaza Pueblo Amigo (Av. Via Oriente, near the border crossing), and Plaza Agua Caliente (Av. Agua Caliente, adjacent to the Hotel Fiesta Americana).

Southern Alta Californians who don't want to venture far from home territory can shop at **Viva Tijuana,** a big indoor-outdoor mall only about 150 meters from the border gate. In fact, all pedestrians entering or exiting the country are forced to walk through this mall. Neither the restaurants nor the shops at Viva Tijuana offer anything very special—it's strictly a place to pick up last-minute souvenirs.

Markets

For a more Mexican shopping experience, seek out Tijuana's public markets. The large **Mercado de Artesanías** at the intersection of Av. Ocampo and Calle 1a offers thousands of pottery items at low prices (always bargain). Much of what's stacked up in row after row is junk, but worthwhile pieces can be uncovered with diligent searching.

Opposite the Tijuana Cultural Center at Paseo de los Héroes and Independencia is the more atmospheric **Mercado Hidalgo.** This outdoor municipal market features dozens of vendor stalls arranged in a large square. Items for sale vary from year to year but generally include fresh fruits and vegetables (sometimes sold from the back of trucks), spices,

and various other grocery items. A couple of loncherías and crafts shops make it more than just a grocery stop.

The **Mercado de Todos**—"Market of Everything"—is out on the 1800 block of Blvd. Agua Caliente/Díaz Ordaz, about four km east of the racetrack. Vendors here offer bargains on clothing, housewares, electronics, and just about anything else you might need to set up house on the peninsula. If you get hungry while strolling from booth to booth, several extra-clean loncherías offer cheap eats. This market doesn't really get rolling until around 1000 on weekdays, or 0900 weekends; it stays open until dark.

Auto Upholstery And Body Work

Tijuana is as legendary for auto work as Hong Kong is for tailoring. As in Hong Kong, patience in arranging for custom work and waiting for it to be completed always pays off. The Tijuana Convention and Visitors Bureau (tel. 84-05-37) maintains a list of reputable upholsterers and body shops—check this list first if you don't already have a recommendation from someone you know.

Typical of the better upholstery shops is **Richard's Upholstery** at Calle 2a and Av. Madero, which offers tuck-and-roll, diamonds, plaids, squares, and just about any other style in leather, vinyl, or fabric. Prices are half, or less, of what a U.S. auto upholsterer would charge; a complete auto interior starts at around US$200 and takes a full day. Check the quality of the upholstery fill in advance—less reputable shops may use low-quality materials (e.g., newspaper in place of foam) to cut corners. Several other upholstery shops can be found along Calle 3a between avenidas Ocampo and Pío Pico. If prices are verbally quoted, they're usually negotiable.

Body shops, or *carroceros*, are mostly found on streets near Parque Teniente Guerrero, down Calle 3a about six blocks past Av. Revolución. Carroceros can do an excellent job of banging out dents and applying primer, but if you only need a fender or door painted, you can usually match the paint better at a North American auto dealer. For an all-new paint job, **Javier's Body Shop,** Av. Baja California 1347, has been recommended ("Pearlescent" is the house specialty.)

Furniture And Tile
Mexican-made furniture—wood or wrought-iron—and tile are considerably less expensive in Tijuana than in the U.S. or Canada. Most of the larger tile and furniture stores are located along Blvd. Agua Caliente between Av. Revolución and the Caliente Race Track. A few stores specialize in high-quality, handmade wood furniture, but generally the wrought-iron pieces are a better bargain.

One of the widest wall and floor tile selections (including imported tiles from Europe, Brazil, and Japan) in the city is at Tile Express (tel. 81-82-87, 81-83-05) at Ave. Salinas and Aviacion. Be sure to check the latest U.S. Customs regulations before buying huge amounts of furniture or tile for U.S. import.

Hunting Ammunition
Tijuana has one of only three stores in Baja authorized to sell ammunition to the public. Since Mexican law limits the importation of hunting ammunition to 50 cartridges per registered firearm (weapons are limited to two per person), anything beyond this number must be purchased in Mexico. Prices are slightly higher than in the U.S. or Canada. The store,

Alcampo Tijuana, is at Calle 10 de Juan Sarabia 2029.

SERVICES

Changing Money
The best place to exchange foreign currency for pesos is at any of the many casas de cambio found along the pedestrian route from the border to about halfway down Av. Revolución. The banks in Tijuana aren't accustomed to changing small amounts of foreign currency since just about everyone uses casas de cambio exclusively. As usual in Mexico, hotels offer low exchange rates but fast service.

Every business and service in Tijuana except public buses and government offices accepts U.S. currency.

Post And Telephone
The **main post office** is at Calle 11a (P.E. Calles) and Av. Negrete; it's open Mon.-Fri., 0800-1700. The **long-distance telephone and telegraph office** is at Calle 10a and Av. Pío Pico; hours are Mon.-Fri., 0800-1400 and 1600-1900.

Tijuana's area code is 66.

Immigration And Customs
Immigration and customs matters are handled at the Tijuana border crossing. These offices are open 24 hours a day. For specific information on visas and tourist permits, see "Immigration and Customs," p. 101.

Green Angels
The Green Angels automotive assistance service is headquartered in the Garita Federal Building (Edificio Federal Garita) at the Otay Mesa border crossing. For assistance or information in Tijuana, call 23-38-77.

TIJUANA INFORMATION

Tourist Assistance And Information
The **Tourist Information Booth** (tel. 83-14-05, 83-13-10) at Av. Revolución between Calle 4a and 5a distributes maps and useful infor-

CONSULATES IN TIJUANA

Austria
   Blvd. Agua Caliente 3401, desp. 803,
   Edificio Gallego (tel. 86-36-25)
Belgium
   Av. Constitución 720-16 (tel. 85-49-57)
Canada
   Germán Gedoviou 5-202, Zona Río (tel./fax
   84-04-61)
China
   Av. Hidalgo 312, Col. Cacho (tel. 84-27-56,
   fax 84-09-56)
Finland
   Calle 9, 2022, desp. 2 (tel. 85-52-73)
France
   Calle Baladezo and Av. 16 de Septiembre
   (tel. 86-55-54)
Germany
   Av. Mérida 221, Col. Hipódromo
   (tel. 21-81-55)

Honduras
   Germán Gedoviou 11, Zona Río
   (tel. 84-01-68)
Nicaragua
   Av. Revolución 1232-107 (tel. 85-22-5)
Norway
   Calle E, 4, fracc. Rubio, La Mesa (tel. 89-29-
   86, fax 89-23-09)
El Salvador
   Av. México 103-1 (tel. 85-56-66)
Spain
   Av. de los Olivos, Col. Cubillas (tel. 86-57-
   80, 81-70-20)
Switzerland
   Av. Revolución 606-8 (tel. 606-8)
United States
   Calle Tapachula 96, Col. Hipódromo
   (tel. 81-74-00, 86-00-01)

mation brochures on Tijuana as well as northern Baja; the bilingual staff can also handle simple inquiries about where to go and what to see in Tijuana. It's open 0900-1900 daily. Similar booths are in place at the Tijuana border crossing and at Tijuana International Airport. Any questions about Tijuana they can't answer should be referred to the **Tijuana Tourism and Convention Bureau** (tel. 84-05-37, 84-05-38) at the intersection of Calle Mina and Paseo de los Héroes in the Zona Río. This office is open Mon.-Fri. 0900-1400 and 1600-1900.

For more tourist information on Baja California Norte, contact the **State Secretary of Tourism** (tel. 81-94-92, 81-94-93, fax 81-95-79) in Plaza Patria, 3rd floor, Blvd. Díaz Ordaz. Legal problems should also be referred to this office.

The Tijuana Chamber of Commerce and Tijuana Tourism and Convention Bureau jointly publish Baja Visitor, a free monthly filled with hotel, dining, and sightseeing information. Most of the publication is oriented toward Tijuana.

Every Sunday at noon the *Jan Wood Show,* a talk-show program telecast on San Diego television channel 6, focuses on Tijuana. Discussion topics include the latest info on border waits, art shows, Tijuana restaurants, and coming city events. The program can be picked up by most TVs in Tijuana as well as in the San Diego area.

GETTING TO TIJUANA

By Air
Four airlines service Tijuana (Abelardo Rodriguez) International Airport (TIJ): Aeromexico, Aero California, Air L.A., and Mexicana. See "Getting There" in the general introduction.

Taxis from the airport (about eight km east of the city) to anywhere in the city cost a flat US$10 for up to five passengers. Public buses to downtown Tijuana (marked "Centro") leave regularly from in front of the airport for about US$.50 per passenger.

By Land
Bus: Several intercity bus lines operate out of Tijuana (see "Getting There" in the general introduction). The main terminal for Mexico-

based lines is the **Central Camionera** (tel. 80-90-60, 96-95-15) at Lázaro Cárdenas and Blvd. Arroyo Alamar, about five km east of the city. Taxis from the Central Camionera to the downtown area cost a flat US$5 per person; public bus fare is around US$.30

The U.S.-based **Greyhound** buses from San Diego and Los Angeles terminate at a downtown depot at Av. Madero and Calle 1a. This same terminal also serves Mexican buses running between Tijuana and Ensenada (US$2), Rosarito (US$1), and Tecate (US$1). **Mexicoach** (from San Diego and San Ysidro) has its own depot next to the Jai Alai palace at Av. Madero and Calle 7a.

Auto: See "Getting There" in the general introduction for specifics on driving to Tijuana.

GETTING AROUND TIJUANA

Much of the downtown area of Tijuana can easily be seen on foot—avenidas Revolución and Constitución, the cathedral, the Jai Alai Palace, and the Mercado Artesanías. Unless you're driving your own vehicle, outlying attractions (e.g., Zona Río, the racetrack) can be reached by city bus or taxi.

Buses
City buses in Tijuana come in several colors, shapes, and sizes. The route destination—usually the name of a district (e.g., "Centro" or "La Mesa")—is displayed on a marquis over the windshield or whitewashed directly on the windshield. Fares are around US$.30, payable only in pesos.

Two of the most useful bus lines are the "green and cream" *(verde y crema),* which operates between the city center and the La Mesa district, east of Caliente Race Track, and the "blue and white" *(azul y blanco),* running between the city center and the Playas district (Plaza Monumental). The "Baja P" is the bus to take for jaunts to the Zona Río, including the Tijuana Cultural Center, Plaza Fiesta, and Plaza Río Tijuana.

Taxis
Most trips by hired taxi within the city cost US$4-6. From the city center to the Hotel Fiesta Americana/racetrack area costs as much as US$7, while to the airport or Central Camionera expect to pay up to US$10. Taxis hired from hotels generally cost a bit more than taxis hired on the street, but the rates are usually posted. If in doubt about a fare, inquire at the tourist information booths at the border or on Av. Revolución at Calle 4a. Drivers are happy to accept U.S. currency.

Bargaining usually isn't necessary—drivers generally quote the standard price immediately, with the exception of the yellow border taxis. You shouldn't have to pay more than US$3 from the border-taxi stand to Av. Revolución, but drivers will often ask gringos for more. (A better deal is to take the Mexicoach bus from San Ysidro on the U.S. side of the border directly to Av. Madero, one block east of Av. Revolución, for only US$2.)

Route taxis *(taxis de ruta)* in Tijuana are large American-made station wagons that can hold up to 12 passengers. These taxis operate along set routes, much like city buses, but stop wherever they're flagged down. Fares are around US$.40 per person, only a tad higher than city buses—as on buses, only pesos are accepted. Route taxis are one of the best ways to get around Tijuana cheaply, since you can tell the drivers exactly where you want off along their route (instead of waiting for a bus stop to come along).

Like the city buses, route taxis are painted according to their routes. Red-and-black taxis operate between Calle 2a (between Revolución and Constitución) and La Mesa, along Blvd. Agua Caliente; brown-and-white route taxis run to the Zona Río.

Driving Your Own Vehicle
The traffic in Tijuana is fairly stiff all day long, so it's not one of the most pleasant cities in Baja to drive in. On the other hand, lots of visitors do manage to drive themselves around the city, the author included—all it takes is a good map and plenty of patience. Generally speaking, streets in the downtown area are well-marked; the biggest difficulty comes in trying to navigate one's way out of the city to Rosarito, Mexicali, or beyond.

Another problem is parking, although the situation is not nearly as bad as most larger cities in the United States. In the Av. Revolución area, street parking is hard to come by; it's best to choose one of the fee parking lots (e.g., at the Jai Alai Palace/Mexicoach terminal or next door to Woolworth's).

Leaving Tijuana: To get back across the border, simply drive north on Av. Revolución and follow signs to San Diego. To drive to Rosarito, Ensenada, or other destinations south along Mexico 1, you must first decide whether you want to take the toll road or the free road.

For the toll road (Mexico 1-D), take Calle 3a west and follow the signs for Ensenada; traffic is often very slow until the toll-road entrance is reached near Playas. The free road can be more difficult to find; some visitors say they've had to give up looking for it and resort to the toll road. One of the problems in accessing the free road out of Tijuana is there's only one sign indicating the way; if you drive south along Av. Revolución until it curves east into Blvd. Agua Caliente, you'll soon see a sign reading "A Rosarito" ("To Rosarito") over the road with an arrow pointing to the right. The next right-hand turn, Blvd. Cuauhtémoc, is the correct turnoff. You can also connect with Blvd. Cuauhtémoc by driving east on Paseo de los Héroes. Once on Blvd. Cuauhtémoc, take no other turns, wade through a seemingly endless succession of stoplights and stop signs, and you'll eventually find yourself on Mexico 1.

For Tecate, Mexicali, and other points east, simply follow Blvd. Agua Caliente out of town (southeast) until it turns into Blvd. Díaz Ordaz and, finally, Mexico 2.

Car Rental

Tijuana has seven different car rental operations: AMCA, Avis, Budget, Central, Dollar, Hertz, and National. All offer day, weekend, and weekly deals either with per-kilometer charges added in (best rates for local driving only) or as flat rates only (most economical if you plan to drive long distances in Baja). Car rentals are less expensive in Tijuana than anywhere else on the peninsula. Especially for auto tours of northern Baja, you'll enjoy considerable savings if you rent a car here rather than in Ensenada or Mexicali.

Advance reservations are a good idea as most agencies don't keep lots of cars on hand. With or without reservations, a credit card is a prerequisite for car rental.

AIRLINE OFFICES IN TIJUANA

Aero California
  Paseo de los Héroes C-19-1, Plaza Río Tijuana (tel. 84-20-06, 84-20-07; toll-free in the U.S.: 800-258-3311)
Aeromexico
  Av. Revolución 1236 (tel. 85-44-01, 85-44-02; 800-237-6639 toll- free in the U.S.)
Air L.A.
  Tijuana International Airport (tel. 95-800-01-0413 toll-free in Mexico; 800-933-5952 toll-free in the U.S.)
Mexicana de Aviacion
  Gobernador Balarezo 2800, Col. Davila (tel. 81-72-11; toll-free in the U.S.: 800-531-7921, in Canada: 800-531-7923)
Noroeste
  Tijuana International Airport (tel. 83-13-36, 82-48-57)

TIJUANA TO TECATE (MEXICO 2 EAST)

The scenery along Mexico 2 between Tijuana and Tecate, once you're beyond the eastern city limits, mostly consists of boulders, rolling hills, and the occasional rancho. At Km 166, the highway crosses over the impressive **Presa Rodriguez** (Rodriguez Dam, usually called simply La Presa, "The Dam"), constructed in 1937. In the vicinity of **El Florido**, a small farm community near Km 158, are several dairy farms; look for "Hay Queso" signs if you'd like to buy some fresh cheese.

A few kilometers east of El Florido, a scenic unpaved road dating from the Spanish colonial period heads north to Valle Redondo. On the south side of Mexico 2, another road leads to Presa El Carrizo, a dam with a sizable lake. This gravel road continues south, past a cou-

TIJUANA AUTO RENTAL AGENCIES

AGENCY	ADDRESS	TELEPHONE
AMCA	Tijuana International Airport	83-16-44
AMCA	Av. Madero 1330	85-89-13, 85-23-12
Avis	Tijuana International Airport	83-23-10
Avis	Blvd. Agua Caliente 3310 (opposite Hotel Paraíso Radisson)	86- 37-18, 86-15-07, 86-20-75
Budget	Tijuana International Airport	83-29-05
Budget	Paseo de los Héroes 77, Zona Río	84-02-53, 84-02-63
Central	Paseo de los Héroes 104, Zona Río	84-22-57, 84-22-68
Dollar	Tijuana International Airport	83-18-61
Dollar	Av. Guanajato 102-D, Col. Cacho	84-24-01
Hertz	Tijuana International Airport	83-20-80
Hertz	Hotel Palacio Azteca	86-22-16, 86-43-71
Hertz	Hotel Fiesta Americana	81-70-00
Hertz	Blvd. Agua Caliente 3402	81-72-20, 81-75-53
National	Tijuana International Airport	82-44-33
National	Blvd. Agua Caliente 5000	86-21-03, 82-44-36

ple of ranchos, to connect with Mexico 3 at Valle de las Palmas (see "Tecate to Ensenada," p. 207).

Just before the border town of Tecate, between Km 136 and 135, is the turnoff for **Rancho La Puerta,** one of the world's most highly rated health resorts (see p. 210 for details). Mexico 2 then becomes Av. Juárez, the main west-east thoroughfare through Tecate. Once through Tecate, the highway resumes its eastward direction toward Mexicali and the state of Sonora.

TIJUANA TO ENSENADA

DRIVING FROM TIJUANA TO ENSENADA

The drive from Tijuana to Ensenada (or any points between) is fairly straightforward—even for drivers who would never consider navigating the Transpeninsular all the way to the Cape. One can choose between two roadways, a modern, four-lane toll expressway (Mexico 1-D, also called the Carretera Cuota or "Toll Highway") and a slightly more challenging two-lane highway (the original Mexico 1, called the Carretera Libre or "Free Highway" along this stretch).

Both are scenic drives of around 100 km (60 miles). Mexico 1, the free road, begins just south of Tijuana and winds through a mountainous area for 18 km before reaching the coast at Rosarito. From Rosarito it hugs the narrow coastal plain for the next 50 km, providing plenty of opportunities for beach stopovers, then turns inland again at La Misión. The final 31 km threads through mountain scenery before joining Mexico 1-D just north of Ensenada at San Miguel.

Mexico 1-D, the toll highway, parallels the coast the entire distance from Tijuana to Ensenada. The roadbed is set along the slopes and cliffs of the inland sierra, so coastal views are from a higher perspective than along the free road. On the negative side, there are limited opportunities for stopovers since highway exits can be as far apart as 18 km.

Tolls are collected at three toll gates (*casetas de cobro*) along Mexico 1-D: at Playas de Tijuana, Rosarito, and San Miguel. At each gate, the toll is approximately US$2 for passenger cars (US$3-5 for cars with trailers, motorhomes, or large trucks), for a total of US$6 (or US$9-15 for trailers, etc.) all the way to Ensenada. Both U.S. and Mexican currency is accepted at the toll gates; change is given in pesos, dollars, or a mixture of the two.

ISLAS LOS CORONADOS

The four Los Coronados islands lie only 11 km west of San Antonio del Mar (a mostly American residential area 12 km south of Tijuana). The Spanish explorer Juan Cabrillo passed by in 1542 and called them Las Islas Desiertas (Desert Islands) because of their apparent lack of vegetation; Vizcaíno (in 1602) renamed them Los Cuatros Coronados, "Four Coronados," after four brothers who died as Christian martyrs during the era of the Roman Empire.

Too steep and rugged for inhabitation, in ensuing years the islands were briefly used as a pirate hideaway and then later as a rendezvous for smugglers who brought rum and Chinese immigrants into the United States. In 1931 a short-lived hotel and casino called the Coronado Islands Yacht Club was built at the edge of a cove on the largest island, Coronado del Sur. The establishment closed when Prohibition was repealed in 1933, and the decaying three-story building now lodges a few Mexican navy personnel who protect the island from intruders.

Geography And Natural History

All four of Los Coronados are the tips of undersea mountain ridges. The largest island, Coronado del Sur, is about three km long and reaches 204 meters at its highest point while the second largest, Coronado del Norte, is about a kilometer long and 142 meters high. The remaining two, Roca Media ("Middle Rock") and Coronado del Medio ("Middle Coronado"), lie between the larger islands and are little more than rock outcroppings.

The islands and the area immediately surrounding them are protected by the Mexican government; commercial fishing (with the exception of a few lobster and sea urchin concessions) isn't permitted nor can visitors land on any of the islands without government permission. As a result, the islands represent one

TIJUANA -
TECATE -
ENSENADA

© MOON PUBLICATIONS, INC.

of the most important brown pelican rookeries on the Pacific coast, and over 160 other bird species have been identified as well. Along the west side of Coronado del Norte is a large sea lion colony; harbor seals are common along the same shoreline, and elephant seals are occasionally seen. Plant varieties on the islands number around 100, mostly cactus, mimosae, and other species suited to arid climates.

Fishing
Yellowtail fishing is usually excellent in the vicinity of the Coronados, although the high season runs April-October. Rock cod, bonito, halibut, barracuda, calico bass, and white seabass are also frequently taken. Favorite fishing spots are just north of Roca Media, at the southeast tip of Coronado del Sur, and inshore along the western side of the same island.

Diving
Los Coronados is the most heavily dived area in Baja waters. Many San Diego novices make their first open-water dives here and spearfishers have long extolled the abundance of underwater game among these islands. In some places the moray eels are so accustomed to being fed they immediately approach any diver who happens along.

Good dive sites for divers of all levels include "The Slot"—an area of rich marinelife between the two middle islands; a rocky cove called the "Lobster Shack" (named for an old shack on shore used by lobstermen) along the northeastern coast of Coronado del Norte; the large kelp bed just south of the southern tip of Coronado del Sur; and the rock-reef at the northern end of Coronado del Sur. Advanced, open-ocean divers can tackle "Eighty-five-foot Reef," named for the depth at which much of the reef begins (the shallowest portion is about 18 meters/60 feet below the ocean surface).

Transport And Tours
No regular boat service to Islas Los Coronados exists (most visitors navigate their own craft), although charters in San Antonio del Mar might be possible if you ask around.

Several fishing outfitters in San Diego offer fishing tours of the islands. **Diving Charters**

(see "Sports and Recreation" in the general introduction for address and phone number) operates twice-monthly diving trips

ROSARITO

Rosarito's multiple personality—ranch-town, beach-town, and boom-town rolled into one—reflects a short but varied history. During the mission era, it was virtually uninhabited since it was out of the reach of Dominican missions to the north and Franciscan missions to the south. Although the Camino Real ("Royal Road") passed nearby, it wasn't until a parallel road began snaking its way southward along the coast from Tijuana that anyone but ranchers developed an interest in the area. The huge beach at Rosarito—one of the widest and longest on Baja's Pacific coast—was discovered by early Baja travelers in the '20s and has become more popular with each passing decade.

History
In 1827, as Mexico was transacting its independence from Spain, Juan Machado received a land grant of 407,000 acres in the Rosarito area (then called El Rosario). The Machado family raised cattle and sheep on the property and leased land to other ranchers. In 1914 the family sold 14,000 coastal acres of El Rosario to a land development corporation, which in turn sold it to a New York attorney in 1920.

In 1924 the attorney opened "El Rosario Resort and Country Club" next to the beach. Initially the resort was little more than a rustic hunting cabin. A dirt road between Tijuana and Ensenada passed El Rosario, however, and it became a popular stopover (especially since free camping was allowed on the property) for North Americans sampling the casinos at either end of the road. Manuel Barbachano bought the property around 1930 and built the Rosarito Beach Hotel, at first only a 10-room hotel with a small lobby, one bathroom, and a casino to take advantage of the Prohibition boom in gambling. (Apparently no record exists as to why Barbachano changed the name from El Rosario to Rosarito—perhaps it was because "Rosarito" is easier for gringos to pronounce. Another theory has it that he named the hotel after Lee J. Rose, developer of one of Tijuana's first racetracks.)

For most of the next 40 years, all development in Rosarito focused around the Rosarito Beach Hotel. After Prohibition ended and the Mexican government banned casino gambling in the mid-'30s, Barbachano closed the casino but enlarged the hotel, employing a Belgian architect and Mexican muralist to turn it into a major attraction. During the '40s and 50s, Rosarito became a favorite haunt of Hollywood celebrities, Latin American presidents, and well-heeled international travelers.

The completion of a four-lane toll road to Rosarito in 1967 brought many more Alta Californians into town and modified the exclusive nature of the resort. Other hotels were built and, although the Rosarito Beach Hotel remained the beach centerpiece for some time, the town grew from a weekend resort to include a large residential community of retirees and self-employed expatriates.

Today a four-lane roadway with lighted traffic islands passes through the center of Rosarito, lined with shopping plazas, neon-lit restaurants, high-rise hotels, and condominiums. Vacation and retirement homes, an estimated 10,000 owned by North Americans, stretch along the ocean for miles in either direction. Off the impressive main drag, however, side streets remain unpaved, much to the chagrin of local residents. The city of 80,000 doesn't yet have a central sewer system.

Many residents would like to see Rosarito become BCN's fifth municipality (joining Tijuana, Ensenada, Tecate, and Mexicali). As part of the municipality of Tijuana (26% of the total area, 5.4% of the population), comparatively wealthy Rosarito provides a large portion of Tijuana's annual budget. If the town were to secede from municipal Tijuana, Rosarito residents argue, more money could be used for local urban improvements.

If Rosarito becomes an independent municipality, one would hope that some kind of zoning restrictions might be developed. New high-rise hotels are being added to the Rosa-

Rosarito Beach Hotel
(JOE CUMMINGS)

rito skyline one by one, pushing the once-sleepy beach town closer and closer toward a Miami Beach fate.

Sights
Rosarito's main draw is its eight-km-long, sandy beach. Several beachwear and surf shops in town offer swimming, snorkeling, floating, and surfing equipment for rent or purchase.

The **Rosarito Beach Hotel** is an attraction in itself. For nearly a half century it was the only place to stay in Rosarito, and for many repeat visitors it's still the first choice. During its heyday in the '40s and '50s, the hotel gained a reputation among the Hollywood set as a romantic retreat. Frequent guests included Victor Mature, Mickey Rooney, Joan Bennett, Lana Turner, Orson Welles, Rita Hayworth, Debbie Reynolds, Robert Stack, Gregory Peck, Robert Preston, Spencer Tracy, Jack Palance, and Vincent Price. International playboy Ali Khan (son of Aga Khan) and actress Gene Tierney, along with an entourage of 24, took over the entire hotel for several weeks in 1955; Kim Novak and Dominican Republic President Rafael Leonidas Trujillo had a tryst here during the same era. Not all Hollywood rendezvous were of the illicit variety; Burgess Meredith and Paulette Goddard married at the hotel.

The original owner's nephew, Hugo Torres, acquired the property in 1974. Following his uncle's example, Torres continues to expand the facilities and is currently adding 150 rooms (for a total of over 300). Although no longer a celebrity hideaway, a tour of the Belgian-designed architecture and Mexican murals (by Matía Santoyo) in the central part of the hotel and a visit to the seaward-facing Beachcomber Bar are on the itineraries of virtually every Rosarito visitor.

Accommodation—In Town
Most of Rosarito's hotels are strung out along Av. Juárez, the main thoroughfare. Room rates range from US$20 s, US$25 d at the cheapest motels to US$70 at the most expensive hotels (over US$100 for a suite, condo, or townhouse)—high for Mexico but bargain rates for most southern Alta Californians. Rates are usually discounted during the low season, Nov. through April. During high season, July-Aug., reservations are highly recommended; on any weekend they may also be necessary.

South of town are a few newer, more expensive (US$100+) condo-style hotels (see "Hotels—Out of Town" below). Currently under construction along Av. Juárez is the towering **Corona del Mar,** a resort hotel that will have 500 rooms when completed.

Accommodation—Out Of Town

At **Hotel Las Rocas** (tel. 2-21-40; mailing address: P.O. Box 1948, San Ysidro, CA 92073), an isolated resort hotel 9½ km south of Rosarito at Km 37, all rooms have ocean views, fireplaces, and kitchenettes. Other facilities include a restaurant, pool, jacuzzi, and tennis courts. During the week, rates range from US$50 for a standard room to US$100 for a deluxe suite (US$75-150 weekends and holidays). **Calafia Ocean Resort** (tel. 12-15-81) at Km 35.5 is a timeshare condo development that frequently has one- or two-bedroom units for rent in the US$100-120 range.

Popotla Trailer Park (tel. 2-15-04), a mobile-home community about 3½ km south of Rosarito, sometimes has permanently sited trailers for rent for US$25-30 a night. See below for the address.

Camping And RV Parks

About two km north of Rosarito at Km 25 is the relatively new, deluxe **El Oasis Resort** (mailing address: P.O. Box 2631, Chula Vista, CA 91912; tel. 3-32-55, 800-225-6001 in the U.S.). Beachfront RV sites cost US$25 a night, back row sites are US$20; add US$5 for June-Sept. rates. Facilities include two pools, jacuzzis, tennis courts, individual BBQ pits, satellite cable TV at each site, a mini-market, and two restaurants.

The **KOA Rosarito** (tel. 86-14-12, A.P. 2082, Tijuana), three km farther north at Km 22, offers tent/camper/RV sites with full hookups for US$12. Facilities include showers, flush toilets, ice, laundry room, pool, tennis courts, and boat ramp.

About three km south of Rosarito is **Costa del Sol,** with full hookups for US$15 per night. Most of the slots at **Popotla Trailer Park,** in the same vicinity, are occupied by long-term residents; when vacant, a space costs US$12 a night.

Food

Rosarito's Av. Juárez is jammed with restaurants of all description. The area specialties are carnitas and Puerto Nuevo-style lobster; every block seems to have at least one taco stand and one seafood restaurant. Some of the better choices are listed below.

$ **La Flor de Michoacán,** Av. Juárez 146: The Ochoa family has been making the best carnitas in town since 1950. Besides carnitas by the kilo, the menu offers tacos, tortas, burritos, and quesadillas, all served with bowls of fiery salsa, lime sections, and pickled chiles and vegetables. The service is excellent; some nights a roving group of *músicos* performs norteña music on request. A second location is at the Centro Artesanal. Open daily except Wed., 1000-2200, for breakfast, lunch, and dinner.

$$ **Derby Restaurant** (tel. 2-14-22), opposite the Rosarito Beach Hotel on Av. Juárez: This is one of Rosarito's oldest eateries and a favorite among local expats. The mostly ranchero-style Mexican menu features carne asada, chiles rellenos, enchiladas, and steak. Open daily for breakfast, lunch, and dinner.

$$ **Giuseppi's** (tel. 2-16-08), Av. Costa Azul 75, next to Chuy's Trailer Park: Formerly George's, now serving pizza, pasta, seafood, and steak.

$$ **La Fachada** (tel. 2-17-85), Av. Juárez 2884: Another expat favorite featuring steak, seafood, and Mexican plates. The ravenous can fill up on the "Sky, Sea, and Earth" platter—a quail, lobster, and steak combo. Open daily except Tues. for breakfast, lunch, and dinner.

$$ **La Leña** (tel. 2-08-26), Quinta Plaza shopping center, Av. Juárez: A branch of the well-known Tijuana steak house, specializing in Sonoran-style, mesquite-grilled meats. Most meals come with an appetizer of *machaca* (dried, shredded beef). Open daily for lunch and dinner.

$ **Los Arcos** (no phone), Av. Juárez, next to the Rosarito Beach Hotel gate: An overgrown taco stand serving tasty flautas, tacos, burritos, queso fundido, gorditas, and Mexican breakfasts. Open daily for breakfast, lunch, and dinner.

$$ **Ortega's Place:** (tel. 2-00-22) Av. Juárez 200: The Ortega family started out serving lobster dinners to tourists at their home in nearby Puerto Nuevo in 1945. As at the other Ortega's restaurants (five at last count—four

ROSARITO HOTELS AND MOTELS

Rates quoted are for peak season (May through September). Off-season rates may be discounted 30-50%. Add 15% hotel tax to all rates (some hotels may charge an additional 10% service charge).

Area code: 661

NAME	ADDRESS	TELEPHONE	RATES	FEATURES
Baja Village Motel	Blvd. Juárez and Via de las Olas	2-00-53	US$30-50	
Castillas del Mar	south of Rosarito Beach Hotel on Blvd. Juárez (P.O. Box 1772, San Ysidro, CA 92073)	2-10-88	US$50-70	ocean view
Hotel Los Pelicanos	Calle Cedros 115	2-04-45	US$35-55	some rooms with ocean view
Hotel Sonia	Blvd. Juárez next door to Panadería La Espiga	no phone	US$20-25	
Hotel El Tucan	south end of Blvd. Juárez	2-05-94	US$35	
Hotel Villanueva	Blvd. Juárez and Calle Acacias	no phone	US$20	
Marsella's Motel	Calle del Mar 75	2-04-68	US$28-30	
Motel Baja del Sol	south end of Blvd. Juárez	2-13-50	US$35-50	
Motel Colonial	Calle 1a de Mayo 71	2-15-75	US$30	kitchenettes in some rooms
Motel Don Luis de Rosarito	Blvd. Juárez 11	2-11-66	US$35	
Quinta del Mar Resort Hotel	north end of Blvd. Juárez P.O. Box 184, Rosarito, BCN)	2-13-01 (in U.S. 619-428-5500)	US$36-65 s/d, US$75-95 1-br US$115-150 2-br, US$160 3-br	condos & townhouses restaurants, pools, tennis, jacuzzi, some, rooms with ocean view
Rosarito Beach Hotel*	south end of Blvd. Juárez P.O. Box 145, San Ysidro, CA 92073 (in CA, 800-343-8582)	2-11-06	US$55 s, US$65 d	restaurants, pool, tennis and racquetball courts, fitness course, gym, sauna

* Special weekday rates of US$44 available during off-peak periods,
US$75-80 jr. suites and bungalows (with kitchenettes),
US$86-126 ocean suites (up to six persons)

in Puerto Nuevo and two in Rosarito), the house specialty is Puerto Nuevo-style lobster—split lengthwise, dropped briefly into hot oil, grilled a few minutes, and served with frijoles, rice, and tortillas. There's no better way to eat lobster. Open daily for breakfast, lunch, and dinner.

$$-$$$ Los Pelicanos (no phone), Calle Ebano and Av. Costa Azul: One of the few restaurants in town with an ocean view; good seafood, quail; upscale ambience.

$-$$ Palacio Royal (tel. 2-14-12) Plaza Comercial Ejido Mazatlán, Av. Juárez: Rosarito has three Chinese restaurants and this is the best. The menu features a variety of southern and northern China cooking styles. Open daily for lunch and dinner.

$$ Pedrin's and **La Costa:** These seafood houses owned by the Pedrin family occupy the same corner complex on Av. Juárez. Good bets are lobster burritos, fish tacos, boiled shrimp, and steak; Pedrin's also has Italian dishes.

$$-$$$ Popotla (tel. 2-15-04), Km 33 (8 km south of Rosarito): Good ocean views; good seafood. Open Mon.-Sat. for lunch and dinner, Sun. for brunch, lunch, and dinner.

$$ Rosarito Beach Hotel: The hotel's coffeeshop serves a reasonable US$7 Sunday brunch (0730-1400) that includes ceviche, chilaquiles, tamales, seafood, Mexican egg dishes, and fresh fruit. Upstairs, the **Azteca** offers more expensive lunch and seafood and Mexican fare.

$ Tacos Sonora, Centro Artesanal, next to El Nido: Serves burritos, tacos, carne asada, and quesadillas with large, Sonora-style flour tortillas.

$ Tamales Rosarito, Juárez 119: This corner stand makes great tamales, tacos, and burritos.

$$ Vince's Lobster Trap (tel. 2-12-53), Av. Juárez 39: This lobster house/seafood market is one of the contenders for best seafood restaurant in town. Lots of daily specials. A smaller version, **Vince's Grill-Bar El Calamar,** is at Av. Juárez 77.

Bakeries
Three Rosarito establishments serve the pastry cravings of tourists and local residents.

Bibi's Bakery in the Quinta Plaza shopping center makes breads, cakes, and other North American-style baked goods. **La Baguette** at Av. Juárez 137 (between Hotel Colonial and Baja Village Motel) is part of a northern Baja chain that bakes European-style fare. For Mexican pastries and bolillos, your best choice is **Panaficadora La Espiga,** across Av. Juárez from (and just a bit north of) the Rosarito Beach Hotel.

Entertainment
On weekend nights and any night in July or Aug., Rosarito throbs with a disco beat. Several clubs are concentrated just north of the Rosarito Beach Hotel, on the beach side of Av. Juárez. **Papas and Beer,** at the end of Calle Nogal, has indoor and outdoor bar areas, plus a sand volleyball court; it's packed on warm summer nights, all but deserted during the winter. Opposite Papas and Beer is the similar **Rosarito Village Beach Club.** Other dance clubs in the area change names from season to season.

The **Rosarito Beach Hotel** hosts a "Fiesta Mexicana" every Fri. evening from 1900 to 0200 in one of the ground-floor lounges. The show features folk dancing, mariachis, and charro rope tricks. The hotel's **Beachcomber Bar** overlooks the beach and is good choice for a quiet sunset drink.

Sports And Recreation
During the winter, intermittent **surf**—usually nothing huge, but surfable—may appear at either end of the beach. (Better breaks are usually found south of Rosarito, starting at Km 33, from Punta Descanso to Punta Mesquite.) **Rosarito Surf'n Sport** sells surf gear, including boards, at their shopping-mall stores attached to the Rosarito Beach and Quinta del Mar hotels.

Horseback riding on the beach is a favorite tourist activity. Local wranglers wait for customers on the beach near the Rosarito Beach Hotel and at the north end of Av. Juárez. Rates start at around US$4 per hour but are negotiable when business is slow.

Gamblers can indulge in off-track betting and sports book at **LF Race and Sports Book,** La Masia Restaurant, Hotel Quinta del

BAJA CALIFORNIA LOBSTERS

Of the several species of lobster scooting about in Baja seas, the two most numerous are *Panulirus interruptus* (known as red lobster or *langosta roja*), found as far south as the 25th parallel on both the Pacific and Sea of Cortez sides, and *P. inflatus* (blue lobster or *langosta azul*) in the Pacific and lower Cortez as far south as Tehuantepec, Oaxaca. None of the lobster species found in Baja waters are related to the cold-water type (genus *Homarus*) found off the coast of the northeastern U.S. and southeastern Canada. Baja's warm-water lobsters are sometimes referred to as "spiny lobsters" because their shells bear spiny projections (the *Homarus* shell is smooth). Spiny lobsters also have smaller pincers than the cold-water varieties.

Adult spiny lobsters reach up to 61 centimeters (24 inches) in length and weigh as much as six kilograms (13 pounds). Most varieties are nocturnal and tend to frequent depths of five to 30 meters. During the daytime they stay beneath or between rocks to hide from their natural enemies (sharks, octopus, rays, and a few larger finfish). Their diet consists mostly of crustaceans, mollusks, and other small sea organisms.

Lobstering is a major part of the fishing industry in Mexico, the world's eighth-largest harvester of lobster. In 1989, 700 metric tons were harvested; about half of the total catch was exported, earning around US$9 million in foreign revenues. The official lobstering seasons are: 16 March to 30 Sep. (red lobster) and 1 June to 15 Sep. (blue lobster). It is illegal to take lobsters out of Mexico unless accompanied by a receipt that shows they were purchased from a store or a *cooperativa de pesca* (fishing cooperative).

Mar or at **Caliente Race And Sports Book,** Quinta Plaza shopping center.

Charreadas are occasionally held at small charro rings near town—check with the tourist office on Av. Juárez for the latest schedule.

Events

Twice yearly on the last Saturday in April and October, Rosarito kicks off the **Rosarito-Ensenada 50-Mile Bicycle Ride.** For details, see "Holidays, Festivals, and Events," p. 83. Bajacalifornio food fans won't want to miss the **Mexican Food Festival** held in early May or the **Rosarito Beach Seafood Fair** in late June (usually Father's Day), when chefs from the Rosarito area compete for your palate. For up-to-date information on Rosarito's ongoing schedule of events, call (661) 2-03-96.

Shopping

Rosarito has a representative sampling of the same kinds of retail outlets found in Tijuana—liquor stores, pharmacies, curio shops, furniture stores, leather shops, and boutiques—specializing in North American tastes. **Tile Express** (tel. 2-19-13, Av. Juárez 54A), for example, is a branch of the larger Tijuana store. Many shops are grouped in shopping plazas, e.g., Plaza Ejido Mazatlán, Quinta Plaza, and the arcade attached to the Rosarito Beach Hotel.

On the east side of Av. Juárez, about midway between the Quinta del Mar and Rosarito Beach hotels, is the **Mercado de Artesanías,** a crafts market with around 200 vendors selling ceramics, textiles, wood carving, sculpture, and other handmade items. Just south of town is a string of vendor stalls where handicraft prices tend to be a bit lower. Bargaining is expected; most vendors are open 0900-1800.

Transport

Mexicoach (tel. 619-232-5049 in the U.S.; 800-628-3745 in Alta California) has a direct daily service from their Tijuana terminal (Av. Madero and Calle 7a) to Rosarito for US$10 roundtrip. Buses leave the Av. Madero terminal every two hours 1000-1600 and return on a similar schedule 1100-1700. (Call to confirm departure times as they may vary seasonally.) In Rosarito the bus leaves and picks up passengers at the Quinta del Mar and Rosarito

Beach hotels; the trip takes about an hour each way.

Public buses from Tijuana (45 minutes, US$1) and Ensenada (1½ hours, US$2) arrive hourly from dawn to dusk at Rosarito's Av. Juárez terminal.

Driving to Rosarito: The drive from Tijuana to Rosarito is 31 km via the toll road, 27 km via the free road. The toll road (Mexico 1-D) is much faster since it has four lanes in each direction, no traffic lights, and a maximum speed limit of 110 km per hour (about 65 mph). The toll-road entrance is situated just south of the Río Tijuana; the toll as far as Rosarito costs about US$2.

To take the free road (Mexico 1) from Tijuana you'll need to find Blvd. Cuauhtémoc by driving east on either Paseo de los Héroes or Blvd. Agua Caliente, then turning south on Cuauhtémoc. Coming from San Diego, you can avoid Tijuana altogether by crossing the border at Otay Mesa (east of Tijuana), then following signs for Tecate. Instead of taking the turnoff for Mexico 2 to Tecate, continue straight on Blvd. Lázaro Cárdenas (which becomes Blvd. Independencia or "Libramiento-Oriente") until the road intersects with Mexico 1—follow signs reading "Ensenada Libre."

Gasoline: Rosarito has two PEMEX stations, both offering unleaded gas; the one near the Hotel Quinta del Mar is open 24 hours.

Rosarito Information

The city tourist office (tel. 2-03-69), next to the police station on Av. Juárez between Calles Olivo and Acacias, distributes Rosarito area tourist information; the staff can also assist with hotel reservations. If you need information on other destinations in northern Baja, the state tourist office (tel. 2-10-65) at Calle Cipres and Av. Costa Azul may be able to help. There is also an information kiosk at Quinta Plaza on Av. Juárez, but it appears to be closed most of the time.

The monthly *Baja Times,* published out of an office in the Rosarito Beach Hotel shopping arcade, is an excellent source of information on local events. It's distributed free at several shops and hotels in town.

Rosarito's telephone area code is 661.

ROSARITO TO ENSENADA

South of Rosarito along the coast are a string of beaches, ejidos, and residential communities: Popotla, Las Gaviotas, Puerto Nuevo, Cantamar, El Descanso, La Fonda, La Misión, La Salina, Bajamar, and San Miguel. Real estate developers call it the "Gold Coast," but except for the coves and beaches they're sometimes built around, the communities themselves are not particularly attractive.

Between Punta Descanso and Punta Mesquite (especially Km 33-38, Km 48, Km 56 on the free road), and as far south as La Misión, are several surfing spots with decent reef or beach breaks. An area of sand dunes near Km 54 south of Cantamar is frequented by handgliding enthusiasts.

Puerto Nuevo

This tiny seaside town is known as Baja's lobster capital. Although the actual lobster harvest in the area isn't what it once was, lobster restaurants are more plentiful than ever (the lobster served in Puerto Nuevo is mostly harvested in areas south of Ensenada). When Baja travelers first discovered Puerto Nuevo in the '50s, one dined in the houses of two or three local families. Now the village has close to 30 seafood restaurants, some of them quite modern.

The typical Puerto Nuevo-style lobster platter includes lobster, beans, rice, and tortillas. The lobster is usually lightly fried in oil and then briefly grilled before serving, but it can also be ordered in a *ranchera* (tomato and chile) sauce, or boiled, new England-style. The Ortega family was the first to serve lobster platters to the public and their original **Ortega's** still stands, along with three other branches nearby (and two in Rosarito). Other family-run favorites include **Ponderosa, Chela's,** and **La Perlita.**

Accommodations: The recently completed **Hotel New Port Baja** (tel. 661-4-11-66; 619-422-6918 or 800-678-7244 in the U.S.) has deluxe ocean-view rooms starting at US$50 a night midweek, US$80 on weekends and holidays. Facilities include a pool, jacuzzi, volleyball court, tennis courts, and coffeeshop.

RV Parks: Just south of Puerto Nuevo are two RV facilities, **Cantamar** (P.O. Box 295, San Ysidro, CA 92073), at Cantamar Beach, and **Rancho Reynosa** (A.P. 640, Rosarito, BCN), about 2½ km north of the Cantamar toll road exit on the free road.

La Fonda And La Misión

This area, approximately 60 km south of the border (take La Misión exit from the toll road), features the best beaches between Rosarito and Ensenada. At one time the valley surrounding La Misión sheltered Mission San Miguel Arangel de la Frontera, founded by Dominican Padre Luis Salles in 1788 and secularized in 1833. The only remains of the mission are two adobe walls standing in a schoolyard on the east side of the free road as it passes through the village.

Accommodations: Two small, comfortable, well-run hotels offer opportunities for overnights in the area. **Hotel La Fonda** (no phone; mailing address: P.O. Box 268, San Ysidro, CA 92073) has rooms for US$35 and ocean-front apartments that accommodate up to four persons for US$50. La Fonda's restaurant serves good seafood with an ocean view. Overlooking the broad beach at La Misión is **Hotel La Misión** (tel. 213-420-8500 in the U.S.), a newer establishment with 10 large rooms, all with fireplace, for US$45 a night Sun.-Thurs. or US$58 Fri.-Saturday. The hotel has a restaurant and a small grocery store.

San Miguel

A unique cross between retirement-oriented trailer park and surf camp, San Miguel is the legacy of a Polish-Mexican-American family, the Robertsons, who have been in northern Mexico and southern Alta California for most of this century. The late Tomás Robertson, who founded the Villa de San Miguel residential community in the '50s, was a mission historian and an active member of the Comite por Conservación de Misións de Baja California. His son Glen now manages the trailer park, bar, and restaurant with aplomb.

The bay formed by Punta San Miguel is the most popular surfing locale in Baja (Mexico's first surfboard manufacturer—San Miguel—is named after the point). A few hard-core surfers live in San Miguel on a semipermanent basis, and during the winter a small legion takes up residence on the beach or in rented trailers. On winter evenings, those who aren't partying in Ensenada (or exhausted by the day's surfing) hang out in the San Miguel Restaurant bar and tell war stories about the three-story waves at Islas de Todos Santos.

Accommodations and Food: Camping is permitted on the beach for US$5 per night; full-hookup trailer sites are US$8. Trailers on the hill above the beach are sometimes for rent at US$25-30 a night (inquire at the restaurant, call 4-62-25, or write: San Miguel Village, A.P. 55, El Sauzal, BCN), but check to see if the water supply is working before accepting an offer. The water pressure in the trailers near the top of the hill is sometimes low or even absent altogether. (For permanent trailers with their own water storage tanks, this isn't a problem; for the rest, the village has plans to upgrade the community system.) Occasionally a trailer slot on the hill opens up.

The San Miguel Restaurant serves good northern Mexican dishes (including excellent chiles rellenos), steak, seafood, and frog legs. A fireplace adds to the cozy atmosphere on chilly winter evenings.

Another lodging possibility is **Motel Sausalito** (tel. 667-4-61-88) at Km 102+ on Mexico 1 in nearby El Sauzal. Although it has no beach or scenic views, the hotel is comfortable enough and has a pool and restaurant. Rooms are US$35 s/d per night. Also in El Sauzal is the **California Trailer Park & Motel** (tel. 667-4-60-33), where RV sites are US$8 a night, basic rooms US$30. About four km north of San Miguel at **Playa Saldamando** is a campground with tent/camper sites (water only) for US$6-8 a night.

Events: The **Flojo Mexican Surf Fiesta,** sponsored by a maker of Mexican fisherman-style sandals, is usually held in San Miguel the last weekend in April and features surfing competitions, food, and bikini contests. The village celebrates **San Miguel's feast day** on

ISLAS DE TODO SANTOS

RADIO TOWER/
LIGHTHOUSE

ISLA
NORTE

FISH CAMP

ISLA SUR

PACIFIC OCEAN

100m/313 ft

FISH
CAMP

NOT TO SCALE

LIGHTHOUSE

© MOON PUBLICATIONS, INC.

the nearest weekend to Sept. 29; sometimes a group of Paipai Indians from San Miguel Valley joins the festivities. Another big party is held in late October at San Miguel in honor of **Oktoberfest,** when the restaurant opens an all-you-can-eat, all- you-can-drink bar and buffet.

Getting There: San Miguel can be difficult to locate on the first attempt. Driving south on the toll road, take the Tijuana Libre exit just past the tollgate at Km 99, then follow the road west (across the toll road) until it curves south and begins to merge with the toll road a half-km farther. Instead of returning to the highway, follow the unpaved road to the right and you'll come to San Miguel Village. (If you're arriving via the free road, just remember to take this unpaved road almost immediately before merging with the four-lane highway.)

From Ensenada, you can make a U-turn immediately before the tollgate to find the road into the village. To get here by public transport from Ensenada, take a Tijuana-bound bus and get off at the tollgate; then follow the above directions on foot.

Islas De Todos Santos

These twin islands about 20 km (12 miles) southwest of San Miguel (or west of Ensenada the same distance) offer a variety of recrea-

tional opportunities. Fishing is good along the western shores of both islands, especially for yellowtail, halibut, and seabass. For longer visits, boats can safely anchor in three coves along the eastern shore of the southern island; the middle cove offers the best shelter overall. Local anglers stay at seasonal fish camps at the southern ends of both islands.

For hikers, the southern island has the most interesting terrain, with cliffs along the perimeter and a hilly interior. The highest elevation, just below the island's midpoint, is approximately 100 meters. Near the northern end of this island are several caves and at the southern tip are a few tidal pools worth exploring. The northern island is mostly flat, with a radio tower and two lighthouses (one abandoned, one in use). Both islands are nesting grounds for brown pelicans, cormorants, blue herons, ospreys, and various other bird species.

Surfing: Islas de Todos Santos is perhaps most well-known as site of the Pacific coast's biggest, baddest surf. November through Feb., a deep-water northwest swell sweeps the skinny northwestern point (partially submerged at high tide) of Isla Norte to produce powerful, eight- to 10-meter (25-30 feet) waves. Dubbed "Killer's," this is a break best attempted only by experienced gunners—unless it's running small. As a rule of thumb, Todos surfers estimate that whatever height the surf at San Miguel is running, waves at Isla Norte will be double plus 2½ meters (eight feet).

The northwest corner of the southern island also has an excellent winter break. When the northwest swell is rolling hard, the channel between the two islands conjures up a monumental, long-riding right called Thor's Hammer, formed by the confluence of direct swell movement toward this point and refracted swell as it wraps eastward around the north island, then bounces off the south island and into the channel. This same channel pumps a grinding left break during the summer southwest swell, making the islands a year-round surf destination. Surfers sometimes camp on the flat northern island, but most boat in for the day from San Miguel or Ensenada.

Getting There: Small-boat charters can be arranged for approximately US$20 roundtrip at Gordo's Landing in Ensenada, at fish camps in Punta Banda (south of Ensenada), or sometimes in San Miguel. San Miguel surfers with their own boats will usually agree to take along a passenger or two if they buy gas for the trip and beer for the day's survivors.

ENSENADA

INTRODUCTION

Every summer an estimated four million visitors—most of them North Americans—pass through Ensenada, far more than any other non-border town (the border is 104 km north) on the peninsula. Yet as a busy trade center for northern peninsula fishing and agriculture, the city retains a Bajacalifornio identity in spite of weekend and summer tourism.

Ensenada is the capital of the Municipio de Ensenada, Mexico's largest municipality (roughly corresponding to a county in the U.S.), extending all the way to the BCS border for 52,511 square km and covering two-thirds of Baja California Norte. The municipality has a population of around half a million; estimates for the city itself vary from 150,000 to 250,000. It's difficult to keep an exact count since there are so many semipermanent residents in the Ensenada area, including an estimated 36,000 North Americans.

Baja California's third-largest city (after Tijuana and Mexicali) is also the peninsula's largest seaport due to its position on the wide Bahía de Todos Santos. The main industries in the area—aside from tourism—are fishing, fish processing, and agriculture, all of which rely on the bay as a shipping point for sending their products to mainland Mexico, the U.S., Canada, and Asia. Olives and grapes are the principal crops produced in the Ensenada area; the huge Oliveres Mexicanos plantation (48 km northeast of Ensenada, near Guadalupe) is the world's largest single olive producer, with over 120,000 trees under cultivation. Yellowtail and halibut are the top fish harvests, followed by various bottom fishes, lobster and other shellfish, and anchovies.

Although some old Baja hands buzz right past Ensenada in a rush to get to the "real Baja" farther south, for many repeat visitors a Baja trip simply doesn't get off to a good start without a ritual *cerveza* at Hussong's or a couple of *tacos de pescado* from the harbor fish market. Is Ensenada Americanized? Undeniably a hybrid culture, Mexican tourists prefer the town to San Felipe or Cabo San Lucas; once you escape the waterfront area, though, you'll find neighborhood *panaderías,* quiet residential streets—and few tourists of any nationality.

CLIMATE AND TOURIST SEASONS

Ensenada's climate is similar to San Diego's. Yearly rainfall amounts to about 25 centimeters (10 inches), most of which falls Oct.-May. Temperatures are mild year-round, averaging 7-18° C (45-64° F) in January and 17-24° C (63-75° F) in August.

The high tourist season is June-Aug., when the weather is warm and rain is a rare occurrence. Christmas-New Year's holidays (late Dec. through early Jan.) and spring break (late March through early April) are also peak periods. To avoid the crowds, consider visiting Ensenada in Oct.-Nov. or April-May.

HISTORY

In pre-Hispanic times, nomadic Yumano Indian tribes occasionally stopped at Bahía de Todos Santos to fish and gather clams, but no permanent Indian settlements existed in the area upon the initial arrival of Spanish missionaries in the 18th century. The first Spaniard to lay eyes on the bay was explorer Juan Cabrillo, who in 1542 named it San Mateo. Sebastián Vizcaíno's subsequent voyage in 1602 lent a different name to this piece of

California coastal geography—Ensenada de Todos Santos, or "All Saint's Cove." Most likely this referred to a smaller cross-section of the bay—possibly the estuary where the Río San Carlos empties into the bay's south end—but eventually the entire bay came to be known as Bahía de Todos Santos.

Following a Spanish land grant to José Manuel Ruíz in 1804, several small farms and ranches were established in the hills east of the bay, including Ruíz's own Rancho Ensenada. A Spanish sergeant, Francisco Gastelum, bought and expanded the ranch in 1824. Following Mexican independence, the discovery of gold at nearby Real del Castillo in 1870 brought miners to the area; the miners needed supplies, and Ensenada (named for Gastelum's ranch) bloomed into a port practically overnight.

In 1882 Ensenada was made capital of the Territory of Baja California, and the town continued to attract miners, farmers, and a variety of entrepreneurs who came to take advantage of the town's increasing prosperity. The boom lasted until the early 1900s, when few significant gold deposits remained and the political

ENSENADA

situation in the border area was becoming increasingly unstable. In order to counter growing Anglo-American influence along the border, the territorial capital was moved to Mexicali in 1915.

Ensenada faded into a farming and fishing village again until the U.S. Prohibition years revived the economy. In the late '20s, heavyweight boxer Jack Dempsey and a number of other Americans opened the Playa Ensenada Hotel and Casino, a grand Spanish-style structure overlooking the bay. Along with Tijuana and Mexicali, Ensenada became a favorite destination for the American drinking-and-gambling set until Prohibition's repeal in 1933 and Mexico's closing of all casinos in 1938. The Playa Ensenada casino-hotel was converted to a resort hotel under a new name, the Riviera del Pacífico, but, unable to attract guests in sufficient numbers, it soon closed. About this same time, Valle de Mexicali agriculture expanded rapidly (following the government's agrarian reforms), and Ensenada's function as a port was steadily upgraded.

Throughout the '40s and '50s the Ensenada area became a favorite destination for sportfishers and earned its title as "Yellowtail Capital of the World." Although increased commercial fishing and shipping have lowered the bay's value as a sportfishing destination, over-all economic development has fostered a cosmopolitan atmosphere, as Ensenada continues to cultivate its split personality as both tourist center and seaport.

SIGHTS

Ensenada's dual character—half resort, half commercial center—is split into two grids by Av. Juárez in the center of the city. The portion of the city south of Juárez, toward the bay, is mostly given over to tourist-oriented businesses, while the portion to the north consists of local businesses that might be found in any Mexican city. Most of the city's hotels, restaurants, and gift shops are found along Blvd. Costero and Av. López Mateos, two parallel streets close to the waterfront.

Many of Ensenada's visual attractions are out of town—at Estero Beach, Punta Banda, and La Bufadora—but a number of places of interest in the city can be visited on foot.

Riviera Del Pacífico
Ensenada's most impressive edifice opened in 1929 as the Playa Ensenada Hotel and Casino, owned and operated by Jack Dempsey and his financial backers (Al Capone was reputed to be a silent partner). The opening act in the hotel's ballroom was Bing

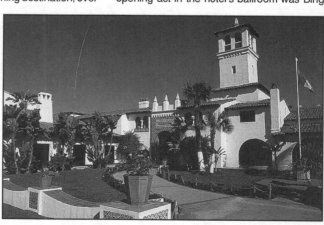

Riviera del Pacífico
(JOE CUMMINGS)

Crosby, backed by the Xavier Cugat Orchestra; the orchestra included a singer named Margarita Carmen Cansino, a Baja native later known as Rita Hayworth. Facing the bay, the hotel's massive white-walled, red-roofed, palm-encircled exterior became a prime symbol of the city's prosperity.

Like Tijuana's El Casino del Agua Caliente and Rosarito's Rosarito Beach Hotel, Playa Ensenada was a big hit with the Hollywood crowd until Prohibition was repealed in 1933. The casino's management converted it into the Hotel Riviera del Pacífico but, deprived of its gambling clientele and suffering the effects of the '30s Depression, the hotel closed and fell into disrepair shortly thereafter.

In 1977 the city decided to restore the structure and turn it into the **Centro Social Cívico y Cultural de Ensenada** ("Social, Civic, and Cultural Center of Ensenada"). The various ballrooms and halls of the former hotel are now hired out for civic events, conventions, weddings, art exhibits, and other public and private occasions. One of the wings houses several municipal agencies and another a small public library. The city is planning to erect a new convention center adjacent to the former hotel.

Much of the building's original interior tilework, murals, and painted ceilings remain intact; a bar in the rear portion of the building, near the parking lot, is an excellent place for a quiet drink. Visitors are welcome to tour the premises daily between 0900 and 1700. The Riviera del Pacífico is located at the corner of Avenidas Costero and Riviera—it's hard to miss since it's the largest structure along Av. Costero.

Wineries

Two Ensenada wineries are open to the public. **Bodegas de Santo Tomás** (tel. 8-25-09, 4-08-36, Av. Miramar 666) is the oldest winery on the peninsula, a direct descendant of the Dominicans' first Valle de San Tomás harvest in 1791. The winery sold its first wine to the public, by the barrel, in 1888. In 1934, the Bodegas moved its winemaking operation to Ensenada, where it has remained ever since. The grapes used in their wines continue to be grown in the Santo Tomás area as well as other northern Baja valleys.

The winery's current facilities cover 1½ city blocks in downtown Ensenada and produce over a half million cases of wine annually. Master vintners employ around 30 different varietals to produce wine, sherry, port, brandy, and champagne-style sparkling wine. Public tours of the winery (in English) are offered daily at 1100, 1300, and 1500. The tours last about an hour and cost US$2 per person; each tour ends in the wood-paneled tasting room, where a variety of vintages can be tasted (bread and cheese are served along with the wines). Bottles of Santo Tomás wine can be purchased in the tasting room for prices ranging from US$3 for a table wine to US$12 for a 1978 private-reserve cabernet. (The '84 cab is a steal at US$5.50.)

On Friday evenings during the summer, the Bodegas hosts jazz and classical music performances in the winery's Barrel Room.

The other Ensenada winery open to the public is **Cavas Valmar** (tel. 8-64-05, Calle Ambar 810), at the northern edge of town. Although Valmar's history (and range of wines) can't compare with that of Bodegas de Santo Tomás, its wine products are worth investigating. Winetasting tours leave hourly on Thursday and Saturday between 1100 and 1400 (no charge).

Nuestra Señora De Guadalupe

This cathedral at Av. Floresta and Calle 6a exhibits a standard-issue, Mexican colonial-style architecture, though the stained-glass windows are well executed. The best times to visit the cathedral are during the Fiesta Guadalupano (Día de Nuestra Señora de Guadalupe, 12-13 Dec.) or Las Posadas (16-25 Dec.), when the interior is filled with candles and worshipers.

El Mirador ("Viewpoint")

The Chapultepec Hills rise along the city's west side and afford a city and bay view. To find the viewpoint, follow Calle 2a west until it terminates at Av. Alemán; then turn right and follow the road to the top.

BAJACALIFORNIO WINE

Ensenada is the unofficial capital of Mexico's finest winemaking region, northern Baja. Most North Americans are unaware of the quality of Mexican wines and assume rum and tequila are all the bar has to offer. Bajacalifornio wines are, in fact, shipped all over Mexico and western Europe, but because of current U.S. trade policies, they are not exported to the United States. This may change if the U.S.-Mexico-Canada free-trade agreement, presently under discussion, is passed. Meanwhile, if you want to taste wines produced in northern Baja, you can go to the source.

History

Although the first wine produced on the peninsula was made by Jesuit monks at Misión San Javier near Loreto in the early 1700s, as the missionaries moved northward it became clear that the best areas for viniculture were the temperate valleys of northern Baja.

In 1791, Dominican Padre José Lorieto founded Misión Santo Tomás and planted the first Spanish vinifera in the Valle de Santo Tomás (45 km south of Ensenada). The product, a variety simply called "Mission," was used mainly for sacramental purposes but was high-

ly regarded by padres throughout the mission system. (In many places in Mexico, mission wine had to be imported.) Following secularization of this mission, Bodegas de Santo Tomás took over the vineyards and in 1888 started selling wine by the barrel in booming Ensenada. In 1906, some 500 Russian immigrants settled the Valle de Guadalupe and cultivated extensive vineyards; other winemakers, including the Italian family of oenologist Angel Cetto, followed the success of the Santo Tomás and Guadalupe operations and began viniculture in valleys near Tecate, San Vicente, Guadalupe, Mexicali, and Ensenada.

Wines And Winemakers

Today some 28 viniculturists and labels compete in northern Baja, among them Bacco, Calafia, Cetto, Domecq, Santo Tomás, Valmar, Don Miguel, Sol de España, Champbrulé, and Viña Real. The highest-producing valleys, in descending order, are Ensenada, Guadalupe, San Vicente, Mexicali, Tijuana, and Tecate. Smaller ejido operations exist in El Porvenir, Ajusco, and Chapultepec.

Among the varietals produced in Baja are Mission, Zinfandel, Cabernet Sauvignon, Barbera, Valdepeñas, Cariñana, Grenache, Ruby Cabernet, Petit Sirah, Merlot, Pinto Noir, Gamay, Chenin Blanc, Palomino, French Colombard, Muscatel, White Riesling, and Pinot Blanc. The best Bajacalifornio wines are said to be made from grapes cultivated in the Guadalupe and San Vicente valleys, where red varietals predominate.

To learn more about Baja wines (and to sample some vintages), join one of the daily tours offered at Bodegas de Santo Tomás or Cavas Valmar in Ensenada.

ACCOMMODATION

Hotels And Motels
See the "Ensenada Hotels and Motels" chart.

Camping And RV Parks
Trailer parks are scattered north and south of the city. Because of competition, rates tend to be a bit lower than at many other tourist centers in Baja; if occupancy is low, or if you plan to stay longer than a night or two, you can negotiate to receive even lower rates.

About two km south of the town center is **Campo Playa RV Park** (tel. 6-29-18), at Av. Lázardo Cárdenas (Blvd. Costero) and Av. Delante (Calle Sangines). Although the nearby boulevards mean this isn't the quietest trailer park in the area, it's the closest to downtown Ensenada—within walking distance, in fact. Tent/RV sites are US$8 per night for two persons, plus US$1 for each additional person.

At Ejido Chapultepec, eight km south of town between Estero and Hermosa beaches, are **Corona Beach, Playa Mona Lisa,** and **El Faro,** all with full hookups for US$8-10 a night depending on the season. Frequent buses, marked "Chapultepec," ply the route between this neighborhood and the city center.

The **Joker Hotel and Trailer Park** (tel. 6-72-01), across the highway from El Ciprés Airport in Ejido Chapultepec, has around 30 full-hookup sites (no tents) with cable TV for US$10 a night. RVers are permitted to use hotel facilities, including the pool and jacuzzi.

For information on camping and RV parks at Estero Beach, La Jolla, and Punta Banda—12-20 km south of Ensenada—see "Vicinity of Ensenada" below. See "San Miguel," p. 170, for information on camping/RV parks north of Ensenada.

FOOD

Ensenada has just about every kind of restaurant imaginable, but seafood and Northern Mexican (ranchero-style) food are the city's culinary strong suits. *Tacos de pescado* (fish tacos) are an Ensenada specialty, usually made from fresh yellowtail or halibut fillets cut in strips, deep-fried in a light batter, and served in folded corn tortillas with salsa, guacamole, and a touch of mayonnaise or sour cream.

Seafood stands are scattered throughout the city, many of them selling *cocteles* (spicy shellfish cocktails) and **ceviche** (a lime-marinated seafood salad). Clams *(almejas),* abalone *(abulón),* shrimp *(camarones),* and oysters *(ostiones)* are the most popular cocktails. The healthiest stands are those using purified water (usually clearly displayed in large bottles) to wash ingredients and utensils before preparing each dish.

Speaking of cocktails, the *clamato,* a beverage made from clams, tomato and lime juice, Mexican spices, and vodka, was probably invented in Ensenada. They're nothing like the pale imitations served north of the border—a good one will come half-filled with fresh clams.

If you don't like seafood on your plate or in your glass, try other Ensenada specialties like *tacos de carne asada* (grilled beef tacos), Sinaloa-style grilled or roasted chicken, or one of the many varieties of burritos available. Several restaurants also specialize in American and continental cuisines.

Seafood
$$ **Casamar** (tel. 4-04-17), Blvd. Costero 987: Offers a wide selection of reasonably priced, freshly prepared seafood in a tourist-oriented atmosphere. Open daily for lunch and dinner.
$$ **Haliotis** (tel. 6-37-20), Calle Delante 174: The name sounds Greek but is actually the Latin genus term for abalone, the house specialty. Other seafood here is consistent as well; the family owners frequently fly fresh fish in from Isla Cedros, where they have another restaurant. Open daily except Tues. for lunch and dinner.
$$ **Hussong's Pelicano** (tel. 4-45-75), three km north of town, off Mexico 1 at Quintas Papagayo Beach Resort Motel: Juan Hussong of Hussong's Cantina fame opened this restaurant to offer Baja regional cuisine with an emphasis on fresh seafood, including lobster, shrimp, clams, and scallops. The Mexican combos are good, too. Open daily for

ENSENADA HOTELS AND MOTELS

Rates quoted are for midweek, peak season (May through Sept.). Off-season rates may be discounted; weekend and holiday rates may be higher. Add 15% hotel tax to all rates (some hotels may charge an additional 10% service charge). Area code: 667

NAME	ADDRESS	TELEPHONE	RATES	FEATURES
DOWNTOWN				
America	Av. López Mateos 1309	8-27-15	US$20-30	kitchenettes, parking
Bahia	Av. López Mateos between Riveroll and Alvarado	8-21-01 (fax 8-14-55)	US$55 US$75-100 suites	restaurant, parking, some rooms with bay view (winter midweek rates as low as US$28)
Balboa	Av. Vicente Guerrero 172	6-10-77	US$25	
Best Western Casa del Sol	Av. López Mateos 1001 (A.P. 557, Ensenada, BCN)	8-15-70 (in U.S. 800-528-1234)	US$48 s, US$55-65 d	a/c, restaurant, pool, parking
Best Western Cortez	Av. López Mateos 1089 (A.P. 396, Ensenada, BCN)	8-23-07 (in U.S. 800-528-1234)	US$50-60	a/c, restaurant, pool, parking
Corona	Blvd. Costero 1442	6-09-01 (fax 6-40-23)	US$55-65	bay view, a/c, heat, restaurant, pool, parking
Coronado	Av. López Mateos 1275	6-16-16	US$30	
El Cid	Av. López Mateos 993	8-24-01	US$52-72	a/c, refrigerators, restaurant, coffee shop, parking
Ensenada Travelodge	Av. Blancarte 130	8-16-01 in U.S. (900-255-3050)	US$50	restaurant, pool, parking
Fiesta Inn	Av. Sangines 237	6-13-61	US$30	pool, parking, discounts for long-term stays
Gonzalez	Av. Pedro Loyola 150	6-34-77	US$15-18	parking
La Pinta	Av. Floresta and Blvd. Bucaneros (P.O. Box 120637, Chula Vista, CA 92012)	6-26-01 (in U.S. 800-336-5454)	US$58 s, US$69 d	restaurant, pool, parking
Las Palmas	Calle 3a 326	8-27-88	US$18	kitchenettes in some rooms, restaurant, pool, jacuzzi, parking
Mexico	Av. Ruíz and Calle 4a (P.O. Box 1817, San Ysidro, CA 92073)	8-30-93, 4-05-73 (fax 8-32-95)	US$36-54	historic building, coffee shop, parking

ENSENADA HOTELS AND MOTELS (CONT.)

NAME	ADDRESS	TELEPHONE	RATES	FEATURES
Misión Santa Isabel	Av. Castillo 1100 (A.P. 76, Ensenada, BCN)	8-36-16 (in U.S. (619-942-9108)	US$45-65, US$75 for jr. suite	restaurant, pool, parking
Playa	Av. López Mateos 1487	6-14-30	US$30-35	parking
Rudi's	Av. Hidalgo 450	6-32-45	US$25	parking
San Nicolás	Av. López Mateos and Blancarte (P.O. Box 4C, San Ysidro, CA 92073)	6-19-01	US$70-80 s, US$80-90 d	a/c, restaurant, coffee shop, pool, jacuzzi, many rooms with bay view
Villa Marina	Av. López Mateos and Blancarte (P.O. Box 727, Bonita, CA 92002)	8-33-21	US$55-65	coffeeshop, pool, parking
Villa Fontana	Av. López Mateos 1050	8-34-34, 8-38-37	US$45-55	a/c, heat, coffeeshop, parking
OUT OF TOWN				
Costa Mar	Calle Veracruz 319 (1½ km south of town)	6-64-25	US$35	parking, near beach (Playa Hermosa)
Estero Beach	Estero Beach, 12 km south of town (A.P. 86, Ensenada, BCN)	6-62-35 (in U.S. (800-762-2494), fax 6-69-25	US$40-80 US$62-250 for suites	restaurant, tennis courts, boat ramp, boat rentals, horseback riding, all rooms with beach view
Joker	Mexico 1, eight km south of town (Ejido Chapultepec)	6-72- 01		restaurant, pool, jacuzzi, opposite Cipres Airport
Joya Mar	Av. Veracruz 360	6-74-30	US$35	restaurant, pool, parking, near Playa Hermosa
Las Rosas	Mexico 1, six km north of town (A.P. 316, Ensenada, BCN)	4-43-10, 4-43-20, (in U.S. 800-829-2252) fax 4-45-95	US$85-110	restaurant, pool, jacuzzi, sauna, exercise center, racquetball court, all rooms with ocean view
Punta Morro	Mexico 1, five km north of town (mailing address: P.O. Box 4263, San Ysidro, CA 92073)	8-35-07	US$60-90 with kitchens, US$95-115 2-br apts., US$140-155 3-br apts.	pool
Quintas Papagayo	Mexico 1, three km north of town (A.P. 150, Ensenada, BCN)	4-45-75	US$40-60 US$80 for 2-br apts.	restaurant, pool, jacuzzi, tennis courts

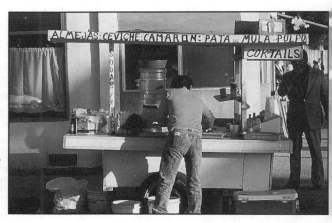

mariscos vendor
(JOE CUMMINGS)

breakfast, lunch, and dinner. A varied Mexican brunch buffet is served Sat.-Sun. 0800-1600. $-$$ **Kiki's** (tel. 6-54-60), Calle Sangines 6 (near Blvd. Costero). Dependable seafood, plus steaks and Mexican, but most known for its inexpensive breakfasts. Open daily for breakfast, lunch, and dinner.

$$-$$$ **La Cueva de Los Tigres ("The Tiger's Cave")** (tel. 6-64-50) Calle Acapulco and Las Palmas, Playa Hermosa: Driving south toward Estero Beach, you can't miss the signs for the Tiger's Cave, about two km out of town. A favorite with the old-timers, this beachfront restaurant is famous for abalone in crab sauce. Some folks rave about this place while others say it's overpriced and overrated. Open daily 0900-2330.

$-$$ **Los Manueles** (no phone), two locations: Calle Sangines at Bucaneros, and Av. Cortés at Belisario Dominguez. Reliable Sinaloa-style seafood with another overriding attraction: both locations are open 24 hours.

$-$$ **Mariscos Playa Azul** (tel. 4-06-22), Av. Riveroll 113: This plain but clean, family-run restaurant is a personal seafood favorite for quality and value. A plate of three lobster burritos—the best around—with all the trimmings costs only US$8. (Other dishes start at US$3.60.) Also on the menu are abalone, octopus, squid, fish filleted or whole—steamed, fried, or roasted—oysters on the

halfshell, and several delicious seafood soups. Very popular with locals, so consider eating during North American dining hours (i.e., noon-1300 and 1800-2000 rather than 1400-1800 and 2000-2200) to avoid the crowds. Open daily for lunch and dinner.

$ **Mercado de Mariscos ("Seafood Market"),** Blvd. Costero and Miramar, on the harbor: A real fish market, not a restaurant, where vendors serve fresh shrimp, octopus, squid, clams, lobster, tuna, abalone, halibut, yellowtail, and more. This is the best, and most inexpensive, place in town for fish tacos. Open daily from late morning until early evening.

Mexican

$$ **Acambero (El Refugio Ensenadense)** (tel. 6-52-35), Av. Iturbide 528 (off Av. Juárez between Calles 5a and 6a): Traditional northern Mexican dishes—pozole, mole, birria, chilaquiles, chiles rellenos, enchiladas—are freshly prepared and served with bowls of limes, oregano, and salsas, in a rustic but tasteful wood-and-brick decor. No alcohol is sold in this off-the-tourist-track restaurant, but Sangría Señorial makes a delicious stand-in. Delicious Mexican *postres* (desserts), too. Open daily for breakfast, lunch, and dinner.

$-$$ **Domico's** (tel. 8-13-75) Av. Ruíz 283 (between Calles 2a and 3a): Known for authentic Sonoran *machaca* (jerked meat) and seafood. Open daily for breakfast, lunch, and dinner.

$$ Carlos 'n Charlie's (tel. 8-15-54), Blvd. Costero 253: A branch of the famous Puerto Vallarta gringo-Mexican venture, with at least a few of the same attributes—flea-market decor, a raucous atmosphere, strong drinks, and large servings of Mexican food, seafood, or steak. Open daily noon-midnight.

$-$$ El Charro (tel. 8-38-81), Av. Mateos 475: Popular with locals and tourists alike for tasty roast chicken, homemade chicken tamales, *pollo pipian* (chicken cooked in a pumpkin-seed mole), burritos, and botanas of all kinds. Fresh tortillas are handmade on the spot. Beverages include *jamaica,* a refreshing Mexican drink made from crushed seeds. Open daily for lunch and dinner till 0200.

$ El Pollo Real (tel. 8-31-11), Av. Macheros and Calle 2a: A fast-food spot cranking out their own Sinaloa-style roast chickens—whole or half—for eating on the premises or *para llevar* ("to go") with tortillas, beans, and salsa. Open daily 1000-2200.

$-$$ Fubar de Ensenada (no phone), Av. López Mateos between Riveroll and Macheros. A small, outdoor bar/café with crab tacos and inexpensive Mexican breakfasts. Open daily for breakfast, lunch, and dinner.

$ Las Brasas (tel. 8-11-95), Av. López Mateos 486 (between Av. Gastelum and Ruíz): Sinaloa-style, marinated-and-mesquite-grilled chicken is the major draw here, but they also serve steak, seafood, and Mexican platters, all at reasonable prices. Open daily except Tues. for lunch and dinner.

$-$$ Las Cazuelas (tel. 6-10-44), Calle Sangines 6 (near Blvd. Costero): An old standby serving ranchero-style dishes, including *codorniz* (quail) and hearty Mexican breakfasts. Open daily 0700-2300.

$ McTaco (no phone), on Av. López Mateos between Riveroll and Macheros: In the heart of the tourist district, this simple taco stand serves some of the best tacos de carne asada in town, along with an array of self-serve condiments. Open late morning till early evening.

$$ Plaza Mexico (tel. 4-06-35), Av. Macheros and López Mateos: A large patio restaurant

with a festive atmosphere and lots of tourists. All the typical Mexican dishes and beverages North Americans expect, plus a first: jelly-filled *churros* (deep-fried, doughnut-like Mexican pastry). Open daily for lunch and dinner.

European

$$-$$$ El Rey Sol (tel. 8-17-33), Av. López Mateos 1000 (at Av. Blancarte): The renowned Doña Pepita, a native of Santa Rosalía, opened this elegant French restaurant in 1947 after spending 16 years in France, where she studied French cuisine at the famous Cordón Bleu cooking school (Pepita died in 1989). Recently renovated, the kitchen prepares a variety of seafood, poultry, and meat dishes, served with herbs and vegetables grown on the family's farm in Santo Tomás. The menu also includes a few Mexican dishes. Open daily for breakfast, lunch, and dinner.

$$-$$$ Enrique's (tel. 8-24-61), on Mexico 1 about a km north of town: Advertising "the smallest bar in the world," Enrique's is an old-timers favorite with a romantic atmosphere and a reputation for consistent quality. The mostly continental menu features chateaubriand, lobster Newburg, quail, frog legs, and abalone prepared to order. The small dining room is a good spot for a quiet celebration. Open daily for breakfast, lunch, and dinner.

$$-$$$ La Taberna Española (tel. 4-03-16), Blvd. Costero near Calle Sangines: A Spanish-style pub serving seafood tapas with Spanish and Mexican wines. Open daily except Tuesday 1300-0200.

American And Pizza

$-$$ Cha-Cha Burger (tel. 6-54-51), two locations: Blvd. Costero 609 between Av. Miramar and Macheros, and Blvd. Costero at Calle Sangines: This American-owned-and-operated burger joint is also a headquarters for Amigos de Ensenada, a gringo service club. Besides burgers, the offerings include corn dogs, fish, chicken, french fries, milk shakes, tacos, and ice cream. Open daily 1000-2200.

$-$$ La Fábula Pizza (tel. 6-55-22), Blvd. Costero and Av. Riviera: Part of a Mexican chain that serves reliable American-style pizza in a family atmosphere. Open daily for lunch and dinner.

Oriental
$-$$ **China Land** (tel. 6-86-44), Av. Riveroll 1149 (between Calles 11a and 12a): Good selection of Sichuan, Mandarin, and Cantonese dishes at reasonable prices. Open daily for lunch and dinner.

$$ **Ebisu** (tel. 6-05-11), Av. López Mateos and Balboa: A decent, reasonably priced Japanese place with fresh sushi, sashimi, tempura, and teppanyaki. Open daily except Wed. for lunch and dinner.

$-$$ **Muy Lam** (tel. 6-11-18), Av. Diamante and Reforma: The most popular Chinese restaurant in Ensenada, serving mostly Cantonese dishes. Open daily for lunch and dinner.

Groceries
The **Gigante** at Av. López Mateos and Calle Delante is a huge supermarket with just about anything you might need for picnics or camping, or for an epic Transpeninsular road trip (e.g., ice and coolers). The store also has a takeout buffet with tasty Mexican dishes that you won't find in most Ensenada restaurants, including spicy moles and Oaxacan cheese.

Scattered along Av. Diamante are a number of inexpensive panaderías, tortillerías, and dulcerías. For European-style baked items, you could investigate **La Baguette** (tel. 8-28-14) on Blvd. Costero near Av. Blancarte. Prices at La Baguette are about double what you'd pay in an Av. Diamante bakery, however; if you're pinching pesos, stick with the latter.

On Mexico 1, a few km south of town between Estero Beach and La Bufadora, is a row of vendors selling fresh tamales stuffed with corn *(elote),* olives *(aceitunas),* or red chiles. Vendors along this road also sell jars of olives, chiles, and honey.

La Milpa (tel. 6-10-05, Calle 4a 1329, between Espinoza and Floresta) is a health-oriented store carrying natural foods, nonalcoholic wine and beer, herbs, dried fruits, and natural remedies.

ENTERTAINMENT

Bars And Discos
Many of the hotels and motels in the main tourist district, along Av. López Mateos and Blvd. Costero between Calle Sangines and Av. Macheros, have bars or lounges with occasional live music—usually *trovadores* (troubadours) or mariachis playing Mexican standards. **Bananas** (tel. 8-20-04, Blvd. Costero 277) and **Ibis** (tel. 6-14-40, Blvd. Costero and Av. Alvarado) offer nightly dancing to recorded music and light shows—not on a par with Tijuana's high-tech discos but good enough for vacationing gringos.

West of Av. Macheros, the city leaves behind the middle-class tourist zone and revels in cheap seafood joints, bars, and dance halls with a slightly seedy air. In this area is one of Baja's most famous landmarks, **Hussong's Cantina** (tel. 8-32-10, Av. Ruíz 113), quite justifiably advertised as "the bar that built a town," (This could be amended to "the bar that built a shopping center" now that the neighborhood is studded with Hussong's souvenir shops.)

At the same location since Johan Hussong, a German immigrant, opened shop in 1892 (and still owned by his son, Juan Hussong), hardly anything about the clapboard structure has changed in a hundred years except for the addition of electricity. Always crowded, on any given night tourists are outnumbered two to one by regulars, a mixture of expats and Baja-californios. Unamplified norteña ensembles sometimes play polkas and *rancheras* as *gritos* (shouts) pierce the smoky air. Come in the early afternoon if you hope to claim a table. 1992 should be a special year, as it's Hussong's 100th anniversary (Rumor has it Oktoberfest '92 will be big here.)

Across the street from Hussong's is **Papa and Beers,** a slightly more sedate bar with recorded music and a collegiate atmosphere. It lacks character but is a reasonable alternative for folks who find Hussong's too rowdy. Another favorite watering hole for the young-and-boisterous is **Plaza Mexico** (Blvd. Costero and Av. Macheros), an outdoor restaurant-bar that packs them in on warm weekend nights.

A wander north along Av. Ruíz or especially Av. Gastelum will turn up a number of Mexican-oriented bars and cantinas, many of the red-light sort but spirited nonetheless. **Anthony's** (Blvd. Costero and Av. Miramar), a classic in this category, is a large bar-dance hall with a bawdy, boy's-town reputation. Beyond the curtained entrance revolves a merry-go-round of ranchers, surfers, painted ladies, and other lost (at least for the night) souls.

EVENTS

February

Carnaval (Mardi Gras): Ensenada has been observing this pre-Lenten festival since 1918, and it seems to get bigger every year (over 300,000 visitors attended in 1990). Usually held for six days before Ash Wednesday (the second week in February), festivities start with the Quema de Mal Humor, or "Burning of Bad Humor," in which an effigy (usually modeled after an unpopular politician of the day) is hanged and burned. Throughout the week, a nightly street fair stretches for 12 downtown blocks, offering food vendors, carnival rides, live music, and a steady flow of Mexican beer, brandy, and tequila. Carnaval parades, consisting of flowered floats and legions of costumed dancers, wind through the streets amid clouds of confetti every afternoon.

Events with a local flavor include a *juegos florales* contest, in which poets compete to see who can compose the best "flowery verse"—Spanish students shouldn't miss this one. Another local highlight is the selection of the Reina de Carnaval ("Carnaval Queen") and El Rey Feo ("Ugly King") at a mid-festival "coronation ball" on Saturday night. The Monday following this weekend is El Día del Marido Oprimido, the "Day of the Oppressed Husband," in which married men are to be allowed 23½ hours of freedom to do whatever they wish.

Carnaval's grand finale is a masquerade ball held on the Tuesday night before Ash Wednesday. Prizes are awarded for best costumes as well as for other attainments over the course of the week—best float, best dance troupe, etc. For specific information on Carnaval scheduling and venues for individual events, pick up a copy of the *Baja Sun*.

March

Three Sister Cities Bike Ride: On the last weekend of the month, cyclists race along a triangle course between Ensenada, Rosarito, and Tijuana; sponsored by Monday International (tel. 619-275-1384 in the U.S.).

April

Rosarito-Ensenada 50-Mile Bicycle Ride: Last Saturday in April; for details, see "Holidays, Festivals, and Events" in the general introduction.

Newport-Ensenada Yacht Race: See "Holidays, Festivals, and Events," p. 83.

Taco, Tamal, and Mole Fiesta: A culinary event held the last weekend in April that draws the best antojitos chefs. Sponsored by CAN-IRAC (tel. 4-04-48, 4-04-35) and the Amigos de Ensenada.

May

Sucro Motocross Series: An off-road motorcycle race usually held the second week of May. Sponsored by SUCRO (contact Alberto Herediu, tel. 6-47-47, Av. México 843).

Tecate-Ensenada Bike Ride: Third week in May. Sponsored by Monday International (tel. 619-275-1384 in the U.S.).

June

Baja 500: A 500-mile offroad race out of Ensenada, held in early June by SCORE International. See November entry for **Baja 1000** below.

July

Gran Carrera de Ensenada: Yet another off-road race, this one sponsored by Baja Promotions (tel. 818-340-5750 in the U.S.) and extending 250 miles out of Ensenada.

August

Hobie Cat Fleet Four Todos Santos Regatta: A Hobie-sponsored catamaran regatta held on Bahía de Todos Santos the first weekend of August.

Seafood Fair: Usually held the last weekend of the month, this is one of the city's most well-attended fiestas. Many local restaurants participate. Sponsored by CANIRAC (tel. 4-04-48, 4-04-35).

September
Mexican Independence Day ("Fiesta Patria de la Independencia"): See "Holidays, Festivals, and Events," p. 83.

Rosarito-Ensenada 50-Mile Bicycle Ride: Last Saturday in September (same as in April); for details, see "Holidays, Festivals, and Events" in the main introduction.

October
SUCRO Supercross Series: Another offroad motorcycle race sponsored by SUCRO (see May entry for contact). First weekend of the month.

Juan Hussong International Chili Cookoff: A real ICS-sanctioned (International Chili Society) cookoff and one of Ensenada's biggest events, usually held on the second weekend in October. The cookoff winner is eligible to compete in the annual ICS World Championship Chili Cookoff held in Alta California.

In addition to chili cooking competitions, entered by individuals, clubs, and local restaurants, the day's activities typically include a chile-pepper-eating contest, a tequila "shoot-and-holler" contest, live music and dancing, and the selection of Ms. Chile Pepper and Mr. Hot Sauce. You can extinguish the fire with beverages provided by Cuauhtémoc Brewery (brewers of Tecate, Carta Blanca, and several other popular Mexican beers), Viuda de Romero (tequila), and Bodegas de Santo Tomás (wine). Last year the cookoff was held at Patios PRONAF behind LF Race and Sports Book; a small admission fee is charged (part of the proceeds goes to charity). For up-to-date information on scheduling and venue, contact Juan Hussong (tel. 4-41- 55) at Quintas Papagayo Resort.

Fiesta Viva: A four-day exposition held the second week of October. Exhibitors are from all over the Ensenada *municipio*.

November
SCORE-Presidente Baja 1000: The granddaddy of all offroad races takes place over a four-day interval during the first or second week of the month. For a race schedule, contact the Ensenada tourist office or pick up a current issue of the *Baja Sun*. For entry information, contact SCORE International (see "Baja 1000" for address and phone number).

BAJA 1000

Every November desert rats from around the globe gather in Ensenada for the grueling Baja 1000 ("Baja Mil"), the world's most prestigious offroad race. The first organized contest took place in October 1967, though informally dirt bikers had been racing from Ensenada to La Paz since the '50s. In 1962, Dave Ekins and Bill Robertson, Jr. were the first to record their efforts when they raced two Honda 250 motorcycles from Tijuana to La Paz, establishing their times by having sheets of paper stamped at telegraph offices in Tijuana and La Paz. Ekins pulled into La Paz after 39 hours, 54 minutes; Robertson made it an hour later.

From 1967 until the present, the event has taken place yearly except in 1974, when the National Off Road Racing Association lost Mexican permission to operate the race. Since 1975, SCORE International has organized the race, most recently with the sponsorship of Mexico's Presidente Brandy. Participants can enter in one of 20 categories—15 car and truck classes, six motorcycle, and two ATV. The course alternates year to year between a straight 1,000-mile Ensenada-La Paz run and a shorter 1,000-km loop beginning and ending in Ensenada; the latter course offers more spectator opportunities and pitstops.

Recently SCORE has added a separate Baja 1000 Endurance Safari on a course parallel to, but rougher than, the usual 1,000-mile Ensenada-La Paz route. A rally rather than a race, in this event contestants aren't rated on their time achievements but rather on endurance (a quality of obvious interest to automotive manufacturers and marketers seeking the imprimatur "Baja-proven").

December
SUCRO Motocross Series: See May entry for contact.

Las Posadas: 16-25 December. See "Holidays, Festivals, and Events" in the main introduction.

SPORTS AND RECREATION

Fishing
Although commercial fishing (both local and foreign) has depleted the overall supply of gamefish in the Ensenada area, sportfishing here can still be rewarding, especially from June through mid-Sept. when several species make coastal runs from the south. Bahía de Todos Santos catches include lingcod, rockfish, calico bass, sand bass, barracuda, bonito, and yellowtail. Living up to Ensenada's reputation as the "yellowtail capital of the world," local yellowtail catches are generally in the 7-14 kilogram (15-30 lbs.) range.

Long-range fishing trips from Ensenada—to Punta Colonet, Isla San Geronimo, or Isla San Martín—yield bluefin, yellowfin, and albacore tuna, skipjack, white seabass, salmon grouper, and the occasional dorado.

Several companies operate sportfishing trips from the Ensenada Sportfishing Terminal, off Blvd. Costero near the end of Av. Macheros. **Ensenada Clipper Fleet** (tel. 8-21-85, 8-20-62, fax 8-19-63; mailing address: 2630 E. Beyer Blvd., Suite 676, San Ysidro, CA 92143-9011) runs day-trips for US$30 a person, overnights for US$75, and multi-day, long-range trips by charter. Rates for local trips (day and overnight) include license and tackle; live bait and added services (e.g., cleaning and fish-filleting) cost extra.

Gordo's Sportfishing (tel. 8-35-15, 8-23-77, fax 4-04-81) is slightly cheaper at US$25 per person for local day-trips, US$75 for long-range party boats. Gordo's also offers a package deal that includes one night's motel room, a fishing trip (including license and tackle), and breakfast for US$84 for two persons.

Tackle: Ensenada Clipper Fleet has a tackle shop at the sportfishing pier that's open to the public 24 hours a day. Just north of town in El Sauzal, **Anzuelos Universales de Ensenada** (tel. 4-62-29, Mexico 1, Km 102) carries a full line of fishing tackle, including their own Baja-tested Anzuelos gear.

Boating
For the moment, Ensenada's public anchorage is little more than a set of breakwaters, a section of rickety piers, and a parking lot. As Ensenada is an offical Mexican port of entry, arriving boaters must check in with the COTP (see "Sports and Recreation" in the main introduction for details on check-in procedures).

A new marina with 220 slips is currently under construction; daily rates are expected to be in the US$5-7 range. A nearby boatyard, **Baja Naval,** offers a few slips and accepts foreign boats for servicing or repair at lower rates than for comparable work done in the United States. Fuel is available at this boatyard.

For outboard motor repairs, inquire at **Motores de Baja California Norte** (tel. 6-30-25, Calle 6a 1990), which specializes in sales and service of American-made motors.

Surfing
The nearest consistent surfing areas are at Punta San Miguel, several kilometers north of Ensenada off Mexico 1 (see p. 170) and Islas de Todos Santos, 20 km west by boat (see p. 171). Playa La Jolla, approximately 16 km south of town via Mexico 1 and BCN 23, occasionally benefits from the winter northwest swell.

Surf gear, including Ensenada-made San Miguel boards, can be purchased at **San Miguel Surf Design** in the Edificio Hussong, a small shopping center next door to Hussong's Cantina on Calle Ruíz. **Cactus Surfboards,** another local surfboard manufacturer, has a shop on Av. López Mateos between Ruíz and Gastelum. San Miguel and Cactus boards run around US$175-220.

Diving
The best local diving spots are at Punta Banda and Islas de Todos Santos (see p. 189 and p. 171 respectively). Ensenada has three dive shops: **Promapa** (tel. 4-06-37, Av. Ruíz 42), **Almar** (tel. 8-30-13, Av. Macheros 149), and **El Yaqui** (no phone, Blanco Shopping Center, Fracc. Valle Dorado).

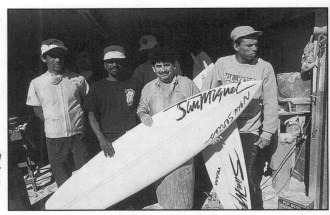

San Miguel surfboard factory
(JOE CUMMINGS)

Bullfights And *Charreadas*
During the summer, bullfights and Mexican rodeos are occasionally held at a modest **Plaza de Toros** on Calle Sangines between Av. Pedro Loyola and los Bucaneros. For current scheduling, contact the state tourist office (tel. 6-22-22).

Race And Sports Book
LF Race and Sports Book has an outlet at the Hotel San Nicolás, Av. López Mateos and Blancarte. **Caliente Foreign Book** is on Av. López Mateos behind the Riviera del Pacífico.

SHOPPING

You'll find the usual assortment of tourist-oriented souvenir and beachwear shops along Av. López Mateos and Blvd. Costero. The government-operated **FONART,** next to the state tourism office on Av. López Mateos, offers a collection of Mexican handicrafts. The **Centro Artesanal** on Blvd. Costero caters mostly to cruise-ship passengers in town for a few hours, but is worth a look for neo-Casa Grandes pottery (made in Chihuahua's Valle de Casas Grandes) and Oaxacan folk art.

The best bargains for everyday items are found deeper in the downtown area, away from Blvd. Costero or Av. López Mateos. The locals do much of their shopping in the vicinity of the Av. Juárez and Ruíz intersection, where bookstores, record shops, and zapaterías are particularly numerous. Ensenada's zapaterías specialize in boots made from "exotic" skins like lizard or ostrich—don't buy anything prohibited by U.S. Customs (e.g., alligator or other endangered species) if you plan on taking it across the U.S.-Mexico border. **Librería El Spaña** (Av. Ruíz 217) and **Librería Banuelos** (Av. Ruíz 370) carry English-language books and magazines.

A large flea market called **Los Globos,** on Calle 9a three blocks east of Av. Reforma, has vendor stalls selling everything from housewares to sandals. It's open daily 0900-1800. A similar market at Calle 6a and Av. Riveroll is open only on weekends.

SERVICES

Money Changing
Most banks in Ensenada refer visitors to a casa de cambio for foreign-exchange services. **La Moneda** casa de cambio in the Blanco Bahía shopping center, at Juárez and Reforma, has one of the best exchange rates in town. Another casa de cambio with a good rate is located in the Gigante shopping center at Calle Delante and Mexico 1.

Post And Telephone

The most convenient post office for visitors staying near the waterfront is at the corner of avenidas López Mateos and Riviera, near the state tourist office. Open Mon.-Fri. 0800-1900, Sat. 0800-1300.

The **Message Center** (tel. 8-29-83, fax 4-07-61), next door to Hussong's Cantina (Edificio Hussong, Av. Ruiz 105, No. 13), also handles U.S. mail service. Open Mon.-Fri. 0900-1900, Sat. 0900-1700.

Ensenada has a number of public telephones in the downtown area. For both local and long-distance calls, these are less expensive than hotel phones. If you need a phone line installed, pay a visit to the municipal telephone office at the intersection of Blvd. Ramirez Mendez and Av. Reforma, near the Blanco Bahía shopping center.

Ensenada's area code is 667.

Immigration Office

The Ensenada immigration office is in a nondescript building just around the corner from COTUCO's information booth, near the waterfront at the northern entrance into town. If you haven't had your tourist card validated yet and are planning to travel farther south than Maneadero, this is the place to accomplish that chore. The office is usually open daily 0900-2000; on Sunday afternoons the office may close for about an hour while the only officer on duty has gone to the pier to meet a cruise ship from San Diego.

Language Schools

Two private institutes in Ensenada offer intensive Spanish-language courses. The long-established **International Spanish Institute of Ensenada** (tel. 6-01-09, 6-65-87, or 213-316-1300 in the U.S.) is at Blvd. Rodriguez 377, near the Gigante shopping center. ISIE's program includes six hours of classroom instruction per day, plus a Mexican family homestay. Tuition is a reasonable US$20 per day (the same for weekends or weekdays), plus US$20 a day for a homestay and three meals. ISIE's U.S. mailing address is 5329 Ruby St., Unit C, Torrance, CA 90503.

A newer institute, the **Center of Languages and Latin American Studies** (tel. 6-70-76, or 619-279-0996 in the U.S.), has a similar program but offers one less hour of classroom instruction per day. Tuition at CLLAS is US$25 per day (US$65 for a weekend course), plus US$20 daily for private homestay and meals (US$15 in a shared room). CLLAS is at Calle San Carlos 242, Fracc. Buenaventura (near Av. Reforma and Calle Diamante); the institute's U.S. mailing address is 5666 La Jolla Blvd., Suite 116, La Jolla, CA 92037.

Amigos De Ensenada

This service club, consisting mostly of resident norteamericanos, organizes fundraising community events throughout the year (e.g., Juan Hussong's Chili Cookoff, the Christmas parade) for charitable purposes. The club meets twice monthly at Calle Mazatlan 526, Playa Hermosa; for information, contact John Dixon (tel. 6-54-51, 6-79-31).

Real Estate

Century 21 (tel. 4-46-48, fax 4-45-36, Km 108; mailing address: P.O. Box 309, Ensenada, BCN) has information on houses, condos, and lots for sale in the Ensenada area.

Emergency

The public hospital (tel. 6-17-01, 6-17-05) at Calle Sangines and Av. Pedro Loyola has 24-hour emergency services. For medical

---

USEFUL ENSENADA TELEPHONE NUMBERS

Police	134
Red Cross	132
Highway Patrol	6-13-11
IMSS Hospital	6-17-01
	6-17-05
Tourist Attorney	6-36-86
State Tourism Office	6-22-22
Customs	8-24-77
Immigration	4-01-64

problems that require emergency treatment at San Diego medical facilities, contact **Transmedic** (tel. 8-14-00, Av. Obregón at Calle 11a), a 24-hour ambulance service that can provide either air or surface transport to San Diego.

ENSENADA INFORMATION

Tourist Offices

The SECTUR-sponsored state tourism office (tel. 6-22-22, 6-37-18; fax 6-36-86), at Av. López Mateos at Espinoza, dispenses information on Ensenada events, dining, and hotels as well as BCN travel. The English-speaking staff is very competent and helpful; the Attorney for Tourist Protection also works out of this office. Open Mon.-Fri. 0900-1900, Sat. 0900-1500, Sun. 1000-1400.

The city-sponsored Convention and Visitors Bureau (COTUCO, tel. 8-24-11) is at Blvd. Costero 540, opposite the PEMEX station at the north entrance to town. They distribute much of the same information as the state tourist office and can also make hotel bookings. Open Mon.-Sat. 0900-1900, Sun. 0900-1400.

Business Offices

Ensenada has an active chamber of commerce (CANACO, tel. 4-09-06, Av. López Mateos 693) and restaurant association (CANIRAC, tel. 4-04-48, Av. López Mateos 885-7) with many North American members.

Newspapers

The English-language *Baja Sun,* a free monthly newspaper, is full of information on current Ensenada events, local business, beaches, entertainment, and dining out. It's available at several locations throughout the city, including tourist offices and larger hotels. For information on subscriptions or advertising, drop by the office at Calle Obregón 1099 (at Calle 11a), open Mon.-Fri. 1000-1800, or call 8-73-33.

Bilingual visitors, or those who want to practice their Spanish, should pick up a copy of *Vivir en Ensenada* ("Living in Ensenada"), a free Spanish-only weekly covering cultural events from a local perspective.

Consulates

Most countries with consulates in Baja have established them in Tijuana or Mexicali. Daring to be different, Denmark has a consulate in Ensenada at Av. Virgilio Uribe 496 (tel. 6-60-35, 6-62-49).

TRANSPORT

Getting There

Air: There are no regularly scheduled flights in or out of Ensenada. Aeropuerto El Ciprés (tel. 6-63-01), just south of town off Mexico 1, has a paved airstrip suitable for small plane arrivals and departures.

Bus: Intercity buses use the bus terminal (tel. 8-67-70) at Av. Riveroll and Calle 11a. For details on scheduling and fares, see "Ensenada Bus Departures."

Driving: Ensenada is the southernmost terminal for Mexico 1-D, the four-lane toll road from Tijuana. Beyond Ensenada, Mexico 1 is, for the most part, a two-lane highway with road conditions varying from kilometer to kilometer.

Mexico 3 from Tecate also terminates in Ensenada, then resumes east of town on its way across the Sierra Juárez to join Mexico 5 (for San Felipe). Finding Mexico 3 east out of Ensenada can be difficult, as the route is not well signposted in the city. The simplest way to get there is to follow Av. Juárez until it meets Av. Reforma (at the Benito Juárez statue). The street directly across Av. Reforma is Calzada Cortés; after crossing Av. Reforma, follow Calzada Cortés until it curves to the left and feeds into Mexico 3.

Getting Around

City Bus: Several varieties of buses and vans ply the main avenues of the city, e.g., López Mateos, Juárez, Ruíz, Diamante, Delante, Reforma, and Calle 9a. The route—designated by the street name—is usually whitewashed on the windshield or printed on a marquis over the windshield. Fares are roughly US$.30, depending on the size of the vehicle (bigger is cheaper). Buses to outlying districts (e.g., Ejido Chapultepec) leave from Av. Juárez.

Taxi: Most of the city's taxis park along López Mateos or Juárez, or near the bus depot at Calle 11a and Av. Riveroll. Fares are negotiable; most trips in the city cost around US$3. A taxi to La Bufadora costs US$10-15.

Car Rental: Ensenada is an expensive place to rent a car compared to Tijuana or Los Cabos. The highest rates are charged by the independents: **Ensenada Rent-A-Car** (tel. 8-18-96) and **Scorpio Rent-A-Car** (tel. 8-32-75), both on Av. Alvarado just off Av. López Mateos. Rates for a Nissan Sentra at either of these two agencies are around US$45 per 24 hours plus US$.25 per km. **Hertz** (tel. 8-37-76, 800-654-3001 in the U.S.), in the Bahía shopping center at Calle 2a and Av. Riveroll, has considerably lower rates (US$24 a day, plus US$.18 per km, for a VW bug) if you reserve in advance, but you must return the car to one of their Tijuana offices .

Driving Your Own Vehicle: Driving in Ensenada is fairly straightforward as long as you are prepared to stop at *every* intersection. Even if you don't see a stop sign, chances are a stop is required. The Ensenada traffic police don't go out of their way to hassle visitors, but fines are stiff for speeding, running stop signs, or drinking while driving. Fines must be paid in cash at the municipal police station, Calle 9a and Av. Espinoza.

Tours
Viajes Guayacura (tel. 8-37-18) offers a three-hour "Discover Ensenada" tour of the city and nearby countryside for US$14 per person. Guayacura's air-conditioned bus departs daily at noon from next to the Best Western Cortez Hotel on Av. López Mateos; the tour includes stops at Santo Tomás Winery and La Bufadora.

VICINITY OF ENSENADA

Estero Beach
This huge, estuarial beach at the junction of Bahía de Todos Santos and Río San Carlos is about 12 km south of the center of Ensenada via Mexico 1, behind Ejido Chapultepec. Except during July and August, the beach is surprisingly uncrowded.

The **Estero Beach Museum,** part of the Estero Beach Resort complex, has natural history exhibits and a display of Mexican folk art. Nominal admission fee; open daily 0900-1700.

Punta Banda And La Bufadora
This rocky peninsula juts into the Pacific at the south end of Bahía de Todos Santos and is

ENSENADA BUS DEPARTURES

Destination	Departures	Duration	Fare
Tijuana	hourly 0500-2300	1½ hours	US$2.20
Mexicali	every 30 minutes 0530-0800, 1030, 1100, 1300, 1400, 1530, 1700, 1730, 1830, 2000	4 hours	US$5.50
San Felipe	0800, 1800	4 hours	US$4.65
San Quintín	hourly 0600-2100	3 hours	US$3.20
El Rosario	0600, 0900, 1600	4 hours	US$4.35
Guerrero Negro	1000, 1900, 2130	8 hours	US$10.50
La Paz	0930, 1230, 1600, 2000, 2230	22 hours	US$25

largely undeveloped except for a few campgrounds and the members-only Baja Beach and Tennis Club. Hikers can explore the peninsula's windswept spine by means of a number of unmarked trails leading from turnouts along the only paved road, BCN 23. From lookout points on Punta Banda, you can often see spouting gray whales as they pass by during their annual Jan.-March migration.

One of the Ensenada area's prime tourist sites, the scenic blowhole at the tip of Punta Banda, is about 25 km (16 miles) from the city via Mexico 1 and BCN 23. During incoming tides, waves rush into an underground cavern and force spumes as high as 25-30 meters through a hole in the top of the cavern. Loosely translated, La Bufadora means "Buffalo's Snort," referring to the sound created as water spews from the blowhole.

La Bufadora is favorite weekend excursion among local Ensenadenses as well as visiting gringos. Vendors selling snacks and souvenirs line the road from the parking lot to the blowhole. This spot could be nicknamed "Baja's *churro* capital" since there are probably more churro (a sweet, fried pastry, sometimes called a "Mexican doughnut") vendors here than anywhere else on the peninsula. Below the blowhole is Bahía Papalote, a bay and small residental-recreational community.

Scuba Diving: Detached rocks, underwater pinnacles, sea caves, and kelp beds below the cliffs on Punta Banda's south shore are popular among scuba enthusiasts, and are accessible by boat or from the shore. Easiest access is at the bay below La Bufadora, Bahía Papalote, which is sheltered enough for intermediate divers or supervised novices; an underwater hot springs at a depth of 25-30 meters warms the bottom of the bay.

Off the northwest tip of Punta Banda is an underwater ridge—accessible by boat only—topped by a 1½-mile chain of small islands. The ridge is dotted with underwater cliffs, caves, rock reefs, and kelp beds. Cold-water upwellings along the ridge stimulate marinelife and help maintain good visibility. Because of swells and currents in this area, only divers with open-ocean experience should consider diving here, unless accompanied by someone who knows local diving conditions well. Dive shops in Ensenada can arrange guided trips to any Punta Banda dive spot; there is also a small dive shop at Bahía Papalote.

Getting There: To drive to Punta Banda from Ensenada, take Mexico 1 south to BCN 23 (just north of Maneadero), then follow this road west through olive orchards and the La Jolla community onto the peninsula. After La Jolla, the road begins to climb and wind its way toward La Bufadora, ending at a parking lot for the blowhole.

Non-drivers can hire a taxi from the city to La Bufadora for US$10-15.

Camping And RV Parks

The deluxe **Estero Beach Trailer Park** (tel. 6-62-65) is adjacent to the Estero Beach Resort Hotel. RVers are permitted to use all of the facilities of the hotel, including a boat ramp, tennis courts, and clubhouse. Full-hookup sites are US$14.

La Bufadora   (JOE CUMMINGS)

A short distance along the road to La Bufadora (BCN 23), in the North American retirement enclave of La Jolla, is the large **La Jolla Trailer Park** facing Bahía de Todos Santos. Electric-water hookups or tent sites are US$5 for two, plus US$1 for each additional person. Additional facilities include hot showers, boat ramp, tennis court, disposal station, market, and restaurant.

The adjacent **Villarino Camp** (tel. 6-13-09) has tent/camper sites with electricity for US$6, full hookups for US$8. Other facilities include hot showers, boat ramp, and market. A couple of ejido-operated campgrounds with minimal facilities (toilets and water only), **Tres Hermanas** and **Rancho La Bufadora,** are farther out on Punta Banda en route to La Bufadora—look for signs along BCN 23. Rates are usually US$5 night for tent or RV, less for long-term stays.

ENSENADA TO SAN FELIPE (MEXICO 3)

Mexico 3 stretches 198 km (123 miles) between Ensenada and San Felipe. The first two-thirds of the highway traverses high chaparral along the gradually ascending western slopes of the Sierra Juárez. Just past Km 39 is a short paved road leading north into the **Ojos Negros,** a small farming center with a PEMEX station, a couple of cafés and markets, an auto parts dealer, and a pharmacy. A network of dirt roads out of Valle Ojos Negros link farms, the old mining settlement of Real del Castillo, and a longer road to Parque Nacional Constitución de 1857.

A natural spring issues forth from a steep hillside on the east side of the highway between Km 73 and 74—a good place to stock up on drinking water.

Parque Nacional Constitución De 1857
The most commonly used road to this national park branches northeast off Mexico 3 at Km 55. Although ungraded much of the way, this 35-km (22-mile) dirt road is usually traversable by ordinary passenger car all the way to the park entrance if caution is taken. As the road climbs, passing a number of ranchos, the chaparral gradually gives way to conifer forests and the temperature drops. At the park entrance, rangers collect a fee of US$1.50.

Most of the park covers a subalpine plateau at the center of the Sierra Juárez with an average elevation of around 1,200 meters (3,950 feet); several granite peaks reach over 1,500 meters (5,000 feet). Laguna Hanson (named for an American settler who disappeared here in 1880—legend has it he was cooked in a cauldron by a friend) is the for all intents the center of the park. In years when rainfall is plentiful, the scenic lake is filled with bass and catfish; in the fall, ducks are common. Fishing is permitted; hunting isn't. A campground at the lake has raked grounds and neat firepits, some furnished with firewood and grills. Except for a 10-km path around the lake, there are no established hiking trails in the park as such.

Most of the year the park receives few visitors. The only time of year it should be avoided is Easter, when enough jeepsters arrive to dispel all peace and quiet around the lake.

The road from Mexico 3 continues northeastward through the park and ends at Mexico 2—60 km (30 miles) from Laguna Hanson—near La Rumorosa. (See "Vicinity of Mexicali," p. 230, for details on the northern approach to Laguna Hanson.)

Independencia
This pueblo of around 500 ejidatarios, at Km 92 on Mexico 5, is part of Ejido Heroes de la Independencia. It makes a good rest spot as if you're driving Mexico 3 straight through, as it's roughly halfway between Ensenada and the Mexico 5 junction (to Mexicali or San Felipe). Among the scattered buildings—some abandoned—are a Conasupo, a PEMEX station, a church, an auto shop, and a couple of handicraft shops.

The latter sell pottery and other crafts made by Paipais who live in nearby **Santa Catarina,** a former mission settlement eight km east of Independencia via a graded dirt road. The adobe ruins—foundations only—of Misión Santa Catarina de los Paipais, founded by

Dominican padres in 1797 and destroyed by Yumanos in 1840, are still visible in the village.

Valle De La Trinidad-Mike's Sky Ranch

A paved road south to Valle de Trinidad branches south from Mexico 5 at Km 155. This farming community of around 5,000 offers a PEMEX station, a bank, several markets, cafés, and auto shops. Southwest of Valle de la Trinidad, a dirt road (sturdy, high-clearance vehicles only) continues southward some 48 km (30 miles) past a few ranchos to the northern boundary of Parque Nacional Sierra San Pedro Mártir; see "Ensenada to San Quintín," p. 193, for more information on the park.

Just beyond Km 138, a dirt road leads 35½ km (22 miles) south to **Mike's Sky Ranch,** an off-the-beaten-track resort at the northwestern edge of Parque Nacional Sierra San Pedro Mártir (elevation: 1,200 meters/ 3900 feet). Named for its late founder, Mike Leon, the ranch has long served as a checkpoint for the Baja 500 and Baja 1000 offroad races; nearby are hiking trails to year-round waterfalls and Río San Rafael. Ranch accommodations include rooms for US$40 a night (includes swimming pool access) and campsites for US$6 a night (water and shower privileges only). Guests eat family-style meals together (US$12 for dinner, US$6.50 for breakfast and lunch). Information or reservations: Mike's Sky Ranch (tel. 66-85-49-95 in Tijuana; 213-560-2119 in the U.S.), P.O. Box 5376, San Ysidro, CA 92073.

The road to Mike's is rough in spots, though drivers with passenger cars and RVs can accomplish it with patience. Beyond the ranch, this road continues southwestward to join the better, graded road between Mexico 1 and the national park (and Rancho Meling). For more information on this route, Rancho Meling, and Parque Nacional San Pedro Mártir, see "Ensenada to San Quintín," p. 193.

San Matías Pass To Crucero La Trinidad

Southeast of Valle de la Trinidad, Mexico 3 climbs through the San Matías Pass (900 meters/2,950 feet), and as the road descends the eastern escarpment of the Sierra San Pedro Mártir, the scenery shifts from chaparral to desert. Between Km 160 and 170, ocotillos increase rapidly in number and size (up to five meters tall).

At Km 164, a dirt road leads southeast toward Rancho Villa del Sol, than south through the dry Laguna Diablo to the eastern approach to Picacho del Diablo, via Cañon del Diablo (see "Ensenada to San Quintín," p. 193, for details). This road also connects with a dirt track east to San Felipe.

Mexico 3 meets Mexico 5 at Crucero La Trinidad (PEMEX, café); from here it's 109 km (65 miles) north to Mexicali, 48 km (29 miles) south to San Felipe.

ENSENADA TO SAN QUINTÍN

Maneadero

This farming community 20 km (12 miles) south of Ensenada is unremarkable except for the fact that it's the southernmost limit of Baja's "free zones." Beyond Km 23, all visitors are supposed to be in possession of a valid tourist permit or visa (see "Immigration and Customs" in the main introduction for more information). The immigration checkpoint at Km 23 has been closed for the last few years; if the Mexican government decides to re-open it, anyone driving through Maneadero should be prepared to show identification and travel documents on demand.

Restaurants, small grocery stores, auto parts shops, and other small businesses line Mexico 1 in the middle of Maneadero. A car wash on the east side of the highway does an excellent exterior and interior cleaning for US$4 (something to consider if you're on the way north after extensive offroad driving in the interior).

Ejido Uruapan

Just south of Km 41 (19 km south of Maneadero) is the turnoff for Ejido Uruapan, a farming village set in a deep valley. During quail season, Nov.-Feb., Uruapan is popular among North American hunters, most of whom stay at a hunting lodge operated by the regional wildlife inspector, Billy Cruz. During the rest of the year, non-hunting visitors are welcome to stay here as well. Guests can explore the Uruapan valley, visit nearby vineyards and dairy farms, or make day-trips to beaches at Punta Santo Tomás, 31 km west of the village.

Uruapan itself has little to see. A stream in the valley floor is linked to a hot springs where *ejidatarios* bathe and wash clothes (at a cement structure built for this purpose). The ejido also operates a sea-urchin processing plant. Established with Japanese assistance, the plant prepares the tiny marine creatures for export to Japan, where they're a popular sushi ingredient.

Accommodation: Cruz's simple, red-brick lodge is built around a courtyard; guests dine in front of a huge fireplace. The Spartan rooms cost US$15 per person during the off-season, including the use of a modern kitchen. A cook can be arranged at extra cost. During hunting season, the lodge rents for US$130 a day, which includes a hunting guide, transport to hunt sites, and a large evening meal. For further information on staying at the lodge, contact the state tourist office in Ensenada.

At the junction of Mexico 1 and the turnoff for the village is a campground with well-shaded tent/camper sites and a few fire pits. Campers can bathe at the village hot springs.

La Bocana-Puerto Santo Tomás

Off Mexico 1 at Km 48, an unpaved graded road follows the Río Santo Tomás 29 km west to the seaside fishing villages of La Bocana and Puerto Santo Tomás, both on the south side of Punta Santo Tomás. The Río Santo Tomás drains into the Pacific at La Bocana ("The Mouth"); during the Dominican era, Puerto Santo Tomás served as a supply port for nearby Misión Santo Tomás.

The scenic coastal topography along Punta Santo Tomás and the coves to the south have attracted a small gringo settlement, but for the most part you'll have the beach all to yourself. Camping is free; rustic cabins can be rented at either village. The villagers also rent fishing pangas.

The shoreline in front of La Bocana offers occasional beach and reef breaks. Determined surfers can brave an ungraded dirt road that runs south off the graded road from Mexico 1 (the turnoff is approximately 20½ km west of the highway) and straggle 11 km southwest to Punta San José, where there are often good reef and point breaks.

Santo Tomás

The Valle de Santo Tomás, cleft by the Río Santo Tomás, is one of Baja's prime agricultural regions and a visual highlight of any transpeninsular journey. Winding up, down, and around olive-green hills, the highway repeatedly suspends drivers over vignettes of tidy olive groves, vineyards, fields of flowers, and the occasional herd of goats. For some visitors, a day's stopover turns into weeks or months, perhaps because Santo Tomás has the ambience of Alta California's Sonoma or Napa valleys without the tourists and high prices. The valley community of around 1,500 is friendly and welcoming.

History: The valley was originally settled in 1790 by Dominican missionaries as an inter-mediate point between Misión San Miguel to the north and San Vicente to the south. In 1791 the Dominican padres established **Misión Santo Tomás de Aquino,** which by 1800 boasted over 3,000 cattle, sheep, and goats, plus an estimated 200 acres of grapes, corn, and wheat. The Mission wine produced at Santo Tomás was famous throughout the Californias mission system, and is now one of several wines produced by Ensenada's Bodegas de Santo Tomás. The Santo Tomás mission was secularized in 1849.

Mission Sites: The mission ruins are in two locations. The original site is on a low mesa off the unpaved road to La Bocana-Puerto Santo Tomás; the second site, where the mission was moved in 1794, is just off the east side of Mexico 1 in the village of Santo Tomás, north of El Palomar Trailer Park. At both sites, the only remains are a few ruined adobe walls and a foundation.

Accommodations and Food: The family-owned **El Palomar** (tel. 667-8-23-55, A.P. 595, Santo Tomás, BCN) in Santo Tomás started out as a restaurant in 1948 but now includes a motel, trailer park, and PEMEX station. Comfortable, heated rooms at the motel are US$25 s, US$35 d. Full-hookup RV sites in the trailer park cost US$8 a night. The swimming pool at El Palomar is a treat during the summer months.

Ejido Eréndira-Puerto San Isidro

At Km 78 a paved road leads west off Mexico 1 to the fishing and farming community of Ejido Eréndira. Although the village itself isn't par-ticularly attractive, the beaches north of here offer plenty of opportunity for camping and surf or boat fishing. The road to Puerto Isidro (two km north of Ejido Eréndira) and beyond is unpaved, ungraded, sandy, and potholed—a passenger car can manage it, but very slowly. Surfers can find a number of decent point and reef breaks in the vicinity of Puerto Isidro.

Castro's Place (tel. 667-6-28-97, A.P. 974, Ensenada, BCN) in Puerto Isidro is a fish camp with simple cabins for US$25 a night. The owner, Fernando Castro Ríos, leads guided fishing trips in the vicinity for around US$18 a day. Camping is permitted at

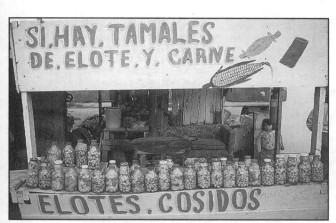

tamal stand
(JOE CUMMINGS)

Castro's for a nominal fee; a few kilometers north of here are plenty of free camping spots. Ejido Eréndira has a small grocery store, but the PEMEX station has been abandoned (the nearest working pumps are in Santo Tomás and San Vicente).

San Vicente
The scenic Valle de San Vicente and adjacent Llano Colorado ("Colorado Plain"), like the Río Santo Tomás valley, are heavily cultivated with olives, grapes, wheat, and corn. Just south of the Km 88 marker, a dirt road leads west off Mexico 1 to the ruins of **Misión San Vicente Ferrer,** a Dominican mission in use from 1780 to 1833. During its half-century tenure, the mission came under repeated attacks by Yumano warriors living in the Sierra Juárez. On a small mesa near the adobe walls of the mission are a mission-established cemetery (still in use) and the remains of a Spanish presidio.

Along Mexico 1 in the small town of San Vicente are a sprinkling of cafés, markets, a PEMEX station, and the **Motel El Camino,** a 10-room motel with basic accommodations for US$12 a night.

San Antonio Del Mar
At Km 126, just north of Colonet, an unpaved graded road leads 12½ km northwest to this seaside settlement, little more than a collection of trailers, rustic beach houses, and a couple of beach camps that charge US$5-8 a night. The beach at San Antonio del Mar, wedged into a large gap between high cliffs created by a tidal estuary, is wide, windy, and backed by sand dunes. (If you can stand the wind, you can camp for free on the beach.) Surfcasting and clamming are usually excellent here; the estuary is an added attraction.

The main road in from Mexico 1 becomes softer as it gets closer to the beach. Unless you have 4WD, stick to the most well-worn, hardened tracks and leave the many branching roads to drivers with SUVs or ATVs.

Colonet
Like San Vicente, Colonet is a small farming center with a PEMEX station and a couple of cafés and markets. Travelers spending time at San Antonio del Mar, Rancho Meling, or Parque Nacional Sierra San Pedro Mértir often use the town as a supply depot.

A graded dirt road leads southwest out of town 14 km to a fish camp on Bahía Colonet. Cabo Colonet, at the north end of the bay, offers a point break during winter northwest swells. The town, bay, and cape are reputedly named (Hispanicized version) for Capt. James Colnett, a British sea captain who explored this section of the Pacific coast in the late 18th century. At **Cuatro Casas,** about 4½ km south of Cabo Colonet on the bay, campsites are available for US$4 a day. Surfcasters will find barred surfperch, halibut, and bass to be plentiful.

San Telmo-Rancho Meling

Between Km 140 and Km 141, an unpaved graded road branches east to San Telmo, the Rancho Meling, and Parque Nacional San Pedro Mártir (see below). San Telmo, six km (3½ miles) east of Mexico 1, is a small farming-ranching settlement with little of interest to the traveler; supplies for extended trips into the interior, including gas, should be procured in Colonet or Colonia Vicente Guerrero on Mexico 1.

Rancho Meling (also known as Rancho San José) is 42 km farther southeast along the road. Founded in 1893 by Texas miner Harry Johnson as a base for his gold-mining operations in the western Sierra San Pedro Mártir, the ranch was destroyed by Magonistas during the 1911 border rebellion. A Norwegian family, the Melings, helped rebuild the ranch shortly thereafter and turn it into a 10,000-acre cattle ranch.

Today, in addition to raising cattle, the ranch takes in paying guests who want to experience Baja's high country. Visitors are accommodated in a comfortable lodge for US$50 s, US$90 d (US$30 for children ages 8-11, US$20 four to seven) per day, including three family-style meals. Optional activities include swimming (the ranch has a spring-fed pool), horseback riding, quail and dove hunting, and excursions into the Sierra San Pedro Mártir—an excellent opportunity to see the national park with experienced guides. Guests with their own planes may use the ranch's 1,064-meter (3,500-foot) airstrip. For reservations or further information, write Rancho Meling, A.P. 1326, Ensenada, BCN, or call (619) 758-2719 in the United States.

Punta San Jacinto-Camalú

Between Km 149 and Km 150, a dirt track suitable for ordinary passenger vehicles in good weather, proceeds west nine km to a sandy beach at Punta San Jacinto. A somewhat popular point break, known as "Freighters" because of the nearby wreck of the huge freighter *Isla del Carmen,* has occasioned the establishment of the rustic **El Parador Surf Camp.** The camp offers few facilities—water (sometimes) and a couple of fire pits. You can camp for free among the dunes behind the beach.

Camalú, beginning at Km 157, offers a variety of markets, pharmacies, cafés, a mechanic's shop, and a PEMEX station. A side road (unpaved) leads west to Camalú Via la Mar, a fish camp, and areas suitable for overnight camping. Surfers report occasional reef and point breaks at Punta Camalú to the north.

Misión Santo Domingo-Colonia Vicente Guerrero

Colonia Vicente Guerrero is a growing agricultural center with a post office, Conasupo, motel, two banks, restaurants, police station, panadería, PEMEX station, *butano* (butane/propane) plant, clinic, and two trailer parks. The surrounding fields produce a variety of vegetables and fruit.

The ruins of **Misión Santo Domingo,** named for the founder of the Dominican Order, are north of town, eight km east of Mexico 1, in a canyon formed by Arroyo de Santo Domingo. An earlier mission, established in 1775, was sited eight km farther east along the arroyo and was moved to the current site in 1782; the mission was closed in 1839 after most of the Indians in the area had either died in battle or succumbed to smallpox. The meter-thick adobe walls at Santo Domingo are more extensive than those at Santo Tomás or San Vicente; the outline of the mission quadrangle and several rooms are clearly visible.

The mission road parallels Arroyo de Santo Domingo for several kilometers beyond the ruins, offering a scenic, if rough, drive past two ranchos. Originating in the high reaches of the Sierra San Pedro Mártir, this arroyo is said to carry the largest volume of water of any stream on the peninsula.

Accommodations: The **Motel Sanchez,** in the middle of town on the west side of Mexico 1, has basic rooms for US$12-20 a night. At the south end of town, also on the west side of the highway (next to the butane facility), is the nicely landscaped **Mesón de Don Pepe RV Park** (tel. 666-6-22-16). Tent sites are US$4 a night, full hookup sites US$6 for two persons (US$1 for each additional person); discounts are readily given for long-term stays. Don Pepe's restaurant serves Mexican standards and seafood.

Follow the same turnoff to Don Pepe's farther west, toward the beach, and you'll come to the quiet **Posada Don Diego Trailer Park** (tel. 666-6-21-81). Full hookups are US$7-8 a night, tent space US$5 (discounts for long-term stays are possible). The park also has a few small trailers for rent (US$20), in case you didn't bring your own. Coin-operated washers (but no dryers) are available. The restaurant and bar at Posada Don Diego enjoy a good reputation, especially for the clam chowder. Or go dig up your own pismo clams on the beach and ask Señora Martinez, who operates the park with her husband José, to steam them for you.

Camping on the beach among the dunes is a possibility, but the sandy track gets a bit dodgy once you pass Posada Don Diego. Passenger cars can make it, but RVs—except those with 4WD—risk getting stuck.

PARQUE NACIONAL SIERRA SAN PEDRO MARTIR

Founded in 1947, this 170,000-acre national park is centered on the Sierra San Pedro Mártir—the highest mountain range in the peninsular cordillera. Like other Baja sierras, the San Pedro Mártir tips toward the west, with its highest peaks thrusting out along the precipitous eastern escarpment. The sierra's (and the peninsula's) highest peak, Picacho del Diablo, or "Devil's Peak"—also known as Cerro de la Encantada, "Enchanted Mountain," and La Providencia, "Providence"—looms over the San Felipe Desert at 3,086 meters (10,154 feet), a challenging Class 3-5 climb.

Three prominent canyons radiate eastward from the base of the mountain—Cañon del Diablo, Cañon Providencia, and Cañon Teledo—and provide magnificent bouldering and scrambling opportunities, sheer cliffs, waterfalls, fan palms, Indian petroglyphs, and several approaches to Diablo's twin granitic summits. Hikers interested in these eastern canyons, which lie just outside the park boundaries, usually approach them from Mexico 3 to the northeast.

Within the park, hikers and backpackers can choose from a network of trails and campsites on a pine-and-juniper forested plateau—approximately 70 km by 15 km—at the heart of the range. Because much of the park exceeds 1,800 meters (6,000 feet) in elevation, annual precipitation averages 60 cm (24 inches); thus water sources are abundant and shady conifers predominate. Only a few hundred people visit San Pedro Mártir each year, making it one of the most under-visited national parks in Mexico and an extraordinary opportunity for wilderness solitude. The mountain hiking conditions enjoyed here are similar to that available in Alta California's Sierra Nevada, but shared with much fewer people.

National Observatory

Because the air is exceptionally clear and potential sources of light pollution are remote, the Mexican government selected the San Pedro Mártir Plateau in 1967 as the site for its Observatorio Nacional. The observatory facilities are at the end of the park access road (20 km past the park entrance), at an elevation of 2,830 meters (9,286 feet). A locked gate just before the observatory means that visitors will have to park and walk two km to reach the domed buildings themselves. Several telescopes are in use at the observatory, including Mexico's largest, a 2.11-meter (83-inch) reflector.

Tours of the facilities are not given to the public except by special arrangement with the Mexican government, but a viewpoint nearby offers an inspiring glimpse of the eastern escarpment and canyons. At night, stars appear over the plateau like a sea of diamonds—who needs a telescope?

Climate

Temperatures on the plateau, 1,800+ meters above sea level, average 26° C (80° F) in July and Aug. during the daytime, down to 4.5° C (40° F) at night. From Dec. through March, temperatures run from 4.5° C (40° F) down to -12° C (10° F). Freezing nights sometimes occur in the spring and fall, with daytime temperatures in the 15-21° C (60-70° F) range.

Snowfall is common above 2,000 meters during the winter (Picacho del Diablo is often snowcapped Nov.-April), and occasional heavy rains fall in late summer. Spring, early summer, and fall are usually dry.

The best hiking seasons are mid-April through mid-June (good for wildflowers) and late Sept. through early Nov. (when quaking aspen puts on its best show). For backpackers, April-June is optimal because water sources (from snowmelt) are more abundant. Late summer rains can cause flashfloods in the arroyos.

Flora And Fauna

About 53 km east of Rancho Meling, the San Telmo road begins ascending rapidly as the terrain changes from arid coastal plains to scrubby high chaparral. At 900 to 1,500 meters (3,000 to 5,000 feet), stands of pine, oak, and juniper appear, mixed with a dwindling number of desert and chaparral species—sagebrush, verbena, yucca, and fan palm. Above 1,500 meters, thickly forested glens leave the Baja desert mythos behind with piñon pine, Jeffrey pine, incense cedar, white fir, sugar pine, and at least three species not found elsewhere in Baja—quaking aspen, lodgepole pine, and the endemic San Pedro Mártir cypress.

Streams in the sierra's western canyons carry an endemic trout species, the Nelson rainbow trout *(Salmo nelsonii,* named for E.W. Nelson, who discovered the fish in 1905). In the early '80s, a group of Mexico City naturalists transplanted Nelson rainbows to several other canyon streams in the park. (Fishing without a license is permitted.) Mule deer, mountain lion, coyote, and the rare *borregon* (bighorn sheep) inhabit some of the canyons.

Domestic animals—cattle and sheep—are often seen in the park, especially along the east side where two ranches are located within park boundaries. Unfortunately, overgrazing is destroying much of the vegetation in this portion of the park, with the full consent of the Mexican government. (On the positive side, the Mexican park service—unlike its U.S. counterpart—forbids logging in all national parks.)

Park Facilities And Regulations

The park entrance is 78 km (47 miles) from Mexico 1 via an unpaved but graded roadway

MOUNTAIN OF MANY NAMES

Devil's Peak, Enchanted Mountain, Providence, and Mt. San Pedro Mártir are a few of the map designations Baja's highest peak has been given over the last four centuries. Whether the Yumano or Cochimí Indians had a name for the soaring peak isn't known today, but they must have been acquainted with its serrated profile, which is visible from 160 km (100 miles) away in Sonora, on the Mexican mainland.

The first recorded mention of the jagged, sparsely vegetated, twin-summited mountain dates from 16th-century Spanish explorations of the Sea of Cortez. As the Spanish sailed into the thirsty upper reaches of the Cortez in late spring, the snowcapped peak hanging over the searing San Felipe Desert to the west must have seemed a mirage, a gift from God. Hence they called it La Providencia, a name that was sustained through the early 1900s.

La Providencia's semantic opposite, El Picacho del Diablo, or "Devil's Peak," surfaced during the missionary period, probably in reference to the peak's formidable appearance when viewed from the west. Misión San Pedro Mártir, perhaps the most remote mission on the peninsula, was established some 25 km to the southwest. Anyone approaching the mountain from its western side is met with a deep chasm, Cañon del Diablo, at its base; the geographical separation makes Diablo seem all the more unassailable. Another possible explanation is that the mountain might have been revered by local Indians; to divert Indian attention away from the peak and toward the mission, the San Pedro Mártir padres may have consigned it to the Devil.

The padres called a large, open valley meadow between the mission and the mountain La Encantada, "The Enchanted," perhaps because it appears in the midst of heavy pine and juniper forests as if cleared by supernatural forces. The meadow appeared on Spanish maps thereafter, and Mexican cartographers in the 1920s, whether by mistake or intention (perhaps they felt a reference to the Devil ran contrary to their religious beliefs), applied the name to the mountain.

Other names have made brief appearances this century, including El Picacho Blanco, a reference both to the peak's mostly white coloring and its snowbound condition in the winter. But El Picacho del Diablo is the most common term used among Sierra San Pedro Mártir residents and mountaineers; it's also the most common name found on English-language maps of Baja. The official Mexican government name, however, remains Cerro de la Encantada.

The Climbers

Called "the unchallenged retreat of lions and mountain sheep, the unscaled lookout of eagles and mighty condors" by author A.W. North in 1910, Devil's Peak was successfully challenged by American cartographer Donald McLain the very year following this colorful statement. The next recorded climb was by a U.S. Sierra Club group in 1932, who bestowed the names Campo Noche and Arroyo Noche ("Night Camp" and "Night Wash") to the area in Cañon del Diablo where they were forced to spend the night after struggling with the mountain's west face.

The peak was ascended by another American climber (Randall Henderson, editor of *Desert* magazine) in 1937, by several more in the '50s, and by the early '70s over 50 persons a year (both Mexicans and foreigners) were scaling the heights—with as many attempting the climb and turning back short of the summit. Today the class-3 Slot Wash approach is a straightforward but challenging ascent for experienced climbers, while the other six proven approaches comprise some of the toughest climbing in Mexico.

(follow signs marked "Observatorio"). In winter, the occasional snowstorm may force temporary road closure, but during most of the year the road is passable by passenger car. The entrance station, at a forested meadow called La Corona de Abajo ("Lower Crown"), is open daily 0700-1900; during these hours an entry fee of US$1.50 is collected.

A number of established campsites and trails are minimally maintained by park staff. Overall, the park is most suited to wilderness hiking and camping. Although there are no facilities for car or trailer camping as such, it is safe to leave a vehicle parked anywhere within the park boundaries (unless otherwise posted).

Neither hunting nor the possession of firearms is permitted within the park boundaries. When the occasional sanctioned deer hunt is held in adjacent Cañon del Diablo, the canyon may be closed to hiking and backpacking. Offroad driving is banned at all times. Fires are permitted (using fallen deadwood) only within established fire-rings at a few campsites on the plateau; backpackers should carry their own portable camp stoves. Before leaving on an overnight hike, you should let park rangers know where you're going and how long you intend to be gone.

Preparations And Precautions

Park trails are not well-marked; don't consider even a day hike without carrying a compass. The observatory road bisects the park, east to west, and makes a useful mental landmark. When embarking on a hike, note whether you're heading north or south of this road. If you get lost anywhere west of the eastern escarpment, simply head directly north (or south) from your current location, and you should intercept the roadway.

Canyon hiking along the eastern escarpment is rugged and should only be attempted by experienced climbers, or in the company of someone who knows the terrain. You may be able to arrange for a guide through Rancho Meling (A.P. 1326, Ensenada, BCN).

Maps: The Mexican government publishes two topographic maps (20-meter contour), San Rafael H11B45 and Santa Cruz H11B55, which cover an area that includes the park (and more). They're available by mail from the Map Centre (tel. 619-291-3830, 2611 University Ave., San Diego, CA, 92104-2894).

More up-to-date and easier to use is a 1988 topo map published by Centra Publications (4705 Laurel St., San Diego, CA 92105) and titled *Parque Nacional San Pedro Mártir: Topographic Map and Visitor's Guide to Baja's Highest Mountains.* This well-designed, easy-to-read map is based on the Mexican topos, but adds many physical features never

mapped before. Also printed on the map are brief descriptions of 17 different hiking trails, including seven Picacho del Diablo climbing routes.

Water: Except during midsummer, streams are abundant on the plateau, and are generally considered clean enough to drink from. In the eastern arroyos and canyons, water is usually available year-round, though it may be contaminated by livestock. Whether on the plateau or in the canyonlands, you should always treat local water just to be sure. Wherever you go in the San Pedro Mártir, carry extra water and a water purification system (filter, iodine, or halazone).

Trails

The park is honeycombed with footpaths and hiking trails, particularly in the vicinity of Picacho del Diablo at the edge of the eastern escarpment. Longer, more isolated trails connect the large meadow areas of Vallecitos, Los Llanitos, La Encantada, La Grulla, and Rancho Viejo, making a 50-km loop. The three trails described below, on the park's scenic northeastern edge, are well-traveled and thus relatively easy to follow. For a more complete inventory, get Centra Publications' detailed topo map of the park (see "Preparations and Precautions" above).

Vallecitos-Blue Bottle Peak (9.5 km): Vallecitos is the name given to a complex of little flats (literally, "Little Valleys") southeast of the observatory road via a dirt track that begins 16.5 km from the park entrance. About 3.5 km from the observatory road, a footpath branches left (east) up an arroyo for 1.7 km, then into an aspen-studded meadow. A smaller path leads north from the meadow to an excellent escarpment-edge view of Cañon del Diablo.

Two km farther southeast on the main trail is another north-branching path that leads to Scout Peak (2,850 meters), where there are primitive campsites and an unobstructed view of Picacho del Diablo's western face. (From this point, climbers can scramble down the side of the Cañon del Diablo to Campo Noche below, and continue on to Blue Bottle Peak via the arroyos at the southern end of the canyon.) Meanwhile, the main trail below Scout Peak continues south and then east a couple of kilometers more to a point just northwest of Cerro Botella Azul ("Blue Bottle Peak"); a smaller trail ascends the peak itself. At 2,950 meters (9,680 feet), Blue Bottle is the highest point on the plateau and a reasonable alternative to Picacho del Diablo for the less adventurous. On a clear day—perhaps 85% of the time—you can see both the Pacific and the Sea of Cortez.

Observatory-Cañon del Diablo (5.3 km): Just below the observatory gate, a trail branches east from the main road and leads into Cañon del Diablo, the deepest and longest canyon in the Sierra San Pedro Mártir. Along the way, this trail passes through a scenic aspen meadow at 2500+ meters, where a short path branches north to a rocky viewpoint over the canyon. Beyond the meadow, the trail becomes a demanding Class 3-4 descent that negotiates brush and boulders along an arroyo intersecting with the larger canyon. Near the bottom of the canyon this trail joins the Cañon del Diablo-Campo Noche Trail, the beginning of one of the east-

SIERRA SAN PEDRO MÁRTIR (PLATEAU)

VIEWPOINT

NATIONAL OBSERVATORY

GATE

RESIDENCES

VIEWPOINT

ASPEN GROVES

CAÑON DIABLITO

CAÑON DEL DIABLO

= VEHICLE TRACK
= ESTABLISHED TRAIL
= OBSCURE CROSS COUNTRY TRAIL OR CLIMBING ROUTE

VALLECITOS

CAÑON PROVIDENCIA

VIEWPOINT

ASPEN GROVES

SCOUT PEAK

CAMPO NOCHE

(3,095m / 10,154ft)

PICACHO DEL DIABLO

SLOT WASH   (3,094m / 10,152ft)

NIGHT WASH

CERRO BOTELLO AZUL

CAÑON TELEDO

LOS LLANITOS

VIEWPOINT

0   1m
0   1km

© MOON PUBLICATIONS, INC.

ern approaches to Picacho del Diablo. (This latter trail, though rated only Class 2-3, involves a four-day hike in desert conditions; it's best undertaken with a guide who knows the terrain.) Water is available at several streams and waterfalls in the canyon.

Slot Wash Ascent of Picacho del Diablo: This is the easiest of the seven routes used to climb Baja's highest mountain (a Class 3 climb—the other six ascents are rated Class 4 and 5). To get to Slot Wash, an arroyo that descends Diablo's west face, follow the Vallecitos-Blue Bottle Peak Trail until you've passed the saddle northwest of Blue Bottle; then continue along the peak's north flank until the trail narrows and descends into Cañon del Diablo.

Near the bottom of the canyon, on the east side, is Campo Noche, a large campsite with a fire ring and nearby pools. The ascent to Slot Wash begins at a shallow arroyo, next to Campo Noche, called Arroyo Noche or "Night Wash," which segues into Slot Wash at an elevation of 2,240 meters. The way is well marked with ducks (stone trail markers). At about 2,500 meters, the route forks. The little-used south branch leads out of Slot Wash, through a brushy side ravine, to the lower of Diablo's twin peaks (3,094 meters). The north route, which most climbers take, continues through Slot Wash, over large stone slabs, until ducks point out a sharp left (north) up a rocky slope. This leads to a steep-walled arroyo nicknamed "Wall Street," which in turn proceeds directly to the higher of the peaks (3,095 meters). Continuing straight up Slot Wash, instead of taking the north branch, leads to the saddle between the two summits.

Starting at Blue Bottle Peak on the plateau, the trip to Picacho del Diablo and back usually takes three days—one night at Campo Noche in each direction, plus one night in the vicinity of the summit.

Approaching Picacho Del Diablo From Mexico 3

The network of trails below Picacho del Diablo can be approached from Mexico 3 (the section between Ensenada and Crucero La Trinidad), to the northeast of the park, via Cañon del Diablo. The road to the canyon area is 164 km southeast of Ensenada (or 34 km northwest of Crucero La Trinidad, if you're driving from Mexicali or San Felipe), south off Mexico 3. The road is graded as far as Rancho Villa del Sol, about eight km south of the Mexico 3 junction, then joins vehicle tracks southeast across the salt flat Laguna Diablo.

Approximately 24 km south of Mexico 3, another set of tracks branches straight west toward Rancho Santa Clara. At Rancho Santa Clara, a dirt track passes just south of the ranch and leads nine km west until it ends at Cañon Diablito. You can park here, but don't leave valuables in the vehicle.

From Diablito, a three-km trail heads northeast to the mouth of Cañon del Diablo. Perhaps the greatest obstacle in the canyon is only about 800 meters into the mouth—a sizable waterfall tumbling down smooth granite walls. A cable bolted to the wall allows hikers to scramble up one side; sometimes accumulated sand creates a temporary platform high enough to surmount the wall without the assistance of the cable. The canyon itself is mostly a Class 2 hike with a few Class 3 bouldering exercises along the way; there are plenty of year-round pools and waterfalls to cool off in along the way.

Campo Noche is 11 km (seven miles) into the canyon, at an elevation of 1,915 meters (6,300 feet). A roundtrip hike from the end of the vehicle track to Picacho del Diablo, at a comfortable pace, usually takes four days, including stops at Campo Noche each way. (See "Slot Wash Ascent of Picacho del Diablo" above for a description of the tried-and-tested route from Campo Noche.)

VALLE DE SAN QUINTÍN-BAHÍA DE SAN QUINTÍN

The Valle de San Quintín, actually more a coastal plain than a valley, is a broad flat between a row of five extinct volcano cones to the west (four on the peninsula, one on Isla San Martín just offshore) and the Sierra San Miguel to the east. Two small rivers, Río San Miguel and Río Santa Maria, bisect the flat east to west and feed an irrigation system that has made the valley an important vegetable-farming center. Many Indians from the interior of Mexico, especially Oaxaca and Chiapas, work on the farms and live in shacks on San Quintín's outskirts.

For visitors, San Quintín's main attraction is a complex coastal environment, the chief features of which are three large, interconnecting bays: Bahía San Quintín, Bahía Falsa, and Bahía Santa Maria. The innermost bay, surrounded by tidal flats and salt-marshes, is referred to both as Bahía San

Quintín and Puerto San Quintín. The outermost bay, facing the Pacific, is called Bahía Santa Maria as far south as the tip of Cabo San Quintín; beyond this point it's usually called Bahía San Quintín. (Yes, it can be confusing—two Bahías San Quintín.)

The town of **San Quintín** itself is little more than a collection of shops, motels, restaurants, and other businesses clustered along Mexico 1. Useful services include a long-distance telephone booth, 24-hour medical clinic, and two banks. Five km south of San Quintín is a another town of similar size, **Lázaro Cár-**

denas, consisting of Mexico's 67th Infantry battalion camp, the intercity bus terminal, a few shops, restaurants, and two motels.

Most visitors staying more than one night in the area are anglers or hunters. Although the beaches are pristine, an almost-constant summer fog has prevented San Quintín from becoming a popular beach-going spot.

History

In the 1880s, a British land company with plans for a wheat empire purchased much of the San Quintín area from the U.S.-based International Land Company (at the time, the ILC owned most of northern Baja). In response to promises of agricultural wealth, around a hundred English colonists purchased subdivided land tracts from the parent company, wheat was planted, and a grist mill constructed. For transport of the flour, the English built a pier on the inner Bahía San Quintín and began construction on a railway that was to link up with Southern Pacific Railway in Alta California. Thirty km of track were laid, including a rail causeway from the west bank of inner Bahía San Quintín, before the colony failed.

A drought devastated one of the colony's first wheat harvests, and by 1900 all of the colonists had abandoned San Quintín. Although the individual farmers were economically ruined, the U.S. and British land companies walked away all the richer, a pattern that was to recur several times in northern Baja. Remains of the grist mill, railroad causeway, pier, and English cemetery can be seen along the perimeter of the inner bay.

Climate

While most of northwestern coastal Baja has a climate similar to San Diego's, with regard to Valle de San Quintín, San Francisco would make a better comparison. As in the San Francisco area, Pacific influences combine with the insulating effect of a large bay (in this case, three bays) to keep average temperatures within a narrow year-round range: from 12° C (54° F) Dec.-Jan. to 20° C (68° F) Aug.-September.

Annual precipitation averages 31 centimeters (12 inches); December usually records

the most rainfall (average six centimeters), with Feb.-March second (four to five centimeters); summer months are usually rain-free but foggy.

Beach And Bay Access

Several dirt roads south of Lázaro Cárdenas lead directly west from Mexico 1 to the inner bay; follow signs to the Old Mill Motel and Old Pier Restaurant. Car-topped or trailered boats can be launched here, or from a boat launch on the west shore of the bay. To reach the latter site, drive west out of Lázaro Cárdenas on the gravel road that leaves Mexico 1 between the PEMEX station and military camp (a sign here reads "Bahía San Quintín"). Fourteen km from Mexico 1, just past Monte de Kenton (a cinder cone immediately to the west), a lesser dirt road forks left and leads to Pedregal, a bayside settlement where small boats can easily be launched.

If, instead of turning south to Pedregal, you continue west along the road from Lázaro Cárdenas, you'll pass an oyster farm on Bahía Falsa and reach the road's end at a fish camp on the Pacific.

To reach Bahía Santa Maria or the larger, Pacific-facing Bahía San Quintín, drive 16 km south of Lázaro Cárdenas and turn right (west) on the paved road to Santa Maria (the turn is marked by signs advertising Hotel La Pinta and Motel Cielito Lindo). Follow the signs along this pine-tree-lined road to Hotel La Pinta; Playa Santa Maria, the largest, longest beach in the area, is behind the hotel.

Hotels And Motels

Motel Chavez (tel. 5-20-05, A.P. 32, San Quintín, BCN) is the only place to stay in the town of San Quintín. Although it's far from bays and beaches, if you're just stopping for the night, it's a clean, economical choice, with well-maintained rooms for US$18-23. Some rooms have kitchenettes.

In Lázaro Cárdenas, near the military camp, are **Las Hadas** and **Hotel Romo,** both with basic, nondescript motel rooms for US$10-15. Southwest of Lázaro Cárdenas, on the inner bay next to the Old Pier Restaurant, is the **Motel San Carlos** (P.O. Box 11, Valle de San Quintín, BCN). Simple rooms, all with bay views, cost US$25. Farther north along the same dirt road, on the site of a former grist mill, is the **Molino Viejo** (Old Mill, A.P. 90, Valle de San Quintín, BCN), a long-time favorite among hunters and anglers. Rustic rooms are US$20-35; some rooms have kitchenettes. The electricity at Molino Viejo is usually turned off during the hours 1000-1800. Reservations at Molino Viejo can be made by contacting Baja Outfitters (tel. 619-428-2779 in the U.S.).

Farther south, next to Bahía Santa Maria, is the **Motel Cielito Lindo** with large, comfortable rooms for US$30 s, US$35 d; the electricity is turned off 1100-1500. A restaurant, bar, and RV park are adjacent to the motel (see "Camping and RV Parks" below). Also on Bahía Santa Maria is **Hotel La Pinta** (tel. 667-6-2601 in Ensenada; 800-336-5454 in the U.S.). Spacious heated rooms, all with sea views and terraces, cost US$55 s, US$60 d. Hotel facilities include a restaurant, bar, tennis court, and private airstrip.

Camping And RV Parks

Primitive camping is possible at a number of spots in the San Quintín area, including the west side of inner Bahía San Quintín (at Pedregal), the Pacific shore below the cinder cone Picacho Vizcaíno, and Playa Santa Maria.

On the east side of inner Bahía San Quintín, the Old Mill Restaurant/Motel San Carlos allows RVs to park nearby for no charge. Farther north along this same shore, beyond the Motel Molino Viejo, **Campo Lorenzo** has sites with full hookups for US$7 a night.

At Bahía Santa Maria, Motel Cielito Lindo offers tent/camper sites, no hookups, for US$5. A more remote choice, **Honey's RV Campground,** is 15 km south of Lázaro Cárdenas and 1.6 km west of Mexico 1, on a secluded beach. Sites with water and sewage (no electricity) cost US$5 per night for tents or RVs. Other facilities include hot showers and flush toilets.

Food

The well-known **Old Pier,** next to Motel San Carlos on the inner bay, offers rather expensive (for Mexico) seafood, from unimpressive clam dinners for US$9.30 to abalone or lobster for US$16. Meals include a generous appetizer tray of salami, soup, marinated mussels, cheese, and olives, but the entrees themselves are disappointing.

In the town of San Quintín, **El Alteño** and **Costa Azul** serve fresh continental- and Mexican-style seafood respectively; both accept credit cards and are open for breakfast, lunch, and dinner. El Alteño also has a bar. The **Hacienda** in Lázaro Cárdenas offers standard Mexican food for breakfast, lunch, and dinner.

The seafood at the Motel Cielito Lindo's restaurant (open for dinner only) is as good as any in San Quintín and prices are quite reasonable. An adjoining coffee shop serves breakfast and lunch. **Las Cazuelas,** the restaurant at Hotel La Pinta, serves the usual La Pinta menu for breakfast, lunch, and dinner.

Groceries are available at a number of tiendas in San Quintín and Lázaro Cárdenas. There's also a panadería in San Quintín and a tortillería in Lázaro Cárdenas.

Sports And Recreation

Fishing: The unusually varied marine environment, caused by the intersection of the Pacific and three bays, makes the San Quintín coast an excellent area for surfcasting and inshore fishing. Because the entrance to the two inner bays, Bahía Falsa and Bahía San Quintín (Puerto San Quintín), is blocked by steady surf year-round, the bays are inaccessible to any commercial fishing fleet. This means more gamefish is available for casual anglers, who can launch small boats from inside (see "Bay and Beach Access" above for details) or from the Pacific shore.

In general, San Quintín attracts the same fish species found north to Ensenada—except they're more highly concentrated here. Flatfish are common in the shallows of the inner bays, bottomfish in the deeper sections. Perch and croaker run along the Pacific beaches. (According to Tom Miller, author of *Angler's Guide to Baja California,* nowhere in their range are croakers as large as the ones typically caught along San Quintín's beaches.)

Farther out in the Pacific, particularly near the south end of volcanic Isla San Martín and at the tip of Cabo San Quintín, yellowtail, yellowfin, white and black seabass, rock cod, and ling cod are common catches (in season,

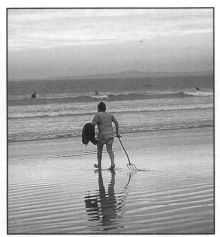

(JOE CUMMINGS)
clam diggers, Playa Santa Maria

of course, among properly equipped anglers). On Isla San Martín are a fish camp and a mussel farm; sheltered anchorages are possible in two coves found at either side of a rocky cape at the southeast end of the island.

Light fishing tackle can be rented at the Hotel La Pinta.

Clamming: All three bays are well endowed with clams and mussels. The most scenic (and easiest) spot for digging up the large pismo clams is Playa Santa Maria, behind Hotel La Pinta. If you come here at low tide, you'll most likely be joined by a legion of local clam-diggers. You can use your fingers to dig the huge clams out of the sand, or bring along a mesh bag and a pitchfork (available in Lázaro Cárdenas) as the locals do. The pros thresh the sand at the surf line with a pitchfork, tossing the clams into the bag tied around their waists. A mesh bag works best because it holds the clams but allows water and sand to drain away. Remember not to take more clams than you can eat that day, and not to take any clams smaller than your hand.

Boat Rentals: The Hotel Molino Viejo (Old Mill) is the best place to rent a boat for bay fishing. Aluminum pangas (18-foot) rent for US$12 a day and will carry up to three. A 22-foot, outfitted fishing cruiser can be chartered for US$225 a day. The Motel Cielito Lindo also rents pangas and is well located for Bahía Santa Maria launches.

Hunting: The tidal flats and marshlands around the inner bays attract migrating duck and Pacific brant (a small, black goose) during the winter, and quail most of the year. The Molino Viejo and Cielito Lindo hotels organize local hunting trips.

Scuba Diving: Johnston's Seamount, 9½ km southwest of Cabo San Quintín, is a renowned site for underwater photography and spearfishing. Sixteen km northwest of Cabo San Quintín, Isla San Martín is surrounded by kelp beds as well as several rock reefs and underwater pinnacles. Roca Ben, five km south of the island, rises within three meters of the surface, with intermediate depths of 30 meters. Encrusted with hydrocoral formations, the rock is a habitat for abundant abalone, scallop, lobster, and other shellfish. Due to cold water upwellings, visibility ranges 15 to 25 meters (50 to 80 feet).

San Quintín has no diving facilities at this writing. Diving Charters (see "Sports and Recreation" in the main introduction for phone and address) leads periodic dive trips to Isla San Martín and Johnston's Seamount. The latter was named for one of Diving Charters' skippers who pioneered diving in this area.

Transport

Fuel: Three PEMEX stations offer regular and unleaded gas, one each in San Quintín and Lázaro Cárdenas, and one at Hotel La Pinta. A fourth, at the junction of the old highway (part of Mexico 1 that was destroyed in a flood) and the road to Playa Santa Maria, is abandoned.

Buses: Intercity buses arrive and depart from a bus depot in Lázaro Cárdenas, on the west side of Mexico 1.

TECATE TO ENSENADA

TECATE

During his 1964 presidential campaign, Gustavo Díaz Ordaz referred to Tecate as *la ventana mas limpia de México*, "the cleanest window of Mexico." He may have been fishing for the Tecate vote (which he didn't get—Díaz was unpopular in northern Baja), but as Mexican border towns go, this one is easily the most inviting.

Set in a bowl-shaped valley in the lower Sierra Juárez (known as the Laguna Mountains on the Alta California side), Tecate is insulated from industrial Tijuana and Mexicali to the west and east. The fresh, unpolluted air in the valley lured the developers of North America's first and longest-running health spa, Rancho La Puerta. Tecate's other claim to fame is its namesake *cerveza*, brewed here for nearly 50 years.

The border crossing, four blocks north at the end of Calle Lázaro Cárdenas, is one of Baja's most relaxed. Savvy Alta Californians use this crossing instead of Tijuana's when returning from an Ensenada holiday; the wait is much shorter, and the drive along Mexico 3 between Ensenada and Tecate provides an alternative to Mexico 1's coastal scenery. (See "Transport," below, for more details.) The town on the U.S. side of the border is also called Tecate.

Town life is centered around **Parque Hidalgo,** a shady plaza at the intersection of Av. Juárez and Calle Lázaro Cárdenas, Tecate's main thoroughfares. At the southeast corner of the park is a statue of Miguel Hidalgo, the Dolores priest who issued the call for Mexican independence in 1810. In the vicinity of the small plaza are a number of restaurants, taco stands, *paleterías y neveterías* (popsicle and ice-cream stands), craft shops, and the tourist office.

Tecate's general ambience is more that of a provincial Mexican town than that of a border town. Yet in spite of the many pleasantries Tecate has to offer, the area gets relatively few tourists compared with Tijuana, Mexicali, Rosarito, or Ensenada.

Climate

Tecate is famous for its mild summers, thanks to an elevation of 514 meters (1,690 feet) and distance from both cold Pacific breezes and high temperatures of the San Felipe Desert. The average temperature in the warmest months, July-Aug., is 22° C (72° F); on a particularly hot afternoon, temperatures may approach 38° C (100° F), but by nightfall temperatures will have dropped to the low 20s C (70s F).

In winter, Tecate records lower temperatures than either Tijuana or Mexicali; during the coolest months, Dec.-Feb., the average temperature is 10° C (50° F), with an occasional frost. Average annual precipitation in the Valle de Tecate is 49 centimeters (19 inches). Typically, over half the rainfall occurs Dec.-February.

History

Tecate has the distinction of being the oldest border town in Baja, though in terms of peninsular history it is still relatively young. In the early 1800s, a few mestizo farmers began working the valley lands, and, as word got around that the valley was fertile and water was abundant (supplied by the Tecate and Las Palmas rivers), more followed. In 1831 Peruvian Juan Bandini received a land grant of 4,500 hectares from the Mexican government, and two years later laid out a town to serve the budding farming community.

Long before Bandini's arrival, the valley surrounding Tecate had been sporadically inhabited by Yuma Indians, who called it Zacate. The Yumas revered 1,520-meter (5,000-foot) Monte Cuchumá, the valley's most outstanding geographic feature, which today straddles the U.S.-Mexico border. Surviving Kumyais, a sub-tribe of the Yumas, still revere the mountain, and in 1982 they were successful in obtaining a U.S. agreement to dismantle radio towers on Cuchumá's Alta California side.

Most likely the name Tecate developed from a Spanish corruption of the Indian name for the valley, Zacate. Another theory, rather unlikely, has it that Tecate comes from the English "to cut," since Anglos to the north often came to the valley to cut wood in the late 19th century (but the vegetation in the valley has always been mostly treeless chaparral). The settlement became the capital of a new Mexican municipality in 1892, just after a railroad was built to connect Tijuana, Tecate, and Mexicali with the national rail system.

Tecate became a household word in Mexico after the founding of the Tecate Brewery in 1943. This is the town's only real industry, however, and Tecate today remains primarily dependent on agriculture. Tourism, though relatively limited, is also a source of local revenue. The year 1992, Tecate's centennial, promises to be a good year for local fiestas.

Tecate Brewery

Tecate beer, the only beer in Mexico named for a town, was first brewed by Tecate entrepreneur Alberto Aldrete in 1943. Aldrete started the brewery as a sideline to his *mal-tería* (malt factory). The first bottles distributed to the public carried a label that read "Rubio Tecate" over a silhouette of Monte Cuchumá. Although the beer sold well in the local area, Aldrete went bankrupt after 10 years, and in 1954 the brewery was sold to Cervecería Cuauhtémoc, brewers of two other well-known Mexican beers, Carta Blanca and Bohemia.

Today, Cuauhtémoc operates breweries in six other Mexican cities and has added the Chihuahua, Indio, and High Life labels to its output (plus Dos Equis and Sol as subsidiaries). The Tecate brand, however, is brewed only in Tecate and Monterrey. The Monterrey brewery produces canned Tecate (in the red-and-silver can familiar to many North Americans), much of it for export; at the Tecate plant, only bottles and kegs are produced. Mexican beer-drinkers mostly drink Tecate in long-necked deposit bottles or liter-size *ballenas* ("whales"). On both cans and bottles, every label still carries the profile of Cuchumá, the Kumyai's sacred mountain.

Beer aficionados claim the best Tecate comes from Tecate (rather than Monterrey) because the water used at the brewery, tapped directly from local springs, is considered the purest in Mexico. According to Cuahutémoc brewers, Tecate is brewed as a lager, with an alcohol content of 3.6% and sufficient hops to rate a 20 on the international bitterness scale. Tecate exported to the U.S. is lowered to 3.2% alcohol—a major reason the brand tastes so different north of the border (along with the fact that U.S.-consumed Tecate is usually canned product from Monterrey).

Carta Blanca, the only other label produced at the Tecate brewery, is a lighter pilsner with a bitterness grade of 16 and an alcohol content of 3.5%. Bajacalifornios overwhelmingly prefer Tecate to Carta Blanca, partially out of loyalty to Baja California (Carta Blanca originated in Monterrey) but also because they perceive the latter to be a bland brew. Incidentally, the custom of drinking Tecate with salt and a squeeze of lime, now part of Cuahutémoc's Tecate advertising campaign, was probably introduced by gringo Baja hands (who squeeze lime over everything they consume in Mexico) concerned with killing bacteria on the top of the can. Lime juice also tends to neutralize the "can" taste. (Follow the *mexicano* example and drink bottled Tecate; it's cheaper, if you return the bottles for a deposit refund, better-tasting, and more ecologically responsible.)

Tours: Brewery tours are offered only on Saturday mornings and only for groups of 20 or more. Sometimes individual visitors are permitted to join a scheduled group tour—contact the state tourist office on the plaza or call the brewery (tel. 665-4-17-09) to see whether this is possible. The usual tour takes around 45 minutes and includes a look at all stages of the brewing and bottling process. A few facts, in case you miss the tour: the present brewery complex stands on the same site as Aldrete's original keg brewery; high-tech German equipment is used to produce 250,000 hectoliters per month (6.6 million U.S. gallons); and the brewery employs around 850 persons, who have their own recreational and cultural center south of town.

PRACTICALITIES

Hotels And Motels
Just west of town on the north side of Mexico 2, **La Hacienda** (tel. 4-12-50, Av. Juárez 861) offers clean rooms with TV and a/c for US$35-40. **El Dorado** (tel. 4-11-01, 4-10-84; fax 4-13-33, Av. Juárez 1100), a wood-and-stucco motel near the western entrance to Tecate (at Av. Juárez and Calle Esteban), has rooms with TV, a/c, and phone for US$43 s, US$50 d, or US$80 suite. Both hotels feature motel-court parking.

Two blocks east of Motel El Dorado at Calle Aldrete and Av. Juárez, closer to the center of town, is the inexpensive **El Paraíso** (tel. 4-17-16). The rooms are basic but clean, with a/c (old window units) and attached hot shower for US$15 s, US$23-28 d. In winter, if necessary, you can ask for a space heater *(calentador)* for your room. Guests can park in the garage beneath the hotel.

Ranch Resorts
The luxurious **Rancho Tecate Resort Country Club** (tel. 4-00-11, 4-02-60; 619-234-7151 in the U.S.), 9½ km (six miles) southeast of Tecate off Mexico 3, is a sprawling ranch resort with a golf course (currently being upgraded to pro status), tennis courts, a swimming pool, and a lake stocked with freshwater gamefish. Rates for standard rooms, in a building constructed in the typical Tecate hacienda style, are US$59 s, US$64 d. Suites cost US$59-95 a night (depending on the floor plan—each is unique) and include kitchens.

Hacienda Santa Veronica (tel. 66-85-97-93 in Tijuana, 619-341-9811 or 619-298-4105 in San Diego) is a newish ranch resort off

Mexico 2, about 30 km east of Tecate near Km 98. Guest rooms, in mission-style condos, cost US$45 and come with fireplace and patio. Recreational facilities include six tennis courts, offroad racetracks for motorcycles and four-wheelers, equestrian trails, swimming pool, volleyball court, and basketball court. Originally a *ganadería* for breeding ranch for fighting bulls *(ganados bravos),* the Hacienda also offers elementary bullfighting lessons for ranch guests. Other facilities include a restaurant, bar, and RV park open to the public. Hacienda Santa Veronica's mailing address is 74818 Vellie Dr., Suite 4, Palm Desert, CA 92260.

Rancho La Puerta

The most famous spa in North America, La Puerta ("The Door") is not open to the public as simple lodgings; the prices, in fact, tend to limit the clientele to CEOs and Hollywood celebrities. Enrolled guests participate in an all-inclusive, week-long health regime designed for physical and spiritual rejuvenation that includes mountain hiking, low-impact aerobics, yoga and t'ai chi, swimming, and weight-training. The site was chosen for its location in one of the Californias' last "safe zones" for the environmentally sensitive, and for its proximity to Monte Cuchumá, viewed by spa's founders as a source of spiritual power.

Originally founded as the Essene School of Life by Hungarian Edmond Szekeley and his wife Deborah in 1940, guests paid US$17.50 a week to pitch their own tents, talk philosophy, climb Monte Cuchumá, get massages, and eat organic food. In the '50s, the spa inspired Michael Murphy to start Big Sur's Esalen Institute. Today Szekeley's son Alex oversees the ranch (and its sister spa, the Golden Door in Escondido, Alta California), which has been transformed into a beautifully landscaped, 300-acre health resort.

The hacienda-style architecture includes cottages and suites for a maximum 150 guests, each unit with its own garden (most with fireplaces). A recently renovated dining hall serves organic fruits and vegetables grown at the subsidiary Rancho Tres Estrellas, along with occasional fresh fish. State-of-the-art recreational facilities include six aerobic gyms with sliding glass walls, a weight-training gym, four swimming pools, five whirlpools, three saunas, and gender-separated centers for massage, herbal wraps, and private sauna-steam baths (the latter services aren't included in the basic weekly rate).

All-inclusive prices for the daily health program, meals, and accommodations range from US$1,200 per week in a studio cottage to US$1,900 for a villa with separate living, bedroom, and kitchen. (In other words, it costs about the same as a deluxe seven-day cruise but is a good deal healthier.) For reservations or more information, contact Rancho La Puerta, P.O. Box 2548, Escondido, CA 92033 (tel. 619-744-4222 or 800-443-7565; fax 619-744-5007).

Camping And RV Parks

The **Intercalifornias Trailer Park** (tel. 4-08-61), Av. Revolución, 3½ blocks west of Calle Lázaro Cárdenas, has 10 trailer sites with full hookups (including cable TV). When spaces are vacant, the daily rate is US$10. Facilities include rest rooms and a telephone.

Costa RV Park at Rancho Santa Veronica (30 km east of Tecate at Km 98, Mexico 2) has full-hookup slots for US$15, tent spaces for only US$2.50. Guests have access to all the ranch's recreational facilities (see "Ranch Resorts" above).

Food

For its size, Tecate has an unusually high number of places to eat. Among the most renowned culinary attractions are the long-established *taquerías* surrounding Parque Hidalgo, which serve a variety of better-than-average tacos, burritos, and tostadas. Each has its unique way of assembling the basic ingredients, but you can hardly go wrong if you choose one of the following: **La Placita** (facing the east side of the plaza on Calle Ortiz Rubio); **El Asadero No. 2** (facing the north side of the plaza on Av. Juárez); **Doña Magi** (a half block east of the plaza on Av. Juárez, next to the bus terminal). The taquerías are typically open from after morning till late evening; the Doña Magi usually opens around 0600 to serve waiting bus passengers (in case you crave a breakfast taco).

For quick, inexpensive, sit-down meals, the **Plaza Jardin Tecate** is a good choice. This tiny diner on the south side of the plaza, a few doors west of the tourist office, offers Mexican standards at reasonable prices for lunch and dinner, plus a large variety of breakfasts. During warm weather, the Jardin places a few tables outside and instantly becomes the only sidewalk café in Tecate.

Another inexpensive, diminutive place is **El Serape,** next door to Motel El Paraíso on Av. Juárez. The short menu includes Mexican breakfasts, tacos, enchiladas, and mole poblana. Open daily for breakfast, lunch, and dinner.

Mariscos Victor (no phone, Av. Hidalgo 284) serves very reasonably priced Mexican-style seafood, including ceviche tostadas, fish tacos, seafood cocktails, and shrimp, as well as ranchero standards like *burritos de machaca, gorditas,* quesadillas, *bistek* (steak). A choice of nine different full breakfasts are available, starting at 0700, for US$2.20-2.35. Open for breakfast, lunch, and dinner.

For more elaborate meals, **La Carreta** (tel. 4-04-62, Av. Juárez 270, at Calle Santana) is often recommended by the locals, who favor the dark, brick-walled interior. The menu features all kinds of Mexican, with an emphasis on norteña cooking, at moderate prices. It's open daily for breakfast, lunch, and dinner. One block west of La Carreta, attached to

Motel El Dorado, is the slightly more expensive restaurant-bar **El Tucán,** specializing in Mexican and continental; open daily for breakfast, lunch, and dinner.

Another local favorite is **El Pueblo Viejo,** moved from its old location near the brewery to the north end of Calle Lázaro Cárdenas at Callejón Reforma, close to the border crossing. Offerings include Mexican, steak, and seafood. The tourist traffic has boosted prices here a bit; open daily for lunch and dinner.

Hidden away on an alley to the west of the plaza is **El Passetto** (tel. 4-13-61, Callejón Libertad 200), which serves mostly Italian pasta, along with seafood and a few Mexican dishes. Prices are moderate; open for lunch and dinner.

Noodle addicts can switch from Italian to Chinese in **El Dragón Cuchumá,** at Av. Hidalgo and Calle Obregon, opposite the brewery. The Cantonese cuisine here won't win any awards, but portions are huge and the table sauce is hotter than most Mexican salsas by several degrees. Open daily for lunch and dinner.

Groceries: A number of tiendas on Av. Juárez and Av. Hidalgo sell basic foodstuffs; there's also a medium-size supermarket on Av. Juárez near the Calle Carranza intersection. For excellent pan dulce, bolillos, and other Mexican bakery items, grab tray and tongs at **Panadería El Mejor Pan,** on the

downtown Tecate
(JOE CUMMINGS)

north side of Av. Juárez between Calles Rodriguez and Portes Gil. Some folks claim it's the best Mexican bakery in all of Baja; it's certainly a contender, a major advantage being that it's open 24 hours.

Entertainment

Tecate is not big on nightlife; the main source of evening entertainment seems to be promenading back and forth along Av. Juárez until around 2100, when the streets become practically deserted. Perhaps the healthy air sends everyone to bed early.

El Passetto and El Tucán restaurants each have attached bars; the bar at El Passetto usually stays open till after midnight. Tecate has only one movie theater, Cine Variedades on Av. Juárez. A solitary dance hall, Los Candiles (Av. Hidalgo 327), books a variety of traveling Latin pop and norteña groups on weekends or during fiestas. During the week, recorded music sometimes transforms the hall into an ersatz disco.

Although it almost seems out of place in this low-key town, LF Race and Sports Book, at the corner of Calle Rodriguez and Av. Juárez, offers the usual betting lounge, restaurant, and bar; it's open Wed.-Sun. 0900-2300, Tues. 0900-2030.

Events

The Tecate-Ensenada Bike Ride, sponsored by Monday International (tel. 619-275-1384, P.O. Box 99120, San Diego, CA 92109), has been a tradition since 1969; it usually takes place the third Sunday of April. Participation is limited to 10,000 entrants. The hilly, 116-km (72-mile) Mexico 3 route, some of it through valley farmlands, is one of the better bike rides in northern Baja.

The Santa Veronica Offroad Park and Roadway, a series of dirt racetracks at Hacienda Santa Veronica, 30 km east of Tecate off Mexico 2, is the site of several racing events throughout the year. The biggest is the three-day Gran Carrera de Tecate, held in late May and sponsored by Baja Promotions (tel. 818-340-5750, P.O. Box 8938, Calabasas, CA 91302). Several classes of four-wheelers, as well as motorcycles and ATVs, participate in a series of multi-lap races scheduled over the three-day interval. Most of the entrants are from Alta California or Arizona. The Tecate Brewery also sponsors smaller offroad races at Santa Veronica in March, July, and October (contact Baja Promotions for information).

More popular among Bajacalifornios is Santa Veronica's Gran Carrera de Caballos (also sponsored by Baja Promotions), which takes place the last weekend in March. The 80-km horse race enters mounts (horse with rider) by weight in heavy, medium, and light classes; riding tack must be either charro or texana (Mexican or Western) style. A fiesta is held at Hacienda Santa Veronica on the Saturday evening following the race.

The SCORE Tecate Baja 500 is held in June (see "Ensenada," p. 172, for information on SCORE activities).

Until recently Tecate hosted a pamplonada—a "running of the bulls" inspired by the famous fiesta in Pamplona, Spain—every August. As in the original, a herd of bulls was loosed to chase participants through the streets of the town. The crowds—as many as 50,000 (almost twice the town population) at the most recent pamplonadas—grew increasingly unruly with each year; pressure from local merchants in 1990 led municipal authorities to cancel the event. The state tourist office in Tecate suggested the pamplonada might be resurrected in the future under a new set of guidelines, but for the moment, it seems doubtful.

Shopping

A few alfarerías (pottery and tile works) and vidrierías (glassworks) sell their products in local stores. As in Tijuana and Rosarito, several shops in town depend on sales to U.S. residents who cross the border for bargains on tile and other building materials.

Visitors crossing into Baja at Tecate can't miss the highly visible Patio del Sol on the east side of Calle Lázaro Cárdenas, two blocks south of the gateway. The outdoor display features a large selection of unglazed pottery, plus a smaller number of decorative sculptures.

The government-sponsored Centro Artesanal, south of the railway and Río Tecate on

Mexico 3 (about 1½ km south of Av. Juárez), houses two shops, **Tecate Handicraft Center** and **Artesanías Mexicanas**. Besides glasswork and pottery, the vendors offer blankets, rugs, folk art, and other crafts from elsewhere in northern Mexico. **Rosita's Curios,** west of Calle Lázaro Cárdenas on the south side of Av. Juárez, is a private shop with an interesting collection of handicrafts.

Information
The state tourist office (tel. 4-10-95) faces the south side of Parque Hidalgo and is open Mon.-Fri. 0900-1900, Sat. 0900-1500, Sun. 1000-1400. There is also a tourist information booth near the border crossing at Calle Lázaro Cárdenas and Callejón Madero. Next to the state tourist office is a police station.

Post and Telephone: Tecate's post office is on the south side of Av. Juárez between Carranza and La Huerta. The telephone area code for Tecate and vicinity is 665.

Transport
The railway that passes through Tecate now carries freight trains exclusively (the nearest passenger railway begins in Mexicali). Most visitors arrive by bus or private vehicle.

Buses: Tecate's bus depot is on Av. Juárez at Calle Rodriguez. Departures include buses to Mexicali (every half-hour), Guadalajara (daily), Tijuana (every half-hour), Ensenada (five times daily), and Mazatlán (twice daily).

Driving: To drive to Tecate from San Diego, take U.S. 94 east 66 km (41 miles) to the Tecate turnoff near the border. From Arizona and points east, take I-8 west to the U.S. 94 junction at Jacumba or Boulevard, then follow U.S. 94 west to the Tecate turnoff. The Tecate border gate is open 0600-midnight.

Tecate lies at the intersection of Mexico 2 (to Tijuana or Mexicali) and Mexico 3 (to Ensenada).

TECATE TO ENSENADA (MEXICO 3)

The two-lane highway between Tecate and Ensenada winds through the rolling, boulder-studded western slopes of the Sierra Juárez. Traffic is generally light, and the boulders offer plenty of opportunities to view modern rock art, including political slogans, evangelical exclamations (¡Cristo viene pronto!—"Christ is coming soon!"), declarations of love, and Catholic iconographs.

Except for the occasional valley, the terrain along Mexico 3 is mostly uninhabited chaparral. Valle de las Palmas, a small farming community at Km 27-28, has a café and a PEMEX station. Roll up the windows at Km 32, location of a large, smoldering trash dump.

Valle De Guadalupe
The next settlement of note along Mexico 3 is historic Guadalupe (Km 77), centered in a large valley created by the Río Guadalupe. The last and most short-lived of the Baja California missionary efforts, **Misión Guadalupe,** was established west of the current village by Dominican padres in 1834. In 1836 the mission was successfully defended against an attack by 400 Yumanos; four years later a much smaller force, led by a Neji Indian who had been baptized at the mission, chased away the last Dominican padre. The remains of the mission have been incorporated into other buildings and are now difficult to identify.

Vineyards: Although a variety of grains, fruits, and vegetables are grown in the Valle de Guadalupe, grapes have been the major crop ever since a colony of Russian immigrants established the valley's first vineyards early this century. Guadalupe grapes are sold to a number of wineries and fruit distributors throughout northern Baja, including the valley's own Domecq winery (not open to the public). The section of the Valle de Guadalupe devoted to viniculture is sometimes called **Valle de Calafia.**

Colonia Rusa: A small Russian cemetery and around 25 Russian-style homes can be seen in a part of the village known as Colonia Rusa. The original Russian immigrants were Molokans (the word means "milk-drinkers," presumably in reference to the sect's abstinence from alcohol), a strait-laced Christian sect that had broken from the Russian Orthodox Church. Around 105 Russian families (approximately 500 individuals) migrated to Guadalupe in 1905 after fleeing religious persecution in czarist Russia.

The group purchased 13,000 acres of valley land from the Mexican government on which they planted grapes and wheat, raised geese, kept honey bees, and built whitewashed adobe-and-wood homes, complete with thatched roofs and glass windows. As in their Russian homeland, the Molokan houses were built along a main street with the front doors facing away from the street. Their simple chapel held no religious decorations or icons, but the Molokans worshiped with such fervor that to the local Mexicans they were known as "the Spirit Jumpers."

In 1938, following President Cardenas's seizure of all foreign-owned lands, the community was engulfed by 3,000 Mexican squatters (and renamed Francisco Zarco), and many Russians left the valley. Of those that stayed on, most ended up intermarrying with the Mexicans; today only four families of pure Russian lineage remain in the area. In almost every respect they've become ordinary Mexican citizens; Russian is spoken as a first language only among a few elders.

Physical, if not cultural, evidence of the Russian colony remains. Around 25 of the original Molokan houses are intact. In the cemetery, the older tombstones at the back are engraved in Russian, while later stones toward the front show a combination of Russian and Mexican names (e.g., Juan Samarin, Pedro Pavloff).

Guadalupe-El Sauzal

At Km 96 is a gravel road west to the Valle San Marcos, a scenic area of cattle ranches and small farms. This gravel road meets paved Mexico 1, the "free road," after 12 km (7½ miles). Mexico 3 links with Mexico 1-D, the toll road, at El Sauzal (Km 105), a tiny coastal community supported by a fish cannery. No toll is charged for the final nine km south to Ensenada.

(BOB RACE)

NORTHEASTERN BAJA

MEXICALI

Driving or walking into Mexicali from Calexico, a visitor's first impression of the city focuses on the congested downtown area—the "old" Mexicali. Like other large Mexican border districts, it's chock-a-block with street vendors, souvenir shops, and *casas de cambio* (money changers). But a few blocks away from the border in any direction are broad, palm-lined boulevards and tidy residential areas that could have been lifted from San Diego or Phoenix. Definitely not Tijuana or Cuidad Juárez.

The only Mexican border town that's a state capital, Mexicali also has Baja's largest population, 850,000 at the official count. (It's probable that more people—uncounted by the federal census—actually live in Tijuana, where the official count is only 800,000.) City promoters make much of the fact that the city is considerably less tourism-dependent than Tijuana; you won't find any zebra-painted burros

on Mexicali street corners, or anyplace resembling Tijuana's Bar San Marcos.

As citizens of Baja Norte's capital, Mexicalienses view themselves as one step closer to Mexico City, while at the same time true *cachanillas*. Like the cachanilla, a sturdy desert plant that flowers in arid, saline soil, Mexicali has flourished at the edge of the harsh San Felipe and Sonora deserts and bloomed as one of Mexico's most prosperous communities. Today, any northern Bajacalifornio can claim to be a cachanilla, but as the verse from Antonio Valdez's famous corrido *El Cachanilla* says, "Mexicali, fue mi cuna" ("Mexicali was my cradle").

THE LAND

The nearly flat Valle de Mexicali extends westward from the Río Colorado delta to the Sierra de Cucapá. Millenniums ago the entire area was covered by a northern extension of the Sea of Cortez; Alta California's Salton Sea (or Salton Sink) and Baja Norte's Laguna Salada are vestiges of the Cortez that were trapped by the gradual silting of the Colorado delta. The city of Mexicali, in fact, is a foot below sea level.

South of the valley lies the San Felipe Desert, an extension of the Sonora Desert—the valley itself can be classified as desert since it averages less than 25 cm (10 inches) of rainfall a year. Quite unlike most deserts, centuries of river silting have made the soil here nutrient-rich; earth that once filled the Grand Canyon was carried into the delta at a rate of 160 million tons per year. Yet the overall lack of water sources meant that agriculture outside the Colorado flood plain was almost impossible before U.S. land companies established a canal system early this century to irrigate Alta California's Imperial Valley and the Valle de Mexicali.

Before the damming of the Colorado River in the U.S., the floodplain was enormous; in fact, the tidal bore at the mouth of the river, where it fed into the Cortez, was strong enough to sink ships. The outflow slowed with the U.S. dams and was further reduced to almost a trickle by the 1950 construction of Mexico's Morelos Dam near Los Algodones, which diverts water into the Valle de Mexicali to supplement the American-built canal system.

With irrigation, a 2½-km-thick layer of river silt, and an abundance on sunshine, most of the valley today is under intensive cultivation, producing cotton, wheat, grapefruit, lemons, oranges, carrots, corn, asparagus, onions, broccoli, potatoes, lettuce, cauliflower, and grapes.

CLIMATE

During December and January, Mexicali's coolest months, temperatures average 12° C (54° F). In July, temperatures reach 35-38° C (95-100° F) in the daytime (occasionally as high as 48° C/120° F), dropping to around 24 C (75° F) at night. The lack of humidity means that perceived temperatures in the summer are significantly lower; since the Mexicali area is primarily agricultural, air pollution is not an appreciable problem. Rainfall averages a scant 12 cm (4.7 inches) a year.

The best overall months for a Mexicali visit are Sept.-Oct., when the temperature averages 23° C (73° F) and desert plants are usually in bloom. March through late May are also quite pleasant. Peak periods for visitors from the north are Nov.-Feb., especially those on their way to San Felipe. July and August are the least hospitable months, as soaring temperatures bring the city all but to a standstill.

HISTORY

Pre-Hispanic Indian Cultures
In pre-Columbian times, the Río Colorado delta (which, at the time, included the Valle de Mexicali) was inhabited by a centuries-long succession of Yumano tribes. When the Spanish first stumbled upon the delta after traversing, with great difficulty, the Sonora Desert's Camino del Diablo ("Devil's Road"), a sophisticated Río Colorado culture was cultivating squash, melons, peas, and five colors of corn: yellow, blue, white, red, and blue-white. The Indians also reportedly had an impressive knowledge of medicinal herbs and a vast inventory of uses for desert plants like mesquite and agave. Along with their neighbors the Kiliwas, the Cucapás' numbers were greatly reduced by Spanish missionization in northwest Mexico.

One of the major Yumano groups in the region was the Cucapás, who navigated the difficult Río Colorado on reed rafts. Today Cucapá descendants inhabit a small government-protected corner of the delta near the junction of the Hardy and Colorado rivers, an area marked by names like Colonia Indígena, Colonia Cucapá El Mayor, Terrenos Indios, and Mestizos. For the most part, the Indians make their living on agricultural ejidos or from fishing the rivers, although many have migrated to Mexicali. Few indigenous customs have survived both the Spanish and Mexican eras; both the Kiliwas and the Cucapás continued to practice cremation rituals, for example, until they were banned by the Mexican government early this century.

NORTHEASTERN BAJA

The Building Of An Agricultural Empire

After the Jesuits left, the Spanish and later the Mexicans had little to do with northeastern Baja, perceiving it as an untamable, flood-prone desert delta. Around the time of the American Civil War, a Yale geologist, while surveying a route for the Southern Pacific Railroad, wandered into the delta and discovered what the dwindling population of Yumanos had known for centuries: that the 2½-km-thick sediment was prime farming soil. The sediments extended far to the west of the river itself, accumulating in a shallow basin below the Sierra de Cucapá. All it needed was the addition of water to become an overnight agricultural miracle.

In 1900 the U.S.-based California Land Company received permission from the Porfirio Díaz government to cut a canal through the delta's Arroyo Alamo, thus linking the dry basin with the Colorado River. To attract farmers to the area, the developers named the basin the "Imperial Valley." In March, 1903, the first 500 farmers arrived; by late 1904, 100,000 valley acres had been irrigated and 10,000 people were settled on the land and harvesting cotton, fruits, and vegetables. A collection of huts and ramadas that straddled the border was named Calexico on the U.S. side, Mexicali on the Mexican side.

Seeing that the equally fertile Valle de Mexicali lay undeveloped, another American land syndicate, the Colorado River Land Company, moved in. Led by Harry Chandler, then publisher of the *Los Angeles Times,* the syndicate already controlled some 800,000 acres of northern Baja, and in 1905 the CRLC began constructing a Valle de Mexicali irrigation system. Instead of using Mexican labor, as the Imperial Valley developers had, Chandler imported Chinese coolies by the thousands. After a major 1905 rainfall, however, the major channel Chandler's company had dug from Arroyo Alamo ended up diverting the entire outflow of the Colorado River into the Imperial Valley, taking Mexicali with it—unknowingly, they had tapped into one of the river's original routes. The Salton Sink, a dried-up remainder of the Sea of Cortez, became the Salton Sea virtually overnight.

Neither the U.S. nor Mexico wanted to take responsibility for the growing "New River" created by Chandler's mistake. As both valleys became increasingly inundated, the Southern Pacific Railroad stepped in and, to protect its tracks, dumped a sufficient amount of rock into the river to head the Colorado back into the Cortez, leaving a canal to the Valle de Mexicali. From then on, both valleys became highly productive agricultural centers.

A New Capital, Prohibition, And The Postwar Boom

In 1911, both Mexicali and Tijuana were briefly occupied by American and Mexican *filibusteros* (see "Tijuana," p. 139). In order to defend the border from similar threats, the Mexican government moved the Baja California Norte capital from Ensenada to Mexicali in 1920. That same year, the U.S. government passed Prohibition, forbidding the manufacture, sale, and consumption of alcohol; although Mexicali received fewer of the Hollywood high-rollers than did Tijuana, Americans nonetheless developed a romance with the city (as embodied in the popular song of the time, "Mexicali Rose").

Many of the Prohibition-era businesses were operated by *chinos,* Chinese laborers and farmers who moved into the city and spent their hard-earned savings to open bars, restaurants, and hotels. As people from both sides of the border were drawn to the burgeoning town, Mexicali's urbanization accelerated.

Like Tijuana, Mexicali suffered an economic recession with the repeal of Prohibition in 1933 and the Mexican ban on casino gambling in 1938. With a flourishing agricultural base and a federal presence, however, Mexicali bounced back sooner than its border counterpart. After Baja California Norte attained statehood in 1952, the capital began receiving a steady rotation of *chilangos* (Mexico City residents), some of whom stayed on and started new businesses after their terms of office were concluded. Although the local residents might hesitate to admit it, part of Mexicali's postwar success in shedding its border-town image should probably be credited to the influx of outsiders—from the coming of the Chinese in the early 1900s to the post-war arrival of the chilangos.

Today the main source of Mexicali income remains agriculture, primarily cotton, wheat, alfalfa, and vegetables. Another is the geo-thermal plants at nearby Cerro Prieto, the world's third-largest producer of geothermal power (electricity generated by the plants powers most of northeastern Baja and is also sold north of the border.) A third major industry

is the growing complex of in-bond plants, or *maquiladoras,* which currently number around 160. Major multinational firms with Mexicali in-bond plants include Rockwell International, Hughes Aircraft, Emerson Electric, ITT, and Goldstar.

The economic symbiosis evident all along the U.S.-Mexico border is especially visible in the Mexicali-Los Algodones area. Laborers alternately work at Imperial Valley or Valle de Mexicali farms on either side of the border.

And, like Tijuana, Mexicali is a free-trade zone. Television and radio stations in El Centro (Alta California) and Yuma (Arizona) broadcast ads for pharmacies in Mexicali and Los Algodones, where generic equivalents for American drugs are available without prescription at prices several times lower than in the United States. In return, the small Alta California town of Calexico (pop. 15,000) serves as a convenience mart for Mexicalienses shopping for discounted American-made apparel and housewares.

Tourism is important to Mexicali but is for the most part limited to short American shopping trips or brief stopovers by San Felipe-bound visitors. A tally of the Mexicali Holiday Inn guest register for 1990 showed that only 26% of hotel guests hailed from the U.S., 73% were from Mexico, and the rest were a mix of visitors from Japan, Central and South America, and Europe. According to the hotel management, most guests are in Mexicali on business.

SIGHTS

Mexicali is not a city with a long list of tourist attractions, nor is it a particularly festive city by Mexican standards. The city seems to focus on creating an amenable environment for government- and business-oriented activities, while trying to make the community as comfortable a place to live as possible. As a result, it's one of the cleanest cities in northern Mexico; there are also a number of modern cultural venues of interest.

The city has two hearts: the old downtown area, pushed up against the border and featuring turn-of-the-century architecture (the Hotel del Norte—almost Texan or New Mexican in appearance—is a prime example), and the newer **Mexicali Civic-Commercial Center** (Centro Civico-Comercial de Mexicali), southeast of downtown along Calzada Independencia. Ambitiously dubbed the *zona rosa* (after Mexico City's chic business-entertainment district), the center is a renovated warehouse district containing offices, restaurants, bars, and utilitarian shops selling paint, furniture, stationery, and office supplies. Although it's near the bullring, bus, and train stations,

the Centro Civico has become more of an attraction for Mexicali residents than for foreign visitors.

Linking the various city sectors is a system of wide avenues and *glorietas* (traffic circles), many of which encircle statues of Mexican national heroes.

University Regional Museum ("Museo Regional De UABC")

This University of Baja California-sponsored museum of anthropology and natural history is unequaled on the peninsula. In spite of its compact size, the exhibits manage to pack in a wealth of information on northern Baja's pre- and post-Columbian history as well as the flora and fauna unique to the region. If you can read Spanish (exhibits are labeled in Spanish only), you can learn much about northern Baja ethnology—especially regarding the Yumano and San Dieguito cultures—from the modest displays.

The museum is not located on the main UABC campus, but at Av. Reforma and Calle L. Hours are Tues.-Fri. 0900-1800, Sat.-Sun. 1000-1600. Admission is free. For more information, call 52-57-17 or 54-19-77.

City Gallery ("Galeria De La Ciudad")

This privately owned gallery exhibits works by painters, sculptors, photographers, and other artists from the region and around Mexico. Admission is free. At Av. Obregón 1209, between Calles D and E (tel. 53-50-44, ext. 23).

City Park ("Bosque De La Ciudad")

An oasis of green in a dry city, this park in southwest Mexicali offers picnic areas, a playground, a botanical museum, and a zoo. At Av. Ocotlán and Calle Alvarado; open Tues.-Sun. from 0900-1700.

Colleges And Universities

Mexicali has four institutes of higher learning, including the respected **University of Baja California** (Universidad Autonomía de Baja California). UABC's main campus is off Blvd. Juárez between Calzada Independencia and Blvd. Lázaro Cárdenas; the university rectory and administrative offices (tel. 54-04-00) are

Hotel Del Norte
(JOE CUMMINGS)

housed in the former governor's palace, in an older section of the city between Av. Reforma and Calle S.L. de Tajada, off Calle Irigoyen. Anthropology is one of the university's stronger disciplines.

Other tertiary institutions include the **Instituto Tecnologico Regional** (tel. 61-85-22, Blvd. Lázaro Cárdenas), a federal institute specializing in engineering studies, and the **Centro de Enseñana Tecnica y Superior** (tel. 65-01-16, Calzada Compuertas), a private school that combines upper high-school and college levels.

ACCOMMODATIONS

Hotels And Motels
Room rates for Mexicali hotels and motels range from around US$20 s (Motel El Indio) to US$84 for a suite at the Holiday Inn, the city's top property. See the "Hotels and Motels" chart, below. If you can't find a room to your liking in Mexicali, try the historic **Hotel De Anza** (tel. 619-357-1112, 233 4th St.) across the border in Calexico; rooms in the 1930-vintage hotel are US$27-34.

Youth Hostel
The **Instituto de la Juventud y el Deporte** (tel. 57-61-92), at Calle Coahuila 2050 and Av. Salinas Cruz in the western part of the city (Parcela 36), has dorm beds for US$5 a night. Unlike most government-sponsored youth hostels, the Mexicali facility has no cafeteria.

Camping And RV Parks
The nearest camping area is a cluster of rustic hunting and fishing camps 30-35 km (18-21 miles) south of the city, off Mexico 5 in the Río Hardy area. Tent/camper sites usually go for about US$4 a night; no hookups.

FOOD

The older downtown area near the border has the least expensive, most authentic northern Mexican food—vendors and cafés every other block or so. Another good area for cheap eats is opposite the bus station on Av. Independencia, where a number of taco and torta stands vie for the patronage of arriving and departing passengers. Other recommended dining venues:

Mexican
$ **Restaurant Del Norte,** Hotel Del Norte, corner of Av. Madero and Calle Melgar: This restaurant wedged onto a downtown corner near the border crossing is popular with tourists and locals alike for it's large *platillos tí-*

picos. Prices are very reasonable. Open daily for breakfast, lunch, and dinner.

$-$$ Cenaduría Selecta (tel. 52-40-47), Calle G 1510 at Av. Arista: In a slightly less congested downtown area, the renowned Selecta has been crowding them in since 1945 for some of the best tacos and burritos in town. Open daily for breakfast, lunch, and dinner.

$$-$$$ La Parroquia (tel. 54-23-13), Av. Reforma and Calle D: This large restaurant is oriented toward visiting gringos (a branch of the Caliente Foreign Book is attached) and the

MEXICALI HOTELS AND MOTELS

Add 15% hotel tax to all rates unless otherwise noted
(some hotels may charge an additional 10% service charge). Area code: 65

NAME	ADDRESS	TELEPHONE	RATES	FEATURES
Azteca de Oro	Calle de la Industria 600 (diagonally opposite train station)	57-21-85	US$25 s, US$27 d	a/c, parking, near train and bus stations
Boulevard	Calzada López Mateos (Mexico 5 south, Km 4.5)	57-06-12	US$27 s, US$33 d	a/c, restaurant, bar, parking
Calafia	Calzado Justo Sierra 1495	68-33-11 (fax 68-2010)	US$54 (s or d, tax included)	a/c, pool, restaurant, 24-hour coffee shop, bar
Casa Grande	Av. Colón 612	53-66-51	US$30 s, US$33 d, US$36 t	a/c, pool, restaurant, bar, parking, walking distance from border gate
Cosmos Posada	Calzada Juárez 4257 (south of town on Mexico 5)	6-67-08	US$26 s, US$30 d	a/c, parking
Del Norte	Calle Melgar and Av. Madero	52-81-01	US$25	a/c, restaurant, bar, parking, walking distance from border gate
El Indio	Calzada López Mateos and Av. Fresnillo	57-22-77	US$20 s, US$28 d	a/c, parking
Holiday Inn	Calzada Juárez 2220	66-13-00 (fax 66-49-01), toll-free in Mexico, 91-800-00-999 in U.S. (800) 465-4329	US$65 (tax included)	a/c, pool, restaurant, coffee shop, bar, disco, parking
La Siesta	Calzado Justo Sierra 899	68-20-01	US$32 s, US$38-41 d	a/c, restaurant, parking
Las Fuentes	Calzada López Mateos 1655	57-15-25	US$23 s, US$30 d	parking
Lucerna	Calzada Juárez 2151	66-10-00	US$52-57 s, US$55-60 d	a/c, refrigerator, pools, restaurants, coffee shop, bar, disco

prices are a bit high, but the all-Mexican menu is dependable. Open daily for breakfast, lunch, and dinner.

Steak/Carne Asada
$$-$$$ **Los Búfalos** (tel. 66-31-16), Blvd. Juárez 1616: Along the Blvd. Juárez hotel strip, steak and carne asada are the clear favorites and are usually served in pseudo-rustic, ranch-style surroundings. Los Búfalos, typical of the genre, is a short walk north of the Holiday Inn; its steak platters are highly rated, but the menu also features a few seafood and less meat-oriented Mexican dishes. Los Búfalos has a second location at Plaza La Cachanilla, Calzada López Mateos. Both are open daily for lunch and dinner.
$$ **Cachanilla's** (tel. 66-23-01), Blvd. Juárez 1990: Although the restaurants is billed as "international," the house specialty is carne asada. Other menu items alternate between American and northern Mexican. Open daily for lunch and dinner.
$$ **Villa del Seri** (tel. 53-55-03), Av. Reforma and Calle D: A good steakhouse with lower prices (since it's well removed from the hotel strip) and longer hours; open for breakfast, lunch, and dinner.

Chinese
Mexicali has more Chinese restaurants per capita than any other city in Mexico—well over a hundred at last count. Cantonese cooking predominates, but with few exceptions it's not the sort you'd recognize from Canton or Hong Kong (or Vancouver or San Francisco, for that matter). As in many Chinese restaurants outside of China, Hong Kong, Singapore, and Taiwan, immigrant cooks have adapted their native cuisine to local tastes. Almost every Chinese restaurant in Mexicali, for example, serves each dish with a small bowl of what tastes like generic steak sauce, a distinctly *norteño* touch. Still, the city's Chinese restaurants are among the most economical places to eat, and are worth visiting for their interior decors alone—some represent the ultimate in Chinese restaurant kitsch.
$-$$ **El Dragón** (tel. 66-20-20), Blvd. Juárez 1830: As is typical in Mexico, "Dragon" appears in a good number of local Chinese restaurant names. This Dragon is in a small shopping center just north of the Holiday Inn and features one of the most elaborate Chinese interiors in town. Large portions and fresh ingredients make it one of Mexicali's most popular restaurants; the huge menu features several regional styles. Open daily for lunch and dinner.
$-$$ **Palacio Imperial** (tel. 61-73-91), Blvd. Juárez and Lázaro Cárdenas: Similar to El Dragón. Open daily for lunch and dinner.
$-$$ **La Misión Dragón** (tel. 66-43-20), Blvd. Lázaro Cárdenas 555: More of the same, but the Chinese-style gardens and fountains are a bonus. Open daily for lunch and dinner.
$ **China Town** (tel. 54-02-12), Av. Madero 701: A good choice if you're touring *Chinesca*. Open daily for lunch and dinner.

Vegetarian
$ **Mesón Vegetariano** (tel. 57-12-19), Arcade Chapala 1096 (Centro Civico): One of the few vegetarian restaurants in Baja specializing in Mexican dishes. Open Mon.-Sat., 0800-1800.
$-$$ **El Oasis** (tel. 68-33-11), Calzada Justo Sierra 1495: International vegetarian cuisine. Open daily for breakfast, lunch, and dinner.

American
$ **Mi Burger** (tel. 66-03-02), Blvd. Juárez 221. Burgers, fries, and shakes: Homesick already? Open daily 1500-2300.
$ **Neil's Fried Chicken** (tel. 52-54-48), Calzada López Mateos and Av. Morelos: Reminiscent of a typical American-style chicken joint. Open daily for lunch and dinner.
$-$$ **Pizza Hut** (tel. 53-46-34), Plaza Cachanilla, Blvd. Lázaro Cárdenas: A branch of the famous American pizza franchise—and they deliver. Open daily for lunch and dinner.

Miscellaneous
$$ **Sakura Kotubyi** (tel. 66-48-46), Blvd. Lázaro Cárdenas 200 (at Calzada Montejano): Teppanyaki, tempura, and sushi are among the offerings at Mexicali's only Japanese restaurant. Open daily for lunch and dinner.

$$ **Heidelberg** (tel. 54-20-22), Av. Madero and Calle H: German and continental dishes; convenient to downtown. Open Tues.-Sat. for lunch and dinner.

ENTERTAINMENT

Live Music

Bars at the big three hotels (Lucerna, Holiday Inn, and Calafia) are popular local meeting spots where you can usually count on a *botanas* lay-out most weekdays around 1800, with live music—norteña, Latin pop, international—later on in the evening. **Casa Carmina** (tel. 52-56-48, Av. Reforma and Calle C) also has live music and is one of the most congenial non-hotel bars—for *mexicanos* and *norteamericanos* alike—in town.

Every Sunday afternoon during warmer weather, mariachi groups play outdoors at **Parque Constitución,** a small downtown park bordered by Av. Zuazua, Av. Hidalgo, Calle Mina, and Calle México.

Discos

Top dance spots are **Tempo's Laser Disco** (tel. 57-29-70, Calle Alfareros), **Forum Videotheque** (tel. 52-40-91, Av. Reforma and Calzada Justo Sierra), and the **Rock En Español** (near the post office on Av. Madero). Expect to pay a cover charge of US$5-6.

State Theater (Teatro del Estado

A variety of local and visiting theatrical, dance, and musical performances are held year-round at this modern, 1,100-capacity building

MEXICALI CHINESE

Mexicali is known as having one of the highest per capita concentrations of Chinese residents in Mexico, but the current population of 5,000, in a city of 850,000, hardly compares with a city like San Francisco (where nearly a quarter of the entire city population—roughly equivalent to Mexicali's—is Asian, mostly Chinese). Earlier this century, however, Mexicali was actually more a Chinese than a Mexican town.

Early Chinese Settlement

The first Chinese to arrive in the area came as laborers for the Colorado River Land Company, which designed and built an extensive irrigation system in the Valle de Mexicali. Some of the Chinese immigrants arrived overland from the U.S., fleeing officially sanctioned anti-Chinese policies; others sailed directly from China via the Pacific Ocean and the Sea of Cortez. As in Alta California, thousands of Chinese coolies were lured to the area by the promise of high wages that never materialized.

A 200-meter desert peak near Crucero La Trinidad is named El Chinero in memory of a group of 160 Chinese laborers who perished while crossing the San Felipe Desert in search of work in the valley—the desert itself was

known for a time as El Desierto de los Chinos, "Desert of the Chinese." An unscrupulous boatman had landed the group at a fork in the Rio Colorado, telling them that Mexicali was only a short distance away; 65 km of burning desert lay between them and their goal, which they never reached.

Many of the Chinese laborers who survived the building of the irrigation system stayed on after it was finished, congregating in an area of Mexicali known as Chinesca ("Chinatown"). During the Prohibition years, Chinesca housed many of the city's casinos and bars; an underground tunnel system led to bordellos and opium dens, and under the border to Calexico (the bootlegger's route). By 1920 Mexicali's *chinos* outnumbered the *mexicanos* 10,000 to 700. A group of 5,000 single Chinese males started the Asociación China, a Mexicali social organization (at least partly devoted to the procurement of Chinese wives from overseas); the association still exists.

The Anti-Chinese Movement
And Overseas Refugees

In 1927 a series of Tong wars in northern Mexico erupted over control of gambling and prostitution at Calzada López Mateos and Av. Castellanos. Ticket prices vary according to the performance but are usually quite reasonable. For information on the latest theater schedule, call 52-96-30 or contact the city tourist office (see "Information and Services" below).

Events
The 350-mile (563 km) **Gran Carrera de Mexicali** offroad race is held yearly in mid-March by Baja Promotions (tel. 818-340-5740, P.O. Box 8938, Calabasas, CA 91302).

In mid-June, the Chamber of Restaurants (CANIRAC) sponsors the **Chinese Food Fair,** an event in which the city's Chinese chefs compete in a number of cooking contests. Call CANIRAC at 57-49-00 for scheduling and

venues. A seafood equivalent, the **Sea of Cortez Food Exhibition,** is held in November, also sponsored by CANIRAC.

Radio And Television
Mexicali broadcast media receive a wide variety of transmissions from Mexican, Arizonan, and Alta Californian stations. One of the better local radio stations is XED (1050 AM), which mostly broadcasts Mexican folk music.

SHOPPING

Mexicali has the usual assortment of souvenir shops expected in a border town, many of them clustered along Calle Melgar in the downtown area, near the border crossing. El

---

MEXICALI CHINESE (CONT.)

rings. Mexican alarm over the Chinese control of organized crime led to the government-encouraged Movimiento Anti-Chino in the late 1920s. The wave of anti-Chinese sentiment that swept across the country led to the torture and murder of hundreds of Chinese in northern Mexico—a tragic echo of what had happened on a larger scale in Alta California in the 1880s. To Mexico's credit, the government never enacted an equivalent to the U.S. Chinese Exclusion Act (which prevented all persons of Chinese heritage from holding U.S. citizenship).

Mexicali quickly became a refuge for Chinese fleeing the violence, since in that city the chinos predominated. As the anti-Chinese movement faded away, still more Chinese arrived in Mexicali when it became the Mexican headquarters for the Kuomintang, Sun Yat-sen's nationalist Chinese party. During WW II, the nationalists were pushed out of China first by the Japanese and then by the Communists; the Mexican government loosened its immigration policies to allow a large number of refugees into Mexico. Until Mexico severed diplomatic relations with the nationalist Taiwan government, Mexicali harbored a Taiwan consulate. (The consulate promptly moved across the border to Calexico; when the U.S. in turn withdrew its recognition of

Taiwan, the consular office continued operations under the name "Coordinating Council for North America.")

Hybridization
Postwar Mexicali had two cinemas; both showed Chinese movies almost exclusively. But as the city recovered from the post-Prohibition recession, a steady influx of Mexicans diluted the local population until the Chinese became a minority. Mexicali still boasts more Chinese restaurants per capita than anywhere else in Mexico, and Chinesca survives in part of the downtown area. Local Chinese associations struggle to preserve the arts and culture of the homeland through the sponsorship of Chinese festivals, calligraphy clubs, and language classes.

But in most aspects, Chinese cultural life has blended with local traditions to create a unique, hybrid culture. Only in Mexicali will you find banners of the Virgin of Guadalupe hanging side by side with Chinese paper lamps, or a café called Mexburger where Chinese elders kibitz over hamburgers and green tea, speaking a mixture of Cantonese and Spanish. Surfers, note: Mexicali is probably the only place in the world where you can enjoy the revenge of eating shark-fin tacos.

Sarape and Campo's Curios, both on Calle Melgar, carry a broad selection of Mexican handicrafts. As the name suggests, Taxco (Calle Melgar, next door to Campo's Curios) offers silverwork from the Valle de Mexico.

Something you might not expect to find in Mexicali is a shop specializing in guayaberas, the pleated men's shirt characteristic of Mexico's Yucatán Peninsula. Merida Guayaberas, in the 700 block of Av. Madero (near the post office), does a good business selling these shirts to locals and visitors during Mexicali's furnace-like summers. (In Mexico, the light, short-sleeved guayabera is considered appropriate apparel for any occasion, even in place of coat and tie.)

A bit farther from downtown is another Mexican handicraft dealer, the government-sponsored Desarrollo Artesanal de Mexicali (tel. 61-64-44, Blvd. Lázaro Cárdenas 1190).

SPORTS AND RECREATION

Bullfights

In Baja, Mexicali's Plaza de Toros Calafia (tel. 65-07-81) is second in size only to the Plaza Monumental in Playas de Tijuana. At Blvd. de los Héroes and Calle Calafia (near the Centro Civico), the stadium hosts corridas two or three Sundays a month, Sept.-November. Current schedule information is available from the city tourist office.

Charreadas (Mexican Rodeos)

Mexicali has two charro rings: Lienzo Charro de Mexicali (tel. 66-55-45), six km east of Calzada Justo Sierra on Calle Compuertas (the airport highway) and Lienzo Charro Zaragoza, west of Mexicali on Mexico 2. Regular charreadas are scheduled about once a month Sept.-April, but may also be held during a fiesta anytime of year. Contact the city tourist office for the latest charreada schedules.

Baseball

Mexicali has its own baseball team, Los Aguilas ("The Eagles"), and their local stadium is known as El Nido de las Aguilas ("Eagles' Nest"). The stadium, in the Ciudad Deportiva (City Sports Complex) on Calzada Cuahutémoc east of Calzada Justo Sierra, periodically hosts other teams in the Mexican-Pacific League, as well as the occasional visiting team from North or Central America. The season lasts from the end of the American World Series (usually late Oct.) through late January. Seats cost around US$3; to find out when home games are being played during the season, contact the city tourist office or call the stadium (tel. 68-30-25).

Sports Centers

Two sports centers in the city offer tennis courts and swimming pools open to public use for nominal day fees. Casino de Mexicali (tel. 52-58-93, Av. J.M. Suarez and Calle L) is open Mon.-Fri. 0800-1330 and 1500-1830, while Club Raqueta Britania (tel. 57-13-07, Blvd. Anahuac and Calle Mar Baltico) is open Mon.-Fri. 0900-1500 and 1700-1900. The latter also has a gym, sauna, and steam room. The Mexicali Country Club (see "Golf" below) also has a pool and tennis courts.

The city-sponsored Ciudad Deportiva (tel. 68-26-31, Blvd. Cuahutémoc) has tennis courts, a swimming pool, a jogging track, and a fronton jai alai (jai alai court) that are open to the public Tues.-Sat. 0600-2200. The Instituto de la Juventud y El Deporte (tel. 57-61-92), at Av. Salinas Cruz and Coahuila, also has public tennis courts, basketball courts, and a pool.

Golf

The Club Campestre de Mexicali, or Mexicali Country Club (tel. 61-71-30), at Km 11.5 on Mexico 5, Fracc. Laguna Campestre, has an 18-hole, par 72, 6,628-yard golf course open to the public Tues.-Sat. 0900-1700 and 1800-2200. Greens fees are considerably lower than in Tijuana, about US$10.

Race And Sports Book

The ubiquitous Caliente Foreign Book has two branches in Mexicali: at Calle Melgar 116 (downtown near the border crossing) and Restaurant La Parroquia, Av. Reforma and Calle D. Hours for each are daily 0900-2230.

Hunting

The Río Hardy area south of Mexicali is popular among visiting hunters for dove and waterfowl (see "Vicinity of Mexicali," p. 230). Mexicali has one of only three stores on the peninsula authorized to sell ammunition to the public (the other two are in Tijuana and La Paz): **Tienda Alcampo Aceves** (tel. 52-27-82, Av. Zuazua 515).

INFORMATION AND SERVICES

Tourist Offices

The Mexicali Tourism and Convention Bureau (COTUCO) and the State Secretary of Tourism (SECTUR) share the same building at Calzada López Mateos and Calle Camelias (tel. 52-97-95, 52-43-91; U.S. mailing address: P.O. Box 7901, Calexico, CA 92231). The information counter—with a helpful, English-speaking staff—is open Mon.-Fri. 0900-1900, Sat. 0900-1500, Sun. 1000-1400.

SECTUR's legal assistance department (Attorney for Tourist Protection) is headquartered in the same building as the state and city tourist offices (see above) and can be contacted by calling 56-10-72 or 56-11-72, fax 56-12-81, or CB channel 40.

Mexican Consulate In Calexico

The Mexican government maintains a conveniently located consular office in Calexico, just across the border, at 331 W. 2nd St. (tel. 619-357-3863). If you're entering Mexico via Mexicali, this can save a stop in San Diego for information on tourist cards, visas, and other Mexican immigration or customs information. The consulate is open Mon.-Fri. 0800-1300.

Border Crossing

The Mexicali border gateway is open 24 hours. Although the crossing here is less congested than Tijuana's, it would still be wise to avoid morning and afternoon commute hours. If you're planning to drive east into the state of Sonora (or to other points east of Baja), and don't already have a temporary vehicle import permit, be sure to obtain one from the Mexican customs office at the border.

MEXICALI TELEPHONE NUMBERS

Mexicali area code	65
U.S. Customs	95 (619) 357-3863
Mexican Customs	52-40-18
Green Angels	54-04-43
Municipal Police	52-66-62
Highway Patrol	54-29-09
Red Cross	132
Chamber of Commerce	54-11-81
(CANACO)	53-46-61
Department of Fishing	52-97-32
State Secretary of Tourism	52-43-91
Attorney for Tourists	52-57-44
Protection	56-10-72
Railway Station	57-21-01
	ext. 221/222
Mexicali International Airport	53-67-42
Central de Autobuses	57-24-22
(Bus Depot)	

Changing Money

Bancomer, Banco Internacional, Multibanco, and several other large Mexican banks have branches in Mexicali; as in most Mexican cities, the foreign exchange service closes around noon each day. For better hours, shorter lines, and competitive rates, use any of the several casas de cambio in the vicinity of the Hotel Del Norte downtown. As in most border towns, the best rates are given for cash rather than traveler's checks.

Downtown Calexico, near the border crossing, also has several small money changers. The dollar-to-peso rate is sometimes a bit higher here than in Mexicali, but check to see whether there's a commission charge before exchanging currencies.

Post And Telephone

Mexicali's **main post office,** at the corner of Av. Madero and Calle Morelos downtown, is open Mon.-Fri., 0800-1700. (Mail to points in the U.S. will move more quickly if deposited at a post office in Calexico—the main p.o. is at

Birch St. and George Ave., four blocks west of Imperial Avenue.)

GETTING THERE

By Air

Mexicali International Airport (MXL), 20 km (12 miles) east of the city via Blvd. de las Americas, fields Mexicana flights from Guadalajara and Mexico City, Aviación del Noroeste flights from Mazatlán, Ciudad Obregón, La Paz, and Hermosillo. **Mexicana's** city office is at Av. Madero 833 (tel. 53-54-01); **Aviación del Noroeste** (tel. 52-58-87, 53-67-41) has an office at the airport. Although they have no flights out of Mexicali, **Aeromexico** (tel. 57-25-51) also maintains a ticket office at Callejón Alamo 1008, Centro Civico.

Bus

Mexicali's intercity bus depot (Central de Autobuses, tel. 57-24-22) is on the south side of Av. Independencia, between Calzada López Mateos and Centro Civico. Buses bound for northern Baja destinations leave every hour from around 0600-2100 to Tijuana (US$4.50), Ensenada (US$5.50), Tecate (US$3.40), and San Felipe (US$4.60). Southbound buses, less frequent, go to La Paz (US$25) via Santa Rosalía (US$16), Mulegé (US$17), and Loreto (US$18), as well as to these mainland destinations: Hermosillo, Sonora (US$12.60-14.60), Culiacán, Sinaloa (US$25-28), Guadalajara (US$38-44), and Mexico City (US$50-55).

Autotransportes Tres Estrellas de Oro (tel. 57-24-22, ext. 33) operates a deluxe "executive" commuter bus to Tijuana several times daily, complete with beverage and movie service, for US$10 one way.

To/From Calexico: The Greyhound station in Calexico (tel. 619-357-1895), a few steps from the pedestrian border crossing on 1st St., has frequent daily bus service to/from Los Angeles (US$30), San Diego (US$20), Tucson (US$32), Yuma (US$17), Phoenix (US$42), and El Paso (US$116).

Train

Mexicali is the northwesternmost terminal for Ferrocarriles Nacionales de México, the country's national rail system. The passenger station is on Calle Ulises Irigoyen (north off Calzada López Mateos), near the Centro Civico. For advance ticket reservations, you can call 57-21-01, ext. 221, 223, or write El Jefe de Estación, P.O. Box 231, Calexico, CA 92231 (in Mexico: A.P. 3-182, Mexicali, BCN). The station's advance ticket window is open daily 0630-1300.

Two Guadalajara-bound trains leave Mexicali daily, Tren No. 2 ("Tren Estrella") at 0820 and Tren No. 4 ("Tren Nocturno") at 2050. The faster No. 2 connects with a train to Mexico City at 2055, which arrives in Mexico City at 0810 the following day.

TRAIN FARES FROM MEXICALI (ONE WAY)

DESTINATION	DISTANCE (KM)	1ST-CLASS*	2ND-CLASS
Puerto Peñasco, Son.	250	US$15.65	US$9
Benjamin Hill, Son.	534	US$34	US$19
Hermosillo, Son.	660	US$41	US$23
Ciudad Obregón, Son.	919	US$58	US$33
Culiacán, Sin.	1,340	US$84	US$47
Mazatlán, Sin.	1,559	US$98	US$55
Tepic, Nay.	1875	US$118	US$66
Guadalajara, Jal.	2,149	US$135	US$76
Mexico City	2,753	US$173	US$97

Children ages 5 to 11 ride for 50% of adult fares; children under five ride for free.

*(includes three meals)

The **Mexicali-Guadalajara** line also connects with rail lines to Nogales (at Benjamin Hill, Son.) and Chihuahua (at Sufragio, Sin.).

GETTING AROUND

Bus

Mexicali's city buses are large converted school buses; districts or main streets (e.g., "Centro Civico" for the civic center/zona rosa area, "Justo Sierra" for Calzada Justo Sierra) marked on the bus marquis indicate the final destination. Many city buses start from Calle Altamirano downtown, just two blocks from the border crossing. Fares are around US$.30.

Taxis

As usual, large *taxis de ruta* (route taxis) compete with city buses along popular routes and cost just a few pesos more. A private hired taxi costs US$3-5 within the downtown area, US$6-8 to the Centro Civico area or the Blvd. Juárez hotel strip from the border crossing. Taxis are most concentrated near the pedestrian border crossing and at the Lucerna, Calafia, and Holiday Inn hotels.

Tours

The Mexicali Tourism and Convention Bureau (COTUCO) recently began offering van tours of the city for only US$1 per person. Tours leave from the COTUCO office at Calzada López Mateos and Calle Camelias on the hour Thurs.-Sun., 1000-1700, wheel through the downtown area, and then stop at shopping

MEXICALI AUTO RENTAL AGENCIES

AGENCY	ADDRESS	TELEPHONE
Budget	Blvd. Juárez 2220	66-48-40
Central	Calzada López Mateos 655	52-22-06
Dollar	Blvd. Juárez 1000	65-62-62
Hertz	Blvd. Juárez 1223	68-19-73
National	Blvd. Juárez 1004	68-39-63

centers (Plaza Cachanilla, Plaza Fiesta, and/or Plaza Universidad). You can arrange to be dropped off anywhere along the tour route and picked up later in the day. For more information, call 52-97-95 or 52-43-91.

Driving In Mexicali

Except for the congested downtown area near the border, the traffic in Mexicali moves fairly easily. Parking can be a problem near the border but elsewhere in the city is plentiful. The *glorietas* (traffic circles) are a bane for timid visiting drivers; lanes within the circles aren't generally marked—drivers jockey for position according to where they plan to exit the circle. It's important to stay alert while maneuvering round the circle (always counterclockwise) so that when the desired "spoke" approaches, you're in a position to take it.

To get onto Mexico 5 south for San Felipe, drive southeast on Calzada López Mateos until it meets Blvd. Juárez; follow the signs to the right (south). Just south of this intersection, Mexico 5 crosses Mexico 2, the highway to take for Tecate and Tijuana (west) or Sonora (east).

VICINITY OF MEXICALI

Southeast of Mexicali, the Valle de Mexicali and Río Colorado Delta area is mostly agricultural. Before the Mexican government's expropriation of foreign-owned lands in the '30s, much of the delta belonged to the U.S.-based Colorado River Land Company. Since then, it has been divided among ejidos, many of them named for mainland Mexican states and cities (e.g., Puebla, Cuernavaca, Oaxaca, Quintana Roo, Veracruz). A network of two-lane state highways connects the ejidos with the small farm towns of Nuevo León, Murguia, Victoria, Ledón, Coahuila, Ciudad Morelos, and Los Algodones.

The state border between Baja California Norte and Sonora runs parallel to the Río Colorado as far south as Coahuila. Mexico 2 east enters Sonora at the town of San Luis; once you cross the state line eastward, a temporary import permit is required for your vehicle unless it carries Mexican license plates. (Auto permits are available at the Mexican customs office at the Mexicali border crossing; in Baja, no permit is necessary.) Set your watch an hour ahead when crossing the Colorado—Sonora is on Mountain Time.

One of the more interesting ejido towns in the delta, if only because it straddles the BCN-Sonora line, is **Coahuila.** At the southeast end of BCN 4, past a toll bridge spanning the Colorado, this Baja outpost sits smack in the middle of the delta; the bumpy streets are paved with clay blocks. The popular **Restaurante India Bonita,** renowned for *milanesa* and carne asada, is almost reason enough to make the trip. The only other reason is to be able to say you've crossed the Colorado River in Mexico; in Coahuila, take a stroll over the state line and you'll have paid a visit to Sonora.

Southeast of Coahuila, about 69 km (43 miles) into Sonora via SON 40, is **El Golfo de Santa Clara,** the northernmost town on the Sea of Cortez. This small fishing town has a couple of cafés, markets, a church, motel (Motel Marcia, US$12-15), PEMEX station,

and three campground/RV parks (US$3 tents/campers, US$10 full hookups). A sandy road to the southeast leads into an area of dunes popular with ATV riders. At high tide, dunes become sandy beaches; at low tide, broad mud flats are exposed and large clams are plentiful. Anyone bringing a boat to El Golfo should also have a current set of Cortez tide tables, as the tidal range is extensive. From May through mid-Sept., the desert delta becomes an inferno.

LOS ALGODONES

This *poblado* of around 2,000 inhabitants in the northeast corner of Baja Norte, eight km (five miles) west of Yuma, Arizona, is named for the main cash crop in the region—cotton. In the town itself, however, the biggest business is dentistry for gringos; fees for dental services are 30-50% less than in the United States. Two or three dental clinics appear on virtually ever commercial block.

The most common Baja gateway for Arizona residents, Los Algodones also receives a steady stream of day visitors from Yuma County, one of the top three "snowbird" communities in the U.S. (along with Dade County, Florida and Río Grande Valley, Texas) where retired Americans choose to spend their winters.

Sights
The southern tip of the huge **Algodones Dunes** complex straddles the U.S.-Mexico border just west of town. (Drive west along Mariano Ma Lee until it ends about eight blocks from the border crossing.) Formed at the northeast banks of an extinct Pleistocene sea (a larger predecessor of the Salton Sea), the 650-square-km Algodones Dunes are the driest spot in North America save for Death Valley and the Mojave Desert. Iron-bearing minerals lend a reddish tinge to some of the dunes.

The **Presa Morelos** ("Morelos Dam"), constructed in 1950 as part of the Valle de Mexicali irrigation system, is about 6½ km south of town via Calle 6a. This is Mexico's only dam on the Río Colorado, which runs roughly 160 km (100 miles) south of the border before emptying into the Sea of Cortez. Considering the 10 major dams (not to mention the All-American Canal System) on the U.S. side, it's a wonder any water is left in the river by the time it crosses the border—an issue that has been a sore spot in U.S.-Mexico relations since early this century. Recently the U.S. government has proposed cementing the bottom of the All-American Canal to stop underground seepage—an action that would further decrease Mexico's supply of Río Colorado runoff.

Restaurants
The most popular restaurant in town among day visitors is **Pueblo Viejo** (tel. 4-78-90), a combination Mexican restaurant, souvenir shop, and bar at Calle 2a and Mariano Ma Lee. **La Cabaña,** a casual eatery at Calle 2a and Av. A, is famous for its *burritos de machaca* (jerked-meat burritos).

Shopping
Los Algodones pharmacies and liquor stores, concentrated along Calle 1a directly opposite the border crossing, do a booming business serving Yuma snowbirds. The **Mercado de Artesanías,** at the Parque de la Ciudad (City Park) at Calle 4a and Av. B, offers a variety of Mexican handicrafts, as does **Curios El Sahuaro,** opposite Restaurant La Cabana at Calle 2a and Av. A.

Information And Services
A Mexican insurance company at Calle 1a and Mariano Ma Lee distributes tourist information on Los Algodones and northern Baja. They can also recommend dental clinics.

The border crossing, along with Mexican **immigration** (tel. 4-78-21) and **customs** (tel. 4-78-30) offices, is open 0700-2000.

You can change money at **Los Algodones** casa de cambio on Av. B, between Calle 2a and 3a (near the church and telegraph office). The **post office** is at Calle 5a and Av. D.

Transport
Bus: A bus depot at Av. A and Calle 2a serves buses west to Mexicali (US$3) and Tijuana (US$7.50). Yuma, Arizona, eight km east of Los Algodones, has a Greyhound station and a regional airport.

Fuel: A PEMEX station at the corner of Av. B and Calle 5a pumps diesel and unleaded gasoline.

SAND FOOD AND SIDEWINDERS

In spite of the fact that the Algodones Dunes average less than 7½ cm (three inches) of rainfall a year, the dunes aren't entirely barren. **Evening primrose, sand verbena, desert lily, creosote bush,** and other long-rooted plants grow in the hollows between the dunes, lending shape and structure to the landscape. Even during long rainless periods, extensive root systems enable these plants to survive by tapping into "lenses" of moisture deep below the sandy surface.

Living in symbiosis with these plants is the hidden **sand food** *(Ammobroma sonorae),* a root unique to the Sonoran Desert. It grows beneath the dunes, tapping moisture and sugar from the other vegetation through a network of root hairs barely touching the host plants, but is not quite a parasite. In times when the host plants lack moisture, they receive nourishment from the sand food in turn. The Sonoran Papago Indians, or Hiach-eD-O'odham ("Sand People") as they called themselves, depended on the sand-colored, melon-flavored root as part of their desert diet, and it was known to early European desert travelers as well (hence it's odd English name).

Animate life in the dunes includes the common **desert iguana,** the **sidewinder** *(Crotalus cerastes,* a rattlesnake whose means of locomotion—tossing its body in side-to-side loops—is uniquely suited to sandy environments), and the rare **fringe-toed lizard,** the only reptile species totally limited to sand dunes.

MEXICALI TO TECATE
(MEXICO 2)

West of Mexicali, Mexico 2 skirts the northern edge of the Sierra de los Cucapá and flattens out along the top of **Laguna Salada,** a huge dry salt lake that extends southward nearly 100 km (60 miles).

At Km 24, an unpaved, ungraded road leads south to the northern shore of the lake, where a small fish camp survives on accumulated runoff from the Río Colorado delta; visitors are permitted to camp overnight. A PEMEX station near this junction offers a chance to gas up before proceeding farther along Mexico 2 or south along Laguna Salada. The next gas station is 53 km (33 miles) west, in La Rumorosa.

Palm Canyons

At Km 28, another unpaved road to the south, this one graded (a mixed blessing, since it means washboard surface much of the way), threads between the western edge of Laguna Salada and the eastern escarpment of the Sierra Juárez. Several steep-walled palm canyons cut deeply into the escarpment; the larger Tajo, El Carrizo, Guadalupe, and El Palomar canyons contain year-round streams and tinajas, and are highly desirable hiking and backpacking destinations from Nov. through mid-April. Late April-Oct., temperatures often exceed 37° C (100° F), not the best of conditions for desert hiking.

The Laguna Salada road is passable by ordinary passenger vehicle as far south as the turnoff for Cañon de Guadalupe; beyond that a 4WD vehicle is usually necessary. For overnight hikes, come prepared for wilderness camping.

Cañon Tajo, the most spectacular of the palm canyons, is reached by a dirt road that branches west off the Laguna Salada road 34½ km (21½ miles) south of Mexico 2. From this point, most vehicles can only make it 2½ km (1½ miles) or so before the track's contours become too extreme; after that it's 5½ km (3½ miles) of hard slogging across sand flats to the mouth of the canyon.

Your reward is a wide canyon studded with thousands of fan palms and watered by fresh-water pools with 450-meter (1,500-foot) granite walls in the background. It's 6½ km (4 miles) to the head of the canyon, where an old Indian trail leads north; a number of petroglyphs and Indian relics (don't touch) can be seen along the way. *Borregos* (desert bighorn sheep) and deer wander into the canyon on occasion.

The turnoff west to **Cañon de Guadalupe** is 59 km (36½ miles) south of Mexico 2. Unlike the approach to Tajo, this side road is passable by car or truck all the way to the mouth of the canyon (12½ km/8 miles), where there's a public campground and hot mineral springs. A nominal fee is charged for use of the hot springs (41.5° C/107° F); campsites are US$6 per night.

Although not as large as Tajo, Cañon de Guadalupe is quite impressive, with tiered waterfalls, pools, and plenty of blue fan palms. The main stream through the canyon leads to the "Pool of the Virgin," surrounded on by white granite walls, ferns, *alamo* (cottonwood), and *sauz* (willow). As in Cañon Tajo, an earlier Indian presence is in evidence. Both canyons were used by the Cucapás and Paipais during their seasonal pilgrimages to collect piñon nuts up on the Sierra Juárez plateau.

La Rumorosa

At around Km 44, Mexico 2 begins climbing the Juárez escarpment along the steep Cantú grade (also called "Cuesta de La Rumorosa"). The town of La Rumorosa, topping the grade at Km 68, is named for the constant murmuring of winds through the 1,275-meter (4,200-foot) mountain pass. Many Tijuana and Mexicali residents have summer homes in the vicinity, but the town itself is little more than a wide spot in the road with a café and a self-serve PEMEX station.

Descending along the more gradual western slope of the Sierra Juárez, the environment changes rapidly from the arid, scrubby vegetation east of the mountains to piñon stands and chaparral.

La Rumorosa To Laguna Hanson

West of La Rumorosa at Km 73 is a dirt road that leads 63 km (39 miles) south to **Laguna**

Mexico 3
(JOE CUMMINGS)

Hanson, part of the Parque Nacional Constitución de 1857. The road is graded for the first 37 km (23 miles) or so but rapidly deteriorates as it approaches the national park's northern boundary. High-clearance vehicles, preferably with 4WD, are recommended for this route.

The more popular (and easier) route into the national park is via Mexico 3, southeast of Ensenada. For information on this road, and on the national park itself, see "Ensenada to San Felipe," p. 191.

El Condor To Tecate

At **El Condor** (Km 83), 14½ km (9 miles) west of La Rumorosa, another unpaved road heads south to Laguna Hanson, passing the ranchos of Cisneros, Jacaranda, El Encanto, Tres Pozos, and others. Although this route is slower going than the La Rumorosa road, there's more to see, including several abandoned mines. Just beyond Rancho Jesayo and Mina Margarita (Margarita Mine), about 30 km from Mexico 2, the road joins the La Rumorosa-Laguna Hanson road.

The ejido settlement of **El Hongo** appears off Mexico 2 at Km 99, where a paved road leads southwest toward Hacienda Santa Veronica and a network of unpaved roads and vehicle tracks in the western foothills of the Sierra Juárez. The largest is an 83½-km (52-mile) road, mostly ungraded, that winds southward to join the Mexico 3-Laguna Hanson road near Rancho El Coyote. Along the way are several ranchos and abandoned mines, including **La Rosa de Castilla,** a former gold-mining center that served as the territorial capital (1870-82) before Ensenada. This road is suitable for high-clearance vehicles only.

Beyond El Hongo, Mexico 2 dips through rolling dairy farms and olive groves, a relatively uneventful ride until you arrive in **Tecate** at Km 130. For information on Tecate, see "Tecate to Ensenada," p. 207; for information on Mexico 2 between Tecate and Tijuana, see "Tijuana," p. 139.

MEXICALI TO SAN FELIPE (MEXICO 5)

Mexico 5, the paved, mostly two-lane highway (some parts have four lanes) between Mexicali and San Felipe is flat all the way and has one of the more durable roadbeds in Baja. Gringo rumor says the road was originally built by the U.S. Army Corps of Engineers following WW II to provide access to a radar station at Bahía de San Felipe's south end (now called Punta Radar); local authorities insist it was 100% Mexican-built. It's odd how the highway immediately deteriorates south of San Felipe.

The first 45 km (27 miles) of the highway is flanked by ejido lands with irrigated vegetable and dairy farms. Several *nopal* (prickly-pear cactus) farms can be seen along the highway around Km 15; fresh and pickled cactus is sold from roadside stands.

Just south of **La Puerta,** at Km 38, BCN 4 branches east to Coahuila and the Sonoran state border. La Puerta has a PEMEX station, market, and café. At about Km 48, the pastureland gives way abruptly to desert lands as the southern limit of the delta irrigation system is reached.

Río Hardy

Beginning at around Km 50 off Mexico 5, the marshy Río Hardy is easily accessed by a number of dirt tracks heading east off the highway. Several rustic *campos,* mostly catering to hunters and anglers, have been established along the river as far as its junction with the Río Colorado (about 15 km southeast).

The Río Hardy attracts a number of migrating bird species, including pintails, green-wing teals, egrets, pelicans, coots, cranes, and a dozen or more duck species. The main quarry for visiting hunters are white-wing and mourning doves, along with quail. Dove-hunting season generally runs Sept.-December.

Local Cucapá Indians fish the river for carp, flathead catfish, largemouth and striped bass, and, more recently, for *mojarra* (tilapia), a prolific African species that has come down into the Río Hardy through locks in Colorado River dams. The best fishing is said to be at the junction of the Hardy and Colorado rivers, near Campo Los Amigos. This area is accessible by vehicle track from Río El Mayor (Km 55) or San Miguel (about 12 km farther south, just before the causeway over Laguna Salada).

Camps in the Río Hardy area open and close from year to year (depending on river conditions), but have included Sonora, Las Cabañas, Río Hardy, El Mayor, Muñoz, and Los Amigos. Campos **Sonora, Río Hardy,** and **El Mayor** are usually open and can accommodate RVs; rates are around US$6 a night.

La Ventana-San Felipe

At Km 105 is the one-pump-one-café town of **La Ventana**; sneeze and you'll miss it. Farther south at Km 122 is an unpaved, graded road to the west that leads to three abandoned mines in the Sierra Las Pintas: La Fortuna, Buena Vista, and La Escondida. A fourth, Jueves Santo, is still a working gold mine.

South of this turnoff, the highway crosses the **Llano El Chinero** ("Chinese Plain"), where a large group of Chinese immigrants died of heat and thirst while trying to reach Mexicali on foot early this century. The lone peak east of the highway is 200-meter **Cerro El Chinero.**

Mexico 5 intersects with Mexico 3, the highway to Ensenada, at **Crucero La Trinidad** (Km 140). Just south of the junction is a PEMEX station. A string of signs for beach camps on the east side of the highway, beginning at around Km 172, marks the final approach to San Felipe, which is reached at Km 189.

SAN FELIPE

This unlikely beach community of 11,000 squeezed between the San Felipe Desert and the Sea of Cortez got its name from Jesuit Padre Fernando Consag, who briefly landed four canoes here in 1746 and named the gently curving bay San Felipe de Jesus. In 1797, a padre from Misión San Pedro Mártir de Verona established a supply port at Bahía San Felipe, but it failed, along with the mission, in 1806. In the late-19th and early-20th centuries, virtually the only people who knew of San Felipe's existence were nomadic fishermen who worked the eastern Sea of Cortez coast.

The post-WW II construction of a paved road to a radar station at the south end of the bay (now called Punta Radar) finally linked San Felipe with the outside world. In the late '40s and '50s, North American anglers came in droves to compete for the *totuava (Cynoscion macdonaldi),* a strong-fighting, copper-silver-gray croaker whose weight ranges 16-115 kilograms (35-254 lbs). Old-timers say it's one of the best-eating fishes in the Cortez, but since they fished the species onto the endangered species list, most of us will never get a taste. (Mexican law now forbids the taking of totuava.)

SAN FELIPE HOTELS AND MOTELS

Rates quoted are for peak season (Nov.-April). Off-season rates may be discounted 20-30%. Add 15% hotel tax to all rates (some hotels may charge an additional 10% service charge).

Area code: 657

NAME	ADDRESS	TELEPHONE	RATES	FEATURES
Hotel Aquamarina San Felipe	13 km south of San Felipe on the beach (P.O. Box 2776, Chula Vista, CA 92012)	800-678-7244 (in U.S. 619-422-6918)	US$38 mid-week US$60 weekends	a/c, satellite TV, pool, restaurant, bar, includes buffet breakfast
Chapala Motel	Av. Mar de Cortez 142 (A.P. 331, San Felipe, BCN)	7-12-40	US$22-32	a/c
El Capitán Motel	Av. Mar de Cortez 298 P.O. Box 1916, Calexico, CA 92231)	7-13-03	US$30 midweek, US$36 weekends (rates valid for one to four persons)	a/c, pool
Motel El Cortez	1 km south of town on bay (Local 5, Mexicali, BCN; in U.S. P.O. Box 1227, Calexico, CA 82231)	7-10-55	US$56	a/c, pool, boat launch, palapas, restaurant
Motel El Pescador	Calzada Chetumal and Av. Mar de Cortez	7-10-44	US$23	
Hotel Las Misiones	2½ km south of town near marina, Av. Misión de Loreto 148 (in U.S. P.O. Box 120637, Chula Vista, CA 92012)	7-12-84 (in U.S 800-336-5454; fax 619-422-6910)	US$65	a/c, satellite TV, pools, tennis courts, basketball court, restaurant, bar, includes buffet breakfast
Hotel La Trucha Vagabunda	Av. Los Cedros	7-13-33	US$45 s, US$50 d	a/c, tennis and volleyball courts, restaurant, bar
Hotel Riviera	Av. Los Cedros	7-11-85	US$30	a/c, satellite TV, pool includes breakfast

The bay is protected from north-northeast winds by Punta San Felipe, a jutting headland topped by 240-meter Cerro El Machorro at the north end of the bay. The summit has a good view of the bay and bears a shrine dedicated to the Virgin of Guadalupe. Below the headland is an estuary and boatyard. At the south end of the bay, an artificial harbor shelters the local commercial shrimping fleet, one of five such fleets licensed to net shrimp along Mexico's west coast. The tidal range in the northern Cortez is extreme, so only the outer section of the harbor is usable for larger craft.

SAN FELIPE

PLAYA BONITA TRAILER PARK

RUBEN'S TRAILER PARK

TO MEXICALI

CALZADA CHETUMAL

PUERTO PEÑASCO

ZIHUATANEJO

ACAPULCO

CARIBE

BERMEJO

CORTEZ

GOLFO DE CALIFORNIA

MAR DE CORTEZ

BUS DEPOT

VIRGIN GUADALUPE SHRINE

LIGHTHOUSE

PUNTA SAN FELIPE

MAR

MANZANILLO

MAR BLANCO

MAR NEGRO

BALTICO

AV. PASEO DE CORTEZ

POST OFFICE

ROCKODILE PATIO AND GRILL

CHAPALA MOTEL

MOTEL EL CAPITAN

LA JOLLA TRAILER PARK

TOURIST OFFICE

GEORGE'S RESTAURANT

HOTEL LA TRUCHA VAGABUNDA

MAR

PLAYA DE LAURA TRAILER PARK

MOTEL EL CORTEZ

HOTEL RIVIERA

CLUB DE PESCA TRAILER PARK

BAHÍA SAN FELIPE

PASEO DE LAS MUJERES

HOTEL LAS MISIONES

TO AIRPORT & PUERTECITOS

AV. MISIÓN DE LORETO

MAR DEL SOL RV PARK

MARINA

0   0.25mi
0   0.25km

© MOON PUBLICATIONS, INC.

San Felipe today has become a beach playground for Alta Californians and Arizonans who camp or park their RVs on the many beaches extending north and south of the bay. The nearby dunes attract dune-buggy and ATV enthusiasts who scream up and down the sloping sands with Cerro Juan (1,025 meters/3,369 feet) and Cerro Kino (1,304 meters/4,290 feet) to the west as a backdrop. A number of North Americans have retired in San Felipe but, for most people, the best San Felipe has to offer is a cheap beach and/or fishing vacation within two to three hours drive of the Alta California-Arizona border—and possibly the best fish tacos on the peninsula.

Climate And Tourist Season
Peak tourist season in the San Felipe area is Nov.-April, when temperatures are mild (although Dec.-Feb., the northern Cortez may be a bit chilly for most swimmers). May-Oct., daytime air temperatures frequently break 38° C (100° F), but it doesn't get quite as hot as in Mexicali. During the summer, many North Americans residing in San Felipe go elsewhere—usually the Pacific coast—to cool off. Rainfall, at any time of year, is virtually nil.

Hotel And Motels
Because San Felipe is so popular and so close to the U.S. border, hotel and motel rates tend to be a bit on the high side, at least for Baja. The cheapest hotels are US$23-25 a night but overpriced at that; if you can spend a little more, you'll get better value. See the "San Felipe Hotels and Motel" chart for specifics.

A recent development in the San Felipe are the "condotels" and resort villas that are often part time-share, part hotel, and part year-round condo complex. Ask at the tourist office about renting local condos or apartments by the night—in some cases they're a better deal than the local hotels and motels. Since sales are slow, developers are desperate to get whatever money they can out of them.

A Mexico City contractor is developing an extensive marina and resort south of the current commercial fishing marina. A 180-space RV park is planned for the first phase (completed in the mid '90s), along with a handful of waterfront villas. Eventually this development may include a hotel wing. Then again, it might never get built at all; it wouldn't the first San Felipe development to falter.

Several kilometers south of the semi-functional San Felipe airport, on the way to El Faro beach, is **La Hacienda** (tel. 7-13-81), a resort development in progress with homes for sale or rent.

Camping And RV Parks
Over two dozen beachfront operations in San Felipe, and to the north and south of the town, tout themselves as campgrounds or RV parks. Some—mostly those out of town—have virtually no facilities beyond a graded road be-

tween the highway and beach; others—in town—come with full RV hookups, restaurants, bars, hot showers, and flush toilets.

Those in town generally cost US$10-15 nightly per site for two persons, plus US$2 for each additional person. The beach camps north and south of town typically cost US$5-10 for two per site, depending on the facilities, plus US$1 for each additional person. An exception is **El Faro Trailer Park** at Punta Estrella (16 km south of town), which has full hookups (including 24-hour electricity), tennis courts, and a pool, but no restaurant (and no telephone), for US$17 per site per night. All camps and RV parks in the San Felipe area will give generous discounts for long-term stays.

The most popular campgrounds among the RV crowd are those along the beach just north of Punta San Felipe, on the outskirts of town. This area generally gets a good sea breeze and is thus cooler than parks on the bay itself. In this northern zone, from north to south, are El Jacalito, Playa Bonita, Ruben's, La Palapa, Costa Azul, La Posada del Mar, and Baja Beverly Hills, all decent places to park awhile; if you don't like the first one you try, you can always move to another. **Playa Bonita** (tel. 7-12-15 in San Felipe, 213-413-4272 in the U.S.) and Ruben's (tel. 7-10-91) are particularly popular for their large deck-topped palapas; some people complain about the level of the music at Ruben's restaurant, however. Playa Bonita takes phone reservations; Ruben's doesn't.

South of town next to Hotel Las Misiones is San Felipe's top trailer park, **Mar del Sol** (tel. 7-12-80 in San Felipe; 800-336-5454 or 619-422-6900 in the U.S.). Perhaps the park's best feature is that the management doesn't allow motorcycles, ATVs, or dune buggies, hence it's one of the quietest trailer parks in San Felipe. Facilities include hot showers, flush toilets, pool, restaurant, palapas, boat launch, coin laundry, and groceries. RV sites are US$17 (US$11 for Good Sam members) per night while tent sites are US$9. Discounts are given for long-term stays.

Other camping and trailer parks in town include **La Jolla** (tel. 7-12-22, Av. Manzanillo and Mar Bermejo)—US$12 for RVs or tents,

Campo San Felipe (tel. 7-10-12, Av. Mar de Cortez)—US$10 for tents, US$15 for RVs, **Club de Pesca** (tel. 7-11-80)—US$12 for RVs, and **Playa de Laura** (tel. 7-11-28)—US$10 for tents, US$14 for RVs. All have full hookups, showers, and flush toilets; La Jolla takes phone reservations.

Food

Seafood is what San Felipe restaurants do best. A string of vendors sell fresh seafood cocktails and fish tacos along the *malecón* (waterfront) at the intersection of Calzada Chetumal and Paseo de Cortez. Right on Calzada Chetumal, a block and half east of the malecón, is the **Red Lobster Inn,** the only restaurant in town whose patio receives full sun all day during the winter. Seafood entrees here are moderately priced, delicious ceviche tostadas are only US$1, and the beer is served in chilled mugs. Open for breakfast, lunch, and dinner.

George's (tel. 7-10-57), at Av. Mar de Cortez 336, is a favorite among gringo regulars who come for the dependable seafood dinners and American breakfasts. For something less touristy, try the homey **Puerto Padre** (tel. 7-13-35, Av. Mar de Cortez 316, next to George's). Puerto Padre's Cuban owners try hard to please with a variety of fresh seafood entrees and a large selection of Mexican and American breakfasts; their real brewed coffee makes a nice change from the Nescafe served in many Baja restaurants. George's and Puerto Padre are open for breakfast, lunch, and dinner.

Wherever you find a heavy concentration of gringos in Baja, there's always an **El Nido** steakhouse. San Felipe's is on Av. Mar de Cortez (tel. 7-10-49) in the same area as George's and Puerto Padre. The menu features the usual steak and ranchero standards—dependable, but not particularly inspiring—for breakfast, lunch, and dinner.

Also on Mar de Cortez is **Green House,** a restaurant-bar with Mexican food and gringo prices. The pleasant sidewalk tables at the front only get sun in the morning; a patio has recently been added in the back. Open for 0730-0300 daily.

To the north of Calzada Chetumal are several small, inexpensive cafés, including **Petunia's Café** at the corner of Calle Puerto de Acapulco and Av. Mar de Cortez. Tacos and burritos, along with Mexican and American breakfasts, are the main draw. **El Club,** between Rockodile and Rock N'Roll Plaza on the malecón, is very popular for Mexican breakfasts (including chilaquiles, one of Mexico's best hangover remedies).

La Perla (tel. 7-10-39), on Mar de Cortez opposite Petunia's, serves Mexican-style seafood and, in the afternoons, a reasonable *comida corrida.* **Los Gemelos,** next door to La Perla, has the cheapest and greasiest *comida corrida* in town: US$3 for chile relleno, enchilada queso, taco dorado, beans, and rice. The taco-burrito-hamburguesa stand farther north on the same side of Mar de Cortez is better.

The Hotel La Trucha Vagabunda's **Alfredo's** restaurant, open for breakfast, lunch, and dinner, serves Italian specialties for those bored with seafood and Mexican. The dining room at **Hotel Las Misiones** has an international menu; the all-you-can-eat breakfast buffet is a bargain at US$6 (complimentary for hotel guests).

Rockodile Patio and Grill, on the malecón, serves very tasty fish tacos (two for US$1) along with a tray of six different condiments. They also have burgers, fries, and huge beef tacos ("tacodiles"). Food is served from around noon till midnight.

Away from the waterfront, and from the bulk of the tourist dining crowd, are **John's** (Av. Mar Baltico 150) and **La Glorieta** (on the *glorieta* at Av. Mar Caribe and Calzada Chetumal), both steak and seafood places open for lunch and dinner only.

Groceries: Several tiendas along Calzada Chetumal, on the way into San Felipe, sell fresh vegetables, ice, canned goods, and camping/household supplies. Two bakeries on Av. Mar de Cortez compete for local business: **Panaficadora Singapur,** opposite Motel El Pescador, with the town's widest selection of baked items, and **Pandería El Buen Gusto,** north of Calzada Chetumal near Petunia's.

To buy fresh, locally harvested finfish and shellfish, pay a visit to the **Pescadería Los Temos,** a fishing coop on Calle San Felipe (make a left turn off Av. Mar de Cortez just north of Punta Santa Felipe). The coop is open daily 0700-1900.

Entertainment

At night, the young and not-so-young shake it at **Rockodile** or **Rock N'Roll Plaza,** both large dance clubs on the malecón. Weekdays are usually on the dead side, weekends packed; Rockodile is the more popular of the two (better sound system) and has a sand volleyball court. The **Green House** restaurant-bar also brings in a loud crowd, especially now that the patio has been added. All three bars have happy hours from noon till around 1700, when drinks are US$1.

Gamblers can wager on race and sports book at **Caliente Foreign Book,** in Plaza Cortez (next to the El Cortez Hotel on Av. Mar de Cortez).

Events

Most of San Felipe's yearly events calendar revolves around desert or Sea of Cortez racing. The **Gran Carrera de San Felipe,** a 250-mile offroad race, is held in early February by Baja Promotions (tel. 818- 340-5790, P.O. Box 8938, Calabasas, CA 91302) and usually runs northwest around the Sierra San Felipe, south through Laguna Diablo and Arroyo Chanate, and east around the Sierra Santa Rosa.

March winds bring the **Hobie Cat Regatta,** a catamaran race on Bahía de San Felipe. In mid-April, Monday International (tel. 619-275-1384 in the U.S.) sponsors the annual **San Felipe Triathlon,** a running-cycling-swimming race; the triathlon is repeated in early November. Monday International also organizes a **Mexicali-San Felipe Bike Ride** in late October.

Navy Day (Día de la Marina), observed on June 1, is celebrated in San Felipe with a street festival, music, and dancing.

Sports And Recreation

Fishing: Although the San Felipe fishery is not what it used to be—the magnificent totuava has become a protected species—fishing is still one of the primary local tourist activities. The high fishing season is March-June, when

trailer park, San Felipe
(JOE CUMMINGS)

white seabass runs are common. Croakers are available year-round, corvinas late March-November. Cabrilla, yellowtail, sierra, and grouper are plentiful May-October; in the fall months, pompano are common.

Generally, the best onshore fishing area is from Punta San Felipe north, while inshore fishing is good from Punta Estrella south. The best offshore fishing (and the best overall) is around Roca Consag, 27 km (17 miles) east of Punta San Felipe, especially for croaker and white seabass.

Two sportfishing services at the north end of the malecón, **Alex's** (tel. 7-10-52) and **Tony's** (tel. 7-11-20), offer a variety of guided fishing trips aboard eight-meter (24-foot) pangas. A 0700-1200 bay fishing trip costs US$50 for two (US$80 for four), including bait, guide, license, and tackle. Bay angling usually nets calico bass, small croaker, sierra, or triggerfish. An all-day trip to Roca Consag (45 minutes away by boat) costs US$100-120 for two to four anglers, US$40 for each additional person. Depending on the season, a Roca Consag trip brings back sierra, large croakers and corvina, and yellowtail. On either type of trip, anglers must bring their own lunch.

Fishing tackle can be purchased at **Proveedora de Equipos de Pesca** on Av. Mar de Cortez near the estuary. Tony's and Alex's small offices sell hooks and sinkers. Live bait can be bought from the shrimpers at the commercial marina south of town. As elsewhere in Mexico, a valid fishing license is needed for every person in every boat that carries fishing tackle. You can legally fish from shore without a license.

Windsurfing: Sailboards—but not exactly state of the art gear—can be rented at the Motel El Cortez. Spring is the best wind season on the bay, but there are breezes year-round. The shoreline north of Punta San Felipe gets the best wind.

Boating: Experienced, self-sufficient small-boaters and kayakers often put in at San Felipe for the 258-km (160-mile) coastal cruise to Bahía de los Angeles. Although there are plenty of coves to stop in along the way, only a few places—Puertecitos, Punta Bufeo, and Bahía San Luis Gonzaga—offer limited supplies.

Information And Services

The **state tourist office** (tel. 7-11-55), at Av. Mar de Cortez and Calle Manzanillo, is open Mon.-Fri. 0900-1900, Sat. 0900-1500, Sun. 1000-1400. In addition to handing out the usual hotel brochures and city maps, the staff can be very helpful with suggestions for things to do in the area.

Changing Money: The Banamex on the corner of Calzada Chetumal and Mar Blanco offers foreign currency exchange service Mon.-Fri. 0900-1100. Bancomer and Banco

Internacional each have branches on Av. Mar de Cortez with similar exchange services.

Post and Telephone: San Felipe's post office is on Mar Blanco, a block south of Calzada Chetumal. Hours are Mon.-Fri. 0800-1300 and 1400-1800. San Felipe's area code is 657.

Bathhouses: On Calle Puerto de Acapulco, just off the malecón, are a couple of small public *baños* (bathhouses). A hot shower costs US$1.

Transport

Air Although the sign at the airport, nine km south of San Felipe, reads "Aeropuerto Internacional de San Felipe," there are no regularly scheduled international flights to San Felipe at this writing.

Bus: San Felipe's bus depot is on Av. Mar Tasmania, north of Calzada Chetumal and west of Av. Mar de Cortez. Transportes Norte de Sonora operates buses to and from Mexicali (US$4.60) four times daily, to and from Ensenada (US$5) twice daily (one morning, one evening bus). Bus tickets go on sale an hour before departure.

Taxi: Local taxis wait on Av. Mar de Cortez and at the Hotel Las Misiones for the occasional fare. A taxi can be ordered by calling 7-12-92. Fares in central San Felipe should be under US$5; from the malecón to Hotel Las Misiones costs around US$7.

SAN FELIPE TO BAHÍA SAN LUIS GONZAGA

The road from San Felipe to Puertecitos (85 km/53 miles) is paved but in a fairly constant state of disrepair, especially south of the turnoff for El Faro Trailer Park. In many places, a sand track parallels the paved road and provides a smoother ride for vehicles that can handle sandy surfaces. In some places, giant chunks of the road are missing or there is heavy washboarding, but it's passable by ordinary passenger vehicle—slowly. The *vados* (places where dry culverts intersect the road) along this road bear mention: they're some of the most treacherous in

Baja. Road signs are mostly in English since only gringos seem interested in driving this desert road.

Indications of human habitation grow increasingly scarce the farther south you proceed. Three km south of San Felipe are a handful of condo developments, then the Hotel Aquamarina 10 km farther south (see "San Felipe Hotels and Motels," above). Just past the El Faro turnoff is a huge, unsightly trash dump right off the highway, used by El Faro Trailer Park and other beach camp owners. Around this point begins an enchanting desert landscape of mesquite, ocotillo, cholla, elephant trees, cenizo, and sage. **Punta Estrella,** a good beach for clamming, is six to seven km south of El Faro.

Every so often—all the way to Puertecitos—a beach camp is signed on the left. The going rate to park on the beach is around US$5; facilities are usually limited to drinking water and outdoor toilets. Between Km 38 and 40 is **Playa Mexico,** a more elaborate beach camp with a restaurant and airstrip.

Puertecitos is little more than a cluster of breeze-block buildings and rusting trailers ensconced around a shallow cove. At one time it was probably a beautiful spot, but has become a jumble of mismatched shelters and discarded auto parts only a dune-buggy or fishing fanatic could love. At the hot springs at the northeast side of the cove, prudish local norteamericanos have been known to scold visiting skinny-dippers. The PEMEX station is closed more often than not; a restaurant and bar provide meager sustenance.

South of Puertecitos the road should only be attempted in vehicles with sturdy tires and shocks. About 29 km (18 miles) south along the coast is a small beach camp/retirement community called **El Huerfanito,** and after another 30 km are several more fish camps, including cabins for rent, at **Punta Bufeo.** The onshore fishing here and at the nearby **Islas Encantadas**—five islands and several islets close to shore—is reputedly good for yellowtail, croaker, corvina, and sierra. Several of the Encantadas (San Luis, Pomo, Encantada, Lobos) are of volcanic origin, displaying pumice and lava deposits. The islands are a good kayaking destination although offshore winds can be quite strong in the winter.

About 12 km (seven miles) south of Punta Bufeo is **Punta Willard,** home of **Papa Hernandez Resort,** a campground with gas, meals, and fishing pangas for rent. Just a few kilometers below Punta Willard, at the south end of Bahía Willard, is **Alfonsina's,** the main supply point for visitors and residents enjoying large, pristine **Bahía San Luis Gonzaga,** the next bay south. The entire 72½-km (45-mile) trip from Puertecitos to Alfonsina's takes five to six hours by car. A cot in one of the rustic rooms here costs US$10 a night; no showers are available and toilets are shared.

From Bahía San Luis Gonzaga, a mostly graded but unpaved road leads southwest 64½ km (40 miles) to meet Mexico 1 at Km 230; this drive generally takes about three hours. About 38 km (24 miles) from Bahía San Luis Gonzaga, near Rancho Las Arrastras, the same road intersects an unpaved, partially graded road east to **Bahía de Calamajué,** another nearly untouched bay.

Reportedly, the Mexican government has plans to extend the paved road from San Felipe all the way to Bahía San Luis Gonzaga and eventually to Mexico 1. This would provide an alternative route to Baja Sur, along the east coast via Mexicali, for drivers of ordinary, low-clearance vehicles.

(BOB RACE)

NORTH CENTRAL BAJA

EL ROSARIO AND VICINITY

Near the mouth of a deep valley formed by Río del Rosario is the town of El Rosario, a market center for farms and ranches in the valley as well as fish camps along the nearby Pacific coast. Although the valley has been continuously inhabited for at least 300 years, El Rosario today is little more than a cluster of modest homes, a rustic baseball field, hospital, school, town hall, several markets, two motels, two PEMEX stations, and a few taquerías and cafés. It is, however, the largest town to for 356 km (221 miles) southward, and as such it's an important supply and reconnaissance point for anyone exploring north central Baja.

El Rosario actually consists of two communities: the larger El Rosario de Arriba, along the highway in the upper part of the valley, and the smaller El Rosario de Abajo, south of the highway and the Río del Rosario, toward the coast.

History

Little is known about the Cochimó Indians who lived here when the Spanish arrived except that they subsisted mostly on Pacific shellfish and wild desert plants, and they called their valley community "Viñadaco." In 1774, the Dominican Order established its first and southernmost California mission, **Nuestra Señora del Rosario,** on the east side of the valley facing the Pacific; the mission was moved downstream in 1802 to take advantage of a better water supply. (The adobe ruins of the latter mission can be found by turning right—west—at the supermarket, where Mexico 1 curves east, and then left at the first road. After crossing the riverbed to El Rosario de Abajo, the ruins can be seen on the right.)

At first the mission community thrived, producing the most abundant crops of any northern Baja mission, as the valley was perfectly suited for agriculture. As elsewhere in the

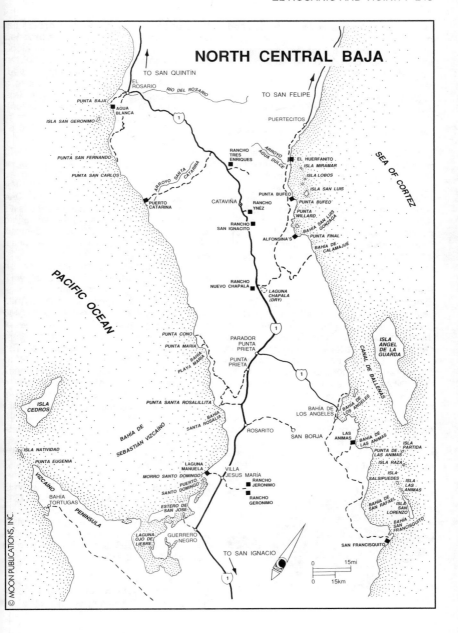

NORTH CENTRAL BAJA

TO SAN QUINTÍN

EL ROSARIO
RÍO DEL ROSARIO

TO SAN FELIPE

PUNTA BAJA
AGUA BLANCA
PUERTECITOS
ISLA SAN GERONIMO

PUNTA SAN FERNANDO
RANCHO TRES ENRIQUES
ARROYO AGUA DULCE
EL HUERFANITO
ISLA MIRAMAR

PUNTA SAN CARLOS
ISLA LOBOS

ARROYO SANTA CATARINA
CATAVIÑA
RANCHO YNEZ
ISLA SAN LUIS

SEA OF CORTEZ

PUERTO CATARINA
PUNTA BUFEO
PUNTA BUFEO

RANCHO SAN IGNACITO
PUNTA WILLARD
BAHÍA SAN LUIS GONZAGA

ALFONSINA'S
PUNTA FINAL

BAHÍA DE CALAMAJUE

PACIFIC OCEAN

RANCHO NUEVO CHAPALA
LAGUNA CHAPALA (DRY)

ISLA ANGEL DE LA GUARDA

PUNTA CONO
PARADOR PUNTA PRIETA
PUNTA MARIA
PUNTA PRIETA
BAHÍA MARIA
PLAYA MARIA

CANAL DE BALLENAS

ISLA CEDROS

PUNTA SANTA ROSALILLITA

BAHÍA DE LOS ANGELES
BAHÍA DE LOS ANGELES

ISLA NATIVIDAD
SANTA ROSALIA
BAHÍA DE SEBASTIÁN VIZCAÍNO
ROSARITO
SAN BORJA
LAS ANIMAS
BAHÍA DE LAS ANIMAS

PUNTA EUGENIA
ISLA PARTIDA
PUNTA DE LAS ANIMAS

VIZCAINO
LAGUNA MANUELA
VILLA JESUS MARÍA
RANCHO JERONIMO
ISLA RAZA
ISLA LAS ANIMAS

BAHÍA TORTUGAS
MORRO SANTO DOMINGO
PUERTO SANTO DOMINGO
RANCHO GERONIMO
ISLA SALSIPUEDES

PENINSULA
ESTERO DE SAN JOSE
BAHÍA DE SAN RAFAEL
ISLA SAN LORENZO

LAGUNA OJO DE LIEBRE
GUERRERO NEGRO
BAHÍA SAN FRANCISQUITO

TO SAN IGNACIO
SAN FRANCISQUITO

0   15mi
0   15km

© MOON PUBLICATIONS, INC.

Californias, the Indians eventually succumbed to diseases brought by the missionaries and, left without converts or laborers, the mission was closed in 1832. A Spanish land grant in the 1840s brought Carlos Espinosa to the valley, where he and his family became successful ranchers and farmers. Italian copper miner Eduardo Grosso arrived at the turn of the century and the union of the two families has been a prime source of El Rosario history ever since.

In the '60s, El Rosario became a checkpoint for the Baja 1000 offroad race and the first landing for the Flying Samaritans, a group of North American doctors who provide volunteer medical service by plane to several northern Baja settlements. El Rosario's Doña Anita Grosso de Espinosa, proprietor of Espinosa's Place café, acted as a liaison between gringos and the local community and was largely instrumental in the initial success of both endeavors.

Punta Baja-Agua Blanca
Sixteen km (10 miles) southwest of El Rosario de Arriba, via an unpaved but all-vehicle road, is **Punta Baja,** a fish camp and headland at the north end of Bahía del Rosario. Pangas can be rented here (or launch your own), and the perch and rock cod fishing is good year-round. Farther offshore, tuna, croaker, bonito, and yellowtail are abundant. During northwest swells, the surfing off Punta Baja is excellent.

Agua Blanca is another fish camp eight km (five miles) south of Punta Baja, toward the middle of the bay. Between Punta Baja and Agua Blanca you may notice piles of sea urchin shells at the roadside. The harvesting

cave painting of a fish   (BOB RACE)

of sea urchins constitutes the bulk of the local fishing industry; 90% of the catch is exported to Japan, mostly for sushi. (The orange-colored "roe" consumed by the Japanese isn't the sea urchin's eggs, as is commonly believed, but the sex organs.) Agua Blanca is also a launching point for scuba excursions to **Isla San Geronimo** (sometimes spelled Jeronimo) and Sacramento Reef.

Accommodations And Food
El Rosario has two motels, **Motel El Rosario** on the east side of the highway as you enter town from the north, and **Motel Sinai,** around the bend in the highway to the east. Both offer adequate rooms for US$15-18 a night. One drawback of staying at Motel El Rosario is it's located at the bottom of a grade leading into town (and next to a PEMEX station); decelerating truckers make quite a roar as they pass, especially when they stop for fuel.

Motel El Rosario has the advantage, on the other hand, of being only a short walk from legendary **Espinosa's Place.** This restaurant, operated by the family of Doña Anita Grosso de Espinosa, has hosted Baja 1000 drivers, Flying Samaritans, and thousands of other Baja travelers since the days before the Transpeninsular was completed. The small dining room has recently been refurbished with plastic, McDonald's-style chairs and tables, but the burritos—from beans to lobster—are as tasty as ever. Profits from the restaurant help support a local orphanage.

Around the bend toward Motel Sinai is **Restaurant Yiyo's,** a popular local hangout with a variety of egg dishes, fish, lobster, and beef machaca, breaded shrimp, and steak. Prices at both restaurants set the standard for what just about every café and rancho between El Rosario and Guerrero Negro charges, US$3 for breakfast, US$8.50 for lunch or dinner.

Camping: Beach camping is possible along Bahía del Rosario. **El Rosario de México,** in town, offers 50 camper/RV slots with full hookups for US$8 a night.

Supplies
Several tiendas in town offer fresh vegetables, baked goods, and a variety of automotive and

(top) bakery, San Felipe; (bottom) fruit vendor, Cabo San Lucas (top left) Bajacalifornio, Tijuana; (top right) Guadalupe Cathedral, Tijuana; (bottom) *norteña* musician, Hussong's Cantina household items. The supermarket at the first bend in the highway, near Espinosa's Place, has the largest selection, including vaquero hats.

El Rosario has two PEMEX stations, one at either end of town.

EL ROSARIO TO BAHÍA DE LOS ANGELES JUNCTION

After El Rosario, the Transpeninsular Highway drifts southeast, toward the center of the peninsula. For many Baja aficionados, this is where the "real" Baja begins, as the population thins out rapidly and the peninsula's most classic desert scenery leaps through the windshield for the next 200 km (120 miles).

Once the Arroyo del Rosario is crossed (Km 62), spindly *cirios* or "boojums" (see "Flora and Fauna," p. 14, for a description of these fascinating plants) begin appearing, gradually increasing in number the farther inland the highway goes. Cardón are also prolific, along with barrel cactus, yucca, and a whole pantheon of Baja desert plants.

A graded road leaves the highway at Km 78 and goes 56 km (35 miles) southwest to **Bahía San Carlos,** a well-known spot among Baja windsurfers and surf anglers.

Misión San Fernando Velicatá

A dirt road at Km 114 leads west off the highway to the ruins of the only mission built by the Franciscans in Baja. The secluded site was first discovered in 1766 by Jesuit Padre Link, but the Jesuits were expelled before they could found a mission. Father Junípero Serra, on his way north, established San Fernando in 1769, and due to its location at a midpoint between the Gulf and Pacific coasts, it became an important way station on the Camino Real. The mission community was wiped out by a 1777-80 epidemic.

Although the adobe ruins themselves aren't much, the arroyo setting is dramatic and the short side trip (eight km/five miles) affords an opportunity for desert solitude and chance to get closer to the regional flora and fauna. Two families have rancherías at the site, living off the slim bounty of the arroyo.

Rock walls near the arroyo bear petroglyphs and pictographs, some created by the Cochimís in the 17th-18th centuries, others possibly older.

Just south of the mission road, at Km 116, is **Rancho El Progreso,** the first of many ranchos along the Transpeninsular that serve food to passing motorists. The menu includes whatever's on the stove that day, usually simple ranchero fare: enchiladas, chiles rellenos, frijoles, and rice.

El Mármol

This abandoned onyx quarry, accessible via a 15-km (nine-mile) graded dirt road branching east off Mexico 1 at Km 143, makes another interesting side trip. "Mármol" means "marble" in Spanish, and for the first half of this century onyx—a brown-and-red-veined calcite or tufa that can be polished to a high gloss—was a popular marble substitute. The El Mármol operation was begun by a San Diego mining company in the early 1900s, and by the late '50s, when it closed (due to the advent of cheaper synthetics), much of the world's onyx inkstands, bathroom fixtures, statues, floor and wall panels, and other decorative objects had been quarried at this site. (Onyx's peak was the art deco period, when celebrities like actress Theda Bara ordered custom-made onyx bathtubs.)

The onyx at El Mármol is easy to quarry since layers of it are sitting right on the desert surface. The problem is transporting it from this isolated site; when the quarry was operative, onyx slabs had to be trucked to Puerto Catarina (80 km east on the Pacific coast), loaded through the surf one by one, and shipped north to San Diego by boat.

Banded onyx blocks remain strewn about the old quarry site. The ruins of a schoolhouse made entirely of thick onyx blocks can be seen to one side of the quarry. About midway between the highway and the old quarry is a huge mesquite tree standing next to a well and an antique Aermotor windmill, a scene that looks like it was plucked straight from West Texas.

Off the El Mármol road, between the highway and the quarry, **Rancho Tres Enriques** offers meals and rustic accommodations.

onyx schoolhouse,
El Mármol
(JOE CUMMINGS)

Rancho Sonora, between Km 144 and 145 on Mexico 1, also has food.

Cataviña-Parque Natural Del Desierto Central

This Mexico 1 way station at Km 174+ lies in the middle of possibly the most spectacular desert scenery on the peninsula, a vast area of Volkswagen-sized boulders, cardón, elephant trees, cirios, and a hundred other desert oddities. The north end of the Desierto Central is marked by the Cataviña Boulder Field, honeycombed with trails and an excellent area for hiking—except in summer when the heat is deadly.

Accommodations, food, and fuel are available at Cataviña's **Hotel La Pinta** (tel. 667-2601 in Ensenada; 800-336-5454 in the U.S.). There's another PEMEX station opposite the hotel. The Parque Natural de Desierto Central operates a trailer park with 60 spots with full hookups adjacent to the hotel; rates are US$7 a night.

A kilometer south of Cataviña is a turnoff east to **Rancho Santa Ynez,** where ranchero food and hot showers are available. A vehicle track (dirt bikes or 4WD only) continues 23 km (14 miles) farther east to the adobe ruins

of Misión Santa María de los Angeles, the last New World mission (1767-69) founded by the Jesuits.

Cataviña To Parador Punta Prieta

About 30 km (18½ miles) south of Cataviña, off the west side of the highway between Km 207 and 208, is **El Pedregoso (Pedregal),** a massive natural rock formation (610 meters/2,000 feet high) that looks as if it were constructed from a pile of boulders.

Rancho San Ignacito, at Km 187, is yet another rancho food stop. A nearby plaque commemorates the completion of Mexico 1, at the spot where road crews from the north and south finally met. Between Km 229 and 230, a graded road heads northeast to Bahía San Luis Gonzaga and Bahía de Calamajué on the Sea of Cortez coast. At this junction, **Rancho Nuevo Chapala** offers traveler's meals. The cirio, cardón, yucca, and cholla in the area are often exemplary specimens.

Parador Punta Prieta is a government-established rest stop at Km 280 with a PEMEX station and a large cafeteria operated by a local ejido. This is also where Mexico 1 splits, with the left fork leading southeast 68 km (42 miles) to Bahía de los Angeles.

BAHÍA DE LOS ANGELES AND VICINITY

The highway to Bahía de los Angeles passes thick stands of copalquín (elephant tree) on its way through the Sierra La Asamblea. At Km 44 a 4WD-only track leads southwest 35 km (21 miles) to the restored Misión San Borja; a better road of similar distance, however, is accessible from Rosarito, off the west branch of Mexico 1 (see "Punta Prieta to Guerrero Negro" below). The final descent to the bay from the sierra affords an inspiring view of the island-studded blue waters.

Beginning in the late '40s, North American sportfishers began flying private planes into Bahía de los Angeles; a few hardy souls even drove here from San Diego and points north. Old Baja hands say in those days the village was nothing more than thatched-roof huts. But novelist John Steinbeck, who sailed into the bay in early 1940 with marine biologist Ed Ricketts, described (in *The Log from the Sea of Cortez*) his feeling of resentment at finding "new buildings, screened and modern, and on a tiny airfield a plane. . . ." Steinbeck wrote that even then there were Americans in Bahía de los Angeles.

The town really hasn't grown much since the pre-Transpeninsular days; telephone service is still nonexistent (the nearest phone is in Guerrero Negro, 197 km/119 miles away by road). Modern concessions brought by tourism include a small power plant, three trailer

parks, a couple of motels, a few cafés, a PEMEX station, and a small park. Behind the park is a **museum** (open Sun., Tues., and Fri. 1400-1600) with gold/silver mining exhibits, shells and fossils, two whale skeletons, and a few Indian artifacts. The toy-like locomotive in front of the museum was once used on the San Juan mine railway, 17½ km (11 miles) south of the current town.

PRACTICALITIES

Accommodations
Motel Villa Vitta is a clean, modern little motel in the center of town whose room rates climb up and down according to the occupancy rate; sometimes it's a great value at US$9-12 s, US$15 d, while at other times it's US$35 and up. Motel facilities include a swimming pool, restaurant/bar, and access to a boat launch. The nearby **Mini Hotel** only has three rather basic rooms; when available, they cost US$25 a night.

La Playa RV Park, across the road on the bay, is under the same ownership as the Villa Vitta and costs US$4 for tent/RV sites with electricity (mornings and evenings only). Showers, flush toilets, and a boat launch are available.

Next to La Playa is the well-run **Guillermo's,** a trailer park and restaurant operation with palapas, full hookups (US$4 a night), boat launch, showers, flush toilets, and a small market/gift shop.

At the south end of town, the long-established **Casa Díaz** has large, funky, bay-front rooms for US$20 s, US$25 d, less for longer stays. The Díaz family operates a fishing and birdwatching guide service to the bay islands, as well as a small market and the town's only PEMEX pump. RV sites with full hookups are available at Casa Díaz for US$5 a night.

BAHÍA
DE
LOS
ANGELES

TO AIRSTRIP &
PUNTA LA GRINGA

TO
MEXICO 1

LA PLAYA
RV PARK

MOTEL
VILLA VITTA

GCC FIELD
CENTER

MARKET

GUILLERMO'S
RV PARK AND
RESTAURANT

MUSEUM

CASA
DÍAZ

TO MINES & BAHÍA
SAN FRANCISQUITO

0   0.2mi

0   0.2km

© MOON PUBLICATIONS, INC.

Camping

Just north of town, near the paved airstrip, is the rustic **Brisa Marina,** a trailer park on the water with its own generator; the area gets a good bay breeze and hence is a good choice in hot weather.

A graded road follows the bayshore as far as **Punta La Gringa,** the end of the bay and a fish camp/retirement community. Along the way are a number of open campsites where camping is free.

Food

Ostensibly because of Bahía de los Angeles' relative isolation, food—whether bought in lo-

cal markets or at restaurants—is pricier here than in many places in Baja. Stock up in Guerrero Negro before coming if you're pinching pennies.

Las Hamacas, just north of the Mini Hotel, serves seafood and ranchero dishes for breakfast, lunch, and dinner; meals are in the US$5-12 range, beer US$1. The restaurant also has used paperbacks for sale; proceeds supposedly go to the town museum.

Guillermo's nicely appointed restaurant-bar has breakfasts for around US$4, dinner US$8, beer US$2. Specialties include fresh fish, shrimp, and lobster; the palapas out front are a nice spot for a margarita.

The dining room at **Casa Díaz,** once the only place to eat in town, is open only intermittently these days.

Hiking

Arroyos east of the bay lead into the Sierra San Borja, and some good day-hikes can be accomplished by picking out a dry wash and following it. As long as you keep the bay in sight, it's impossible to get lost.

Mina Santa Marta, an abandoned mine nearby, makes an interesting hike. Along with the more successful Mina San Juan farther south, Santa Marta was operational during the 1890s and used a cable- and-bucket system to transfer gold and silver ore (mostly the latter) from steep hillsides to a miniature railway below. Access to Mina Santa Marta begins about 3½ km (two miles) south of Casa Díaz next to the town dump. Once you've located the dump alongside the graded road south, walk west until you come across the remains of the railway grade, then follow the grade west until you reach the remains of the mine itself. The roundtrip hike can be accomplished in one day, though many hikers spend a night in the vicinity of the mine.

The San Juan mine is reached by following the same road 17½ km (11 miles) southwest of the bay to Valle Las Flores until you see the remains of a smelter and boiler along the west side of the road. This same road can be followed farther south into the Sierra San Borja, where there are several major Indian rock art sites; inquire at local ranches for trail guides.

The graded road continues southward through the sierra all the way to **Bahía San Francisquito,** approximately 131½ km (83 miles) south of Bahía de los Angeles.

Fishing

Due to heavy local gill-netting, Bahía de los Angeles fishing is not what it once was. The best bets are either onshore angling for sand bass, guitarfish, and triggerfish (or, at Punta La Gringa in spring, croaker and halibut), or farther out at nearby islands—especially near **La Ventana, Cabeza de Caballo, and Coronado**—where yellowtail, white and black seabass, dorado, and grouper are possible. Most of the offshore fish run in the summer months, though yellowtail runs are sometimes seen here Jan.-March.

Guillermo's and Casa Díaz can arrange guided fishing trips to the islands for US$65 a day. Bring your own tackle, as it's scarce in Bahía de los Angeles.

Transport

Bus service to Bahía de los Angeles is nonexistent—to get here you've got to have your own wheels or hitch from the Parador Punta Prieta junction. Once you've arrived, all of the town of Bahía de los Angeles is accessible on foot. For trips to the airfield, Punta La Gringa, or farther afield, a VW van taxi can be hired at Restaurant Las Hamacas.

SPORTS

Boating And Kayaking

Guillermo's, La Playa, and Casa Díaz each have boat launches. Pangas can be rented at the latter. The bay is protected by the 67½-km-long **Isla Angel de la Guarda,** but strong northeasterlies can set up a nasty chop on occasion. Local weather inquiries should be made before venturing any considerable distance from shore.

Bahía de los Angeles is popular among kayakers, who paddle to the nearby coves and islands, including the larger **Isla Coronado** (three km/two miles northeast of Punta La Gringa) and **Isla Angel de la Guarda** (19

km/12 miles from Punta La Gringa). Landings are usually easiest on the westward (leeward) side of the islands; this is generally where the best camping spots are. On Angel de la Guarda, **Puerto Refugio,** at the northern tip (64 km/40 miles from Bahía de los Angeles), is the usual landing. Explorations on Isla Angel de la Guarda can take in cirio stands, 1,200-meter (4,000 feet) peaks, and beaches with basking sea lions.

In **Canal de Ballenas**—the channel between Isla Angel de la Guarda and the peninsula—a variety of whales and dolphins are often seen, including Bryde's, Minke, gray, finback, blue, sperm, pygmy sperm, humpback, orca, pilot, common dolphin, and bottlenose dolphin. Bryde's whale (in winter) and finback whale (summer) are the most common.

East and south of Bahía de los Angeles are several coves worth visiting. Those with beaches and camping areas include **Puerto Don Juan, Ensenada del Quemado,** and **Ensenada del Pescador.**

It's possible to accomplish a "stepping stones" kayak route from Bahía de los Angeles (or from farther south at Bahía San Francisquito) to Isla Tiburón and Bahía Kino on the Mexican mainland. The usual route, once followed by Seri Indians in reed canoes, is Partida-San Lorenzo-San Esteban-Tiburón-Kino, but navigating the currents requires advanced kayaking abilities and knowledge of the local geography.

Because many novice kayakers have had problems in the Bahía de los Angeles area, an Alta Californian kayaking club called San Diego Sea Kayakers has printed a set of Bahía de los Angeles kayaking guidelines which are distributed for free at Guillermo's Restaurant, the mayor's office, and the museum.

Windsurfing

Bahía de los Angeles is a good bay for novice board-sailors because of the lack of large swells. Prevailing northeasterlies are strongest in the northern parts of the bay. A 10- to 12-km (six- to seven-mile) downwind run through the small islands west of Isla La Ventana, then all the way to the town waterfront, can be accomplished from Punta La Gringa.

Birdwatching

The shores of Bahía de los Angeles and the bay islands host a wide variety of birdlife, including terns, pelicans, gulls, egrets, herons, cormorants, petrels, boobies, and ospreys. The most renowned local rookeries for marine birds are **Isla Partida** and **Isla Raza**. The latter, a tiny, guano-covered, sparsely vegetated island of 250 acres, is the site for annual territorial wars between approximately 100,000 Heermann's gulls and 200,000 elegant terns, who battle for nesting grounds on the small island. The conflict—including "war formations" and egg-smashing—takes place in April; Casa Díaz can arrange special boa[trips to view the annual event.

A number of rare royal terns and tropic bird: also inhabit Isla Raza, which was declared national wildlife sanctuary in 1964 to stop egg hunters from destroying the bird populations It's possible the gull-tern wars are related to th elimination of egg-hunting, which local Indian had practiced—albeit at a slower pace tha their Mexican successors—for centuries.

Baja California Field Studies Program

Alta California's **Glendale Community Co lege** sponsors a special field studies progra

VICINITY OF BAHÍA DE LOS ANGELES

ISLA CORONADO

CANAL DE BALLENAS

ENSENADA LA GRINGA

PUNTA LA GRINGA

ISLA EL PIOJO

ISLA LA VENTANA

ISLA CABEZA DE CABALLO

AIRSTRIP

PUERTO DON JUAN

BAHÍA DE LOS ANGELES

PUNTA ARENA

PUNTA LA HERRADURA

ENSENADA EL QUEMADO

PUNTA EL PESCADOR

ISLA EL PESCADOR

ENSENADA EL PESCADOR

PUNTA EL ALACRAN

BAHÍA DE LOS ANGELES

TO MINA SANTA MARTA

TO MINA SAN JUAN & BAHÍA SAN FRANCISQUITO

ENSENADA EL ALACRAN

0   1.5mi

0   1.5km

AIRSTRIP

© MOON PUBLICATIONS, INC.

state border sign
(JOE CUMMINGS)

every summer at Bahía de los Angeles. Courses include Introduction to Marine Biology, Natural History Field Studies, or Introduction to Marine Vertebrates, plus Basic Spanish Conversation. Students stay in the field studies center, a building at the center of town on the bay. For information, contact Dr. José Mercade, GCC, 1500, N. Verdugo Rd., Glendale, CA 91208.

BAHÍA DE LOS ANGELES JUNCTION TO GUERRERO NEGRO

Southwest of the Bahía de los Angeles junction, the main section of Mexico 1 is marked by a new kilometer sequence beginning at Km 0. The ranch community of **Punta Prieta** is reached at Km 13, and between Km 38 and 39 a graded gravel road heads west 13 km (eight miles) to **Santa Rosalillita,** a fish camp below Punta Santa Rosalillita.

The Santa Rosalillita area is a well-known surfing destination; in a northwest swell, the point break at the north end of the bay reportedly offers Baja's longest ride (much depends on current bottom conditions). Windsurfers also enjoy the breaks and the bay's steady breeze. At the bay's south end, **Punta Rosalito** produces decent reef breaks in swells from any direction. If the waves aren't tipping right at either of these spots, breaks at **Punta**

Negra, **Punta Maria,** and **Punta Cono**—all positioned perfectly to catch winter swells—can be reached by following the dirt road north out of Santa Rosalillita within 24-30 km.

Historical note: the wreck of the double-masted schooner *Jennie Thelin* (built in 1869, stranded in 1912) lies buried in the sand dunes along Bahía Santa Maria. The schooner and her captain Alexander McLean were the inspiration for the infamous ship *Ghost* and skipper Wolf Larson in Jack London's novel *The Sea Wolf*. The ship was reputedly often used to transport illegal immigrants and untaxed merchandise between the U.S. and Mexico.

Rosarito-San Borja

Rosarito, a small ranching center, appears at the east side of Mexico 1 at Km 52. The **café** at the northeast end of town, on the highway, is a favorite stop for passing truckers. The ranchero food is good, and reasonably priced, but best of all is the real coffee, filtered through a cloth strainer in the old Mexican style.

A dirt road, suitable for high-clearance vehicles only, leads 34 km (21 miles) east from Rosarito to San Borja, a small farm settlement in the foothills of the Sierra San Borja. **Misión San Francisco Borja de Adác** was founded here by Jesuit padres in 1759, then handed over to the Franciscans in 1767 along with a large number of sheep, goats, cattle, horses, and mules. In 1773, the Dominicans took charge of the mission property and over 1,600 Indian parishioners in the Adác (the original Indian name for the site) community. Although the mission was officially secularized in 1818, it has since been restored and offers weekly services for local residents. The fig, pomegranate, olive, and date orchards planted by the missionaries continue to provide a livelihood.

Northeast of San Borja are at least two major Indian rock art sites, Las Tinajitas and Montevideo. They're difficult to find; inquire in San Borja for a guide if interested in viewing them.

Villa Jesus Maria-Puerto Santo Domingo

The town of Villa Jesus Maria, at Km 95 on Mexico 1, has a PEMEX station and a couple of cafés, including the dependable **Restaurant Campesino.** A paved road runs northwest from town to Ejido Morelos, connecting with a graded dirt road southwest to **Laguna Manuela,** a fish camp on the bay of Puerto Santo Domingo.

The occasional point break off **Morro Santo Domingo,** at the north end of Puerto Santo Domingo, draws a few surfers. Fishing is said to be good in the bay—corvina, croaker, and halibut inshore, and grouper, yellowtail, and white seabass offshore. Trailered or car-topped boats can easily be launched on the beach, or pangas can be rented at Laguna Manuela. The laguna itself can be difficult to navigate due to high winds and unpredictable tidal surges.

Paralelo 28

The northern border of Baja California Sur, at 28° north latitude, is reached at Km 128. A 43-meter-high (140 feet) steel monument—a stylized eagle (it looks more like a giant tuning fork)—marks the border and the change from Pacific to Mountain Time. South of the 28th parallel, kilometer markers on the Trans-peninsular Highway begin at Km 220 and descend toward Km 0 (at Santa Rosalía).

Between the border and the town of **Guerrero Negro** (seven km south of the state border) is an agricultural inspection station. The inspectors usually wave gringos in passenger vehicles through without an inspection or even a single query. Trucks and large vehicles may be stopped briefly.

(BOB RACE)

SOUTH CENTRAL BAJA

GUERRERO NEGRO AND VICINITY

This town of around 10,000 took its name from the *Black Warrior,* a Hawaii-ported whaling barque that foundered in Laguna Guerrero Negro in 1858. Too overloaded with whale oil to leave the lagoon under its own power, the barque sank while being towed out to sea—just a year after Charles Melville Scammon had "discovered" the Baja lagoons where migrating gray whales came to calve.

Within 20 years, tens of thousands of gray whales had been slaughtered and the whalers moved on to other Pacific hunting areas. But the gray has made a remarkable comeback from the brink of extinction (currently numbering around 21,000), and once again the whales of Scammon's Lagoon are attracting visitors. (For a description of gray whale mi-

gration and history of Baja whaling, see "Gray Whales," p. 22).

More important to the local economy than whalewatching tourists is the local saltworks, a large solar-evaporative operation that produces around six million tons of salt a year. Exportadora de Sal, S.A. (ESSA), the town's largest employer, maintains a huge system of diked ponds (southwest of town) which take in seawater from the lagoons and impound it, at a depth of about one meter, until the fierce Vizcaíno Desert sun turns it into thick layers of salt. The salt is then scooped into trucks and driven to Puerto El Chaparrito at the north end of Laguna Ojo de Liebre (Scammon's Lagoon), where it's loaded onto barges and shipped 80 km northwest to Isla Cedros. From Isla Cedros the salt is shipped by freighter to the Mexican mainland, the U.S., Canada, and Japan.

CLIMATE

Temperatures in Guerrero Negro remain fairly steady year-round, due to the overall Pacific influence and the insulating effect of bays and lagoons to the west. Daytime highs are 21°-24° C (70°-75° F) in summer, 15°-18° C (59°-65° F) in winter. Rainfall is very scarce, but an almost-constant fog keeps the air moist during the summer months.

ACCOMMODATIONS

Hotels And Motels

Except for La Pinta, all of Guerrero Negro's hotels and motels are located along Blvd. Zapata, the main street through town, west of Mexico 1. Right below the state border, just off Mexico 1, the **Hotel La Pinta** (tel. 667-2601 in Ensenada; 800-336-5454 in the U.S.) offers large, comfortable rooms for US$58 s, US$69 d, including tax. If you're just stopping off for the night, La Pinta is conveniently situated for getting on and off the highway. It's a seven-km (four-mile) drive into town; if you plan to spend a few days exploring Guerrero Negro, you might look for something in the town itself.

In town, next to the Malarrimo Restaurant, prefab trailer-style units at **Cabañas Don Miguelito** rent for US$20 a night. More amenable and less expensive is the **Motel San Ignacio,** farther west on the same side of the street; cozy rooms here cost US$12 s, US$16 d. **Motel El Morro** (tel. 7-04-14) next door is a bit more modern and costs the same as the San Ignacio. Farther on is the **Dunas Motel** (tel. 7-00-57), where well-scrubbed, off-the-street rooms cost US$12-14 s, US$16 d.

Even cheaper digs are available at the **Motel California** and **Motel Gamez,** west toward the ESSA buildings; rooms at either are US$10, but they're very basic and the hot water supply may be inconsistent.

Camping And RV Parks

Coastal areas around Guerrero Negro offer plenty of free camping spots, but few are accessible by ordinary passenger vehicle.

Camping is permitted along the lagoon in the Parque Natural de la Ballena Gris (see "Whalewatching at Scammon's Lagoon" below); a daily parking fee of US$3 is usually collected during whalewatching season, Jan.-March. A few RVers set up camp near the old salt wharf, about 10 km (six miles) northwest of town on a graded road.

The **Benito Juárez RV Park,** just south of Hotel La Pinta next to the state border of Mexico 1, has full hookups (no shade) for US$5 per vehicle. In town, Malarrimo Restaurant/Cabañas Don Miguelito runs an RV park with full hookups, also for US$5.

FOOD

Guerrero Negro has several places to eat and a couple of supermarkets that supply residents as far away as Bahías Los Angeles and San Francisquito. Like the hotels and motels, most are spread out along Guerrero Negro's main avenue, Blvd. Zapata.

Restaurants

The most popular restaurant in town, especially for gringos, is **Malarrimo,** on the north side of Blvd. Zapata just as you enter Guerrero Negro. The pismo clams, deep-sea scallops, lobster, and other fresh seafood are always good; breakfasts are another highlight here, including lobster omelets, homemade chorizo and eggs, and other diet-busters served with beans, chilaquiles, and tortillas. It's open daily for breakfast, lunch, and dinner; prices are moderate.

Two other restaurants on Blvd. Zapata competing for local and tourist business include **Lupita** (seafood, open for breakfast, lunch, and dinner) and **Figón de Sal** (Mexican, open for lunch and dinner). For something fast and cheap, try **Asadero Las Delicios,** specialists in carne asada and tacos—al pastor, al carbon, or al vapor. **Pizzas Sinaloa,** opposite Malarrimo, serves a variety of pizzas with fresh, homemade crust for lunch and dinner.

Groceries

Guerrero Negro has the only supermarkets south of Ensenada and north of Santa Rosa-

VIZCAÍNO PENINSULA—
LAGUNA
SAN IGNACIO

TO ISLAS.
SAN BENITO
PICO GILL
CERRO
DE CEDROS
CEDROS
ISLA CEDROS
CANAL DE KELLER
PUNTA
MORRO
REDONDO
ISLA NATIVIDAD
CANAL DE DEWEY
PUNTA EUGENIA
BAHÍA
TORTUGAS
BAHÍA TORTUGAS
BAHÍA THURLOE
BAHÍA DE SEBASTIAN VIZCAÍNO
PLAYA
MALARRIMO
PICO
VERA CRUZ
LAGUNA OJO
DE LIEBRE
(SCAMMON'S LAGOON)
GUERRERO
NEGRO
RANCHO
SAN MIGUEL
PUERTO
NUEVO
MONTE
AZUL
RANCHO SAN
JOSE DE CASTRO
PARQUE NATURAL
DE LA BALLENA GRIS
BAHÍA DE SAN CRISTOBAL
PICO LOWRY
PUNTA
SAN ROQUE
PUNTA
ASUNCIÓN
BAHÍA ASUNCIÓN
BAHÍA ASUNCIÓN
PUNTA
PRIETA
SAN HIPÓLITO
CERRO CARDON
PICO ASPERO
PICO EL GATO
PICOS
DOBLES
MONTE
PLANO
BAHÍA SAN HIPÓLITO
LA BOCANA
PUNTA
ABREOJOS
ESTERO
DE COYOTE
PUNTA ABREOJOS
BAHÍA DE BALLENAS
ISLAS
BALLENAS
RÍO SAN IGNACIO
LAGUNA
SAN IGNACIO
CAMPO
PACHICO
ISLA ARENA

PUNTA PRIETA
TO EL
ROSARIO
PUNTA SANTA
ROSALILLITA
BAHÍA SANTA ROSALÍA
PUNTA
ROSARITO
ROSARITO
EJIDO
MORRO MORELOS
SANTO DOMINGO
LAGUNA
MANUELA
VILLA
JESÚS
MARÍA
PUERTO DE
SANTO DOMINGO
ESTERO DE
SAN JOSE
18
EL
ARCO
TO BAHÍA SAN
FRANCISQUITO
RANCHO
SANTA
TERESITA
VIZCAÍNO
JUNCTION
TO SANTA ROSALÍA
SAN IGNACIO
SAN
ZACARIAS
RANCHO
BATEQUI
RANCHO
BAHÍA SAN IGNACIO
TO BAHÍA SAN
JUANICO

MOON

0   20mi

0   20km

© MOON PUBLICATIONS, INC.

lía. **La Ballena** is the most popular of the two on Blvd. Zapata, and is the only store in town that accepts traveler's checks. **Panadería Hermanos (Hnos.) Aguiar,** on the south side of Blvd. Zapata west of Malarrimo Restaurant, has a good selection of Mexican pastries, including fresh bolillos daily.

OTHER PRACTICALITIES

Changing Money
A bank near the ESSA buildings, on the west end of Blvd. Zapata, offers a currency exchange service Mon.-Fri., 0900-1200. On weekends or at other times of day, the only other choice for cashing traveler's checks is La Ballena supermarket. (Naturally, they prefer that you make a purchase and accept change in pesos.) **Novedades Ely,** a sundries store next to Motel San Ignacio, will change cash dollars into pesos.

Telephone
Guerrero Negro has the only public telephone service in a 200-km (120-mile) radius. Two privately operated phone offices in town add a service charge to the cost of any call. Collect calls can be made at the public phone booth in front of Malarrimo Restaurant for no charge (dial 02 or 09). The area code for Guerrero Negro is 685.

Whalewatching At Scammon's Lagoon
During the season, Jan. through March, several whalewatching options at Scammon's Lagoon are available for those interested. The Malarrimo Restaurant organizes small group tours (up to eight persons) for US$25 per person; prospective participants should book at least a day in advance. During the height of the season, a van leaves daily from the restaurant at around 8 a.m. and drives, via an ESSA-owned road, to a shore of the lagoon where a panga takes participants out on the water for about two hours. Lunch (included in the tour fee) is eaten on Isla Arena, a large sandbar island covered in dunes.

A less expensive alternative is to drive to the shore of the lagoon on your own and deal directly with the *pangeros*. To do this, take Mexico 1 south of town nine km (5½ miles) to the turnoff marked **Parque Natural de la Ballena Gris** and turn right (southwest). This 24-km (15-mile) road alternates between washboard and sandy surfaces that sometimes require slow driving. After about six km (3½ miles), the road reaches a salt company checkpoint where you must usually wait for an attendant to open the gate. After the checkpoint, the road runs between two salt evaporation flats; the drying salt looks like packed snow. The road ends at the edge of the lagoon, where a US$3 parking fee is collected.

close encounters of the big and barnacled kind
(COURTESY OF
BIOLOGICAL JOURNEYS)

Once you're at the shore, you can watch the whales from land or sign on with a boat tour. Although with a good pair of binoculars you can see the whales from shore, you can get much closer to them via water, and hear them blowing. From Jan. through March, two or three boats are usually on hand at the park for charters. The going rate is US$10 per person; boats leave 0900-1500 only and stay out about an hour and 15 minutes. After 1500, the wind comes up, fog comes in, and whale-watching conditions are poor.

Private boats, kayaks, sailboards, inflatable rafts, or other floatables aren't permitted anywhere in Scammon's Lagoon during the whale season. The *pangeros* who take tourists out to see the whales are granted seasonal permits to do so. They're also very skilled at running their *pangas* so as not to frighten or threaten the whales, most of whom are mothers and babies (the males, for the most part, cavort near the entrance of the lagoon, farther from shore).

Vizcaíno Peninsula

Jutting northwest into the Pacific, the coast of this huge desert peninsula is renowned among beachcombers, anglers, surfers, and scuba divers for the abundant opportunities to participate in their favorite recreational activities, far from "civilization." The isolation and long distances involved in navigating the peninsula's interior deters the casual visitor, despite the fact that the roads aren't really all that bad. The greatest distance between PEMEX stations on the Vizcaíno Peninsula is 166 km (100 miles). More critical is the lack of automotive and/or medical assistance along lengthy stretches of road.

Although most visitors head straight for the peninsular shores, a leisurely drive through the interior affords close, uninterrupted views of the Vizcaíno Desert. Rainfall is scant and the desert vegetation mostly survives on Pacific fog; yucca trees *(datillos)* are particularly abundant. Several of the cactus and succulent species chosen for Biosphere II—an experimental, self-contained, dome environment in Arizona—were borrowed from this desert. Around a hundred rare berrendo pronghorn antelope) survive on the peninsula.

Fuel, food, and other supplies are available at four cannery towns along the southwest coast of the peninsula and, to a much lesser extent, from a handful of fish camps and ranchos between these settlements. **Bahía Tortugas,** 166 km (100 miles) from Mexico 1 (Vizcaíno Junction), is the largest, with a population of around 3,000. Aside from a cannery and PEMEX station, the town offers several markets, cafés, a clinic, a post office, a modest motel, and an airfield. Aerolineas California Pacificos and Soc. Coop. de Producción Pesquera ("Cannery Airlines") fly here from Guerrero Negro and Ensenada. Bahía Tortugas's harbor is the best between Ensenada and Bahía Magdalena. North of Bahía Tortugas, 26½ km (16½ miles) by graded dirt road, is **Punta Eugenia,** a small fishing village and jumping-off place for boat trips to Islas, Natividad, Cedros, and San Benito.

Bahía Asunción, 56 km southwest of the Vizcaíno Junction-Bahía Tortugas road, is less than half the size of Bahía Tortugas, and has a PEMEX station, airstrip, cannery, clinic, market, and café. **La Bocana** and **Punta Abreojos,** farther southeast along the coast, are smaller yet; both may have gasoline available in barrels, but leaded only. The best onshore/inshore fishing areas are generally found between Bahía Asunción and Punta Abreojos; typical catches include Cortez halibut, corvina, croaker, and sand, calico, and pinto bass.

A loop trip can be accomplished by driving west from Vizcaíno Junction (Mexico 1, Km 144) to Bahía Tortugas and/or Bahía Asunción, then southeast to Punta Abreojos and back to Mexico 1 at Km 98. Beach camping is possible at numerous spots between Bahía Asunción and Punta Abreojos, and rustic rooms are available in Bahía Tortugas for around US$10 a night. **Vizcaíno Junction** (also called Fundolegal) has several cafés and small markets.

A side journey to **Malarrimo Beach** is possible for those with 4WD vehicles. The challenging track to Malarrimo branches north off the Vizcaíno Junction-Bahía Tortugas road 116 km (72 miles) from Mexico 1, at Rancho

San José de Castro. It then winds through arroyos and around mesas for 44 km (27 miles) before fading out at the dunes behind the beach. Malarrimo receives the brunt of northwest Pacific currents (including the Japanese Current, which once carried Manila galleons to Mexico), and hence it's a beachcomber's paradise. It takes a hardened beachcomber to appreciate the beach, since much of the flotsam washed ashore consists of the dregs of civilization—styrofoam and plastic—and garbage jettisoned by ships throughout the North Pacific.

Isla Cedros

Baja's largest Pacific coast island (not of oceanic origin) is 20 km (12 miles) north of the tip of the Vizcaíno Peninsula, or about 72 km (43 miles) northwest of Guerrero Negro. The two main industries on the 24-km-long (14½-mile) island are fishing and off-loading salt from Guerrero Negro's saltworks for long-distance shipping.

Among naturalists, Isla Cedros is known for its small stands of juniper and pine in the center of the island between its tallest peaks, Pico Gill (1,060 meters/3,488 feet) at the north end and Cerro de Cedros (1,200 meters/3,950 feet) toward the south. Like cedars, the island's mistaken namesake, junipers are in the cypress family; even more impressive are the Cedros Island oak, *(Quercus cedrosensis)* and Cedros Island pine *(Pinus radiata* var. *cedrosensis),* both endemic to this island. A rare variety of mule deer reportedly inhabits the island's center.

Fish camps are found at **Cabo San Agustín** (southwest corner of the island) and at **Punta Norte** (at the north). The largest settlement on the island, **Cedros,** is a village of around 5,000 on the southeast coast facing the peninsula. The village has a harbor, port captain's office (COTP), Conasupo, fish cannery, post office, church, bank, school, a couple of cafés, and a sizable residential area. South of the village along the same coast are the docks where salt from Guerrero Negro is off-loaded.

Transport: Aside from sailing there in your own boat, the easiest way to get to the island is by plane. Aerolineas California Pacificos flies from Guerrero Negro; Soc. Coop. de Producción Pesquera ("Cannery Airlines") flies from Ensenada. The island's paved airstrip is south of Cedros village at Punta Morro Redondo. It is sometimes also possible to charter a boat to the island from either Bahía Tortugas or Punta Eugenia.

Isla Natividad

During the Spanish missionary period, a Cochimí subtribe lived on this arid island 10 km (six miles) northwest of Punta Eugenia; they called it Afegua, or "Island of Birds." Eventually a Jesuit padre from Misión San Ignacio convinced them to leave the island and live at the mission. Renamed "Christmas Island," today it's one of the most famous surfing destinations along the Pacific coast of the Americas.

The most popular Natividad break, "Open Doors," is off the southeast tip and catches summer swells from the southwest—peak time is generally July-September. Waves here typically run four to six feet, with occasional sets up to 15 feet. In winter, large breaks—for pros only—are found at the northwest and southwest tips; the former break can only be reached by boat. A small village along the southeast shore of the 22½-square-km island houses about 200 fishermen during the summer. In winter many of them visit relatives on the peninsula or work on farms in the Ensenada area. Thus boats out to the northwest shore break should be arranged in Punta Eugenia (or bring your own boat).

Transport to and from Isla Natividad can be difficult to find in winter, when the island is mostly deserted. In summer, Soc. Coop. de Producción Pesquera sometimes (when there are enough passengers) flies to the island from Ensenada via Isla Cedros; boats can be chartered from Punta Eugenia in summer as well, less easily in winter. The easiest way to accomplish a Natividad surfing vacation is through **Scorpio Surfing Tours,** an Alta California-based organization that has been operating Natividad surf tours every summer since 1984. (For details on the tours, see "Sports and Recreation," in the main introduction.)

What else is there to do on the island besides surf? According to Scorpio, the surf and inshore fishing is good, and if surfing the best tubes on the coast isn't thrilling enough, cliff diving—from 10- to 15-meter-high ocean precipices—provides an alternative. Another is "surging," an activity (invented by bored surfers) in which you jump into a deep tidal pool and allow the wave action to pump your body six to nine meters (20-30 feet) up and down. The island has a small clinic to handle small injuries.

Islas San Benito

This group of three small islands (Isla Benito del Este, Centro, and Oeste), about 25 km northwest of Isla Cedros, is known to have the best yellowtail fishing on the Pacific coast. Boats usually anchor along the leeward (southeastern) shore of Isla Benito del Oeste, opposite the tiny village of Benito del Oeste. Elephant seals, the world's largest pinnipeds (see "Flora and Fauna," in the main introduction), often sun themselves along the coves north of the village.

Rock reefs along the western shores of all three islands provide the best diving and fishing opportunities. Divers may be interested in the wreck of the U.S. tanker *Swift Eagle,* which went aground in 1934 off the north shore of Isla Benito del Oeste; parts of the wreck lie within two meters of the ocean surface.

SAN IGNACIO

In pre-mission days, local Cochimí Indians called the sheltered arroyo formed by the Río San Ignacio *Kadakaamán* or "Creek of Reeds." Fed by an underground stream, this fertile palm oasis on the southeastern edge of the Vizcaíno Desert has supported mission crops of wheat, figs, grapes, pomegranates, oranges, corn, and dates for over 200 years. The sleepy town of San Ignacio (pop. 4,000) is a cluster of stuccoed, pastel-colored, colonial-style buildings and small rancherías centered around **Misión San Ignacio Kadakaamán** and the adjacent plazuela. Hemmed in on all sides by mesas, the town's palm-oasis ambience and ongoing resistance to change have made it a favorite among Baja travelers for decades.

Climate

San Ignacio is very pleasant in the winter months, when daytime temperatures are 18° C (65° F) to 21° C (70° F), nights a bit cooler. During the summer, the surrounding desert reaches as high as 40° C (105° F), although the valley floor may be a few degrees less. Rainfall is nearly nil year-round.

Misión San Ignacio Kadakaamán

Jesuit records indicate the Cochimís of Kadakaamán (San Ignacio Valley) sent several requests for mission assistance to Padre Píccolo of Misión Santa Rosalía de Mulegé in the early 18th century. Píccolo first visited the area in 1716 and stayed in a brush cabaña for a month, apparently converting and baptizing a willing Indian population. In 1728 Jesuit Padre Juan Bautista Loyando constructed a church and mission house on the present site, and then proceeded to build a number of visiting chapels at nearby rancherías. He was succeeded by Padre Sigismundo Taraval, who brought Indians from the Pacific islands off the tip of the Vizcaíno Peninsula into the mission community. Eventually the San Ignacio mission became the largest and most successful in Baja California, with a parish of over 5,000 Indians.

THE DÁTILES OF SAN IGNACIO

The lush date palms of Arroyo de San Ignacio, a welcome sight to those who have driven the Transpeninsular Highway south across Baja's Central and Vizcaíno deserts, have multiplied considerably (around 100,000 at last count) since their introduction to the valley by Spanish missionaries over 200 years ago. First cultivated in Mesopotamia around 1,000 B.C., dates (*dátil* in Spanish) were originally brought to Spain during the Moorish occupation of the Iberian Peninsula. The Middle East is currently the second-highest date producer after the U.S.; Mexico is a distant third.

Although mature date palms are easy to maintain, palm shoots must be planted near the mother tree for several years before they can be separated (if moved too soon, they'll perish). From germination, it takes an average 12 years for a date palm to mature and begin to produce commercially, after which it can yield fruit for 85 years. Dates are very rich in potassium and proteins—the protein content of two dates equals that of one egg.

The annual date harvest is celebrated in San Ignacio on 31 July, which also happens to be the feast day for the town's patron saint, San Ignacio Loyola. During the fiesta, all manner of date products are displayed in the town plaza, La Reina del Dátil ("Date Queen") is crowned, and music and dancing keep things lively well into the night.

date palm
BOB RACE

After the Jesuits were expelled from New Spain, Dominican Friar Juan Crisostomo Gomez took charge of the mission and built a grander church on the original site in 1786. The walls, 1.2 meters (four feet) thick, were constructed of local volcanic stone without the use of mortar. The lumber for the wooden beams used in the construction was transported from Misión Guadalupe in the high sierra to the southwest, and the carved doors at the front of the church were brought from the Mexican mainland. According to Jesuit records, the Queen of Spain paid 1.5 million pesos for the church's construction.

Today the venerable church stands in much its original condition, thanks to a 1976 restoration, and is used by the local community for masses, weddings, funerals, and daily worship. The church's elaborate facade, with its engraved stone plaques and plaster ornamentation, makes it inarguably the most impressive of all Baja's mission churches. The plaque to the left of the main doors, above the lower left window, is emblazoned with two crowned lions (symbol of the Kingdom of León in Spain), two castles (for the Kingdom of Castile), and the crown of Spain. To the right of the portal, over the corresponding lower window, is a simpler plaque with two overlapping globes (representing the Old and New Worlds), flanked by the twin Hercules pillars of Spain and North Africa; the pillars are topped by the crowns of Spain and Portugal, while the globe motif features a hybrid crown combining aspects of both the Portuguese and Spanish crowns.

Inside the church, the statue at the center of the main viceregal-style altar is of the mission's patron saint, St. Ignacius Loyola. Surrounding the statue are paintings of St. Joseph and the infant Jesus (upper left); St. Bernard (lower left); Virgin de Pilar (above the statue); St. John the Baptist (upper right); and St. Dominio (lower right). The two side altars, while not as impressive as the one described above, also date from the mission period.

A sign in the church foyer requests that visitors dress with respect and refrain from chewing gum in the church.

Hotels And Inns

The **Hotel La Pinta** (tel. 667-2601 in Ensenada; 800-336-5454 in the U.S.), 3½ km (two miles) off Mexico 1 on the edge of town, has rooms for US$58 s, US$69 d, including tax. Facilities include a restaurant, pool, billiards room, and PEMEX station.

A more modest choice in town, **La Posada,** has rooms for US$20 per room; each room has two beds, dressers, a hot-water shower, and fan. La Posada can be a bit difficult to find: walk or drive away from the church along Av. Hidalgo (with the plazuela on your left), turn right at Callejón Ciprés, and then after 200 meters, turn left; after passing a street to the right, you'll come to La Posada on the right-hand side of the road.

Camping And RV Parks
On the highway at the turnoff for San Ignacio (Km 74), next to a PEMEX station, is the **San Ignacio Transpeninsular Trailer Park.** Sites with electricity and water, but no shade, are US$5.

Two smaller campgrounds near the Hotel La Pinta are located in palm groves on the Río de San Ignacio. **El Padrino** charges US$2 for tent/camper sites, **La Candelaria** costs US$3. At either, mosquitoes and/or *jejenes* (no-see-ums) are sometimes a problem.

Food
On the plazuela, the family-run **Lonchería Chalita** serves enchiladas, tacos, chilaquiles, and, occasionally, fresh seafood; it's open daily for breakfast and lunch till around 1700 or 1800.

Restaurant Tota, a palapa hut in the south part of town, has inexpensive seafood meals in a congenial atmosphere. To find it, take Calle Cipres past the turnoff for La Posada and continue about 200 meters until you see it on the right-hand side of the road. In the evening Restaurant Tota doubles as the town cantina.

Other than the Hotel La Pinta's restaurant, **Las Cazuelas,** there is nowhere else in town to get a meal. Out on Mexico 1, in nearby Ejido Alfredo V. Bonfil (Km 53, 21 km/12 miles south of San Ignacio), are the **Café Tuxpan** and **Lonchería Sinaloense,** serving mainly *antojitos* and beer for passing truckers. Farther south at Km 39, **Rancho El Mesquitál** serves whatever's on the wood-fired stove that day;

if the family's had hunting luck, it might be *venado guisado* (deer stew).

Groceries: A couple of small tiendas in town, including a Conasupo, supply the basics. As might be suspected, dates are plentiful.

VICINITY OF SAN IGNACIO

Indian Rock Art
San Ignacio is in the middle of the what Indian cave painting expert Harry Crosby has termed the "Great Mural Region" of Baja California. The most extensive and numerous pictograph and petroglyph sites are found in caves and arroyos north of San Ignacio in the sierras of San Francisco and San Juan. The nearest to San Ignacio are those in the Sierra de San Francisco, including the highly developed **Cuesta Palmarito** and **El Batequi** sites, in the arroyos of Palmarito and Batequi respectively.

Misión San Ignacio (JOE CUMMINGS)

THE PREHISTORIC MURALS
OF BAJA CALIFORNIA

In hidden palm oases and remote canyons throughout the sierras of Baja California, far from the Transpeninsular Highway and most of the peninsula's larger towns, the artistic heritage of a lost Indian culture arcs across rock walls. Dubbed the "Painters" by Baja rock art expert Harry Crosby, these anonymous Indian artists painted thousands of figures in hundreds of prehistoric mural sites—most of them concentrated in the central peninsular sierras of San Francisco, San Borja, San Juan, and Guadalupe—that rival the cave paintings of Europe's Lascaux and Altamira. To a lesser extent, paleolithic paintings are also found in northern Baja (at San Jose de Tecate, Palmas de Cantú, Pilitas, and Arroyo Grande) and in the south (Sierra de Cacachillas and Miraflores).

The Paintings

In reality, central Baja's prehistoric murals are larger and more numerous than those found at Lascaux and Altamira. Between Bahía de los Angeles and Comondú alone, there are estimated to be over 400 mural sites. Most paintings are placed high—as high as 10 meters (33 feet)—on the walls or ceilings of arroyos, canyons, and rock overhangs. Scaffolds, probably made of cardón ribs or palm trunks, were used to reach these heights. Styles were codified to such an extent that all human figures have their arms extended upwards, all four-legged animals are depicted in running or leaping poses, fish are shown from a dorsal view, and birds are in flight as seen from below, but with their heads turned in profile.

Ritual purposes are implied by the fact that only the outlines of painted figures are representational, while interiors contain conventionalized abstractions. In some areas of the sierras, human figures are occasionally bicolored, with the left half of the body painted red and the right half painted black. Figures may also be depicted wearing headdresses or top-knotted hair. Rock-art experts have discerned several different schools within the Great Mural Region of central Baja, from north to south: in the Sierra San Borja, *monos* (a Bajacalifornio term for prehistoric painted figures) are painted in red; Sierra San Francisco paintings show red-black bicolors; the Sierra de Guadalupe has monochrome, bicolor, and checkerboard color schemes, along with monos filled in with vertical lines.

One of the more awesome examples of prehistoric rock art is a 166-meter (500-foot) by 10-meter (30-foot) mural at Cueva Pintada in Arroyo de San Pablo (Sierra de San Francisco) consisting of overlapping images of men and women with their arms raised, deer, bighorn sheep, rabbits, and birds. At Arroyo de San Gregorio a four-meter (12-foot) whale is painted onto a rock overhang.

The Painters

Little is known about the Painters except that they belonged to the only culture, in a succession of central peninsula cultures, to leave behind artifacts borne not of economic necessity but from the realm of art and ritual. Ancillary evidence discovered at the rock-art sites—metates (grinding plates), manos (grindstones), bows and ar-

(CONT.)

THE PREHISTORIC MURALS
OF BAJA CALIFORNIA (CONT.)

rows, choppers, scrapers, carved bone, woven fibers, and fire pits—identify the Painters as paleolithic, and the artwork itself, ritualistic paintings of human and animal figures, correlates with art styles found in paleolithic sites the world over.

Eighteenth-century missionary documents from Baja refer to a few mural sites, but the Cochimí Indians living in the central peninsula at the coming of the Spanish padres had no knowledge of the significance of the symbols or motifs in the paintings, nor of the techniques of painting; they themselves didn't paint. Cochimí legends said the paintings were accomplished by a race of giants who inhabited the region well before the time of their ancestors. The Painters must have been giants, according to the Cochimí, because many of the paintings occurred on rock walls up to 10 meters above the ground.

Because archaeological and anthropological research in Baja has been so scant, scholars haven't a clue whether the Painters were a separate cultural group that migrated from the north or whether they represented an early phase of the Cochimí culture. That the Painters were migratory—like all the early Indian cultures of Baja—is certain since they left behind no permanent dwellings or pottery. The desert conditions of central Baja meant they had to move with the migrations of game and the seasonal changes in surface water. Such a culture required highly portable materials made mostly of wood, hide, and fibers. The minerals used for painting, as well as materials for building the scaffolds, could be gathered on site.

Rock-art Research

Although the Spanish missionaries of the 18th and 19th centuries were aware of the murals, the first systematic study of the paintings was carried out by Leon Diguet, a French naturalist working at El Boleo copper—mining company in Santa Rosalía near the turn of the century. Diguet visited several mural sites in 1893-94 and published his findings in a few French journals, but he missed seeing the Painters' most extensive sites in San Francisco.

The next person to delve into the mysteries of the murals was American mystery writer Erle Stanley Gardner of "Perry Mason" fame. Gardner began making trips to Baja in the 1940s and was first led to El Batequi and other Sierra San Francisco sites in 1962 by local ranchers. Realizing he had viewed sites of great archaeological significance, the writer devoted a considerable part of his income to the study of the murals and wrote about them for *Life* magazine and in his book *The Hidden Heart of Baja*.

In 1972, Baja historian Harry Crosby succeeded Gardner in the search for undiscovered sites and made extensive forays into the San Borja, San Francisco, San Juan, and Guadalupe mountain ranges. Crosby compiled the results of his explorations for *National Geographic*, as well as in his excellent 1984 book, *The Cave Paintings of Baja California*, the most authoritative general reference yet to appear on Baja rock art.

Based on an as yet non-integrated assortment of facts and artifacts (including what appears to be a mural rendering of the supernova birth of the Crab Nebula in A.D. 1054), Crosby speculates that the Painters' artistic output extended over a thousand-year period from around A.D. 500 to 1500. To verify or refute this dating, more research in the fields of archaeology, anthropology, geology, and meteorology needs to be carried out at mural sites.

To view these rock-art sites, one needs a guide, not only because of the difficulties involved in finding the sites, but because the state requires it. Wandering around on your own—unless you're a recognized researcher (even most researchers employ local guides)—usually isn't done. The Fischer family at San Ignacio's La Posada offers guided trips from San Ignacio for US$20 per person; during whale season, they also lead a combined whalewatching (at Laguna San Ignacio) and rock-art trip for US$40.

An alternative is to drive to the village of San Francisco de la Sierra and arrange for a guide there (ask at the tienda). The village is approached by a 37-km (22-mile) graded dirt road that branches east off Mexico 1 at Km 118, 45 km (27 miles) north of San Ignacio. **El Batequi** (also known as Gardner's Cave, since it was "discovered" by mystery writer Erle Stanley Gardner during one of his many Baja sojourns), in magnificent Cañon San Pablo, can be visited by mule from the village, usually a three-day trip. Also accessible from San Francisco is the **Serpent Cave** of Arroyo del Parral, with its eight-meter-long (26-foot) deer-headed serpent and bicolored, rabbit-eared *monos* (human figures). Closer but much less impressive is **Cueva Ratón**, just west of the village.

Laguna San Ignacio

Southeast of San Ignacio is a large bay used by calving gray whales January through March every year. Besides the fact that the grays are closer to shore here than at Scammon's Lagoon to the north or Bahía de Magdalena to the south, the grays here seem to exhibit more "friendly" behavior here than at other calving lagoons. Many mothers and calves at Laguna San Ignacio, in fact, actively seek out tactile encounters, i.e., petting and scratching.

During the calving season, only boats with whalewatching permits are allowed on the bay. At **Campo Pachico,** where the road from San Ignacio meets the bayshore, licensed *pangeros* will take visitors out to meet the whales for US$20 per person. The tour lasts about four hours; you must be at the camp by around 0900 to get on one of the boats. Since the 59-km (35-mile) drive from San Ignacio takes up to three hours due to road conditions (most passenger vehicles can make it—slowly), you must leave town early in the morning or spend the previous night at the camp.

Farther south along the bay is **Punta Piedras,** a camp often used by adventure travel organizations for Laguna San Ignacio expeditions. High-clearance vehicles can reach Punta Piedras by road—a stream must be crossed along the way—or you can arrange to be dropped off by boat from Campo Pachico. Food service can also be arranged at Punta Piedras, and there is radio contact with Campo Pachico. The road to Punta Piedras continues south all the way to Bahía San Juanico, but can be recommended only for 4WD vehicles.

In the northern section of the bay, **Isla Pelicano** is a nesting grounds for ospreys and a variety of other birds. The island is closed to visitors during the whale season, but can be visited by boat the remainder of the year.

SANTA ROSALÍA

At Santa Rosalía, the Transpeninsular Highway completes its 215-km (129-mile) journey from Pacific to Cortez coasts. As in San Ignacio, the town is wedged into a deep arroyo between mesas, but the similarity between the two towns ends there. Whereas San Ignacio's architecture is strongly Spanish-flavored due to the mission influence, the buildings along Santa Rosalía's narrow streets—many of them wood-frame houses fronted by long verandas in the French colonial style—were designed by a French mining company in the 19th century.

Other Gallic touches include a French bakery and the only Eiffel-designed church in Mexico. One of the most impressive French-built structures in town, the Palacio Municipal, was once a school. Although many of the town's current residents certainly appear as if they could be of French or part-French ancestry, the locals claim that most French citizens left town when the mines closed in 1954.

Santa Rosalía is a terminus for the SEMATUR ferry to Guaymas, eight hours across the Sea of Cortez, and is the capital of the Município de Mulegé.

History
Copper-bearing deposits, in blue-green globules called *boleos,* were discovered near here in 1868, and in 1885 a French mining company calling itself El Boleo acquired mineral rights to the area. To help build over 600 km (375 miles) of mine tunnels, a large copper-smelting foundry (imported by ship from Europe), a pier, and a 30-km (18-mile) mine railway, the French brought in Yaqui Indians from Sonora; fresh water was piped in from the Santa Agueda oasis, 16 km (10 miles) west. (Two thousand Chinese and Japanese laborers, told they would be able to plant rice, also came to work at El Boleo. When they found that rice wouldn't grow in central Baja, almost all of them left; many ended up in Sinaloa across the Cortez.)

After smelting, the copper ore was shipped to Tacoma, Washington, for refining. Instead

of returning empty, copper transport ships brought lumber from the Pacific Northwest to Santa Rosalía, and, as the town grew, the French filled the arroyo and mesas on either side with wooden buildings to house workers, company officials, and Mexican soldiers. During El Boleo's heyday in the 1940s, a sooty cloud issued constantly from the foundry's smokestack and hung over the town. Eventually the ore began to run out, and in 1954 the French company sold its mining facilities back to the Mexican government. Copper ore from the Mexican mainland is smelted in Santa Rosalía on occasion, but the mines are closed.

Without the mines in operation, Santa Rosalía is probably a far more pleasant place to live than ever before, and today it serves as a government, transport, and market center for central Baja. It's also an important tourist crossroads for visitors making the ferry trip to the mainland or stocking up on supplies for further peninsular explorations.

The **Mahatma Gandhi Public Library** in Parque Morelos, at the east end of town near the harbor, has an exhibit of historic photos from Santa Rosalía's mining days.

Iglesia Santa Bárbara De Santa Rosalía
A novelty in Baja—or anywhere for that matter—is this prefabricated, iron-walled church designed by famous French architect Alexandre Gustave Eiffel in 1884. The church was originally constructed in France in 1887, then exhibited in Paris (along with the with Eiffel Tower) at the 1889 World's Fair, and finally shipped in sections to Santa Rosalía, where it was reassembled in 1897. The exterior is modern, even minimalist, in tone, while the interior resembles that of any Catholic church. The church is still in use, with an Italian padre in residence.

Hotels
The tourist-oriented **Hotel Morro** (tel. 2-04-14), about 1½ km south of town on Mexico 1, overlooking the Sea of Cortez, has a/c rooms

Iglesia Santa Barbara (JOE CUMMINGS)

for US$23 s, US$25 d. Facilities include a restaurant, bar, and swimming pool.

Several hotels in town offer more basic, but comfortable, accommodations at lower rates. The **Hotel Blanco y Negro** (tel. 2-00-80), an old French building with friendly proprietors at Av. Sarabia and Calle 3, has clean rooms with shared bath for US$10 s or d, with private bath for US$11.60 (two or three beds), or with TV for US$15. **Hotel Olvera** (tel. 2-00-57), at the corner of Calle Playa and Av. Montoya, is similarly priced but newer. Nearby on Av. Montoya is the modest **Hotel Del Real** (tel. 2-00-68), with a/c rooms for US$15-20.

Farther west from the harbor is the **Hotel San Victor** (tel. 2-01-77) at Av. Progresso 36, where a/c rooms cost US$20. Overlooking the copper smelter on Mesa Norte, the venerable **Hotel Frances** was once the best hotel in town, but it closed down in 1991. Perhaps someone will come along and re-store the French colonial-style building to its former glory.

Camping And RV Parks
Just south of Santa Rosalía off Mexico 1, the **Las Palmas RV Park** offers hot showers and a dump station, but no hookups, for US$6 a night. Fifteen km (nine miles) south of town off Mexico 1, on Caleta San Lucas, is the secluded **San Lucas RV Park** (mailing address: A.P. 131, Santa Rosalía, BCS). Tent/camper sites (no hookups) cost US$5 per vehicle. Facilities include a restaurant, bar, hot showers, disposal station, and boat ramp. The beach here would be quite nice if someone would take the time to clean it up.

Food
Most of the town's restaurants and cafés are spread out along Av. Obregón. **La Carreta,** on Av. Obregón between Calle Pedro Altamirano and Calle 2, serves a wide variety of moderately priced breakfasts, seafood, steaks, and Mexican standards.

In the next block east, between Calles 1 and 2, **El Cha Cha II** has hamburgers, sandwiches, and American breakfasts (including pancakes and French toast). Next door is **Terco's Pollito,** specializing in barbecued chicken; open daily for lunch and dinner.

Restaurant Tokyo, run by a descendant of a Japanese laborer who worked for El Boleo, offers inexpensive seafood and tacos—but no Japanese food. It's on Av. Obregón between Calle 3 and 4 and is open daily for lunch and dinner.

Groceries: The **Conasuper** (a larger version of a Conasupo) on Av. Obregón at Calle 3 purveys a wide selection of foodstuffs and household supplies. Just west of the Conasuper, on the same side of the street, is the famous **Panadería El Boleo,** which typically has a long line out front when it opens at 1000. The baguettes here are legendary, but they also have a good variety of other Mexican- and French-style baked goods. For fresh tortillas, visit the **Tortillería Cachania** on Av. Obregón near Calle 6.

The government-subsidized **Tienda ISSSTE,** on the south side of Av. Constitución, west of Calle 11 and Arroyo de Santa Rosalía, carries a rotating stock of food, liquor, and toiletries at prices that are as much as 40% lower than Conasuper's. They don't always have the same items two weeks in a row, but what they have is always a bargain.

Fishing
Corvina, pompano, grouper, and snapper are usually plentiful at **Caleta San Lucas,** 15 km (nine miles) south of town. Small boats can be launched here at low tide. Farther offshore in the Canal San Marcos (between Caleta San Lucas and Isla San Marcos), sierra is available, especially in the winter months.

Fisherman's Landing (tel. 2-04-14, 2-08-80; 213-439-9906 in the U.S.), at Av. Obregón 48 (between Calles 5 and 6) in Santa Rosalía, organizes guided fishing trips to nearby bays and islands. A full-day, all-inclusive charter for six costs US$350.

Events
Santa Rosalía's biggest festival is **Carnaval,** a pre-Lenten festival held six days before Ash Wednesday (usually mid-February). For a description of the types of festivities occurring in Carnaval, see "La Paz," under "Cape Region," p. 289 or "Ensenada," under "Northwestern Baja," p. 172.

During the **Fiesta de Santa Rosalía,** held annually around Sept. 4, the townspeople organize concerts, food fairs, and fishing tournaments to honor their patron saint, Santa Rosalía.

Information And Services
A **tourist office** between the ferry terminal and the bus depot distributes tourist brochures on Baja California Sur but doesn't have much information on Santa Rosalía itself.

Foreign traveler's checks or cash can be exchanged for pesos at the **Banamex** at Calle 5 and Av. Obregón, Mon.-Fri., 0900-1200. The

© MOON PUBLICATIONS, INC.

post office is east of the plaza at Calle 2 and Av. Constitución. On the south side of the plaza is a **public telephone** where local and long-distance calls can be made. Santa Rosalía's area code is 685.

Transport
Bus: Santa Rosalía's intercity bus depot is on the west side of Mexico 1, just south of the ferry terminal. Several buses a day go north to Tijuana (US$15) and south to La Paz (US$10), and more frequently to Guerrero Negro and Mulegé.

Ferry: Tickets for the Santa Rosalía-Guaymas ferry can be purchased at the SEMATUR office (tel 2-0013, fax 2-00-14), at the ferry pier, daily 0800-1200 and 1700-2200. For information on fares and departure times, see "Getting There," in the main introduction.

Boat: A marina in the breakwater-protected harbor has a few slips for rent—the city has plans to add more in the near future—and fuel is available. As Santa Rosalía is an official port of entry, the harbor also has COTP, immigration, and customs offices.

VICINITY OF SANTA ROSALÍA

South of Santa Rosalía, on the way to Mulegé via Mexico 1, are two side roads—suitable for high-clearance vehicles—into the Sierra de Guadalupe. At Km 188+, just beyond the state prison, a grade road branches 12 km west to **Santa Agueda** and beyond to several ranchos. Local ranchers may be willing to act as guides to Indian murals at La Candelaria, San Antonio, or Los Gatos. The Guadalupe "school" of Indian rock art shows more variation than the paintings found farther north in the Sierra de San Francisco, and known sites are more numerous. (According to Crosby, more sites can be found in the Guadalupe than at any of Baja's other sierras.) Murals here are typically smaller than in the San Francisco area.

An even more scenic side road leaves Mexico 1 about 20 km (12 miles) south of the Santa Agueda turnoff, and heads 14 km (8½ miles) west to the isolated farming community of **San José de Magdalena.** The winding, rocky road climbs several steep grades with inspiring views of palm-studded canyons, healthy stands of cardón, mesquite, and ocotillo, and picturesque rock outcroppings—you almost expect to see the Lone Ranger and Tonto around the next bend. Beyond San José de Magdalena, the road continues another 48 km (30 miles) to several ranchos. A number of Indian mural sites are accessible in this area, assuming you can find a guide at one of the ranchos, as are the adobe ruins of **Misión Guadalupe de Guasinapi** (1721-95), one of the peninsula's most remote mission sites.

San Bruno, a small fishing community just before the turnoff to San José de Magdalena, has a PEMEX station, bus stop, church, *tienda rural,* and **Costa Serena Trailer Park,** where basic tent/camper sites are US$5 a night. The village ambience is enhanced by wandering cows and chickens, along with fishing nets hanging out to dry or be mended. On the highway near the bus stop, the **Restaurant Peninsular** serves delicious home-cooked seafood platters, meatballs, spaghetti and Mexican dishes.

MULEGÉ

The town of Mulegé (pop. 6,000) straddles a wide arroyo formed by the Río Santa Rosalía (also called Río Mulegé), an estuarial river that feeds into the Sea of Cortez. The abundance of water made it a desirable mission location in the early 1700s, and today the agricultural legacy of the Jesuit padres—dates, figs, bananas, olives, and oranges—comprises most of the local livelihood, along with fishing and tourism.

The quaint mission-style buildings, narrow streets, and riverside palms have made Mulegé a favorite stopover among Transpeninsular travelers. The local facilities, including a first-class dive shop, laundromat, five auto mechanics, two auto parts stores, markets, restaurants, hotels, and campgrounds, provide all the amenities as well as the necessities for a long-term bivouac. Concerned with preserving Mulegé's tourist image, municipal authorities recently forced the closure of all the town brothels (which have since moved to Santa Rosalía).

Although it's well above the Tropic of Cancer, Mulegé is the first point south along the peninsular coast where the climate and ambience begin to feel tropical. Winters are mild, summers are hot and humid, and mosquitoes make an appearance along the river when the wind is still. The river can be explored by canoe (available at the Orchard RV Park for US$2 an hour) though portage is required at the dam by the bridge; the small lagoon where the river meets the sea is a good birdwatching site.

Climate

Weather conditions along the coast from Mulegé to Loreto can be characterized as subtropical. From Dec. through March, daytime temperatures average 15°-21° C (60°-70° F); April through July, daytime temps run 26°-35° C (80°-95° F); and Aug. through Nov., the thermometer ranges 32°-43° C (90°-110° F). Annual rainfall is 10 centimeters (four inches), with much of the precipitation occurring in the late summer and early fall. These weather patterns mean that, for most prospective visitors (divers and anglers excepted), Aug.-Nov. is low tourist season.

Misión Santa Rosalía De Mulegé

Mulegé's original mission was founded on the riverbanks in 1705. In 1770, a flood destroyed most of the community structures, and shortly thereafter the church was rebuilt at its current site, a bluff overlooking the river. Although it's not one of Baja's most striking mission churches, a visit is worthwhile just for the unobstructed views of the town and palm-lined river below. The church is usually locked except when services are held.

The church is best approached by following Calle Zaragoza southwest beneath the highway bridge, then west (right) past Granny's Goodies until the road climbs the bluff by the church, about three km (1.8 miles) from the bridge.

Hotels

Mulegé has four hotels in town, two west of town. One of the most popular is **Hotel Las Casitas** (tel. 3-00-19) on Calle Madero, the town's main east-west street. Formerly the home of Mexican poet Vicente Gorosave, this eight-room establishment offers modest a/c accommodations for US$18-25; facilities include a patio restaurant and bar.

Just east of Las Casitas on the same street is **Hotel Rosita** (tel. 3-02-70), where budget apartments, complete with kitchenette, cost US$18-20 per night for up to four persons. A bit farther east on Calle Madero, the rambling, colonial-style **Hotel Baja Hacienda** (tel. 3-00-21; 714-756-2222 in the U.S.) has recently come under new management and offers rooms for US$25 a night. The hotel pool, long lying in ruin, is operational again.

Hotel Terrazas (tel. 3-00-09), at the north end of Calle Zaragoza, has problems with its hot water and power supply, as well as general cleanliness; even at US$15, it should only be considered if nothing else is available.

Up a notch or two are the two hotels west of town. **Hotel Vista Hermosa** (tel. 3-02-22; 213-578-9680 or 800-336-5454 in the U.S.) has a river view, pool, restaurant, and bar. Room rates fluctuate with hotel occupancy from as low as US$25 to as high as US$50. At the lower rates, it's the best value in town. To get to the hotel, follow Calle Madero east along the river toward the coast and you'll see the sign for the hotel after three km (two miles).

Four km (2½ miles) east of town off Mexico 1 is Mulegé's largest inn, the **Hotel Serenidad** (tel. 3-01-11, fax 3-03-11; mailing address: A.P. 9, Mulegé, BCS). The Serenidad even has its own paved, 1,200-meter airstrip (Unicom 122.8), hence it's a favorite among *yan-*

qui pilots, many of whom fly in for the Saturday night pig roast here. The spacious hotel grounds, which include a pool, tennis court, boat ramp, restaurant, and bar, are impressive-looking, but some of the a/c units in rooms need replacing and the hot water supply can be weak. Noise from the bar is sometimes a problem, continuing well past midnight. Rooms are US$45-50 a night, two-bedroom cottages US$90.

Casas De Huéspedes

Mulegé supports three guesthouses, or *casas de huéspedes:* **Nachita's, Canett,** and **Manuelita,** all of which offer basic rooms with shared bath for US$5-6 a night. Canett, on

© MOON PUBLICATIONS, INC.

Calle Madero opposite a church, is the most livable of the three.

Camping And RV Parks

Several well-run trailer parks compete for Mulegé's campers and RVers. Best of the bunch is the attractively landscaped **Orchard (Huerta Saucedo),** on the river about a kilometer east of town off Mexico 1. Tent sites are US$5 for two persons, full hookups US$8 for two, plus US$2 for each person. Facilities include a boat launch, canoe rentals, free fruit (depending on the season—mangoes, dates, oranges, limes, figs), hot showers, toilets, and a dump station.

Also along the river, in the same vicinity, are **Jorge's, Pancho's, Río Oasis,** and **Villa Maria Isabel,** all decent, well-kept spots with rates similar to the Orchard. Discounted rates are generally given to travel club members and for long-term stays.

The **Hotel Serenidad** (see "Hotels" above) has an RV park with full-hookup slots for US$8 for two person, plus US$2 for each additional person.

Food

The tastefully decorated **Los Equipales,** a second-floor dining room overlooking Calle Moctezuma next to Casa de Huéspedes Nachita's, features the tastiest Mexican specialties and seafood in town; though a bit on the pricey side, for Mexico, it's worth every peso.

For inexpensive, well-prepared meals, the family-run **Restaurant La Palma,** on Av. Martinez near the PEMEX station, is hard to beat. Breakfast selections include oatmeal, cream of wheat, corn flakes, omelettes, huevos rancheros, chilaquiles, and good coffee. For lunch and dinner, the tiny restaurant serves fresh seafood, cheeseburgers, and a few Mexican standards.

Granny's Goodies, in a thatched-roof building strung with Christmas lights below the highway bridge (en route to the mission church), is a restaurant, cantina, and library rolled into one. Granny (a Canadian expat who has lived many years in Mexico) and her loyal staff purvey fresh baked goods, inexpensive breakfasts, homemade pizza (two free margaritas go with the house pizza), and inexpensive cerveza from around 0900 until the last customer is gone, sometimes in the wee hours. As if the food and beer weren't enough, Granny's offers free showers for customers, a book exchange service, and a great selection of music cassettes—including her norteña favorites. A happy hour is in effect from 2000 onward, when the house becomes one of the only places in Mulegé where locals and gringos mix. It's almost too good to last—rumor has it the local authorities are cultivating bureaucratic roadblocks to Granny's continued operation.

Another find is **Café La Almeja,** a palapa hut on the beach at the mouth of the estuary (Punta El Sombrerito). Exemplary tacos and fresh seafood are reasonably priced, especially considering the location.

The restaurants at the **Vista Hermosa, Las Casitas,** and **Serenidad** hotels are popular among the tourist crowd and serve decent, moderately priced Mexican fare. The Serenidad hosts a pig roast every Saturday night; Wednesday night brings mariachis and a Mexican buffet. Las Casitas has its own mariachi night on Fridays. Most of the other restaurants in town aren't really worth trying. The service at **Las Candiles,** on Calle Zaragoza opposite the plaza, is slow and the food's not worth the wait. **La Jungla Bambú,** along the river near the trailer parks, is on-again, off-again. **El Nido,** on Calle Romero Rubio, has the usual steak, Mexican, and seafood prepared for gringo tastebuds—if you haven't grown tired of the El Nido franchise by this point in your transpeninsular journey, then you might like it.

Great fish tacos are available from the taco vendor on the plaza, usually open 0900-1300. **Taquería Doney,** on the road in from Santa Rosalía, has good tacos de carne asada, quesadillas, tostadas, and tamales; it's open only in the evening.

Fishing

Las Casitas, Baja Hacienda, Serenidad, and Vista Hermosa hotels can arrange guided fishing trips to nearby islands, Punta Chivato, and Bahía Concepción. Onshore fishing near the

Misión Santa Rosalía de Mulegé
(JOE CUMMINGS)

estuary (the south side's best) sometimes lands winter catches of yellowtail, roosterfish, sierra, and pargo; farther offshore are summer runs of dorado, yellowfin, and various billfish.

Diving

The marinelife in the Sea of Cortez off the coast of Mulegé and Santa Rosalía is more prolific and colorful than that in the upper Cortez. Many of the tropical or Panamic species begin making their appearance in reef areas, including the green moray eel (much less shy than its Pacific counterpart), angelfish, damselfish, parrotfish, triggerfish, flag cabrilla, several wrasses, and three varieties of lobster (red, spiny Cortez, and slipper). Generally speaking, the best diving season is Aug.-Nov., when visibility extends up to 30 meters (100 feet) and water temperatures near the surface are in the mid-20s C (mid-80s F).

Islas Santa Inés, three small islands in the northern part of Bahía Santa Inés, offer good snorkeling along their eastern shores, where rock reefs can be seen at depths of around 4½ to 12 meters (15-39 feet). Reefs and rock pinnacles extending from the north end of these islands are excellent scuba diving spots, with depths of six to 25 meters (20-85 feet). Scuba diving is also good at a reef at the north end of the bay, about a kilometer northeast of

Punta Chivato. Other possibilities, father north toward Santa Rosalía, include **Caleta San Lucas** and **Isla San Marcos.**

The islands and reefs of **Bahía Concepción,** south of Mulegé, provide plenty of diving and snorkeling opportunities, including **Pelican Reef (Arrecife Pelicano), Isla Santispac, Isla Guapa, Isla Requesón,** and **Roca Frijole.**

Mulegé Divers at Calle Madero 45 in Mulegé offers just about everything scuba and free divers need, including air, equipment, and boat charters. A basic scuba excursion costs US$25 with no equipment; add US$10 for weight belt and two tanks, US$5 for a wetsuit (recommended in winter). Equipment rentals are very reasonable, from US$1 a day for a harness to US$8 for a power-inflated buoyancy compensator; air fills are available for US$3 (2250 psi) and US$4 (3000 psi).

For those needing scuba instruction, Mulegé Divers offers a four-hour basic course for US$50 (including all equipment and transport). Snorkeling equipment is on hand for rent or purchase as well. Of possible interest even to those not planning an immediate dive trip are the shop's selection of fishing and diving guidebooks, waterproof fish chart for identifying marine life underwater, and fishing tackle. The shop is open Mon.-Sat., 0900-1300 and 1500-1800.

Mexigo Adventures, at the Hotel Baja Hacienda, runs snorkeling trips every Saturday morning to Bahía Concepción. The group leaves the hotel at 0800 by van and returns around 1500-1530; the fee of US$25 per person includes van and boat transport, snorkeling equipment, lunch, a bilingual guide, and all the beer, soda, or water you can drink.

Kayaking
Kayaks can easily be launched at the estuary for excursions into Bahía de Santa Inés to the north or Bahía Concepción to the south. Most kayakers intending to paddle in the latter launch farther south—see "Vicinity of Mulegé" below.

Experienced kayakers enjoy the well-known Mulegé to Loreto coastal trip, a 135-km (84-mile), five- to seven-day paddle. Because shore campsites are few and far between, this route should only be attempted in the company of someone who has made the trip before and knows the best stopovers.

Mexigo Adventures operates half-day kayak trips (on easy-to-paddle, open-cockpit kayaks) in the estuary area and at Bahía Concepción for US$25 per person. Mexigo also rents kayaks to experienced kayakers for US$35 a day (less for overnight or long-term rentals), which includes boat, paddle, life-vest, and spray skirt. See "Tours" below for Mexigo's address and phone number, or stop by the Hotel Baja Hacienda for information.

Information And Services
A **post office** and **public phone** (with local and long distance service) are located on the plaza off Calle Zaragoza. There is also a small private long-distance telephone office in the tienda at the corner of Calle Zaragoza and Av. Martinez. The area code for Mulegé and vicinity is 685.

The local **U.S. Consul,** Don Johnson, lives on Calle Madero, near Mulegé Divers. Mr. Johnson, who also owns Hotel Serenidad, has been known to assist Americans with legal or health emergencies.

A **laundromat** at the corner of Calle Zaragoza and Moctezuma is open Mon.-Sat., 0800-1800.

Fuel
The PEMEX station in town, on Av. Martinez, often has vehicles waiting for gas backed up all the way to the end of the block. A quicker alternative—in spite of the drive—is the large, new PEMEX station on Mexico 1, about 15 minutes south of Mulegé by car.

Tours
Mexigo Adventures (tel. 3-00-21), a new outfit affiliated with the renovated Hotel Baja Hacienda, organizes several moderately priced excursions in the Mulegé area. Initial offerings include snorkeling and kayaking in Bahía Concepción and hikes to cave paintings in the Sierra de Guadalupe. The usual fee for a five- to seven-hour trip is US$25. Early reports say the Mexigo trips are a great way to learn a bit more about central Baja and meet other travelers.

VICINITY OF MULEGÉ

Cave Paintings
The Sierra de Guadalupe, east of Mulegé, contain the largest number of known prehistoric mural sites in Baja California. Several of the hotels in Mulegé can arrange excursions to the more accessible sites for US$20-30 per person.

If you prefer to drive into the sierra and arrange your own guide, the easiest site to reach is **San Borjitas.** This site has been known to local residents continuously since mission times; Leon Diguet visited San Borjitas in the 1890s, Erle Stanley Gardner in the 1960s, and Harry Crosby in the 1970s. To get there from Mulegé, drive north on Mexico 1 to the Km 157 marker near Palo Verde (at the turnoff for Punta Chivato), then take the dirt road east into the sierra (high-clearance vehicles only). Keep left at all forks, pass two abandoned ranchos (when you reach a gate, go through it and close it after you), and continue until you arrive at Rancho Las Tinajas (about 30 km/18½ miles from the highway), where you should be able to get a guide. This area is also known as Cerro Gordo. From Las Tinajas, it's a two-hour mule ride and walk to the cave.

The paintings at San Borjitas are unique among Baja rock-art schools in several respects: at least a dozen of the more than 50 large *monos* (human figures) in the rock shelter are apparently transfixed with arrows; some exhibit male genitalia; and about a dozen are filled in with longitudinal stripes, rather than mono- or bicolor schemes. Colors employed at San Borjitas include black, red, ocher, gray, white, and combinations of all five, painted in monocolor, bicolor, and checkerboard patterns. Along the tuff side walls of the cave is a collection of petroglyphs (rock carvings) depicting female genitalia; the fire-blackened back wall shows fish and deer.

Punta Chivato

At the north end of Bahía Santa Inés, 48 km (30 miles) northeast of Mulegé (24 km north via Mexico 1, then another 24 km east on a graded, unpaved road), is the secluded resort of **Hotel Punta Chivato** (tel. 3-01-88; mailing address A.P. 18, Mulegé, BCS). The hotel has its own airstrip (Unicom 122.8), a boat ramp, and pool. Air-conditioned rooms, with private patio, cost US$40 s, US$50 d. The hotel also maintains a campground with tent/camper sites (no hookups) for US$8 on a nearby beach. The Islas Santa Inés lie just southeast of the point; fishing and diving excursions can be arranged.

Bahía Concepción

This huge bay, open to the north and sheltered on the east, has a string of sandy beaches along its west side and a number of small islands anchored in its middle—a perfect setting for anglers, small boaters, windsurfers, and kayakers. Mexico 1 parallels the west bayshore, providing inspiring views of the blue-green bay and conical, flat-topped islands to the east and Sierra Coyote peaks to the west, as well as access to several beaches and coves along the way.

The largest and most popular beach is **Playa Santispac** (Km 118), where tent and trailer camping, next to shade palapas, is available for US$4 per vehicle per night (no hookups). Facilities include toilets, showers, and two cafés, and the famous **Ana's Panadería y Bar.**

Posada Concepción, access at Km 112, is a congested, unpleasant-looking development of houses and trailer homes with a market and tennis courts. Full-hookup slots, when vacant, cost US$10.

Next south is **Playa Los Cocos,** at Km 111, with one of the prettiest beaches along this section of the bay (sometimes called Bahía Coyote); the limestone in the surrounding cliffs lends a turquoise hue to the bay. Camping is permitted here, but there are no facilities as yet. An unpaved road parallels the highway and provides access to other beaches; follow the road over some hills to **Playa Escondido,** a scenic, uncrowded beach with campsites for US$3 a day.

Two kilometers farther along the shore is **Playa Coyote,** a public beach with palapas and trash barrels. El Coyote is divided into two sections: **Rancho Coyote,** with houses and a public beach in bad need of a clean-up, and **Palapas El Burro,** a campground/RV park (pit toilets, palapas, showers, drinking water) that charges US$5 a vehicle. The **Restaurant Estrella del Mar,** opposite El Coyote, serves breakfast, lunch, and dinner. A few hundred meters east of Playa El Coyote is **Isla Bargo,** an elbow-shaped island with a sandy beach in the "elbow."

After El Coyote, Mexico 1 veers away from the coast for a short distance, returning at Km 94.5 to **Playa Buenaventura,** a half-sand, half-rock beach with a market, restaurant, and palapas. A kilometer or so farther south is the nicer **Playa El Requesón.** Tent and RV camping (pit toilets, palapas, no drinking water) is permitted along the broad, sandy beach here for US$3 per vehicle; at the north end a sandbar connects the shore with Isla El Requesón, forming sheltered coves on either side.

Península Concepción, on the east side of the bay, is much less visited than the western shore because access requires a sturdy, high-clearance vehicle, preferably with 4WD. Although there are plenty of camping areas along the peninsula's bayshore, usually deserted, none have toilet or water facilities. The 60-km (37-mile) road north along the bayshore ends just southeast of Punta Concepción at an abandoned manganese mine. The

MULEGÉ-BAHÍA CONCEPCIÓN

TO SANTA ROSALÍA

MULEGÉ

BAHÍA DE SANTA INÉS

PUNTA CONCEPCIÓN

SEA OF CORTEZ

PLAYA SANTISPAC
PUNTA ARENA
CERRO LAS ORILLAS

POSADA CONCEPCIÓN

PLAYA EL COYOTE

PLAYA EL REQUESON

ISLA EL REQUESÓN

PUNTA SANTA TERESA

BAHÍA CONCEPCIÓN

SAN SEBASTIÁN

BAHÍA SAN NICOLAS

TO LORETO

0   10mi
0   10km

© MOON PUBLICATIONS, INC.

beaches and coves of Península Concepción are best visited by boat from **Punta Arena,** west across the bay. (The access road for Punta Arena branches off Mexico 1 at Km 118.)

San Isidro-La Purísima-Comondú
Southeast of Mulegé is a series of volcanic valleys, isolated from the rest of Baja California Sur by the rugged Sierra de la Gigante, that support the historic farm/ranch communities of San Isidro, La Purísima, and Comondú. Although a journey to this region is most easily accomplished via the paved and gravel roads heading north from Ciudad Insurgentes, the road from Mexico 1, from a point south of Bahía Concepción, is shorter and more scenic.

The turnoff for this rough byway into Old Baja branches west from Mexico 1 at Km 60,

75 km (47 miles) south of Mulegé. The first 18 km (11½ miles) of this unpaved roads are graded, and threads through a series of steep-walled arroyos before meeting a four-way junction.

Left is an unpaved, ungraded, 40-km (25-mile) road southwest to San José de Comondú, the larger of the two villages that comprise Comondú. The latter half of the Comondú road is very rough and features steep grades; except for 4WD vehicles, a better approach would be from San Isidro to the northwest or La Poza Grande to the southwest.

The road to the right at the four-way junction is abandoned. Take the unpaved, ungraded road straight ahead to arrive, via a series of switchbacks into Valle de la Purísima, at **San Isidro** (37 km/23 miles west of the junction). San Isidro (pop. 1,500) offers rustic accommodation, a café, clinic, market, clinic, and drinking water, but most visitors continue another five km (three miles) west to the slightly larger **La Purísima.**

Set amidst date, citrus, and mango orchards, and ponds, surrounded by high volcanic cliffs, and backed by a sloped butte (El Pilón), La Purísima represents the quintessential interior Baja settlement. Originally established as a mission community in 1719 (the ruins of Misión de la Purísima Concepción, incorporated into a private residence, lie several kilometers north of the village), the village was abandoned in 1822 and revived in the latter 19th century by Mexican farmers.

Before the completion of the Mexico 1, Todos Santos, San Ignacio, and Mulegé must have resembled this place. If a second highway along the east side of the peninsula, as proposed by a La Paz consortium, becomes a reality, it will most likely pass just west of here. Facilities in La Purísima include gasoline (probably Nova and diesel only), guesthouse accommodations, post office, market (with ice!), auto parts store, drinking water, and medical clinic.

The twin communities of **San José de Comondú** and **San Miguel de Comondú** (known collectively as "Comondú," with a combined population of around 1,000) lie 23 km (14½ miles) southeast of San Isidro via an unpaved, ungraded road. The well-watered, 11-km-long (seven-mile) Arroyo Comondú, wedged between barren volcanic mesas, produces dates, figs, citrus, corn, grapes, sugarcane, and a variety of vegetables. A small plaza in San José is surrounded by stone and

adobe buildings, including a surviving Jesuit missionary house from Misión San José de Comondú (1737-1827), now used as a church. A church bell dating to 1708 is on display next to the edifice.

San Miguel de Comondú, about three km (two miles) west of San José, was originally the site of a **capilla de visita** (visiting chapel). Locally grown sugarcane is still processed in San Miguel using traditional donkey-powered presses. Although smaller than San José, the village has a few more local services because it's on the road southwest to Ciudad Insurgentes. San Miguel has gasoline, a post and telegraph office, and a general store; drinking water is available at either village.

One of the best times of year for a Comondú visit is on the feast day for San Miguel (Sept. 29), when tiny San Miguel de Comondú bursts with music and dancing.

(top) ruins, Misión San Fernando Velicatá; (bottom) city hall, San José del Cabo;
(following page) Puerto Balandra

LORETO

At first sight, it's difficult to believe this unassuming seaside town of 10,000 was the first European settlement in the Californias, and that it served as the Californias' secular and religious capital for 132 years. Superseded by La Paz following an 1829 hurricane, Loreto all but vanished for three-quarters of a century before Mexican fishermen began frequenting the area again. As word of the prolific fisheries spread, a handful of North American anglers began flying to Loreto fish camps in private planes.

Although Loreto never regained its former glory, the 1973 completion of the Transpeninsular Highway finally brought the area within range of the average tourist. Today Loreto is part of a 27-km (17-mile) coastal segment, including **Nopoló** and **Puerto Escondido,** slated by the Mexican government for development as a major tourist resort. In the town itself, a restored cobblestone plaza adjoins the historic mission church and museum, and a new malecón has transformed the old seawall into a picturesque promenade. A small marina with a concrete boat ramp has recently been completed at the north end of the malecón.

Offshore fishing remains the principal tourist attraction. Other major assets include an international airport and a world-class tennis center; an 18-hole golf course at Nopoló and recreational marina at Puerto Escondido are nearing completion. Not entirely reliant on tourism, Loreto also benefits from the saltworks on **Isla del Carmen,** opposite the peninsular coast, where 40,000 tons of salt per year are harvested from a salt basin formed by an extinct volcano crater. Commercial fishing and agriculture are also important local sources of livelihood.

In spite of FONATUR (Fondo Nacional de Fomento del Turismo—National Foundation for Tourism Development) accomplishments, Loreto for the moment remains a sleepy port town if compared with La Paz or Los Cabos. The predicted tourist invasion has yet to appear—a bonus for Baja visitors looking to get away from the crowd.

History
After several unsuccessful attempts—over a 167-year period—to establish a permanent Spanish settlement on the peninsula (then thought to be an island), Jesuit Padre Juan María Salvatierra founded the first mission in the Californias at Loreto in 1697. As the Loreto colony grew, it served as a base for California exploration and for the expansion of the mission system throughout the peninsula. Franciscan Padre Junípero Serra started his journey north to Alta California from here in 1769, eventually founding Alta California's first mission at San Diego Bay.

As the "mother of the California missions" and Spanish California capital, Loreto prospered until a hurricane destroyed much of the town in 1829. The mission church survived, but damage was so extensive, and fear of future hurricanes so high, that the capital was moved from Loreto to La Paz the following year.

The town remained virtually deserted until the 1850s and 1860s, when a small group of intrepid immigrants resettled the area. Several among this second wave of settlers were English immigrants; a surprising number of Loreto residents today bear surnames such as Green, Davis, Cunningham, and Drew. Loreto remained a backwater, frontier village until after WW II, when it began developing a small commercial and sportfishing industry.

Misión Nuestra Señora De Loreto
The first chapel at Loreto was merely a large tent erected at the mouth of Arroyo San Dionísio in October 1697. The building of the mission church proper proceeded in three stages, beginning with a simple rectangular chapel (along with presidio) near the current site in 1699. The foundations for a larger church, with a cruciform floor plan, were laid in 1704, and the church as it now appears reached its basic form in 1752.

After weathering the 1829 hurricane and several subsequent earthquakes, the church was restored in 1976 and is currently in use as

(JOE CUMMINGS)

Misión Nuetra Senora de Loreto

a place of worship. A sign over the massive front doors reads "Head and Mother of the Missions of Lower and Upper California." Other than its historicity, however, it's not a particularly impressive Spanish mission church.

Of equal or greater interest is the adjoining **Museo de los Misiones,** a small but well-endowed historical and anthropological museum with exhibits on regional history and culture, Baja California mission history, and religious art. An anthropological library and small book store offer a variety of literature on Baja and Mexican history. The museum is open Mon.-Fri. 0900-1230 and 1300-1700. Admission is US$1.70.

On the first weekend of every September, the church and town cosponsor a Virgin of Loreto festival with plenty of feasting, music, and dancing. Activities are centered around the plaza.

Nopoló-Puerto Escondido

Loreto—along with Cancún, Huatulco, Ixtapa, and Los Cabos—was chosen for tourist development upon the recommendations of a computer study carried out by the Mexican government during the oil-rich '70s. The prime criterion in Loreto's selection was the fact that the area enjoys an average of 360 sunny days per year. Most of the completed and ongoing projects in the Loreto area have been entirely or partially funded by FONATUR, which has invited investors from around the world to participate in the area's future as a tourist destination. Even gringos looking for an inexpensive vacation home in the Loreto area can receive FONATUR assistance in the form of low-interest, low downpayment loans.

The focus of most ongoing local development is **Nopoló,** eight km (five miles) south of Loreto. Nopoló consists of a hotel zone (so far only one hotel, the Stouffer Presidente, has opened), a recreation zone (tennis center and golf course), and a residential zone, linked by wide, palm-lined boulevards. The Stouffer Presidente is one of the most pleasant hotel stops along the entire peninsula, but what wasn't entered into the computer equation, or so it seems, is the lack of sandy beaches at Nopoló (although Playa Notri and Juncalito, several kilometers south, fill the bill).

Now that the marina at **Puerto Escondido,** 16 km south of Loreto, is nearing completion, FONATUR's hopes lie in attracting boaters since fishing and boating are, and always have been, Loreto's major strengths (see "Sports and Recreation" for details). Rumor has it that the Intercontinental and Paraiso-Radisson hotel chains may soon be building at Puerto Escondido.

Hotels

A favorite among anglers, the **Hotel Oasis** (tel. 3-01-12. 3-02-11, fax 3-07-95; mailing address: A.P. 17, Loreto, BCS) started as a fish camp many years ago but has been transformed into a nicely landscaped, palapa-roofed hotel facing the Sea of Cortez. At the south end of Calle de la Playa (Blvd. López Mateos), the hotel's large, clean, a/c rooms cost US$40 per day without meals, US$80 with three meals. Facilities include a restaurant and bar, pool, tennis court, and the hotel's own sportfishing fleet.

At the north end of Calle de Playa is the **Hotel Misión de Loreto** (tel. 3-00-48; mailing address: A.P. 49, Loreto, BCS), with a pool, two restaurants, and a/c rooms for US$33-40. Farther north along the waterfront, on Calle Davis, the **Hotel La Pinta** (tel. 3-00-25; 800-336-5454 in the U.S.) has spacious a/c rooms with sea views and terraces at US$55 s, US$60 d; facilities include a restaurant, bar, and pool.

Budget: Away from the waterfront is the more basic **Hotel Salvatierra** (tel. 3-00-21), at Calle Salvatierra 125. Room rates vary according to occupancy rate but are usually US$12 s, US$20 d. The Salvatierra has a/c rooms with hot showers but little else in the way of amenities.

Nopoló: The **Hotel Stouffer Presidente** (tel. 3-07-00; fax 3-03-77; toll-free in Mexico 91-800-9-04-44) is on Blvd. Misión de Loreto in Nopoló's hotel zone, eight km (five miles)

south of Loreto. Large, bilevel rooms come with a separate sitting area and all the amenities of an international-class hotel for US$70-80 s, US$90-110 d (rates are lowest May-Jan.). Set among spacious, immaculate, palm-shaded grounds, the hotel features a restaurant, outdoor café, bar, disco, two pools, tennis courts; also on hand are instruction and equipment for windsurfing, boating, and fishing. The Presidente is the only hotel in the Loreto area with telephones in the guest rooms.

Although FONATUR hopes eventually to have several hotels in Nopoló's hotel zone, so far Stouffer Presidente is the only one. Recently the government issued an advance announcement of the opening of a 280-room, four-star hotel called **Hotel Guaycura** in Nopoló in early '92. The municipal tourist office in Loreto should have the latest information on this project.

Puerto Escondido: The **Tripui Motel** (tel. 3-08-18; 512-749-6070 in the U.S.), part of the Tripui Resort complex 24 km (15 miles) south of Loreto, has a/c rooms for US$40—showers are tiny. Facilities include a pool and tennis courts.

Camping And RV Parks

The popular, American-owned **Loremar RV Park** (tel. 3-07-11), 1½ km (a mile) south of town via Calle Madero, has full hookup RV spaces for US$10 a night for two or more nights (US$12 for one night only), tent sites for US$4, hot showers, laundry service, boat launch, and palapas along the waterfront. Discounts for long-term stays are available.

Also in this vicinity is **Las Palmas RV Park** (tel. 3-02-02), with full hookups for US$10 a night, tents for US$3, laundry, and showers.

An unnamed campground at Playa Juncalito, 22½ km (14 miles) south of town costs US$5 a night (no hookups) and features a boat ramp and dump station. North of Juncalito, toward Nopoló, you should be able to camp on the beach for free.

Puerto Escondido: The trailer park at **Tripui Resort** (tel. 3-08-18; 512-749-6070 in the U.S.) has 129 "permanent" (yearly) spaces and only 31 overnight slots. A full-hookup slot is US$12 a night for two persons, plus US$5 for each additional person. Discounts for long-term stays are available. Facilities include boat launch, boat storage, pool, tennis, restaurant, bar, and grocery store. For reservations, call one of the numbers above or write Tripui Resort, A.P. 100, Loreto, BCS.

Food

Loreto doesn't have a great number of restaurants but, among those available, quality is high. **Café Olé**, at Calle Madero 14 (on the plaza), serves a variety of inexpensive breakfasts and lunches, including seafood omelets, *huevos con nopales* (eggs with cactus), tacos and other antojitos, plus burgers, ice cream, and milk shakes. It's open 0700-1400 daily. Next door, **La Casita** serves a similar Mexican and American menu, plus *menudo* (tripe soup) on Sundays.

Another good choice for quick, inexpensive snacks is **McLulu's**, a taco stand just west of Calle Colegio on Calle Baja California. McLulu's fish tacos are legendary; other offerings include tacos de carne asada, homemade chorizo, and *picadillo* (spicy meat-and-chile salad). Lulu, the cook, doesn't mind if you buy beer at the nearby supermarket to drink while eating at her tables.

For more leisurely, atmospheric meals, one of the most popular places in town is palaparoofed **Cesar's** (tel. 3-02-03), on Calle Juárez and Zapata. House specialties are moderately priced and include fresh seafood, Caesar salads, and *carnes rojas,* (barbecued steaks); the bar, to one side of the dining room, is one of Loreto's nicest. Open daily for lunch and dinner.

Playa Blanca (tel. 3-04-28), Hidalgo and Madero, is a seafood house decorated with whale vertebrae, lacquered turtle shells, and a sand floor. Prices are fair and breakfast is also served; in the evenings, the upstairs bar becomes a night club with the only live music in town.

El Nido (tel. 3-02-84), at Calle Salvatierra 154, has the usual menu of mesquite-grilled steaks and seafood, but this is generally known to be one of the better links in the Baja chain. Open daily for breakfast, lunch, and dinner.

Groceries: Loreto has two supermarkets, one each on Calle Salvatierra **(El Pescador)** and Calle Juárez **(Focardi Supermarket).** A bakery on Calle Juárez, near the bus terminal, sells fresh bolillos and Mexican pastries. A number of small tiendas and *ultramarinos* can also be found around town.

Sports And Recreation

Fishing: Although commercial gill-netting has to some extent affected Loreto's coastal fisheries, this section of the Sea of Cortez is still considered one of Baja's hottest sportfishing destinations, and the Mexican government is taking steps to keep commercial operations out of the area. Offshore fishing is best east of Isla del Carmen, where you'll find yellowtail and sierra in winter, dorado, snapper, cabrilla, grouper, tuna, sailfish, and marlin in summer. Inshore fishing, between Loreto and Isla del Carmen (particularly at the north end of Carmen), nets smaller yellowtail, snapper, white seabass, and, in spring, roosterfish.

Fishing trips can be arranged at the Oasis, Misión, La Pinta, and Stouffer Presidente hotels, or at one of the sportfishing outfits in town. **Arturo** (opposite Restaurant Playa Blanca on Calle Madero) and **Alfredo's** (tel. 3-01-65, fax 3-05-90; Calle Juárez and Callejón 2) are two of the longest-established sportfishing fleets. The going rate for a panga trip is US$80-90 per day for up to three anglers. Fishing cruisers run US$250-350.

Boating: Small boats can be launched at the north end of the malecón, at the Loremar RV Park, or farther south at Playa Juncalito and Puerto Escondido. Jaunts to Isla del Carmen (18 km from Loreto, eight km from Puerto Escondido) are popular; the island has several good beaches, but the best anchorages are at Puerto Balandra and Bahía Marquer on the island's west shore or at Bahía Salinas on the east.

Any of the hotels that organize fishing trips can arrange pangas by the day. Pangas can also be rented at the pier at the north end of Loreto's waterfront. The Hotel Stouffer Presidente rents Hobie catamarans for fun sailing. **C & C Ground Services** (tel./fax 3-01-51; mailing address: P.O. Box 1, Loreto, BCS) organizes picnic trips to Isla del Carmen and Isla Coronado beaches, as well as whale-watching excursions (blues, humpbacks, and fins) in nearby waters.

Sea cruisers generally anchor at the sheltered, deep-water marina at Puerto Escondido. A COTP office was recently established at the marina, making Puerto Escondido an official marine entry point. Didn't bring your own yacht? A Florida-based company, **The Moorings,** offers luxury yacht charters from the Puerto Escondido marina. Yachts vary in size and can be charted with or without crew. For details, contact The Moorings (tel. 3-08-32, fax 3-08-35; 800-535-7289 in the U.S.; mailing address: A.P. 133, Loreto, BCS). The Moorings also operates guided fishing trips and a free public boat ramp for trailered boats.

SIERRA CEVICHE

Ceviche (sometimes spelled "cebiche" or "sibiche") is a seafood appetizer in which fish or shellfish is marinated in lime juice until "cooked." It's very popular throughout Baja and there are as many recipes as there are cooks—it can be a wonderful experience in one restaurant and a bad excuse for getting rid of fish scraps in another.

Since it's easy to make even while camping on the beach (no fire necessary), ceviche offers an excellent alternative to the usual fried, baked, or grilled fish dishes that most Baja anglers are acquainted with. One of the best fishes to use for ceviche is the sierra, a common type of mackerel usually caught inshore-offshore; John Steinbeck, during his 1941 Sea of Cortez expedition, pronounced it "the most delicious fish of all." Other great candidates for ceviche are halibut, shark, shrimp, lobster, or just about any other fish whose flesh is not too "dry" (the oilier the better, since the lime juice counteracts the oil). Always use only the freshest fish available.

Recipe:
Serves four
- ½ pound fresh sierra filets, thinly sliced
- ¼ cup fresh lime juice
- one avocado, peeled and cut into half-inch cubes
- eight ripe, red cherry tomatoes cut in half (or 1 large ripe tomato)
- one serrano chile, minced (or more if you want it *really hot*)
- two tablespoons fresh cilantro leaves, minced
- one tablespoon olive oil
- ½ teaspoon salt (optional)

Put the sliced sierra in a large bowl, mix with the lime juice, and marinate in a cooler for a half-hour. Drain; then gently toss the remaining ingredients. Best served with fresh tortilla chips (or spread over *tostadas,* whole fried corn tortillas) and cold cerveza.

Kayakers can put in at Loreto for excursions to Isla Coronado or the north end of Isla Carmen. For the southern or eastern shores of Isla Carmen, as well as for Isla Danzante and Los Candeleros, Puerto Escondido is the most convenient put-in point. Starting from Puerto Escondido, the ambitious, experienced sea kayaker can paddle out to Isla Monserrate or even Isla Santa Catalina. A logical run would be to put in at Puerto Escondido and paddle south with the currents to Bahía Agua Verde (described below in "Vicinity of Loreto") by way of Danzante (13 km/eight miles) and Monserrate (24 km/15 miles).

Diving: The islands off Loreto's coastline offer numerous diving opportunities, including rock reefs, seamounts, and underwater caves. The best local diving areas include: the north end of Isla Coronado; the north and east shores of Isla del Carmen; the 120-foot sunken freighter near del Carmen's Bahía Salinas; Playa Juncalito, where the wreckage of a small, twin-engine plane can be viewed; and the smaller islands of Monserrate, Santa Catalina, and Danzante (northern and eastern shores). South of Isla Danzante is a string of granite islets called Los Candeleros, whose vertical walls make an awesome underwater sight.

Guided excursions and/or scuba equipment rentals can be arranged through **Fantasia Divers de Loreto** (tel. 3-07-00, ext. 412), in the Hotel Stouffer Presidente at Nopoló. In Loreto, **Deportes Blazer** (tel. 3-00-06), Calle Hidalgo 18, has scuba equipment for sale or rent, as well as air fills.

Tennis: The **Loreto Tennis Center** (tel. 3-04-08), attached to the Hotel Stouffer Presidente, has nine lighted courts, a clubhouse, bar, and pro shop; John McEnroe is a touring pro for the center. Stouffer Presidente hotel guests may use the courts at no charge; non-hotel guests pay a court fee of US$3 during the day, US$5 after dark.

Golf: Nine holes of the 18-hole golf course at Nopoló had been completed as we went to press. The entire course should be finished by the end of '92.

Information And Services

The **municipal tourist office** (tel. 3-06-89, 3-03-44) is on the plaza, near the mission church. Also on the plaza are the post office, a bank (Bancomer), and a public phone with long-distance service. The area code for Loreto, Nopoló, and Ciudad Constitución is 683.

Viajes Pedrin (tel. 3-02-04), a travel agency on Calle Hidalgo, can book air tickets, bus tickets, and hotel reservations.

Transport

Air: Aero California (tel. 3-05-00, 3-05-66), the only international airline with service to Loreto at this writing, has daily nonstop flights from Los Angeles, La Paz, and Los Cabos. The airlines has an office in town at Calle Juárez and Zapata.

Bus: Loreto's bus terminal is at the corner of Calle Juárez and Ayuntamiento. Tres Estrellas de Oro has several buses daily to La Paz (US$8 first-class, US$5 second-class) and two buses a day to Tijuana (US$18 express).

Car: Cars can be rented through the **Turismo Los Candeleros** office (tel. 3-07-00, ext. 453) at the Hotel Stouffer Presidente in Nopoló.

Loreto has several mechanics and auto parts shops.

VICINITY OF LORETO

Las Parras-San Javier

The 35-km (22-mile) road to San Javier, one of Baja's most scenic interior drives, is a section of the old Camino Real ("Royal Road") used by Spanish missionaries and explorers. Access to the road is off Mexico 1 at Km 118, south of Loreto. Only drivers with sturdy, high-clearance vehicles should attempt this trip, however, as surfaces are stony and, except in the driest years, it's necessary to ford a winding stream in several places. Following heavy rains, this road shouldn't be driven at all for a few days, unless you have a 4WD vehicle and are skilled at driving through mud. Grades approach 15% in places; the average driving time is two hours.

Along the way, the road passes several palm oases hidden away in narrow arroyos, *zalates* (wild fig trees) clinging to cliffs, and other rewarding vignettes as it winds around Cerro La Gigantica (1,490 meters/4,885 feet). **Rancho Las Parras**—an oasis settlement consisting of a stone chapel, small dam, and orchards of grape, olives, figs, and citrus—appears about midway to the mission (19 km/12 miles from Mexico 1) in the Arroyo de Las Parras. This arroyo provided water and a way into the Sierra de la Giganta for Indians and later missionaries; in the vicinity are a number of old Indian trails and Indian rock art.

About 9½ km (six miles) beyond Las Parras, the San Javier road meets a lesser branch road leading northwest to Comondú (see "Vicinity of Mulegé," p. 273). This route to Comondú is in poor condition, with grades of 20-23%, and hence is recommended only for 4WD vehicles.

San Javier, a village of thatched-roof, stone houses and around 300 inhabitants, contains one of the peninsula's most well-preserved Jesuit mission churches. Misión San Francisco Xavier de Viggé-Biaundó (simply called Misión San Javier nowadays) was originally founded by Padre Francisco Píccolo in 1699, two years after the peninsula's first mission was established in Loreto. In 1701, Padre Juan de Ugarte arrived at Arroyo de San Javier from Mexico City, bringing with him a number of seeds and seedlings from which to plant the Californias' first cultivated fruit orchards. Many of the "mission" varieties of grapes, olives, figs, oranges, and lemons now grown throughout the Californias are descended from Ugarte's original San Javier plantings.

To make room for the orchards, the mission church was moved to its current site in 1720 and rebuilt by Padre Miguel del Barco sometime between 1741 and 1768. Although the church's facade is not as ornate as that of Misión San Ignacio to the north, the side windows are splendid—no two are alike. The gilded altar and statuary inside the church are thought to have been transported from Mexico City by boat and burro in the mid-1700s; two

of the bells in the church's tower are dated 1761, the third 1803.

Practicalities: The only amenities in the village are a couple of small tiendas with beverages and limited foodstuffs. For those without their own vehicles (or without the right kind of vehicle), it's possible to arrange a car and driver from Loreto to San Javier for about US$25—inquire at any Loreto hotel.

Primer Agua

The graded, unpaved road to Primer Agua, a FONATUR-owned palm oasis, begins at Km 114 on Mexico 1. A sign for the road is posted just south of a highly visible electric transformer station next to the highway. The Primer Agua road, a bit better than the San Javier road, reaches the oasis after 6½ km (four miles); ordinary passenger vehicles can make it in dry weather. The main function of this fenced-off section of arroyo (a branch of Arroyo de San Javier) is as a nursery for propagating plants to be used at nearby FONATUR projects. Recently a picnic area, complete with tables and barbecue grills, has been opened to the public near a natural pool at the bottom of the arroyo. If the gate to the facility is locked (it sometimes is, even in the middle of the day), a hike into non-fenced sections of the arroyo, west of the orchards, is still worthwhile.

Bahía Agua Verde

At Km 40, where Mexico 1 veers inland from the Cortez coast, a part graded, part ungraded, gravel-and-dirt road heads southeast for 40 km (24 miles) to the fish camp of **Agua Verde.** The roadbed is steep and winding in places, not at all suitable for trailers or motorhomes. As the road approaches Agua Verde, it flattens out and divides into several tracks running to five small coves scalloped into the bayshore. The turquoise waters—framed by Islas Monserrate and Santa Catalina to the north and east, and hillsides of palo verde, palo blanco, cardón, palm, and mesquite to the west—provide a picturesque setting.

Local residents make their living herding goats, fishing for small shark *(cazón)* (twice weekly a truck comes to transport the catch to city markets), and servicing a steady trickle of outside visitors who brave the road in from Mexico 1. Rocky bayshore campsites, with palapas, cost US$3-5. Panga fishing trips can be arranged for US$50-60 a day.

Isla Santa Catalina, 17½ km (11 miles) east of Isla Monserrate, is known for its endemic "rattleless rattlesnake" *(Crotalus catalinensis),* and for the largest barrel cactus species in Baja, *Ferocactus diguettii,* named for French naturalist Leon Diguet. Individuals of this variety may reach four meters (13 feet) in height and a meter (3.28 feet) in diameter. *(Ferocactus diguettii* is also found on Islas Cerralvo, Monserrate, Danzante, and del Carmen.)

Ciudad Insurgentes

At Ciudad Insurgentes, the kilometer marke countdown from Santa Rosalía reaches Km and starts over again at Km 236. The tow itself has little to recommend it except as a fue and food stop or as a transit point for the "easy road north to La Purísima (102 km/61 miles and Comondú (101 km/60½ miles). About third of this road is paved, and the remainde is graded as far as La Purísima and Sa Miguel de Comondú.

From La Purísima, an ungraded road lead northwest 48 km (30 miles) to **Bahía Sa Juanico** on the Pacific coast. Gas and limite supplies are available at San Juanico. Fishing is said to be good here, and surfers can catch

LORETO-BAHÍA AGUA VERDE

TO MULEGE

ISLA CORONADO

PUERTO DE LA LANCHA

PUERTO BALANDRA

SALT POND

LORETO

NOPOLÓ

BAHÍA SALINAS

ISLA DEL CARMEN

SEA OF CORTEZ

PLAYA JUNCALITO

BAHÍA MARQUER

BAHÍA CHUENQUE

PUERTO ESCONDIDO

PUNTA COYOTE

PUNTA BAJA

ISLA DANZANTE

LOS CANDELEROS

PUNTA CANDELEROS

ISLA SANTA CATALINA

TO CIUDAD CONSTITUCIÓN

ISLA MONSERRATE

0   1mi

0   1km

PUNTA PASQUEL

BAHÍA AGUA VERDE

© MOON PUBLICATIONS, INC.

a point break during summer swells. The road continues north from San Juanico all the way to San Ignacio via Laguna San Ignacio. Portions of the road between San Juanico and Laguna San Ignacio, however, require 4WD vehicles and skilled driving.

CIUDAD CONSTITUCIÓN

Even though it has more hotels than any other town between Santa Rosalía and La Paz, few Baja travelers stop over in Ciudad Constitución (pop. 45,000), the capital of Municipio de Comondú and the second-largest population center in Baja California Sur. Founded in the '60s to serve as a market center for the irrigated Llano Magdalena (Magdalena Plain) agricultural basin, the town has two PEMEX stations, two banks (Banco Serfin and Banco Internacional), three bicycle shops, supermarkets (including Conasuper and Tienda SSSTE), a hospital, an Aero California office, panaderías, tortillerías, auto shops, and a number of other small businesses.

Accommodations

Of the nine hotels in town, the best value is the clean and friendly **Hotel Conchita** (tel. 2-02-56), Blvd. Olachea and Hidalgo; a/c rooms with phones and color TV cost only US$15 s, US$22 d. Nearby, the **Maribel Hotel** (tel. 2-01-55), next to Banco Internacional on Blvd. Olachea at Victoria, offers similar rooms at US$26 s, US$30 d.

Other Ciudad Constitución hotels include the **Hotel Conquistador** (tel. 2-25-25, Calle Bravo 161) at US$20 s, US$26 d, and the economic **Hotel Reforma** (tel. 2-09-08, Calle Obregón 125), US$14-18. The **Motel Plaza Bonita,** a modern American-style motel, is under construction on the west side of the main boulevard in the south part of town. Projected room rates are in the US$30-35 range.

RV Park: The **Campestre La Pila** (tel. 2-05-62), south of town near the power plant, has full hookups, a pool, showers (no hot water), and a picnic area for US$7 for two persons, plus US$2 for each additional person.

Food

The main boulevard—part of Mexico 1—through Ciudad Constitución is dotted with restaurants, *asaderos* (grills), and taquerías. In the northern part of town, before the turnoff for BCN 22 west (to San Carlos), good choices along the boulevard include the **Dragon** (Chinese), **Rincón Jarocho** (seafood and antojitos), and **Super Pollo** (Sinaloa-style barbecued chicken). **Restaurant Queratan,** at the center of town on the east side of the boulevard (within walking distance of the Maribel and Conchita hotels), has inexpensive *comidas corridas* and various *platillos típicos.*

The Maribel and Conchita hotels each have restaurants open for breakfast, lunch, and dinner. Opposite Super Pollo on the boulevard is a supermarket; the town also has several *tiendas de abarrotes* and *ultramarinos.*

Misión San Luis Gonzaga

Ciudad Constitución is a convenient departure point for an excursion to this surviving mission settlement 42 km (26 miles) southeast of Mexico 1. The best of two secondary roads leading from Mexico 1 starts at Km 195 (a sign reads "La Presa Iguajil"). Originally founded in 1737 and rebuilt in 1751, the simple mission church is well maintained by local ranchers and farmers. The surrounding arroyo is planted in figs, dates, pomegranates, citrus, grapes, and olives.

BAHÍA MAGDALENA

This unique marine environment is only a 45-minute drive from Ciudad Constitución, yet many transpeninsular voyagers pass it by. Where the flat Llano Magdalena has sunk lower than the Pacific, the ocean has intruded and created a string of barrier islands over 209 km (130 miles) long, separated from the peninsula by a series of shallow bays (average depth less than 18 meters/60 feet). Arroyos that sank under the Pacific have become *bocas* or "mouths" that let the sea in; these bocas now form channels between the barrier islands.

BAHÍA MAGDALENA

PACIFIC OCEAN

LA POZA GRANDE
BOCA DE LAS ANIMAS
BOCA DE SANTO DOMINGO
ISLA SANTA DOMINGO
BOCA DE SOLEDAD
SANTO DOMINGO
COLONIA PURISIMA
CIUDAD INSURGENTES
TO LORETO
ISLA MAGDALENA
CABO SAN LAZARO
VILLA BENITO JUÁREZ
22
CIUDAD CONSTITUCIÓN
PUNTA HUGHES
BAHÍA SANTA MARIA
PUERTO SAN CARLOS
VILLA MORELOS
PUERTO MAGDALENA
BAHÍA MAGDALENA
TO MISIÓN SAN LUIS GONZAGA
PUNTA ENTRADA
ISLA SANTA MARGARITA
CANAL GAVIOTA
BAHÍA ALMEJAS
PUERTO CANCUN
SANTA RITA
PUERTO CHALE
ISLA CRECIENTE
TO LA PAZ
0   15mi
0   15km
© MOON PUBLICATIONS, INC.

Starting at Boca de las Animas in the north, the most prominent barrier islands are **Isla Santo Domingo, Isla Magdalena, Isla Santa Margarita,** and **Isla Creciente.** The largest of the bays between the islands and peninsula, **Bahía Magdalena** and **Bahía Almejas,** are linked by Canal Gaviota to form a vast, protected waterway—the best on Baja's Pacific coast for boating and windsurfing. Naturalists could spend a lifetime exploring the mangroves and estuaries along the eastern bayshores, which support an astounding variety of marine- and birdlife.

History

Because of the proximity of Bahía Magdalena's natural harbor to the fertile Llano Magdalena, several groups of colonists attempted to settle the coastal plains here. In 1879 the Chartered Company of Lower California, an American land syndicate, settled around 5,000 Americans along the bayshore. For a time the colony made money harvesting orchilla, a lichen growing on many of the plants on the Llano Magdalena that was rendered for use as a commercial dye. The subsequent introduction of synthetic dyes killed the orchilla industry, and the colony along with it.

The shore remained unpopulated throughout the first half of this century except for the occasional visit by Bajacalifornio anglers and a few unplanned visits by passing mariners. Several passing ships foundered on the barrier islands, including the famous steamer *Independence* in 1853. Of the 400 passengers aboard, 150 perished in fires on the ship or by drowning after jumping into the breakers.

In 1920, the U.S. submarine *H-1* ran aground on Isla Santa Margarita. What the sub was doing in Mexican waters—at a time when relations between the two countries were tense—has never come to light. Although all but four of the crew were rescued by a passing ship, the sub was mysteriously looted of all logs and other classified material before U.S. Navy rescue ships could approach it; the Navy scuttled the sub at a depth of nine fathoms just off the island coast and erased virtually all records of its existence. More submarine lore: during WW II, Japanese submarines used Bahía Magdalena as a hiding place. Max Miller, author of *Land Where Time Stands Still,* spotted a Japanese sub in the bay when he made an overland journey to the edge of the Llano Magdalena in 1941.

In the '60s, after Mexico recovered full ownership of the Llano Magdalena basin from foreign investors, the valley was irrigated and farmers began moving in. The harbor settlement of **Puerto San Carlos** soon developed as a relay point for the shipping of agricultural products (principally cotton and alfalfa) from the plains to mainland Mexico and abroad.

Puerto San Carlos

From Ciudad Constitución, paved highway BCN 22 leads west 57 km (34 miles), then crosses a causeway onto a small hooked peninsula. Mangroves fringe the peninsula; a long wharf stretches from the western shore to the only other deep-water port besides Ensenada on the Pacific coast. Often simply called San Carlos, this small port town of 5,000 residents has a PEMEX station, tiendas, a café, and COTP, customs, immigration, and fishery offices. The **Hotel Las Brisas** offers basic rooms; camping and RV parking is possible at the north and south ends of the small peninsula for fees of around US$4 per vehicle.

Boating

Trailered or car-topped boats can be launched from a concrete boat ramp in San Carlos; pangas can easily be launched from the beach. Other put-in points for small boats or kayaks are **Puerto López Mateos** to the north (accessible via Ciudad Insurgentes), **Puerto Cancun** to the south (accessible from Mexico 1 at Km 173), and **Puerto Chale** (via Santa Rita, Km 157, Mexico 1).

Fishing

The bay fisheries have provided steady sportfishing even in recent years due to the relative lack of commercial fishing interests. Onshore catches, near the mangroves, include halibut, occasional yellowtail, red bass (mangrove snapper), corvina, and snook. Farther out in the bay, anglers take grouper, black bass, and yellowtail; offshore, beyond the 100-fathom line, are sailfish, marlin, dorado, wahoo, and giant seabass. Although most of these gamefish frequent the area in lesser or greater numbers year-round, July through Nov. are generally the most productive fishing months. Best places to get live bait are the mackerel holes off Punta Entrada.

Clams can be gathered in the shallows of both bays, although Bahía Almejas lives up to its name with the most extensive clam grounds. In the latter bay, clamming is most accessible at Puerto Cancun.

Windsurfing

Mag Bay, as gringo board-sailors usually refer to Bahía Magdalena, has the best windsurfing on Baja California's Pacific coast. A strong year-round breeze, together with the relatively calm bay surface, create perfect conditions for novices and intermediate windsurfers; experienced wave-sailors can experiment at or near the bocas, where breakers and stronger winds heighten the challenge.

A protected run of 88 km (52 miles) can be made by putting in at Puerto López Mateos and taking out at Puerto Cancun; this run can be lengthened to 113 km (70 miles) by staying in until Puerto Chale.

Whalewatching

During the annual gray whale migration, Jan.-March, the canals, bays, and bocas of the Bahía Magdalena complex are practically filled with the whales' undulating forms. Puerto López Mateos is the usual center for whalewatching activities. Often the grays can be spotted from shore here as they come and go via Boca de Soledad to the north; a public parking and viewing area has been set aside north of the port's fish-processing plant. Pangeros offer two-hour boat tours from this area for US$10-20 per person.

While pregnant female grays venture into shallower parts of the bay for calving, males tend to loiter near bay entrances, where they cavort with other males and nonpregnant females, often breaching and spyhopping. One of the best spots for viewing such activities is **Punta Entrada,** at the southern tip of Isla Magdalena, which forms the north end of the wide channel between Mag Bay and the Pacific. The island is only accessible by boat (best anchorage on the southeast of the point) or small plane (a landing strip is situated just north of Punta Entrada). Camping is possible at the fish camp near the tip or farther north near the village of **Puerto Magdalena.**

Mag Bay whale-watching tours can also be booked in La Paz through Aventuras Turisticas Calafia (tel. 682-2-28-88, Paseo Obregón 220). The agency charges US$70 per person, including a guide, boat, lunch, and roundtrip transport from La Paz.

cave paintings—buzzards (BOB RACE)

Transport

The road to Puerto San Carlos (57 km/35 miles from Ciudad Constitución), one of Baja California Sur's only official state highways, is an easy drive of less than an hour. Buses ply the Ciudad Constitución-Puerto San Carlos route several times daily with a fare of about US$1 per passenger.

El Cien-Punta Conejo

At Km 100, about midway between Ciudad Constitución and La Paz, is the tiny roadside settlement of El Cien ("One Hundred"). As a pit stop, El Cien offers the **Lonchería El 100**, a Conasupo, and a PEMEX station (the only one between Ciudad Constitución and La Paz). A nearby fossil reef reportedly contains whale vertebrae and other marine skeletons inquire at the lonchería for a guide.

Farther south at Km 80, a good dirt road branches west 19 km (12 miles) to **Punta E Conejo.** El Conejo ("The Rabbit") is wel known among surfers for steady point breaks in both northwest and southwest swells. Near the coast, the road to El Conejo intersects a lesser dirt road heading south 17 km (12½ miles) to another surfing spot, **Punta Marquez.** This road continues southward along the coast all the way to Todos Santos (124 km/77 miles from El Conejo)—recommended for 4WD vehicles only—and passes a number of good beach breaks.

(BOB RACE)

CAPE REGION

LA PAZ

Ensconced along the southeastern crescent of Baja's largest Sea of Cortez bay, La Paz is noted for its attractive *malecón* (waterfront) backed by swaying palms and pastel-colored buildings, splendid sunsets, easy-going pace, near-perfect climate, and the proximity of un-crowded beaches and islands. Many Baja travelers—Mexicans and gringos alike—cite La Paz ("Peace") as their favorite city on the peninsula; a few even go as far as to pro-nounce it their favorite in all of Mexico. Nowa-days Cabo San Lucas, 221 km (137 miles) farther south, receives more attention than La Paz in the North American press, which suits La Paz fans fine since it means fewer tourists.

La Paz is also arguably Baja's most Mexi-can city due to the long-time influx of Mexican mainlanders and its history as the first major European settlement on the peninsula. Many *paceños* (La Paz natives) are descendants of mainlanders who sailed to La Paz to avoid the political turmoil of 19th- and early-20th century mainland Mexico. It's not uncommon to meet more recent Mexican emigrés who have re-settled in La Paz after becoming fed up with modern-day political machinations in Mexico City, Guadalajara, or Monterrey. Paceños are proud of the many ways in which their city lives up to its name.

For travelers and tourists, the city of around 180,000 offers a variety of accommodations and dining venues, well-stocked supermar-kets, marine supplies, and a ferry terminal with daily departures for Mazatlán and Topolobam-po across the Sea of Cortez. Traffic snarls are common in *el centro,* the downtown area, but can be avoided by using Blvd. Forjadores, a wide avenue skirting the southern section of the city. Along the bay, La Paz remains much as John Steinbeck described it in 1941:

La Paz grew in fascination as we approached. The square, iron-shuttered colonial houses stood up right in back of the beach with rows of beautiful trees in front of them. It is a lovely place. There is a broad promenade along the water lined with benches, named for dead residents of the city, where one may rest oneself....[A] cloud of delight hangs over the distant city from the time when it was the great pearl center of the world.... Guaymas in busier, they say, and Mazatlán gayer, but La Paz is *antigua*.

CLIMATE

The most pleasant time of year for a La Paz visit is mid-Oct. through May, when days are balmy, evenings cool. In January, maximum temperatures average 22° C (72° F), minimum temperatures 14° C (57° F). Temperatures for July average 35° C (96° F) maximum, 24° C (75° F) minimum. Hot summer afternoons are somewhat moderated by the daily arrival of the *coromuel,* a strong onshore breeze that bedevils yachties trying to escape the harbor but cools down the rest of the population.

La Paz and vicinity averages only around 15 cm (six inches) of rainfall per year, over half of which generally falls during the Aug.-Sept. chubasco (tropical storm) season. Full-fledged *chubascos* with gale-force winds ac-

Bahía de la Paz (JOE CUMMINGS)

tually only reach La Paz every couple of years—most of the time the area receives only the remote influences of storms centered along mainland Mexico's lower west coast.

HISTORY

Early Spanish Contact

When the Spanish first landed on the shores of Bahía de la Paz in the early 16th century, the area was inhabited by migrating bands of Guaycura and Pericú Indians. Hunters and gatherers, these Indian groups lived mostly on shellfish, small game, and wild plants. As artifacts on display at La Paz's Museum of Anthropology demonstrate, they were also skilled weavers and potters.

Into this peaceful scene entered the first European, a Basque mutineer named Fortún Jiménez who commandeered the Spanish ship *Concepción* on the Sea of Cortez in 1533. Originally under the command of Capt. Diego Becerra, the *Concepción* had been sent to explore the sea on behalf of Spain's most infamous conquistador, Hernán Cortés. After executing the captain, Jiménez landed at Bahía de la Paz in early 1534, where he and 22 of his crew were killed by Indians while filling their water casks at a spring. The survivors sailed the *Concepción* back to the mainland, where the ship was immediately captured by Cortés's New Spain rival, Nuño Guzman. At least one crew member managed to escape and returned to Cortés with descriptions of a huge, beautiful bay filled with pearl-oyster beds.

Cortés himself landed at the northeast end of the bay (probably at Pichilingue) in May 1535, naming it Puerto de Santa Cruz. Cortés was able to effect a truce with local Indians, but his attempt at establishing a permanent Spanish colony lasted only through 1538, when the colonists were forced to abandon the peninsula due to supply problems.

The next Spaniard to visit the bay was famed explorer Sebastián Vizcaíno, who landed here in 1596 during his long voyage around the peninsula's perimeter and north to Alta California. Because he and his crew were treated so well by the Pericús, Vizcaíno named the bay Bahía de la Paz ("Bay of Peace").

CAPE REGION

BAHÍA DE LA PAZ

SEA OF CORTEZ

PACIFIC OCEAN

PUNTA COYOTE

PICHILINGUE

PICHILINGUE PENINSULA

PUNTA MARQUEZ

CANAL DE CERRALVO

ISLA CERRALVO

EL CENTENARIO

LA PAZ

LA PAZ INTERNATIONAL AIRPORT

RANCHO LOS INOCENTES

EL SARGENTO

BAHÍA DE LA VENTANA

SAN PEDRO

LA VENTANA

PUNTA ARENA DE LA VENTANA

PUNTA PERICO

SAN JUAN DE LOS PLANES

LAGUNA

EL TRIUNFO

SAN ANTONIO

EL CARDONAL

BAHÍA DE LOS MUERTOS

LA

SAN BARTOLO

PUNTA PESCADERO

DE

LOS BARRILES

19

BUENA VISTA

BAHÍA DE PALMAS

TODOS SANTOS

PLAYA SAN PEDRITO

EL PESCADERO

PLAYA LOS CERRITOS

SIERRA

LAS CUEVAS

PUNTA GASPAREÑO

COLONIA P.E. CALLES

AGUA CALIENTE

SANTIAGO

LA RIBERA

MIRAFLORES

PUNTA COLORADA

CADUAÑO

PLAYA MIGRIÑO

RÍO CANDELARÍA

CABO PULMO

CABO PULMO

RÍO CANDELARÍA

LA CANDELARÍA

SANTA ANITÀ

RÍO SAN JOSÉ

LOS FRAILES

BAHÍA LOS FRAILES

SAN JOSÉ VIEJO

RANCHO LA VINORAMA

PUNTA BOCA DEL TULE

SANTA ROSA

SAN JOSÉ DEL CABO

RANCHO LA FORTUNA

CABO SAN LUCAS

1

CABO FALSO

PUNTA PALMILLA

BAHÍA SAN LUCAS

BAHÍA CHILENO

0   10mi

0   10km

MOON

© MOON PUBLICATIONS, INC.

Pirates And Colonization

Baja California remained free of Spaniards another 100 years before a mission colony was successfully established at Loreto to the north. By this time, English and Dutch pirates were plundering New Spain's Manila galleons as they returned from the Orient weighted down with gold, silks, and spices. One of the freebooters' favorite staging areas was Bahía de La Paz, which contained numerous *ensenadas* (coves) and inlets perfect for concealing their swift corsairs. When Spanish crews put in for water, the pirates raided the galleons, often using their knowledge of strong bay winds to attack the ships when they were effectively pinned down.

Increased pirate activity in the late 17th and early 18th century created the need for a Spanish presence in the Cape Region. In 1719 Padre Juan de Ugarte, then President of the Missions, contracted a master shipbuilder to construct a ship for the specific purpose of exploring the Sea of Cortez coast and improving supply lines with the mainland. The barque *El Triunfo de la Cruz,* assembled of native Baja hardwood at the Mulegé estuary, made its first sailing to Bahía de la Paz in 1720 with Ugarte and Padre Jaime Bravo as passengers.

Ugarte and Bravo founded the mission community of Nuestra Señora del Pilar de la Paz at the current city site. The padres didn't find the Pericús to be as friendly this time

ENGLISH PIRATES ON THE SEA OF CORTEZ

Sir Francis Drake, Thomas Cavendish, William Dampier, Woodes Rogers, Thomas Dover, and other English privateers left behind a colorful Baja legacy. In spite of Spain's repeated attempts to colonize the peninsula, the pirates probably gained more wealth in the Californias than the Spanish themselves throughout the Spanish colonial period. For 250 years they plagued the Manila galleons off the coast of the Californias, finding the bays and lagoons of Baja's Cape Region perfect hiding places from which to launch attacks on the treasure-laden ships.

In La Paz, using their knowledge of a strong breeze that blows into the harbor every summer afternoon, the pirates attacked Spanish galleons while the vessels were effectively trapped in the bay. Four centuries after the first Manila-Acapulco voyages were launched, this afternoon wind is still known as *El Coromuel,* named for the Puritan Cromwells (father and son) who ruled successively as Lord Protectors of England.

The Disappearance Of The *Desire*

The most notorious of the Pacific privateers was Sir Thomas Cavendish, whose biggest capture took place at Cabo San Lucas in 1587. During this episode, his two English vessels, *Desire* and *Content,* commandeered the Spanish galleon *Santa Ana* following a protracted sea battle. After

looting the *Santa Ana's* cargo holds and setting its crew and passengers ashore, Cavendish set fire to the ship. (The Spanish crew later retrieved the burned hulk, and were able to restore the galleon for a return to Acapulco.)

The plundered treasure, meanwhile, was divided between *Desire* and *Content.* The ships set sail for England immediately, but during the first night of their triumphant voyage, the *Content* disappeared. Cavendish reported in England that the captain and crew of the *Desire* must have scuttled the ship on a nearby island and disappeared with the loot. Neither the wreckage of the vessel nor the treasure was ever discovered; some historians speculate that at least part of the missing wealth remains buried near the Cape.

A Visit By Robinson Crusoe

In 1709, famed corsair Woodes Rogers landed in La Paz after rescuing a seaman who had been marooned five years on a deserted island off Chile's coast. The rescued man was Alexander Selkirk, whose island sojourn became the inspiration for Daniel Defoe's *Robinson Crusoe,* published in 1719. Selkirk was aboard Rogers's *Dover* when the crew captured the Spanish galleon *Encarnación* off Cabo San Lucas in 1709; he served as sailing master on the ship's return voyage to England the following year.

around; the mission only lasted until 1749, when it was abandoned following a series of Indian rebellions. By this time, another mission, along with a presidio, had been founded farther south at San José del Cabo—a better location for monitoring pirate activity.

La Paz Reborn

Left with European diseases and without the support of the mission system, the local Indian population dwindled quickly. By 1811, Mexican ranchers and *pescadores* who had settled along the Bahía de la Paz started their own town, which they named La Paz after the bay. After Loreto was severely damaged during a hurricane in 1829, the capital of Baja California Sur was moved to burgeoning La Paz, where it has remained ever since.

During the Mexican-American War (1846-48), the city was occupied by U.S. troops; the soldiers left when the Californias were split by the 1848 Treaty of Hidalgo. But American General William Walker, dissatisfied with the treaty and hoping to add another slaveholder state to counter the growing U.S. abolitionist movement, formed his own army and retook La Paz in November 1853. Proclaiming himself "President of the Republic of Lower California," Walker lasted only six months before he and his mercenaries fled upon hearing that the U.S. wouldn't back their claims, and that the Mexican Army was on its way to La Paz from the mainland. Walker was tried for violation of neutrality laws in U.S., acquitted, and two years later was executed by the Nicaraguan army for attempting a similar takeover of Nicaragua.

La Paz remained a sleepy tropic port, known only for pearl fishing, until declared a duty-free port following WW II. During Mexico's postwar economic boom, mainland Mexicans crossed the Sea of Cortez in droves to buy imported merchandise; enchanted by La Paz itself, many stayed on. In the '50s, La Paz became well-known as a fishing resort and was visited by a succession of North American literati and Hollywood celebrities, thus initiating the city's reputation as an international vacation spot. But until the Transpeninsular Highway was completed in 1973, the city remained for the most part a tourist destination for mainland Mexicans.

Statehood was bestowed on the Territory of Baja California Sur in 1974, with La Paz as its capital. Linked by air, ferry, and highway to mainland Mexico and the U.S., the city has grown considerably yet has managed to maintain its tropic port ambience.

SIGHTS

Museum Of Anthropology ("El Museo Antropología")

Baja history buffs shouldn't miss this well-designed museum (tel. 2-01-62) at Calle 5 de Mayo and Altamirano. Three floors of exhibits cover Cape Region anthropology from prehistoric to colonial and modern times (labels are in Spanish only). On display are fossils, minerals, Indian artifacts, dioramas of Indian and colonial life, and maps of rock-painting sites throughout central and southern Baja. Next to the museum is an older building that has served La Paz as a hospital, prison, and, more recently, as the **Biblioteca Justo Sierra,** a children's library. Behind the library is a recently completed sculpture garden.

Admission to the museum is free; daily hours are 0900-1800.

Plaza Constitución (Jardín Velazco)

La Paz's tidy downtown *zócalo* is enclosed by Calles 5 de Mayo, Independencia, Revolución de 1910, and Madero. At the southwest side of the plaza is the post-missionary-style **Catedral De Nuestra Señora De La Paz,** which replaced La Paz's original mission church in 1861. Although the twin-towered brick edifice looms over the plaza, it has none of the charm of earlier Jesuit missions.

At the northwest side of Plaza Constitución, opposite the cathedral, is the **Biblioteca de Historia de las Californias** ("History of the Californias Library"). Housed in the former Casa de Gobierno ("Government House"), the library is filled with Spanish- and English-language volumes on Alta and Baja California history. The general public is welcome to use the library for research purposes; it's open Mon.-Fri., 0900-1800, Sat. 0900-1500. For library information, call 2-01-62.

La Unidad Cultural Profesor Jesus Castro Agundez

This cultural center at Calle Farías and Legaspi, in the area of the city known as Cuatro Molinos ("Four Windmills"), includes an art gallery, community art school, and city archives. Also part of the complex is the **City Theater** (Teatro de la Ciudad, tel. 5-02-07), a

1500-seat performing-arts facility that hosts musical, theatrical, and dance performances throughout the year.

The four windmills next to the theater pay tribute to a time when La Paz relied on windmills to pump water and generate electricity. Another symbolic display in the complex is **La Rotunda de los Sudcalifornianos Illustres,** a circle of sculpted figures representing Baja California Sur's most illustrious heroes. Most of the historical personages honored at the Rotunda are former teachers or soldiers.

*Catedral Nuestra
Señora de La Paz*
(JOE CUMMINGS)

Malecón

One of the city's major attractions is the pleasant malecón, a seawall promenade along the northwest side of Paseo Alvaro Obregón extending from Calle 5 de Febrero (Mexico 1 south) to the northeastern city limits. Palm-shaded benches are conveniently situated at intervals along the walkway for watching sailboats and yachts coming in and out of the bay. The best time of day for people-watching is around sunset, when the city begins cooling off, the sun dyes the waterfront orange, and paceños take to the malecón for an evening stroll. Snacks and cold beverages are available at several palapa bars along the way.

Universities

As Baja California Sur's educational center, La Paz supports a large number of schools at the primary, secondary, and tertiary levels. Most prominent among the latter is the **University of South Baja California** (Universidad Autonomía de Baja California Sur) on Blvd. Forjadores, with an enrollment of around 2,000 and reputable programs in agriculture, engineering, and business. The **Technological Institute of La Paz** (Instituto Tecnologico de la Paz), also on Blvd. Forjadores, enrolls approximately 3,000 students and is primarily known for its commercial fishing department.

ACCOMMODATIONS

Hotels And Motels

In 1941 Max Miller, author of *Land Where Time Stands Still,* wrote:

> The Hotel Perla is the place to stay. For an American there's no other choice unless he wishes to rent a room with a Mexican family or live in a Mexican board-and-rooming house. . . . [T]he Mexicans themselves expect an American to stay at the Hotel Perla. If he doesn't stay there when he first arrives, then he's in La Paz for no good reason. He's under suspicion.

Time hasn't stood still in La Paz, and although the malecón's Hotel Perla is still one of most popular hotels in the city, it's now only one among many.

Hotel rates in La Paz are quite reasonable for a resort area, with most rooms falling in the US$25-60 range. Another standby around since the dawn of La Paz's tourist industry is Cabañas de Los Arcos. Built in 1954, during La Paz's heyday as an exotic playground for Hollywood celebrities, Los Arcos became the city's first center for sportfishing trips. Paceño-owned Los Arcos now has

LA PAZ HOTELS AND MOTELS

Add 15% hotel tax to all rates (some hotels may charge an additional 10% service charge).
Area code: 682

NAME	ADDRESS	TELEPHONE	RATES	FEATURES
Cabañas de Los Arcos	Paseo Obregón 498 (A.P. 112, La Paz, BCS)	2-27-44; 213-583-3393 (or in U.S. 800-347-2252	US$53 s, US$55 d, US$60 t	a/c, cabaña section with fireplaces, (jr. suites—same rates, no fireplace), telephones, pool
Club El Moro	La Paz-Pichilingue Rd., Km 2 (A.P. 357, La Paz, BCS)	2-40-84	1-br US$57, 2-br US$74;	a/c, refrigerator, pool, restaurant, bar weekly and monthly rates on request
Hospedaje Mareli	Av. Serdán Sur 283	2-10-17	US$13.30 s, US$16.60 d	a/c
Hotel Acuario's Mar de Cortés	Calle Ignacio Ramirez 1665	2-92-66	US$35-40	a/c, telephones, pool, restaurant, bar
Hotel Gardenias	Av. Serdán Norte 520	2-30-88	US$20-30	a/c, pool, restaurant
Hotel Gran Baja	Calle Rangel	2-39-00, 2-38-44, fax 2-07-55	US$51 s/d, US$85 jr. suite	a/c, telephones, bay views, beach, pool, tennis courts, amphibious plane service, restaurant bar, disco
Hotel La Posada de Engelbert	Calle Nuevo Reforma and Playa Sur (A.P. 152, La Paz, BCS or P.O. Box 397, Bonita, CA 91908)	2-40-11, fax 2-06-63 (in U.S. 619-421-2062)	US$52 s, US$57 d court, restaurant, bar	a/c, cottages w/fireplaces, pool, tennis
Hotel Lori	Calle Bravo 110	2-18-19	US$15	a/c
Hotel Los Arcos	Paseo Obregón 498 (A.P. 112, La Paz, BCS)	2-27-44; (in U.S . 213-583-3393 or 800-347-2252)	US$53 s, US$55 d, US$60 t (add US$2 for bay-view rooms)	a/c, telephones, pool, massage, sauna, coffee shop, restaurant, bar, gift shop
Hotel Miramar	Calle 5 de Mayo and Domínguez	2-06-72, fax 2-06-82	US$23 s, US$26 d	a/c, TV w/VCR, bar, refrigerator, restaurant

LA PAZ HOTELS AND MOTELS (CONT.)

NAME	ADDRESS	TELEPHONE	RATES	FEATURES
Hotel Palmira	La Paz-Pichilingue Rd., Km 2.5 (opposite Marina Palmira)	2-40-00, fax 5-39-59; (in U.S. 800-336-5454)	US$45-55 s, US$50-60 d, US$55-65 t	a/c, telephones, pool, tennis court, restaurant, bar, disco
Hotel Perla	Paseo Obregón 1570	2-07-77, fax 5-53-63	US$31 s, US$32 d, US$40 t	a/c, telephones, pool, restaurant, coffee shop, night club
Hotel San Carlos	Calle Revolución and 16 de Septiembre	2-04-44	US$10-15	
Hotel Yeneka	Calle Madero 1520	2-03-35	US$15-25	
La Concha Beach Resort	La Paz-Pichilingue Rd., Km 5	2-65-44, fax 2-62-18; (or in U.S. 213-943-1369 800-528-1234)	US$70-85 d, US$115-125 suite	a/c, telephones, bay views, beach, pool, restaurant, bars, gift shop, aquatic sports center

a hotel section which, like the cabañas, faces the malecón and bay. For specifics on these hotels and others, see "La Paz Hotels and Motels," above.

Pensiones, Casas De Huéspedes, And *Hosterías*

La Paz offers more budget accommodation—*pensiones, hosterías,* and *casas de huéspedes*—than any other city in Baja. Doubles with a private shower are readily available for under US$10—a steal by modern Baja standards. Long-term visitors can often get a room for around US$5 a night. On the downside, accommodations in this price range come without air-conditioning, a significant inconvenience July-Oct., and since most of them are located in the downtown area, they can be a bit noisy (open windows and vented doors contribute to the influx of noise). But if you can do without air-conditioned silence, these are fairly clean, friendly, safe, and economical choices.

As old as the city itself is **Pension California** (tel. 2-28-96), housed in a former 18th-century convent at Calle Degollado 209 between Revolución de 1910 and Madero. The interior courtyard of this rambling Moorish-style building contains a tropical garden of sorts and a display of old and new paintings—some by local artists, some from the mainland (including an 18th-century Silva in a 17th-century baroque frame)—lending a distinctly Bohemian feel to the atmosphere. Rooms are very basic, little more than a few worn sticks of furniture, fan, and (hot) shower. Rates are US$6 s or d, US$9 for up to four persons, or US$11.50 for a room that sleeps six. Discounts are possible for long-term stays.

Just around the corner at Calle Madero 85 is another former convent (operated by the same family that owns Pension California), **Hostería del Convento** (tel. 2-35-08). Room rates here are the same as at Pension California, although the place is a bit more funky and faded. Even less expensive is **Casa de Huéspedes Miriam** (tel. 2-11-04), Calle 16 de Septiembre 202 (between Calles Domínguez and Madero), where a cell-like but clean room costs US$4.50 s, US$6.50 d.

One of the better values in this category is the **Posada San Miguel** (tel. 2-18-02), Calle Domínguez 15140, a colorful colonial-style villa built around a tiled courtyard. The basic, almost bare, rooms cost US$8.50 s, US$10 d but the courtyard entrance is a major plus.

La Paz has an official youth hostel at the *Instituto de la Juventud y El Deporte* (tel. 2-46-15), a sports complex on Blvd. Forjadores (Km 3) near Calle 5 de Febrero. A bed in a gender-segregated, four-person dorm costs US$4 a night; all ages are welcome. Facilities include a pool, gym, cafeteria, and volleyball and basketball courts.

Camping And RV Parks

Free beach camping is possible north of the Pichilingue ferry terminal at Playa Pichilingue, Playa Balandra (Puerto Balandra), Playa El Tecolote, and Playa El Coyote. At none of these beaches are there sources of fresh water; all supplies must be brought from La Paz. (See "Beaches" below for more details.)

In and around La Paz are six trailer parks—five at the western edge of the city off Mexico 1 and one to the south off BCN 286. Starting from the west (Mexico 1 south), the first is **Los Aripes (Oasis de Aripes) RV Park,** just before Km 15 in El Centenario. Popular among Transpeninsular voyagers making short La Paz stopovers, full-hookup slots here cost US$8 for two (no tent sites available), plus US$2 per each additional person; facilities include showers, flush toilets, laundry, restaurant, bar, and access to the shallow Ensenada de Aripes (boat launching possible).

Next along Mexico 1, five km (three miles) west of the city near the state tourism office, is **Casa Blanca RV Park** (tel. 2-51-09, fax 5-11-42), where full hookups are US$10 a night for two persons plus US$2 for each additional guest. Showers, flush toilets, a pool, laundry, restaurant, and small market are available. **El Cardón Trailer Park** (tel. 2-12-61; mailing address: A.P. 104, La Paz, BCS), at Km 4, has well-tended palapa sites with full hookups for US$9 for two, plus US$1 each additional person (tents permitted). El Cardón has a pool, groceries, flush toilets, hot showers, dump station, and laundry.

Just before the Hotel Gran Baja, off Av. Abasolo (Mexico 1) near the VW dealer, is the upscale **La Paz Trailer Park** (tel. 2-87-87; mailing address: A.P. 482, La Paz, BCS). Full hookups or tent sites cost US$12 for two plus US$2 per additional guest; facilities include showers, flush toilets, pool, jacuzzi, tennis court, laundry, restaurant, and bar. The **Hotel Gran Baja Trailer Park,** next to the hotel of the same name, offers full hookups for US$10 per two persons, plus US$2 for each additional person. The park has flush toilets and showers; guests have use of most Hotel Gran Baja facilities, including the pool, beach, and tennis courts.

A bit farther east toward the city center, off Calle Nayarit on the bay, is the **Aquamarina RV Park** (tel. 2-37-61; mailing address: A.P. 133, La Paz, BCS). A favorite among boaters and divers, Aquamarina has its own marina, complete with boat ramp, storage facilities, and air for scuba tanks, plus showers, flush toilets, pool, and laundry facilities. Full hookup sites are US$13 for two persons, plus US$1 per additional guest.

El Carrizal RV Park is about two km south of La Paz off BCS 286, the state highway to San Juan de los Planes. Full hookups at El Carrizal cost US$9; facilities include a large pool, showers, flush toilets, and laundry.

FOOD

Restaurants

La Paz has dining venues for all tastes and budgets; as might be expected for a coastal city, the seafood selection is particularly good. In the evenings, the downtown area centered around the malecón and Calle 16 de Septiembre features a number of street vendors serving fish tacos and *cocteles*. One of the best stands for fish, shrimp, and clam tacos is at the corner of Calle Arreola and Esquerro, opposite the bank.

During the daytime, the cluster of loncherías in the **Mercado Municipal Francisco E. Madero,** Revolución and Degollado, make a very inexpensive grazing spot for antojitos and comidas corridas.

THE PEARLS OF LA PAZ

Pearls develop from sand grains or other small particles that manage to get between an oyster's mantle and its shell. The oyster secretes a substance that cushions it from the irritation of the particle—if the grain moves freely during the secretion buildup, the pearl is more or less spherical; if it stays in one place or is embedded in the shell, it becomes a "baroque" pearl. Even when an oyster doesn't contain a pearl, the interior of the shell is valued for its rainbow luster. Only particular mollusk varieties within the family Pteridae—found only in certain coastal areas in East Asia, Panama, and Baja California—are equipped to form pearls.

Pearl gathering in the New World goes back at least 7,000 years. When the Spanish found Indians along the Sea of Cortez coast wearing pearls and pearl shells as hair ornaments in the early 16th century, they quickly added pearls to the list of exploitable resources in Mexico. Finding the source of the luminescent, milky-white spheres—oyster beds—became a priority of marine expeditions off Mexico's west coast.

After a Spanish mutineer reported the presence of pearls in Bahía de la Paz in 1533, one of Cortés's primary interests in exploring Baja's lower Sea of Cortez coast became harvesting them. Between 1535, when Cortés finally managed to establish a temporary settlement at Bahía de la Paz, and 1697, when Jesuit padres began missionizing the Baja peninsula, untold thousands of pearls from the area were harvested. The Jesuits, however, strongly discouraged any secular exploitation of the peninsula, preferring to keep Baja within the domain of the Church. During the mission period (1697-1768), pearling was restricted to sporadic illegal harvests; still, many pearls found their way to Europe, where they encrusted the robes of bishops and Spanish royalty.

In the mid-19th century, following the secularization of Baja missions, the Baja pearl industry was revived by *armadores* (entrepreneurs) who hired Yaqui divers from Sonora to scour the shallow bays, coves, and island shores between Mulegé and La Paz. The invention of diving suits in 1874 revolutionized pearling by allowing divers access to deeper waters. By 1889 the industry was dominated by Compañía Perlífera de Baja California, based in La Paz. Intensive harvesting rapidly depleted the oysterbeds, and between 1936 and 1941 most of the remaining pearl oysters were wiped out by an unknown disease. Many La Paz residents today believe the disease was somehow introduced by the Japanese to eliminate Mexican competition in the pearl industry, but it's more likely the disease simply took advantage of an already weakened population.

The mystique of La Paz pearls continued long after the industry's demise. John Steinbeck based his novella *The Pearl* on a famous pearl story he heard while visiting La Paz in 1941.

$$-$$$ **Bermejo** (Los Arcos Hotel, Paseo Obregón): One of the better hotel restaurants, enhanced by its location overlooking the malecón (ask for a window table). The menu features mostly seafood, steak, and pasta; open daily for lunch and dinner.

$$ **Bismark II** (tel. 2-48-54, Degollado and Altamirano): A casual, family-run restaurant specializing in lobster, abalone, and carne asada. All meals start with the restaurant's unique *totopos*—instead of chips, they're fried whole tortillas—with a smooth guacamole. The ceviche is also very good. Open daily for lunch and dinner.

$$ **Camarón Feliz ("Happy Shrimp")** (tel. 2-90-11, Obregón and Bravo): A small, cutesy seafood place on the malecón; good *cocteles de camarones* (shrimp cocktails), so-so breakfasts. Open daily for breakfast, lunch, and dinner.

$$-$$$ **El Moro** (tel. 2-40-84, La Paz-Pichilingue Rd., Km 2): Elegant atmosphere, fresh seafood, Sonoran steaks, and international specialties; impeccable service. Open Tues.-Sun. for breakfast, lunch, and dinner.

$$ **El Taste** (tel. 822-8121, Paseo Obregón and Juárez): An old-timer featuring steaks, Mexican, and seafood, patronized by a mostly

tourist and ex-pat clientele. Open daily for breakfast, lunch, and dinner.

$ El Quinto Sol (tel. 2-16-92, Calle Domínguez and Independencia): This natural food/vegetarian store has a café section serving tortas, comida corrida, pastries, salads, granola, fruit and vegetable juices, and yogurt. Open daily 0800-2200.

$-$$ Imperiales (tel. 2-95-96, Calle 5 de Mayo 1345): La Paz's tiny Chinatown harbors five or six Chinese restaurants, of which this is usually considered the best. Basically Cantonese, with Mexican influences; open daily for lunch and dinner.

$$ La Fabula Pizza (three locations: Obregón and Independencia; Obregón and Altos; La Católica and Allende): American-style pizza and Italian specialties. Very popular with young Paceños. Open daily for lunch and dinner.

$$ La Paz-Lapa de Carlos 'n Charlie's (tel. 2-60-25, Paseo Obregón and M. de León): A large palapa restaurant on the malecón with the usual Mexican-kitsch Carlos 'n Charlie's decor. The Mexican and seafood menu is good, but you might want to give it a miss if a cruise ship is in town—the passengers tend to take over this restaurant en masse, flashbulbs popping. Open Wed.-Mon. for lunch and dinner.

$-$$ La Terraza (tel. 2-07-77, Paseo Obregón 1570): This outdoor cafe beneath the Hotel Perla has an extensive menu of seafood, Mexican, steak, and Italian that attracts a steady crowd of both tourists and locals. Besides being the best place in town for people-watching, the food is reasonably priced and reasonably tasty.

$$-$$$ Las Brisas (Paseo Obregón at Calle Heróico Colegio Militar): Upscale palapa restaurant with a romantic atmosphere and a varied menu of steaks, seafood, Mexican, and Chinese. Open daily for dinner only.

$ Los Arcos Cafetería (Hotel Los Arcos, Paseo Obregón): A self-service coffeeshop with inexpensive Mexican and international dishes; open daily 0600-2200.

$ Mr. Taco (no phone, Paseo Obregón and Salvatierra): Though it's a bit removed from the central malecón action, you won't find a larger selection (18 kinds) of tacos in La Paz. Open daily 1100-2200.

$-$$ Palapa Adriana (tel. 2-83-26, on the beach at Paseo Obregón, between 5 de Mayo and Constitución): One of the malecón's original palapa restaurant-bars, with fresh seafood, *carnes rajas* (grilled steak), and Mexican standards.

$ Parilla Norteña (tel. 5-07-70, Calle 5 de Mayo 1007): Northern Mexican specialties—including 20 varieties of seafood, chicken, and beef tacos—and *hamburguesas*. Open daily 1300-2400.

$$ Samalú (tel. 2-24-81, Calle Rangel between Jalisco and Colima): A mostly seafood restaurant housed in a thatched-roof A-frame, popular with Old Baja Hands. Open daily for lunch and dinner.

$ Super Pollo (two locations: Calle 5 de Febrero and Gómez Farías; Blvd. Forjadores and Loreto): A good, economic choice for *pollo asado al carbón estilo Sinaloa,* Sinaloa-style grilled chicken, sold with tortillas and salsa. Eat in or take out; open daily 1100-2200.

Groceries

The **Mercado Municipal Francisco E. Madero,** at Revolución and Degollado, houses a collection of vendor stalls purveying fresh fish, meats, fruit, and vegetables at free-market (non-subsidized) prices—usually posted, no bargaining necessary. Nearby at the corner of Revolución and Bravo is a tortillería.

La Paz has several supermarkets, including the large **CCC** (Centro Comercial California) outlets at Av. Abasolo and Calle Colima and at La Católica and Bravo. These carry American-brand packaged foods as well as Mexican, but prices are about twice what you'd usually pay elsewhere in town. The government-subsidized **ISSSTE tienda** at Calle Altamirano and Bravo has the best grocery prices in the city, although the selection varies according to what ISSSTE has been able to purchase cheaply that week. The **Tienda Militar** ("Military Store") on Calle 5 de Mayo at Padre Kino has a larger selection than ISSSTE tienda and is almost as inexpensive.

Two stores in La Paz specialize in natural foods. **El Quinto Sol** (Domínguez and Independencia) offers natural juices, wheat gluten, soybean meat substitutes (including soybean chorizo), whole wheat flour, herbs, yogurt, and ice cream, as well as a few ready-to-eat items like tortas and salads. **Los Girasoles** (tel. 2-55-90, Calle Revolución between Hidalgo and Morelos) has a bakery, veggie sandwiches, yogurt, granola, vitamins, and various whole grains.

At the other end of the nutritional spectrum are two *dulcerías* (sweet shops) on the corner of Calle Ocampo and Serdán. **Dulcería Perla** has a complete selection of traditional and modern Mexican sweets, while **Dulcería La Coneja** on the opposite corner specializes in candy-filled *piñatas* (including some in the shape of Teenage Mutant Ninja Turtles). #35 Downtown La Paz Map

ENTERTAINMENT AND EVENTS

Bullfights
The municipal stadium at Calle Constitución and Verdad hosts *corridas de toros* in the late winter months (usually Feb.-March). For information on the latest schedule, contact the state tourism office (see p. 305).

Bars, Discos, And Night Clubs
The **Bar Pelicanos,** overlooking the malecón in Hotel Los Arcos, is a large, sedate watering hole popular among tourists and Old Hands. It's worth at least one visit to peruse the old photos along the back wall; subjects include a motley array of unnamed vaqueros and revolutionaries, Pancho Villa, Gen. Blackjack Pershing, Pres. Eisenhower, Emiliano Zapata, and Clark Gable posing with a marlin. The bar is open daily until 0100.

Also on the Paseo Obregón, a few blocks west of Hotel Los Arcos, is the casual and sometimes lively **Tortuga Loca,** where the clientele is predominantly local. Take a seat by the windows to take advantage of bay breezes, unimpeded by glass or screens. Drinks are reasonably priced and sometimes arrive with a complimentary plate of *botanas*.

Living up to its laid-back reputation, La Paz isn't big on discos. The most popular dance

spot among young Paceños is the two-story **OK Maguey** (tel. 2-31-33) at Paseo Obregón and La Paz. An older, mixed tourist-local crowd patronizes the Hotel Palmira's disco, **El Rollo,** which features a mix of international and Latin recordings and occasional live music. The **Cabaña Club,** at the Hotel Perla, usually has live music and attracts a more local, good-time crowd.

Events
La Paz's biggest annual celebration is **Carnaval,** held for six days before Ash Wednesday (mid-February). Carnaval is also held in the Mexican cities of Santa Rosalía, Ensenada, and Veracruz, but Carnaval connoisseurs claim La Paz's is the best—perhaps because the city's malecón makes a perfect parade route.

As at all Mexican Carnavals, the festival begins with the Quema de Mal Humor, or "Burning of Bad Humor," in which an effigy representing an unpopular public figure is burned. Other events include the crowning of La Reina del Carnaval ("Carnaval Queen") and El Rey Feo ("Ugly King"), colorful costumed parades, music, dancing, feasting, cockfights, and fireworks. The festival culminates in El Día del Marido Oprimido, the "Day of the Oppressed Husband"—23½ hours of symbolic freedom for married men to do whatever they wish—followed by a masquerade ball on the Tuesday evening before Ash Wednesday.

Also prominent on the city's yearly events calendar is the **Fiesta de la Paz,** held May 3, the anniversary of the founding of the city. The state tourist office can provide up-to-date details on festival scheduling and venues.

SHOPPING

Until recently, imported merchandise could be purchased in La Paz free of import duties and sales tax. The city's duty-free status was recalled in 1989, however, and sales tax is now commensurate with the rest of Mexico's. But the city still offers some of Baja's best shopping in terms of value and variety, starting with the downtown department stores of **Dorian's** (Calles 16 de Septiembre and Esquerro) and **Perla de la Paz** (Calles Arreola and Mutualismo).

Along Paseo Obregón in the vicinity of the Hotel Perla and Hotel Los Arcos are a number of souvenir and handicraft shops of varying quality. One of the better ones is **Artesanías La Antigua California,** at Paseo Obregón 220, which sells quality folk arts and crafts from the mainland. Away from the downtown area, the **Centro de Arte Regional** (Calles Chiapas and Encinas) produces and sells pot-

tery, while **Artesanía Cuauhtémoc** (Av. Abasolo between Jalisco and Nayarit) weaves rugs, blankets, wall-hangings, tablecloths, and other cotton or wool items. Custom orders are also taken, and customers are welcome to watch the weavers at their looms in back of the shop.

For tourist-variety souvenirs, especially T-shirts, **Bye-Bye** (four blocks east of Hotel Perla on Paseo Obregón) is a good choice. **Soko's Curios** (Obregón and 5 de Septiembre) is strictly for collectors of Mexican kitsch.

DOWNTOWN LA PAZ

© MOON PUBLICATIONS, INC.

For bottom-dollar bargains on clothing and housewares, browse the **Mercado Municipal Francisco E. Madero** at Revolución and Degollado.

SPORTS AND RECREATION

Beaches

Bahía de la Paz is scalloped with nine public beaches. At the northwest end of the bay are **Playa El Comitán** and **Playa Las Hamacas,** both shallow beaches that tend toward mud flats in low tide. More inviting are the seven beaches strung out east of the city along the Pichilingue Peninsula—they get better the farther from the city you go. **Playa Palmira,** around four km (2½ miles) east of downtown La Paz via the La Paz-Pichilingue Rd., is now monopolized by the Hotel Palmira and Marina de Palmira. A kilometer farther, the small but pleasant **Playa El Coromuel** offers restaurant-bar service, palapas, and a waterslide.

Playa del Tesoro, 14 km (8½ miles) from the city, is another casual, semi-urban beach with palapas and a restaurant. At Km 17, just beyond the SEMATUR ferry terminal, is **Playa Pichilingue,** the only public beach in the La Paz vicinity with restrooms available 24 hours (for campers). The beach also has a modest palapa restaurant.

After Pichilingue the paved road ends; the road to the remaining three beaches is sandy, but passable by passenger car except in heavy rains. None of these beaches has palapas (or any natural shade), restaurants, restrooms, or drinking water, so both campers and day-trippers should come prepared. The turnoff for **Playa Balandra** appears five km (three miles) beyond Pichilingue, and then it's another kilometer to the parking area and a short walk to the beach.

Depending on the tide, the large, shallow bay of Puerto Balandra actually forms several beaches, some of them long sandbars. Ringed by cliffs and steep hills, the bay is a beautiful and usually secluded spot (weekends are the exception), perfect for wading in the clear, warm waters. Clams are fairly abundant; a coral reef at the south end of the bay offers decent snorkeling. Climb the rock cliffs (carefully) for sweeping bay views. Camping is permitted at Balandra, but oftentimes a lack of breeze brings out the *jejenes* (no-see-ums), especially in the late summer and early fall.

About three km (1½ miles) beyond the Playa Balandra turnoff is **Playa El Tecolote,** a wide, steep beach backed by vegetated dunes. Because Tecolote is open to the stiff breezes of Canal de San Lorenzo, the camping here is usually insect-free. After Tecolote the road worsens a bit as it passes a small goat ranch before ending at remote **Playa Cachimba,** at the base of a rocky headland. Both Tecolote and Cachimba are good put-in points for kayak trips to **Isla Espíritu Santo,** 6½ km (four miles) away. Because of winds and tidal currents, this isn't a trip for the novice sea kayaker.

Islands

The 22½-km-long (14-mile-long) **Isla Espíritu Santo** and its smaller immediate neighbor to the north, **Isla Partida,** are excellent destinations for all manner of sailing craft from sea kayaks to yachts. Sandy beaches and large coves along the western shores of both islands offer an abundance of opportunities for small-craft landings and camping. **Punta Lupona,** on the southern tip of Espíritu Santo, is just 6½ km (four miles) from Pichilingue Peninsula (see "Beaches" above), and the shallow channel between Espíritu Santo and Partida is only a few hundred meters across.

At the south end of Isla Partida are a couple of fish camps where drinking water and food might be available in an emergency—but don't count on it. There are usually plenty of yachts in the vicinity. Just north of Partida are **Los Islotes,** a group of islets popular among divers, anglers, and sea lions.

Fishing

Outer bay and offshore fishing in the La Paz area are very good; a boat is mandatory since there is little onshore or surf fishing. In the bay or in the canals west of the islands are roosterfish, pargo, cabrilla, needlefish, bonito, amberjack, jack crevalle, yellowtail, sierra, and pompano. Beyond Isla Espíritu Santo are the larger gamefish, including dorado, grouper, marlin, tuna, and sailfish. Yellowtail usually run in the area Jan.-March, while most other gamefish in this area reach peak numbers April-November. Canal de Cerralvo, around the other side of Pichilingue Peninsula, is excellent for roosterfish and pargo colorado Jan.-July.

Any of the major La Paz hotels can arrange fishing trips; one of the longest-running operations is **Dorado Velez Fleet** (tel. 2-27-44) at Hotel Los Arcos. Another established outfit is **Fisherman's Fleet** (tel. 2-13-13), also with a desk at Los Arcos. Guides and boats can also be arranged at the pier just east of the Pichilingue ferry terminal. Panga fishing trips in the bay generally cost US$80-90 a day for two persons, beyond Isla Espíritu Santo or to Canal de Cerralvo around US$160; long-range fishing cruises run US$200-300 a day and can usually accommodate up to four anglers.

Fishing tackle is available at **Deportiva La Paz** (tel. 2-73- 33), Paseo Obregón 1680.

Boating

With a huge, protected bay, four public marinas (plus one private), and several boatyards and marine supply stores, La Paz is Baja California's largest and best-equipped boating center. Northeast of town, on the Canal de la Paz at Km 2.5, **Marina Palmira** (tel. 2- 42-77, fax 5-39-59; mailing address: A.P. 34, La Paz, BCS), currently offers 146 slips, with electricity, for yachts up to 42½ meters (140 feet), as well as dry-storage facilities. This marina also offers crewed and bareboat yacht charters. Slip rates range US$5.75-7.25 per foot, with discounts for long-term moorings. Condos adjacent to the marina are also available for rent by day, week, or month.

At the west end of the malecón (Calles Topete and Legaspi) is the **Marina de La Paz** (tel. 2-16-46; mailing address: A.P. 290, La Paz, BCS), owned by panga-designer Mac Shroyer. Facilities include a launch ramp, fuel dock, water and electricity, laundry, showers, restrooms, chandlery, vehicle storage, and 80 slips. Daily rates range from US$13 for a six- to nine-meter (20- to 30-foot) craft to US$36 for anything over 19 meters (63 feet), up to a max of 22.8 meters (75 feet). The daily rate is discounted June-Oct. and monthly

rates are available. Showers cost US$1. Marina de la Paz is by far the most popular marina in the bay and is often full Nov.-May; call or write in advance to check for vacancies before sailing in.

Next to the Hotel Gran Baja is the **La Paz Yacht Club,** a private marina open to members only. Still under construction is La Paz's fifth docking facility, the government-financed **FIDEPAZ Marina** on the waterfront near the state tourist office. Trailered and car-topped boats can be launched at Marina de la Paz, Marina Palmira, Aquamarina RV Park, and at Pichilingue. Smaller boats and kayaks can also be launched at any of the public beaches.

Pangas: If you're in the market for a new panga, La Paz just happens to be the panga capital of Mexico. American Malcolm ("Mac") Shroyer, the first person to design and build the molded fiberglass panga, produces them at his panga factory at Calle Navarro 960. Until 1968, when Mac started his small factory, many Sea of Cortez fishermen still used dugout canoes of Indian design; now his glass pangas are sold all over Mexico.

The standard panga is sold in 18-, 20- or 22-foot lengths, but the factory can build special orders as long as 36 feet. The standard outboard motor for a panga is the "cinco-cinco caballos" (55 horsepower). Prices run US$3200-4200 each, depending on whether a canopy, stowage compartment, or other options are included. To arrange for a tour of the factory or to inquire about panga sales, call Mac or his wife Mary at Marina de la Paz (tel. 2-16-46).

Parts and Repairs: Marina de la Paz is the best local source of information for boating needs. A booklet by Janet Calvert entitled *La Paz Boater's Guide to Goods and Services,* available at the marina, contains a thorough list of all the boatyards, outboard-motor shops, and marine supply stores in La Paz. Boaters at the marina can also offer recommendations for the best places to acquire boat parts and repairs.

Diving

Some of Baja's best dive sites are in the La Paz vicinity, but most are accessible only by boat. As elsewhere in the Sea of Cortez, the optimum diving months are Aug.-Nov., when visibility reaches 30 meters (100 feet) or more. During the late fall and winter months, visibility is reduced and a light wetsuit is necessary.

One of the most popular diving spots is the wreck of the *Salvatierra,* a 91-meter (300-feet) La Paz-Topolobampo ferry that went down in the Canal de San Lorenzo in 1976. The hull lies about 2½ k,m a half mile southeast of the southern tip of Isla Espíritu Santo at a depth of approximately 10 fathoms (18 meters/60 feet). Encrusted with sponges, sea fans, mollusks, and gorgonians, the wreck attracts numerous varieties of tropical fish, including groupers, barracuda, angelfish, goatfish, parrotfish, moray eels, and rays.

Along the western shores of **Isla Espíritu Santo** and **Isla Partida** are several good diving reefs. Bahía San Gabriel, a large cove along Espíritu Santo's southwest shore, has a shallow boulder reef at its northern end suitable for both scuba diving and snorkeling. A similar reef is found farther north off Espíritu Santo's western shore, extending from the west side of **Isla Ballena.**

The most colorful dive site in the vicinity is **Los Islotes,** the tiny islet group off the north end of Isla Partida. Boulder reefs and underwater pinnacles off the north and northeast draw large marine species, including schools of hammerhead sharks, manta rays, and other pelagic (open-ocean) fish. A nearby cove is home to a large colony of sea lions who seem to enjoy swimming alongside divers and performing tricks for the camera. Late in the breeding season (Jan.-May) is the best time to visit the colony, since this is when the adolescent pups are most playful.

To the southwest of Los Islotes is **El Bajito,** a large rock reef that extends within six meters (20 feet) of the sea's surface; the base of the reef meets a sandy bottom at about 24-28 meters (80-90 feet). The diverse marinelife frequenting the reef includes grouper, cabrilla, and an unusually large number of morays; attached to the rocks are gorgonians, sea fans, and a variety of other invertebrate creatures.

A group of three sea pinnacles called **El Bajo** (also known as Marisla Seamount), about 13 km (8.2 miles) northeast of Los Islotes, is renowned for the presence of large pelagics such as marlin, shark (hammerhead, blacktip, tiger, silvertip), dorado, corvina, and manta rays. Mantas frequent El Bajo from July to mid-Oct., and for unknown reasons they often allow divers in this area to "hitch" rides by holding onto their backs near the pectoral fins. Whale sharks, the largest fish in the world (see "Flora and Fauna" in the main introduction), are occasionally seen near El Bajo during the same months, as are pilot whales.

Due to strong tidal currents, Los Islotes, El Bajito, and El Bajo are best left to experienced open-ocean divers.

Dive Shops: The granddaddy of all dive outfits in La Paz is Fernando Aguilar's **Baja Buceo y Servicio** (tel. 2-18-26, fax 2-86-44) at Av. Independencia 107-B. Besides offering equipment sales and rental, Aguilar organizes dive trips to the *Salvatierra,* El Bajo, and Los Islotes for US$70 a day including a guide, transport, lunch, unlimited sodas and beer, and full gear. Basic scuba certification costs US$90; a complete open-water diving certification course is available for US$280. In addition, BBS offers snorkeling trips for US$25 (beach) and US$35 (sea lion colony), as well as windsurfing equipment and instruction.

Other La Paz dive outfits include **La Paz Diving Service** (tel. 2-37-61), **Baja Expeditions** (tel. 2-89-15), and **Deportes Acuaticos** (tel. 2-39-00). Diving equipment is available at **Deportiva La Paz** (tel. 2-73-33), Paseo Obregón 1680, although this shop doesn't organize dive trips.

LA PAZ INFORMATION AND SERVICES

Tourist Offices

Baja California Sur's SECTUR office (tel. 2-11-99, fax 2-77-22) is between Km 6 and 5 on Mexico 1 (Av. Abasolo) opposite the FIDEPAZ Marina. The friendly staff speak English and can assist with most tourist inquiries; the Attorney for the Protection of Tourists is also stationed here. The office maintains an information booth for the distribution of maps and brochures on the malecón near Calle 16 de Septiembre. Office and booth are open Mon.-Sat., 0800-1900.

Newspapers

Two Spanish-language dailies are published in La Paz: *La Extra* and *El Sudcaliforniano*. The *Baja California News,* an English-language monthly based in Cabo San Lucas but printed in La Paz, usually carries a few tourist-oriented features on the La Paz area.

Librería Contiempo, a bookstore on Calle Arrelo at Paseo Obregón, carries *The News* from Mexico City and day-old editions of the *Los Angeles Times.*

Changing Money

Several banks and money changers are found in the area around Calle 16 de Septiembre. As elsewhere in Baja, the foreign exchange service at banks is only open Mon.-Fri. before noon. Money changers *(casas de cambio)* stay open till early evening and on Saturday, but are closed on Sunday, when your only alternative is to change money at a hotel at lower rates. Pesos are a must for everyday purchases in La Paz; city merchants are not as receptive to U.S.-dollar transactions as their counterparts in Ensenada or Cabo San Lucas simply because they're not as used to them.

Post Office

The main post and telegraph office is at Calle Revolución and Constitución, a block north-

---

USEFUL LA PAZ TELEPHONE NUMBERS

(La Paz area code: 682)

Police	2-07-81
Red Cross	2-11-11, 2-12-22
Highway Patrol	2-03-69, 2-87-98
IMSS Hospital	2-73-77
Tourist Attorney	2-59-39
State Tourism Office	2-11-99
Immigration	2-04-29
Ferry Office	5-38-33, 5-51-17

---

east of the cathedral; it's open Mon.- Fri. 0800-1300 and 1500-1900, Sat. 0800-1300.

Immigration

If you're planning to cross the Sea of Cortez by ferry and haven't had your tourist card validated yet, stop by the immigration office (tel. 2-04-29), opposite the Muelle Fiscal ("Public Pier") at Paseo Obregón and Calle Muelle, for a validation. It's usually open Mon.-Fri. 0800-1500. The immigration office at the Pichilingue ferry terminal is open only an hour or so before each ferry departure.

TRANSPORT

Air

La Paz International Airport (LAP) is 12 km south of the city; the airport access road leaves Mexico 1 at Km 9. **Aeromexico** (tel. 2-00-91, 2-16-36, Paseo Obregón between Hidalgo and Morelos) offers daily nonstop flights between La Paz and Los Angeles, Culiacán, Guaymas, Tijuana, and Mexico City, as well as connecting flights to San Francisco, Tucson, Indianapolis, Baltimore, and a number of Mexican cities.

Aero California (tel. 2-11-13, 2-83-92, Paseo Obregón 550 at Bravo) has daily nonstops to/from Culiacán, Loreto, Los Mochis, Mazatlán, and Tijuana, plus connecting flights to Los Angeles (via Loreto) and Mexico City (via Mazatlán).

Land

Intercity Bus: La Paz has two intercity bus terminals. From Terminal Malecón, Paseo Obregón 125, Transportes Aguila runs deluxe buses between La Paz and Pichilingue (US$.70, every two hours 0800-1200, hourly thereafter till 1800), San José (US$5, five buses a day), and Cabo San Lucas (US$6, five buses a day).

Central Camionera, used mainly by Tres Estrellas de Oro buses, is at Calle Jalisco and Independencia. From here, buses depart regularly for Loreto (US$8.50) Santa Rosalía (US$11), Ensenada (US$21), Tijuana (US$25), and Mexicali (US$28). Transportes

Aguila also has buses from this terminal to the central Cape Region towns of El Triunfo (US$1), San Antonio (US$1), San Bartolo (US$1.50), Santiago (US$2.50), and Miraflores (US$3). Local buses for Todos Santos (US$2) leave from the local bus terminal at Calle Revolución and Degollado, next to the Mercado Municipal, and continue to Cabo San Lucas (US$4).

Driving: For now, Mexico 1 is the only federal highway leading to La Paz. A local consortium sponsored by CANACINTRA (National Chamber of Manufacturing Industries) has recently announced plans to develop a new four-lane toll road that would run along the west coast from Ensenada to La Paz the entire way (instead of turning inland at El Rosario as does Mexico 1).

Fuel: La Paz is blessed with seven PEMEX stations, all of which offer Magna Sin (unleaded) as well as Nova (leaded).

Sea
The ferry port at Pichilingue, 16 km (9½ miles) northeast of downtown La Paz, serves vehicle and passenger ferries between La Paz and two mainland destinations, Topolobampo (for Los Mochis) and Mazatlán. **SEMATUR** (tel. 5-38-33, 5-51-17, fax 2-52-58) runs passenger and vehicle-ferries to and from both cities; **Baja Express** (tel. 5-63-11, fax 5-63-10) operates a passenger-only jetfoil to and from Topolobampo. SEMATUR ferry tickets can be booked in advance at the ferry terminal (tel. 2-51-17, 2-50-05), the city ticket office (tel. 5-38-33, 6-46-66) at Calle 5 de Mayo and Guillermo Prieto, or Turismo La Paz (tel. 2-76-76, 2-83-00) at the Hotel Perla.

The Baja Express office (tel. 5-63-11, 5-63-13, fax 5-63-10) is at Paseo Obregón and 16 de Septiembre. Tickets for the Baja Express jetfoil service can also be booked at several La Paz travel agencies and hotels. For full details regarding fares, schedules, and reservations for both SEMATUR and Baja Express services, see "Ferry and Jetfoil," under the main introduction.

Vehicle Permits: Tourist cards must have a special endorsement (a temporary import permit) for vehicular travel on the Mexican

La Paz-Mazatlan ferry (JOE CUMMINGS)

mainland. These permits aren't needed for Baja California travel, but if you've driven down to La Paz and decide you'd like to take your wheels on a mainland-bound ferry, you'll need to get one before boarding. Fortunately the proper permit can be arranged in advance in La Paz—simply apply at the customs office at the ferry terminal a day or two in advance of departure. Bring your vehicle plus all immigration and registration papers. The Registro Federal de Vehículos, on Calle Domínguez at 5 de Febrero, does not issue temporary import permits.

Private Boats: La Paz is an official Mexican port of entry and, as such, the COTP office at the Muelle Fiscal has authority to clear yachts for movement throughout Mexican waters. The easiest way to arrange this is to check in at the Marina de la Paz and let the marina staff process all port clearance papers. For Marina de la Paz clients, clear-in service is free, clear-out is US$10; for non-clients it's US$5 in, US$15 out. (Only one clearance in and out is needed for entering and exiting the country; between Mexican ports the same papers can be presented.) See "Boating," p. 71, for information on the five La Paz marinas.

Local Public Transport
Most points of interest downtown may be reached on foot. For outlying areas in the city, you can choose among city buses, hire taxis, and route taxis.

Bus: As in other towns on the peninsula, La Paz city buses bear either the name of the principal street along which they run or a district where their route begins and ends. Any bus marked "El Centro," for example, will end up near the Mercado Municipal at Revolución and Degollado. Bus fare anywhere in town is around US$.30. Buses to Pichilingue depart from the Terminal Malecón (Paseo Obregón 125) regularly 0800-1800; the fare is US$.70.

Taxi: Taxi stands are found throughout El Centro (the downtown area between Calles 5 de Mayo and Degollado) and in front of the tourist hotels. The average taxi hire downtown costs around US$3; La Paz taxis don't have meters, so it's sometimes necessary to haggle to arrive at the correct fare. A taxi to the airport should be US$10 (some hotels operate airport vans that cost US$3 per person).

Route taxis *(taxi de ruta)* operate along the main avenues parallel to city buses for about US$.35 per person.

Auto Rental: Several La Paz travel agencies can arrange auto rental, but rates are generally lower if you deal directly with a rental agency. **Servitur Autorento** (tel. 2-14-48), at Calles 5 de Febrero and Abasolo, **Auto Renta Sol** (tel. 2-45-45, Paseo Obregón and 16 de Septiembre), and **Budget** (tel. 2-10-97), at Paseo Obregón and Hidalgo, offer Volkswagens bugs, vans, and Jettas for US$25-40 per day, plus a per-kilometer charge.

VICINITY OF LA PAZ

San Juan De Los Planes-
Punta Arena De La Ventana

State highway BCN 286 begins south of La Paz off Mexico 1 (at Km 211) and leads south-east 43 km (26 miles) to the agricultural center of San Juan de los Planes. Along the way this paved road climbs over the northwestern escarpment of the Sierra de la Laguna and then descends toward the coastal plains with a panoramic view of aquamarine Bahía de la Ventana and Isla Cerralvo in the distance. At Km 38 a graded road branches northeast off BCN 286 eight km (five miles) to the fish camps of La Ventana and El Sargento on **Bahía de la Ventana.**

Windsurfing is good here due to the strong northeasterlies channeled through Canal de Cerralvo to the north. Free beach camping is possible along the bay just south of La Ventana.

San Juan de los Planes, or "Los Planes" as it's usually called, has several markets, a café and around 1,500 inhabitants supported by farming (cotton, tomatoes, beans, and corn) or by fishing at nearby bays. From Los Planes, a graded road runs east 21 km (13 miles) to **Bahía de los Muertos,** a pretty, curved bay with primitive beach camping.

A lesser road branches northeast about three km before los Muertos and leads eight km (five miles) to Punta Arena de la Ventana and the **Hotel Las Arenas,** a fishing and diving resort with its own 1,820-meter (6,000-foot) airstrip (Unicom 122.8). Rooms with fans and sea views cost US$75-85 s, US$115-150 d; facilities at the hotel include a beach, pool, tennis courts, and recreational equipment (pangas, sailboards).

The waters off Punta Arena de la Ventana reputedly offer Baja's best roosterfish angling; wahoo, amberjack, grouper, dorado, and billfish are also said to be in abundant supply. Guided fishing cruises are available at the Hotel Las Arenas for US$200 per day. A bit south of the hotel, at **Punta Perico** ("Parakeet Point"), is a lively reef with varied depths of 3-25 meters (10-82 feet).

Isla Cerralvo

Opposite Bahía de la Ventana and Canal de Cerralvo, **Isla Cerralvo** is one of the largest islands in the Sea of Cortez (about 30 km/18 miles from north to south). At the time of early Spanish exploration, the island featured large pearl-oyster beds and was inhabited by a small group of Pericú Indians. Later the rugged island reportedly became a favored final resting place for *vagabundos del mar,* Mexican-Indians who roamed the Sea of Cortez in dugout canoes until well into this century.

Today Cerralvo remains one of the least visited of Baja's large coastal islands, simply due to its location on the far side of the Pich-

VICINITY OF
LA PAZ

© MOON PUBLICATIONS, INC.

LOS ISLOTES

ISLA PARTIDA

ISLA ESPÍRITU SANTO

SEA OF CORTEZ

CANAL DE SAN LORENZO

PLAYA EL TECOLOTE

PUERTO BALANDRA   PLAYA BALANDRA

PLAYA PICHILINGUE

BAHÍA DE LA PAZ

PICHILINGUE

BAHÍA PICHILINGUE

PLAYA DEL TESORO

11

PLAYA EL COROMUEL

PLAYA PALMIRA

PENÍNSULA EL MOGOTE

PLAYA EL COMITÁN

ENSENADA DE LA PAZ

CANAL DE LA PAZ

LA PAZ

PLAYA LAS HAMACAS

EL CENTENARIO

LA PAZ INTERNATIONAL AIRPORT

TO CABO SAN LUCAS

0   2mi
0   2km

1

---

ilingue Peninsula. Coral-encrusted **Roca Montaña,** off the southeastern tip of the island, is an excellent diving and fishing location, as is **Piedras Gordas** (marked by a navigation light) at the southwestern tip. Depths at these sites range 3-15 meters (10-50 feet). Other good dive sites are the rock reefs off the northern end (average depth 18-21 meters/60-70 feet). One of the reefs, Arrecife de la Foca, features an un-

identified shipwreck with "Mazatlán" marked on its hull.

Access to Isla Cerralvo is easiest from Bahía de la Ventana or Punta Arena, where beach launches are possible. From La Paz, it's a long haul around the Pichilingue Peninsula via Canal de San Lorenzo.

CENTRAL CAPE

Along Mexico 1 between La Paz and San José del Cabo are a number of mining-turned-farming towns with cobblestone streets and 19th-century stone-and-stucco architecture. Nestled among well-watered arroyos of the Sierra de la Laguna, these neglected settlements now support themselves by growing citrus, avocado, mangoes, corn, and sugarcane, and, to a lesser extent, by serving the needs of passing travelers. Many of the families living in the central Cape Region are descended from Spanish settlers of the 18th and early 19th centuries. Others are newcomers—including a few *norteamericanos*—who were drawn by the area's solitude and simplicity.

San Pedro appears (and quickly disappears) just before the junction of Mexico 1 and Mexico 19. Carnitas connoisseurs swear by **El Paraíso de San Pedro,** an unassuming roadside café on the highway's west side. The junction itself is reached at Km 185; if Cabo San Lucas is your destination, you must decide whether to take Mexico 19 via Todos Santos or the Transpeninsular Highway (Mexico 1) via El Triunfo, San Antonio, San Bartolo, Santiago, and Miraflores.

For trailers, RVs and other wide or lengthy vehicles, Mexico 19 is the better choice since it runs along relatively flat terrain. South of San Pedro, Mexico 1 winds through the Sierra Laguna and features a succession of dizzying curves and steep grades. Unless you're in a hurry to reach Cabo San Lucas, Mexico 1 is the most scenic choice for drivers of autos and light trucks.

El Triunfo-San Antonio
During the Jesuit missionary period, this section along the lower northern slopes of the

sierra was earmarked for cattle ranching. Mining concessions moved in following the discovery of silver near San Antonio in 1748, and the settlement quickly grew into a town of 10,000 people. When Loreto was heavily damaged by a hurricane in 1829, San Antonio briefly served as capital of the Californias before the capital was transferred to La Paz in 1830.

Gold and silver were discovered at El Triunfo ("Triumph"), seven km (4½ miles) north of San Antonio, in 1862. Both towns bustled with frontier commerce through the end of the 19th century, when the ore began running out; then a hurricane in 1918 flooded the mines, and by 1925 both towns were virtually abandoned. Today El Triunfo has only around 700 residents, San Antonio around 1,000. A number of historic adobe buildings in both towns have been restored, including San Antonio's unusual 1825 church exhibiting train and paddlewheeler motifs. San Antonio also boasts a PEMEX station, post office, and a few markets.

A fun time to visit San Antonio is June 13, the feast day of St. Anthony, when the whole town (and El Triunfo) turns out for music and dancing.

San Bartolo

Beginning just past Km 128, San Bartolo is the greenest and lushest of the central Cape settings because of a large spring that gushes straight out of a mountainside into the arroyo. To complete the tropical picture, many homes sport thatched roofs. Mangoes, avocados, and other fresh fruits are available at roadside stands or in town. **Restaurant El Paso,** on the east side of highway, serves meals.

San Bartolo's patron saint day is June 19 (conveniently close to San Antonio's).

Santiago

The largest of the central Cape Region towns (pop. 2,500), set in the Arroyo de Santiago among stands of blue fan palms, was originally founded as a mission community in 1723. The mission was abandoned in the latter half of the 18th century following a series of Pericú rebellions, and it has only

been in relatively recent times that agriculture has revived the arroyo community. A handful of *tiendas* line the town plaza; the town also has a PEMEX station, hotel, supermarket, church, and the only zoo on the peninsula south of Mexicali. Among the residents of the small but nicely landscaped **Parque Zoologico** are a peccary, bear, coyote, fox, monkey, parrots, and ducks; some of the animals are Cape Region natives. The park is open daily 0600-1800 and admission is free (donations gladly accepted).

Accommodations and food are available at **El Palomar,** south of the plaza. This eight-room *casa de huéspedes* charges US$20-25 a night; meals—primarily seafood and Mexican standards—are served Mon.-Sat., 0830-2000.

The dirt road to the zoo continues westward nine km (5½ miles) to the village of **Agua Caliente,** where a hot spring in a nearby canyon (about four km/2½ miles west of the village) has been channeled into a concrete tub for recreational purposes. Camping is permitted in the canyon.

At the north end of Santiago, another dirt road leads northwest to Rancho San Dionísio (14½ km/23½ miles), where the Cañon San Dionísio approach to Picacho la Laguna begins. (See "Sierra de la Laguna," below, for information on Laguna hiking routes.)

Santiago celebrates its patron saint day (the feast day of St. James) on July 25.

Three km south of Santiago is a large cement sphere marking the Tropic of Cancer (23.5° north latitude), south of which you are "in the tropics."

Miraflores

A 2½-km (1½-mile) paved road to Miraflores branches west off Mexico 1 at Km 71 next to a PEMEX station. This ranching and farming community is known for leatherwork; **Curtiduría Miraflores** ("Miraflores Tannery"), near the town entrance, sells handmade leather articles.

A dirt road northwest of Miraflores leads to **Boca de la Sierra** ("Mouth of the Sierra"), a settlement at the mouth of Cañon San Bernardo—the second of the three canyons that provide access deep into the Sierra de la Laguna. Another dirt road southwest of town leads to the mouth of Cañon San Pablo, a third Laguna hiking route. Inquire at the tannery about guided trips into the sierra to view Indian rock-art sights.

SIERRA DE LA LAGUNA

The mountainous heart of the Cape Region extends southward from the Llano de la Paz (the plains just south of La Paz) to Cabo San Lucas, a distance of around 135 km (81 miles). Originally named Sierra de la Victoria by the Spanish but renamed Sierra de la Laguna in the early Mexican era, these peaks are unique among sierras in the southern half of Baja California in that they are granitic rather than volcanic. Unlike all the sierras to the north, the entire Laguna range is tilted eastward instead of westward, i.e., its steepest slopes are on the west side of the escarpment rather than the on the east. They're also lined up along a north-south axis instead of in a northwest-southeast direction, the only mountain range on the entire peninsula with this orientation.

Picacho de la Laguna (elevation 2,155 meters/7,090 feet), roughly in the sierra's center, is usually cited as the highest peak in the range, although according to some sources Cerro las Casitas—approximately 6½ km (four miles) southeast of Picacho de la Laguna—is higher. Between these two peaks is a large, flat meadow called La Laguna (elevation 1,700 meters/5,600 feet). This depression held a mountain lake until around 1870 when Cañon San Dionísio became sufficiently eroded to drain away accumulated water.

Relic Environments
This meadow and other flats and high canyons in the Sierra de la Laguna contain a number of "relic environments" which preserve flora and fauna long ago lost to the arid plains below. La Laguna's highlands, in fact, receive more annual precipitation—up to 89 centimeters (35 inches) per year in some microclimates—than any other place in Baja California.

These "islands in the sky" have gathered together a rare mix of desert, tropical, and subalpine species seen growing side by side nowhere else in one place in North America, including mosses and cacti, madrone and monkey flower, palm and willow, and other unlikely combinations. Undisturbed by human progress, deer, coyote, mountain lion, Pacific tree frog, and dozens of hummingbird species also thrive in the highland areas of the sierra.

A growing number of naturalists and outdoor enthusiasts are clamoring for the upper Sierra de la Laguna to be declared a national park. Some Baja maps even optimistically add green shading to the area as if it already had park status. On the darker side, one rumor has it that the state government has plans to allow development in La Laguna meadow. Anyone interested in expressing their support for a Sierra de la Laguna national park should contact offices of Mexico's

(BOB RACE)

SEDUE (Secretaría de Desarollo Urbano y Ecología) and SECTUR (Secretaría de Turismo) in La Paz.

Hiking And Backpacking

The Sierra de la Laguna is a popular hiking area for Cape residents, as it offers the opportunity to leave behind the fig trees and palms of the arid-tropical environment and to walk among cottonwoods and subalpine meadows. Three lengthy east-west canyons provide the principal access into the sierra: Cañon Dionísio, Cañon San Bernardo, and Cañon San Pablo. All three routes enable hikers to tra-

verse the sierra's spine from east to west—or vice versa, although the western escarpment is considerably more precipitous. Primitive campsites are available along each of the three routes.

The best backpacking season for La Laguna is late fall, after the rainy season has passed and sierra streams and tinajas are full. In January and February, temperatures above 1,500 meters (5,000 feet) can dip close to freezing at night; July-Oct. rains may wash out trails and flood the canyons. A compass and good topo map are musts for any trip into the Sierra de la Laguna. (See "Hiking and Backacking," in the main introduction, for recommended maps and map sources.)

The northernmost route, via **Cañon San Dionísio,** leads directly to La Laguna, the range's largest and most impressive meadow. La Laguna also lies between Picacho de la Laguna and Cerro las Casitas, the sierra's tallest peaks, hence the scenery on this hike is impressive. The eastern mouth of the canyon is reached via a dirt road to Rancho San Dionísio from Santiago (19 km/12 miles), from where it's a 13-km (eight-mile) hike west through the canyon to La Laguna at just under 1,800 meters (6,000 feet).

Those wishing to traverse the sierra can descend westward from La Laguna another seven km (11 miles) to San Juan del Aserradero (La Burrera), a village on the sierra's western slopes around 17½ km (11 miles) northeast of Todos Santo. From either side of the sierra (some hikers prefer to begin on the Todos Santos side), count on three days to La Laguna and back with time to explore the area—six days for a complete traverse.

The next route south, via **Cañon San Bernardo,** is a relatively easy hike that crests at around 900 meters (3,000 feet). The canyon trailhead is accessible via an eight-km (five-mile) dirt road from Miraflores to Boca de la Sierra, where the trail skirts a dam and follows the canyon to the crest, 16 km (10 miles) northwest. Several pools along the way provide fresh water year-round. From the 900-meter mark, the trail continues over the sierra to the village of Santo Domingo on the western side, for a total traverse of 22½ km (14 miles). The Cañon San Bernardo crossing makes a good four- to five-day hike, although it's possible to make a quick overnight to the crest and back from the eastern approach.

Cañon San Pablo provides the southernmost route into the sierra, and reaches an elevation of around 1,000 meters (3,250 feet). The canyon mouth is best reached by taking a 6½-km (four-mile) dirt road west from Caduaño, a village four km (2½ miles) south of Miraflores, to Rancho El Salto. From Rancho El Salto, the crest is reached in approximately 10½ km (6½ miles); the trail continues over the ridge and along a steeper 4.8-km (three-mile) westward descent to the village of El Guerigo on the other side, where a network of dirt roads leads west to Mexico 19. A leisurely El Salto-El Guerigo hike takes four to five days.

Guides

Anyone unsure of their backpacking and orienteering skills should consider hiring a local guide for Sierra de la Laguna trips, since Laguna trails are often obscured, and junctions are not always obvious. A guide can also prepare simple camp meals and point out items of natural interest—e.g., Indian rock art, flora, and fauna—that first-timers might otherwise miss along the way. Guides are available in Santiago, Miraflores, and Todos Santos—simply ask around. For the Cañon San Dionísio route, a guide can also sometimes be arranged at Rancho San Dionísio, just before the eastern trailhead.

The going rate for guide hire is US$15-25 per day per person, depending on whether pack animals (horses or burros) are used.

EAST CAPE

The Cabo del Este ("East Cape") consists of a succession of scenic tropical coves and beaches extending from the northern end of Bahía de Palmas south to San José del Cabo, at the tip of the cape.

Beach camping is possible along almost the entire length of the coast, although the area is developing gradually and some of the prettiest beaches now bear rather tasteless housing developments. Coastal development, in fact, is ongoing from Buena Vista all the way around the Cape to Cabo San Lucas, and land prices have skyrocketed in recent years. Fortunately, there are still a few choice spots left where the fishing and camping is free. Not all are mentioned below, in hopes that a certain anonymous few may yet escape the bulldozer.

Bahía De Palmas

The gently curving shore of Bahía de Palmas, stretching 32 km (20 miles) from Punta Pescadero south to Punta Arena, is a Baja fishing and windsurfing mecca. Anglers can reach the 100-fathom line less than a mile from shore in many places along the bay, especially toward Punta Pescadero ("Fisherman's Point") at the north end. Billfish frequent the area June-Dec., yellowtail Jan.-June, and roosterfish, wahoo, tuna, and dorado all year-round. Inshore catches include pargo, cabrilla, grouper, amberjack, wahoo, and pompano, plus the occasional yellowtail or rooster.

The world-famous "Tuna Hole," about 6½ km (four miles) directly south of Punta Pescadero, reaches depths of 50 fathoms and has a year-round population of sizable yellowfin tuna; rocks along the Tuna Hole's submerged canyon walls tend to eat the lines of all but the most skilled sportfishers. Guided fishing trips can be arranged at any of the hotels along the bay—generally US$80-90 a day for a panga, US$200-300 a day aboard a fishing cruiser. Trailered or car-topped boats can be launched off sandy beaches or at the boat ramp just north of the Hotel Spa Buena Vista.

With such favorable fishing conditions, it's little wonder that a small legion of gringo anglers are buying up property along the bay and building vacation and retirement homes. Although the area is still without telephone service, the Barriles-Buena Vista area is starting to look a bit like a San Diego suburb.

Windsurfing: Board-sailors flock to Los Barriles Nov.-April when sideshore winds—aided by thermals from the Sierra de la Laguna—blow 18-30 knots for weeks at a time. The rest of the year, you can settle for around 12-14 knots—not too shabby. During the high wind season, inshore water temperatures average around 22-24° C (72-75° F), with air temps in the 25-29° C (78-85° F) range.

Several hotels on the bay rent windsurfing equipment and provide basic instruction. During the high-wind season, two windsurfing centers in the Barriles-Buena Vista area can arrange package deals that include use of state-of-the-art equipment (bring a wetsuit, harness, and booties—the centers supply the rest), lessons geared to your level, air transportation, and accommodations. **Baja Surf Club** (tel. 800-551-8844 in the U.S.) is based at the Hotel Palmas de Cortez, while **Vela Highwind Center** (tel. 800-223-5443 in the U.S.) uses both Hotel Playa Hermosa and Hotel Rancho Buena Vista.

During the second week of January, Vela Highwind Centers and surf-gear manufacturer O'Neill co-host the annual Baja Championships sailboard race at Los Barriles. (Nonwindsurfing spectators are welcome to watch the event from shore.) The center also offers a race clinic, staffed by world-class instructors, the week before the competition. For more information, contact Vela Highwind Centers, 125 University Ave. No. 40, Palo Alto, CA 94301 (or call 415-322-0613).

1991 Vela-O'Neill Baja Championships
(HOWARD MOREHEAD COURTESY OF VELA HIGHWIND CENTERS)

Surfing: One of Baja's least-known surfing spots—simply because no one expects surf along the Sea of Cortez—is Punta Arena, at the south end of Bahía de Palmas just below Punta Colorada. A left point break can crop up here anytime during the March-Nov. southwest swell, but the peak surf usually comes around in late summer or early fall—chubasco season.

Hotels—Central Bay: Several dirt roads branch east off Mexico 1 between Kms 110 and 105 to hotels and trailer parks—most owned by North Americans—scattered along the central section of Bahía de Palmas. None have local phone service, so reservations must be made through their U.S. reservations office. In the center of the bay at Los Barriles are the **Hotel Playa Hermosa** (tel. 408-375-2251, P.O. Box 1827, Monterey, CA 93942) and **Hotel Palmas de Cortez** (tel. 818-887-7001, P.O. Box 9388, Canoga Park, CA 3109). Playa Hermosa has a restaurant, bar, and rental fishing tackle; rooms cost US$45 s, US$50 d. The hotel is closed in September.

South of Playa Hermosa, the Hotel Palmas de Cortez has air-conditioned rooms for US$55 s, US$85 d; facilities include a restaurant and bar, pool, tennis court, a 1,000-meter (3,250-foot) landing strip (Unicom 122.8), windsurfing gear, and equipment for both fishing and hunting (dove and quail hunting in the nearby Sierra de la Laguna is reportedly good).

About 6½ km (four miles) south of Los Barriles, at Buena Vista, is the **Rancho Bueno Vista** (tel. 818-303-1517, 800-258-3200 outside CA, P.O. Box 673, Monrovia, CA 91016). The resort has a restaurant and bar, pool, tennis courts, fishing tackle (including fly-fishing equipment) and cruisers, windsurfing gear, a boat ramp, and air-conditioned cottages for US$75-130 per night for two, plus US$45 for each additional guest.

Hotel Spa Buena Vista (tel. 714-524-6656 or 800-752-3555 in CA only, P.O. Box 218, Placentia, CA 92670), about a kilometer farther south, has rooms in a converted hacienda for US$55-70 s, US$80-100 d (additional persons pay US$25 each); facilities include a pool, tennis court, mineral spa, and equipment for fishing and hunting. The Spa Buena Vista also offers special package deals that include accommodations, all meals, and several days of guided fishing.

Hotels—North and South Bay: At the extreme north end of Bahía de Palmas (13 km/ eight miles north of Los Barriles via an unpaved road from Mexico 1 signed "El Cardonal") is the **Hotel Punta Pescadero** (tel. 415-948-5505, 800-426-2252, P.O. Box 1044, Los Altos, CA 94022), a small fishing resort on 125 palm-studded acres overlooking a sandy beach. Rooms cost US$55 s, US$75 d and come with sea views, a private veranda, television, and refrigerator; some also have fireplaces. The resort has a restaurant and bar, pool, tennis court, golf course, landing strip (1,160 meters/3,500 feet, Unicom 122.8), and rental equipment for scuba and free diving, boating, and fishing. The unpaved road to Punta Pescadero is not recommended for RVs or trailers.

Punta Colorada, at the south end of the bay (16 km/10 miles east of Mexico 1 via the La Ribera road), has the **Hotel Punta Colorada** (tel. 818-703-1002, P.O. Box 2573, Canoga Park, CA 91306). Roosterfish fanatics often choose to stay here since the roosterfishing off nearby Punta Arena is usually the best in Baja. Large rooms cost US$50 s, US$80 d; like the competition to the north, Hotel Punta Colorada has its own airstrip (1,060 meters/ 3,300 feet, Unicom 122.8). Guided hunting and fishing trips are available. The hotel is closed September and the first week of October.

North of Punta Colorada is the palapa-style, 12-room **Inn at Rancho Leonero** (tel. 818-703-0930, same U.S. address as Hotel Punta Colorada) with restaurant and bar, jacuzzi, fully equipped dive center, and rental fishing gear. Rates are US$55 s, US$85 d, US$120 t, US$144 quad. Rancho Leonero's restaurant is considered one of the best on the East Cape.

Camping and RV Parks: North of Hotel Playa Hermosa in Los Barriles are **Martin Verdugo's Trailer Park** (A.P. 477, La Paz, BCS) and **Playa de Oro RV Resort** (A.P. 4, Santiago, BCS; tel. 818-336-7494 in the U.S.).

WHAT'S A GRINGO?

The Latin-American Spanish word *gringo*, reportedly a corruption of the Spanish word *greigo* or "Greek," has different meanings in different parts of Latin America. In Argentina or Uruguay, for example, it is used to refer to anyone of Italian descent. In Mexico and Central America, it is almost always reserved for persons of northern European descent, especially North Americans. In Cabo Pulmo, I once heard a naive, newly arrived white Canadian archaeologist comment that it would be easy for him to carry out his research in Baja because he wasn't a gringo. (Sorry pal, but you're a gringo, too.) In spite of contrary, linguistic evidence to the contrary, many non-Spanish speakers insist that only Americans are gringos. The Mexicans, however, have a more precise epithet for Americans: *yanquis* or "Yankees."

Is *gringo* a derogatory term? It can certainly be used that way. Most of the time, however, it's simply an unconscious racial identification of neutral value. Educated Mexicans tend not to use it; instead they would typically say *norteamericano* or *americano* for Americans—some Mexicans insist on the former even though the term is a slight to Canadians who, after all, are North Americans, too—*canadiense* for Canadians, *alemán* for Germans, and so forth. Expatriate North Americans and Europeans living in Baja frequently refer to themselves and their expat friends as gringos.

Both have flush toilets, showers, laundry, boat ramps, and full hookups for US$6-8 (depending on the size of the vehicle) for two, plus US$1.50 for each additional person; tent sites cost US$5 a night at Verdugo's, US$6.50 at Playa de Oro. Verdugo's has a restaurant; Playa de Oro has an ocean view and bonded boat storage. Both parks can arrange fishing trips.

Free primitive camping is possible in the area north of these two parks, usually referred to by gringos as the "North Shore."

About two km south of Hotel Spa Buena Vista is modest **La Capilla Trailer Park,** with flush toilets, showers, and full hookups for US$6 a day.

El Camino Rural Costero ("The Rural Coastal Road")

About halfway down the infamous Coastal Road is a brass plaque commemorating the road's May '84 grading. For first-time drivers who have braved washouts and sandpits to read it, the sign never fails to elicit a few chuckles. Big plans claim the road will soon be paved—such claims have been around for several years now. In spite of the rough access, certain areas along the Coastal Road—e.g., Cabo Pulmo and Los Frailes—are being consumed by small, half-finished housing developments. Yet plenty of open space for beach camping is still available.

Contrasting strongly with the budding resort development are several ranchos along the road that raise cattle, goats, pigs, and sheep—mostly without fencing. If you substitute fiberglass pangas for dugout canoes, the ranchos today appear much like they must have to John Steinbeck in 1941, when he described Cabo Pulmo:

> On the shore behind the white beach was one of those lonely little *rancherías* we came to know later. Usually a palm or two are planted nearby, and by these trees sticking up out of the brush one can locate the houses. There is usually a small corral, a burro or two, a few pigs, and some scrawny chickens. The cattle range wide for food. A dugout canoe lies on the beach, for a good part of the food comes from the sea. Rarely do you see a light from the sea, for the people go to sleep at dusk and awaken with the first light.

In general, driving conditions along the Coastal Road are suitable for passenger cars of average road clearance; even smaller RVs sometimes manage to make it all the way. Sand can be a problem in places, and shoulers are invariably soft. Weather plays an important role in day-to-day conditions; following late-summer or early-fall storms, parts of the Coastal Road can be impassable. (An October 1990 hurricane wreaked havoc on southern portions of the road.) Make inquiries before embarking on the trip and be prepared to turn back if necessary. The 88½-km (55-mile) stretch between La Ribera and San José del Cabo can take up to four hours of driving.

La Ribera-Cabo Pulmo: To reach the Coastal Road from the north, take the paved road signed "La Ribera" east at Km 93 off Mexico 1. This 12-km (7½-mile) road terminates in La Ribera (La Rivera), a small town of around 2,000 with markets, houses, a PEMEX station, church, and **Restaurant Villy's Tres Banderas.** Another paved road branches south from La Ribera, meeting the unpaved road east to Punta Colorada (see "Bahía de Palmas," p. 313), and the Coastal Road. The section of the Coastal Road from here to Cabo Pulmo, 26½ km (16½ miles) south of La Ribera, is usually in fair condition.

Extending south from Cabo Pulmo is **Bahía Pulmo,** noted for its reef-building corals. The bay's **Pulmo Reef,** one of only three coastal reefs in North America (including two Pacific coast locations off Costa Rica and Panama), is rich with Panamic marinelife and hence a favorite snorkeling and scuba-diving destination. Adding to its attraction is the fact that it's easily accessible from shore.

The reef has eight fingers that extend northeastward from the bay shore. The reef system here is very delicate; reef corals can't tolerate temperatures lower than 21° C (70° F) and must have clear water since debris settling on their disks and tentacles will kill them. The Mexican government has declared Pulmo Reef an underwater nature preserve—no fishing or anchoring at the reef is permitted. Shore development remains the reef's biggest ecological challenge, since the corals rely on unpolluted (and unimpeded) runoff. If resorts or housing developments are permitted along Bahía Pulmo, the reef will perish quickly.

Another system, **Outer Pulmo Reef,** lies roughly 3.2 km (two miles) east of Cabo Pulmo (the cape, not the village). Ask for Juan Castro in Cabo Pulmo if you're interested in a guided dive or boat service. **Tito's,** a casual palapa restaurant in the small settlement of Cabo Pulmo, can provide meals and drinking water. Beach camping is permitted along the bay—a nominal fee is collected at campsites near Cabo Pulmo.

Bahía los Frailes-San José del Cabo: About eight km (five miles) south of Cabo Pulmo village is a sandy spur road east to Bahía los Frailes, with one of the best camping beaches along the East Cape in spite of the conspicuous housing development underway behind the beach. Onshore and inshore fishing is usually good—surfcasters have even reportedly landed tuna here. Windsurfers will find a steady cross-shore breeze at the bay's south end. A restaurant in Los Frailes serves breakfast, lunch, and dinner.

South of Los Frailes, the Coastal Road deteriorates rapidly but those with sturdy vehicles and steady nerves will be rewarded by secluded arroyo campsites and vignettes of disappearing ranch life. About 12½ km (7½ miles) south of Los Frailes is **Rancho Tule,** followed after 5½ km (3½ miles) by **Rancho Boca Vinorama,** then another five km (three miles) and 1½ km (one mile) respectively to **Rancho San Luis** and **Rancho Santa Elena.** Following another 5½-km (3.3-mile) section is the small dairy farm of **La Fortuna,** after which the road improves a bit for 24 km (15 miles) before terminating at **Pueblo la Playa,** a fishing village on the eastern outskirts of San José del Cabo. On the coast before Pueblo la Playa is **Punta Gorda,** known for fishing and, in a southwest swell, surfing.

The last couple of kilometers between Pueblo la Playa and San José del Cabo is more tropical than the entire East Cape, passing mango trees, huge banyan trees, and wild sugarcane.

SAN JOSÉ DEL CABO

Los Cabos ("The Capes") is a marketing term of rather recent origin applied to the twin resort towns of San José del Cabo and Cabo San Lucas at Baja California's southernmost tip. Although closer to Los Cabos International Airport, San José represents the quieter, more traditional resort of the two. A somewhat older tourist crowd frequents San José (pop. 22,000), leaving Cabo San Lucas to partying singles and young couples.

HISTORY

Spanish galleons first visited Estero San José, at the mouth of the Río San José, to obtain fresh water near the end of their lengthy voyages from the Philippines to Acapulco in the late-17th and early-18th centuries. As pirate raids along the coast between Cabo San Lucas and La Paz became a problem, the need for a permanent Spanish settlement at the tip of the cape became increasingly urgent. The growing unrest among Guaycura and Pericú Indians south of Loreto was also threatening to engulf mission communities to the north; the Spanish had to send armed troops to the Cape Region to quell Indian uprisings in 1723, 1725, and 1729.

In 1730 Jesuit Padre Nicolás Tamaral traveled south from Misión La Purísima and founded Misión San José del Cabo on a mesa overlooking the Río San José, some five km north of the current town site. Due to the overwhelming presence of mosquitoes at this site, however, Tamaral soon moved the mission to the mouth of the estuary, on a rise flanked by Cerro del Vigía and Cerro de la Cruz.

Tamaral and the Pericús got along fine until he pronounced an injunction against polygamy, long a tradition in Pericú society. After Tamaral punished a Pericú shaman for violating the anti-polygamy decree, the Indians rebelled and burned both the San José and Santiago missions in October 1734; Tamaral was killed in the attack. Shortly thereafter, the Spanish established a presidio, which serve the dual purpose of protecting the communit from insurgent Indians and the estuary from English pirates.

By 1767, virtually all the Indians in the area had died either of European-borne diseases or in skirmishes with the Spanish. Surviving mission Indians were moved to missions farther north, but San José del Cabo remained an important Spanish military outpost until the mid-19th century when the presidio was turned over to Mexican nationals.

During the Mexican-American War (1846-48), marines from the U.S. frigate *Portsmouth* briefly occupied the city. A bloody siege ensued, but the Mexicans prevailed under the leadership of Mexican naval officer José Antonio Mijares (Plaza Mijares, San José's town plaza, is named for him). But as mining in the Cape Region gave out during the late-19th and early-20th centuries, San José lost population along with the rest of the region. A few farmers and fishermen began trickling into the San José area in the '30s, and in 1940 the church was rebuilt.

San José remained largely a backwater until the Cape began attracting sportfishers and later the sun-and-sand set in the '60s and '70s. Since the late '70s, FONATUR (Fondo Nacional de Fomento del Turismo—National Foundation for Tourism Development) has sponsored several tourist development projects along San José's shoreline. Fortunately the development has done little to change San José's Spanish colonial character, and local residents have taken pride in restoring the town's 18th-century architecture and preserving its quiet, laidback ambience.

SIGHTS

Plaza Mijares

The shady town plaza at the intersection of Blvd. Mijares and Zaragoza—San José's two main streets—is a well-tended expanse of brick with a number of benches and a gazebo. At the west end of the plaza is the twin-towered **Iglesia San José,** built in 1940 on the site of the original 1730 Misión San José del Cabo. A mosaic over the main entrance depicts a scene from the infamous 1734 Pericú uprising (Indians are shown dragging Padre Tamaral toward a fire, presumably to be burned alive).

Since December 1990, the town has held a fiesta every Saturday evening in Plaza Mijares. (See "Entertainment and Events" below.)

Estero San José

The freshwater Río San José meets the Pacific Ocean at this estuary, just east of the Stouffer Presidente Hotel. A sandbar at the mouth of the river forms a scenic lagoon sur-

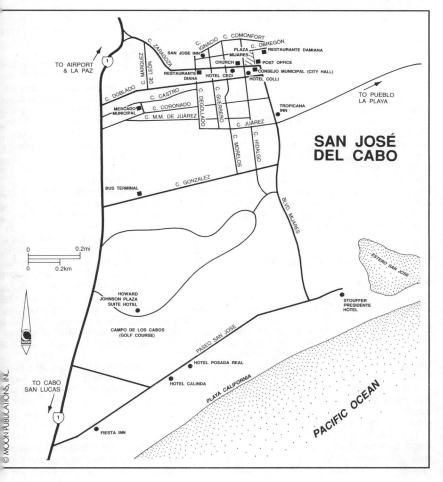

rounded by tall palms and marshgrasses, a habitat for over 200 species of birds. Canoes can be rented at the Stouffer Presidente for paddling around the lagoon.

Zona Hotelera

FONATUR has developed 4,000 shoreline acres adjacent to San José into a hotel-recreation zone. Thus far, the zone contains six resort hotels, a nine-hole golf course, and several condominium developments. The wide, sandy beach here, known either as Playa Hotelera or Playa California, is perfect for sunbathing, but the undertow is very strong.

La Playita

Just east of San José via Calle Juárez is a beach area called the La Playita ("Little Beach"), adjacent to the village Pueblo La Playa. Besides being an ocean beach away from the hotel zone, La Playita has pangas for rent, a reputable seafood restaurant, and free camping. Along the dirt road from here to Pueblo la Playa and beyond to the East Cape are a number of large banyan *(zalate)* and mango trees as well as wild sugarcane. Earlier this century much of the Río San José valley was planted in sugarcane.

ACCOMMODATIONS

Hotels In Town

Besides the major hotels and condotels in the Zona Hotelera (see "San José del Cabo Hotels and Condos" chart), San José offers a number of smaller, moderately priced inns in the town itself. Top of the list is the hospitable **Posada Terranova** (tel. 2-05-34), on Calle Degollado (just south of Zaragoza), a converted home with five, clean, air-conditioned rooms for US$30 s, US$45 d. The owners say they will soon be expanding to 18 rooms. The inn also has an intimate dining room with an outdoor eating section and a bar.

The **Hotel Colli** (no phone) on Calle Hidalgo, between Zaragoza and Doblado, is a mostly residential hotel with occasional rooms—simple but comfortable—for US$20-

25. More modest is the **Hotel Ceci,** around the corner at Calle Zaragoza 22 (opposite the church), with rooms for only US$9.50 s US$13.50 d, US$18 t. At night, busy Calle Zaragoza might make this small hotel an economical but noisy choice.

Farther off the beaten track is the **San José Inn** (tel. 2-09-24), on Calle Obregón between Degollado and Verde. Formerly the Hotel Pagamar, the inn has large, somewhat bare rooms with basic furnishings and hot showers for US$20 s, US$25 d. If the Ceci and Colli are full, you can usually count on finding a room here simply because it's not well-known.

A new town hotel, the **Tropicana Inn** (tel. 2-25-80, fax 2-25-90, 415-652-6051 in the U.S.), was built around the Tropicana Bar and Grill on Blvd. Mijares in 1991. Room rates are US$75 s/d Nov.-March, US$65 s/d the rest of the year. All rooms come with air-conditioning and telephones; other hotel facilities include a swimming pool and complimentary transport to La Playita and Playa Palmilla.

Camping And RV Parks

Brisa del Mar Trailer Park (mailing address A.P. 45, San José del Cabo, BCS), 3.2 km (two miles) southwest of San José off Mexico 1 at Km 30, is the only beachfront RV park in the Cabos area (so far). As such, it's often full in the high tourist season, mid-Nov. through mid February. For two persons/one vehicle, full hookup RV slots are US$12, tent spaces US$6, plus US$1.50 per additional guest. Facilities include flush toilets, showers, laundry pool, restaurant, and bar. Farther southwest at the east end of Playa Palmilla (Km 26), a new campground called **Montañas de Palmilla RV Park** is reportedly under construction.

Free beach camping is possible at La Playita (between San José and Pueblo La Playa and between Brisa del Mar Trailer Park and the water.

FOOD

Almost all of San José's fashionable restaurants are found along Blvd. Mijares and Calle Zaragoza in the vicinity of the plaza. As a

SAN JOSÉ HOTELS AND CONDOS

All hotels and rental condos listed below are on the beach (Paseo Malecón) in the Zona Hotelera.
For a listing of hotels in town, see the Accommodations section.
Rates quoted are for peak season (Nov. through May); some hotels may offer a 15-20% discount
June-October. Add 15% hotel tax to all rates (some hotels may charge an additional
10% service charge). Area code: 684

NAME	TELEPHONE	RATES	FEATURES
Colony Inn Las Misiones	2-14-01, fax 2-09-85 (in U.S. 800-777-1700)	2-bedroom condos with kitchenettes, US$125-240	a/c, pool, tennis courts, golf course, bar
Fiesta Inn	2-07-01 (in U.S. 800-343-7821)	US$35	a/c, pool, telephones, restaurant
Hotel Calinda Aquamarina	2-00-77, fax 2-02-87 (in U.S. & Canada, 800-228-5151 in Mexico 91-800-90-000)	US$80 s/d	a/c, pool, restaurant, bar
Hotel Best Western Posada Real Cabo	2-01-55 (in the U.S. 800-336-5454 or 800-528-1234)	US$80 s/d	a/c, telephones, jacuzzis, pool, tennis court, snack bar, restaurant, gift shop
Howard Johnson Plaza Suite Hotel	2-09-99, fax 2-08-06 (in U.S. 800-654-2000	US$90 d, US$140 deluxe suite	a/c, telephones, kitchen, pool, restaurant, bar
Stouffer Presidente Los Cabos	5-25-00, fax 2-02-32 (in U.S., 800-468-3571, in Mexico 91-800-90-444)	US$100 standard, US$140 deluxe, US$240 jr. suite	a/c, telephones, pools, tennis courts, gift shop, aquatic equipment, restaurants, bars, disco, travel agency, auto rental

general rule, the closer a restaurant is to the plaza, the more expensive the menu becomes. To save money and/or experience local flavor, seek out the spots where San José residents eat—most are in the western part of town toward Mexico 1. At the west end of Calle Doblado are several inexpensive taco stands and *fruterías*. The Mercado Municipal has a section of side-by-side *loncherías*.

Boulevard Mijares
$-$$ **Sandrick's** (tel. 2-12-70): Informal late-lunch, aprés-beach kind of place, specializing in fajitas, burgers, and chimichangas. Open daily 1400-2100.
$$ **Tropicana Bar & Grill** (tel. 2-09-07): Large, touristy restaurant-bar with outdoor patio, big-screen sports TV, and music and dancing at night. The menu is basic Tourist-Mex/

Fake Caribbean, but the drinks are strong. Open daily for lunch and dinner.

$$ **Andre Mar** (tel. 2-03-74): Mostly seafood (excellent *tostadas de ceviche)* plus a good selection of Mexican standards. Open daily for lunch and dinner. .

$$ **Iguana Bar** (tel. 2-02-66): A relatively recent addition to Blvd. Mijares's restaurant row, the Iguana serves a variety of well-prepared seafood, ribs, chicken, and Mexican dishes. In the evenings, the restaurant transforms into a night club with live music. Open daily 1100-0100.

$$-$$$ **Damiana** (tel. 2-04-99): Named for the Cape Region's legendary herbal aphrodisiac, and housed in a restored 18th-century townhouse, this is one of the most romantic settings in either San José or San Lucas. The front room is a tastefully decorated bar, followed by an indoor dining area in the middle room, and a patio dining area—candle-lit in the evening—in the lushly foliated rear courtyard. House specialties include shrimp, lobster, abalone, and steak. A complimentary taste of *damiana* liqueur is served to guests upon request. Open daily 0900-midnight *(almuerzo,* lunch, and dinner).

$$ **Café Europa** (no phone): Tucked away near the northeast corner of Plaza Mijares, this friendly, cozy café-bistro offers espresso coffees, omelets, pastries, a fully stocked deli counter, and daily specials such as kielbasa and *croque monsieur.* Open daily 0830-2200.

Calle Zaragoza

$$ **Plaza Principal** (no phone): A good choice if you're in the mood for a lighter menu, e.g., pasta, tortilla soup, or seafood. Opposite the plaza; open daily for lunch and dinner.

$$-$$$ **La Fogata** (no phone): Despite the name, this well-touristed restaurant specializes in steaks and seafood, plus a few Mexican dishes. Popular for its huge, gringo-style portions. Opposite Bancomer; open daily for breakfast, lunch, and dinner.

$$-$$$ **Pietro** (tel. 2-05-58): Near La Fogata, this tastefully decorated restaurant-bar serves Italian food for dinner only.

$-$$ **Diana** (no phone): A second-story place with a view of Calle Zaragoza, this tiny dining room is very popular among locals and visitors for its reasonable prices and authentic Mexican food, including fresh mariscos. The TV in the corner is tuned not to American sports but to Mexican variety shows and novellas, always a good indication. Open daily for breakfast, lunch, and dinner.

$-$$ **Restaurant Canton** (no phone): Another upstairs place, reached by spiral staircase. Best (only) Chinese food in San José. Open daily for lunch and dinner.

$$ **Los Arcos** (tel. 2-07-93): A bit west of Calle Zaragoza's restaurant row, opposite Banco Serfin, this small, family-run restaurant focuses on serving exemplary Baja-style seafood. Open daily for breakfast, lunch, and dinner.

$ **Cafetería Rosy** (no phone): A local place away from the tourist district altogether at the west end of Zaragoza. Inexpensive Mexican antojitos, plus a fixed-price comida corrida. Open daily for breakfast, lunch, and dinner.

$ **Lonchería Ophelia** (no phone): Another local eatery with basic Mexican dishes. Opposite Cafetería Rosy; open daily from around noon to 1700.

Other Locations

$ **Cafetería Arco Iris** (no phone), Calle Morelos near Zaragoza: A quick-stop place with inexpensive licuados, tortas, and burritos.

$$ **Posada Terranova** (tel. 2-05-34), on Calle Degollado (just south of Zaragoza): This family-run inn has a small dining room and bar, plus outdoor seating; good variety of Mexican and American breakfasts. Open daily for breakfast, lunch, and dinner.

$$ **Kepy's Pizza** (tel. 2-14-26), Calle Obregón: A decent pizzeria on one of San José's back streets, with a mix of local and tourist clientele. Open daily 1600-2300; delivery orders accepted.

$$-$$$ **Cafetería Frutas y Flores,** Stouffer Presidente Hotel: The Sunday champagne brunch here is quite popular, as is the Italian buffet on Friday's "pasta night." On other nights the house specialty is grilled seafood. Open daily 1900-2300, plus 1000-1400 for Sunday brunch.

$$ **La Playita** (no phone), La Playita, Pueblo la Playa: Many people swear this big palapa-

roofed restaurant has the best seafood in San José. Try the barbecued shrimp and become an instant rooter. Also good are the grilled cabrilla and snapper. The bar is a great spot for a casual drink. Open daily 1100-2200.

Groceries

The **Mercado Municipal,** between Calles Castro and Coronado in the west part of town, has fresh fruits and vegetables, fish, meats, a licuado stand, and a cluster of loncherías; it's open daily from dawn to dusk. More expensive canned and imported foods, plus beer and liquor, are available at **Almacenes Goncanseco,** Blvd. Mijares 14-18 (opposite city hall); this supermarket accepts credit cards. A couple of smaller grocery stores are found along the west end of Calle Zaragoza as well.

Also toward the west end of Calle Zaragoza is **Pastelería y Panaderí La Princesa,** with a good selection of Mexican cakes, pastries, and bread. Pricier European-style baked items are available at **La Baguette,** Blvd. Mijares 10 (east side of the plaza, near Café Europa).

ENTERTAINMENT AND EVENTS

Bars And Discos

While San José isn't as much of a nighttime party scene as Cabo San Lucas, neither does the town close down at sunset. The current hotspot is the **Iguana Bar** (tel. 2-02-66) on Blvd. Mijares, where live bands play a mix of Latino and international pop. Also popular is the **Tropicana Bar & Grill** (tel. 2-09-07) across the street, although the music isn't as good (lounge-lizard folk music in the front room, canned music in the back). Both bars host a two-drinks-for-the-price-of-one happy hour in the late afternoon.

The **Club Eclipse,** near the Iguana on Blvd. Mijares, is a sizable video disco pushing "Daks" (daiquiris) and "Margs" (margaritas). The Stouffer Presidente has its own **Cactus Video Disco** for folks who don't want to leave the Zona Hotelera.

Events

Every Saturday evening since December 1990, San José has hosted a fiesta in Plaza Mijares. Although it's mostly put on for the benefit of tourists, lots of locals attend as well. Typical events include folk dances, mariachi performances, cockfight demonstrations, piñata breaking, as well as food vendors and arts-and-crafts sales. Profits from food and beverage sales go to local charities and service clubs.

San José's biggest annual festival is held 19 March, the feast day of its patron saint. In addition to music, dancing, and food, celebratory activities include horse races and parades.

SHOPPING

Near the intersection of Blvd. Mijares and the road to Pueblo la Playa (about halfway between the Zona Hotelera and the plaza) is a large open-air market selling inexpensive Mexican handicrafts; it's generally open 1100-2100. Higher-quality (and higher-priced) arts and crafts are offered in shops along the east end of Calle Zaragoza and north end of Blvd. Mijares, including **Antigua Los Cabos** (handmade furniture, antiques, rugs, and ceramics), **Bye-Bye** (T-shirts and souvenirs), **La Casa Vieja** (folk art, jewelry, beachwear), **Galería El Dorado** (modern sculpture), and **La Mina** (silver jewelry).

Galería Los Cabos, on Calle Obregón (one block north of Zaragoza), has a unique assortment of antique furniture, stoneware, crafts, decorator items, and locally made barrel-back chairs. Also on this street is **Zapatería Evelyn,** a shoe store with a good selection and reasonable prices.

SPORTS AND RECREATION

Fishing

All hotels in the Zona Hotelera can arrange guided fish trips. Since San José has no harbor or marina, all trips use *pangas,* fiberglass skiffs with outboard motors. Pangas can also be hired directly from the pangeros at the beach next to Pueblo la Playa (in front of Restaurante La Playita).

Onshore and inshore catches include cabrilla, grouper, roosterfish, sierra, snapper, toro, pompano, and occasional yellowtail. Far-

Calle Zaragoza,
San Jose del Cabo
(JOE CUMMINGS)

ther offshore tuna, dorado, and sailfish are possible. One of Baja's best marlin and wahoo grounds is Bancos Gordos ("Gordo Banks"), about 16 km (10 miles) southeast of San José. Striped marlin are seen year-round in Cape Region waters; dorado, roosterfish, and sailfish are best fished in the late summer and early fall.

Golf And Tennis
Surrounded by FONATUR condotel projects, the **Campo de Los Cabos** (Los Cabos Country Club) features a well-groomed, nine-hole golf course with a sea view. Despite having only nine holes, the course is challenging (the third hole extends 540 yards, with a lake in the middle of the fairway). The greens fee is US$18; carts (US$14) and clubs (US$12) are available for rent. Tee-offs can be scheduled daily 0700-1600.

The club also has tennis courts, a pool, a clubhouse with changing rooms, a pro shop, restaurants, and a bar.

SERVICES

Changing Money
Two banks in town offer foreign exchange services, open Mon.-Fri. 0830-1130. The lines at **Bancomer** (one block west of plaza) are generally longest; if you're not in line by 1100, you might not make it to the foreign-exchange window before it closes. **Banco Serfin,** two blocks west of Bancomer, usually has shorter lines. There don't appear to be any casas de cambio in San José, although the major hotels will gladly take your dollars—at a low exchange rate.

Post And Telephone
San José's post and telegraph office, on Plaza Mijares, is open Mon.-Fri. 0800-1700. The public telephone office on Calle Doblado, opposite the hospital, offers direct-dial long-distance phone service.

TRANSPORT

Air
Los Cabos International Airport (SJD), 12.8 km (eight miles) north of San José del Cabo, services both San José and Cabo San Lucas. Three airlines—Aero California, Alaska, and Mexicana—fly into Los Cabos. **Aero California** (tel. 3-08-27, 3-08-48) has daily nonstop flights to Los Cabos from Los Angeles, Phoenix, and San Diego. **Alaska** (tel. 95-800-426-0333 in Mexico) has nonstop flights to Los Cabos from Los Angeles and San Diego, plus connecting flights from Anchorage, Bellingham, Fairbanks, Portland, San Francisco, Se-

attle/Tacoma, Spokane, Victoria (B.C.), Walla Walla, and Yakima.

Mexicana (tel. 2-02-30) offers nonstop flights to Los Cabos from Denver, San Francisco, Guadalajara, and Mazatlán, with connecting flights from Chicago, Los Angeles, Sacramento, San Diego, Mexico City, Monterrey, Puerto Vallarta, and Tokyo. Mexicana has a ticket office on Paseo San José in the Zona Hotelera; Aero California's office is in the Centro Comercial Plaza in Cabo San Lucas. Alaska handles ticket sales only at the airport.

Airport Transport: A taxi from the airport to any destination in San José del Cabo costs US$4 pp or US$11 for an entire taxi.

BEACHES BETWEEN SAN JOSÉ DEL CABO AND CABO SAN LUCAS

Beach	Km marker	plus number (of meters*)
Costa Azul	29	(+500)
Acapulquito	27	(+800)
Arroyo Seco/ Punta Palmilla	26	(+400)
Punta Bella	24	(+400)
Buenos Aires	22	(+400)
El Mirador	20	
San Carlos	19	
El Zalate	17	(+500)
Costa Brava	17	(+100)
Canta Mar	16	(+700)
Del Tule	15	(+400)
Punta Chileno	14	
Santa María	12	(+200)
Twin Dolphin	11	(+500)
Barco Varada ("Shipwreck")	9	
Cabo Bello	6	(+200)

*refers to the approximate number of meters west of the kilometer marker, with San José as the starting point

---

Departure Tax: the Los Cabos airport collects a US$12 departure tax from every passenger, payable in cash only.

Bus

From San José's bus station (tel. 2-11-00) on Calle Valerio Gonzales, there are nine buses per day to La Paz (US$5) and 10 buses to Cabo San Lucas (US$1.30). The last bus to Cabo San Lucas leaves around 2000. Each morning a bus also leaves for the 24-hour trip all the way to Tijuana (US$25).

The bus station has a small cafeteria and a licuado stand.

Vehicle Rental

Several auto rental agencies (Budget, Hertz, Avis, Servitur) have desks at Los Cabos International Airport. Rates average US$24 a day for VW bug (plus US$.18 per km), US$34 for a Golf (plus US$.20/km), US$44 for a Jetta (plus US$.23/km), US$48 for a Combi van (plus US$.30/km), and US$56 for a Caravelle (plus US$.33/km).

Servitur (tel. 3-08-97, 2-05-50) also has an office in the Stouffer Presidente Hotel. **Vagabundos** (no phone), next to the Stouffer Presidente, rents motor scooters and ATVs for US$8 an hour or US$22 per day.

SAN JOSÉ DEL CABO-CABO SAN LUCAS

The Transpeninsular Highway's 29-km (18-mile) stretch between San José del Cabo and Cabo San Lucas provides access to numerous beaches, points, and tidal pools along the Pacific Ocean (or Sea of Cortez, depending on where you choose to draw the boundary). Most of the roads branching south of the highway are unpaved; almost all of these can be negotiated by ordinary passenger vehicles, although walking may be required. To locate beaches, follow the SEDUE signs along Mexico 1 marked "Acceso a Playa" (sometimes these signs include the name of the beach, sometimes not). The key, above, lists all of those accessible from the highway.

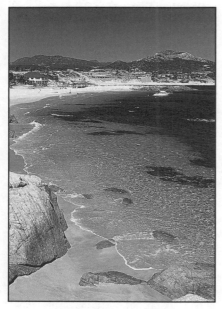

Playa Palmilla   (JOE CUMMINGS)

Hotels

Three of Los Cabos's priciest and most well-situated hotel properties grace the coast along the "corridor." Even if you have no plans to stay in this area, the bars in these hotels are worth stopping at for a drink and an ocean view.

Covering 900 acres of Punta Palmilla (Km 27) is the **Hotel Palmilla,** the Cape's first major resort (built in 1956 by "Rod" Rodríguez, son of former Mexican President Abelardo Luis Rodríguez). Coconut palms, clouds of hibiscus, and sweeping sea views dominate the grounds; facilities include a chapel (used for weddings), 1,500-meter (4,500-foot) illuminated airstrip (Unicom 122.8), pool, tennis courts, croquet court, giant outdoor chessboard, horse stables, restaurant, and bar. The hotel maintains its own sportfishing fleet, offering panga trips (one to three anglers) for US$75-150 per day or long-range cruises (one to four anglers) for US$395 per day. A Jack Nicklaus-designed 18-hole golf course is expected to open in October 1992.

The Palmilla's room rates vary from US$95 s, US$110 d in the Garden section in winter to US$250 s, US$340 d for a Vista Suite in summer. Two-bedroom suites sleeping up to four are also available for US$345 (summer) or US$700 (winter), five-bedroom villas for US$650-1090. For information contact Hotel Palmilla Reservations (tel. 714-833-3033 or 800-637-2226 in the U.S; mailing address: 4343 Von Karman Ave., Newport Beach, CA 92660-2083). In Baja, dial (684) 2-05-83.

If even the Hotel Palmilla's La Cantina bar seems beyond your budget, you might at least enjoy the beach below the hotel by stopping in at **Restaurant-Bar Pepe's** on Playa Palmilla, where the first drink is on Pepe (or if he's not in attendance, the first two drinks are on the house).

Farther southwest at Km 15-14 is the **Hotel Cabo San Lucas** (tel. 213-205-0055 or 800-733-2226 in the U.S.), on Playa Chileno. Another heavy hitter in the colonial-luxury league, the Cabo San Lucas has its own hunting ranch, as well as sportfishing excursions, horseback riding, a three-level swimming pool, a dive center, a 1,200-meter (3,600-foot) airstrip, and an Asian art gallery. The reef below the hotel is suitable for snorkeling and surfing. Rooms cost US$70-90 in summer, US$118-140 in winter. One- and two-bedroom apartments that sleep up to four guests are available for US$260 a night, three-to seven-room villas for US$920-1410.

The third and most expensive of the corridor's royal triumvirate is the **Twin Dolphin Hotel** (tel. 3-04-96 in Los Cabos; tel. 213-386-3940 or 800-421-8925 in the U.S.) at Km 11. Like the Palmilla, the Twin Dolphin has splendid ocean views; Playa Santa María, to the immediate north, is one of Los Cabos's best snorkeling/diving beaches. The hotel has its own fishing fleet, an 18-hole putting green, dive center, pool, tennis courts, horseback riding, restaurant, and bar. Rooms are US$180 s, US$225 d, plus US$20 for each additional guest.

Surfing

Although Los Cabos is less famous than Baja's northern and central Pacific coast for surf, the summer southwest swell brings decent wave action to the tip of the peninsula—when most of the west coast points are flat—reaching peak height during the chubasco season, late summer to early fall. Probably the best surfing area between San José and Cabo San Lucas is **Playa Costa Azul,** at Km 29-28, where a grinding shore-breaker called "Zippers" is sometimes backed by Hawaii-style outside breaks in heavy swell. **Punta Palmilla,** below the Hotel Palmilla at Km 28-27, whips out a decent point break, while the bay to the point's immediate north gets a good reef break in heavy swell.

Reef breaks sometimes crop up at **Playa Buenos Aires,** at Km 22, and **Playa Cabo Real,** Km 20, after which there's a gap until **Playa Canta Mar** at Km 16 and **Punta Chileno** at Km 14, both offering workable point breaks. **Playa Cabo Bello,** Km 6-5 (near the Hotel Cabo San Lucas), is known for a consistent reef break nicknamed "Monuments" (for the H-shaped concrete monument on the highway near here). This break is fueled by northwest swell refracted off Cabo San Lucas, and as such is the easternmost break for winter surfing.

Diving

Several beaches along the corridor feature rock reefs suitable for snorkeling and scuba diving, particularly **Playa Santa María** (Km 12) and **Playa Barco Varado** (Shipwreck Beach, Km 9-10). Santa María features rocky reefs at either end of a protected cove at depths of 13 meters (40 feet) or less. The north point displays sea fans and gorgonians, along with the usual assortment of tropical fish. The south end has sea caves, coral outcroppings, and large rocky areas inhabited by reef fish and lobster.

The remains of the Japanese tuna boat *Inari Maru No. 10,* stranded on rocky shoals in 1966, is the main diving focus at Shipwreck Beach. The hull and other wreckage are within 2-26 meters (6-48 feet) of the bay surface; there are also scenic rock reefs in the vicinity. Tidal pools containing starfish and sea urchins along the beach are of interest to non-divers.

TODOS SANTOS

One of the more lushly vegetated arroyo settlements in the Cape Region, Todos Santos started as a mission community founded by Jesuit Padre Sigismundo Taraval about two km inland from the Pacific in 1734. The Guaycura

Playa Santa Maria
(JOE CUMMINGS)

Todos Santos
(JOE CUMMINGS)

population in the vicinity was soon wiped out by smallpox and Pericús were brought in to work the fields irrigated by springs connected to Arroyo la Reforma. Misión Santa Rosa de Todos Santos somehow weathered the Pericú rebellions to the southwest in Santiago and San José del Cabo and lasted until secularization in 1854. Unfortunately the original chapel (at Misión Vieja just north of present-day Todos Santos) was replaced by a newer one around that same time.

In the post-mission era, Todos Santos thrived as Baja's sugarcane capital, at one time supporting five sugar mills. All but one mill closed when the most abundant freshwater spring dried up in 1950; the remaining mill closed in 1965. Around 1980 the spring came back to life, and the arroyo now produces avocados, mangoes, citrus, coconuts, papayas, and a variety of other fruits and vegetables.

Today's Todos Santos is a sleepy town of around 8,000 with semi-historic architecture and a growing artists' colony of Mexicans and North Americans. For Cabo San Lucas-or La Paz-bound travelers on Mexico 19, the town makes a good mid-point stopover with several restaurants and cafés, two decent hotels and RV parks, fruit stands, and a PEMEX station. Longer-term visitors can explore the nearby as-yet-undeveloped Pacific beaches and the western escarpment of the

Sierra de la Laguna (see "Todos Santos to Cabo San Lucas," below, and "Sierra de la Laguna," p. 312). The feast day of the town's patron saint, Virgen del Pilar, is celebrated on 12 October.

Hotels And Motels

The Spanish colonial-style **Hotel California** (tel. 4-00-02, 415-768-0614 in the U.S.; mailing address: 407 Miner Rd., Orinda CA 94563), on Calle Juárez between Morelos and Marquez de León, has 16 clean, renovated rooms for US$29 s, US$36 d, plus a small pool, bar, and restaurant. The management can arrange pack excursions into the Sierra de la Laguna as well as nearby scuba, fishing, and hunting trips.

Opposite the Hotel California on Calle Juárez is the very basic **Motel Guluarte** with rooms for US$10 a night. A better alternative is the **Todos Santos Inn** (tel. 4-91-33) at Calle Obregón 17A. This 1850-vintage house features a terrace and view, a swap library, and three rooms at US$30 s, US$40 d, or US$45 t, including breakfast. As at the Hotel California, the Todos Santos Inn staff can arrange pack trips into the nearby sierras.

Camping And RV Parks

El Molino Trailer Park (tel. 4-01-40, 818-986-7420 in the U.S.), at the southeast edge of town off Mexico 1, rents RV spaces for US$10

a night per vehicle for up to four persons, plus US$1 per additional guest. Facilities include flush toilets, showers, laundry, and a café. **San Pedrito RV Park** (tel. 4-01-47), about 6½ km (four miles) south of town off Mexico 1 (3.2 km west of Km 59), has full hookups for US$10, tent sites for US$3 a night. The park has flush toilets, showers, laundry facilities, a pool, bar, and restaurant.

Free, primitive beach camping is possible on Playa San Pedrito (2½ km/1.6 miles west of Km 57).

Food
For a small, relatively "undiscovered" town, Todos Santos has a surprising number of places to eat. Popular among gringos for seafood and Mexican are the **Santa Monica** and **El Progresso** restaurants, just north of the PEMEX station on Mexico 1 (Calle Degollado). **El Molino,** next to El Molino RV Park on the old mill grounds, is also reportedly good.

Steaks and seafood are house specialties at **La Langosta Loca,** on Calle Colegio Militar near Obregón; the "Crazy Lobster" is also known for its American and Mexican breakfasts. The **Café Santa Fé,** on Calle Centenario off Marquez de León, offers Italian food; open for dinner only.

The small, shaded patio behind the **Sweetwater Café** (Calle Juárez between Marquez de León and Hidalgo) is a pleasant spot to savor the tiny café's milkshakes, ice cream, breakfasts, burgers, or Mexican antojitos.

Fish tacos and other seafood delights, as well as fresh fruit, are available in the afternoon from street vendors along Mexico 1 between Morelos and Degollado.

Groceries
The usual assortment of staples can be bought at any of several markets in town, including: **Conasupo** (Calle Colegio Militar near Obregón), **Minisuper Salgado** (opposite the Sweetwater Café), **Supermercado Guluarte** (next to Motel Guluarte), and **ISSSTE tienda** (Calle Juárez between Zaragoza and Morelos). Buy tortillas by the kilo at the tortillería on Calle Colegio Militar (Mexico 1) between Morelos and Marquez

de León. A public seafood market on Calle Zaragoza, just south of Mexico 1, sells fresh fish and shellfish.

Information
Todos Santos' **post office** is on Colegio Militar (Mexico 1) between Hidalgo and Marquez de León. Long-distance phone calls can be made from the **public telephone booth** at Mexico 1 and Calle Zaragoza; for long-distance calls to Todos Santos, the area code is 682.

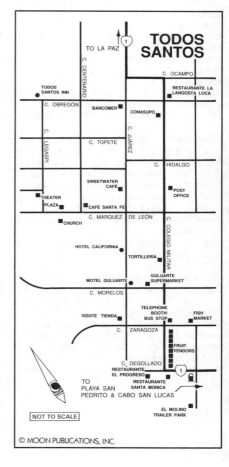

Transport

Six to seven intercity buses a day run between Todos Santos and La Paz to the north and Cabo San Lucas to the south. Either bus trip takes about two hours and costs US$2 per person; buses depart from the corner of Mexico 1 (Calle Colegio Militar) and Calle Zaragoza.

TODOS SANTOS TO CABO SAN LUCAS

The 140-km (87-mile) stretch of Mexico 19 between Todos Santos and Cabo San Lucas passes several undeveloped beaches and small coastal communities. Wags are fond of saying it's only a matter of time before this area is dotted with resorts; housing developments are already slowly appearing along the southern end of the highway outside Cabo San Lucas. Local resistance to development is growing, so perhaps the area farther north will remain preserved and relatively pristine.

Playa San Pedrito-Playa Los Cerritos

Just north of El Pescadero between Km 56 and 57 is a 2½-km (1½-mile) dirt road west to **Playa San Pedrito.** Backed by coconut palms, this scenic beach offers good camping, fishing, and a steady beach break for surfing.

Rancho Nueva Villa, just before Km 60, is a well-known farm that produces fruits and vegetables without the use of chemical pesticides or fertilizers. Organic produce can be purchased from the farm's roadside stand. **El Pescadero** (pop. 1,500), at Km 62, is little more than a plaza lined with tiendas and a café. East of El Pescadero, a network of dirt roads leads southeast approximately 56 km (35 miles) across the Sierra de la Laguna to Mexico 1 between Santa Anita and Caduaño; parts of the road are graded but the middle section is passable only by sturdy, 4WD vehicles.

At Km 64 a good dirt road branches 2½ km (1½ miles) southwest to **Playa los Cerritos,**

another fine beach for camping and fishing. A campground with no facilities charges US$3.50 per vehicle for tent or trailer camping. Access to free beach campsites is available via several dirt roads branching off Mexico 19 at Km 70-71, Km 75, and Km 86. **Punta Gaspareño,** near Km 73, catches a right point break.

Playa Migriño-Cabo Falso

Playa Migriño, accessed at Km 94 or 97, is a long section of beach next to Estero Migriño, a small estuary linked with Río Candelaría. In winter, surfers can catch a point break at the north end of the beach. Several spots along the beach are suitable for camping.

After Migriño, a small ranching settlement, the highway begins climbing over the southwestern foothills and coastal plateaus of the Sierra de la Laguna. Southeast of Migriño is an 11-km (six-mile), ungraded dirt road inland that connects with a road north (eight km/five miles) to **La Candelaría.** This small, picturesque village is known throughout the Cape Region for its Indian *curanderos* (healers); tourism flacks in Los Cabos call the curandero culture "white magic." Irrigated by an underground stream, the village produces mangoes, corn, and bamboo. La Candelaría can also be approached from Cabo San Lucas via a 24-km (15-mile), mostly graded dirt road.

About three km before the Cabo San Lucas city limits is **Cabo Falso,** once incorrectly thought to be the Baja California's southernmost point. The wide beach along Cabo Falso is protected as a nesting grounds for sea turtles; visitors aren't permitted within 50 meters (150 feet) of the surf line. The dunes behind the beach, however, are a popular destination for rented ATVs from Cabo San Lucas. The abandoned lighthouse here, **El Faro Viejo,** signaled ships from 1895 to 1961; the original lens is now installed in a newer lighthouse higher on the beach.

CABO SAN LUCAS

The resort town of Cabo San Lucas (named for the slender cape extending eastward from Baja's southernmost tip) has been a long time developing into a tourist hot spot. During the Spanish colonial era, its natural harbor was periodically used by passing mariners, but since it offered no source of fresh water and scant protection during the late summer storm season (when chubascos roll in from the southeast), it was largely ignored by the Spanish. Although English pirates were known to use the harbor as a hiding place for attacks on Manila galleons, many of the historical incidents ascribed to Cabo San Lucas may actually have taken place near present-day San José del Cabo, where ships often watered at the Río San José estuary.

By the 1930s, a small fishing village and cannery had grown up at the north end of the Cabo San Lucas harbor, inhabited by around 400 hardy souls. The Cape sportfishing craze of the '50s and '60s—when the waters off the peninsula's southern tip earned the nickname "Marlin Alley"—had expanded the population to around 1,500 by the time the Transpeninsular Highway was completed in 1973. Once the highway link between North America and Cabo San Lucas was established, the town transformed from a fly-in/sail-in resort into an auto-and-RV destination.

The construction of Los Cabos International Airport near San José del Cabo in the '80s brought the area within reach of vacationers who didn't have the time for a six-day drive from border to Cape and back. The establishment of a water pipeline between San José and San Lucas further loosened the limits on development. Los Cabos—the area stretching between and including San José del Cabo and Cabo San Lucas—is currently the seventh most popular tourist destination in Mexico (ahead of Cozumel, behind Mazatlán). With a permanent population of only around 25,000, many of whom are retirees, the tourist-resident ratio is quite high, especially during the peak Nov.-Feb. tourist season.

San José del Cabo and Cabo San Lucas have equal access to the great beaches along the "corridor" between the two towns; but because the Cabo San Lucas harbor provides shelter for a large sportfishing and recreational fleet, the preponderance of the 250,000-plus yearly Los Cabos visitors center themselves here rather than in San José or along the corridor. In spite of all the tourists, Cabo has managed to retain something of a small-town feel.

Besides the harbor, Cabo San Lucas's main attractions include an underwater nature preserve only a few minutes' boat ride from the harbor and the striking Land's End rock formations at one end of the bay, with a pristine beach right around the corner. Without the tenacity of a few of the town's original residents, who demanded this land be preserved, hotels and condos would probably fill the town's entire perimeter. San Lucas has the fortunate distinction of being the only coastal resort in Mexico with such a nature preserve within its city limits.

Outside of this area, however, hotel and condo development is marching ahead. Pedregal, a fashionable hillside district to the west, the marina, and Playa Médano to the east are all chock-a-block with condos and villas. Next to undergo development will probably be the large section of unused harbor-front property near the inner harbor entrance, where an old cannery and ferry pier lie abandoned. Rumor has it this will become a new docking area for cruise ships; in 1991 five cruise lines—Princess, Carnival, Royal Cruise, Bermuda Star, and Seabourn—had Cabo San Lucas on their itineraries.

While Cabo nightlife isn't on a par with Acapulco's, the town attracts a young, energetic crowd who help create a more vibrant ambience than is found at relatively staid San José del Cabo, 29 km (18 miles) northeast.

CABO SAN LUCAS

TO TODOS SANTOS

ORTEGA

MORALES

EL FARO VIEJO TRAILER PARK

ALIKAN

12 DE OCTOBRE

OBREGÓN

CARRANZA

REVOLUCIÓN

20 DE NOVIEMBRE

LIBERTAD

16 DE SEPTIEMBRE

MATAMOROS

ABASOLO

OCAMPO

ZARAGOZA

MORELOS

LEONA VICARIO

MENDOZA

GÓMEZ FARIAS

16 DE SEPTIEMBRE

CABO SAN LUCAS

HIDALGO

1

TO SAN JOSÉ DEL CABO

HOTEL CASABLANCA

LOS CABOS INN

COTP

IMMIGRATION OFFICE

LÁZARO CÁRDENAS

BUS TERMINAL

PATY'S TACOS

LAUNDROMAT

NIÑOS HÉROES

POST OFFICE

PLAZA ARAMBURO

HOTEL MAR DE CORTEZ

CENTRAL COMERCIAL PLAZA

GUERRERO

MADERO

GIGGLING MARLIN RESTAURANT-BAR

EL CORAL RESTAURANT

MARINA BLVD.

PLAZA LAS GLORIAS

RESTAURANT BAR LAS PALMAS

HOTEL MELIÁ SAN LUCAS

GALEÓN RESTAURANT

MARINA

HACIENDA BEACH RESORT

PLAYA EL MÉDANO

BAHÍA SAN LUCAS

HOTEL FINISTERRA

0   0.25mi

0   0.25km

ASTON TERRASOL CABO

HOTEL SOLMAR

PLAYA SOLMAR

PACIFIC OCEAN

PLAYA DEL AMOR

© MOON PUBLICATIONS, INC.

CLIMATE

Another major Cabo San Lucas advantage is its sunny and mild year-round climate. The town's location at the confluence of the Pacific Ocean and the Sea of Cortez means ocean currents and airstreams from both sides of the peninsula tend to moderate the general climatic influences of each; neither the cool Pacific nor the warm Cortez completely dominates in any given season. Hence summers aren't as hot as in La Paz (220 km north on the Cortez side), for example, and winters aren't as cool as in El Pescadero (62 km north on the Pacific).

The average August temperature is 27° C (81° F), in January 18° C (64° F). Maximum temperatures rarely exceed 33° C (92° F) and minimum temps Nov.-Feb. seldom fall below 13° C (56° F).

Cabo San Lucas boasts an average of 360 days of sunshine a year. Annual rainfall averages a scant 19 cm (7½ inches), most of which falls Aug.-Oct. although brief showers are sometimes encountered as late as November or early December.

SIGHTS

Cabos San Lucas has virtually nothing of historical or cultural interest; people fly, drive, and boat here to soak up the plentiful sunshine and to enjoy fishing, diving, and other aquatic activities as described under "Sports and Recreation," below.

Beaches

Beachgoers have a choice of four beaches close to the downtown area, plus a string of beaches and coves along the San José del Cabo-Cabo San Lucas Corridor.

Playa Médano: The most popular and easily accessible local beach, Playa El Médano ("Dune Beach"), extends several kilometers northeast from the inner harbor's southeast corner along Bahía San Lucas. This heavily used beach is Baja's closest equivalent to Hawaii's Waikiki Beach in terms of the concentration of swimmers and sunbathers on hand during peak vacation periods. Besides swimming (Médano is one of the few local beaches where swimming is safe year-round) and lying on the sand, a variety of other beach activities are available to beachgoers. Pangas, jetskis, inflatable rafts, sailboards, snorkeling equipment, volleyball equipment, palapas, and beach furniture are for rent from beach vendors; several palapa bars and restaurants (Playa Brujita Beach Club, El Sinaloense, El Delfin, and Las Palmas) strung out along the beach offer cold beverages and seafood.

Minor annoyances at Playa Médano include the jewelry and rug vendors who plod up and down the beach (fortunately they don't persist if you show no interest) and the condo developments in the background, marring the view of the Sierra de la Laguna foothills from the water.

Playa del Amor: Cabo's next most popular beach can only be reached by boat or by a difficult climb over two rock headlands along the ocean. Playa del Amor ("Love Beach," also known as Playa del Amante, "Lover's Beach") is near the tip of Cabo San Lucas (the cape itself, not the town), just northwest of the famous arch-shaped rock formation seen in virtually every Los Cabos advertisement. The wide, sandy, pristine beach actually extends across the cape (behind the arch) to the other side, to form two beachfronts—one on the Bahía San Lucas and one on the Pacific. (The latter is sometimes whimsically called "Divorce Beach.")

Only the beachfront facing the bay is generally safe for swimming. Bring along a cooler full of beverages, as the entire area is kept free of vendors and commercial enterprises. Unless you have a portable beach umbrella, go early in the day to command one of the shady rock overhangs. The southeast end of the bay features a series of coral-encrusted rocks suitable for snorkeling; a deep submarine canyon lying only 45½ meters (150 feet) offshore is a popular scuba-diving site.

Playa del Amor can be reached by water taxi from the marina for US$3, or take a glass-bottom boat tour (US$5) and arrange a drop-off at the beach; any tour boat in the vicinity

El Arco, Cabo San Lucas
(JOE CUMMINGS)

will give you a ride back to the marina upon presentation of your ticket stub (the last tour boat leaves the marina at 1500). Those skilled at bouldering can reach the south side of the beach by climbing from the east end of Playa Solmar (in front of the Hotel Solmar) over two rocky points that separate the two beaches. The climb is best accomplished during low tide, when the cove between the rock formations has a sandy beach—useful as a midway rest-stop. The second set of rocks, to the east, is more difficult than those to the west; turn back after the first set if you've reached the limit of your climbing skills.

Playa Solmar: This huge beach running along the southwestern edge of the cape is accessible via the road to Hotel Solmar. The strong undertow makes it a sunbathing-and-wading only beach. Solmar's biggest advantage is its lack of people, even during peak tourist seasons.

Corridor Beaches: Northeast of Cabo San Lucas—on the way to San José del Cabo—are a number of uncrowded, relatively pristine beaches suitable for swimming, fishing, camping, snorkeling, and scuba diving. See "San José del Cabo-Cabo San Lucas Corridor," p. 325, for names and locations.

Beach Equipment: Desportes Baja (Baja Sports) on Calle Guerrero rents surfboards (US$10 per day), boogie boards (US$4), snor-kels, mask, and fins (US$4 each or US$10 together), and coolers (US$3.50).

Rock Formations
El Arco ("The Arch"), a rock outcropping at the tip of the cape, has become Cabo San Lucas's most immediately recognizable symbol. Also called **Finisterra,** or "Land's End," the 62-meter (200-foot) rock formation has an eroded passage through the middle. Just offshore are **Los Frailes** ("The Friars"), two rock islets frequented by sea lions.

A smaller, bird-limed rock pinnacle off the northeast side of the cape, **Roca Pelicanos** ("Pelican Rock"), is a crowded pelican roost. The base of the pinnacle, about six meters (20 feet) down, is richly endowed with marinelife, including coral, sea fans, gorgonians, sea urchins, and numerous tropical fish varieties. Recent reports from divers say visibility at the rock is declining, however, due to discharge from boats moored in the outer harbor.

ACCOMMODATIONS

Hotels And Condominiums
Cabo San Lucas has a greater number and variety of hotels than neighboring San José. Most are in the US$50-110 range although there are four hotels with rooms under US$35

a night and several that cost well over US$100 in winter and early spring. Some of the best deals for families or small groups are rental condos, which usually sleep up to four for US$80-125 per night. For names, addresses, rates, and facilities, see "Cabo San Lucas Hotels and Condos," below.

Camping And RV Parks

El Faro Viejo Trailer Park, at Matamoros and Morales in the northwestern section of town (on the way to Todos Santos), has full hookups for US$8 for two, flush toilets, showers, laundromat, and a reputable restaurant-bar. The only other RV park in town is **El Marlin Trailer Park,** next to the Giggling Marlin Restaurant on Blvd. Marina. Rates and facilities are on a par with El Faro Viejo. Both of these parks tend to fill up Nov.-May.

Three km northeast of Cabo San Lucas off Mexico 1, the **Vagabundos del Mar RV Park** (tel. 3-02-90; 707-374-5511 in the U.S.), has full hookups for US$15 for two plus US$3 per additional guest; discounts are available for members of the Vagabundos del Mar travel club. Facilities include flush toilets, showers, a pool, and laundry.

Also northeast of town, at Km 4 on the south side of Mexico 1, is **Cabo Cielo RV Park,** with full hookups for US$8, flush toilets, and showers. On a rise at Km 5.5 on the highway, **El Arco Trailer Park** (tel. 3-06-13) commands a view of the town and Bahía San Lucas even though it's on the north side of the highway. Full hookups cost US$8, tent sites US$5; the park has flush toilets, pool, and a large palapa restaurant with distant bay views.

Beach camping is possible at beaches farther northeast along Mexico 1 (see "San José del Cabo-Cabo San Lucas Corridor," p. 325) or northwest along Mexico 19 (see "Todos Santos to Cabo San Lucas," p. 330).

FOOD

Downtown Cabo San Lucas is riddled with restaurants and bars, most of them open-air designs, with menus that attempt to cover all the bases—seafood, Mexican, and steak. Because Cabo is a Baja's number-one resort town, prices are above what you'd find in La Paz, Ensenada, Tijuana, or other touristed areas. Quality is also generally high since Cabo attracts chefs from all over Mexico and beyond. One complaint: Cabo restaurants sometimes hold back on the chiles in Mexican dishes and table salsas, hence picante-lovers may be forced to request extra chiles or a fresh salsa cruda just to bring things up to par.

Mexican And Seafood

$$-$$$ **Caballo Blanco** (tel. 5-59-52, Calle Abasolo and Jalisco): Charbroiled meats from Sonora are the house specialty, plus over 35 varieties of tequila. Open daily for lunch and dinner.

$$ **Cilantro's Bar & Grill** (tel. 3-07-44, Playa El Médano): One of the better tourist-oriented Mexican restaurants in town, featuring mesquite-grilled seafood and homemade tortillas. Open daily for lunch and dinner.

$$ **El Camarón Feliz** (tel. 3-08-66, Calle 16 de Septiembre at Morelos): As at its sister restaurant in La Paz, the best menu items at "The Happy Shrimp" are the neither-happy-nor-sad shrimp. Open daily for lunch and dinner.

$-$$ **El Coral** (no phone, opposite Plaza Las Glorias on Blvd. Marina): This rambling outdoor restaurant serves reasonably priced meals from early till late. The food's not bad, and nowhere else in town can you get huevos rancheros for US$2 or a lobster dinner for US$12. Open daily for breakfast, lunch, and dinner.

$ **La Perla** (no phone, Calle Lázaro Cárdenas at Guerrero): One of the few Cabo restaurants that has maintained a local flavor, with inexpensive desayuno, comida corrida, tortas, tacos, burritos, quesadillas, and licuados. Open daily for breakfast, lunch, and dinner.

$$ **Giggling Marlin** (tel. 3-06-06, Calle Matamoros near Blvd. Marina): Better for appetizers and booze than entrees, most tourists come here to snap photos of themselves hanging upside down—like landed marlins—from the restaurant's block-and-tackle rig. Others come for the big-screen satellite TV.

CABO SAN LUCAS HOTELS AND CONDOS

Rates quoted are for peak season (Nov. through May); some hotels may offer a 15-20%
discount March-October. Add 15% hotel tax to all rates
(some hotels may charge an additional 10-15% service charge). Area code: 684

NAME	TELEPHONE	RATES	FEATURES
Bahía Condo/Hotel (Playa El Médano)	3-18-88, fax 3-18-91 (800-932-5599 in the U.S.)	US$95-120	a/c, kitchenettes, pool, bar, ocean view, beach access
Aston Terrasol Cabo (Playa Solmar)	3-03-83, fax 3-18-04 (in CA, 800-794-6835 elsewhere in U.S. 415-652-6051)	studio US$120, 1-br US$170, 2-br US$240 (up to four persons)	a/c, full kitchens, pools, sauna, health club, restaurant, bar, ocean view, beach access
Giggling Marlin Inn (Blvd. Marina at Matamoros)	3-06-06 (in U.S. 818-907-7219)	US$85-110 s/d	a/c, kitchenettes, restaurant, bar
Hacienda Beach Resort (Playa El Médano)	3-01-22 (in CA, 213-205-0055 or 800-282-4809 elsewhere in U.S. 800-421-0645)	US$120-170 s/d	a/c (some rooms), pool, tennis court, aquatic center, anchorage, restaurant, bars, ocean view, beach access
Hotel Casablanca (Calle Revolución at Morelos)	3-02-60	US$15 s, US$20 d, US$23 t	
Hotel Clarion Cabo San Lucas (Km 6, Playa Cabo Bello)	3-00-44 (in U.S. 800-228-5151)	US$125 s/d	a/c, telephones, pools, jacuzzi, tennis courts, ocean view, beach access
Hotel Dos Mares (Calle Zapata s/n)	3-03-30	US$17 s, US$19.50 d, US$22 t	a/c
Hotel Finisterra (Blvd. Marina)	3-00-00, 3-01-00 (in U.S. 714-827-3933 or 800-347-2252)	US$80-95 s, US$95-110 d, US$105-125 t, 1-br suites US$125, 2-br suites US$220	a/c, pools, tennis courts (charge for night play), spa, horseback riding, travel agency, chapel (for weddings), restaurant, bars, ocean and marina views
Hotel Mar de Cortez (Calle Lázaro Cárdenas and Guerrero)	3-00-32 (in U.S. 408-375-4755 or in CA 800-347-6847)	US$29-38 s, US$33-41.50 d, suites US$41-51.50	a/c, patios, pool, restaurant, bar

CABO SAN LUCAS HOTELS AND CONDOS (CONT.)

NAME	TELEPHONE	RATES	FEATURES
Hotel Meliá San Lucas (Playa El Médano)	3-10-00	US$140-160 s, US$150-170 d	a/c, telephones, in-room safe, pool, tennis court, restaurants, bars, ocean view, beach access
Hotel Solmar (Playa Solmar)	3-00-22 (in U.S. 213-459-9861 or 800-878-4115)	US$90 s, US$99 d, US$115 t, suites US$142-196	a/c, pool, tennis court, restaurant, bar, gift shops, aquatic center, ocean view, beach access
Las Ventanas de Cabo Condominiums San Lucas	no local phone (in U.S. 408-375-2252 or in CA800-347-6847)	2-br villas US$200 (up to four persons)	a/c, full kitchens, pool, jacuzzi, bay view
Los Cabos Inn (Calle Abasolo and 16 de Septiembre)	3-05-10	US$25 s/d	
Marina Cabo Plaza (Blvd. Marina)	3-08-98, (in CA., 800-794-6835 elsewhere in U.S. 415-652-6051)	US$70 s/d, US$80 s/d with kitchenette	a/c, pool, gift shop, marina view, Playa El Médano access
Medusa Suites (Calle Ocampo and Alikan)	3-08-80	US$46	a/c, telephones, kitchenettes
Plazas Las Glorias (Blvd. Marina)	3-12-20, fax 3-10-18 (in U.S. 713-448-2829 or 800-342-2644)	US$60-90 s/d, suites US$110-2210 (up to four persons), US$280-290 (up to six), US$250-260 (up to eight)	a/c, telephones, refrigerators, in-room safety box, pool, restaurants, bars, shopping center, travel agency, beach club at Playa El Médano, marina view
Villa Alfonso's (Playa El Médano) (P.O. Box 3, Cabo San Lucas, BCS)	3-07-39	US$100-125 s/d	complimentary breakfast, a/c, pool, jacuzzi, beach access, restaurant, bar

$$ **Las Palmas** (tel. 3-04-47, Playa El Médano): This was the first palapa restaurant on Médano, and most residents agree it's still the best in spite of the ugly concrete addition. The grilled seafood is always a good choice. Open daily for lunch and dinner.

$$-$$$ **Río Grill** (tel. 3-13-35, Blvd. Marina, near Calle Zapata): One of the nicer outdoor restaurant-bar combinations in the central marina area, with live music nightly and well-prepared steak, lobster, shishkebob, and Mexican combos. Open daily 1200-2400.

$$ Salsitas (tel. 3-17-40, Plaza Bonita, Blvd. Marina): This mall restaurant is mostly a tourist scene serving Mexican adapted for gringo palates, but is one of the only restaurants outside Plaza Las Glorias with marina views. Open daily 0630-2230.

$-$$ San Lucas (Broken Surfboard) (no phone, Calle Hidalgo at Zapata): A casual, second-story place overlooking the street with reasonably priced breakfasts, sandwiches, seafood, and licuados. Open daily for breakfast, lunch, and dinner.

$$-$$$ Señor Sushi (tel. 3-13-23, Blvd. Marina and Guerrero): A sushi bar in Cabo? You bet, and not bad either. The energetic staff also serves seafood platters, ribs, fajitas, and huge drinks from the Tai Won On Bar. Open daily for lunch and dinner.

$$$ Villa Alfonso's (tel. 3-07-39, Playa El Médano): The elegant dining room at this small hotel specializes in *nacional novelle,* or "Nouvelle Mexicain" cuisine, served a la carte or as a seven-course, fixed-price meal. The changing menu also features several international dishes. Open daily for lunch and dinner; reservations suggested.

Tacos And Fast Food

The local food scene is concentrated along Calle Morelos, where a string of stands offer tacos, carne asada, mariscos, and the lowest prices in town. Tamal fans shouldn't miss the Yucatán-style, banana-leaf-wrapped chicken tamales at the small stand diagonally opposite Castro's Market on Morelos. A trolley cart at the corner of Calle Lázaro Cárdenas and Guerrero assembles delicious custom fruit salads for US$1.30 a cup, including your choice of sliced papaya, watermelon, cucumber, mango, orange, cantaloupe, and jicama, with a squeeze of lime (salt and chile powder optional).

$-$$ Ali's Burger (Calle Morelos and 16 de Septiembre): Popular among tourists and residents alike for quick American breakfasts and burgers. Open daily 0630-2200.

$ El Pollo de Oro (Blvd. Lázaro Cárdenas at Morelos): A long-time favorite for Sinaloa-style barbecued chicken. Open daily 1200-2200.

$ Ocho Tostadas (opposite the Giggling Marlin): This street vendor specializes in tasty seafood tacos stuffed with oysters, shrimp, scallops, or octopus; the ceviche is also good. Usually open midday till mid-evening.

$$ Paty's (Calle Niños Héroes and Zaragoza): The huge tacos and barbecued chicken at this casual palapa restaurant are gringo favorites, but not particularly cheap. Open daily 1100-2200.

$ Supertacos de Baja California (Calle Morelos between 20 de Noviembre and Revolución): Reliable, inexpensive seafood or carne asada tacos. Open daily 1100-2200.

$ Tacos Chido's (Calle Zapata): A tiny diner with great fish tacos, *torta milanesa,* and breakfasts at low prices. Open for breakfast, lunch, and dinner.

$ Tacos Toño (Calle Morelos next to Paletería Michoacana): Ranchero-style carne asada, *carne adobada,* and *birria.* Open daily for lunch and dinner.

$$ Taco Wabo (Calle Guerrero): During the day this Van Halen-owned night club serves excellent taco platters (try the Chihuahua cheese and *rajas poblanos* combo), tortas, tortilla soup, and other antojitos on its outdoor patio, with New York radio station WNEW 102.7 pumping from the first-class sound system. Even the nachos come with no fewer than five homemade salsas. Open daily for lunch and dinner.

$ Taquería El Pastorcito (Calle Matamoros near Lázaro Cárdenas): Features 20 kinds of tacos at rock-bottom prices. Open daily for lunch and dinner.

$ Super Pollo (tel. 3-07-88, Calle Morelos and Ortega): Part of the Sinaloa-style chicken chain found throughout Baja. Very reliable. Open daily 1100-2200.

European

$$$ Galeón (tel. 3-04-43, Blvd. Marina): Elegant restaurant with harbor views, specializing in Neapolitan cuisine and pizzas baked in wood-fired ovens. Open daily for dinner only.

$$$ Pavo Real (Peacocks) (no phone, next to Hotel Meliá Cabo): Highly regarded continental kitchen presided over by a German chef. Open daily for dinner only.

$$-$$$ **Romeo y Julieta** (tel. 3-02-25, Blvd. Marina near Hotel Finisterra): An Italian menu featuring fresh pasta and wood-fired pizzas. Open daily for dinner only.

Trailer Park Restaurants

$$ **El Arco** (Km 5.5, Mexico 1): A large, airy restaurant with a distant view of Bahía San Lucas. The menu includes a variety of seafood, Mexican, and American dishes. Open Wed.-Mon. for breakfast, lunch, and dinner.

$$ **El Faro Viejo** (Calle Matamoros and Morales): Renowned for steak, seafood, and ribs. Open daily for breakfast, lunch, and dinner.

Groceries

Cabo's several supermarkets stock a variety of Mexican and U.S. foodstuffs—from fresh Mexican cheeses to Sara Lee frozen cheesecake—plus cooking and cleaning supplies, and even motor oil. Ranging from small to huge, these include **Castro Market** (Calle Morelos and Revolución), **SanLiz Supermarket** (Blvd. Marina and Madero), **Chany's Supermarket** (Blvd. Marina near the boat launch), **Koala Supermercado** (off Blvd. Marina, behind Restaurante Romeo y Julieta), and **Supermercado Plaza** (at Plaza Aramburo, Calles Lázaro Cárdenas and Zaragoza). Chany's has the longest hours, 0600-2400.

Panadería San Angel (Calle Morelos between Niños Héroes and 16 de Septiembre) carries all your favorite Mexican bakery items, including *bolillos* and *pan dulce,* plus dairy products. The best shopping area for beer and liquor is the string of *subagencias* and *licores* along Calle Matamoros.

ENTERTAINMENT AND EVENTS

Bars And Discos

Nightlife in Cabo starts in the bars downtown near the marina and after midnight moves to the discos, which stay open till 0300 or 0400. Among the bars, quieter types prefer the **Río Grill** (Blvd. Marina at Zapata), while the loud crowd hangs at the **Giggling Marlin** (Calle Matamoros and Blvd. Marina) or the two-story **El Squid Roe** (Calle Lázaro Cárdenas at Zaragoza). Squid Roe's dance floor (with bleachers) distinguishes it from the surrounding bar scene.

Cabo's discos begin filling up around 2300 but the crowd doesn't really break a sweat till around midnight or later. The town's first dance club, **El Oasis** (northeast edge of town near the PEMEX station on Calle Lázaro Cárdenas), is still in vogue but is facing serious competition from the newer **Lukas** at Plaza Bonita, which features a state-of-the-art laser show and sound system. Also at Plaza Bonita is the considerably more casual **Corona Beach Club,** which closes earlier (0200) than the others.

Alta Californians tend to prefer **Cabo Wabo** on Calle Guerrero, a dance club owned by the rock group Van Halen; the music here alternates between a recorded mix with video and live bands (yes, members of Van Halen put in the occasional—make that rare—appearance). The atmosphere is loose, though not "beach-y."

Events

Cabo San Lucas hosts several sportfishing tournaments throughout the year. The largest is the **Black and Blue Marlin Jackpot Tournament,** held for three days each October. The purse for the contest exceeds US$100,000, with proceeds going to local charities.

Another notable yearly event falls around the Festival of San Lucas on 18 Oct., part of a week of music, dancing, and feasting in the Mexican tradition.

SHOPPING

The streets of Cabo are filled with souvenir shops, street vendors, clothing boutiques, and galleries—probably more shops of this type per capita than anywhere else in Baja. For inexpensive handicrafts—rugs, blankets, baskets, leatherwork—from all over Mexico, check the outdoor **Mercado Mexicano** on Calle Hidalgo at Obregón; for the best prices you'll have to bargain. Another place where bargaining is useful is the **Tianguis Marina,** an outdoor souvenir market on the southwest

THE LA BAMBA SYNDROME

In Mexico, all it takes is the right combination of circumstances—a hotel lounge or tourist bar, plus plenty of tequila or Tecate and a table full of sunburned gringos—and sooner or later someone will be stricken by what might be called the La Bamba Syndrome. Initial symptoms are a desperate urge to hear or sing the song "La Bamba." If a live Mexican band (it doesn't matter whether they're mariachis or *norteños)* or even a lone guitarist is present, those afflicted by the syndrome will begin shouting at the musician(s) "La Bamba! La Bamba! Play La Bamba!" Victims are convinced they must hear La Bamba or else they'll die.

The desperation appears very convincing, as the victim's face becomes increasingly flushed if the strains of La Bamba don't ring out immediately. Finally, the *músicos* give in—perhaps hesitating just a bit longer than necessary in order to relish the victim's suffering—and begin banging out those three chords that would bring relief to the sufferer. But in order to prolong recovery, the LBS victim usually begins singing along with the music, shouting out an unintelligible mixture of mispronounced Spanish, pseudo-Spanish, and improvised English lyrics to the song. The syndrome is sometimes contagious, but if others in the room don't join in on their own, the original victim will often cajole other gringos to follow his (it's almost always a guy) example.

When the song's over, some LBS sufferers are temporarily cured, but in others the condition only becomes aggravated and they may demand other gringo chestnuts like "Guadalajara" or, in the worst cases, even "La Cucaracha." When it goes this far, even the musicians begin to suffer, along with all the gringos (and locals, if they haven't already made hasty exits) who were hoping to hear something a little more authentic or up-to-date, or who hoped that they might at least be able to enjoy themselves without the distractions of a raging La Bamba maniac.

If you're ever in a bar or restaurant that has musical entertainment and an organized tour from the States arrives, consider calling in the tab and leaving, as conditions are ripe for a mass LBS outbreak. And should you become afflicted yourself, at least try to get the lyrics halfway right. (Certain variations are acceptable.) "La Bamba," incidentally, is a Veracruz-style song; if you want to hear something local, ask for la música norteña.

"La Bamba"

Para bailar la bamba
Para bailar la bamba
se necesita una poca de gracia
una poca de gracia y otra cosita
Ay arriba y arriba
Ay arriba y arriba
Arriba ire
Yo no soy marinero
Yo no soy marinero, soy capitan
Soy capitan, soy capitan
Bamba, bamba . . . bamba, bamba . . .
Para subir al cielo
Para subir al cielo
Se necesita una escalera larga
Una escalera larga y otra chiquita
Ay arriba y arriba
Ay arriba y arriba
Arriba ire
Yo no soy marinero
Yo no soy marinero, soy capitan
Soy capitan, soy capitan
Bamba, bamba . . . bamba, bamba . . .
En mi casa me dicen
En mi casa me dicen el inocente
El inocente porque tengo chamacas
De quince a veinte
Ay arriba y arriba
Ay arriba y arriba
Arriba ire
Yo no soy marinero
Yo no soy marinero, por ti sere
Por ti sere, por ti sere
Bamba, bamba . . . bamba, bamba . . .

side of the inner harbor (toward the old ferry pier). Typical items here include black-coral sculptures, T-shirts, and costume jewelry.

Among the better shops in town are **La Bamba** (folk art, hand-painted T-shirts) on Calle Guerrero near Cabo Wabo, **Joyería Albert** (a branch of the reputable Puerto Vallarta jeweler) on Calle Matamoros, **Galería El Dorado** (modern sculpture) on Blvd. Marina at Madero, and **Zen-mar** (Oaxacan folk art, weavings, pottery, masks) on Calle Lázaro Cárdenas near the Hotel Mar de Cortez.

Plaza Bonita, Cabo's newest shopping center, faces the marina and contains a number of shops offering tourist-oriented sportswear, jewelry, and souvenirs. **Plaza Candidos,** near the Hotel Mar de Cortez, consists almost exclusively of clothing boutiques.

SPORTS AND RECREATION

Fishing
After swimming and lying on the beach, sportfishing is Cabo's number-one outdoor activity. Known as "the marlin capital of the world," an average of 10,000 billfish (marlin, sailfish, and swordfish) a year are hooked off the cape. The biggest trophy of all, the *marlín azul* (blue marlin), can reach five meters (15 feet) long and weigh close to a ton; in the Cape area, it's not unusual to hook 200- to 400-kilogram (440- to 880-pound) blues. A smaller species, the *marlín rayado* (striped marlin), grows to over 270 kilograms (600 pounds), while the *marlín negro* (black marlin) is almost as big as the blue.

To catch a glimpse of these huge gamefish, stop by the sportfishing dock on the marina's west side around 1500-1600, when sportfishing boats return with their catches. Note the flags flown over the boats; a triangular blue flag means a billfish has been bagged while a red flag with a T means one has been tagged and released. All Cabo sportfishing outfits request that anglers release billfish to fight another day; some even require it. Instead of skinning and mounting these beautiful fish, they recommend bringing a video camera along to record the catch from start to finish.

Good marlin-fishing spots include **Banco San Jaime,** 29 km (18 miles) southwest of Cabo Falso and **Banco Golden Gate,** 31 km (19 miles) west of Cabo Falso. Dorado and wahoo are also common in the same areas. Sportfishing cruisers—power boats equipped with electronic fish-finders, sophisticated tackle, fighting chairs and harnesses, and wells for keeping live bait—are the angler's best chance for landing large gamefish.

Almost unbelievably, marlin are also somewhat common just beyond the steep dropoffs between Los Frailes and Cabo Falso, an area easily reached by panga or skiff. Without the technology of a fishing cruiser, panga marlin-fishing becomes the most macho hook-and-line challenge of all—the resulting fish stories reach *Old Man and the Sea* proportions. For anglers with more humble ambitions, black seabass, cabrilla, sierra, and grouper are available in inshore waters; surfcasters can take corvina, ladyfish, sierra, and pargo.

Guided cruiser trips are easy to arrange through any major Cabo hotel (Solmar, Finisterra, and Meliá Cabo Real each have their own fleets) or through **Pisces Fleet** (tel. 3-12-88, fax 3-05-88, opposite SanLiz Supermarket), **Pesca Tours** (tel. 3-01-09, fax 5-44-99, Calle Matamoros and Lázaro Cárdenas, or **Los Dorados Sportfishing** (tel. 3-16-30, 3-06-30, Plazas Las Glorias). Rates average US$300 a day on a 28-foot cruiser, US$250 a day on a 26-footer (around US$100 per half-day), or US$175 per couple on 31-foot party boat. Charter boats can generally hold up to six anglers.

Pangas are available in Cabo San Lucas, but most panga-fishing trips operate out of San José del Cabo. When inquiring about rates—panga or cruiser—ask whether the quote includes filleting of edible gamefish. The better outfits include fish preparation among their services at no extra charge.

Fernando's Taxidermía (tel. 3-00-23, Calle Morelos and 20 de Noviembre or Hotel Solmar) can mount gamefish and ship the completed trophy anywhere in the world.

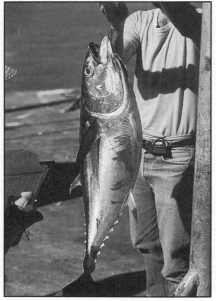

(JOE CUMMINGS)

yellowfin tuna, Cabo San Lucas

Boating

Cabo San Lucas is a major Baja California boating center although harbor size and facilities don't match those of La Paz. The outer harbor anchorages are mostly occupied by sportfishing cruisers; recreational boaters can moor off Playa El Médano to the northeast.

Within the inner harbor, first dredged in the early '70s, is the **Cabo Isle Marina** (tel. 3-12-51, 3-12-52, fax 3-12-53), with showers, pool, snack bar, and 200 slips that can accommodate boat lengths of up to 45 meters (148 feet). Permanent and monthly renters at Cabo Isle Marina have priority over short-term visiting boaters; daily rentals are available on a first-come, first-served basis for US$20 per day for the first 30 feet of boat length, plus US$.80 for each additional foot. Visiting boaters should call the marina within 15 days of arrival to check on the availability of slips. The marina's 14 condos are occasionally available as rentals.

Also in the inner harbor are two boat ramps, one near the old ferry pier and one at the northeast end of the harbor near Plaza Las Glorias. A fuel dock is located between the old ferry pier and abandoned cannery, just inside the entrance to the inner harbor. Cabo San Lucas is an official Mexican port of entry; the COTP office is on Calle Hidalgo between Libertad and 16 de Septiembre.

Boat Cruises: Dos Mares operates a fleet of glass-bottom tour boats that depart frequently from the marina (and from Playa Médano) between 0800 and 1500 each day. The standard 45-minute tour costs US$5 pp and covers Pelican Rock, the famous Land's End arch, and the sea lion colony. For no extra charge, the crew will also let passengers off at Playa del Amor near the arch; you can flag down any passing Dos Mares boat and catch a ride back to the marina later in the day.

Sunset bay cruises with all the beer and margaritas you can drink are also popular and usually last around two hours and 15 minutes. Reservations can be made at the marina or at most hotels; tickets cost US$20-40 pp depending on whether dinner is included.

Diving

Cabo is a unique diving destination in that several snorkeling and scuba sites are only a 15- to 25-minute boat ride from the marina. Snorkelers will find the base of the cliffs on each side of Playa del Amor, about three meters (nine feet) deep, worth exploring for coral and tropical fish. Nearby Pelican Rock, at six meters (18 feet) depth, is a bit more challenging. Strong divers, on calm days, can swim south around the arch to the seal colony at Los Frailes and frolic with the seals.

Divers with experience below 30 meters (100 feet) can visit a vast submarine canyon that begins just 50 meters (164 feet) off Playa del Amor. Part of a national marine preserve, the canyon is famous for its "sand falls," streams of sand tumbling over the canyon rim at a depth of around 26 meters (85 feet) and forming sand "rivers" between rock outcroppings. At a depth of around 40 meters (130 feet), the outcroppings give way to sheer granite walls, where the sand rivers drop vertically for hundreds of meters (to around 2,750 meters/9,000 feet).

The phenomenon was first documented by a Scripps Institute of Oceanography expedition in 1960 and later made famous in one of Jacques Cousteau's television documentaries. The edges of the canyon walls are also layered with colorful coral, sea fans, and other marinelife. These in turn attract schools of tropical fish, including many open-ocean species that aren't ordinarily seen this close to shore.

As with sportfishing, many Cabo hotels can arrange guided dive trips and equipment rentals. Independent outfitters include **Amigos del Mar** (tel. 3-05-05, 3-06-46) opposite the sportfishing pier on the marina), **Cabo Divers** (tel. 3-07-47, Blvd. Marina at Madero), **J&R Baja Divers** (tel. 3-15-70, Zapata at Guerrero, near Tacos Chido's), and **Cabo Acuadeportes** (tel. 3-01-17, fax 3-06-66, VHF radio 69, Playa El Médano or Playa Chileno). Typical rates are US$25-45 pp for snorkeling tours (the more expensive tours go to Playa Santa María), US$40-60 pp for a guided scuba dive (to Shipwreck Beach or the sand falls), and US$225 for NAUI/PADI certification for two persons.

Divers seeking equipment rentals only can expect the following rates: wetsuit US$6-10; mask and snorkel US$4-5; fins US$4-5; wetsuit, fins, and mask US$15; weight belt and weights US$4-5; regulator US$12; tanks US$10 each; BCD vest US$6-9; Hawaiian-sling spearguns US$7; underwater camera (and film) US$20; air fills US$5.

Horseback Riding

Marcos's Horse Rentals (tel. 3-01-23, Hacienda Beach Resort, Playa El Médano) offers horseback riding by the hour or on trail rides. The hourly rate is a relatively high US$15; better value is the three-hour trail ride to El Faro Viejo ("The Old Lighthouse," built in 1890) for US$30, best undertaken in the morning or at sunset for maximum scenic effect. A 1½-hour, US$20 beach ride or four-hour, US$50 beach and Faro Viejo ride are also available.

ATV Trail Rides

The sandy beaches and dunes in the Cabo San Lucas area are open to ATVs (all-terrain vehicles) as long as they're kept away from swimming areas (Playa El Médano) or turtle-nesting areas (Cabo Falso). **Chubasco's** (tel. 3-04-04, Blvd. Marina, Plaza Las Glorias, and Hotel Meliá San Lucas) operates ATV tours for US$40 pp per half-day (four hours), US$70 pp all day (six hours). The basic route visits sand dunes, the ruins of El Faro Viejo, and a 1912 shipwreck; the six-hour tour adds La Candelaría, an inland village known for its mango trees and *curanderos* (traditional healers).

Whalewatching

A variety of whales pass within a few hundred meters of Cabo San Lucas throughout the year, but the most activity occurs during gray whale migration season, Jan.-March. The Dos Mares tour-boat fleet operates whalewatching trips from the marina during the migration season for US$25 pp. With binoculars you can also see passing whales from the Hotel Finisterra's Whale Watcher's Bar.

INFORMATION AND SERVICES

Tourist Information

Cabo San Lucas has no government tourism offices or information booths, although FONATUR maintains an office on the marina; FONATUR representatives are always interested in speaking with potential investors but they don't distribute general tourist information. The Los Cabos Tourism Board, a private consortium, has a toll-free information number in the U.S.: tel. 800-765-2226.

El Tiempo Los Cabos ("Los Cabo Times"), a bilingual monthly newspaper distributed for free throughout the city, contains a number of ads and announcements concerning restaurants, clubs, and recreational events as well as local social and business news. The similar *Baja California News* is English-language only and contains information on La Paz as well. Also widely available is *Los Cabos Baja!,* a semi-annual booklet packed with tourist information and ads.

Post And Telephone

Cabo's post office, on Calle Matamoros just north of Lázaro Cárdenas, is open Mon.-Fri., 0800-1100, 1500-1800. The recently established **Centro de Comunicación,** Calles Revolución and Morelos, offers telephone, fax, and telex services 0800-1900. A long-distance telephone office in Centro Comercial Plaza, Calles Lázaro Cárdenas and Hidalgo, is open 0800-2200. Cabo's area code is 684.

Immigration

Cabo's *migración* office is on Calle Lázaro Cárdenas between Gómez Farías and 16 de Septiembre.

Changing Money

U.S. dollars are readily accepted throughout Cabo, although in smaller shops and restaurants you'll save money if you pay in pesos. Three banks offer foreign exchange services (0830-1200): **Banco Somex** (Calle Lázaro Cárdenas opposite Centro Comercial Plaza), **Banamex** (Calle Hidalgo), and **Banco Serfin** (Plaza Aramburo). Hotel cashiers will also gladly change dollars for pesos, albeit at a lower rate than the banks.

Laundry

A laundromat on Calle Lázaro Cárdenas, opposite Cabo Isle Marina, has coin-operated machines for self-service laundry or you can pay (by weight) to have it done by the staff. Open Mon.-Sat. 0900-1700.

Travel Agencies

Cabo's major hotels (Solmar, Finisterra, Hacienda, Plaza Las Glorias) have their own travel agencies for making air reservations and flight changes, or arranging local tours. In town, the most reliable and long-running independent is **Los Delfines** (tel. 3-13-96, 3-13- 97), next to Panadería San Angel on Calle Morelos; it's open Mon.-Fri. 0830-1800, Sat. 0830-1500.

TRANSPORT

Air

See "Transport" under "San José del Cabo" p. 324, for details on domestic and international service to Los Cabos International Airport, 12.8 km (eight miles) north of San José del Cabo. **Mexicana** (tel. 3-04-11) has a Cabo San Lucas office at Calles Niños Héroes and Zaragoza; **Aero California** (tel. 3-08-27, 3-08-48) is in Centro Comercial Plaza, Calle Lázaro Cárdenas.

Sea

The Cabo San Lucas-Puerto Vallarta ferry service was suspended some years ago;

harbor, Cabo San Lucas
(JOE CUMMINGS)

SEMATUR, the private corporation that took control of the formerly government-owned ferry line between Baja and the mainland, has no plans to reinstate service in the near future. The nearest ferry service to the mainland operates from La Paz to Mazatlán (see "Transport" under "La Paz," p. 306).

Cabo Isle Marina is the main docking facility for visiting recreational boats (see "Boating," above, for details); bow-stern anchorages are also possible in the outer bay.

Land

Buses to/from La Paz: Autotransportes Aguila and Tres Estrellas de Oro operate 13 buses a day (0600-1830) to La Paz from Cabo's main intercity bus depot, Calle 16 de Septiembre at Zaragoza. Buses run via Todos Santos, cost US$4 pp, and take about 3½ hours. About half these departures stop in Todos Santos (two hours); the fare to/from Todos Santos is US$2.

Autotransportes de la Paz runs six buses (0600-1730) daily to La Paz, via San José, from its terminal two blocks east on Calle 16 de Septiembre (at Calle Leona Vicario); the fare on this route is US$6.

Buses to/from San José: Autotransportes de Aguila (main depot) has 15 buses a day (0645-2000) to San José del Cabo; the trip takes 30-45 minutes and costs US$1.30 pp.

Driving: If you've driven down from the U.S. border, congratulations—you've reached "Land's End!" If you're contemplating the drive and have limited time, you can figure on making it from Tijuana to Cabo in three eight-hour days (Cataviña first night, Santa Rosalía or Mulegé second night) or 2½ dawn-to-dusk days (Guerrero Negro first night, La Paz sec-

ond night). If you stretch your itinerary to include a week's driving time each way, you'll have a safer trip and more of an opportunity to enjoy the sights along the way.

Local Transport

Taxi: A taxi from Los Cabos International Airport to Cabo San Lucas costs US$7 pp or US$24 for the whole cab. In Cabo itself, you can easily get around on foot, bicycle, or scooter.

Water Taxi: Harbor skiffs can be hired from the marina (in front of Plaza Las Glorias) to Playa El Médano (US$2.50 pp) and Playa del Amor (US$3). In the reverse direction, skiffs are plentiful at El Médano, but for del Amor, advance arrangements for a pickup are necessary.

Auto Rental: VW sedans or vans are easily rented at Los Cabos International Airport (see "Transport" under "San José del Cabo," p. 324). In Cabo, they can also be rented at **Auto Rentas Baja Sol** (tel. 3-16-46, Paseador del Pescador, near the northeast entrance to town), **Servitur** (tel. 3-08-97, Hacienda Beach Resort), or **Budget** (tel. 3-02-41, Plaza Aramburo). Rates vary from around US$24 a day plus US$.18 per km for a no-frills VW bug to US$56 and US$.33/km for a Caravelle.

Two-wheel/Three-wheel Rental: Chubasco's (tel. 3-04-04, Blvd. Marina and Hotel Meliá San Lucas) has cornered the market on mopeds (US$22.50/day), ATVs (US$39/day), and motorcycles (US$49/day). This agency also rents bicycles for US$2.50 per hour or US$10 per day. **Baja Sports Bicycle Rentals** (no phone, Calle Madero and Guerrero) has bicycles for US$2 an hour or US$10 a day.

BOOKLIST

DESCRIPTION AND TRAVEL

Burleson, Bob, and David H. Riskind. *Backcountry Mexico: A Traveler's Guide and Phrase Book*. University of Texas Press, 1986. Part guidebook, part anthropological study of Northern Mexico with some relevance to Baja California backcountry travel.

Cudahy, John. *Mañanaland: Adventuring with Camera and Rifle Through California in Mexico*. Duffie and Co., 1928. Provides an interesting glimpse of pre-WW II Baja, with no outstanding revelations.

Gardner, Erle Stanley. *The Hidden Heart of Baja*. Morrow and Co., 1962. Gardner, the mystery novelist who created Perry Mason, is one of the key persons responsible for pulling Baja out of its "forgotten peninsula" status among North Americans in the '60s. The book describes his findings as an amateur archaeologist in Baja's central sierras, including "discoveries" of El Batequi and other now-famous prehistoric murals. Of Gardner's Baja travelogues, this is arguably the best, in spite of minor inaccuracies.

Mackintosh, Graham. *Into A Desert Place*. Graham Mackintosh Publications, P.O. Box 1196, Idyllwild, CA 92549. A thoroughly engaging report of Mackintosh's walk around the entire coastline of Baja California over the course of two years. Destined to become a classic of gringo-in-Baja travel literature for its refreshingly honest style and insights into Baja fish-camp and village life.

Miller Max. *Land Where Time Stands Still*. Dodd, Mead, and Co., 1943. A classic travelogue that chronicles Baja life during WW II, when Mexicans alternately fell prey to German and American propaganda.

Miller, Tom, and Carol Hoffman. *The Baja Book III*. Baja Trail Publications, 1987. One of the original "road log"-style guidebooks. The NASA "space maps" aren't always effective, but the authors show a great sensitivity for Baja wildlife.

Steinbeck, John. *The Log from the* Sea of Cortez. Viking Press, 1941. This surprising chronicle of a Baja research voyage with marine biologist Ed Ricketts (the inspiration for *Cannery Row's* protagonist) shows Steinbeck to be a bit of a scientist himself. Annotated with Latin, the book is full of insights into Pacific and Cortez marinelife as well as coastal Bajacalifornio society. Sprinkled throughout are expositions of Steinbeck's personal philosophy, implicit in his novels but fully articulated here. The source for his novella *The Pearl* is also revealed.

HISTORY AND CULTURE

Crosby, Harry. *The Cave Paintings of Baja California*. Copley Books, 1984. A seminal work on prehistoric Baja California art, written with a poetic perspective. Includes numerous photos and maps.

Crosby, Harry. *The King's Highway in Baja California: An Adventure into the History and Lore of a Forgotten Region*. Copley Books, 1974. Another excellent reference work by Baja historian Crosby, tracing the original trails used by Jesuit, Dominican, and Franciscan missionaries.

Paz, Octavio. *The Labyrinth of Solitude: Life and Thought in Mexico*. Grove Press, 1961. Paz has no peer when it comes to expositions of the Mexican psyche, and this is his best work.

Robertson, Tomás. *Baja California and its Missions*. La Siesta Press, 1978. Robertson was the patriarch of an old Baja California-Sinaloa family of north European extraction as well as a patron of Baja mission restoration. His useful amateur work synthesizes Baja mission history from several sources; like its sources, it contains a few minor contradictions and muddy areas.

Weisman, Alan. *La Frontera: The United States Border with Mexico.* University of Arizona Press, 1986. Only the last chapter, "Las Californias," is concerned with northern Baja, but scattered therein are several gems of history and pop sociology.

NATURAL HISTORY

Krutch, Joseph Wood. *The Forgotten Peninsula: A Naturalist in Baja California.* University of Arizona Press, 1986 (reprint from 1961). Combines natural history and a curmudgeonly travelogue style to paint a romantic portrait of pre-Transpeninsular Highway Baja.

Nickerson, Roy. *The Friendly Whales: A Whalewatcher's Guide to the Gray Whales of Baja California.* Chronicle Books, 1987. A light study, with photographs, of the "friendly" whale phenomenon in Laguna San Ignacio, where gray whales often initiate contact with humans.

Roberts, Norman C. *Baja California Plant Field Guide.* Natural History Publishing Co., 1989. Contains concise descriptions of over 550 species of Baja flora, more than half illustrated by color photos.

Scammon, Charles Melville. *The Marine Mammals of the Northwestern Coast of America.* Dover Publications reprint, 1968. Originally written in the 19th century by the whaler who almost brought about the gray's complete demise, this is *the* classic, pioneering work on Pacific cetaceans, including the gray whale.

Wiggins, Ira L. *Flora of Baja California.* Stanford University Press, 1980. For the average layperson with an interest in Baja vegetation, Norman Roberts's *Baja California Plant Field Guide* will more than suffice, but for the serious botanist, this weighty work, with listings of over 2,700 species, is a must.

Zwinger, Ann Raymond. *A Desert Country near the Sea.* Truman Talley Books, 1983. A poetic succession of essays centered around Baja natural history, with sketches by the author and an appendix with Latin names for flora and fauna.

SPORTS AND RECREATION

Fons, Valerie. *Keep It Moving: Baja by Canoe.* The Mountaineers, 1986. Well-written account of a canoe trip along the Baja California coastline; recommended reading for sea kayakers as well as canoeists.

Franz, Carl, with Steve Rogers. *RV Camping in Mexico.* John Muir Publications, 1989. Contains 50 pages (out of 308) on Baja camping. A bit out of date, but the introductory chapters would be useful for anyone planning his or her first RV trip to Mexico.

Lehman, Charles. *Desert Survival Handbook.* Primer Publishers, 1990. A no-nonsense guide to desert survival techniques that ought to be part of every pilot's or coastal navigator's kit.

Miller, Tom. *Angler's Guide to Baja California.* Baja Trail Publications 1984. Contains complete descriptions and sketches of common Pacific and Cortez fishes, as well as extensive commentary on tackle and seasons. Still the best Baja fishing guide in print.

Peterson, Walt. *The Baja Adventure Book.* Wilderness Press, 1987. Packed with information on outdoor activities in Baja, with an emphasis on fishing, hunting, and scuba diving. Contains very little on towns and cities.

Williams, Jack. *Baja Boater's Guide, Vols. I and II.* H.J. Williams Publications. 1988. These ambitious guides, one each on the Pacific Ocean and the Sea of Cortez, contain useful aerial photos and sketch maps of Baja's continental islands and coastline.

Wong, Bonnie. *Bicycling Baja.* Sunbelt Publications, 1988. Written by an experienced leader of Baja cycling tours, this book includes helpful suggestions on trip preparation, equipment, and riding techniques as well as road logs for 17 different cycling routes throughout the peninsula.

Wyatt, Mike. *The Basic Essentials of Sea Kayaking.* ICS Books, 1990. A good introduction to sea kayaking, with tips on buying gear, paddling techniques, safety, and kayak loading.

GLOSSARY

abarrotes—groceries
aduana—customs service
arroyo—canyon, dry wash, or stream
bahía—bay
basura—trash or rubbish; the sign No Tire Basura means "Don't throw trash."
calle—street
callejón—alley or lane
cañon—canyon
casa de huéspedes—guest house
cerro—mountain peak
cerveza—beer
CONASUPO—Compañía Nacional de Subsistencias Populares (National Company for Popular Subsistence)
correo—post office
COTP—Captain of the Port
ejido—collectively owned agricultural lands
ensenada—cove or small bay
IMSS—Instituto Mexicano del Seguro Social (Mexican Social Security Institute)
FONATUR—Fondo Nacional de Fomento del Turismo (National Foundation for Tourism Development)
hostería—hostelry, inn
ISSSTE—Instituto de Seguridad y Servicios Sociales para Trabajadores del Estado (Security and Social Services Institute for Government Workers)
laguna—lagoon, lake, or bay
llano—plains
mercado—market
palacio municipal—literally "municipal palace," equivalent to city or county hall in the U.S.
palapa—thatched umbrella-like shade shelter or roof
panadería—bakery
parrada—bus stop
PEMEX—Petroleos Mexicanos (Mexican Petroleum)
pensión—boarding house
playa—beach
punta—point
ramal—branch road
SECTUR—Secretaría de Turismo (Secretariat of Tourism)
SEDUE—Secretaría de Desarollo Urbano y Ecología (Secretariat of Urban and Ecological Development)
tienda—store
tinaja—pool or spring
topes—speed bumps
ultramarinos—delicatessen-liquor store

INDEX

Page numbers in **boldface** indicate the primary reference to a given topic. *Italicized* page
numbers indicate information in callouts, charts, illustrations, or maps.

THE METRIC SYSTEM

1 inch = 2.54 centimeters (cm)
1 foot = .304 meters (m)
1 mile = 1.6093 kilometers (km)
1 km = .6214 miles
1 fathom = 1.8288 m
1 chain = 20.1168 m
1 furlong = 201.168 m
1 acre = .4047 hectares (ha)
1 sq km = 100 ha
1 sq mile = 2.59 sq km
1 ounce = 28.35 grams
1 pound = .4536 kilograms (kg)
1 short ton = .90718 metric ton
1 short ton = 2000 pounds
1 long ton = 1.016 metric tons
1 long ton = 2240 pounds
1 metric ton = 1000 kg
1 quart = .94635 liters
1 US gallon = 3.7854 liters
1 Imperial gallon = 4.5459 liters
1 nautical mile = 1.852 km

To compute centigrade temperatures, subtract 32 from Fahrenheit and divide by 1.8. To go the other way, multiply centigrade by 1.8 and add 32.

Moon Handbooks—The Ideal Traveling Companions

Open a Moon Handbook and you're opening your eyes and heart to the world. Thoughtful, sensitive, and provocative, Moon Handbooks encourage an intimate understanding of a region, from its culture and history to essential practicalities. Fun to read and packed with valuable information on accommodations, dining, recreation, plus indispensable travel tips, detailed maps, charts, illustrations, photos, glossaries, and indexes, Moon Handbooks are ideal traveling companions: informative, entertaining, and highly practical.

To locate the bookstore nearest you that carries Moon Travel Handbooks or to order directly from Moon Publications, call: (800) 345-5473, Monday-Friday, 9 a.m.-5 p.m. PST

The Pacific/Asia Series

BALI HANDBOOK by Bill Dalton
Detailed travel information on the most famous island in the world. 12 color pages, 29 b/w photos, 68 illustrations, 42 maps, 7 charts, glossary, booklist, index. 428 pages. **$12.95**

BANGKOK HANDBOOK by Michael Buckley
Your tour guide through this exotic and dynamic city reveals the affordable and accessible possibilities. Thai phrasebook, 16 color pages, 55 b/w photos, 30 maps, 19 illustrations, 9 charts, booklist, index. 214 pages. **$10.95**

BLUEPRINT FOR PARADISE: How to Live on a Tropic Island by Ross Norgrove
This one-of-a-kind guide has everything you need to know about moving to and living comfortably on a tropical island. 8 color pages, 40 b/w photos, 3 maps, 14 charts, appendices, index. 212 pages. **$14.95**

FIJI ISLANDS HANDBOOK by David Stanley
The first and still the best source of information on travel around this 322-island archipelago. 8 color pages, 35 b/w photos, 78 illustrations, 26 maps, 3 charts, Fijian glossary, booklist, index. 198 pages. **$8.95**

INDONESIA HANDBOOK by Bill Dalton
This one-volume encyclopedia explores island by island the many facets of this sprawling, kaleidoscopic island nation. 30 b/w photos, 143 illustrations, 250 maps, 17 charts, booklist, extensive Indonesian vocabulary, index. 1,000 pages. **$19.95**

MICRONESIA HANDBOOK:
Guide to the Caroline, Gilbert, Mariana, and Marshall Islands by David Stanley
Micronesia Handbook guides you on a real Pacific adventure all your own. 8 color pages, 77 b/w photos, 68 illustrations, 69 maps, 18 tables and charts, index. 300 pages. **$11.95**

NEW ZEALAND HANDBOOK by Jane King
Introduces you to the people, places, history, and culture of this extraordinary land. 8 color pages, 99 b/w photos, 146 illustrations, 82 maps, booklist, index. 546 pages. **$14.95**

OUTBACK AUSTRALIA HANDBOOK by Marael Johnson
Australia is an endlessly fascinating, vast land, and *Outback Australia Handbook* explores the cities and towns, sheep stations, and wilderness areas of the Northern Territory, Western, and South Australia. Full of travel tips and cultural information for adventuring, relaxing, or just getting away from it all. 8 color pages, 39 b/w photos, 63 illustrations, 51 maps, booklist, index. 355 pages. **$15.95**

PHILIPPINES HANDBOOK by Peter Harper and Evelyn Peplow
Crammed with detailed information, *Philippines Handbook* equips the escapist, hedonist, or business traveler with thorough coverage of the Philippines's colorful history, landscapes, and culture. 8 color pages, 2 b/w photos, 60 illustrations, 93 maps, 30 charts, index. 587 pages. **$12.95**

SOUTHEAST ASIA HANDBOOK by Carl Parkes
Helps the enlightened traveler discover the real Southeast Asia. 16 color pages, 75 b/w photos, 11 illustrations, 169 maps, 140 charts, vocabulary and suggested reading, index. 873 pages. **$16.95**

SOUTH KOREA HANDBOOK by Robert Nilsen
Whether you're visiting on business or searching for adventure, *South Korea Handbook* is an invaluable companion. 8 color pages, 78 b/w photos, 93 illustrations, 109 maps, 10 charts, Korean glossary with useful notes on speaking and reading the language, booklist, index. 548 pages. **$14.95**

SOUTH PACIFIC HANDBOOK by David Stanley
The original comprehensive guide to the 16 territories in the South Pacific. 20 color pages, 195 b/w photos, 121 illustrations, 35 charts, 138 maps, booklist, glossary, index. 740 pages. **$15.95**

TAHITI-POLYNESIA HANDBOOK by David Stanley
All five French-Polynesian archipelagoes are covered in this comprehensive guide by Oceania's best-known travel writer. 12 color pages, 45 b/w photos, 64 illustrations, 33 maps, 7 charts, booklist, glossary, index. 235 pages. **$11.95**

THAILAND HANDBOOK by Carl Parkes
Presents the richest source of information on travel in Thailand. Color and b/w photos, illustrations, maps, charts, booklist, glossary, index. 600 pages **$16.95**

TIBET HANDBOOK by Victor Chan
This remarkable book is both a comprehensive trekking guide and a pilgrimage guide that draws on Tibetan literature and religious history. Color and b/w photos, illustrations, maps, charts, booklist, glossary, index. 1,200 pages. **$24.95**

The Hawaiian Series

BIG ISLAND OF HAWAII HANDBOOK by J.D. Bisignani
An entertaining yet informative text packed with insider tips on accommodations, dining, sports and outdoor activities, natural attractions, and must-see sights. 12 color pages, 72 b/w photos, 73 illustrations, 22 maps, 5 charts, booklist, glossary, index. 347 pages. **$11.95**

HAWAII HANDBOOK by J.D. Bisignani
Winner of the 1989 Hawaii Visitors Bureau's Best Guide Book Award and the Grand Award for Excellence in Travel Journalism, this guide takes you beyond the glitz and high-priced hype and leads you to a genuine Hawaiian experience. 12 color pages, 86 b/w photos, 132 illustrations, 86 maps, 44 graphs and charts, Hawaiian and pidgin glossaries, appendix, booklist, index. 879 pages. **$15.95**

KAUAI HANDBOOK by J.D. Bisignani
Kauai Handbook is the perfect antidote to the workaday world. 8 color pages, 36 b/w photos, 48 illustrations, 19 maps, 10 tables and charts, Hawaiian and pidgin glossaries, booklist, index. 236 pages. **$9.95**

MAUI HANDBOOK: Including Molokai and Lanai by J.D. Bisignani
"No fool-'round" advice on accommodations, eateries, and recreation, plus a comprehensive introduction to island ways, geography, and history. 8 color pages, 60 b/w photos, 72 illustrations, 34 maps, 19 charts, booklist, glossary, index. 350 pages. **$11.95**

OAHU HANDBOOK by J.D. Bisignani
A handy guide to Honolulu, renowned surfing beaches, and Oahu's countless other diversions. 12 color pages, 93 b/w photos, 67 illustrations, 18 maps, 8 charts, booklist, glossary, index. 354 pages. **$11.95**

The Americas Series

ALASKA-YUKON HANDBOOK by Deke Castleman and Don Pitcher
Get the inside story, with plenty of well-seasoned advice to help you cover more miles on less money. 8 color pages, 26 b/w photos, 95 illustrations, 92 maps, 10 charts, booklist, glossary, index. 384 pages. **$13.95**

ARIZONA TRAVELER'S HANDBOOK by Bill Weir
This meticulously researched guide contains everything necessary to make Arizona accessible and enjoyable. 8 color pages, 194 b/w photos, 74 illustrations, 53 maps, 6 charts, booklist, index. 505 pages. **$14.95**

BAJA HANDBOOK by Joe Cummings
A comprehensive guide with all the travel information and background on the land, history, and culture of this untamed thousand-mile-long peninsula. 8 color pages, 40 b/w photos, 28 illustrations, 41 maps, 29 charts, booklist, index. 356 pages. **$13.95**

BELIZE HANDBOOK by Chicki Mallan
Complete with detailed maps, practical information, and an overview of the area's flamboyant history, culture, and geographical features, *Belize Handbook* is the only comprehensive guide of its kind to this spectacular region. 8 color pages, 65 b/w photos, 43 illustrations, 25 maps, 30 charts, booklist, index. 212 pages. **$11.95**

BRITISH COLUMBIA HANDBOOK by Jane King
With an emphasis on outdoor adventures, this guide covers mainland British Columbia, Vancouver Island, the Queen Charlotte Islands, and the Canadian Rockies. 8 color pages, 56 b/w photos, 45 illustrations, 66 maps, 4 charts, booklist, index. 381 pages. **$13.95**

CANCUN HANDBOOK and Mexico's Caribbean Coast by Chicki Mallan
Covers the city's luxury scene as well as more modest attractions, plus many side trips to unspoiled beaches and Mayan ruins. 12 color pages, 76 b/w photos, 25 illustrations, 24 maps, 12 charts, Spanish glossary, booklist, index. 257 pages. **$10.95**

CATALINA ISLAND HANDBOOK: A Guide to California's Channel Islands
by Chicki Mallan
A complete guide to these remarkable islands, from the windy solitude of the Channel Islands National Marine Sanctuary to bustling Avalon. 8 color pages, 105 b/w photos, 65 illustrations, 40 maps, 32 charts, booklist, index. 245 pages. **$10.95**

COLORADO HANDBOOK by Stephen Metzger
Essential details to the all-season possibilities in Colorado fill this guide. Practical travel tips combine with recreation—skiing, nightlife, and wilderness exploration—plus entertaining essays. 8 color pages, 92 b/w photos, 15 illustrations, 57 maps, 10 charts, booklist, index. 422 pages. **$15.95**

IDAHO HANDBOOK by Bill Loftus
A year-round guide to everything in this outdoor wonderland, from whitewater adventures to rural hideaways. 8 color pages, 35 b/w photos, 21 illustrations, 42 maps, booklist, index. 275 pages. **$12.95**

JAMAICA HANDBOOK by Karl Luntta
From the sun and surf of Montego Bay and Ocho Rios to the cool slopes of the Blue Mountains, author Karl Luntta offers island-seekers a perceptive, personal view of Jamaica. 8 color pages, 21 b/w photos, 35 illustrations, 16 maps, 7 charts, booklist, glossary, index. 213 pages. **$12.95**

MONTANA HANDBOOK by W.C. McRae and Judy Jewell
The wild West is yours with this extensive guide to the Treasure State, complete with travel practicalities, history, and lively essays on Montana life. 8 color pages, 62 b/w photos, 43 illustrations, 49 maps, 10 charts, booklist, index. 393 pages. **$13.95**

NEVADA HANDBOOK by Deke Castleman
Nevada Handbook puts the Silver State into perspective and makes it manageable and affordable. 34 b/w photos, 43 illustrations, 37 maps, 17 charts, booklist, index. 400 pages. **$12.95**

NEW MEXICO HANDBOOK by Stephen Metzger
A close-up and complete look at every aspect of this wondrous state. 8 color pages, 85 b/w photos, 63 illustrations, 50 maps, 10 charts, booklist, index. 375 pages.   **$13.95**

NORTHERN CALIFORNIA HANDBOOK by Kim Weir
An outstanding companion for imaginative travel in the territory north of the Tehachapis. 12 color pages, 200 b/w photos, 54 maps, 36 illustrations, booklist, index. 759 pages.   **$16.95**

OREGON HANDBOOK by Stuart Warren and Ted Long Ishikawa
Brimming with travel practicalities and insider views on Oregon's history, culture, arts, and activities. 8 color pages, 113 b/w photos, 26 illustrations, 28 maps, 20 charts, booklist, index. 422 pages.   **$12.95**

TEXAS HANDBOOK by Joe Cummings
Seasoned travel writer Joe Cummings brings an insider's perspective to his home state. 8 color pages, 79 b/w photos, 60 maps, 45 illustrations, 18 charts, booklist, index. 483 pages. **$13.95**

UTAH HANDBOOK by Bill Weir
Weir gives you all the carefully researched facts and background to make your visit a success. 8 color pages, 102 b/w photos, 61 illustrations, 30 maps, 9 charts, booklist, index. 452 pages. **$12.95**

WASHINGTON HANDBOOK by Dianne J. Boulerice Lyons and Archie Satterfield
Covers sights, shopping, services, transportation, and outdoor recreation, with complete listings for restaurants and accommodations. 8 color pages, 92 b/w photos, 24 illustrations, 81 maps, 8 charts, booklist, index. 433 pages.   **$13.95**

WYOMING HANDBOOK by Don Pitcher
All you need to know to open the doors to this wide and wild state. 16 color pages, 30 b/w photos, 42 illustrations, 64 maps, 19 charts, booklist, index. 427 pages.   **$12.95**

YUCATAN HANDBOOK by Chicki Mallan
All the information you'll need to guide you into every corner of this exotic land. 8 color pages, 154 b/w photos, 55 illustrations, 57 maps, 70 charts, appendix, booklist, Mayan and Spanish glossaries, index. 391 pages.   **$12.95**

The International Series

EGYPT HANDBOOK by Kathy Hansen
An invaluable resource for intelligent travel in Egypt. 8 color pages, 20 b/w photos, 150 illustrations, 80 detailed maps and plans to museums and archaeological sites, Arabic glossary, booklist, index. 510 pages.   **$14.95**

MOSCOW-LENINGRAD HANDBOOK by Masha Nordbye
Provides the visitor with an extensive introduction to the history, culture, and people of these two great cities, as well as practical information on where to stay, eat, and shop. 8 color pages, 36 b/w photos, 20 illustrations, 16 maps, 9 charts, booklist, index. 205 pages. **$12.95**

NEPAL HANDBOOK by Kerry Moran
Whether you're planning a week in Kathmandu or months out on the trail, *Nepal Handbook* will take you into the heart of this Himalayan jewel. 16 color pages, 76 b/w photos, 45 illustrations, 46 maps, 9 charts, booklist, glossary, index. 378 pages. **$12.95**

NEPALI AAMA by Broughton Coburn
A delightful photo-journey into the life of a Gurung tribeswoman of Central Nepal. Having lived with Aama (translated, "mother") for two years, first as an outsider and later as an adopted member of the family, Coburn presents an intimate glimpse into a culture alive with humor, folklore, religion, and ancient rituals. 67 b/w photos. 165 pages. **$13.95**

PAKISTAN HANDBOOK by Isobel Shaw
For armchair travelers and trekkers alike, the most detailed and authoritative guide to Pakistan ever published. 28 color pages, 86 maps, appendices, Urdu glossary, booklist, index. 478 pages. **$15.95**

Moonbelts

Made of heavy-duty Cordura nylon, the Moonbelt offers maximum protection for your money and important papers. This all-weather pouch slips under your shirt or waistband, rendering it virtually undetectable and inaccessible to pickpockets. One-inch-wide nylon webbing, heavy-duty zipper, one-inch quick release buckle. Accommodates traveler's checks, passport, cash, photos. Size 5 x 9 inches. Black. **$8.95**

**New travel handbooks may be available that are not on this list.
To find out more about current or upcoming titles,
call us toll-free at (800) 345-5473.**

IMPORTANT ORDERING INFORMATION

FOR FASTER SERVICE: Call to locate the bookstore nearest you that carries Moon Travel Handbooks or order directly from Moon Publications:

  (800) 345-5473 · **Monday-Friday** · **9 a.m.-5 p.m. PST** · **fax (916) 345-6751**

PRICES: All prices are subject to change. We always ship the most current edition. We will let you know if there is a price increase on the book you ordered.

SHIPPING & HANDLING OPTIONS:

  1) Domestic UPS or USPS first class (allow 10 working days for delivery):

    $3.50 for the first item, 50 cents for each additional item.

Exceptions:

  · **Moonbelt** shipping is $1.50 for one, 50 cents for each additional belt.

  · Add $2.00 for same-day handling.

  2) UPS 2nd Day Air or Printed Airmail requires a special quote.

  3) International Surface Bookrate (8-12 weeks delivery):

    $3.00 for the first item, $1.00 for each additional item. Note: Moon Publications cannot guarantee international surface bookrate shipping.

FOREIGN ORDERS: All orders which originate outside the U.S.A. must be paid for with either an International Money Order or a check in U.S. currency drawn on a major U.S. bank based in the U.S.A.

TELEPHONE ORDERS: We accept Visa or MasterCard payments. Minimum order is US $15.00. Call in your order: 1 (800) 345-5473. 9 a.m.-5 p.m. Pacific Standard Time.

ORDER FORM

Be sure to call (800) 345-5473 for current prices and editions or for the name of the bookstore nearest you that carries Moon Travel Handbooks · 9 a.m.-5 p.m. PST
(See important ordering information on preceding page)

Name:_____Date:_____

Street:_____

City:_____Daytime Phone:_____

State or Country:_____Zip Code:_____

Quantity	Title	Price

Taxable Total	
Sales Tax (7.25%) for California Residents	
Shipping & Handling	
TOTAL	

Ship: ☐ 1st class   ☐ UPS (no P.O. Boxes)   ☐ International Surface

Ship to: ☐ address above   ☐ other_____

_____

_____

Make checks payable to:
Moon Publications Inc., 722 Wall Street, Chico, California 95928 U.S.A.
We Accept Visa and MasterCard
To Order: Call in your Visa or MasterCard number, or send a written order with your Visa or MasterCard number and expiration date clearly written.

Card Number: ☐ **Visa**   ☐ **MasterCard**

☐ ☐ ☐ ☐ ☐ ☐ ☐ ☐ ☐ ☐ ☐ ☐ ☐ ☐ ☐ ☐

Exact Name on Card: ☐ same as above   expiration date:_____

☐ other_____

signature_____

WHERE TO BUY THIS BOOK

Bookstores and Libraries:
Moon Publications Handbooks are sold worldwide. Please write our sales manager for a list of wholesalers and distributors in your area that stock our travel handbooks.

Travelers:
We would like to have Moon Publications Handbooks available throughout the world. Please ask your bookstore to write or call us for ordering information. If your bookstore will not order our guides for you, please write or call for a free catalog.

MOON PUBLICATIONS INC.
722 WALL STREET
CHICO, CA 95928 U.S.A.
tel: (800) 345-5473
fax: (916) 345-6751

ABOUT THE AUTHOR

Joe Cummings has been writing about travel and culture for over a decade. Attracted to geographical extremes, his first in-depth journeys were in the river deltas and rainforests of Southeast Asia, where he worked as a Peace Corps volunteer (Thailand) and university lecturer (Malaysia), and later contributed to popular guidebooks on Thailand, Malaysia, Singapore, Burma, Indonesia, and China.

Joe became infatuated with desert terrains while exploring the Sierra del Carmen and Chihuahuan Desert reaches of Texas' Big Bend Country for Moon's *Texas Handbook*. His love of South Texas border culture, including *norteña* music and food, eventually spilled over into Mexico; in preparation for his research travels in Baja California, he undertook an intensive Spanish language course and lived with a Mexican family. Safe and sound after clocking several thousand miles by VW bug on peninsular roads, Joe is now a confirmed Baja fanatic.

When not on the road or sequestered with his word processor in Alta California, Joe likes to cook, play guitar, swim, boogie-board (preferably in tropical surf), read/re-read Graham Greene novels, and ride mountain bikes.